D0876042

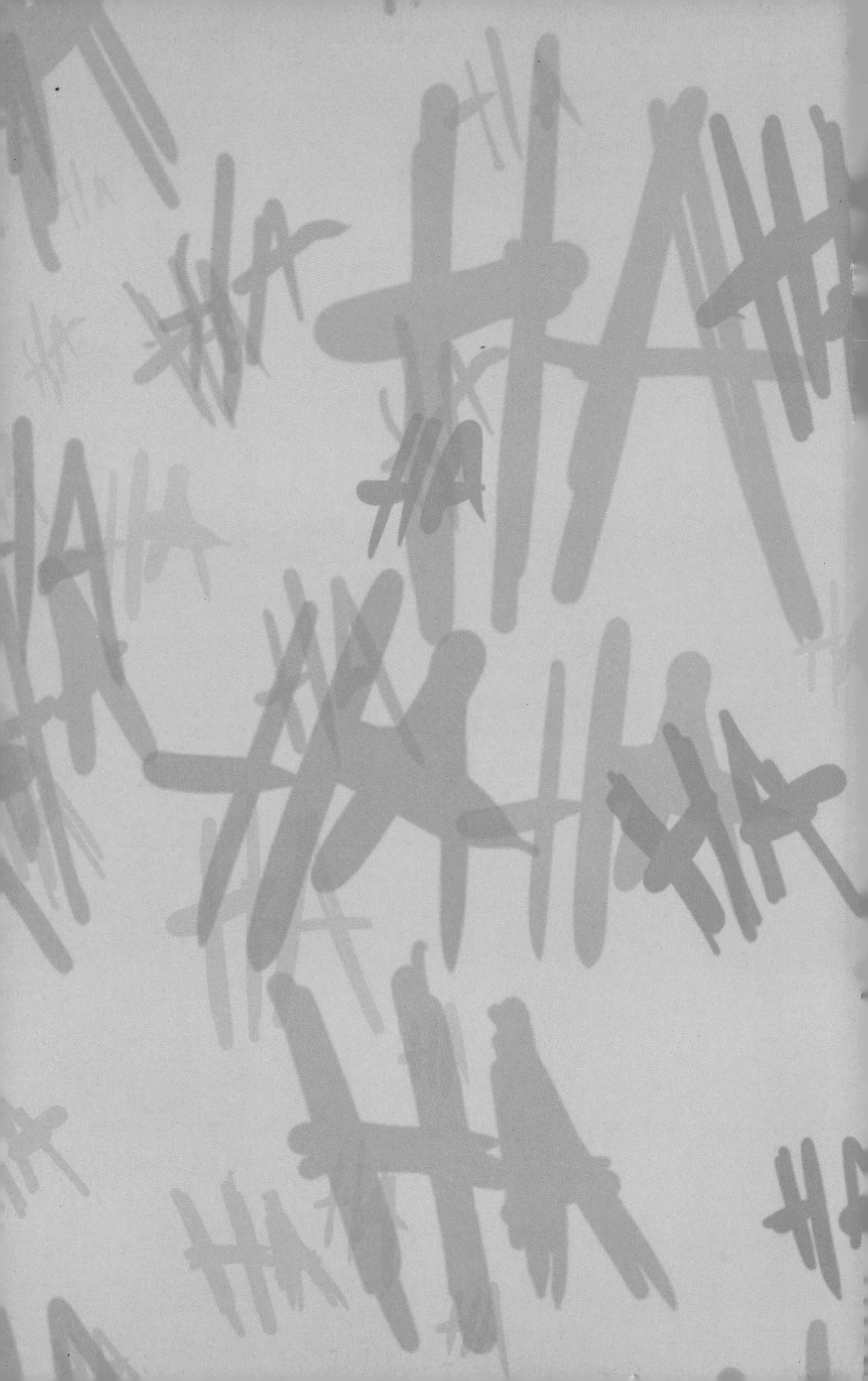

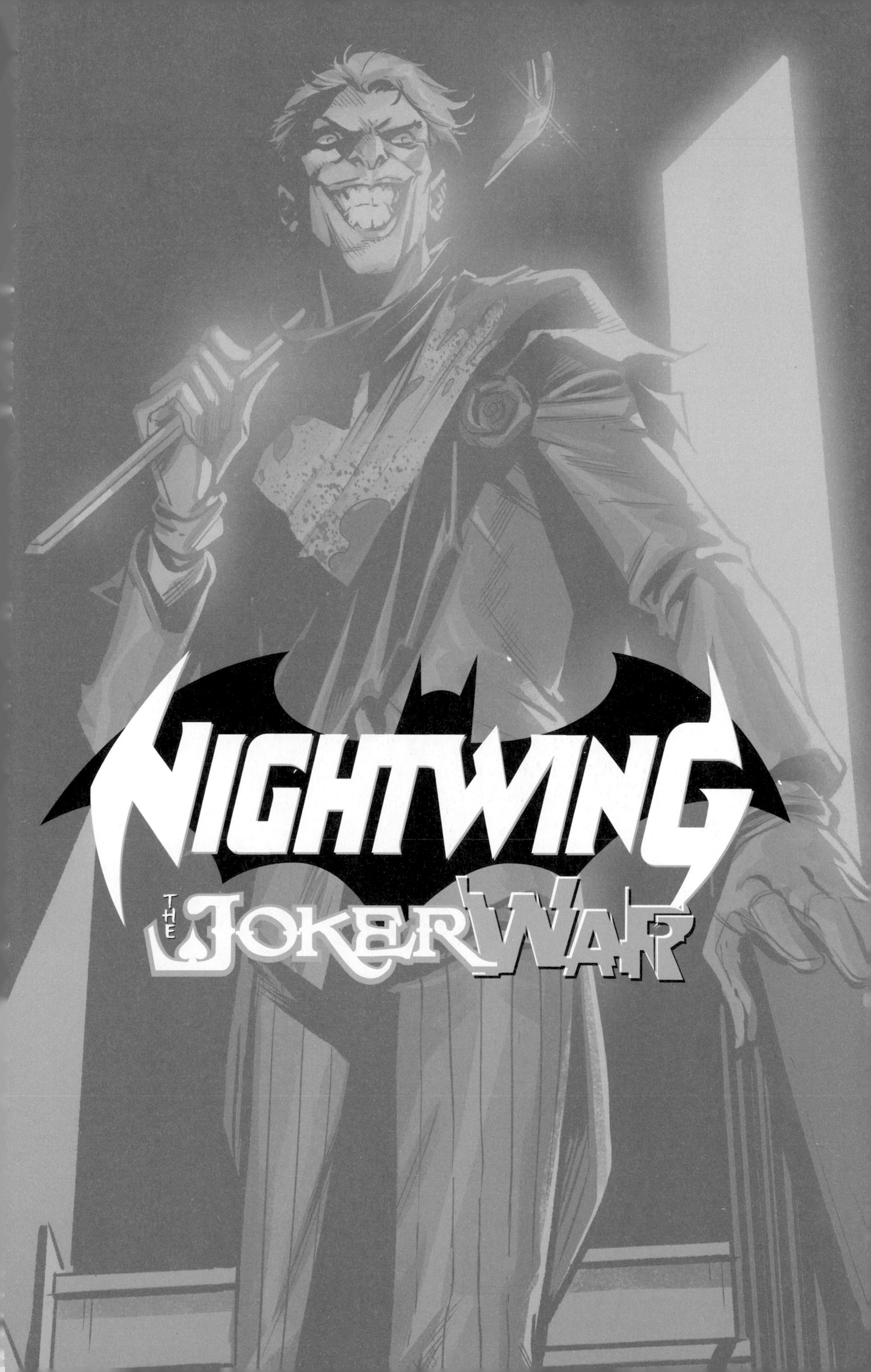
NIGHTWING
THE JOKER WAR

NIGHTWING

THE JOKER WAR

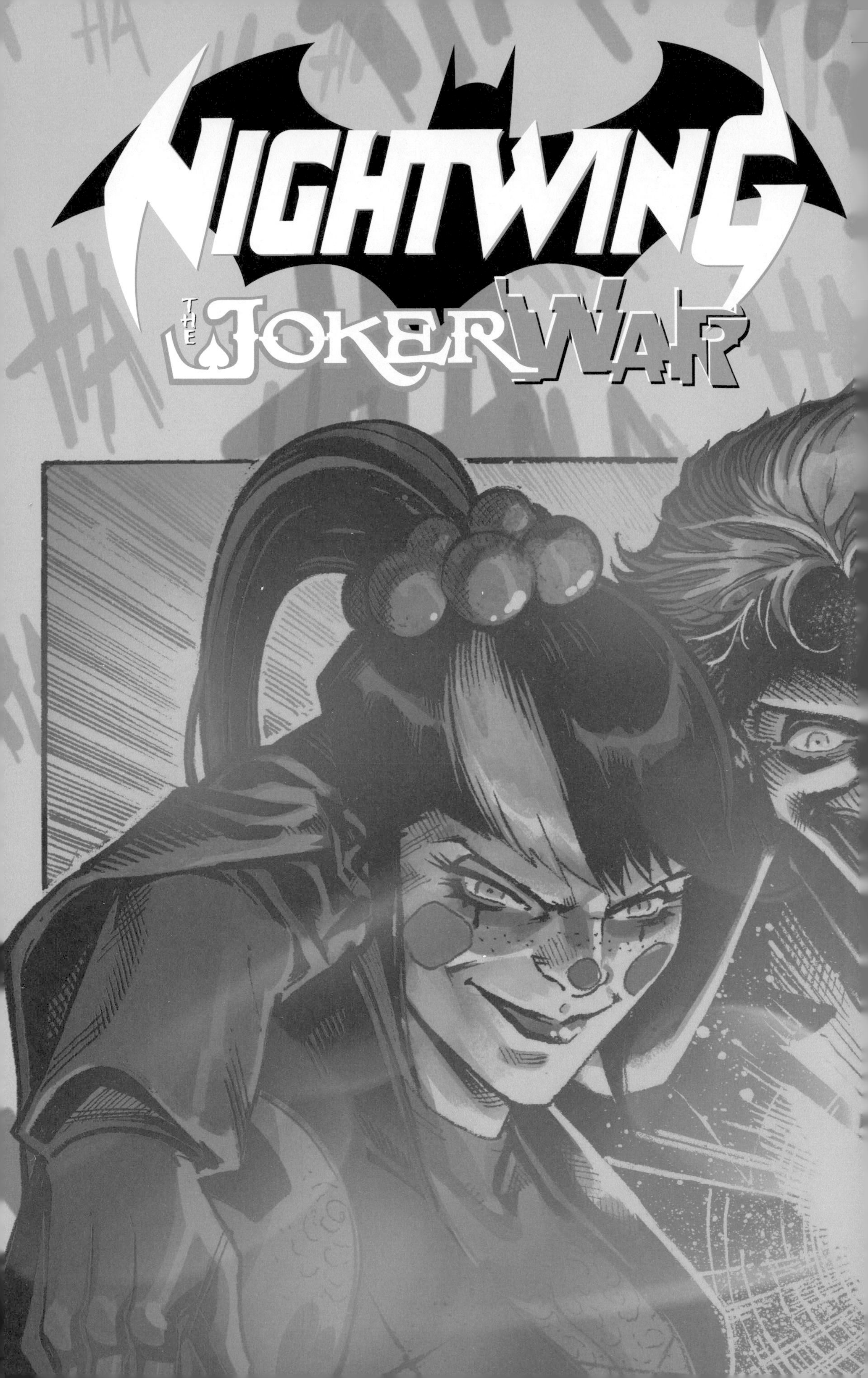

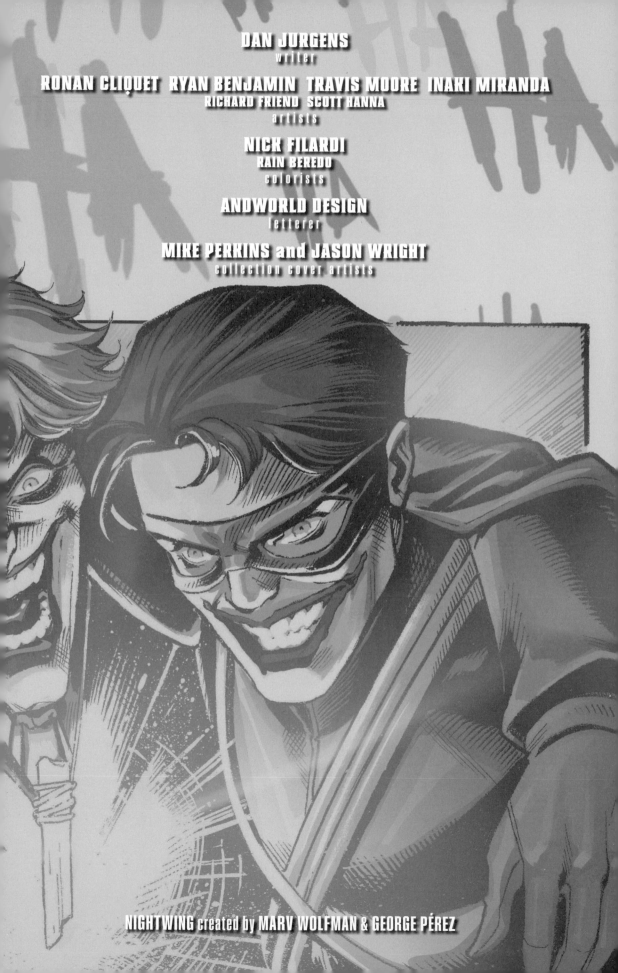

DAN JURGENS
writer

RONAN CLIQUET   RYAN BENJAMIN   TRAVIS MOORE   INAKI MIRANDA
RICHARD FRIEND   SCOTT HANNA
artists

NICK FILARDI
RAIN BEREDO
colorists

ANDWORLD DESIGN
letterer

MIKE PERKINS and JASON WRIGHT
collection cover artists

NIGHTWING created by MARV WOLFMAN & GEORGE PÉREZ

JESSICA CHEN	Editor – Original Series
BEN MEARES	Assistant Editor – Original Series
JEB WOODARD	Group Editor – Collected Editions
JESSICA CHEN	Editor – Collected Edition
STEVE COOK	Design Director – Books
CURTIS KING JR.	Publication Design
SUZANNAH ROWNTREE	Publication Production
MARIE JAVINS	Editor-in-Chief, DC Comics
DANIEL CHERRY III	Senior VP – General Manager
JIM LEE	Publisher & Chief Creative Officer
DON FALLETTI	VP – Manufacturing Operations & Workflow Management
LAWRENCE GANEM	VP – Talent Services
ALISON GILL	Senior VP – Manufacturing & Operations
NICK J. NAPOLITANO	VP – Manufacturing Administration & Design
NANCY SPEARS	VP – Revenue
MICHELE R. WELLS	VP & Executive Editor, Young Reader

NIGHTWING: THE JOKER WAR

DC Comics, 2900 West Alameda Ave., Burbank, CA 91505
Printed by LSC Communications, Willard, OH, USA. 1/22/21. First Printing.
ISBN: 978-1-77950-569-9

Library of Congress Cataloging-in-Publication Data is available.

PEFC Certified
This product is from sustainably managed forests and controlled sources
PEFC
PEFC/29-31-337
www.pefc.org

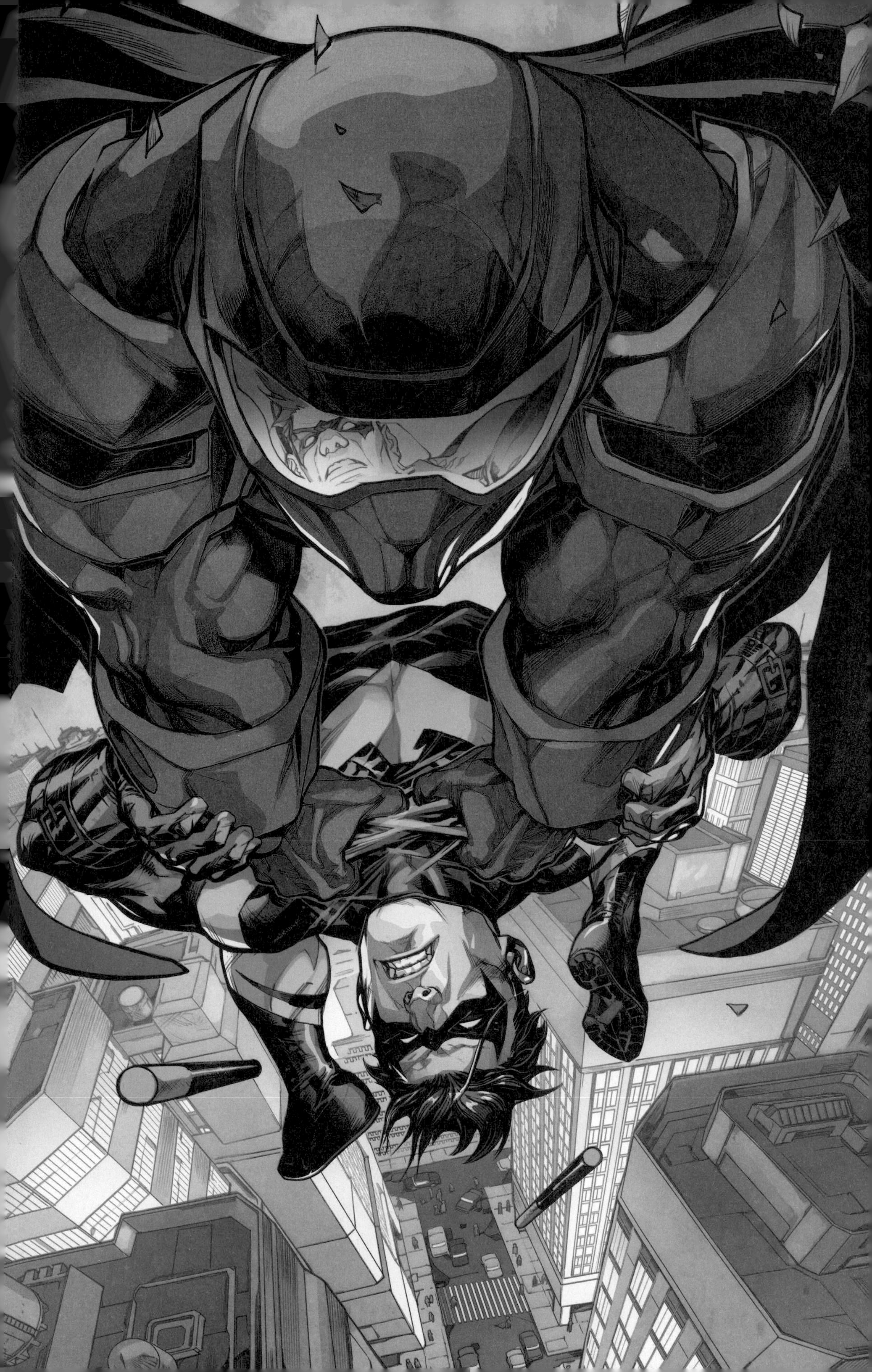

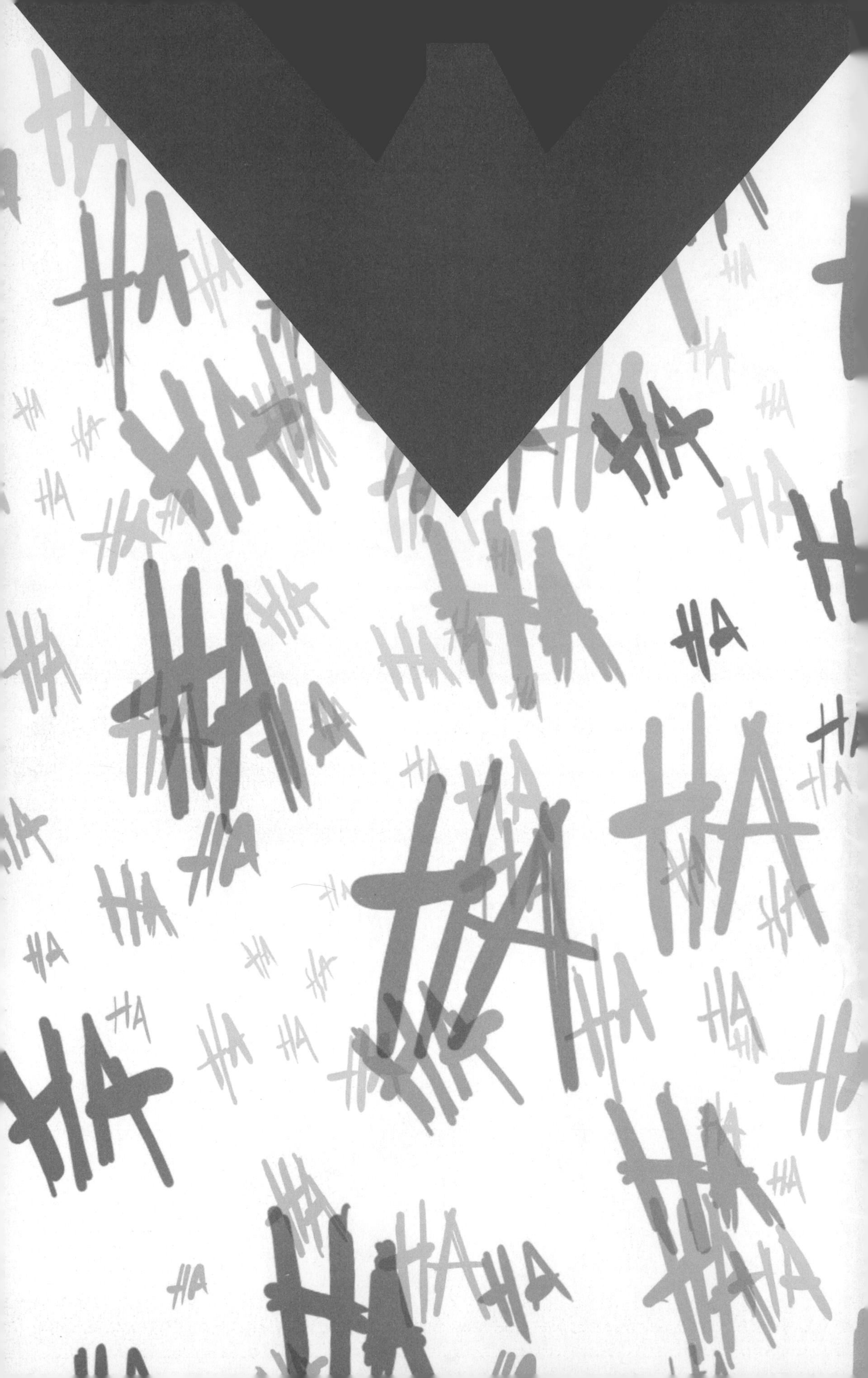

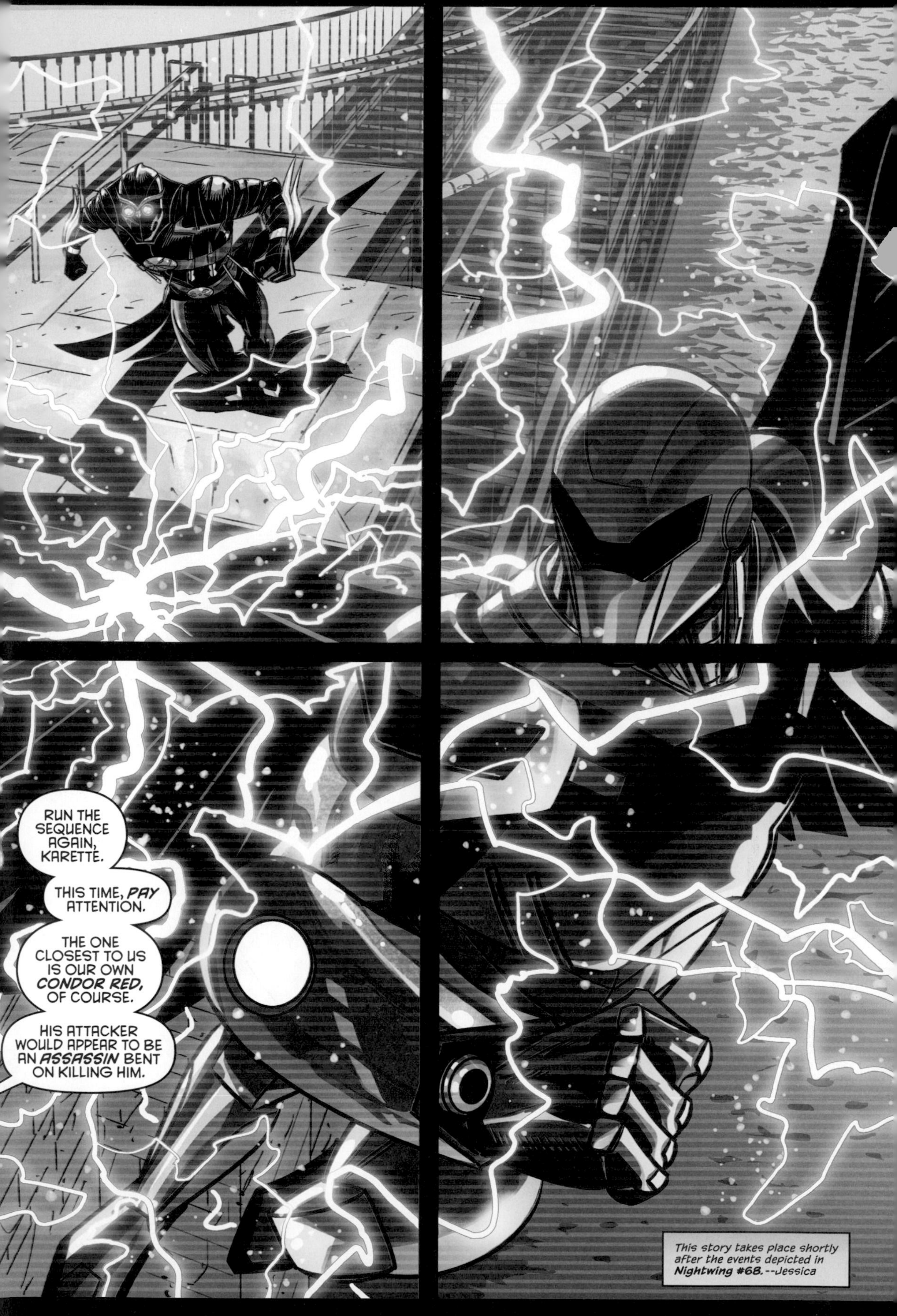
RUN THE SEQUENCE AGAIN, KARETTE.
THIS TIME, *PAY* ATTENTION.
THE ONE CLOSEST TO US IS OUR OWN *CONDOR RED,* OF COURSE.
HIS ATTACKER WOULD APPEAR TO BE AN *ASSASSIN* BENT ON KILLING HIM.
This story takes place shortly after the events depicted in **Nightwing #68.**--Jessica

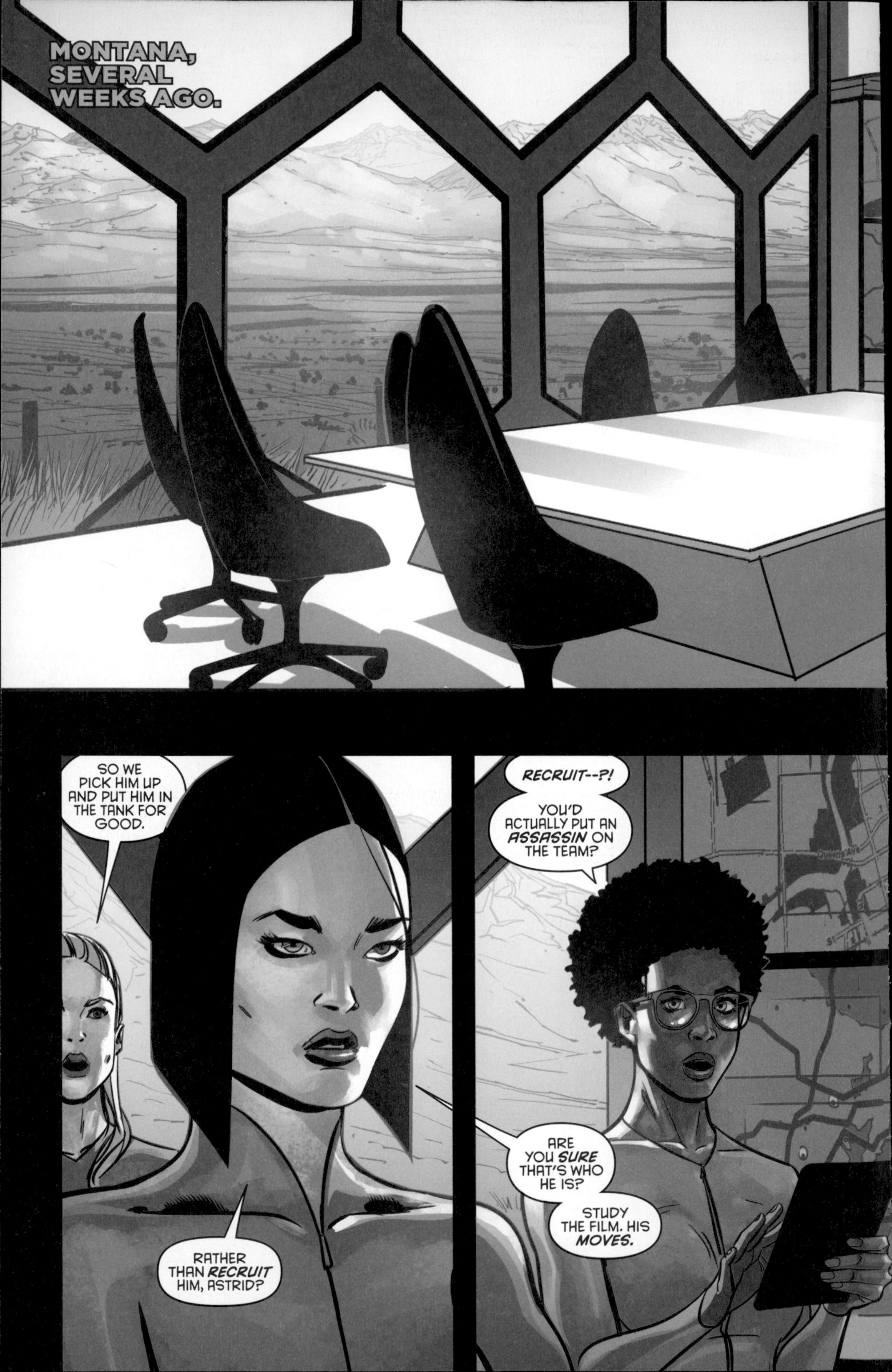
MONTANA, SEVERAL WEEKS AGO.
SO WE PICK HIM UP AND PUT HIM IN THE TANK FOR GOOD.
RATHER THAN *RECRUIT* HIM, ASTRID?
RECRUIT--?!
YOU'D ACTUALLY PUT AN *ASSASSIN* ON THE TEAM?
ARE YOU *SURE* THAT'S WHO HE IS?
STUDY THE FILM. HIS *MOVES.*

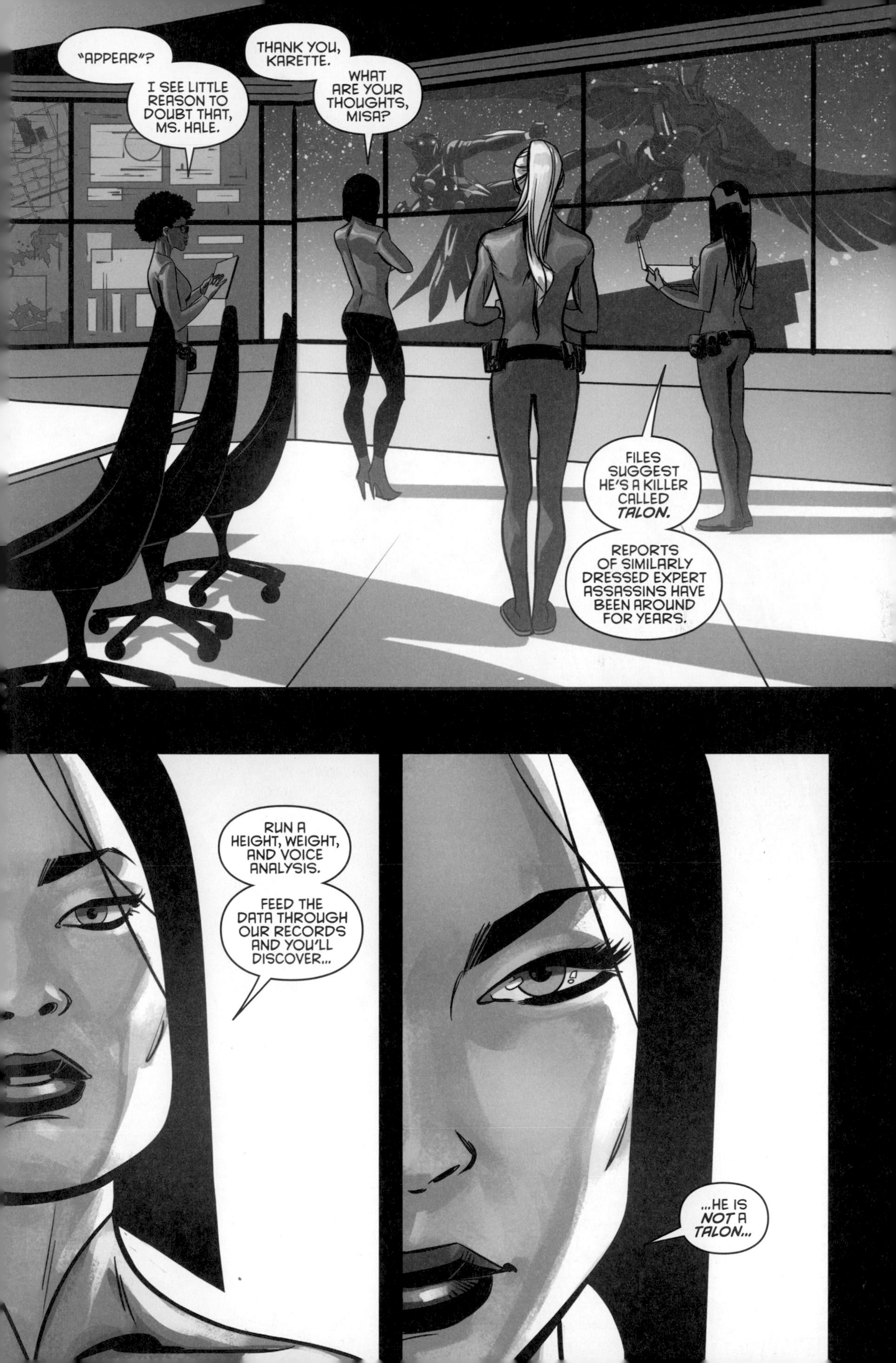
"APPEAR"?
I SEE LITTLE REASON TO DOUBT THAT, MS. HALE.
THANK YOU, KARETTE.
WHAT ARE YOUR THOUGHTS, MISA?
FILES SUGGEST HE'S A KILLER CALLED *TALON.*
REPORTS OF SIMILARLY DRESSED EXPERT ASSASSINS HAVE BEEN AROUND FOR YEARS.
RUN A HEIGHT, WEIGHT, AND VOICE ANALYSIS.
FEED THE DATA THROUGH OUR RECORDS AND YOU'LL DISCOVER...
...HE IS *NOT* A *TALON...*

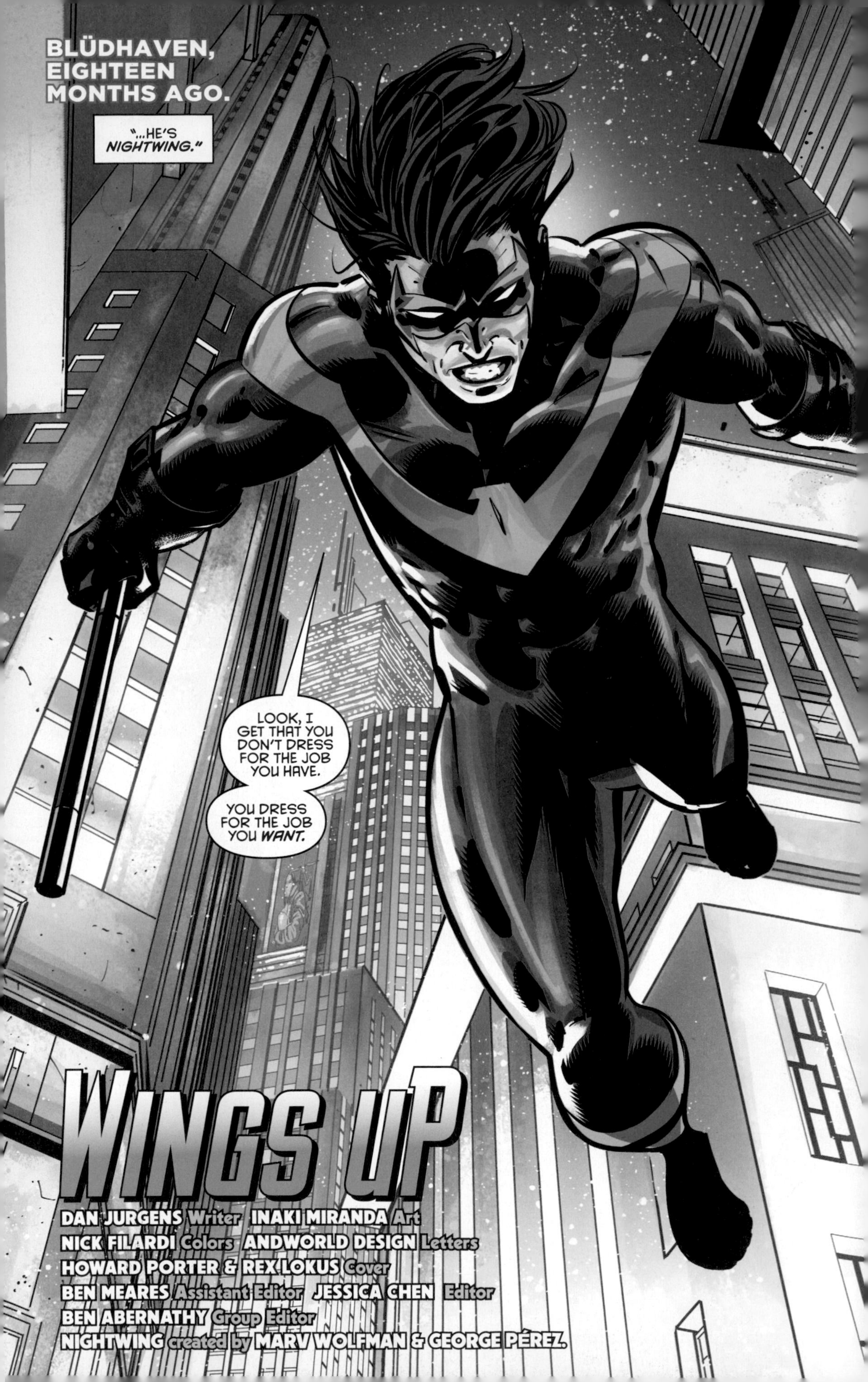
BLÜDHAVEN, EIGHTEEN MONTHS AGO.
"...HE'S NIGHTWING."
LOOK, I GET THAT YOU DON'T DRESS FOR THE JOB YOU HAVE.
YOU DRESS FOR THE JOB YOU WANT.
WINGS UP
DAN JURGENS Writer INAKI MIRANDA Art
NICK FILARDI Colors ANDWORLD DESIGN Letters
HOWARD PORTER & REX LOKUS Cover
BEN MEARES Assistant Editor JESSICA CHEN Editor
BEN ABERNATHY Group Editor
NIGHTWING created by MARV WOLFMAN & GEORGE PÉREZ.

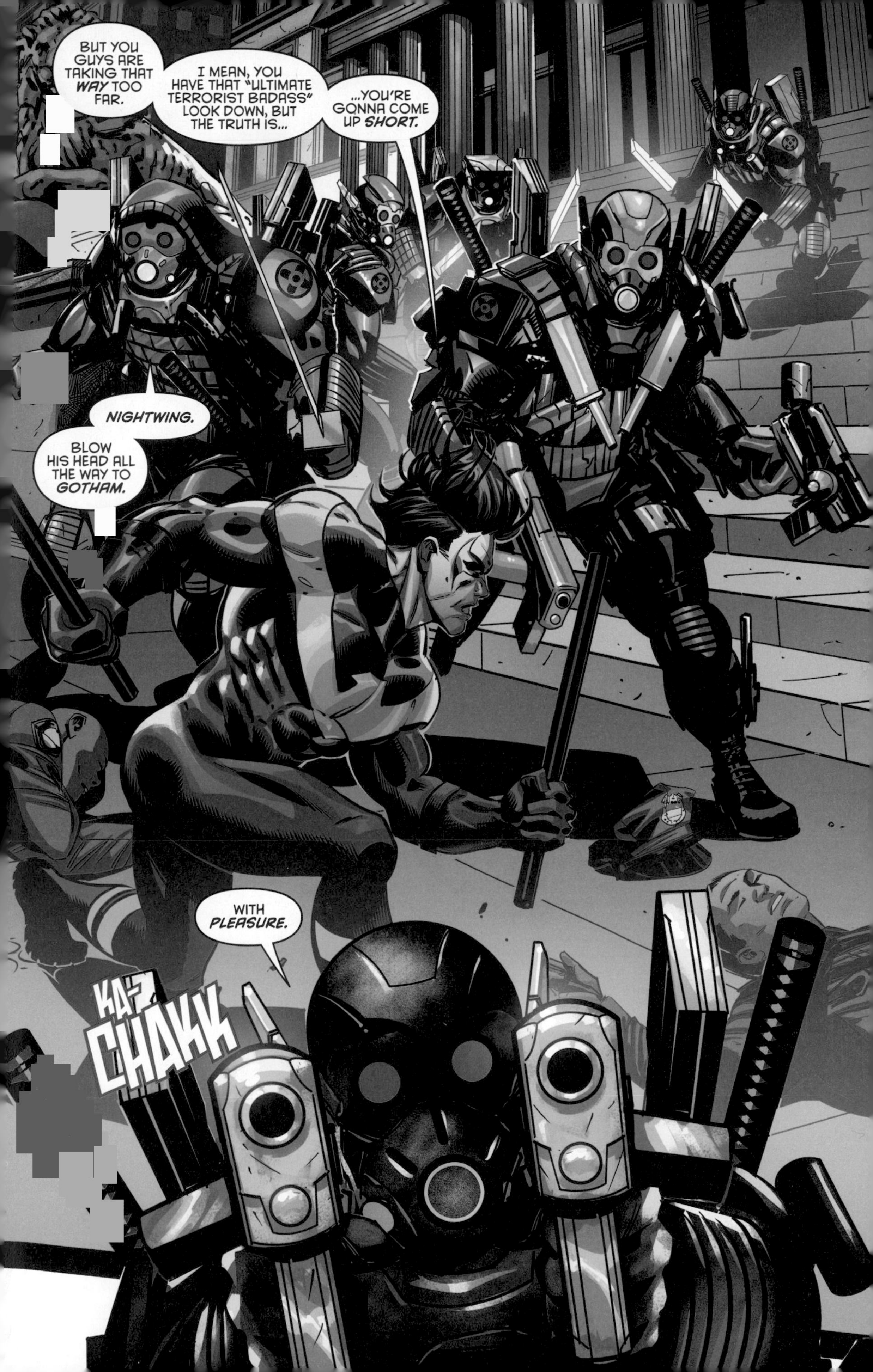
BUT YOU GUYS ARE TAKING THAT WAY TOO FAR.
I MEAN, YOU HAVE THAT "ULTIMATE TERRORIST BADASS" LOOK DOWN, BUT THE TRUTH IS...
...YOU'RE GONNA COME UP SHORT.
NIGHTWING.
BLOW HIS HEAD ALL THE WAY TO GOTHAM.
WITH PLEASURE.
KA-CHAKK

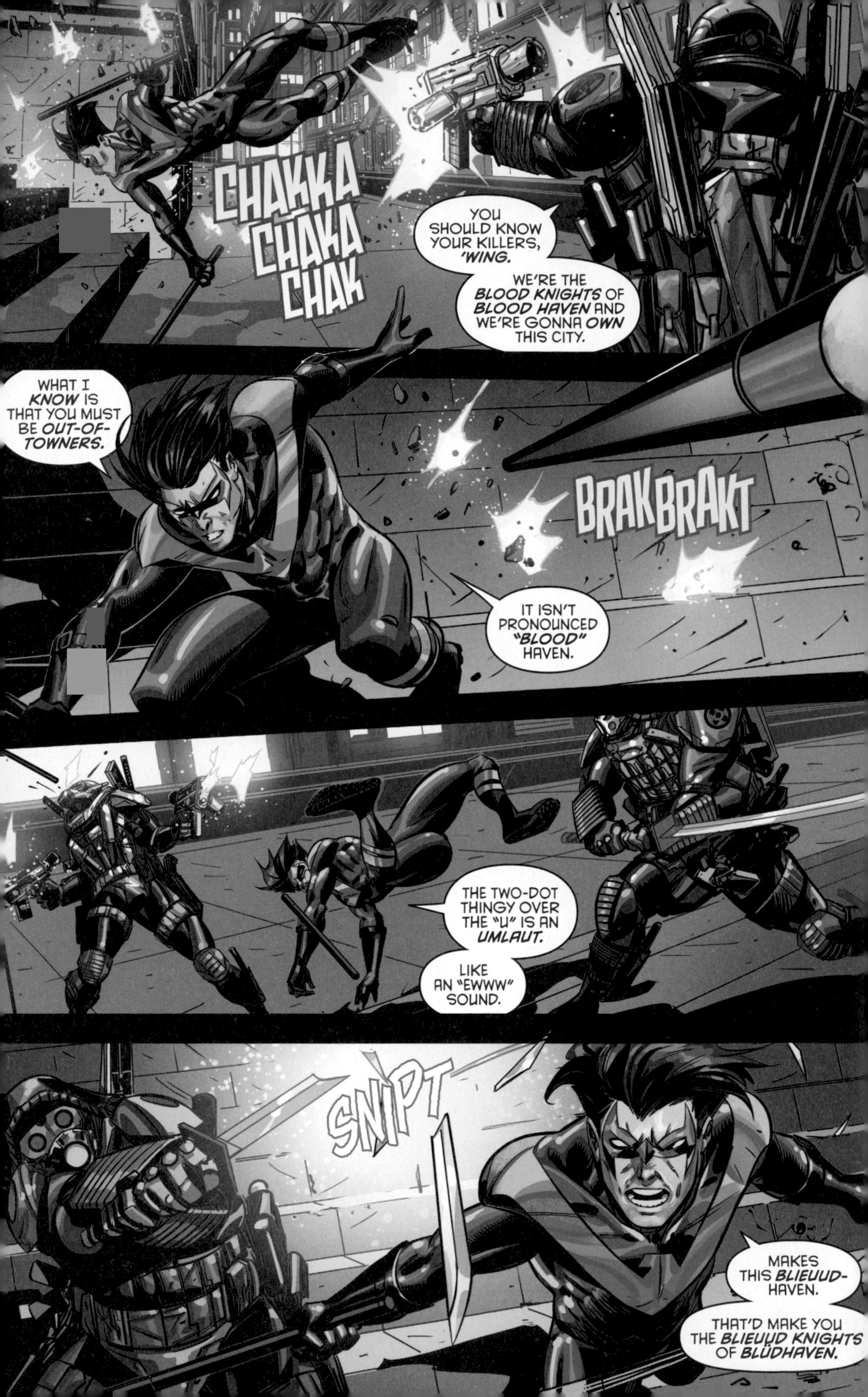
CHAKKA CHAKA CHAK
YOU SHOULD KNOW YOUR KILLERS, 'WING.
WE'RE THE BLOOD KNIGHTS OF BLOOD HAVEN AND WE'RE GONNA OWN THIS CITY.
WHAT I KNOW IS THAT YOU MUST BE OUT-OF-TOWNERS.
BRAKBRAKT
IT ISN'T PRONOUNCED "BLOOD" HAVEN.
THE TWO-DOT THINGY OVER THE "U" IS AN UMLAUT.
LIKE AN "EWWW" SOUND.
SNIPT
MAKES THIS BLIEUUD-HAVEN.
THAT'D MAKE YOU THE BLIEUUD KNIGHTS OF BLÜDHAVEN.

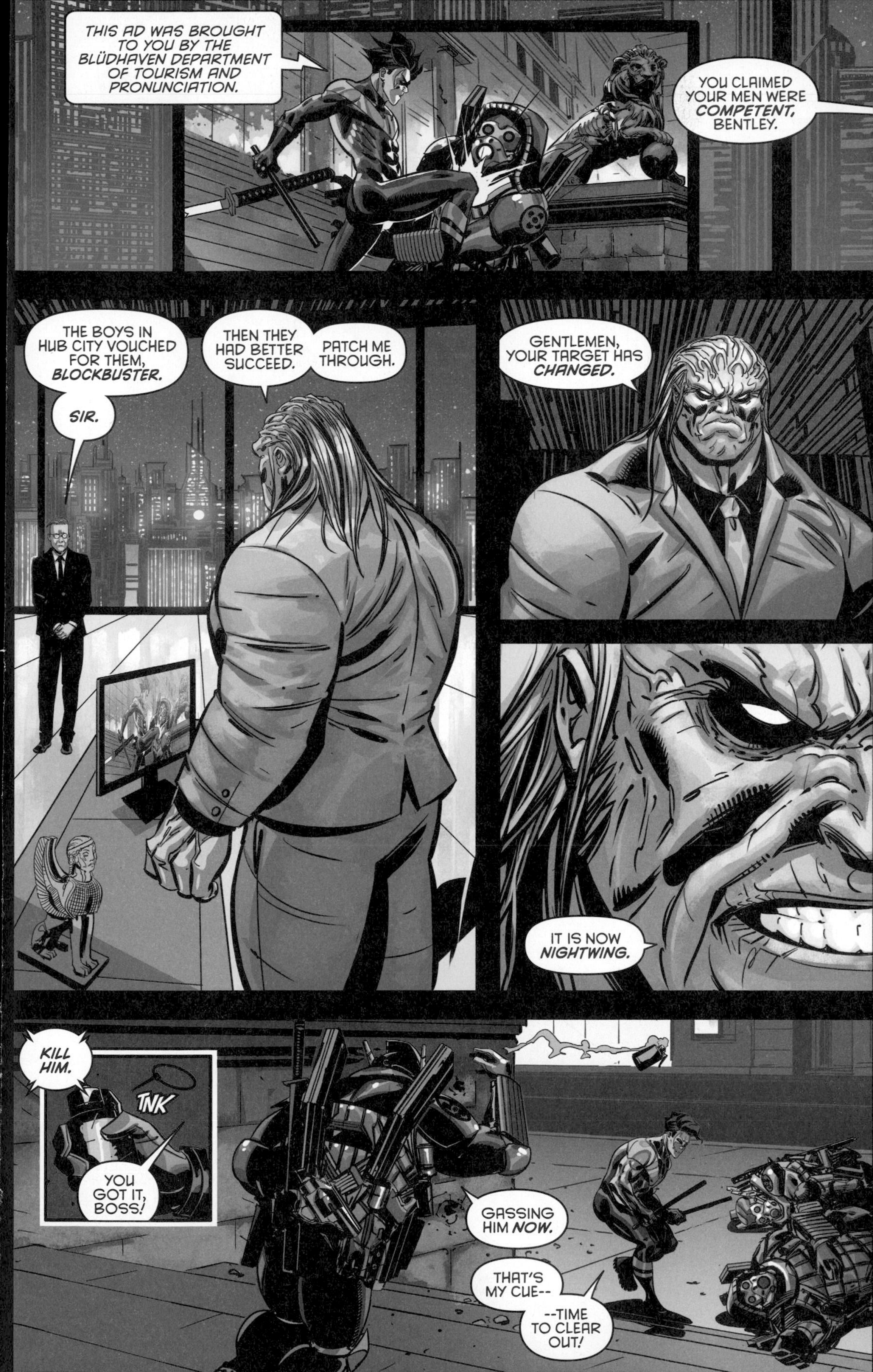
THIS AD WAS BROUGHT TO YOU BY THE BLÜDHAVEN DEPARTMENT OF TOURISM AND PRONUNCIATION.
YOU CLAIMED YOUR MEN WERE COMPETENT, BENTLEY.
THE BOYS IN HUB CITY VOUCHED FOR THEM, BLOCKBUSTER.
SIR.
THEN THEY HAD BETTER SUCCEED.
PATCH ME THROUGH.
GENTLEMEN, YOUR TARGET HAS CHANGED.
IT IS NOW NIGHTWING.
KILL HIM.
TNK
YOU GOT IT, BOSS!
GASSING HIM NOW.
THAT'S MY CUE--
--TIME TO CLEAR OUT!

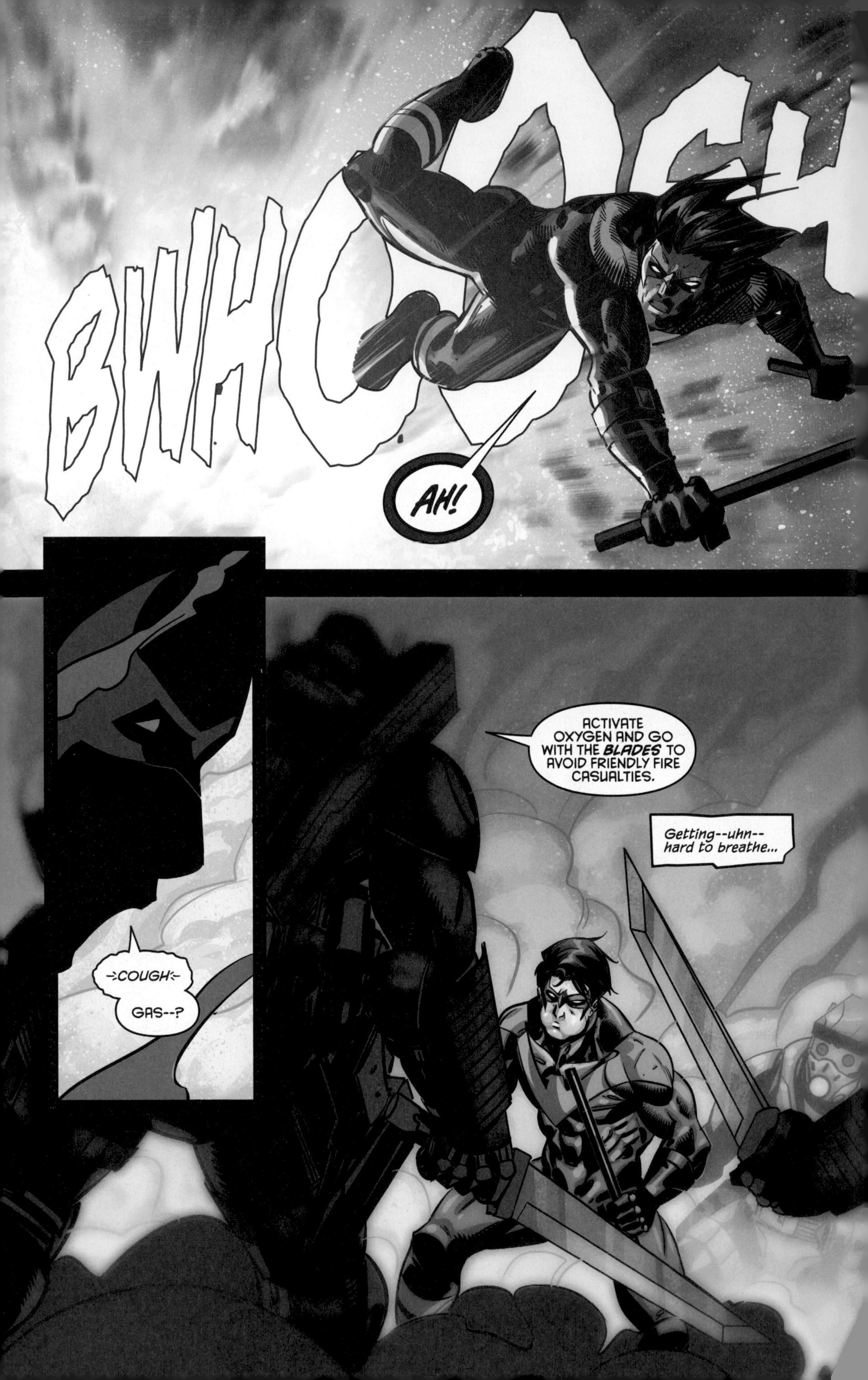
BWHOOOSH
AH!
ACTIVATE OXYGEN AND GO WITH THE *BLADES* TO AVOID FRIENDLY FIRE CASUALTIES.
Getting--uhn--hard to breathe...
COUGH
GAS--?

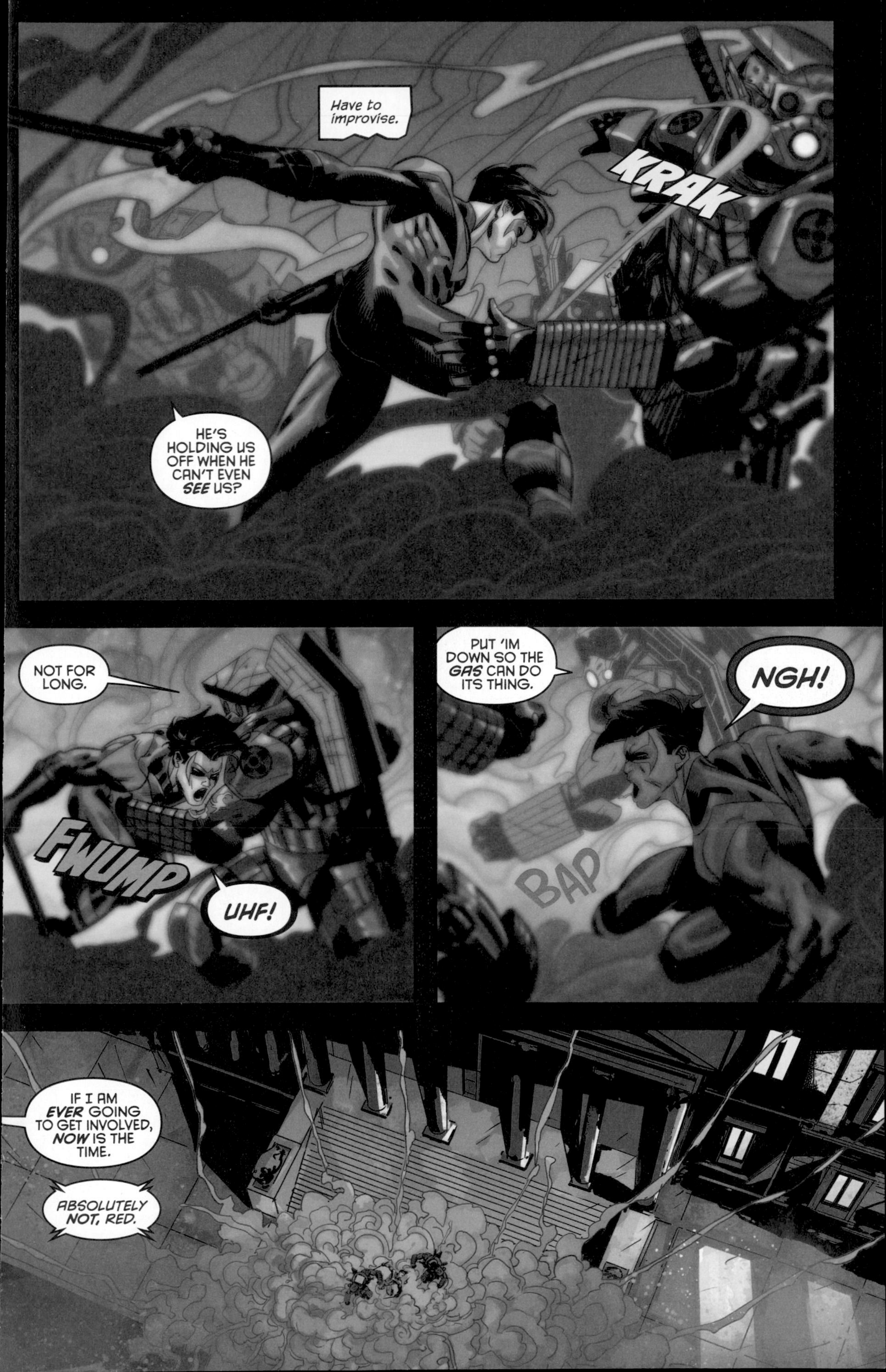
Have to improvise.
KRAK
HE'S HOLDING US OFF WHEN HE CAN'T EVEN SEE US?
NOT FOR LONG.
FWUMP
UHF!
PUT 'IM DOWN SO THE GAS CAN DO ITS THING.
NGH!
BAP
IF I AM EVER GOING TO GET INVOLVED, NOW IS THE TIME.
ABSOLUTELY NOT, RED.

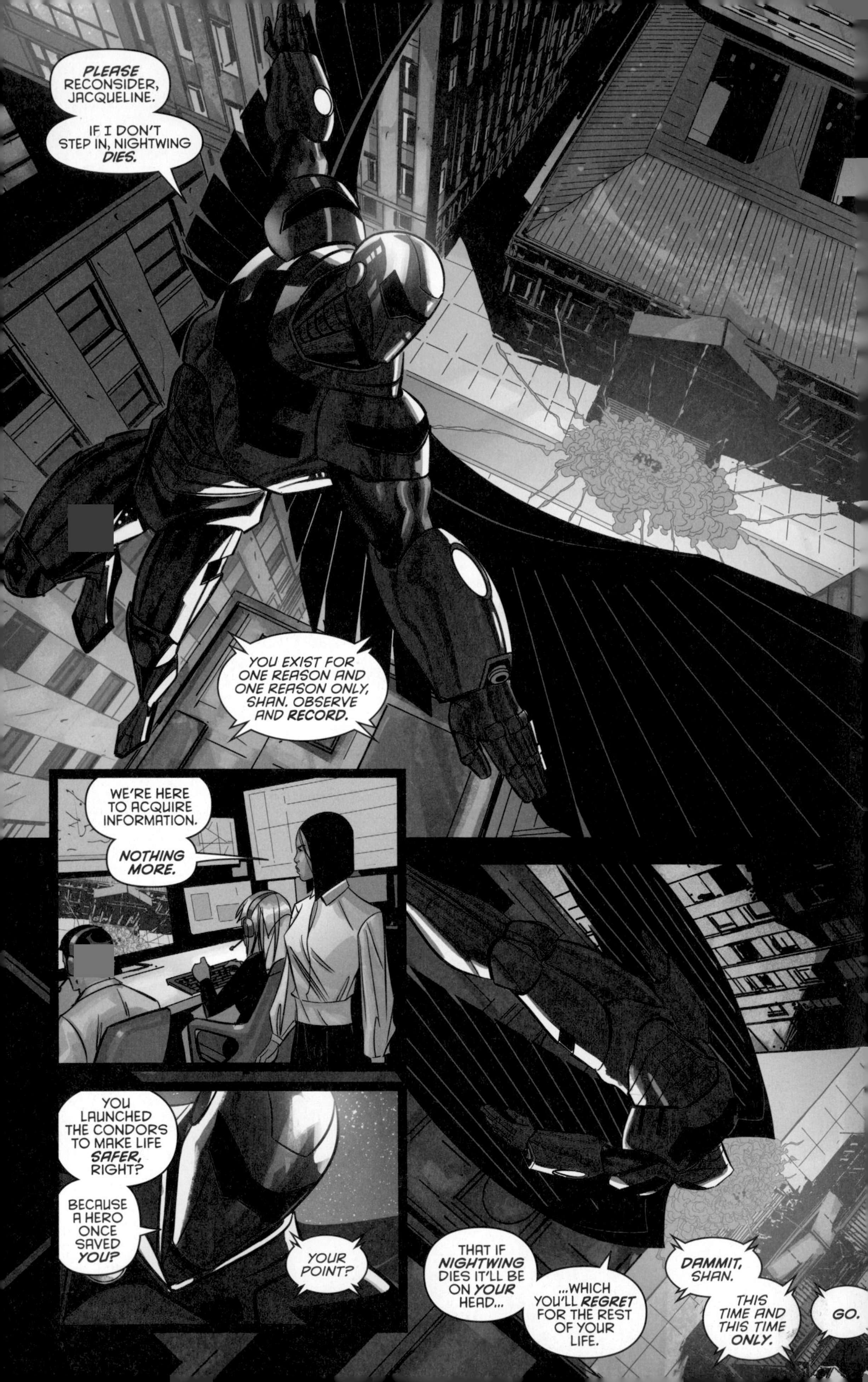
PLEASE RECONSIDER, JACQUELINE.
IF I DON'T STEP IN, NIGHTWING DIES.
YOU EXIST FOR ONE REASON AND ONE REASON ONLY, SHAN. OBSERVE AND RECORD.
WE'RE HERE TO ACQUIRE INFORMATION.
NOTHING MORE.
YOU LAUNCHED THE CONDORS TO MAKE LIFE SAFER, RIGHT?
BECAUSE A HERO ONCE SAVED YOU?
YOUR POINT?
THAT IF NIGHTWING DIES IT'LL BE ON YOUR HEAD...
...WHICH YOU'LL REGRET FOR THE REST OF YOUR LIFE.
DAMMIT, SHAN.
THIS TIME AND THIS TIME ONLY.
GO.

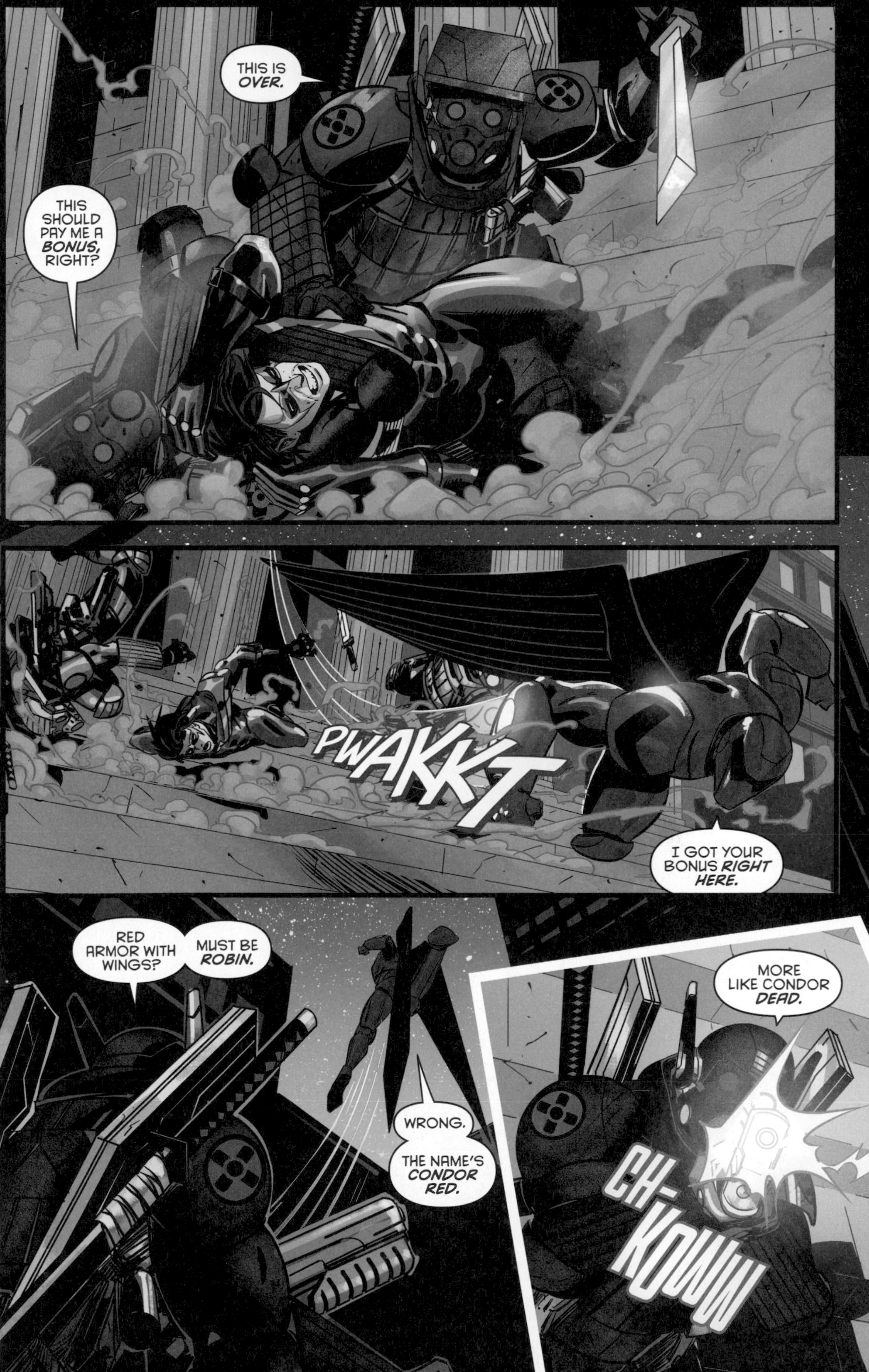
THIS IS *OVER.*
THIS SHOULD PAY ME A *BONUS,* RIGHT?
PWAKKT
I GOT YOUR BONUS *RIGHT HERE.*
RED ARMOR WITH WINGS?
MUST BE *ROBIN.*
WRONG.
THE NAME'S *CONDOR RED.*
MORE LIKE CONDOR *DEAD.*
CH-KOWW

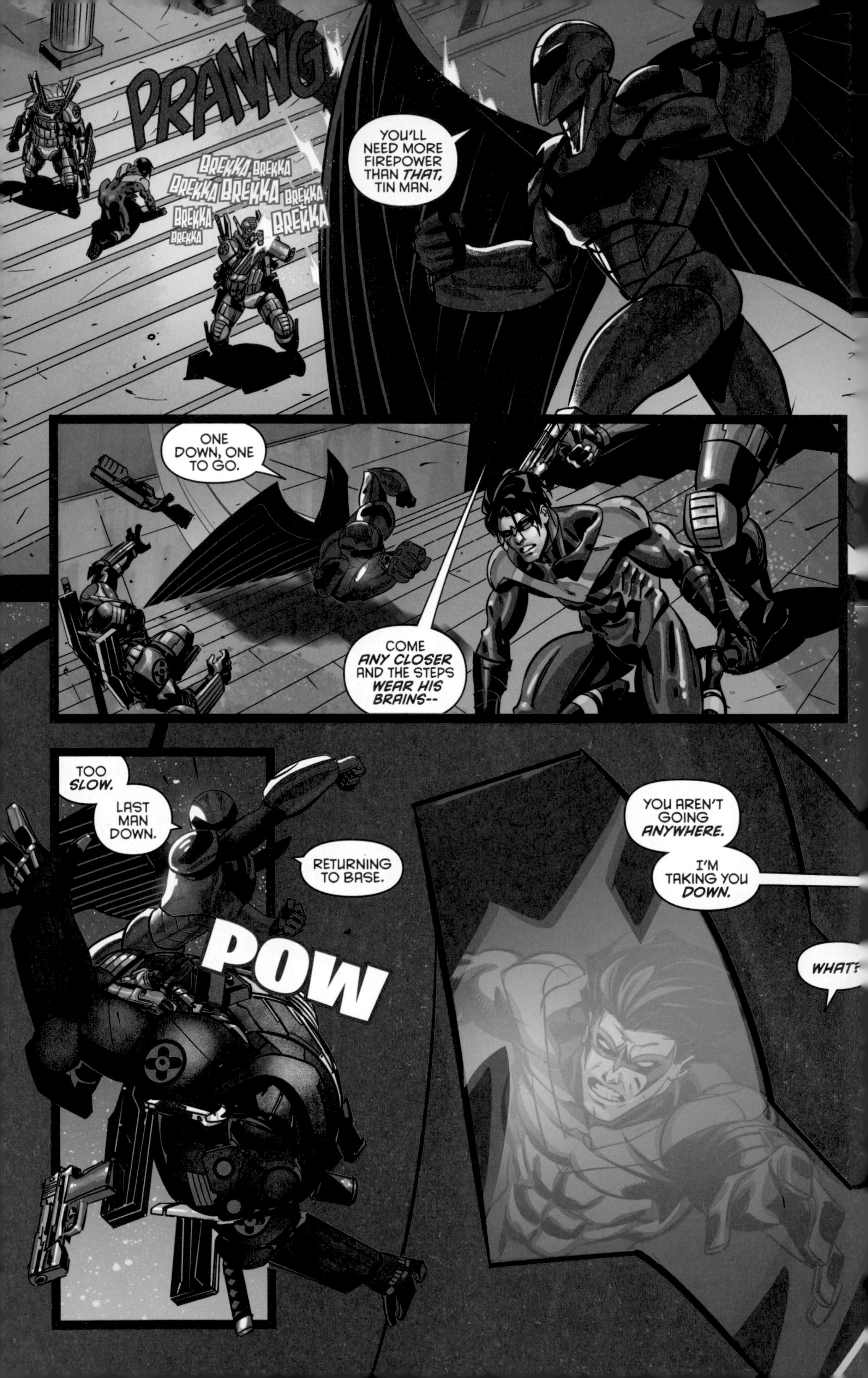
PRANNG
BREKKA BREKKA
BREKKA BREKKA BREKKA
BREKKA
BREKKA BREKKA
YOU'LL NEED MORE FIREPOWER THAN *THAT,* TIN MAN.
ONE DOWN, ONE TO GO.
COME *ANY CLOSER* AND THE STEPS *WEAR HIS BRAINS--*
TOO *SLOW.*
LAST MAN DOWN.
RETURNING TO BASE.
POW
YOU AREN'T GOING *ANYWHERE.*
I'M TAKING YOU *DOWN.*
WHAT?

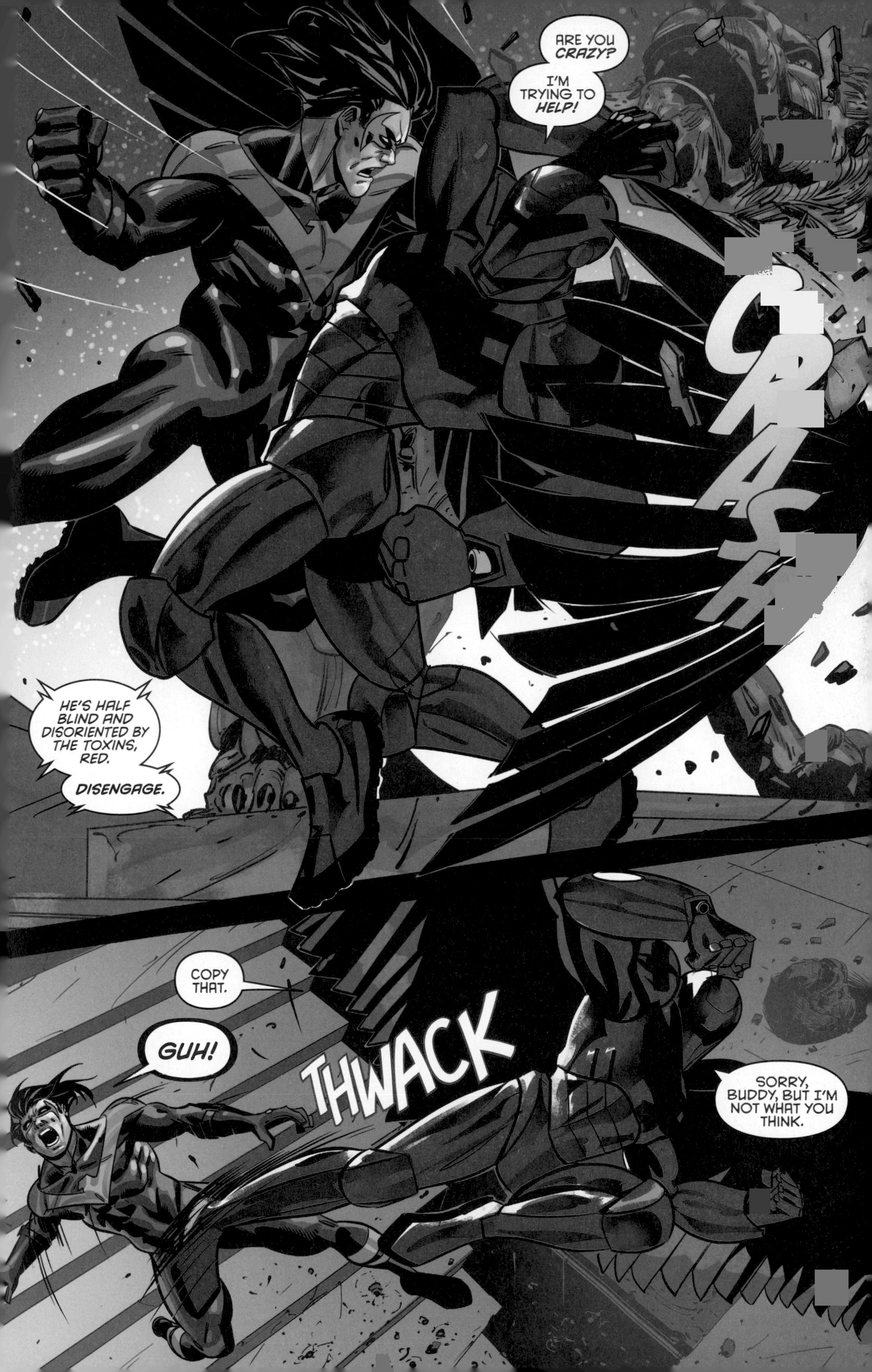
ARE YOU CRAZY?
I'M TRYING TO HELP!
CRASH
HE'S HALF BLIND AND DISORIENTED BY THE TOXINS, RED.
DISENGAGE.
COPY THAT.
GUH!
THWACK
SORRY, BUDDY, BUT I'M NOT WHAT YOU THINK.

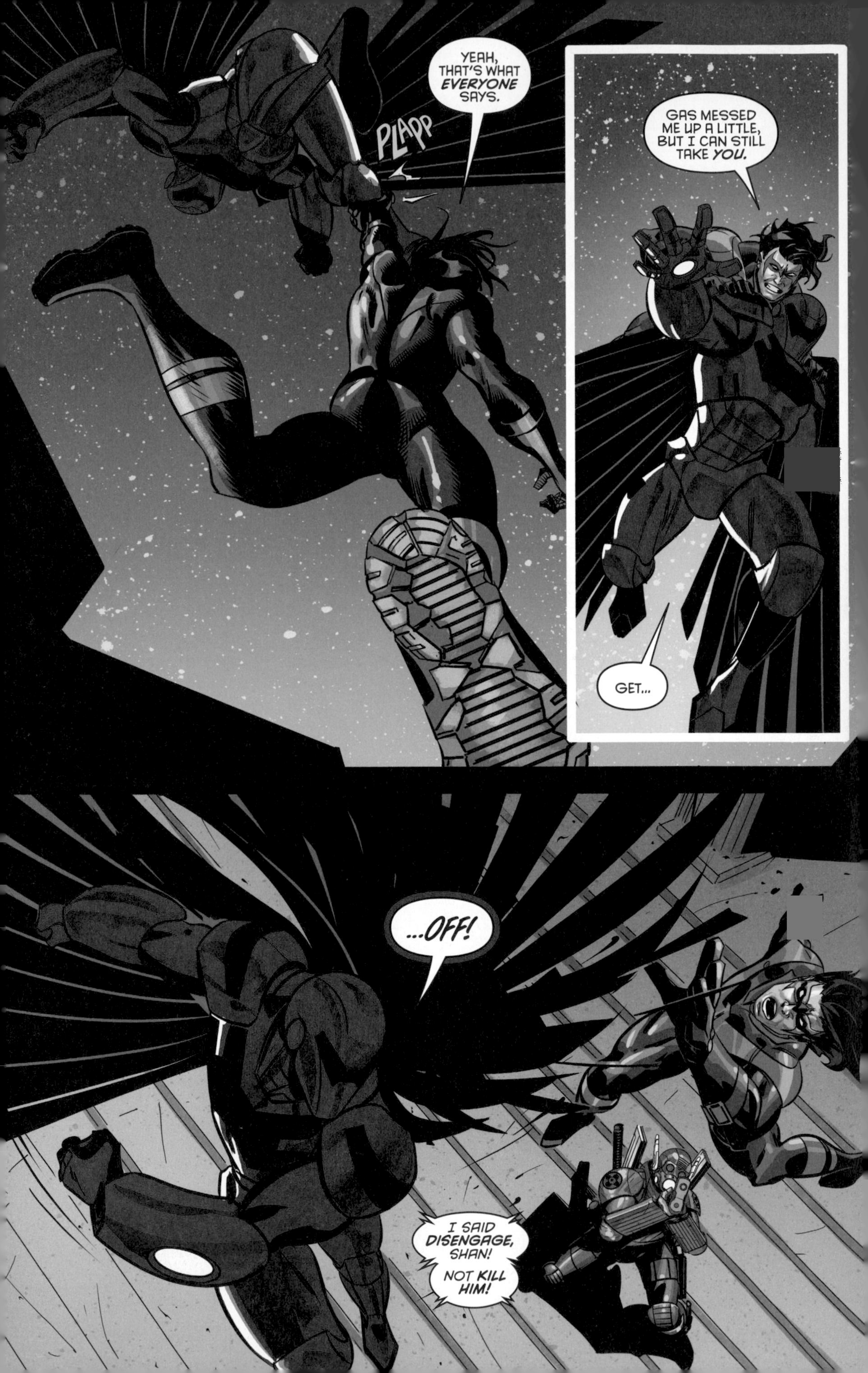

YEAH, THAT'S WHAT EVERYONE SAYS.
PLAPP
GAS MESSED ME UP A LITTLE, BUT I CAN STILL TAKE YOU.
GET...
...OFF!
I SAID DISENGAGE, SHAN!
NOT KILL HIM!

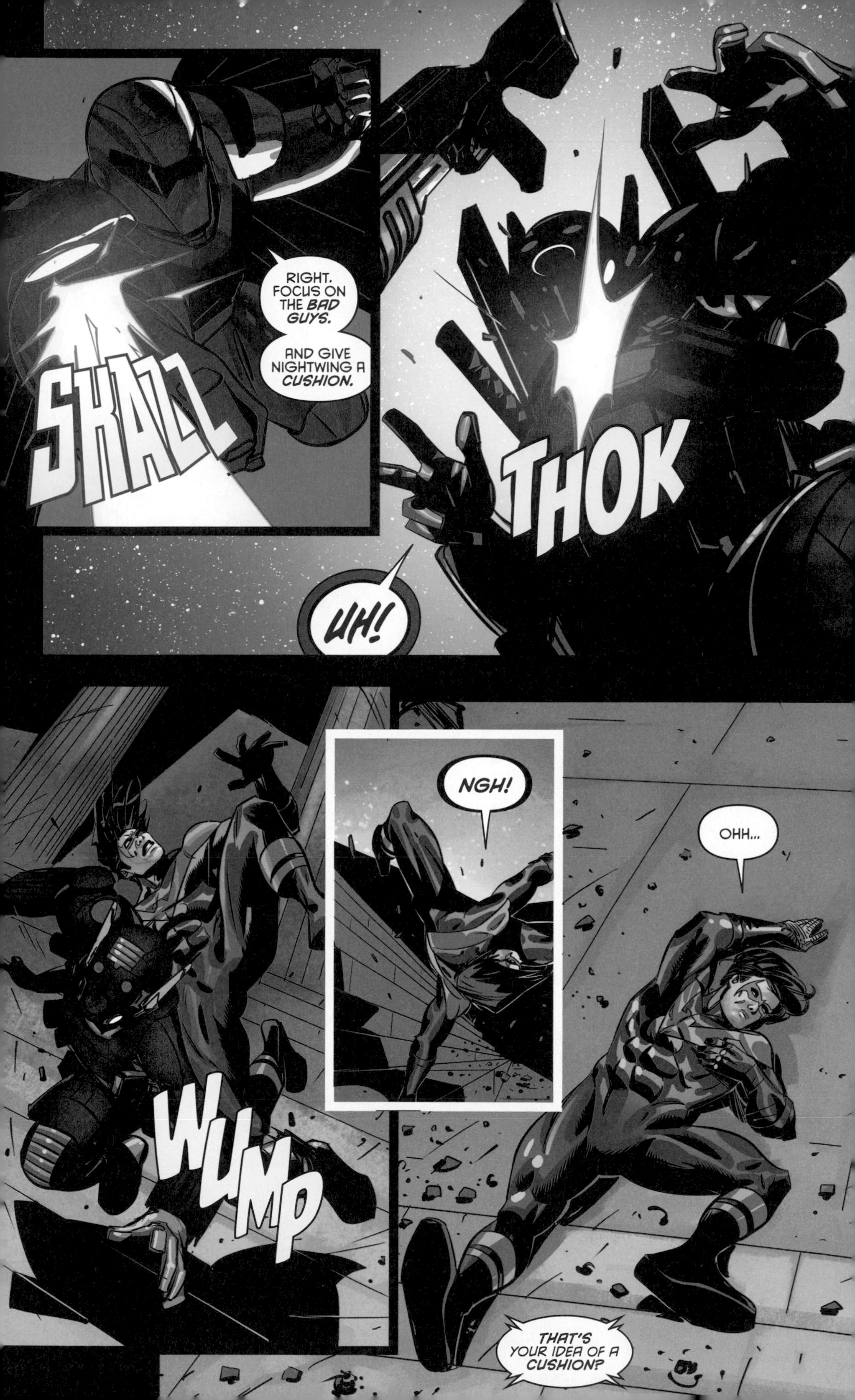
RIGHT. FOCUS ON THE BAD GUYS.
AND GIVE NIGHTWING A CUSHION.
SHAZZ
THOK
UH!
WUMP
NGH!
OHH...
THAT'S YOUR IDEA OF A CUSHION?

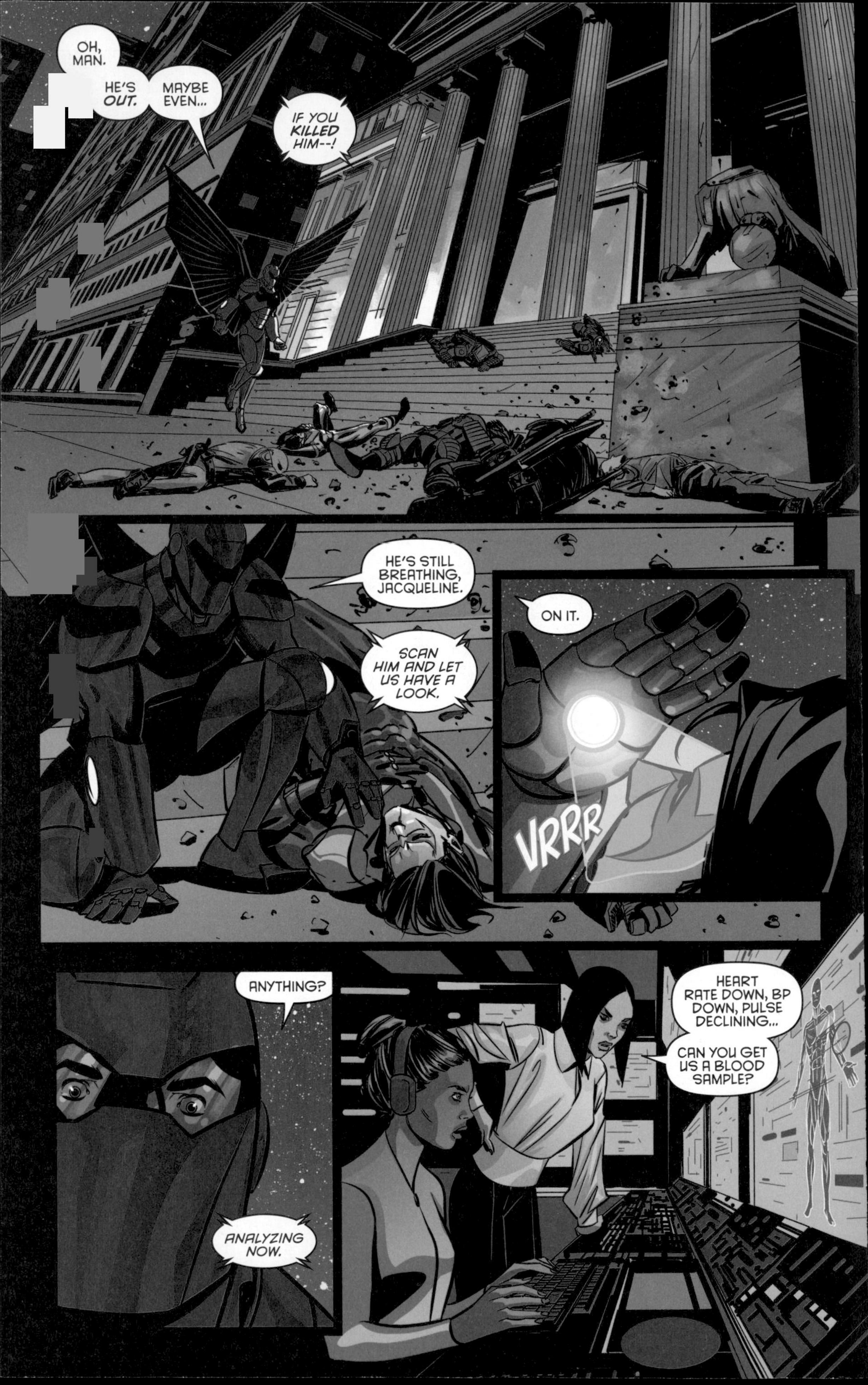
OH, MAN.
HE'S *OUT.*
MAYBE EVEN...
IF YOU ***KILLED*** HIM--!
HE'S STILL BREATHING, JACQUELINE.
SCAN HIM AND LET US HAVE A LOOK.
ON IT.
VRRR
ANYTHING?
HEART RATE DOWN, BP DOWN, PULSE DECLINING...
CAN YOU GET US A BLOOD SAMPLE?
ANALYZING NOW.

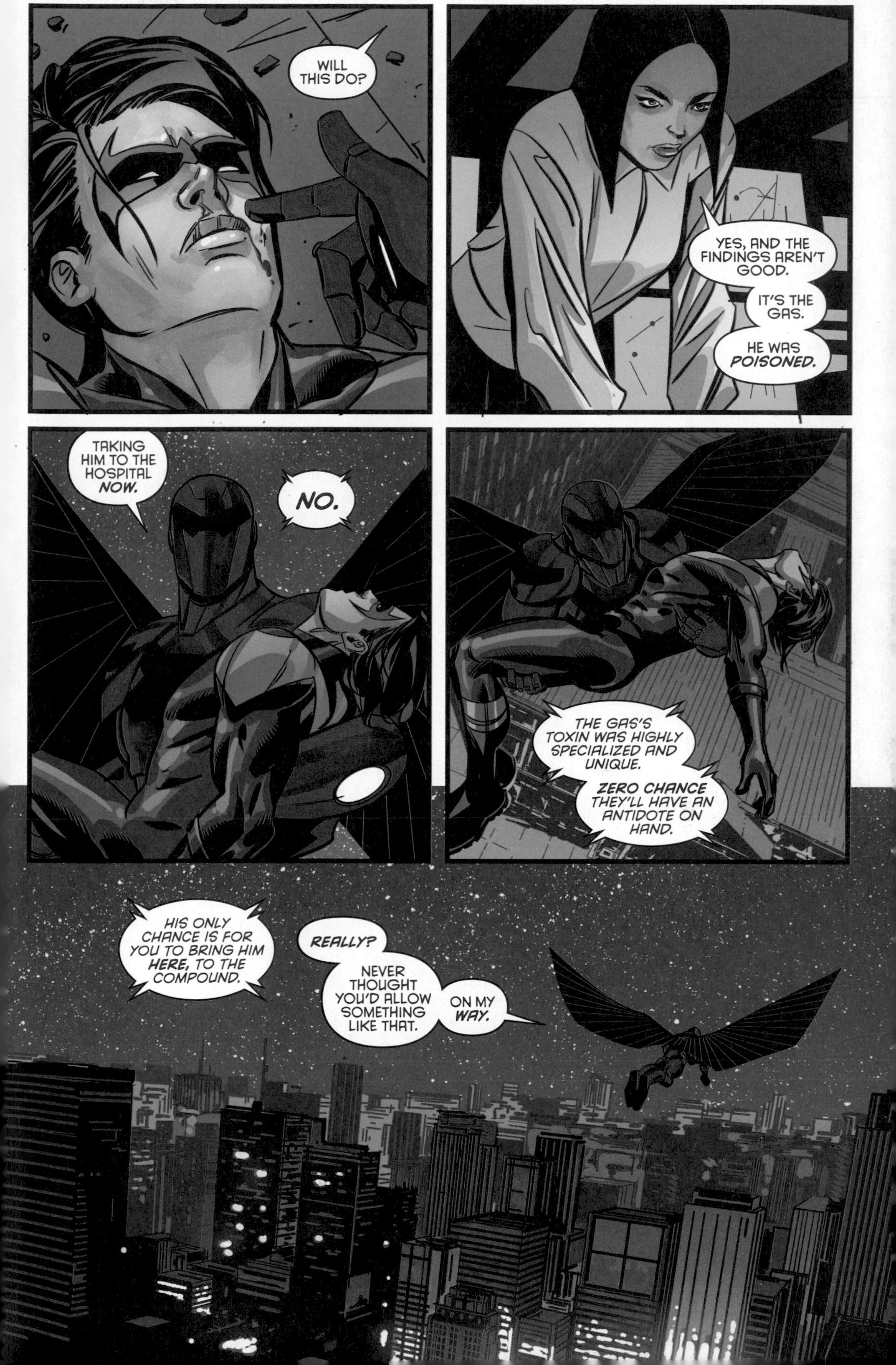
WILL THIS DO?
YES, AND THE FINDINGS AREN'T GOOD.
IT'S THE GAS.
HE WAS POISONED.
TAKING HIM TO THE HOSPITAL NOW.
NO.
THE GAS'S TOXIN WAS HIGHLY SPECIALIZED AND UNIQUE.
ZERO CHANCE THEY'LL HAVE AN ANTIDOTE ON HAND.
HIS ONLY CHANCE IS FOR YOU TO BRING HIM HERE, TO THE COMPOUND.
REALLY?
NEVER THOUGHT YOU'D ALLOW SOMETHING LIKE THAT.
ON MY WAY.

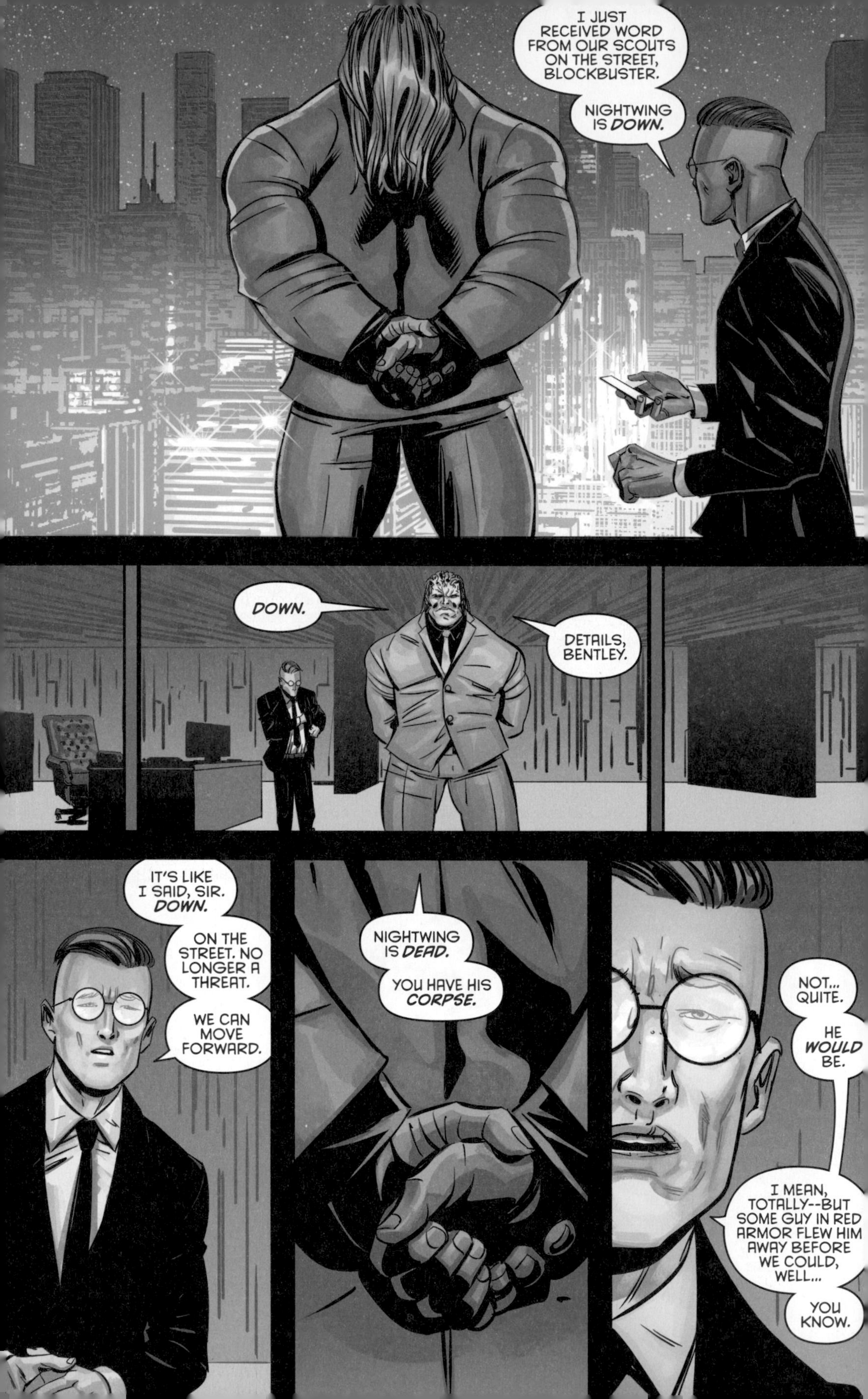
I JUST RECEIVED WORD FROM OUR SCOUTS ON THE STREET, BLOCKBUSTER.
NIGHTWING IS *DOWN.*
DOWN.
DETAILS, BENTLEY.
IT'S LIKE I SAID, SIR. *DOWN.*
ON THE STREET. NO LONGER A THREAT.
WE CAN MOVE FORWARD.
NIGHTWING IS *DEAD.*
YOU HAVE HIS *CORPSE.*
NOT... QUITE.
HE *WOULD* BE.
I MEAN, TOTALLY--BUT SOME GUY IN RED ARMOR FLEW HIM AWAY BEFORE WE COULD, WELL...
YOU KNOW.

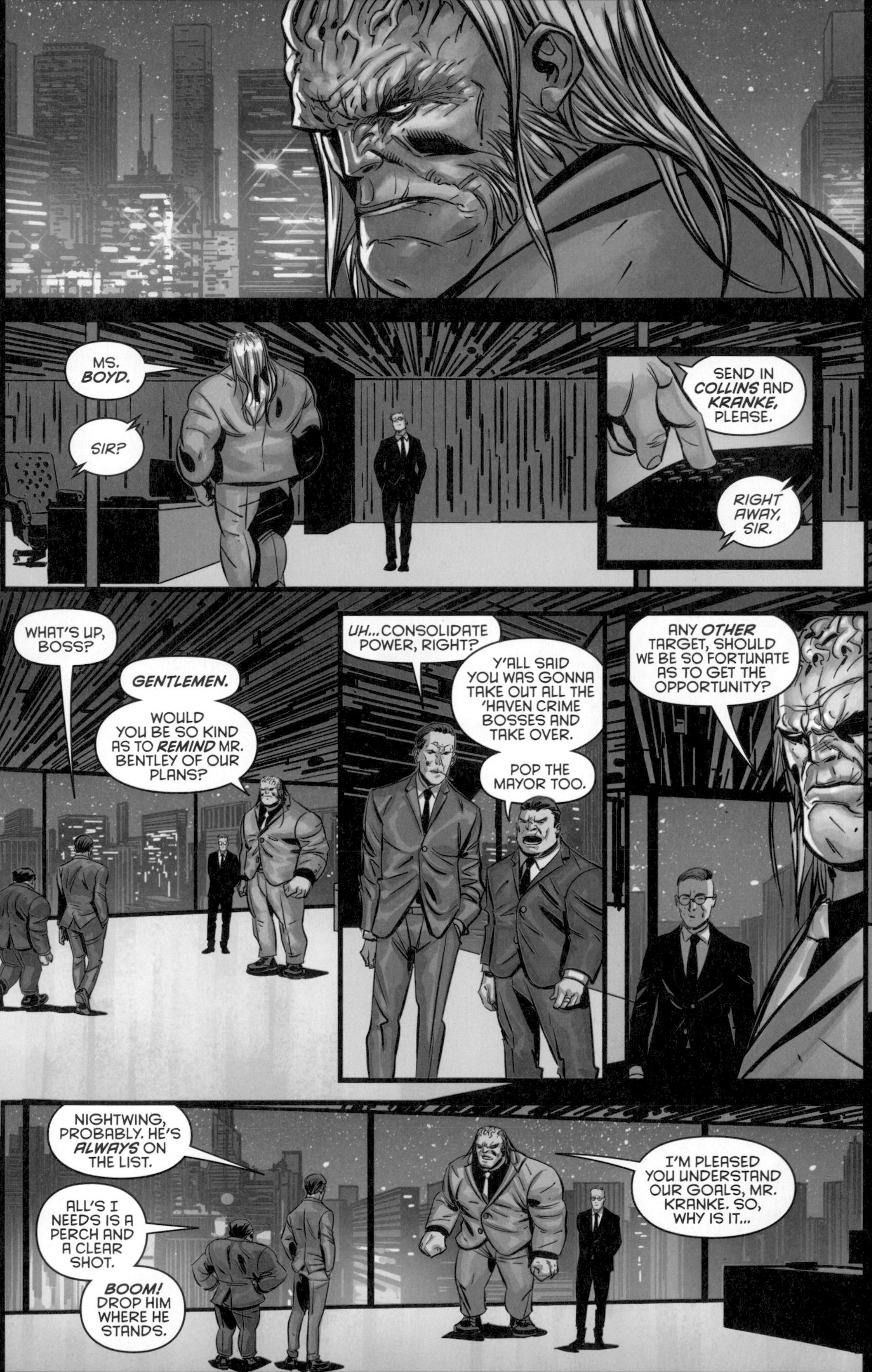

MS. *BOYD.*
SIR?
SEND IN *COLLINS* AND *KRANKE,* PLEASE.
RIGHT AWAY, SIR.
WHAT'S UP, BOSS?
GENTLEMEN.
WOULD YOU BE SO KIND AS TO *REMIND* MR. BENTLEY OF OUR PLANS?
UH... CONSOLIDATE POWER, RIGHT?
Y'ALL SAID YOU WAS GONNA TAKE OUT ALL THE 'HAVEN CRIME BOSSES AND TAKE OVER.
POP THE MAYOR TOO.
ANY *OTHER* TARGET, SHOULD WE BE SO FORTUNATE AS TO GET THE OPPORTUNITY?
NIGHTWING, PROBABLY. HE'S *ALWAYS* ON THE LIST.
ALL'S I NEEDS IS A PERCH AND A CLEAR SHOT.
BOOM! DROP HIM WHERE HE STANDS.
I'M PLEASED YOU UNDERSTAND OUR GOALS, MR. KRANKE. SO, WHY IS IT...

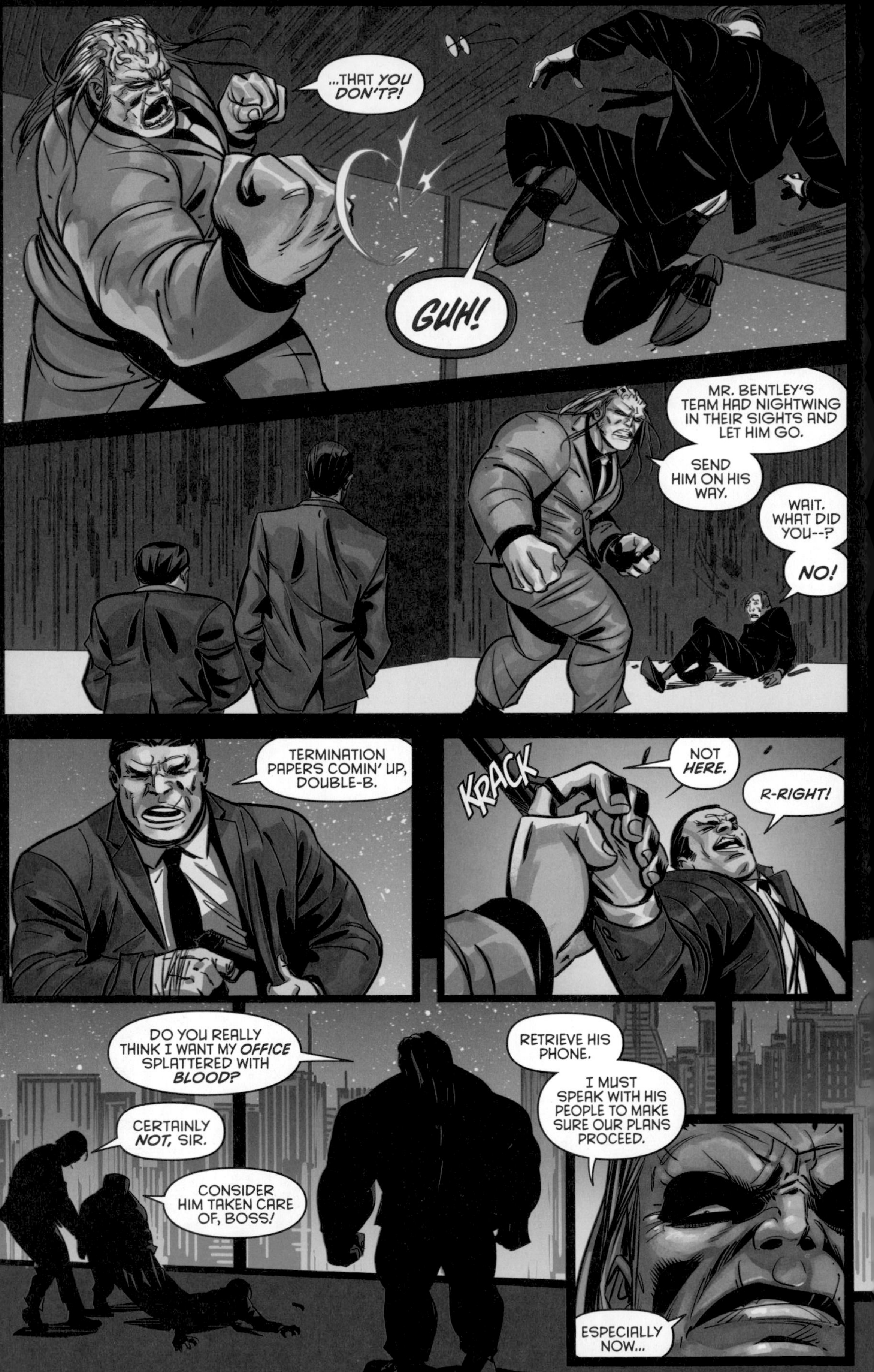
...THAT *YOU* *DON'T*?!
GUH!
MR. BENTLEY'S TEAM HAD NIGHTWING IN THEIR SIGHTS AND LET HIM GO.
SEND HIM ON HIS WAY.
WAIT. WHAT DID YOU--?
NO!
TERMINATION PAPERS COMIN' UP, DOUBLE-B.
KRACK
NOT *HERE.*
R-RIGHT!
DO YOU REALLY THINK I WANT MY *OFFICE* SPLATTERED WITH ***BLOOD?***
CERTAINLY *NOT,* SIR.
CONSIDER HIM TAKEN CARE OF, BOSS!
RETRIEVE HIS PHONE.
I MUST SPEAK WITH HIS PEOPLE TO MAKE SURE OUR PLANS PROCEED.
ESPECIALLY NOW...

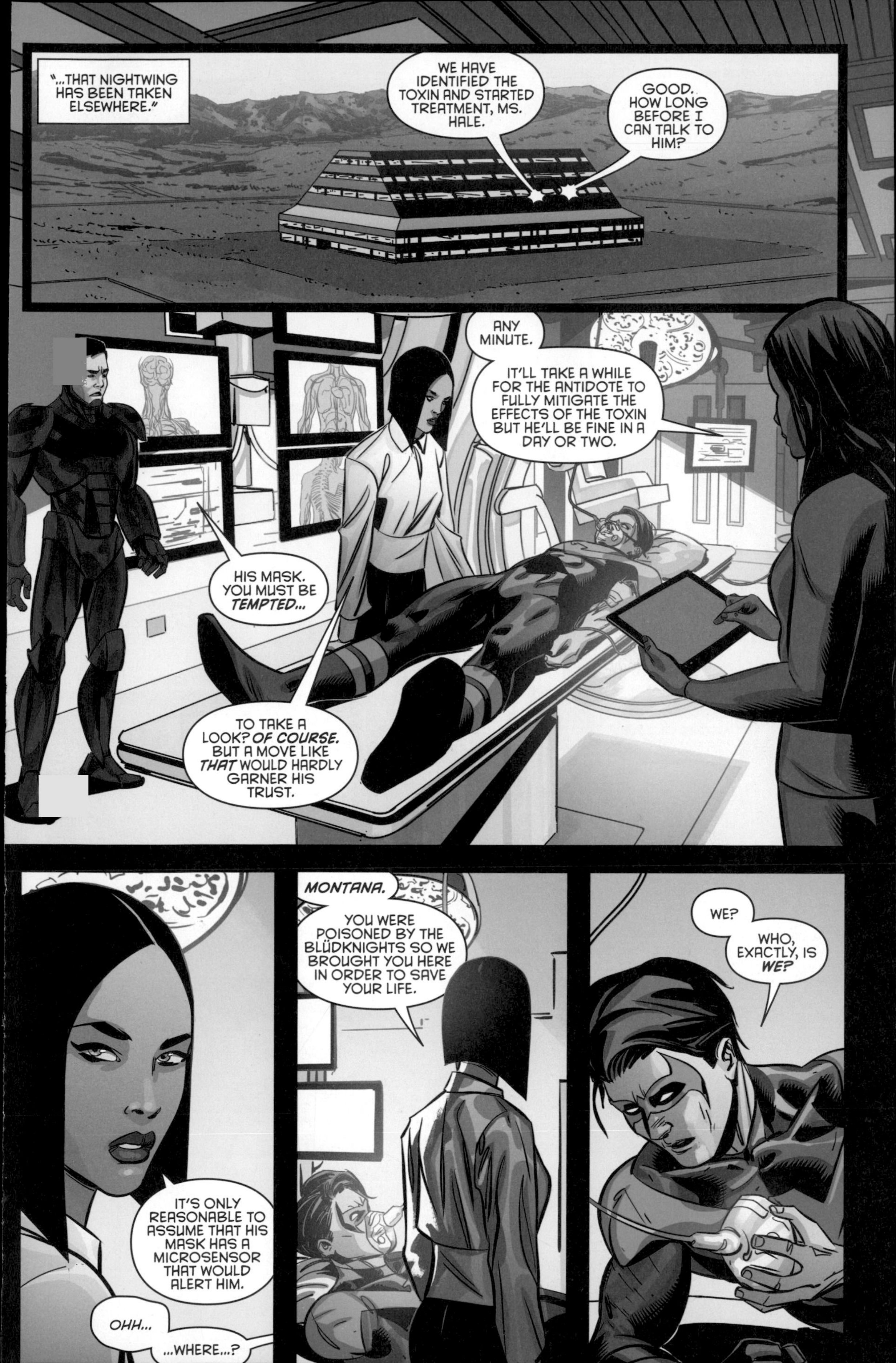
"...THAT NIGHTWING HAS BEEN TAKEN ELSEWHERE."
WE HAVE IDENTIFIED THE TOXIN AND STARTED TREATMENT, MS. HALE.
GOOD. HOW LONG BEFORE I CAN TALK TO HIM?
ANY MINUTE.
IT'LL TAKE A WHILE FOR THE ANTIDOTE TO FULLY MITIGATE THE EFFECTS OF THE TOXIN BUT HE'LL BE FINE IN A DAY OR TWO.
HIS MASK. YOU MUST BE TEMPTED...
TO TAKE A LOOK? OF COURSE. BUT A MOVE LIKE THAT WOULD HARDLY GARNER HIS TRUST.
IT'S ONLY REASONABLE TO ASSUME THAT HIS MASK HAS A MICROSENSOR THAT WOULD ALERT HIM.
OHH...
...WHERE...?
MONTANA.
YOU WERE POISONED BY THE BLÜDKNIGHTS SO WE BROUGHT YOU HERE IN ORDER TO SAVE YOUR LIFE.
WE?
WHO, EXACTLY, IS WE?

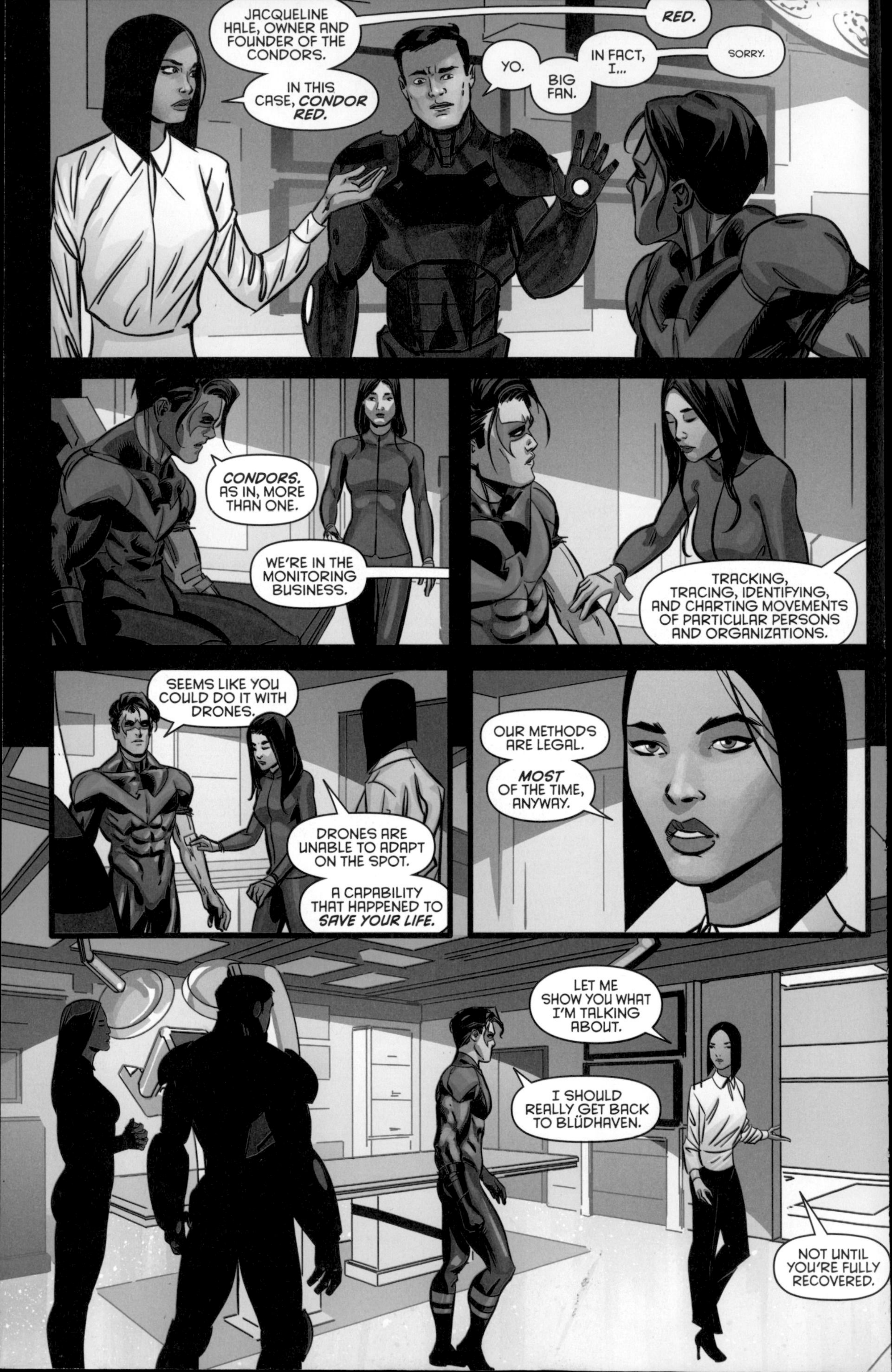
JACQUELINE HALE, OWNER AND FOUNDER OF THE CONDORS.
IN THIS CASE, CONDOR RED.
RED.
YO.
BIG FAN.
IN FACT, I...
SORRY.
CONDORS. AS IN, MORE THAN ONE.
WE'RE IN THE MONITORING BUSINESS.
TRACKING, TRACING, IDENTIFYING, AND CHARTING MOVEMENTS OF PARTICULAR PERSONS AND ORGANIZATIONS.
SEEMS LIKE YOU COULD DO IT WITH DRONES.
DRONES ARE UNABLE TO ADAPT ON THE SPOT.
A CAPABILITY THAT HAPPENED TO SAVE YOUR LIFE.
OUR METHODS ARE LEGAL.
MOST OF THE TIME, ANYWAY.
LET ME SHOW YOU WHAT I'M TALKING ABOUT.
I SHOULD REALLY GET BACK TO BLÜDHAVEN.
NOT UNTIL YOU'RE FULLY RECOVERED.

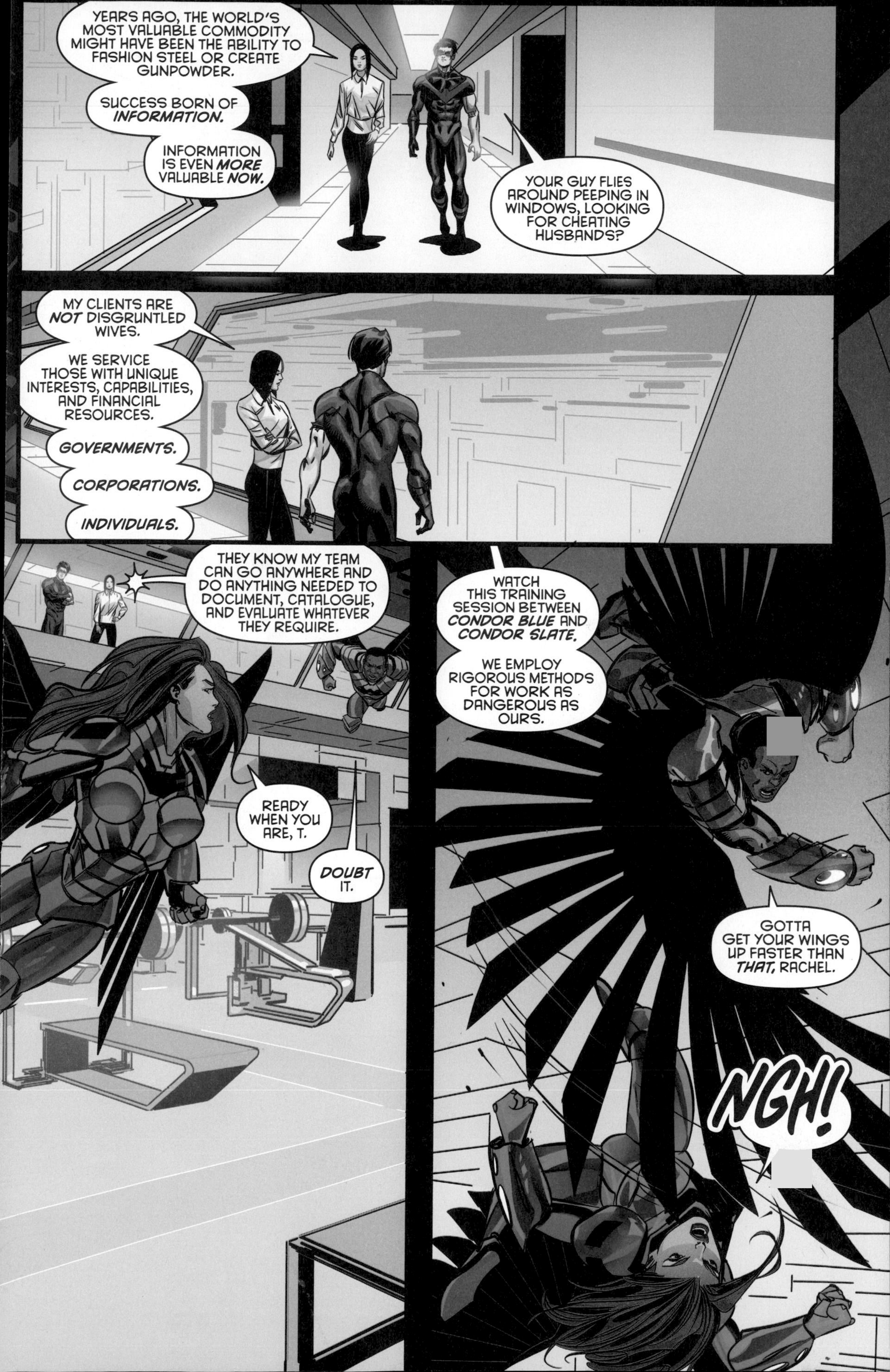
YEARS AGO, THE WORLD'S MOST VALUABLE COMMODITY MIGHT HAVE BEEN THE ABILITY TO FASHION STEEL OR CREATE GUNPOWDER.
SUCCESS BORN OF *INFORMATION.*
INFORMATION IS EVEN *MORE* VALUABLE *NOW.*
YOUR GUY FLIES AROUND PEEPING IN WINDOWS, LOOKING FOR CHEATING HUSBANDS?
MY CLIENTS ARE *NOT* DISGRUNTLED WIVES.
WE SERVICE THOSE WITH UNIQUE INTERESTS, CAPABILITIES, AND FINANCIAL RESOURCES.
GOVERNMENTS.
CORPORATIONS.
INDIVIDUALS.
THEY KNOW MY TEAM CAN GO ANYWHERE AND DO ANYTHING NEEDED TO DOCUMENT, CATALOGUE, AND EVALUATE WHATEVER THEY REQUIRE.
READY WHEN YOU ARE, T.
DOUBT IT.
WATCH THIS TRAINING SESSION BETWEEN *CONDOR BLUE* AND *CONDOR SLATE.*
WE EMPLOY RIGOROUS METHODS FOR WORK AS DANGEROUS AS OURS.
GOTTA GET YOUR WINGS UP FASTER THAN *THAT,* RACHEL.
NGH!

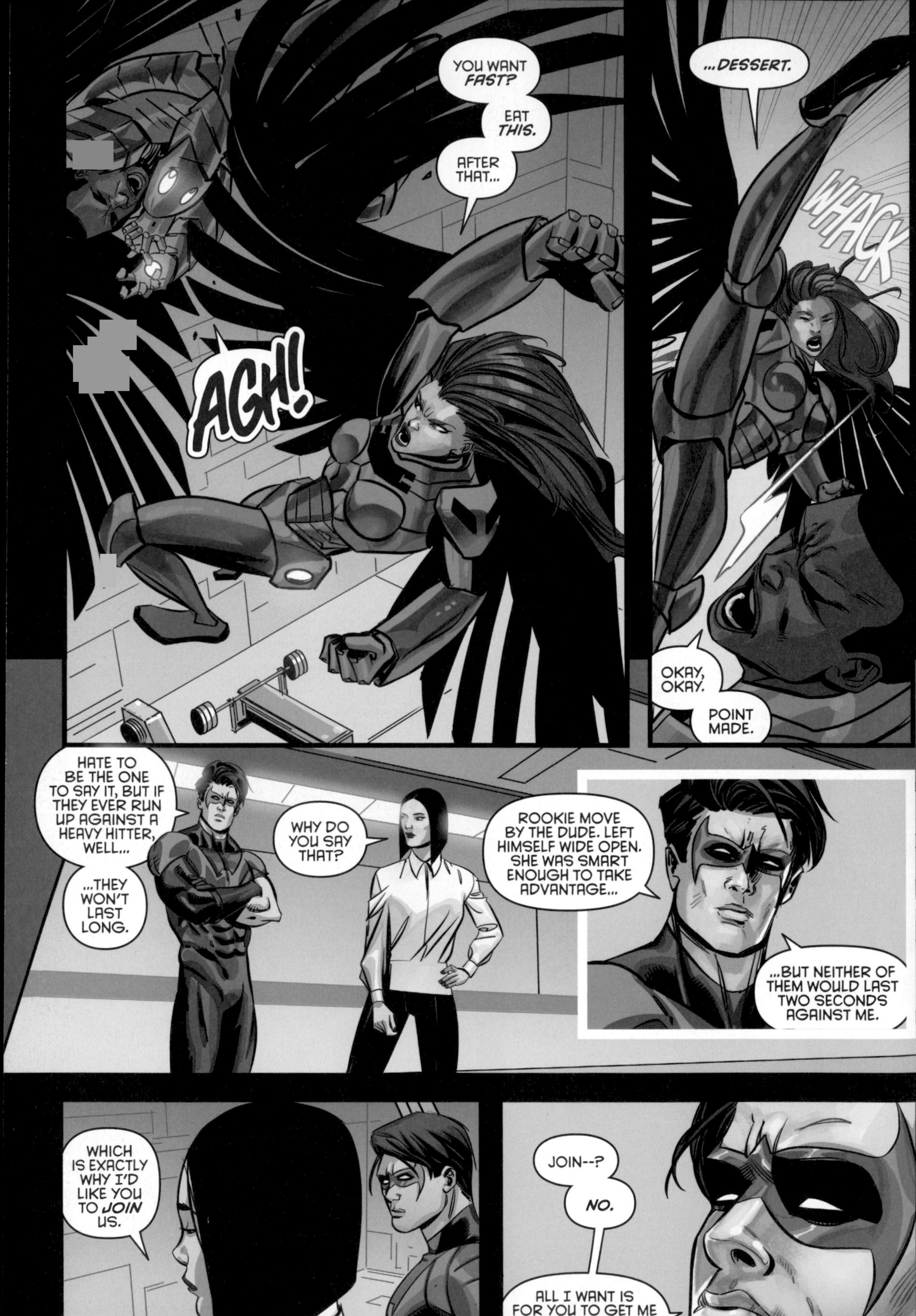
YOU WANT *FAST?*
EAT *THIS.*
AFTER THAT...
AGH!
...DESSERT.
WHACK
OKAY, OKAY.
POINT MADE.
HATE TO BE THE ONE TO SAY IT, BUT IF THEY EVER RUN UP AGAINST A HEAVY HITTER, WELL...
...THEY WON'T LAST LONG.
WHY DO YOU SAY THAT?
ROOKIE MOVE BY THE DUDE. LEFT HIMSELF WIDE OPEN. SHE WAS SMART ENOUGH TO TAKE ADVANTAGE...
...BUT NEITHER OF THEM WOULD LAST TWO SECONDS AGAINST ME.
WHICH IS EXACTLY WHY I'D LIKE YOU TO *JOIN* US.
JOIN--?
NO.
ALL I WANT IS FOR YOU TO GET ME BACK HOME SO I CAN TAKE CARE OF THE BLÜDKNIGHTS.

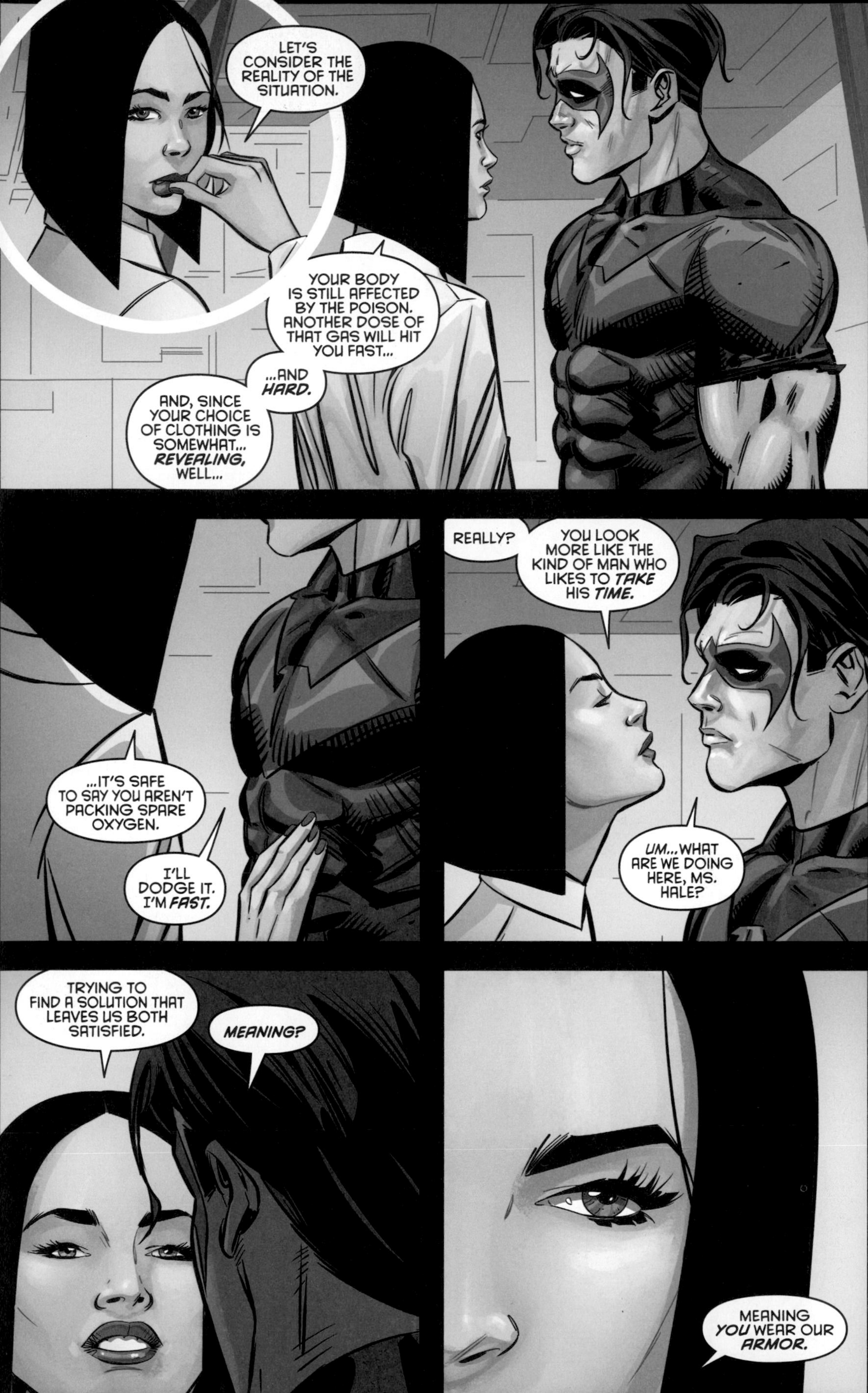
LET'S CONSIDER THE REALITY OF THE SITUATION.
YOUR BODY IS STILL AFFECTED BY THE POISON. ANOTHER DOSE OF THAT GAS WILL HIT YOU FAST...
...AND *HARD.*
AND, SINCE YOUR CHOICE OF CLOTHING IS SOMEWHAT... *REVEALING,* WELL...
...IT'S SAFE TO SAY YOU AREN'T PACKING SPARE OXYGEN.
I'LL DODGE IT. I'M *FAST.*
REALLY?
YOU LOOK MORE LIKE THE KIND OF MAN WHO LIKES TO *TAKE* HIS *TIME.*
*UM...*WHAT ARE WE DOING HERE, MS. HALE?
TRYING TO FIND A SOLUTION THAT LEAVES US BOTH SATISFIED.
MEANING?
MEANING *YOU* WEAR OUR *ARMOR.*

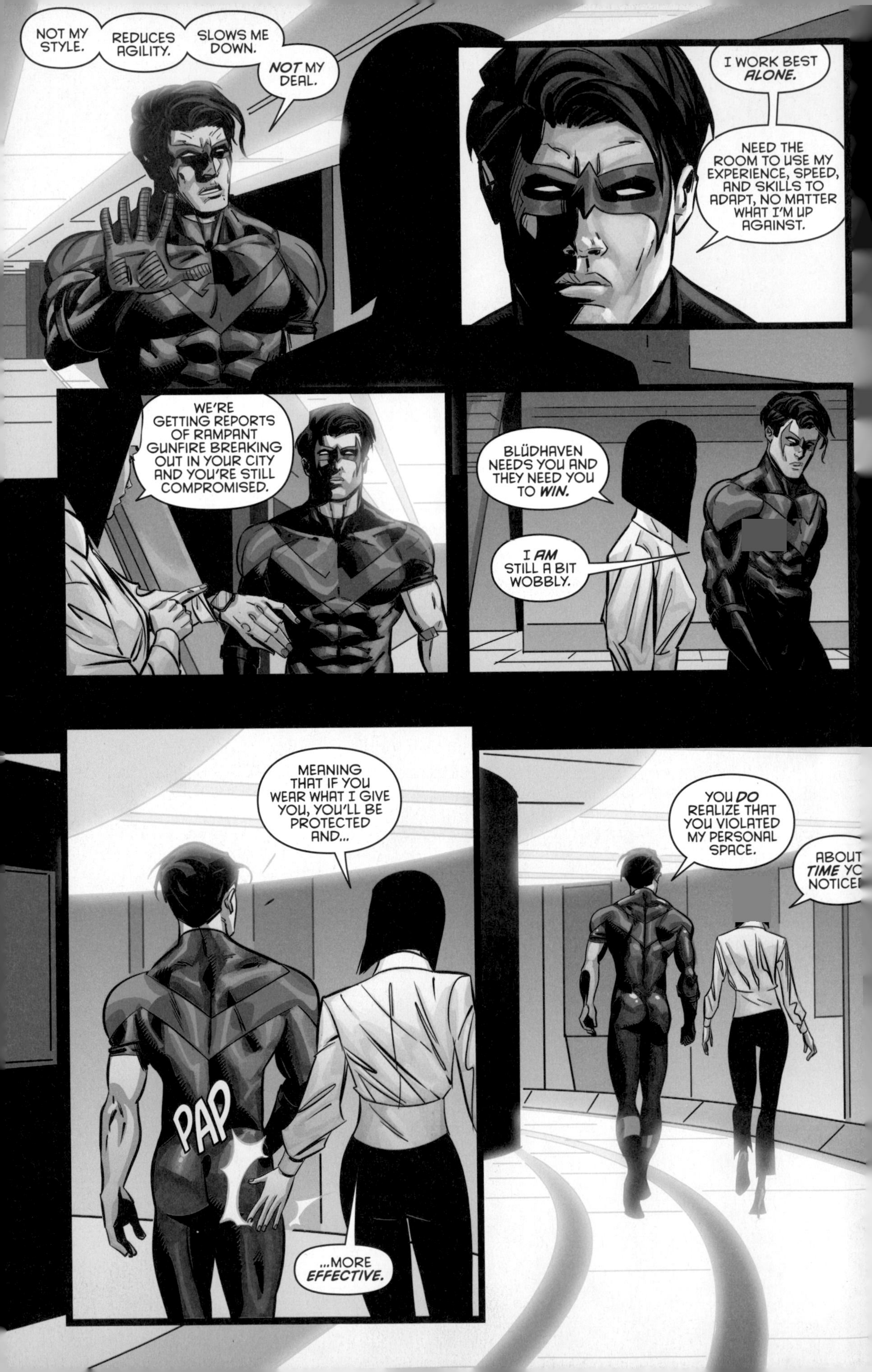
NOT MY STYLE.
REDUCES AGILITY.
SLOWS ME DOWN.
NOT MY DEAL.
I WORK BEST ALONE.
NEED THE ROOM TO USE MY EXPERIENCE, SPEED, AND SKILLS TO ADAPT, NO MATTER WHAT I'M UP AGAINST.
WE'RE GETTING REPORTS OF RAMPANT GUNFIRE BREAKING OUT IN YOUR CITY AND YOU'RE STILL COMPROMISED.
BLÜDHAVEN NEEDS YOU AND THEY NEED YOU TO WIN.
I AM STILL A BIT WOBBLY.
MEANING THAT IF YOU WEAR WHAT I GIVE YOU, YOU'LL BE PROTECTED AND...
PAP
...MORE EFFECTIVE.
YOU DO REALIZE THAT YOU VIOLATED MY PERSONAL SPACE.
ABOUT TIME YO NOTICE

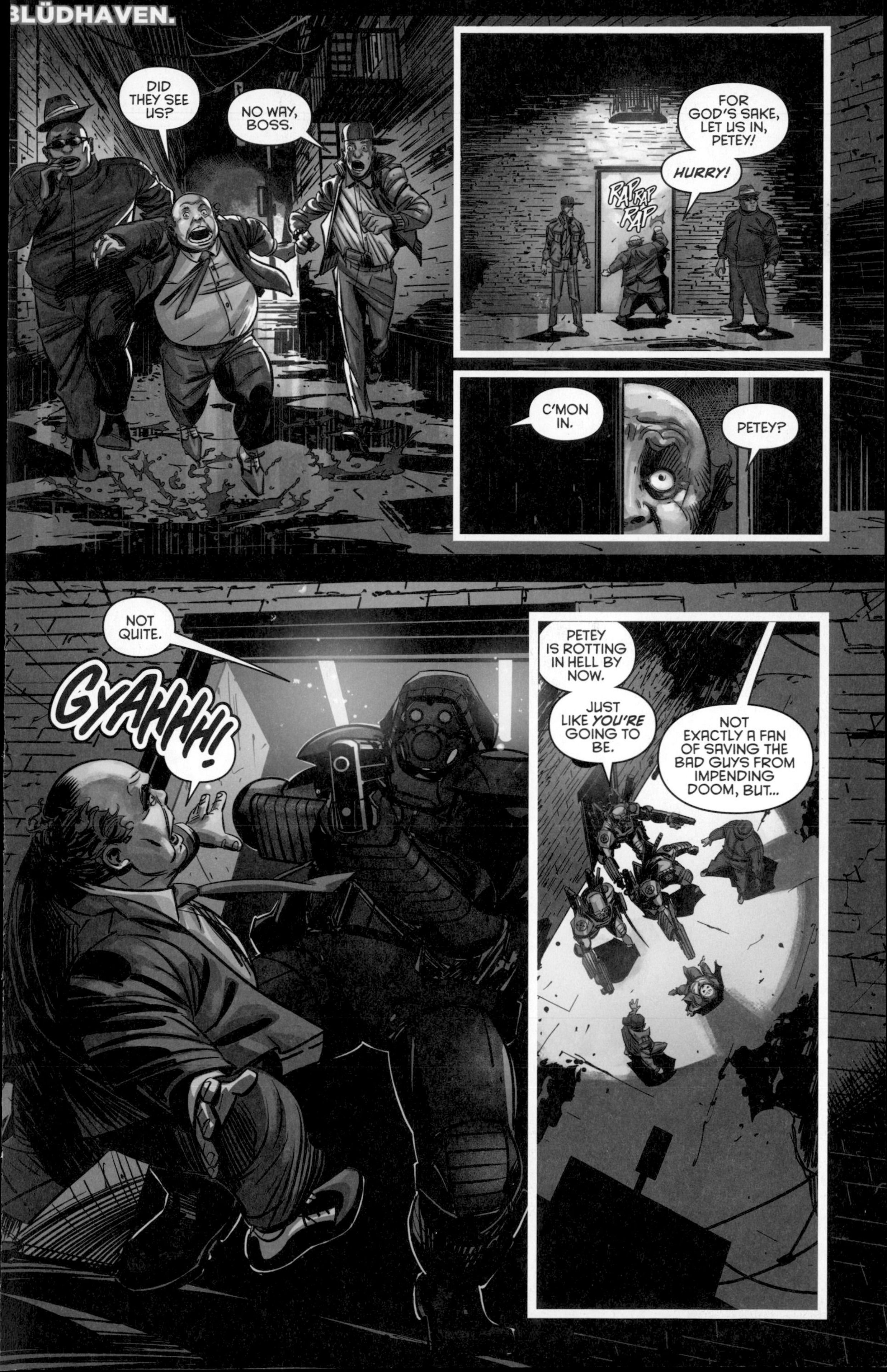
BLÜDHAVEN.
DID THEY SEE US?
NO WAY, BOSS.
FOR GOD'S SAKE, LET US IN, PETEY!
HURRY!
RAP RAP RAP
C'MON IN.
PETEY?
NOT QUITE.
GYAHHH!
PETEY IS ROTTING IN HELL BY NOW.
JUST LIKE YOU'RE GOING TO BE.
NOT EXACTLY A FAN OF SAVING THE BAD GUYS FROM IMPENDING DOOM, BUT...

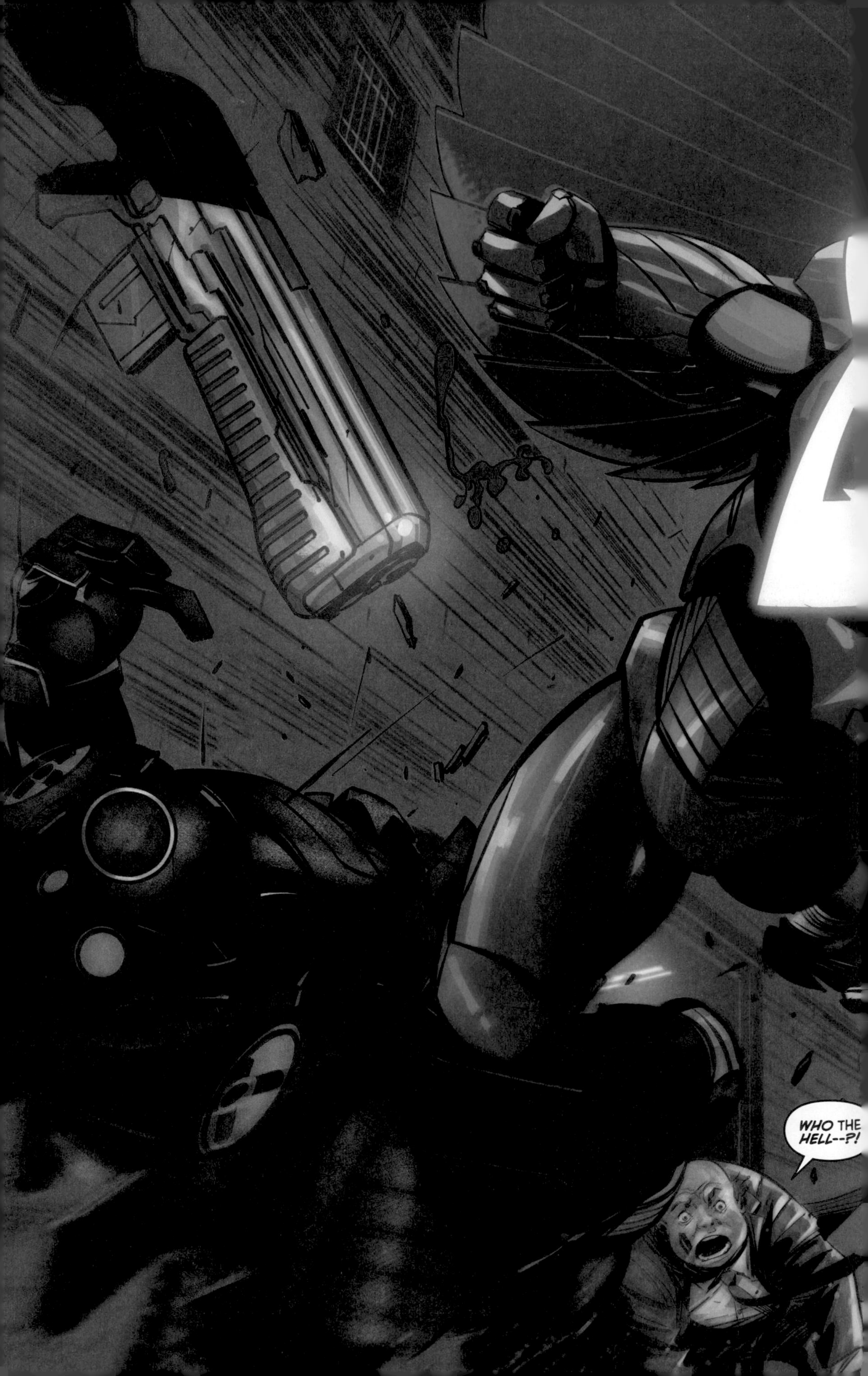
WHO THE HELL--?!

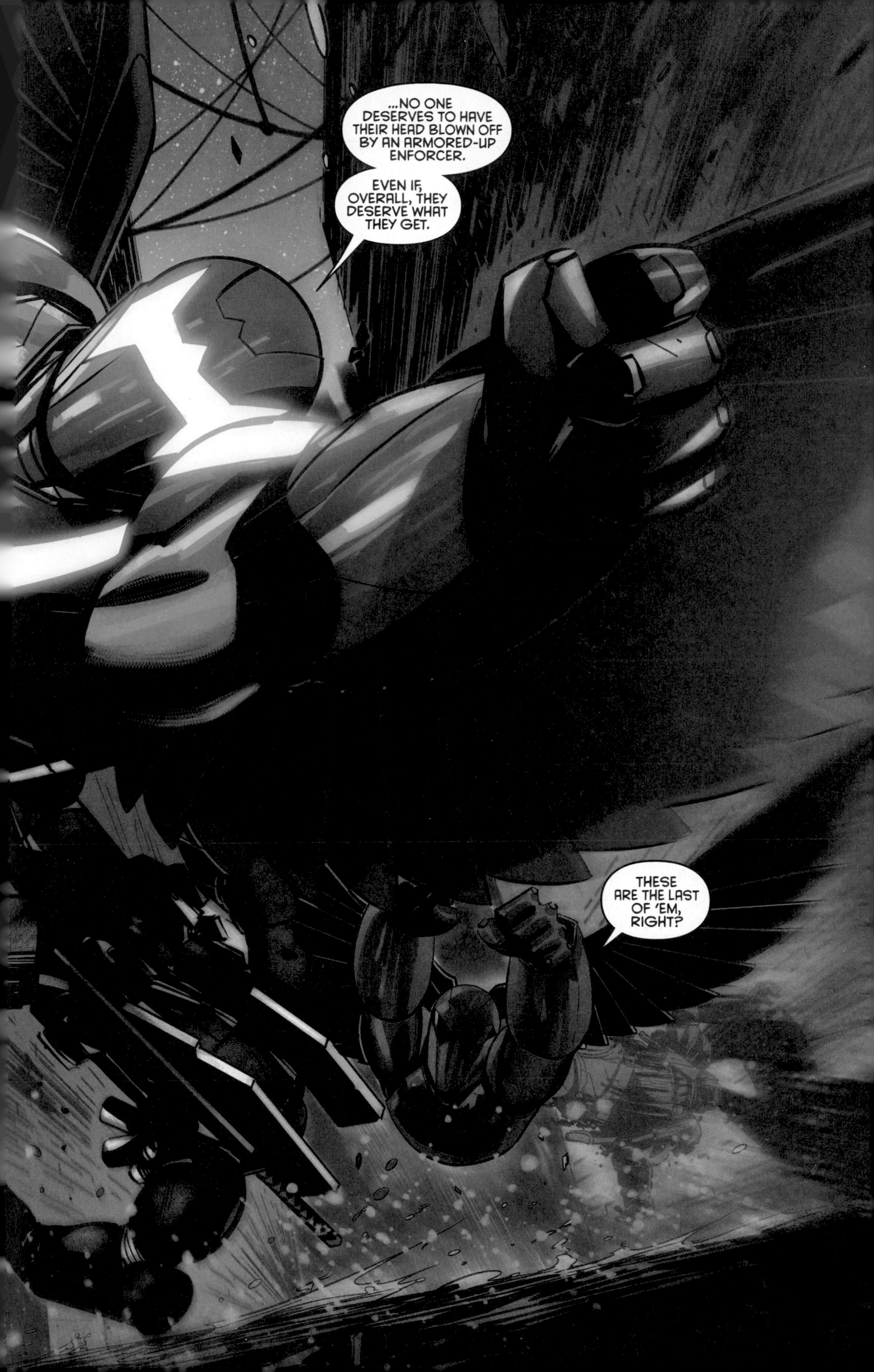
...NO ONE DESERVES TO HAVE THEIR HEAD BLOWN OFF BY AN ARMORED-UP ENFORCER.
EVEN IF, OVERALL, THEY DESERVE WHAT THEY GET.
THESE ARE THE LAST OF 'EM, RIGHT?

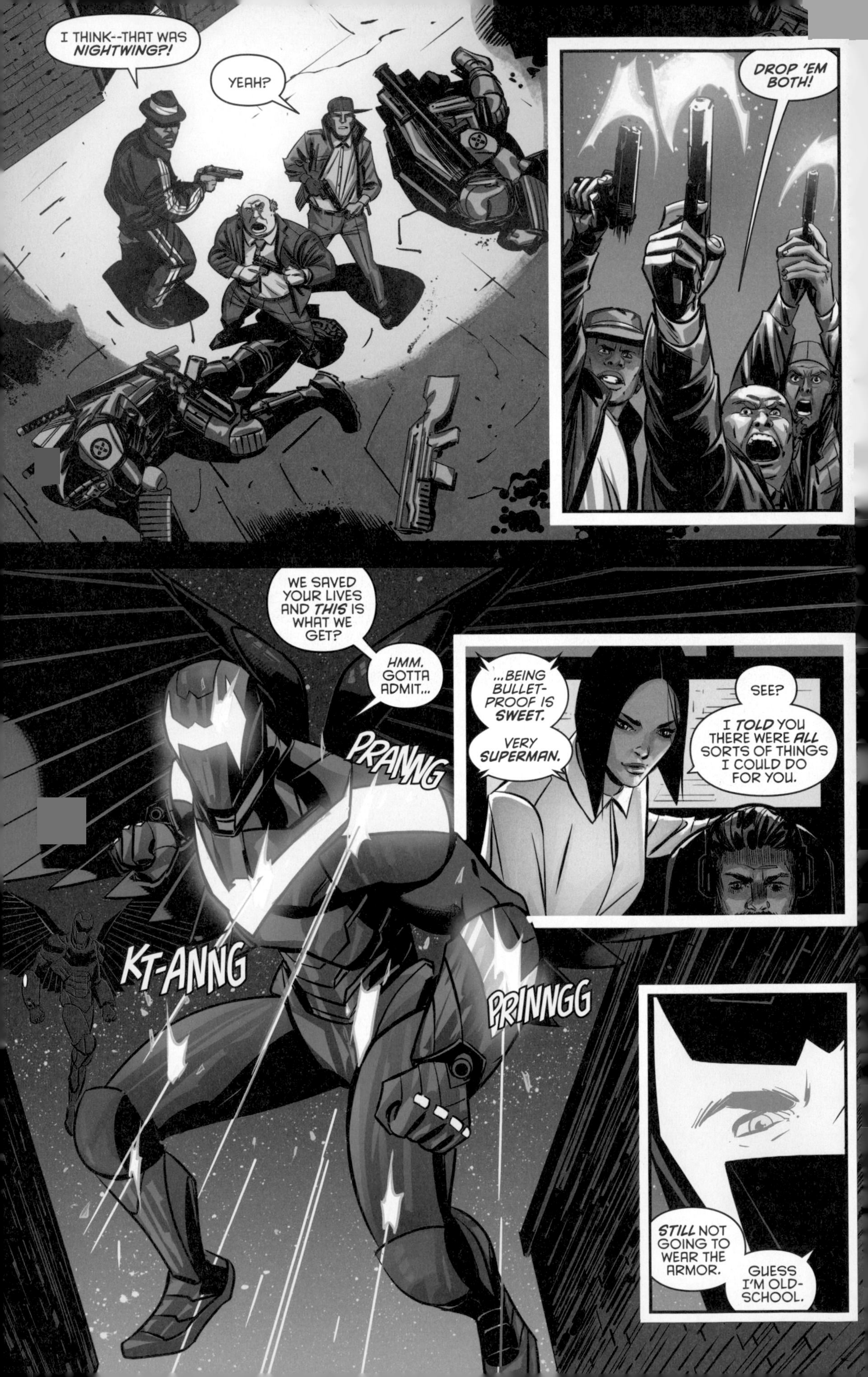
I THINK--THAT WAS NIGHTWING?!
YEAH?
DROP 'EM BOTH!
WE SAVED YOUR LIVES AND THIS IS WHAT WE GET?
HMM. GOTTA ADMIT...
...BEING BULLET-PROOF IS SWEET.
VERY SUPERMAN.
SEE?
I TOLD YOU THERE WERE ALL SORTS OF THINGS I COULD DO FOR YOU.
PRANNG
KT-ANNG
PRINNGG
STILL NOT GOING TO WEAR THE ARMOR.
GUESS I'M OLD-SCHOOL.

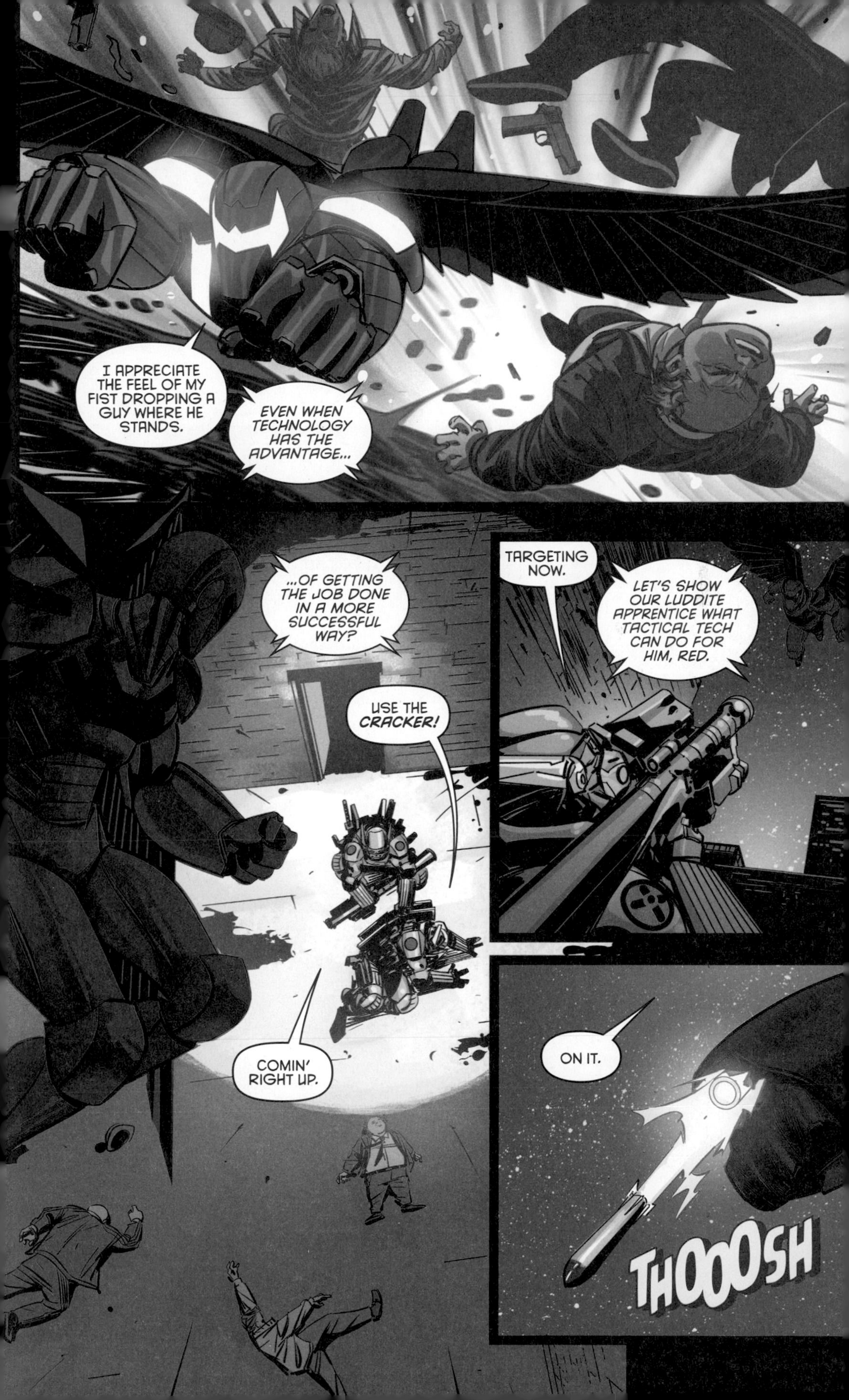
I APPRECIATE THE FEEL OF MY FIST DROPPING A GUY WHERE HE STANDS.
EVEN WHEN TECHNOLOGY HAS THE ADVANTAGE...
...OF GETTING THE JOB DONE IN A MORE SUCCESSFUL WAY?
USE THE CRACKER!
COMIN' RIGHT UP.
TARGETING NOW.
LET'S SHOW OUR LUDDITE APPRENTICE WHAT TACTICAL TECH CAN DO FOR HIM, RED.
ON IT.
THOOOSH

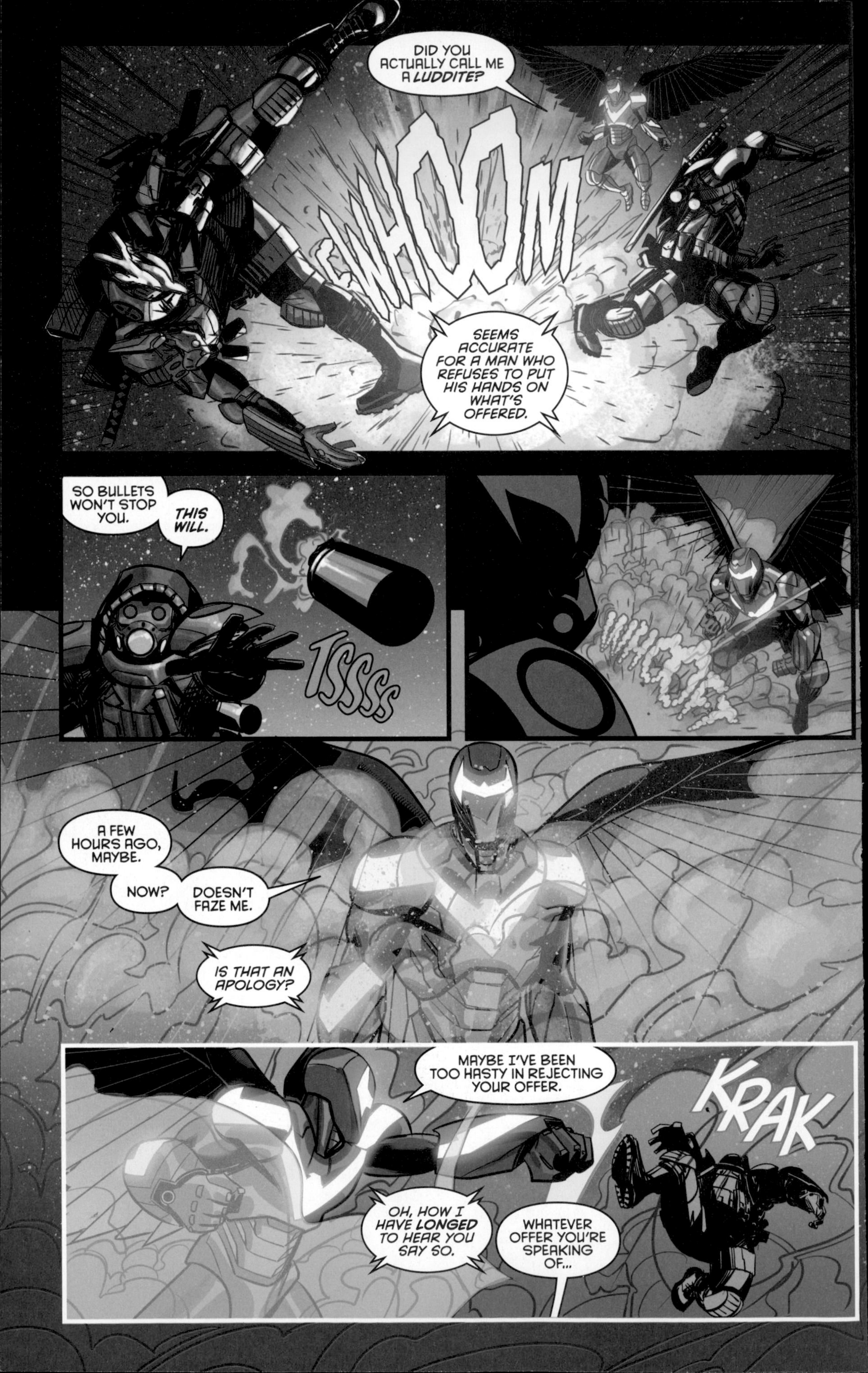
DID YOU ACTUALLY CALL ME A *LUDDITE?*
WHOOM
SEEMS ACCURATE FOR A MAN WHO REFUSES TO PUT HIS HANDS ON WHAT'S OFFERED.
SO BULLETS WON'T STOP YOU.
THIS WILL.
TSSSs
A FEW HOURS AGO, MAYBE.
NOW?
DOESN'T FAZE ME.
IS THAT AN APOLOGY?
MAYBE I'VE BEEN TOO HASTY IN REJECTING YOUR OFFER.
KRAK
*OH, HOW I HAVE **LONGED** TO HEAR YOU SAY SO.*
WHATEVER OFFER YOU'RE SPEAKING OF...

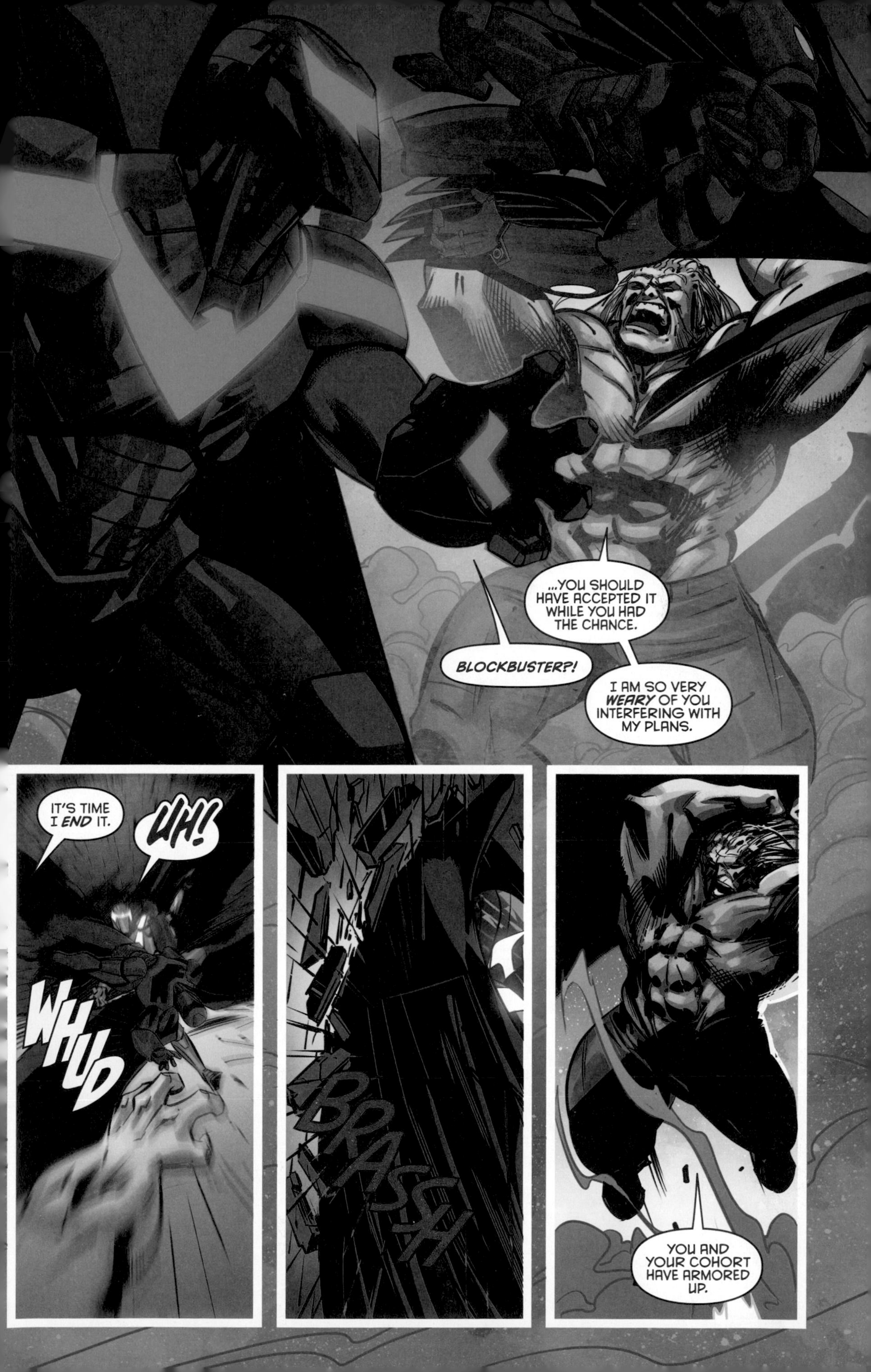

...YOU SHOULD HAVE ACCEPTED IT WHILE YOU HAD THE CHANCE.
BLOCKBUSTER?!
I AM SO VERY WEARY OF YOU INTERFERING WITH MY PLANS.
IT'S TIME I END IT.
UH!
WHUD
BRASSH
YOU AND YOUR COHORT HAVE ARMORED UP.

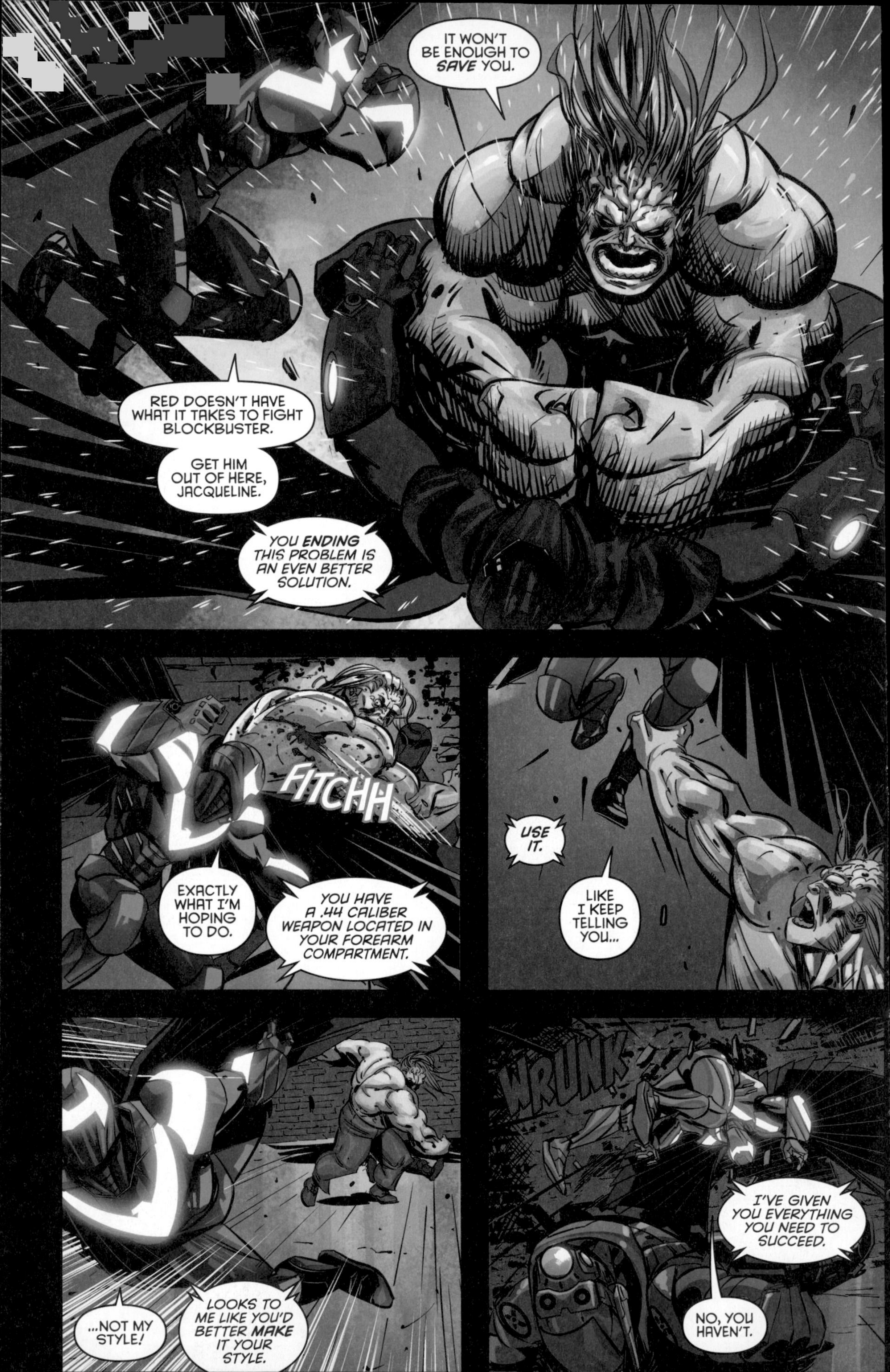

IT WON'T BE ENOUGH TO SAVE YOU.
RED DOESN'T HAVE WHAT IT TAKES TO FIGHT BLOCKBUSTER.
GET HIM OUT OF HERE, JACQUELINE.
YOU ENDING THIS PROBLEM IS AN EVEN BETTER SOLUTION.
FITCHH
EXACTLY WHAT I'M HOPING TO DO.
YOU HAVE A .44 CALIBER WEAPON LOCATED IN YOUR FOREARM COMPARTMENT.
USE IT.
LIKE I KEEP TELLING YOU...
...NOT MY STYLE!
LOOKS TO ME LIKE YOU'D BETTER MAKE IT YOUR STYLE.
WRUNK
I'VE GIVEN YOU EVERYTHING YOU NEED TO SUCCEED.
NO, YOU HAVEN'T.

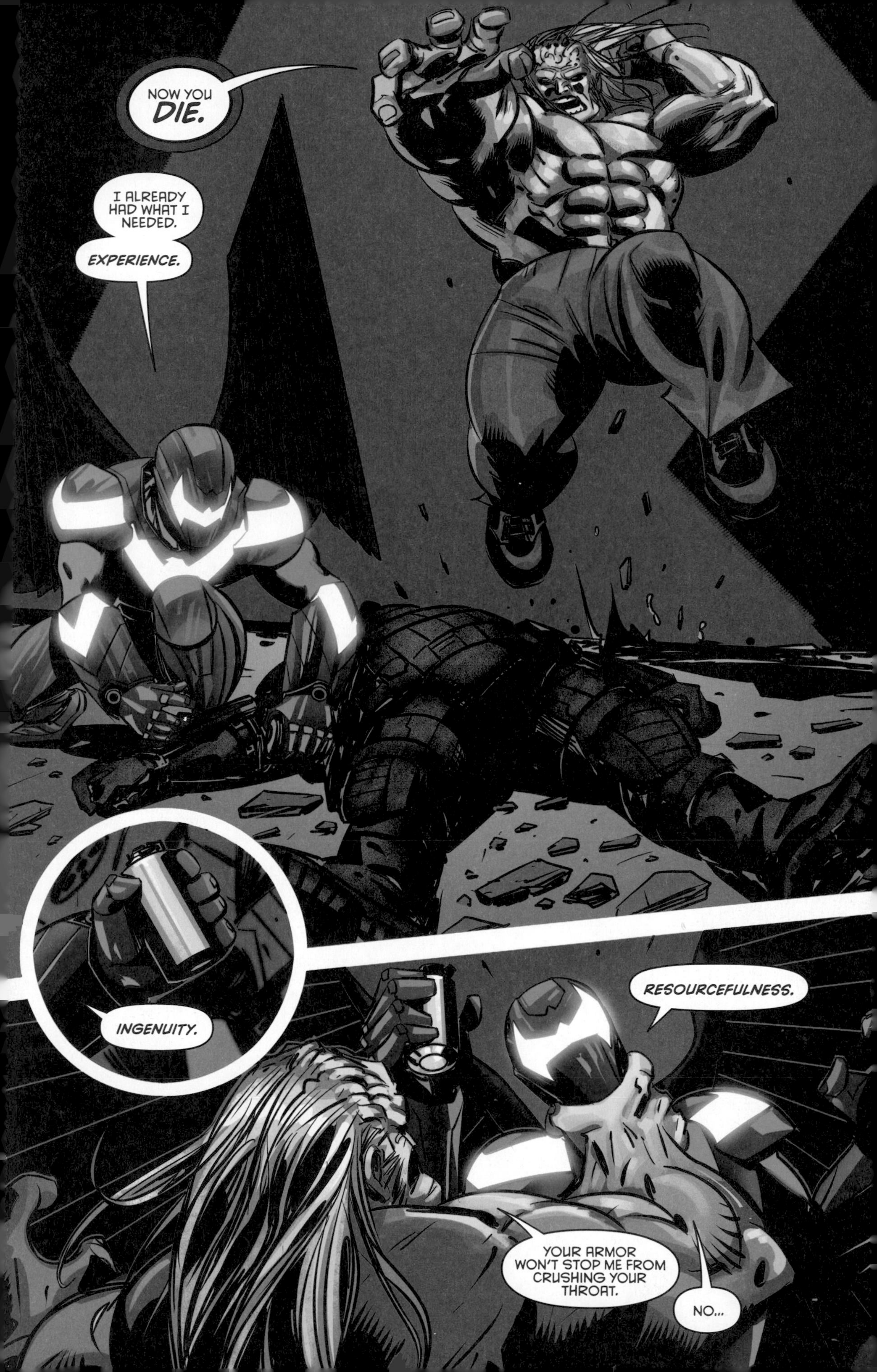
NOW YOU DIE.
I ALREADY HAD WHAT I NEEDED.
EXPERIENCE.
INGENUITY.
RESOURCEFULNESS.
YOUR ARMOR WON'T STOP ME FROM CRUSHING YOUR THROAT.
NO...

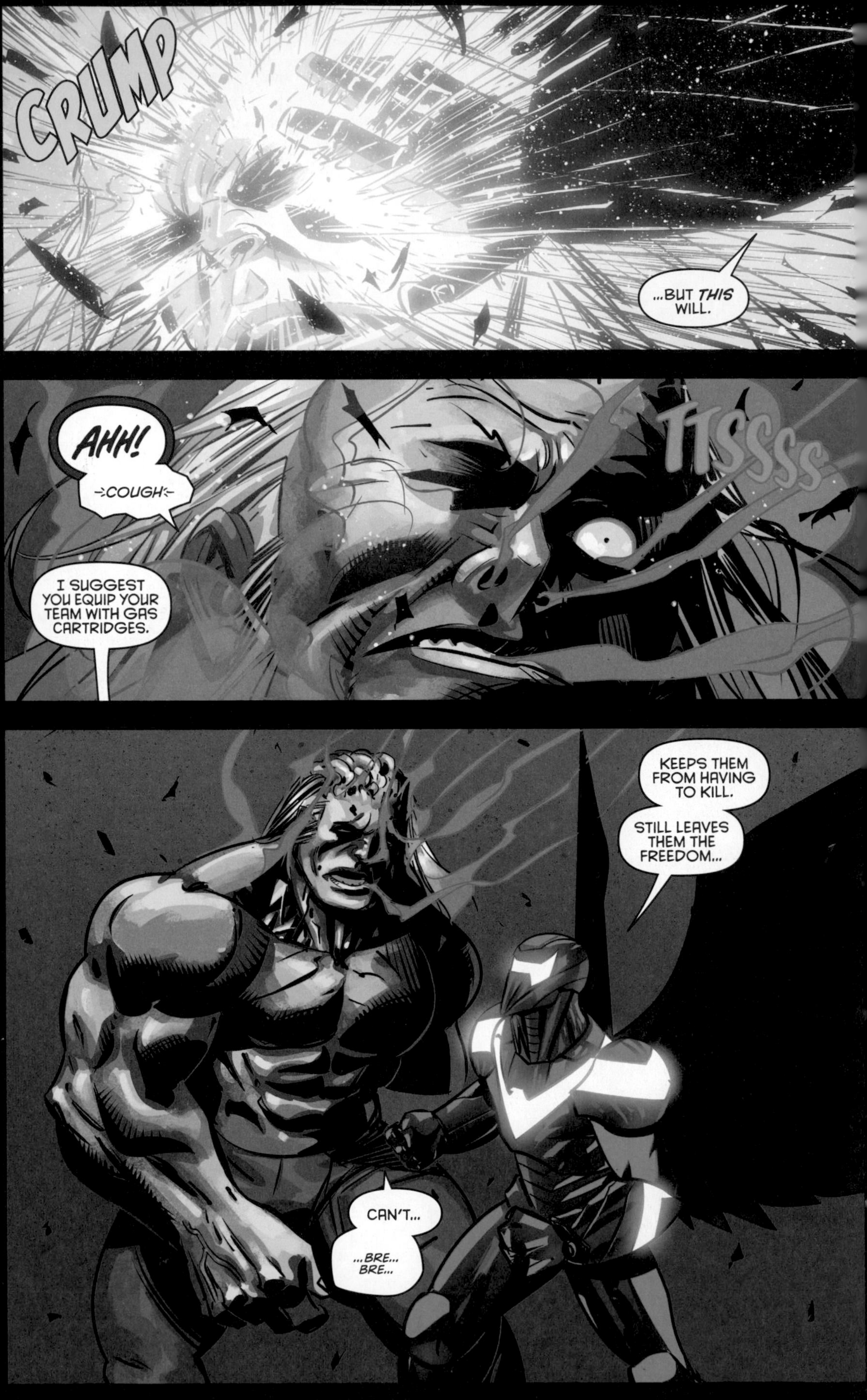
CRUMP
...BUT THIS WILL.
AHH!
COUGH
TTSSSS
I SUGGEST YOU EQUIP YOUR TEAM WITH GAS CARTRIDGES.
KEEPS THEM FROM HAVING TO KILL.
STILL LEAVES THEM THE FREEDOM...
CAN'T...
...BRE... BRE...

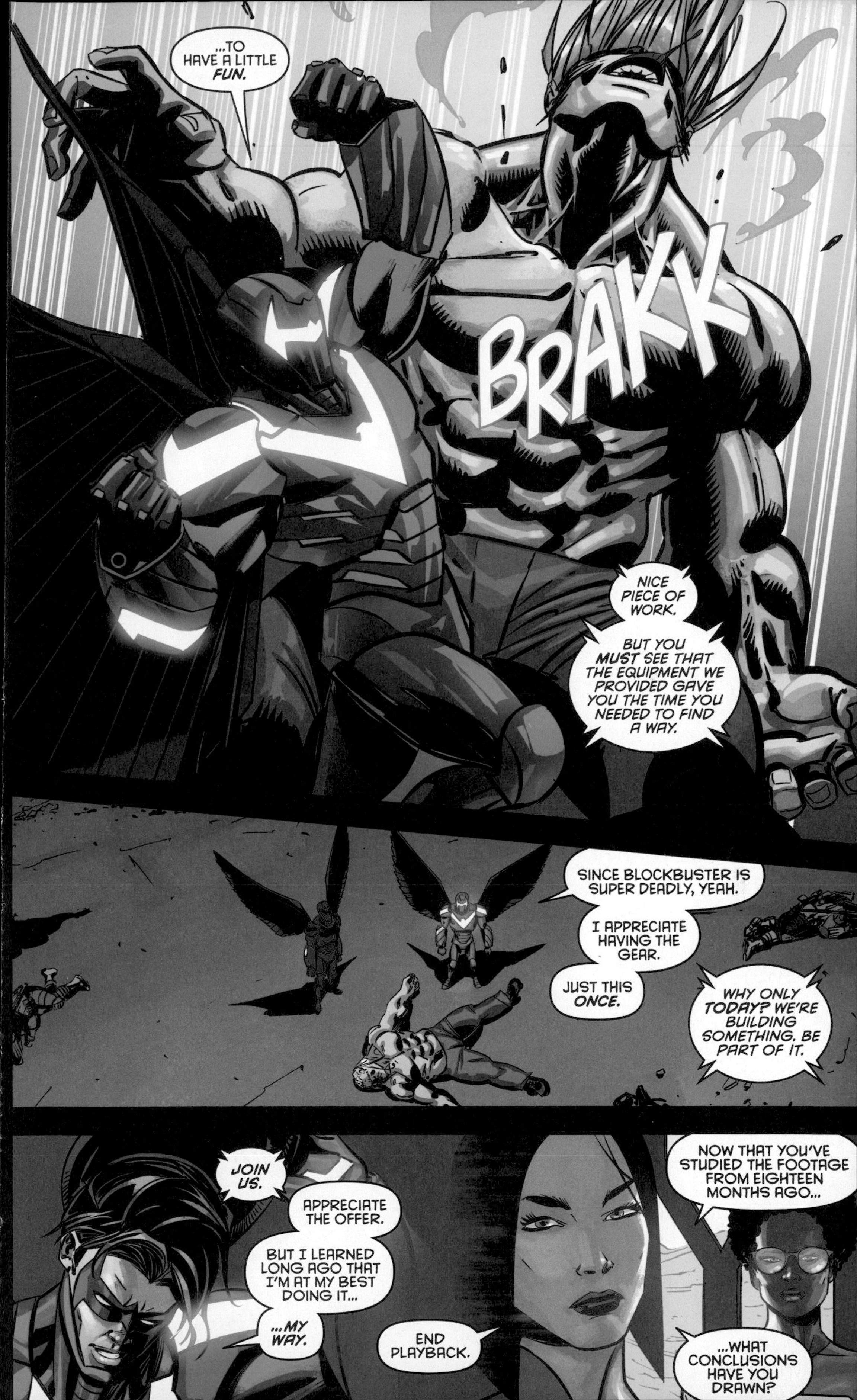
...TO HAVE A LITTLE FUN.
BRAKK
NICE PIECE OF WORK.
BUT YOU MUST SEE THAT THE EQUIPMENT WE PROVIDED GAVE YOU THE TIME YOU NEEDED TO FIND A WAY.
SINCE BLOCKBUSTER IS SUPER DEADLY, YEAH.
I APPRECIATE HAVING THE GEAR.
JUST THIS ONCE.
WHY ONLY TODAY? WE'RE BUILDING SOMETHING. BE PART OF IT.
JOIN US.
APPRECIATE THE OFFER.
BUT I LEARNED LONG AGO THAT I'M AT MY BEST DOING IT...
...MY WAY.
END PLAYBACK.
NOW THAT YOU'VE STUDIED THE FOOTAGE FROM EIGHTEEN MONTHS AGO...
...WHAT CONCLUSIONS HAVE YOU DRAWN?

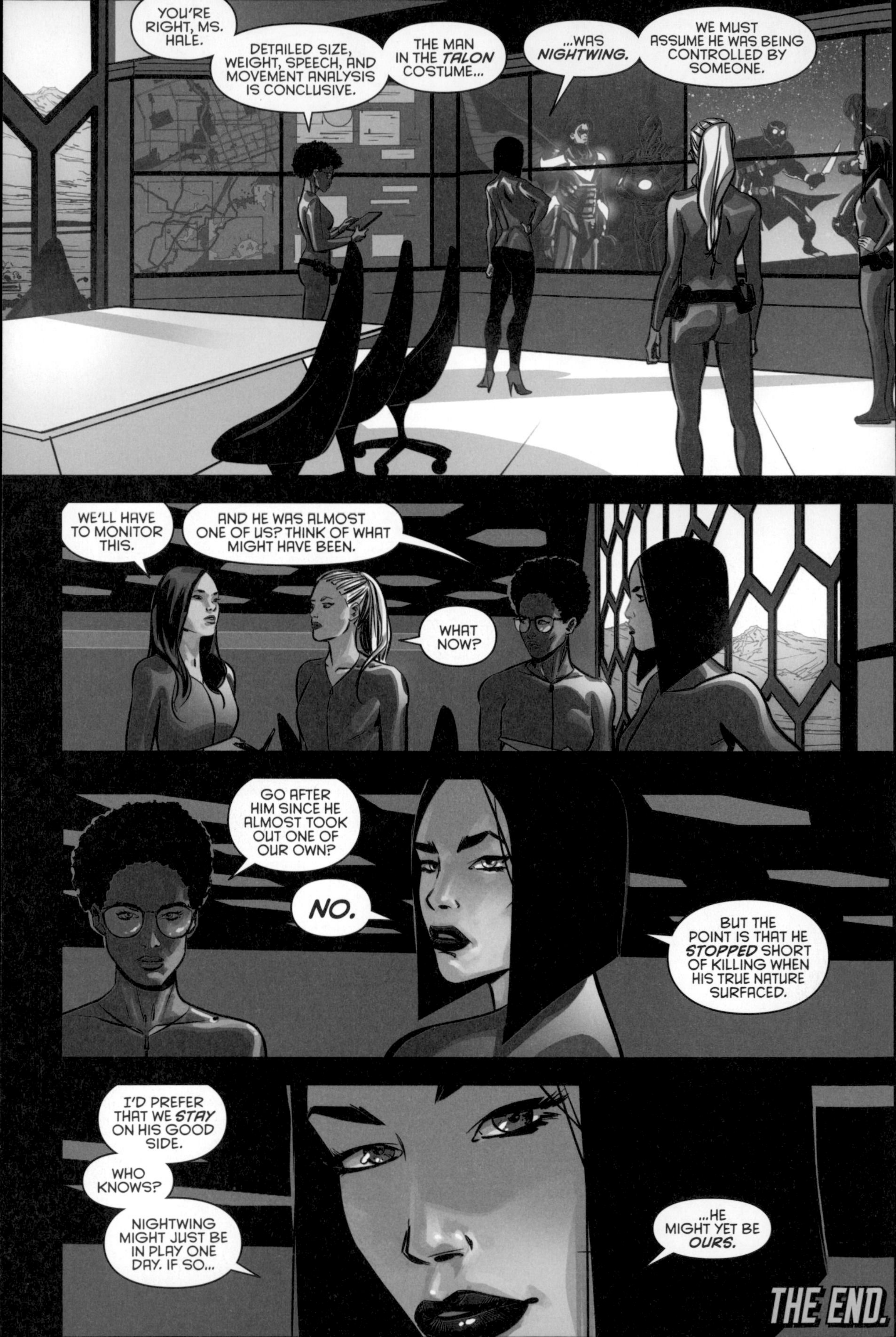
YOU'RE RIGHT, MS. HALE.
DETAILED SIZE, WEIGHT, SPEECH, AND MOVEMENT ANALYSIS IS CONCLUSIVE.
THE MAN IN THE *TALON* COSTUME...
...WAS *NIGHTWING.*
WE MUST ASSUME HE WAS BEING CONTROLLED BY SOMEONE.
WE'LL HAVE TO MONITOR THIS.
AND HE WAS ALMOST ONE OF US? THINK OF WHAT MIGHT HAVE BEEN.
WHAT NOW?
GO AFTER HIM SINCE HE ALMOST TOOK OUT ONE OF OUR OWN?
NO.
BUT THE POINT IS THAT HE *STOPPED* SHORT OF KILLING WHEN HIS TRUE NATURE SURFACED.
I'D PREFER THAT WE *STAY* ON HIS GOOD SIDE.
WHO KNOWS?
NIGHTWING MIGHT JUST BE IN PLAY ONE DAY. IF SO...
...HE MIGHT YET BE *OURS.*
THE END.

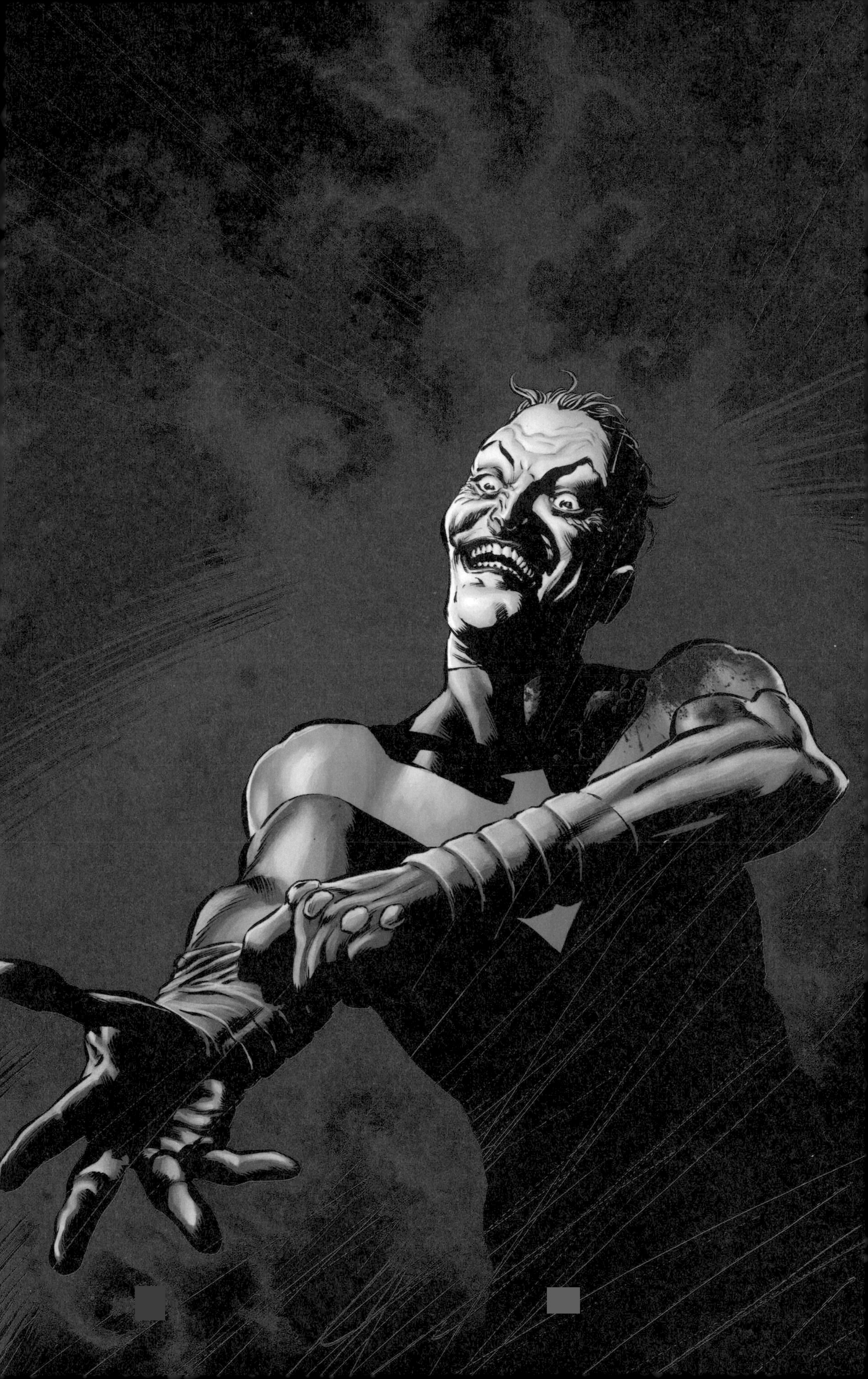

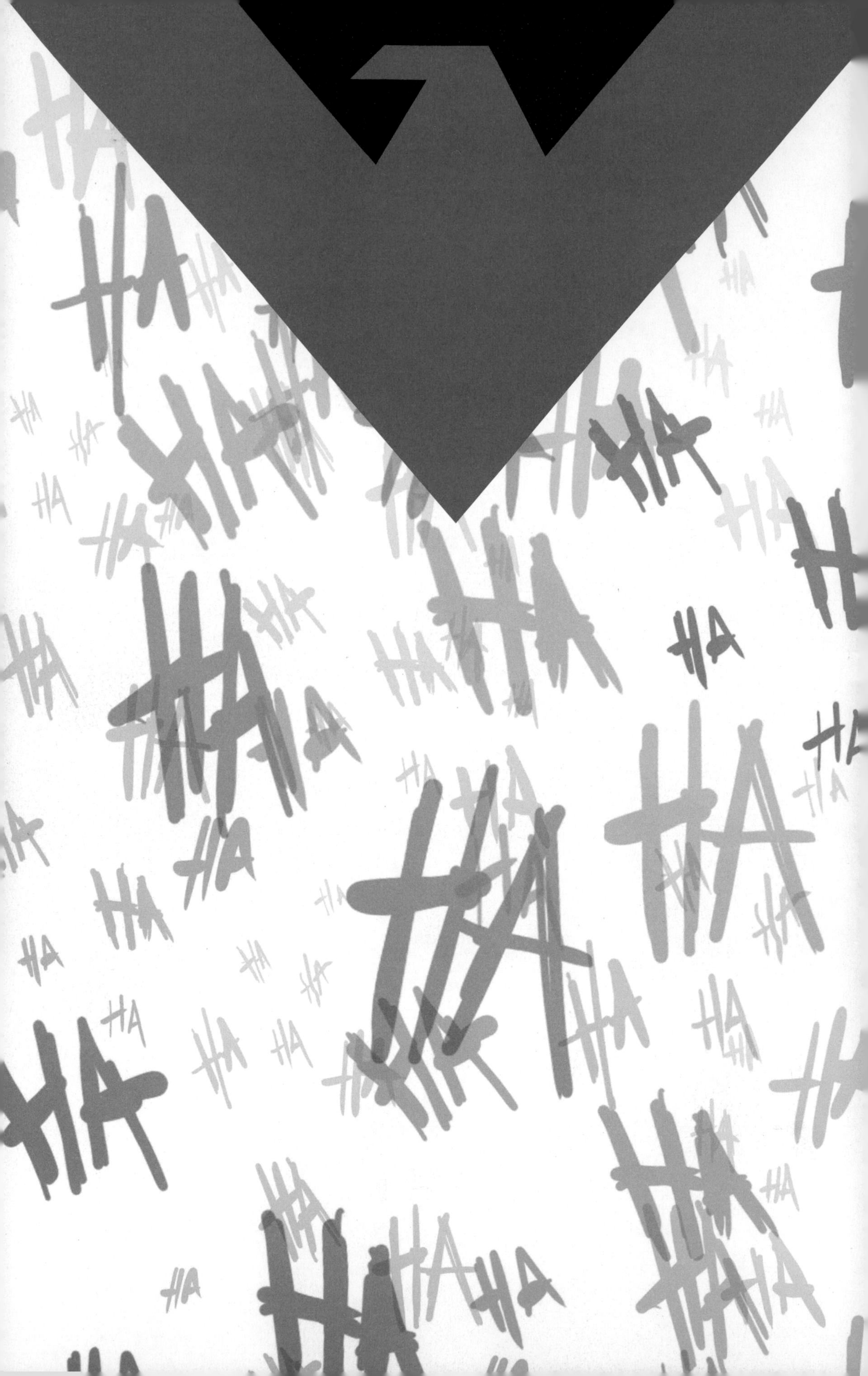

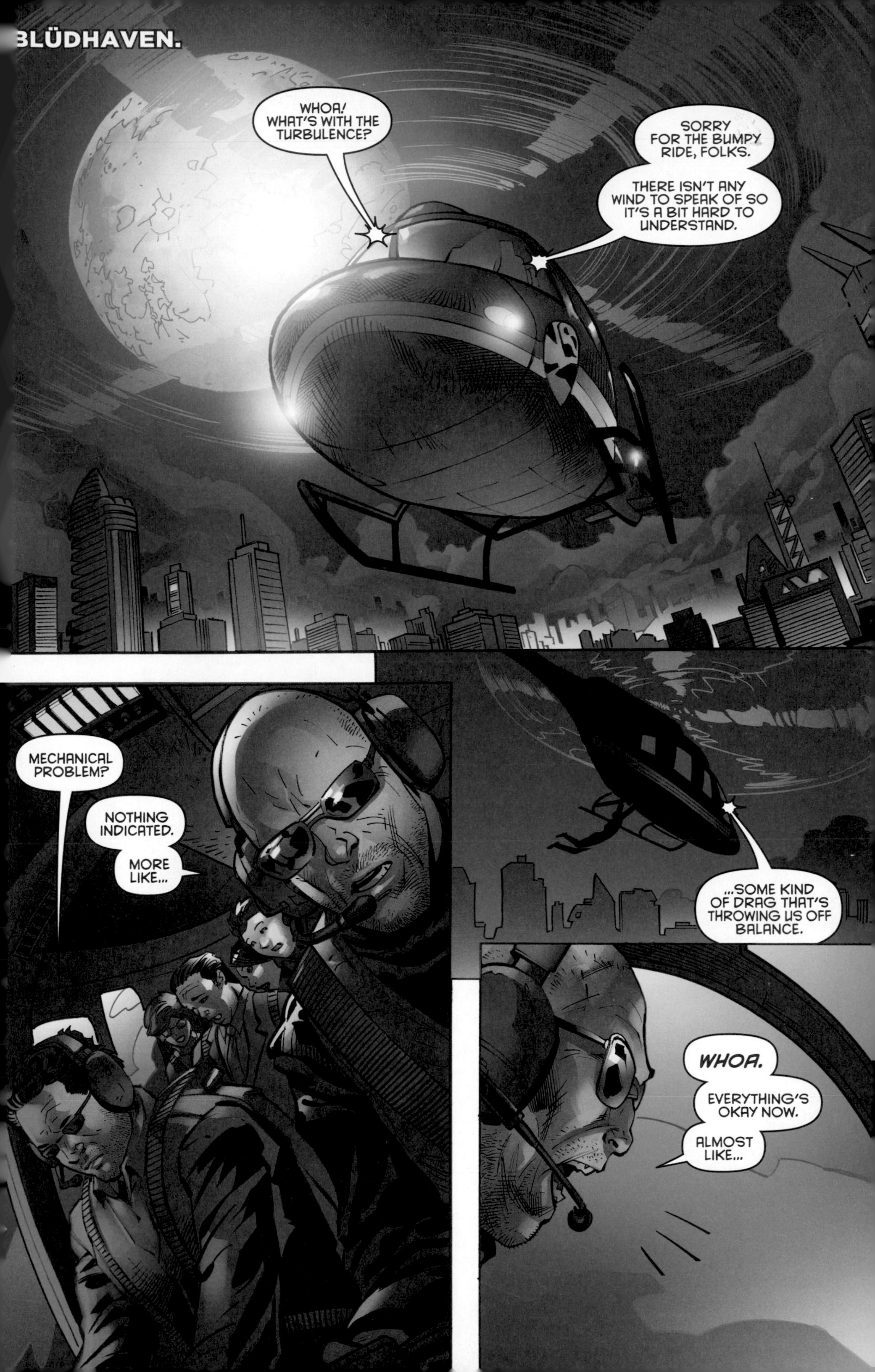

BLÜDHAVEN.
WHOA! WHAT'S WITH THE TURBULENCE?
SORRY FOR THE BUMPY RIDE, FOLKS.
THERE ISN'T ANY WIND TO SPEAK OF SO IT'S A BIT HARD TO UNDERSTAND.
MECHANICAL PROBLEM?
NOTHING INDICATED.
MORE LIKE...
...SOME KIND OF DRAG THAT'S THROWING US OFF BALANCE.
WHOA.
EVERYTHING'S OKAY NOW.
ALMOST LIKE...

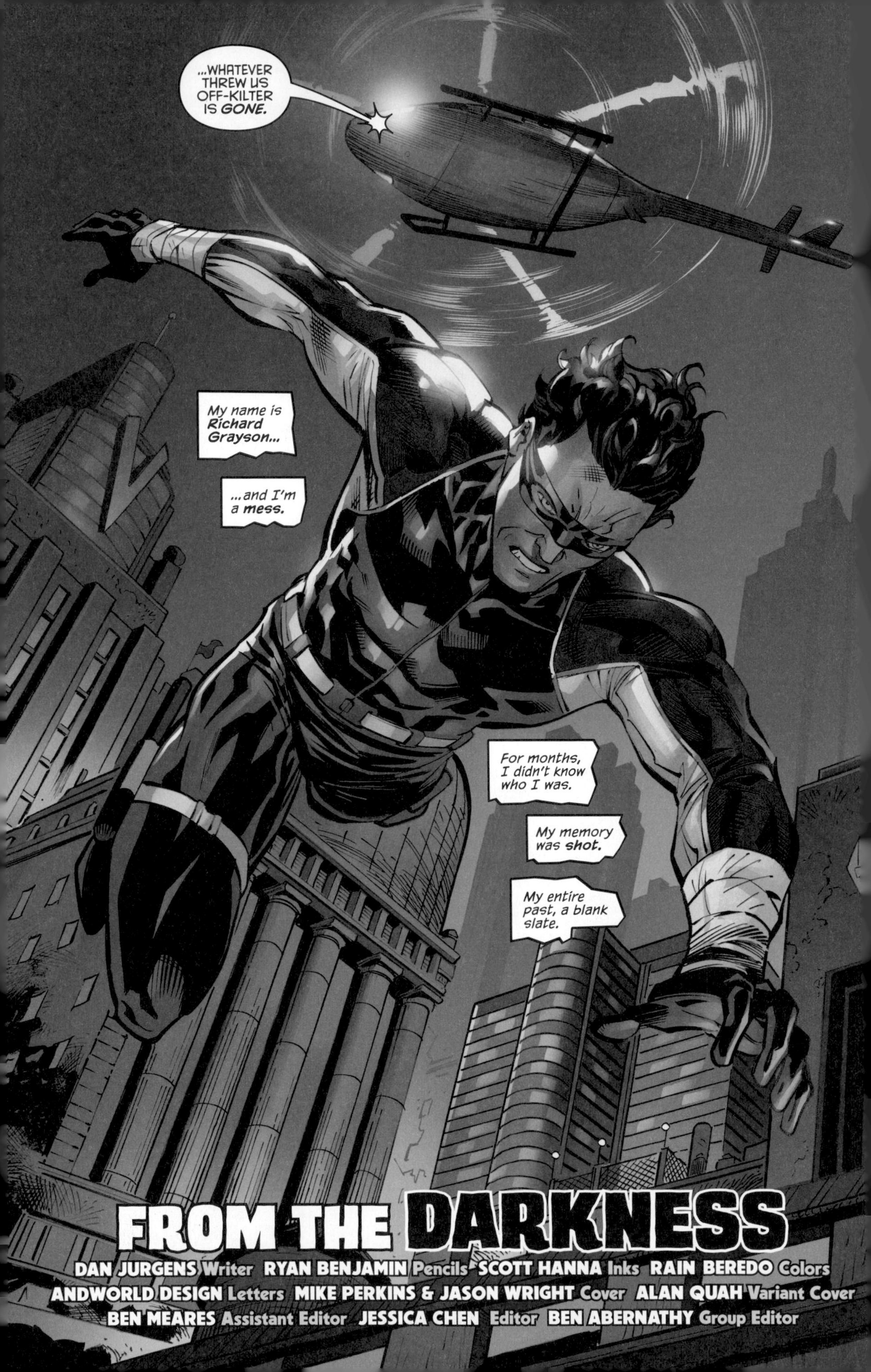
...WHATEVER THREW US OFF-KILTER IS GONE.
My name is Richard Grayson...
...and I'm a mess.
For months, I didn't know who I was.
My memory was shot.
My entire past, a blank slate.
FROM THE DARKNESS
DAN JURGENS Writer RYAN BENJAMIN Pencils SCOTT HANNA Inks RAIN BEREDO Colors
ANDWORLD DESIGN Letters MIKE PERKINS & JASON WRIGHT Cover ALAN QUAH Variant Cover
BEN MEARES Assistant Editor JESSICA CHEN Editor BEN ABERNATHY Group Editor

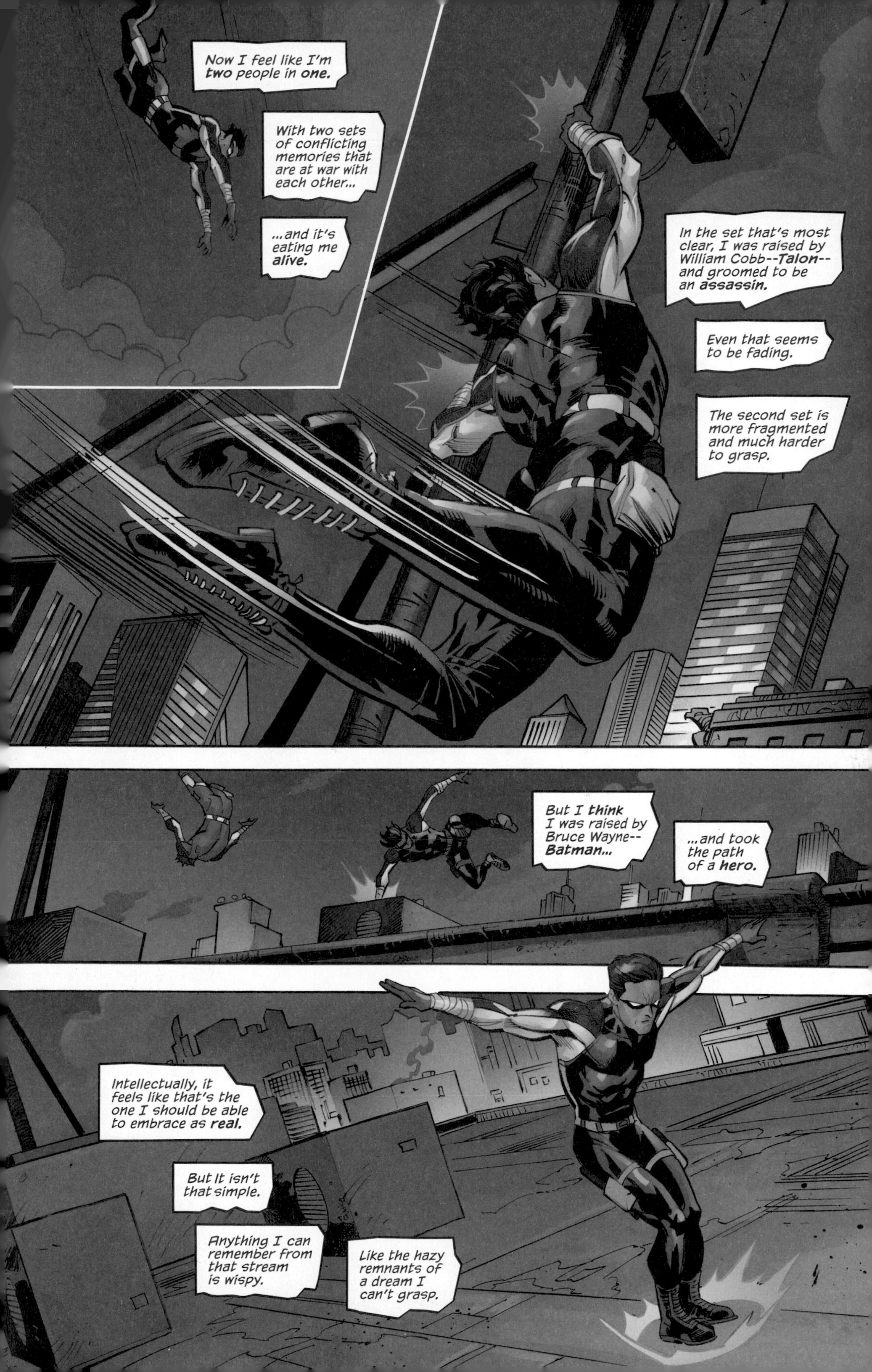

Now I feel like I'm **two** people in **one.**
With two sets of conflicting memories that are at war with each other...
...and it's eating me **alive.**
In the set that's most clear, I was raised by William Cobb--**Talon**--and groomed to be an **assassin.**
Even that seems to be fading.
The second set is more fragmented and much harder to grasp.
But I **think** I was raised by Bruce Wayne--**Batman**...
...and took the path of a **hero.**
Intellectually, it feels like that's the one I should be able to embrace as **real.**
But it isn't that simple.
Anything I can remember from that stream is wispy.
Like the hazy remnants of a dream I can't grasp.

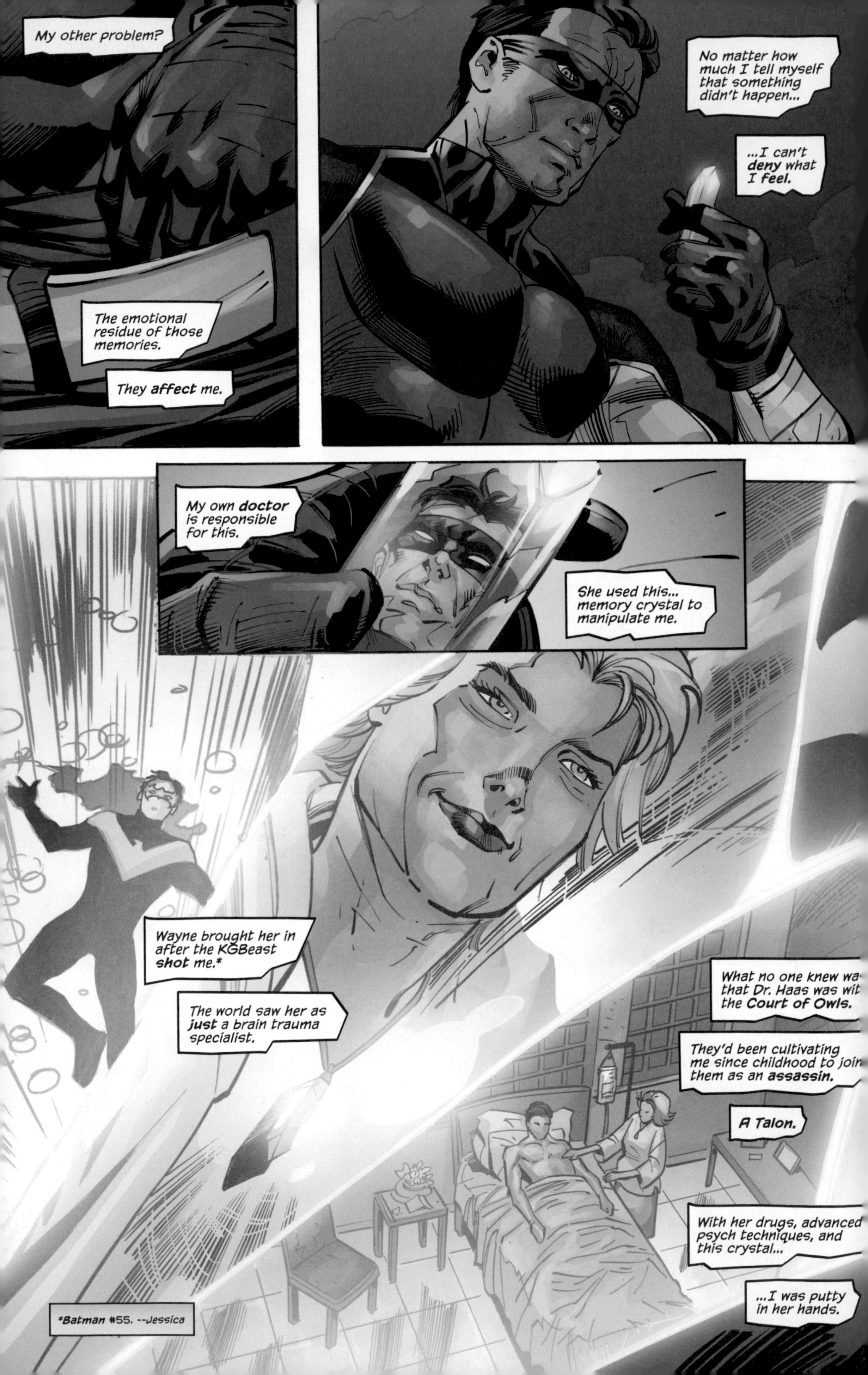
My other problem?
The emotional residue of those memories.
They affect me.
No matter how much I tell myself that something didn't happen...
...I can't deny what I feel.
My own doctor is responsible for this.
She used this... memory crystal to manipulate me.
Wayne brought her in after the KGBeast shot me.*
The world saw her as just a brain trauma specialist.
What no one knew wa that Dr. Haas was wit the Court of Owls.
They'd been cultivating me since childhood to join them as an assassin.
A Talon.
With her drugs, advanced psych techniques, and this crystal...
...I was putty in her hands.
*Batman #55. --Jessica

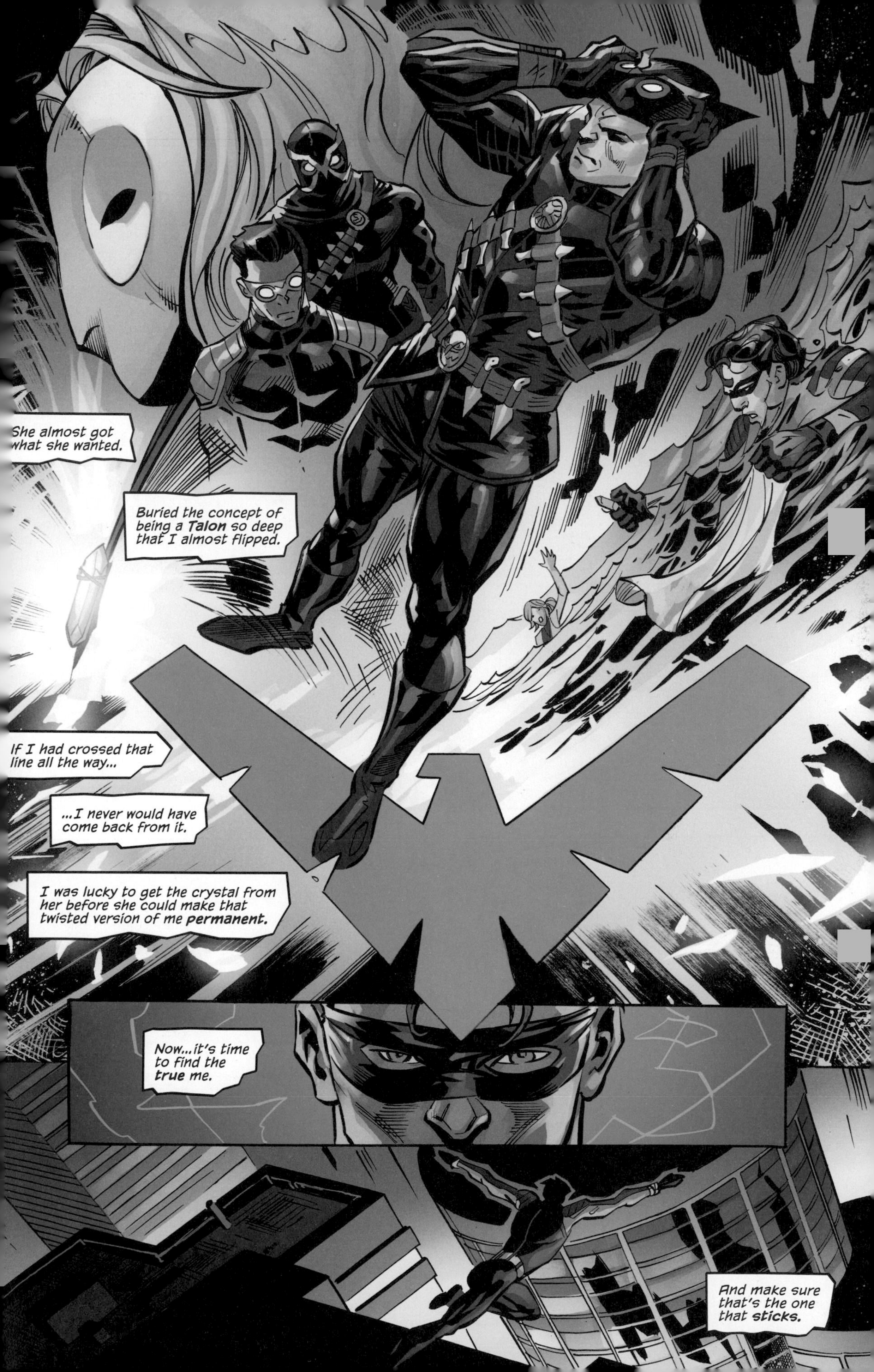
She almost got what she wanted.
Buried the concept of being a **Talon** so deep that I almost flipped.
If I had crossed that line all the way...
...I never would have come back from it.
I was lucky to get the crystal from her before she could make that twisted version of me **permanent.**
Now...it's time to find the **true** me.
And make sure that's the one that **sticks.**

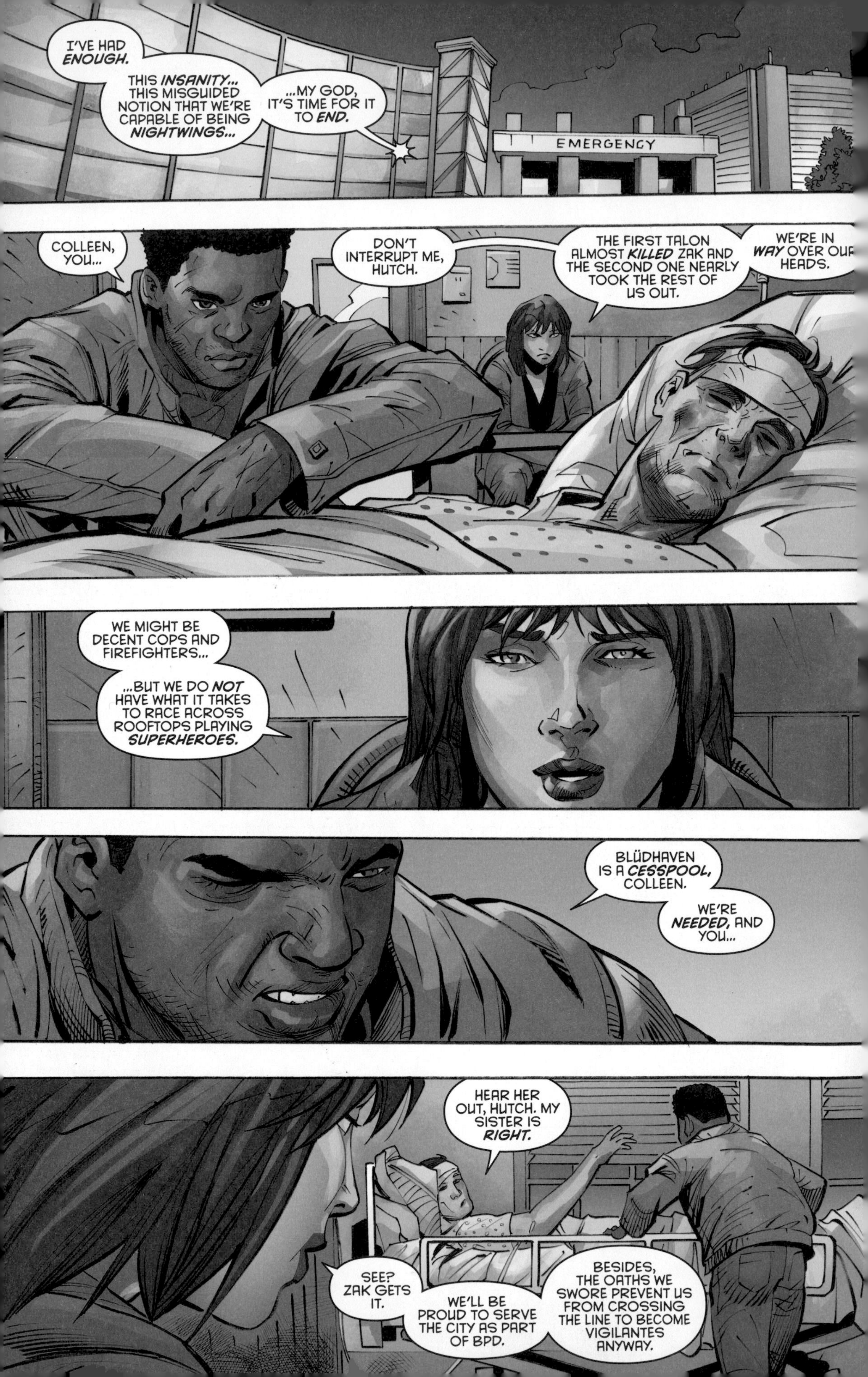
I'VE HAD ENOUGH.
THIS INSANITY... THIS MISGUIDED NOTION THAT WE'RE CAPABLE OF BEING NIGHTWINGS...
...MY GOD, IT'S TIME FOR IT TO END.
EMERGENCY
COLLEEN, YOU...
DON'T INTERRUPT ME, HUTCH.
THE FIRST TALON ALMOST KILLED ZAK AND THE SECOND ONE NEARLY TOOK THE REST OF US OUT.
WE'RE IN WAY OVER OUR HEADS.
WE MIGHT BE DECENT COPS AND FIREFIGHTERS...
...BUT WE DO NOT HAVE WHAT IT TAKES TO RACE ACROSS ROOFTOPS PLAYING SUPERHEROES.
BLÜDHAVEN IS A CESSPOOL, COLLEEN.
WE'RE NEEDED, AND YOU...
HEAR HER OUT, HUTCH. MY SISTER IS RIGHT.
SEE? ZAK GETS IT.
WE'LL BE PROUD TO SERVE THE CITY AS PART OF BPD.
BESIDES, THE OATHS WE SWORE PREVENT US FROM CROSSING THE LINE TO BECOME VIGILANTES ANYWAY.

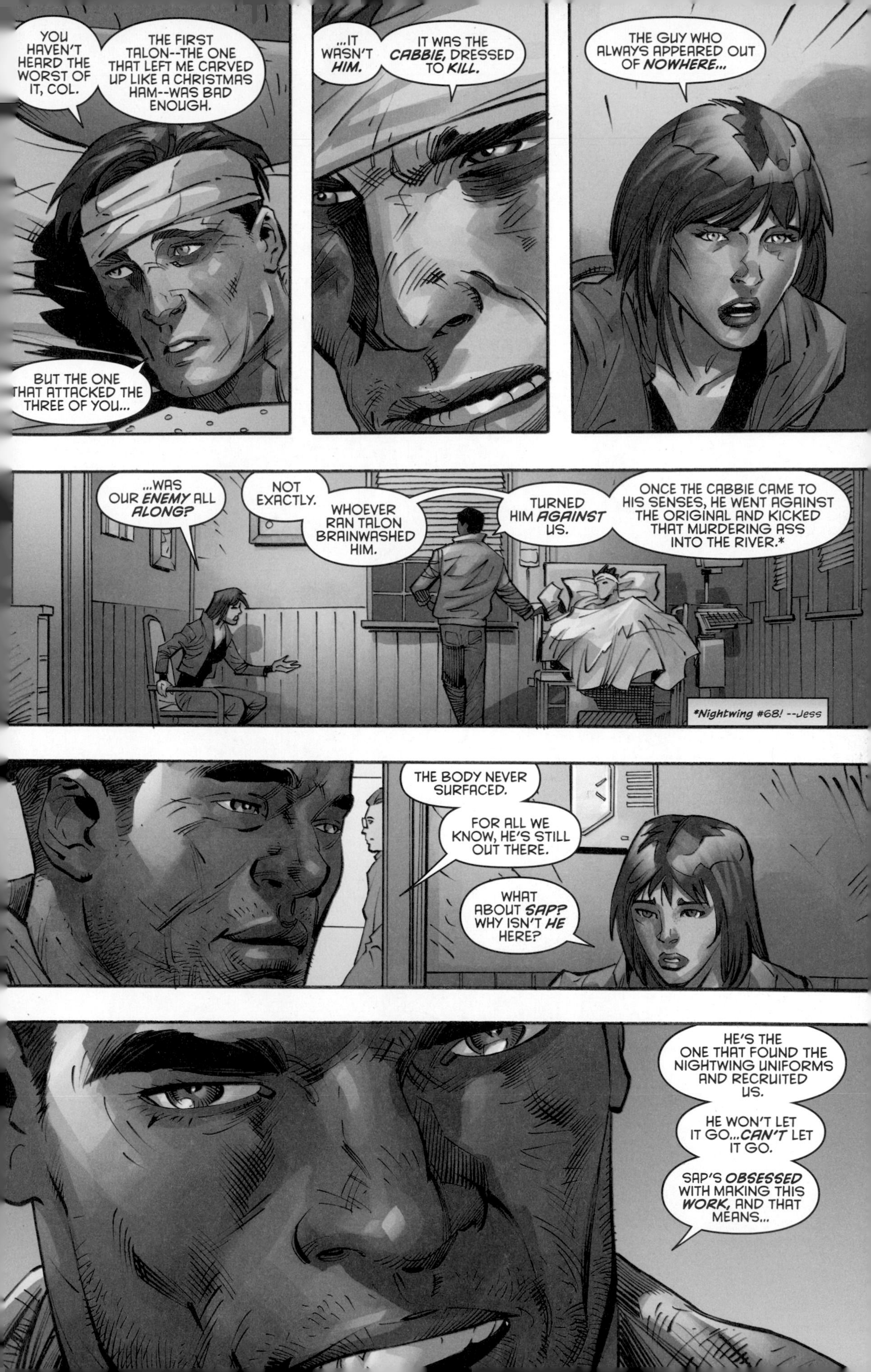

YOU HAVEN'T HEARD THE WORST OF IT, COL.
THE FIRST TALON--THE ONE THAT LEFT ME CARVED UP LIKE A CHRISTMAS HAM--WAS BAD ENOUGH.
BUT THE ONE THAT ATTACKED THE THREE OF YOU...
...IT WASN'T HIM.
IT WAS THE CABBIE, DRESSED TO KILL.
THE GUY WHO ALWAYS APPEARED OUT OF NOWHERE...
...WAS OUR ENEMY ALL ALONG?
NOT EXACTLY.
WHOEVER RAN TALON BRAINWASHED HIM.
TURNED HIM AGAINST US.
ONCE THE CABBIE CAME TO HIS SENSES, HE WENT AGAINST THE ORIGINAL AND KICKED THAT MURDERING ASS INTO THE RIVER.*
*Nightwing #68! --Jess
THE BODY NEVER SURFACED.
FOR ALL WE KNOW, HE'S STILL OUT THERE.
WHAT ABOUT SAP? WHY ISN'T HE HERE?
HE'S THE ONE THAT FOUND THE NIGHTWING UNIFORMS AND RECRUITED US.
HE WON'T LET IT GO...CAN'T LET IT GO.
SAP'S OBSESSED WITH MAKING THIS WORK, AND THAT MEANS...

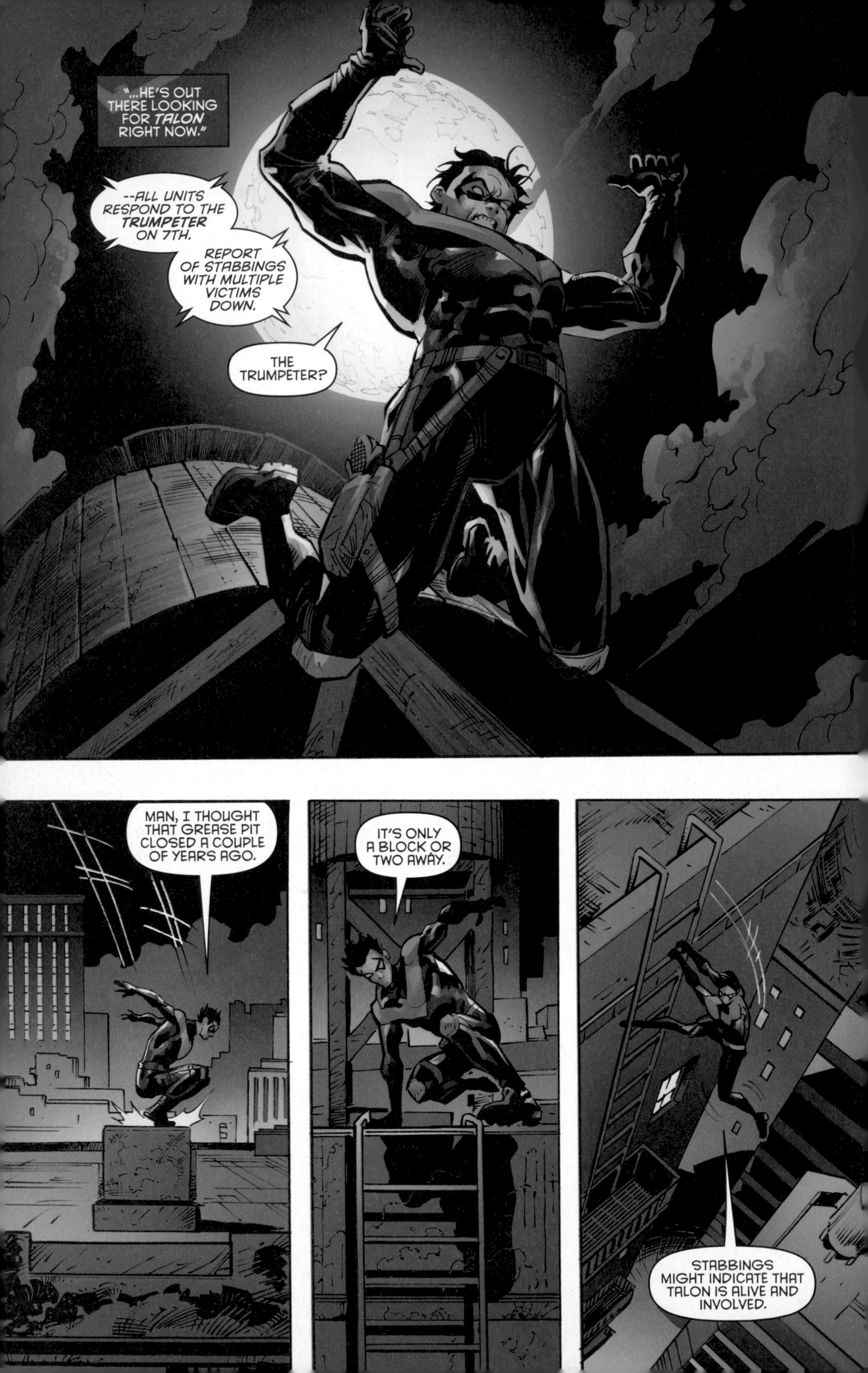
"...HE'S OUT THERE LOOKING FOR *TALON* RIGHT NOW."
--*ALL UNITS RESPOND TO THE* ***TRUMPETER*** *ON 7TH.*
REPORT OF STABBINGS WITH MULTIPLE VICTIMS DOWN.
THE TRUMPETER?
MAN, I THOUGHT THAT GREASE PIT CLOSED A COUPLE OF YEARS AGO.
IT'S ONLY A BLOCK OR TWO AWAY.
STABBINGS MIGHT INDICATE THAT TALON IS ALIVE AND INVOLVED.

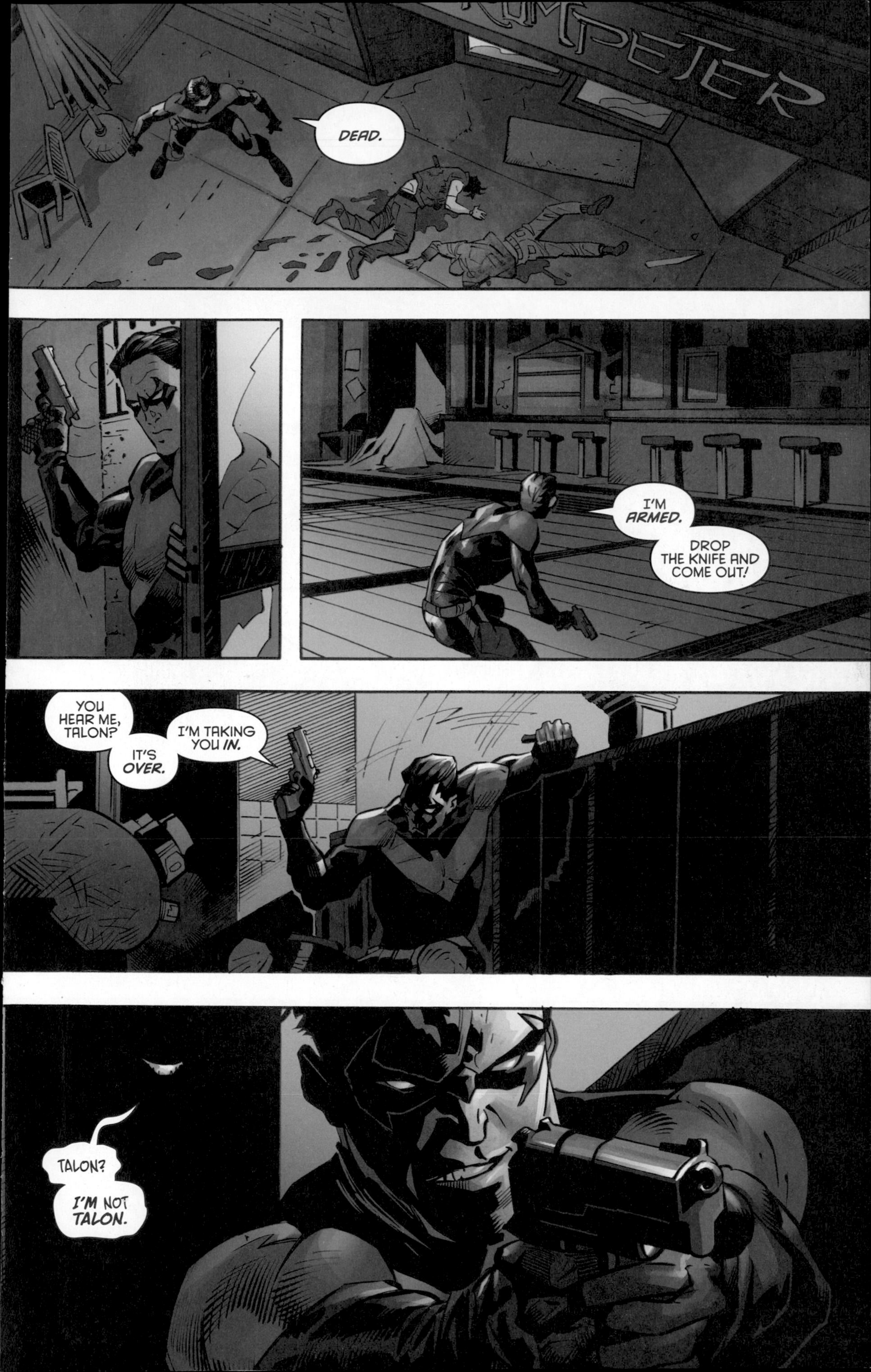

DEAD.
I'M ARMED.
DROP THE KNIFE AND COME OUT!
YOU HEAR ME, TALON?
IT'S OVER.
I'M TAKING YOU IN.
TALON?
I'M NOT TALON.

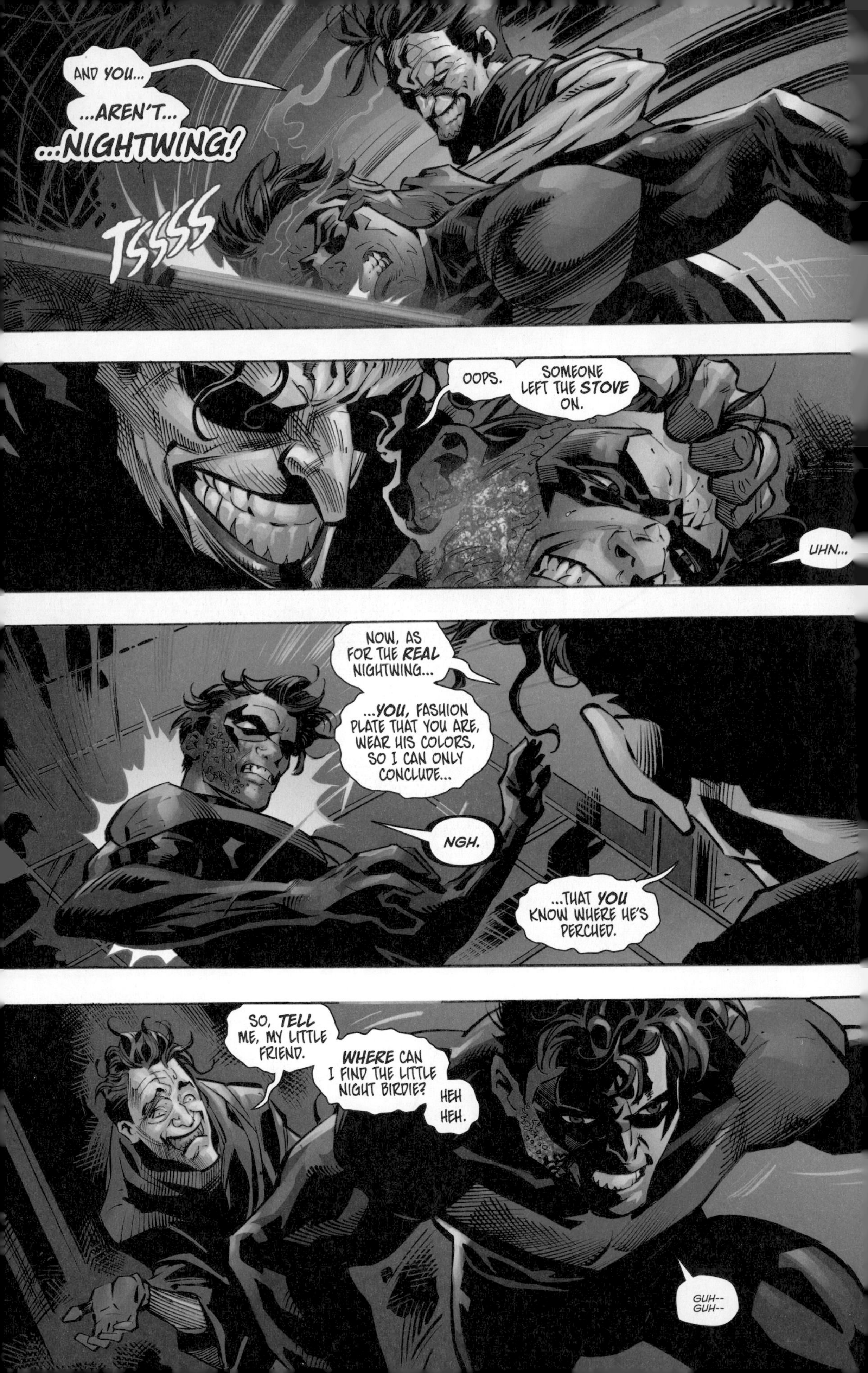

AND YOU...
...AREN'T...
...NIGHTWING!
TSSSS
OOPS.
SOMEONE LEFT THE STOVE ON.
UHN...
NOW, AS FOR THE REAL NIGHTWING...
...YOU, FASHION PLATE THAT YOU ARE, WEAR HIS COLORS, SO I CAN ONLY CONCLUDE...
NGH.
...THAT YOU KNOW WHERE HE'S PERCHED.
SO, TELL ME, MY LITTLE FRIEND.
WHERE CAN I FIND THE LITTLE NIGHT BIRDIE?
HEH HEH.
GUH-- GUH--

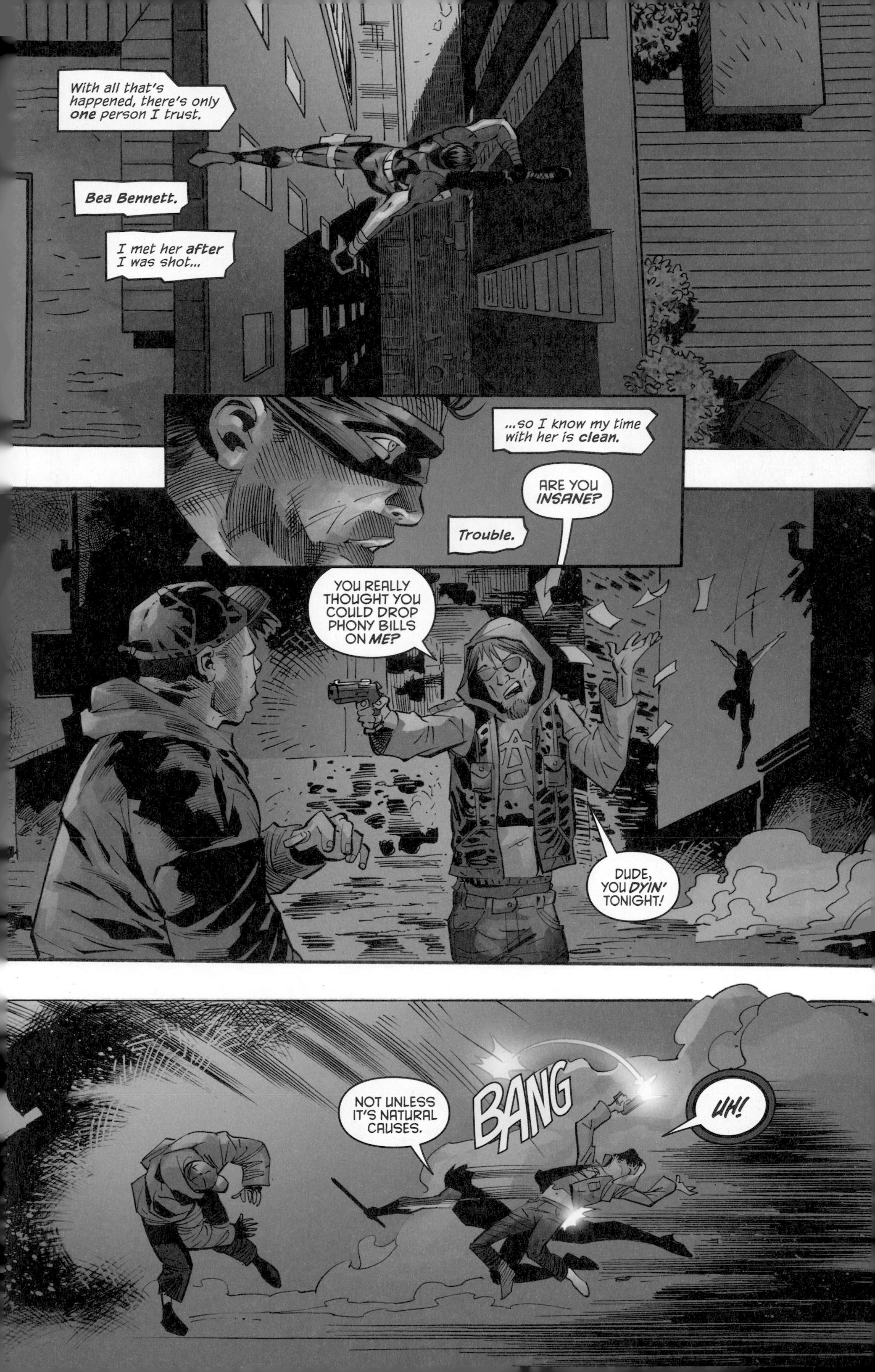
With all that's happened, there's only one person I trust.
Bea Bennett.
I met her after I was shot...
...so I know my time with her is clean.
Trouble.
ARE YOU INSANE?
YOU REALLY THOUGHT YOU COULD DROP PHONY BILLS ON ME?
DUDE, YOU DYIN' TONIGHT!
NOT UNLESS IT'S NATURAL CAUSES.
BANG
UH!

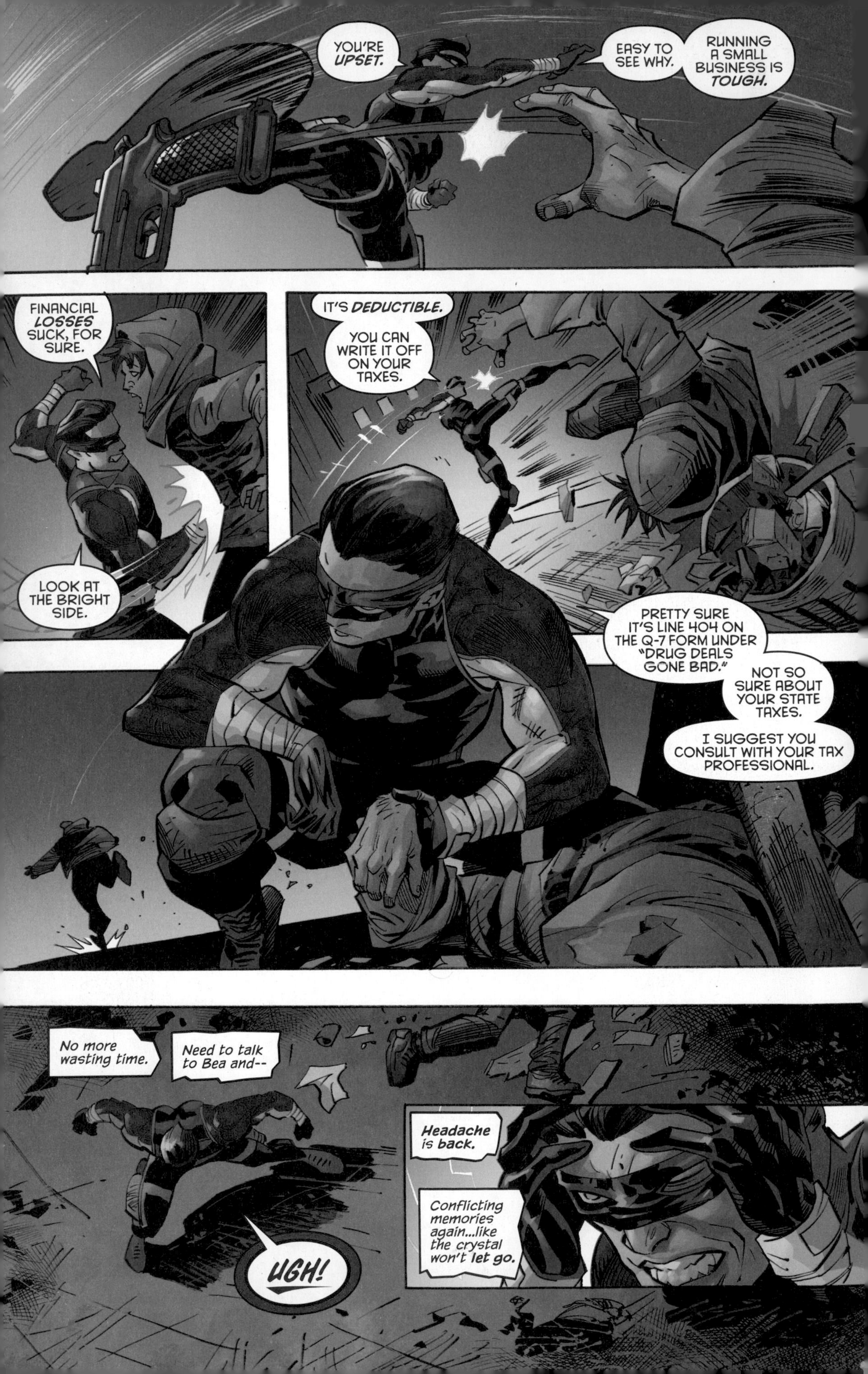

YOU'RE UPSET.
EASY TO SEE WHY.
RUNNING A SMALL BUSINESS IS TOUGH.
FINANCIAL LOSSES SUCK, FOR SURE.
LOOK AT THE BRIGHT SIDE.
IT'S DEDUCTIBLE.
YOU CAN WRITE IT OFF ON YOUR TAXES.
PRETTY SURE IT'S LINE 404 ON THE Q-7 FORM UNDER "DRUG DEALS GONE BAD."
NOT SO SURE ABOUT YOUR STATE TAXES.
I SUGGEST YOU CONSULT WITH YOUR TAX PROFESSIONAL.
No more wasting time.
Need to talk to Bea and--
UGH!
Headache is back.
Conflicting memories again...like the crystal won't let go.

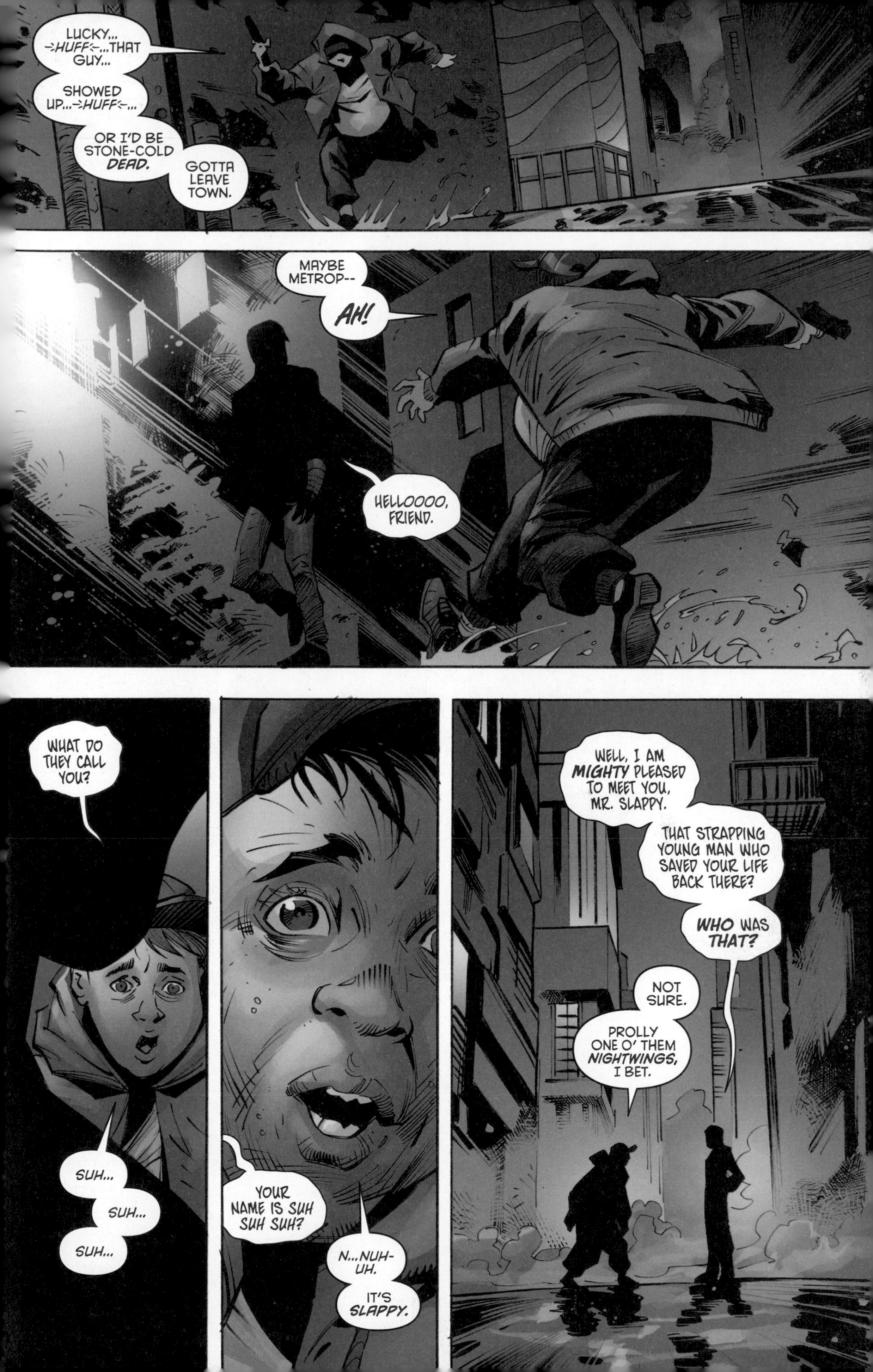

LUCKY... ~HUFF~...THAT GUY...
SHOWED UP...~HUFF~...
OR I'D BE STONE-COLD DEAD.
GOTTA LEAVE TOWN.
MAYBE METROP--
AH!
HELLOOOO, FRIEND.
WHAT DO THEY CALL YOU?
SUH...
SUH...
SUH...
YOUR NAME IS SUH SUH SUH?
N...NUH-UH.
IT'S SLAPPY.
WELL, I AM MIGHTY PLEASED TO MEET YOU, MR. SLAPPY.
THAT STRAPPING YOUNG MAN WHO SAVED YOUR LIFE BACK THERE?
WHO WAS THAT?
NOT SURE.
PROLLY ONE O' THEM NIGHTWINGS, I BET.

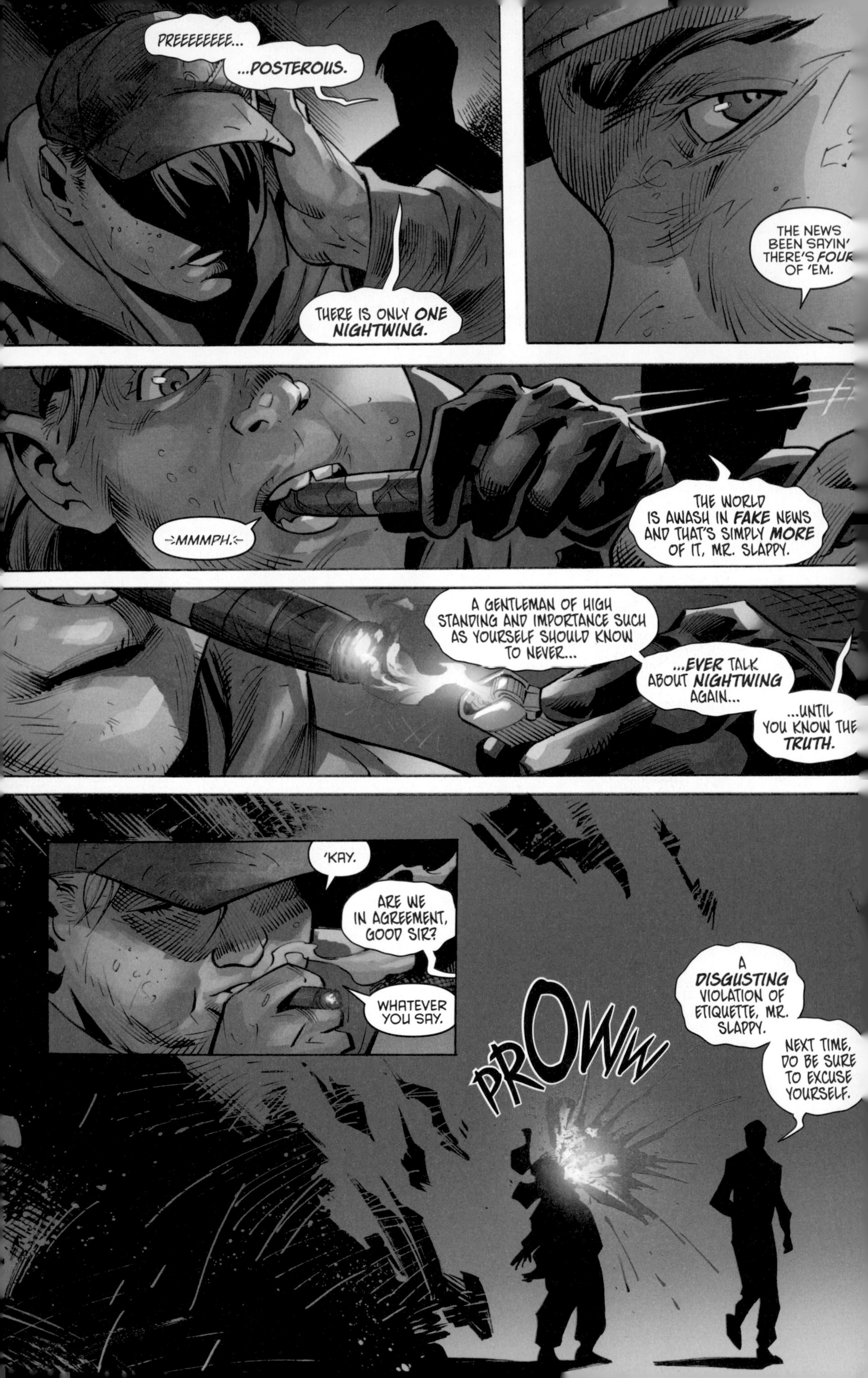
PREEEEEEEE...
...POSTEROUS.
THERE IS ONLY ONE NIGHTWING.
THE NEWS BEEN SAYIN' THERE'S FOUR OF 'EM.
MMMPH.
THE WORLD IS AWASH IN FAKE NEWS AND THAT'S SIMPLY MORE OF IT, MR. SLAPPY.
A GENTLEMAN OF HIGH STANDING AND IMPORTANCE SUCH AS YOURSELF SHOULD KNOW TO NEVER...
...EVER TALK ABOUT NIGHTWING AGAIN...
...UNTIL YOU KNOW THE TRUTH.
'KAY.
ARE WE IN AGREEMENT, GOOD SIR?
WHATEVER YOU SAY.
PROWW
A DISGUSTING VIOLATION OF ETIQUETTE, MR. SLAPPY.
NEXT TIME, DO BE SURE TO EXCUSE YOURSELF.

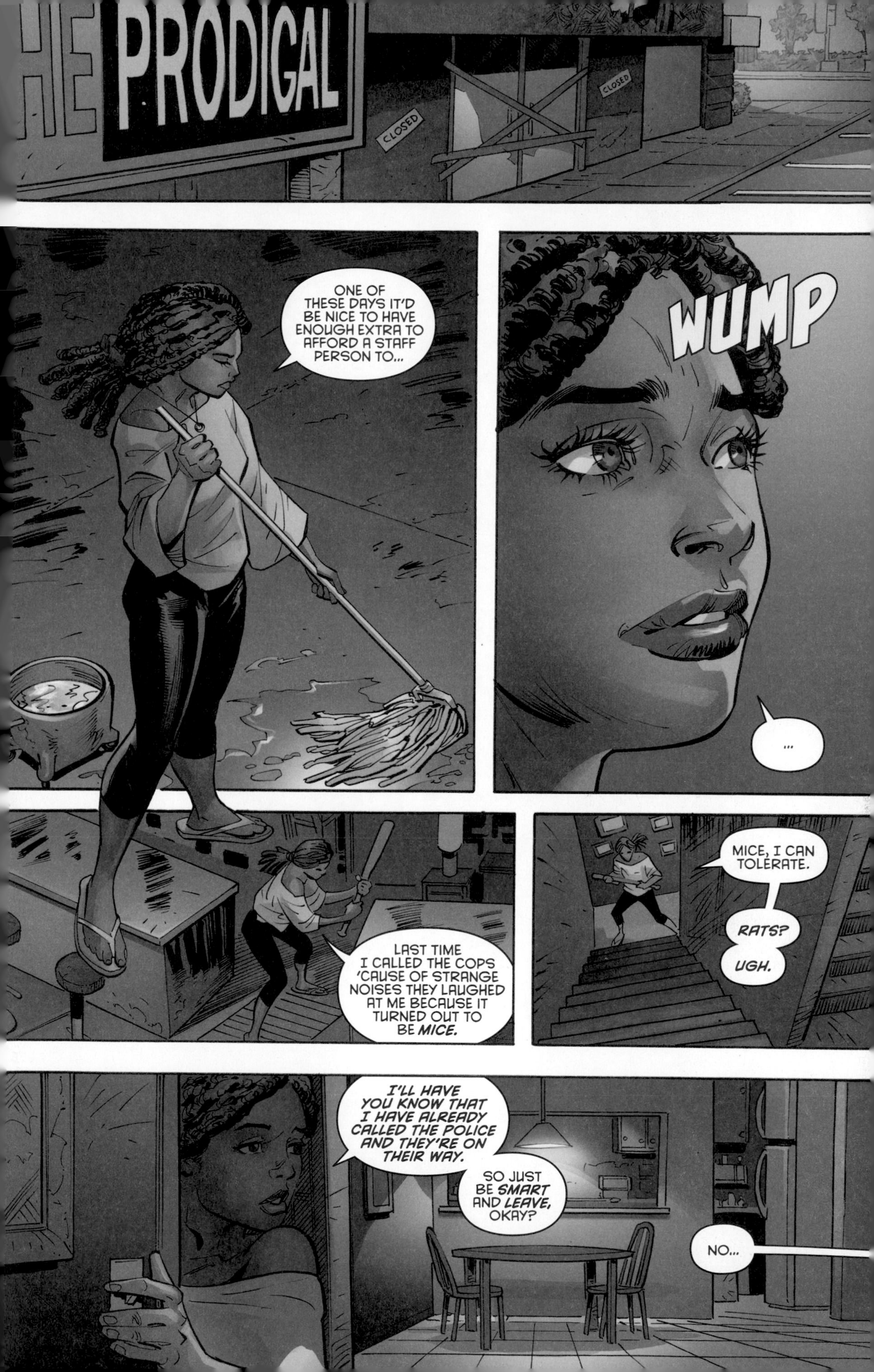
THE PRODIGAL
CLOSED
CLOSED
ONE OF THESE DAYS IT'D BE NICE TO HAVE ENOUGH EXTRA TO AFFORD A STAFF PERSON TO...
WUMP
...
LAST TIME I CALLED THE COPS 'CAUSE OF STRANGE NOISES THEY LAUGHED AT ME BECAUSE IT TURNED OUT TO BE *MICE.*
MICE, I CAN TOLERATE.
RATS?
UGH.
I'LL HAVE YOU KNOW THAT I HAVE ALREADY CALLED THE POLICE AND THEY'RE ON THEIR WAY.
SO JUST BE *SMART* AND *LEAVE,* OKAY?
NO...

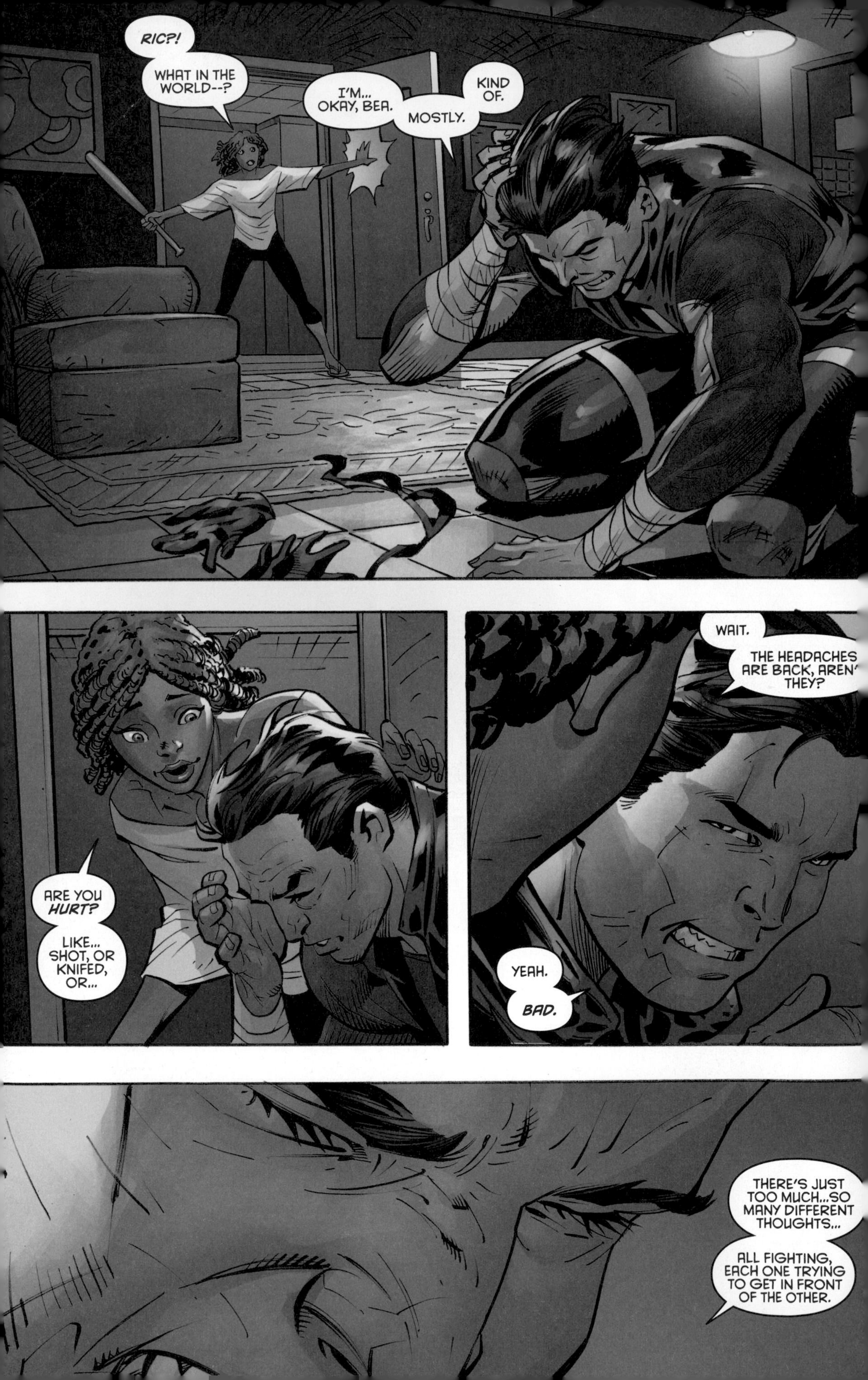
RIC?!
WHAT IN THE WORLD--?
I'M... OKAY, BEA.
MOSTLY.
KIND OF.
ARE YOU HURT?
LIKE... SHOT, OR KNIFED, OR...
WAIT.
THE HEADACHES ARE BACK, AREN'T THEY?
YEAH.
BAD.
THERE'S JUST TOO MUCH...SO MANY DIFFERENT THOUGHTS...
ALL FIGHTING, EACH ONE TRYING TO GET IN FRONT OF THE OTHER.

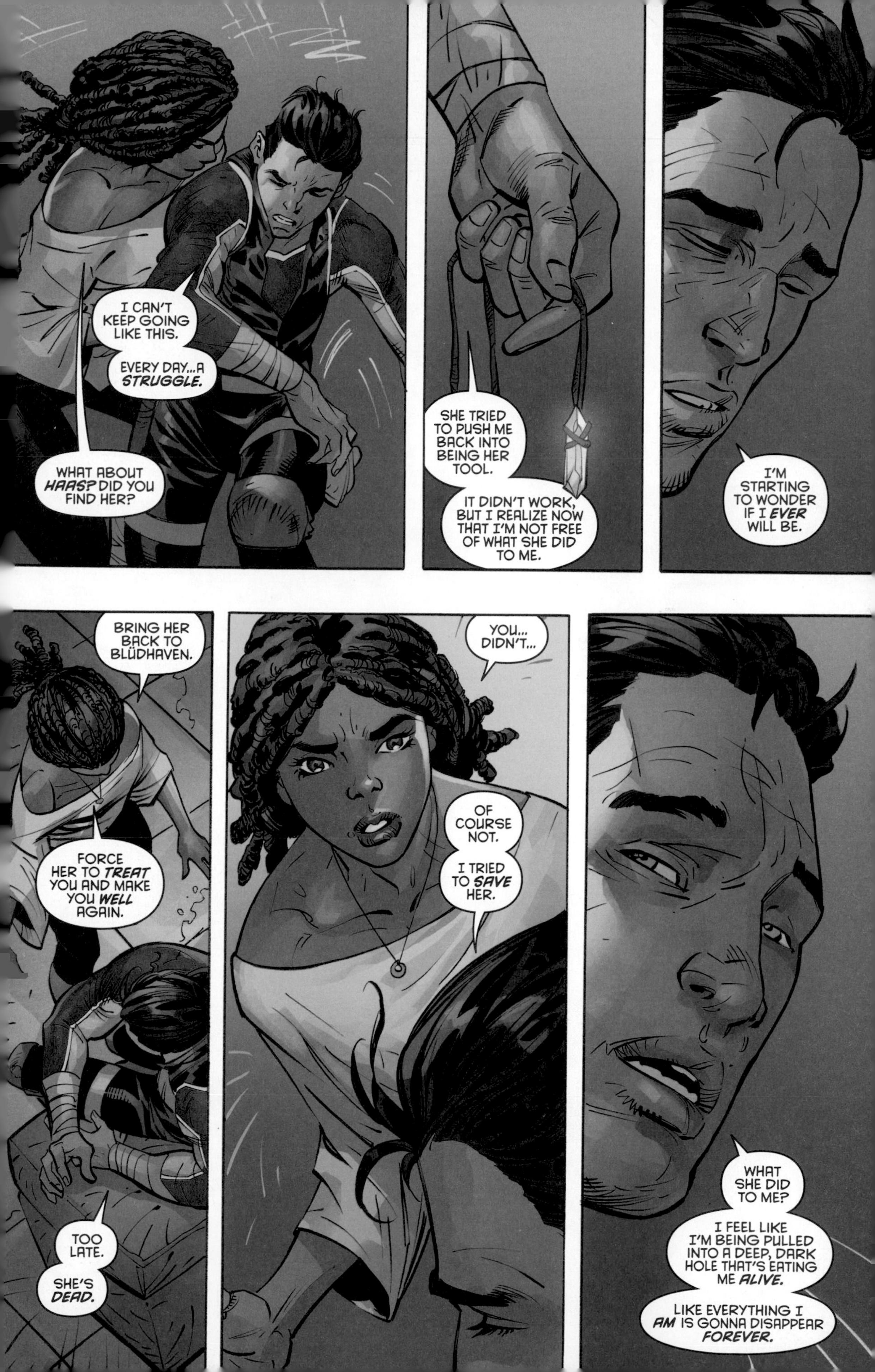
I CAN'T KEEP GOING LIKE THIS.
EVERY DAY...A STRUGGLE.
WHAT ABOUT HAAS? DID YOU FIND HER?
SHE TRIED TO PUSH ME BACK INTO BEING HER TOOL.
IT DIDN'T WORK, BUT I REALIZE NOW THAT I'M NOT FREE OF WHAT SHE DID TO ME.
I'M STARTING TO WONDER IF I EVER WILL BE.
BRING HER BACK TO BLÜDHAVEN.
FORCE HER TO TREAT YOU AND MAKE YOU WELL AGAIN.
TOO LATE.
SHE'S DEAD.
YOU... DIDN'T...
OF COURSE NOT.
I TRIED TO SAVE HER.
WHAT SHE DID TO ME?
I FEEL LIKE I'M BEING PULLED INTO A DEEP, DARK HOLE THAT'S EATING ME ALIVE.
LIKE EVERYTHING I AM IS GONNA DISAPPEAR FOREVER.

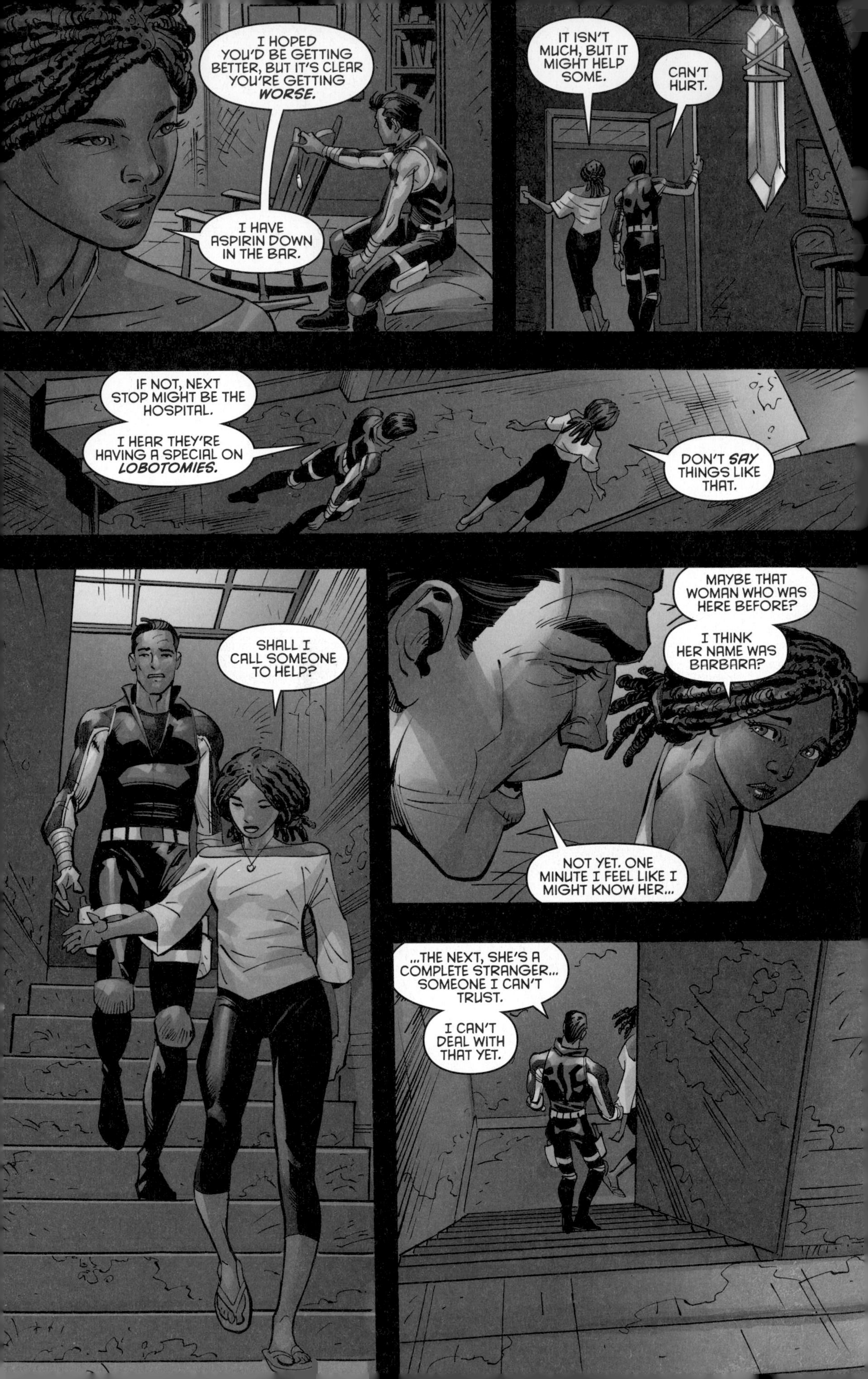
I HOPED YOU'D BE GETTING BETTER, BUT IT'S CLEAR YOU'RE GETTING WORSE.
I HAVE ASPIRIN DOWN IN THE BAR.
IT ISN'T MUCH, BUT IT MIGHT HELP SOME.
CAN'T HURT.
IF NOT, NEXT STOP MIGHT BE THE HOSPITAL.
I HEAR THEY'RE HAVING A SPECIAL ON LOBOTOMIES.
DON'T SAY THINGS LIKE THAT.
SHALL I CALL SOMEONE TO HELP?
MAYBE THAT WOMAN WHO WAS HERE BEFORE?
I THINK HER NAME WAS BARBARA?
NOT YET. ONE MINUTE I FEEL LIKE I MIGHT KNOW HER...
...THE NEXT, SHE'S A COMPLETE STRANGER... SOMEONE I CAN'T TRUST.
I CAN'T DEAL WITH THAT YET.

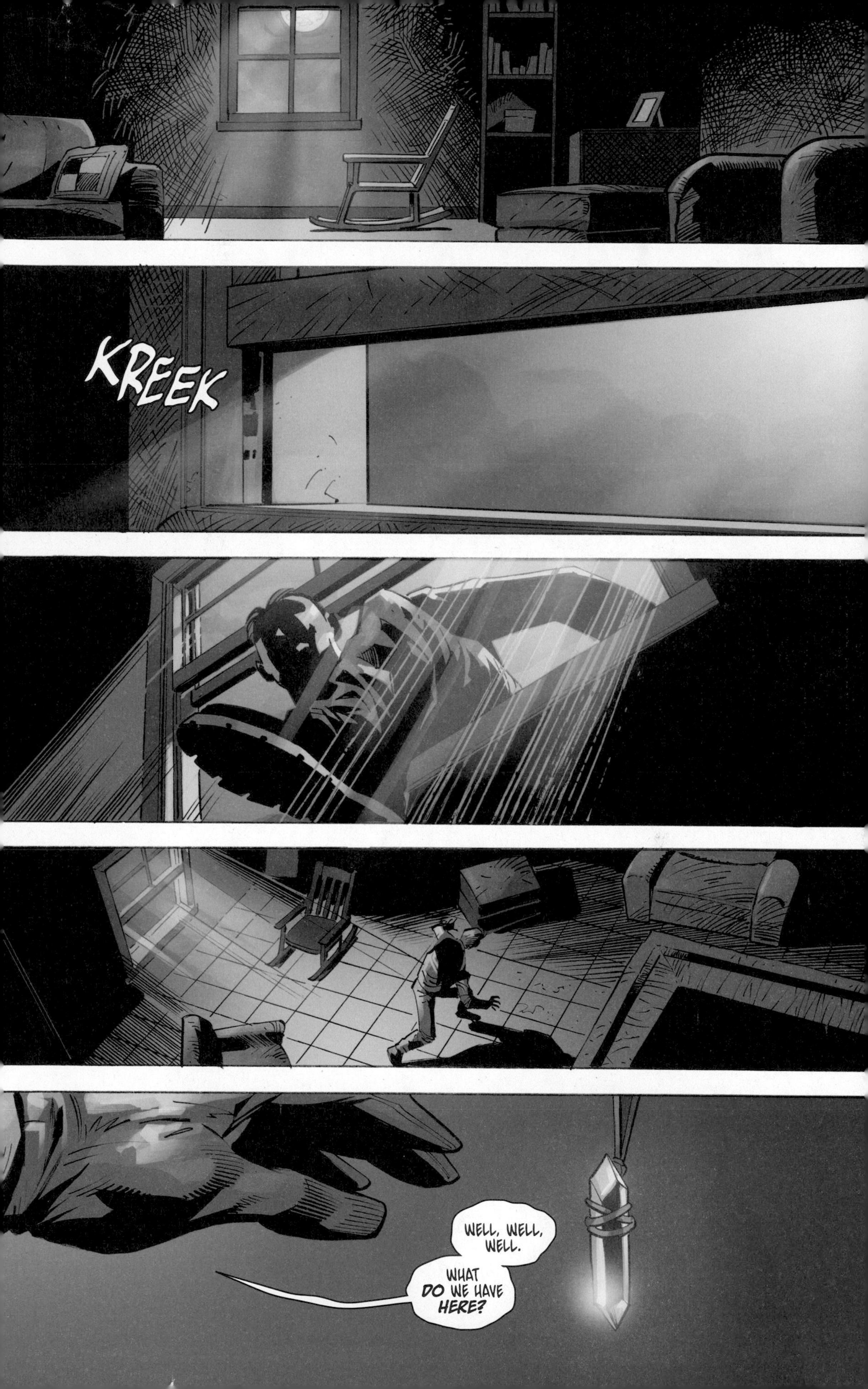
KREEK
WELL, WELL, WELL.
WHAT DO WE HAVE HERE?

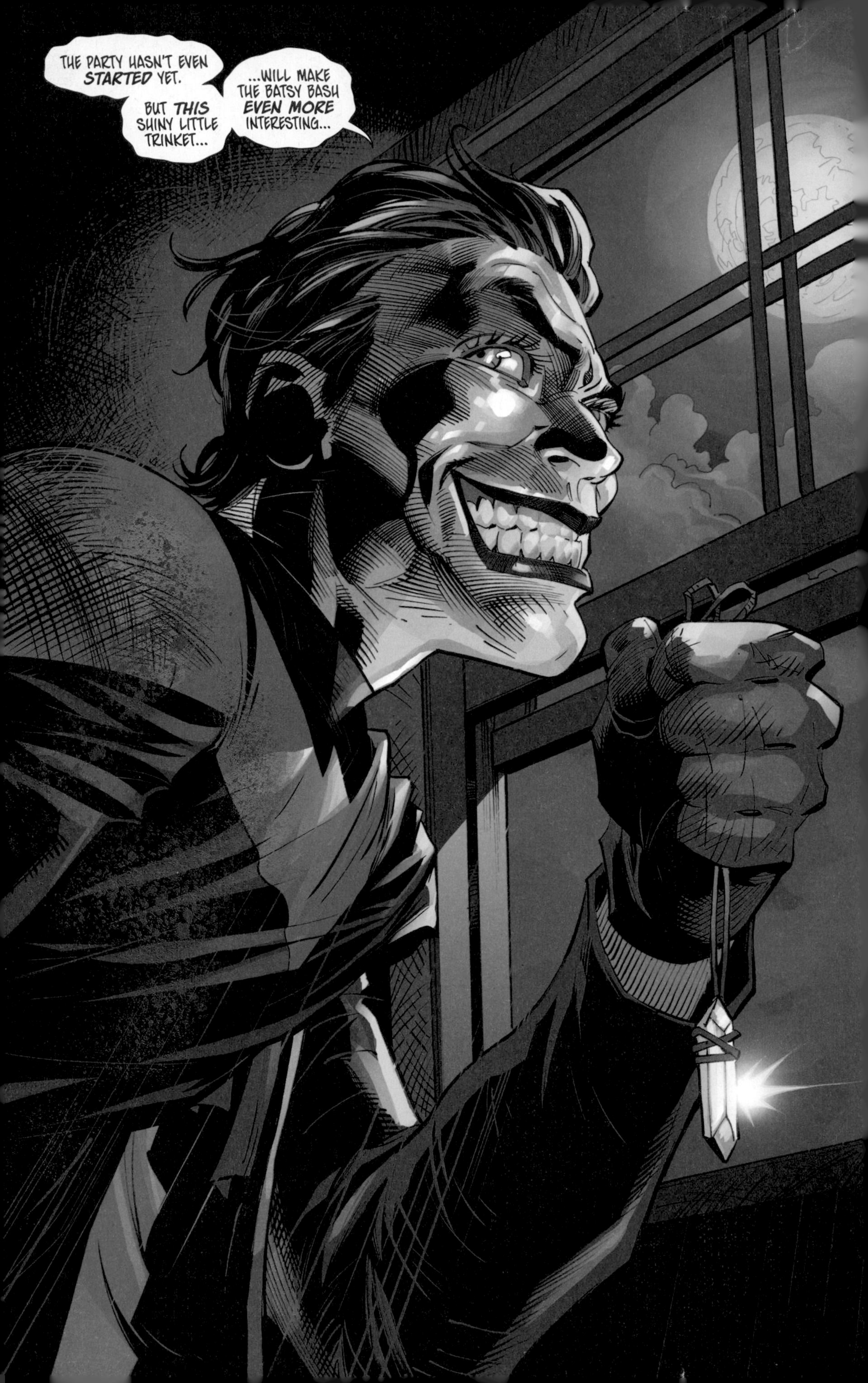
THE PARTY HASN'T EVEN STARTED YET.
BUT THIS SHINY LITTLE TRINKET...
...WILL MAKE THE BATSY BASH EVEN MORE INTERESTING...

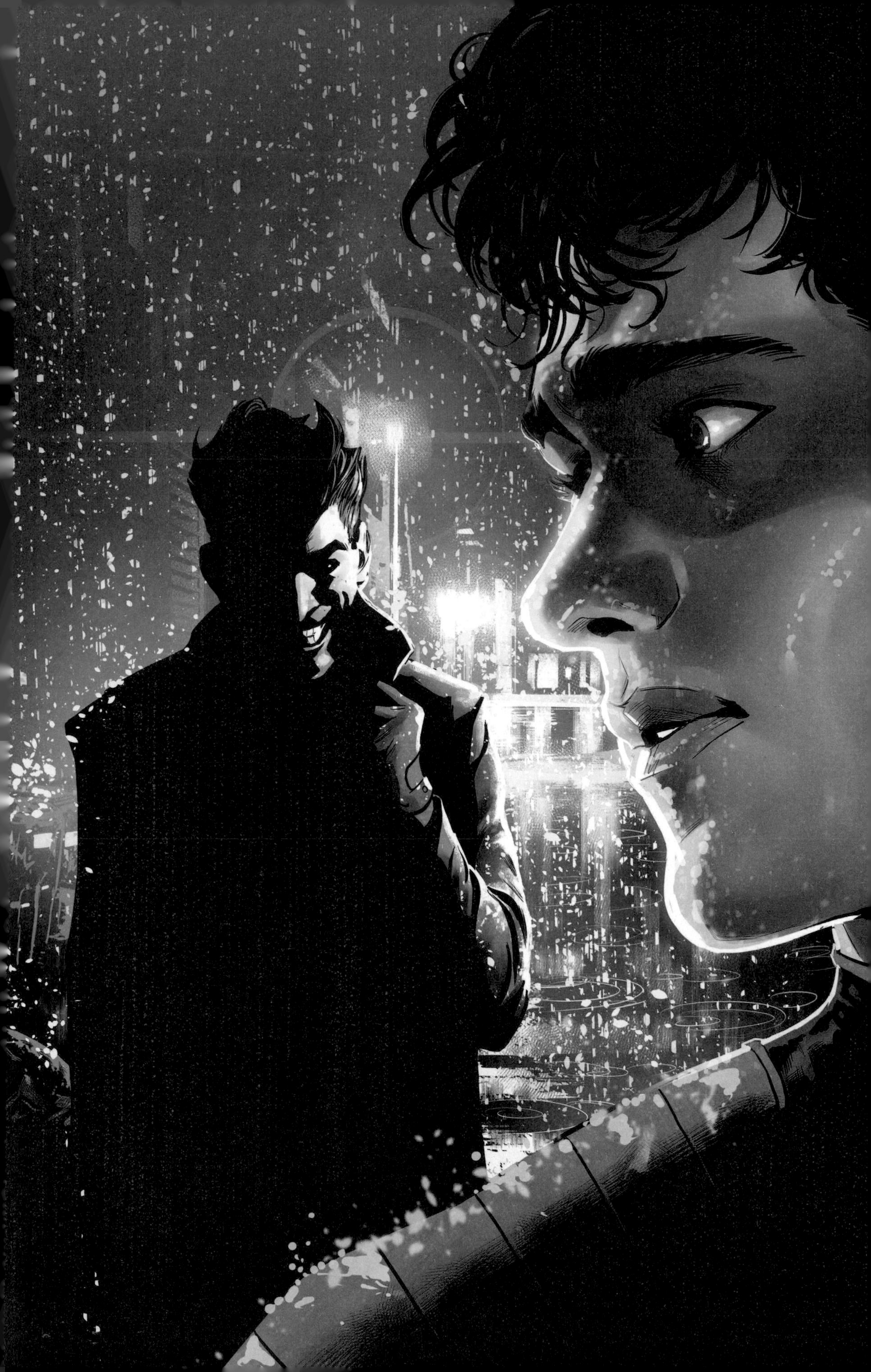

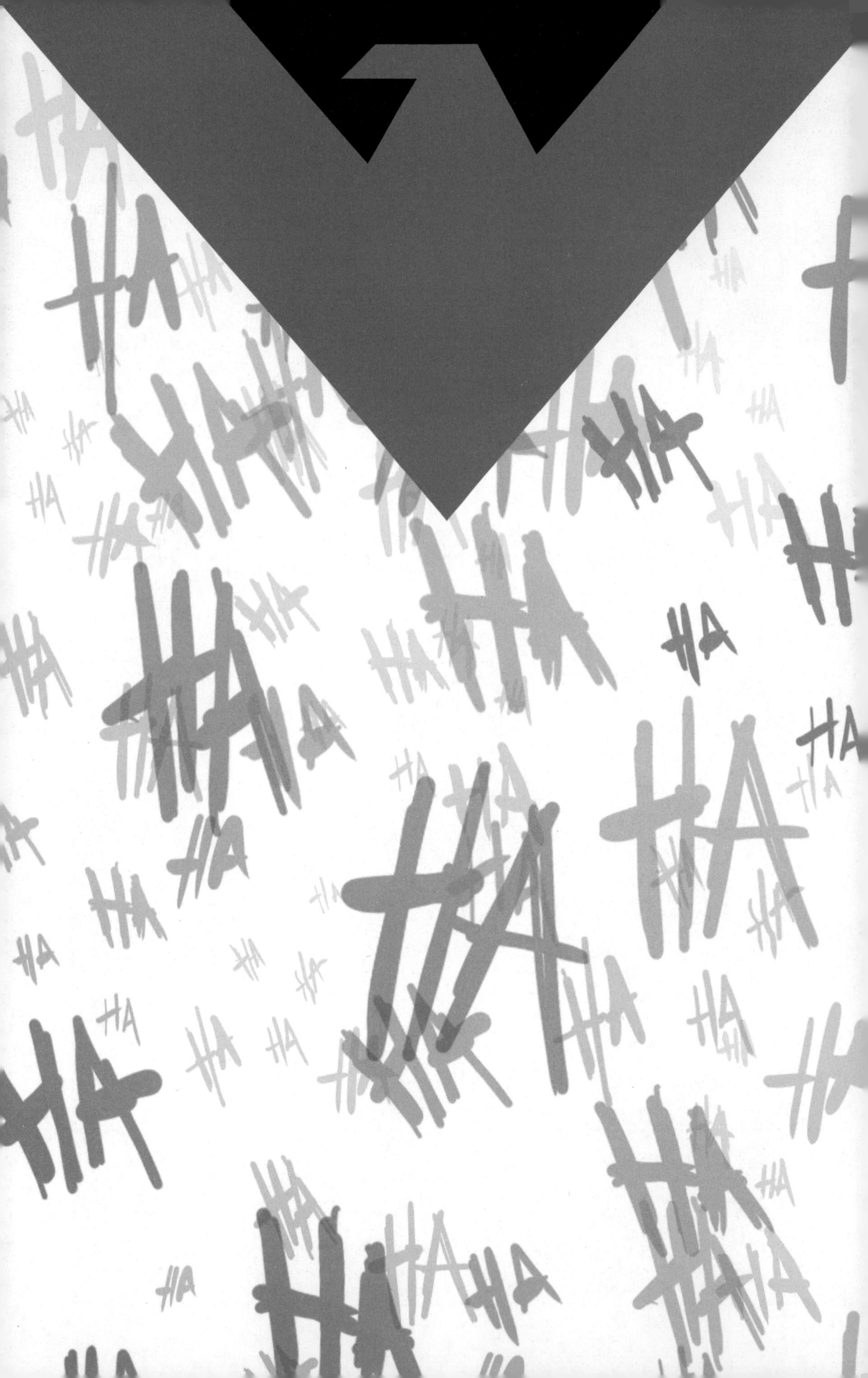

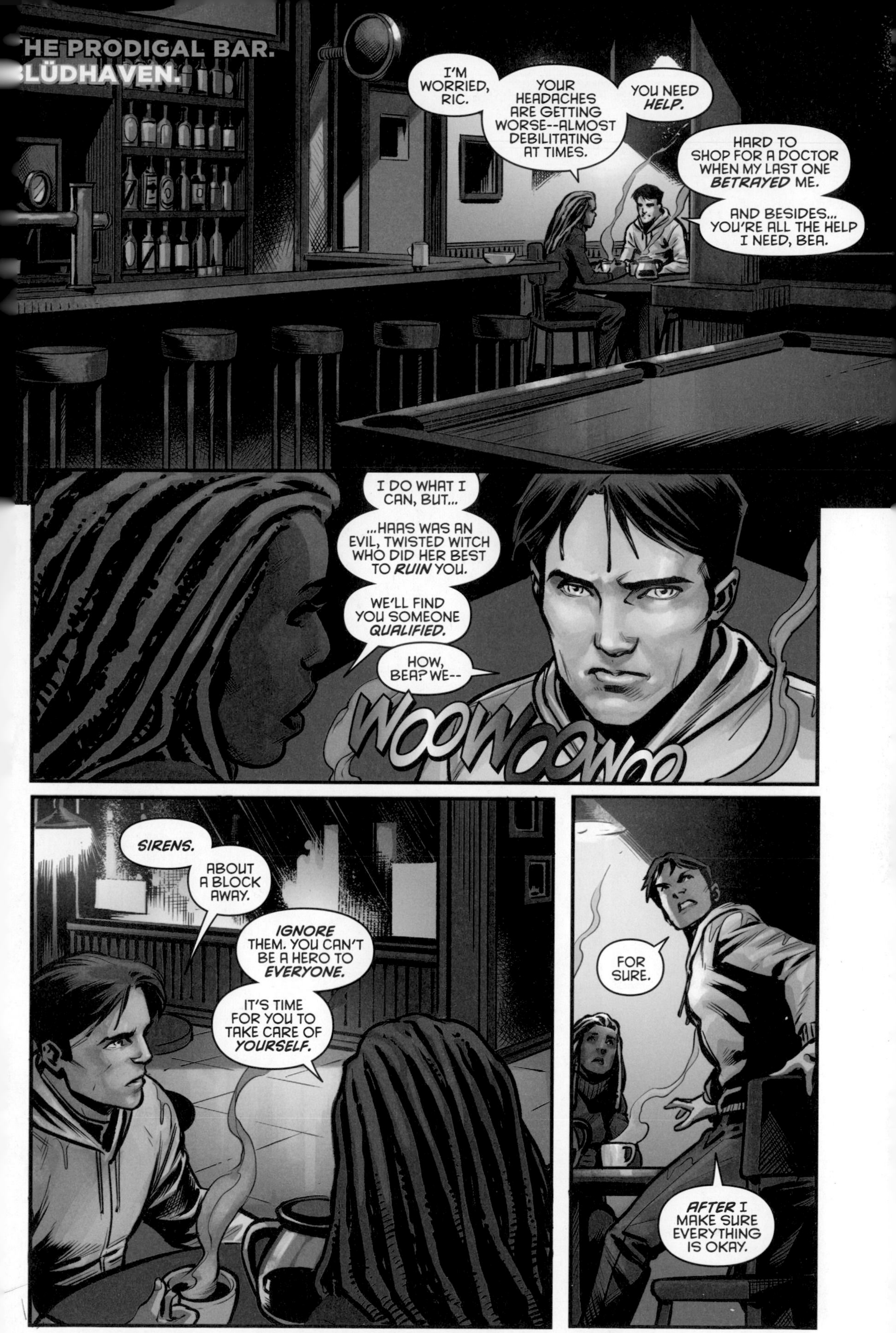
THE PRODIGAL BAR. BLÜDHAVEN.
I'M WORRIED, RIC.
YOUR HEADACHES ARE GETTING WORSE--ALMOST DEBILITATING AT TIMES.
YOU NEED HELP.
HARD TO SHOP FOR A DOCTOR WHEN MY LAST ONE BETRAYED ME.
AND BESIDES... YOU'RE ALL THE HELP I NEED, BEA.
I DO WHAT I CAN, BUT...
...HAAS WAS AN EVIL, TWISTED WITCH WHO DID HER BEST TO RUIN YOU.
WE'LL FIND YOU SOMEONE QUALIFIED.
HOW, BEA? WE--
WOOWOOWOO
SIRENS.
ABOUT A BLOCK AWAY.
IGNORE THEM. YOU CAN'T BE A HERO TO EVERYONE.
IT'S TIME FOR YOU TO TAKE CARE OF YOURSELF.
FOR SURE.
AFTER I MAKE SURE EVERYTHING IS OKAY.

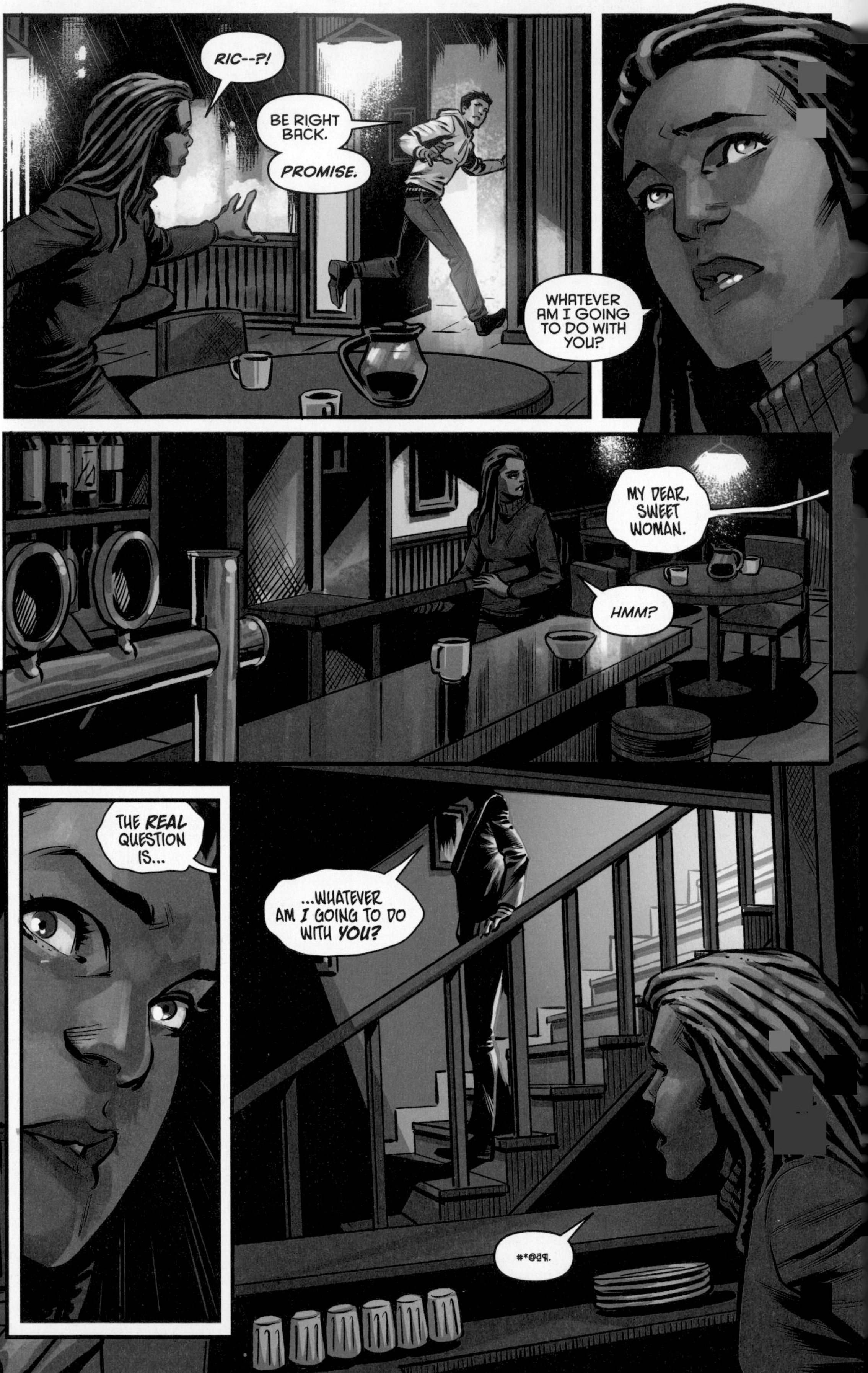
RIC--?!
BE RIGHT BACK.
PROMISE.
WHATEVER AM I GOING TO DO WITH YOU?
MY DEAR, SWEET WOMAN.
HMM?
THE REAL QUESTION IS...
...WHATEVER AM I GOING TO DO WITH YOU?
#*@ª¶.

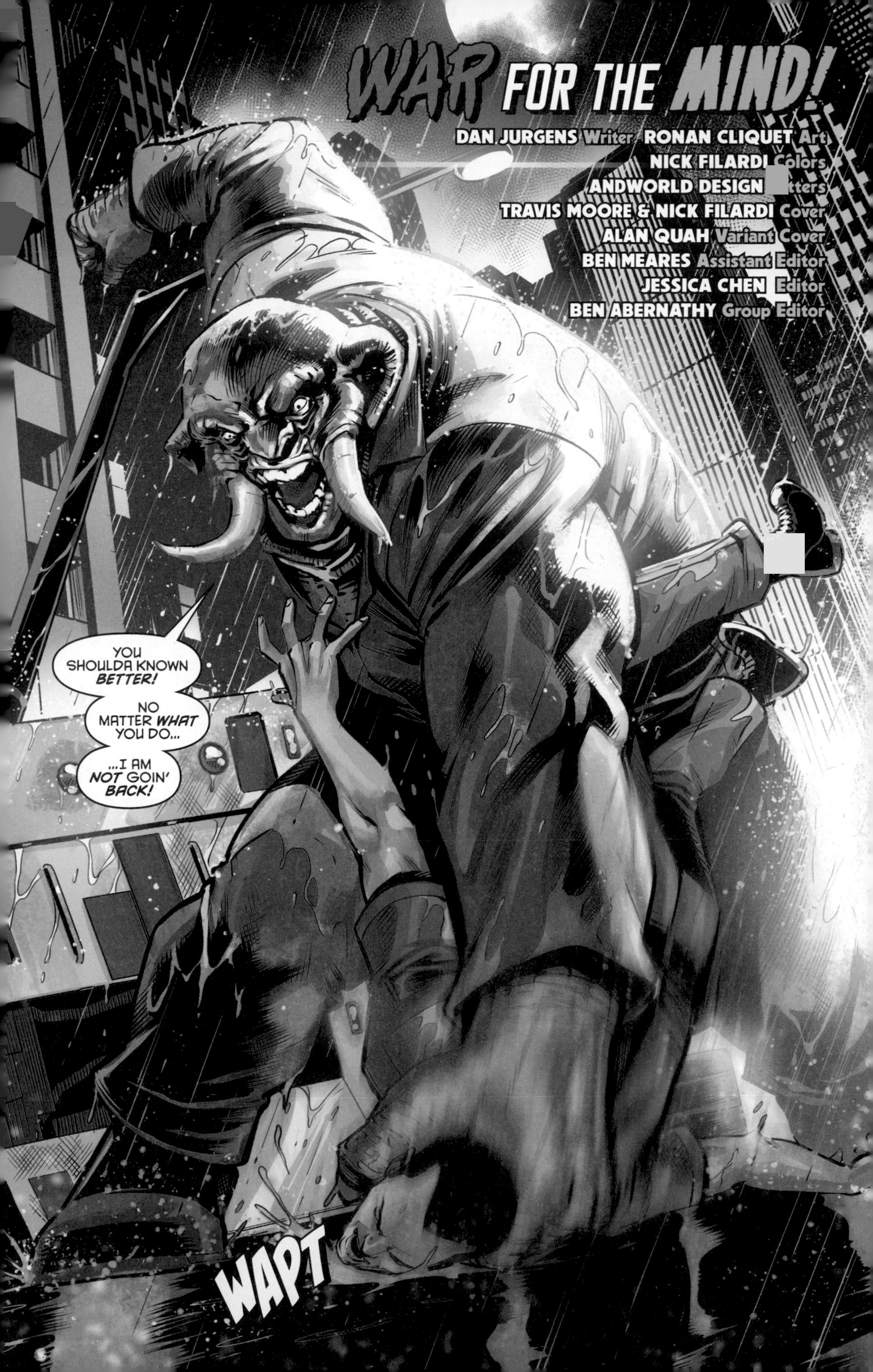
WAR FOR THE MIND!
DAN JURGENS Writer RONAN CLIQUET Art
NICK FILARDI Colors
ANDWORLD DESIGN tters
TRAVIS MOORE & NICK FILARDI Cover
ALAN QUAH Variant Cover
BEN MEARES Assistant Editor
JESSICA CHEN Editor
BEN ABERNATHY Group Editor
YOU SHOULDA KNOWN BETTER!
NO MATTER WHAT YOU DO...
...I AM NOT GOIN' BACK!
WAPT

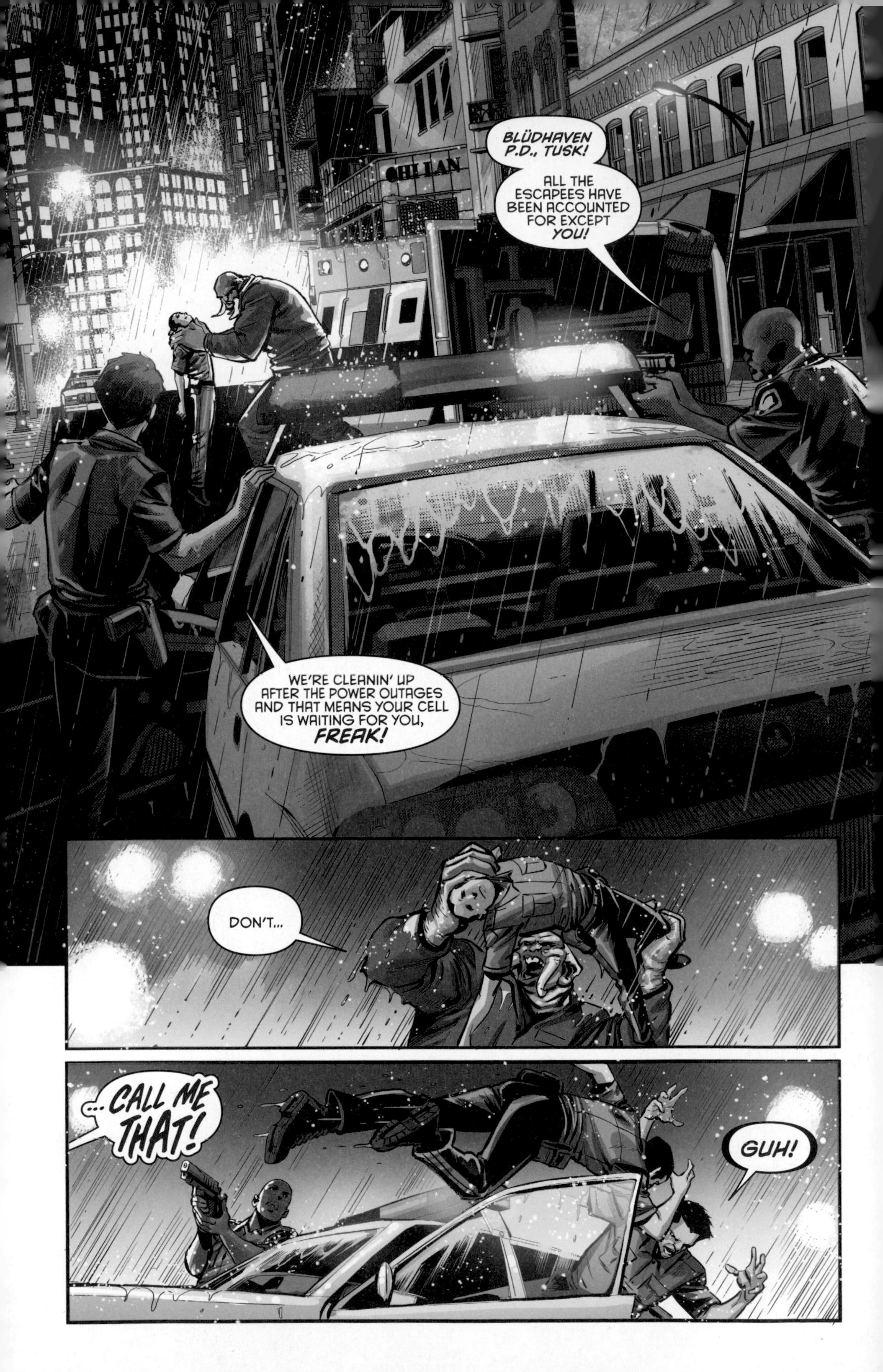

BLÜDHAVEN P.D., TUSK!
ALL THE ESCAPEES HAVE BEEN ACCOUNTED FOR EXCEPT YOU!
WE'RE CLEANIN' UP AFTER THE POWER OUTAGES AND THAT MEANS YOUR CELL IS WAITING FOR YOU, FREAK!
DON'T...
...CALL ME THAT!
GUH!

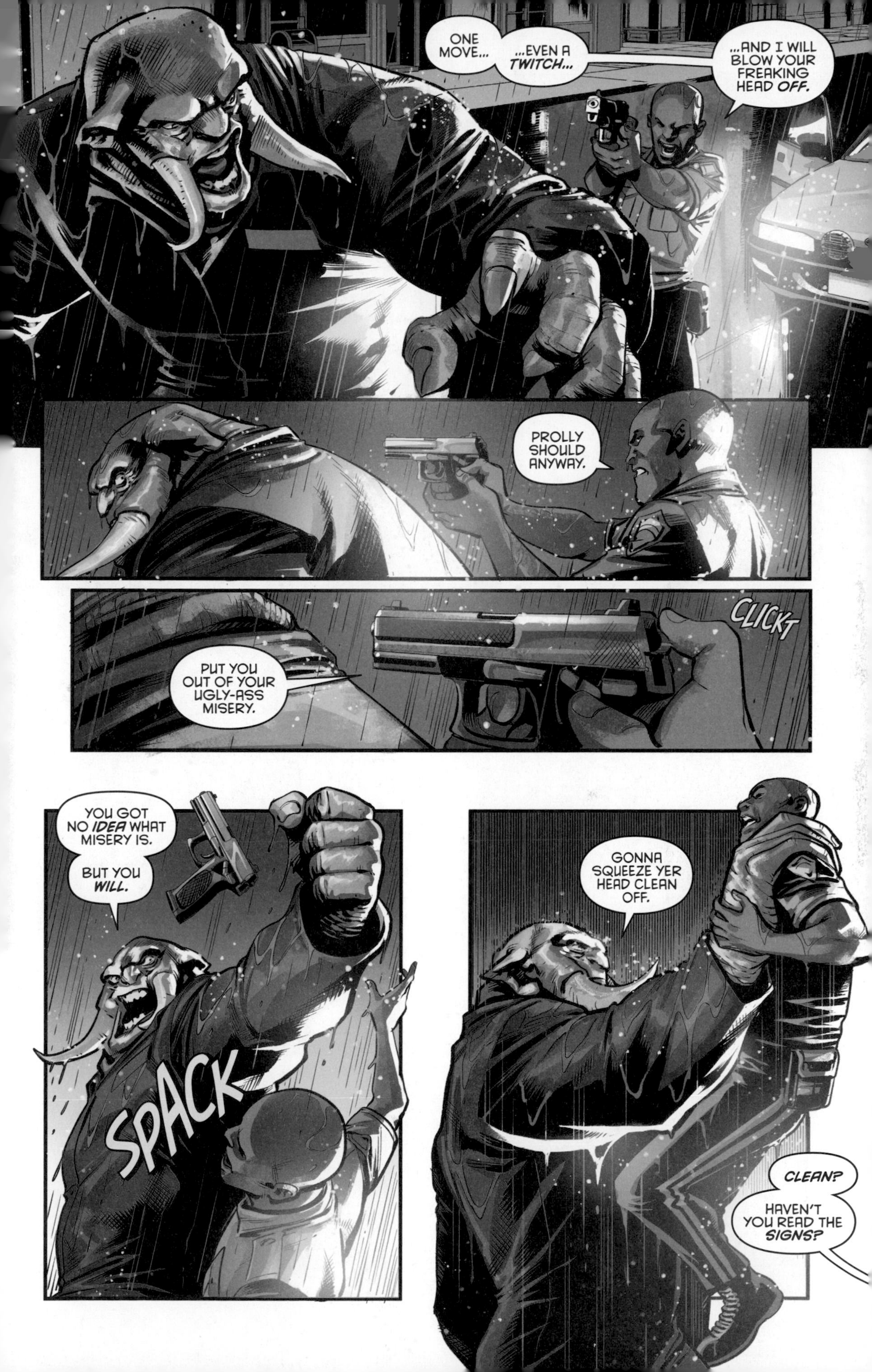
ONE MOVE...
...EVEN A *TWITCH*...
...AND I WILL BLOW YOUR FREAKING HEAD *OFF.*
PROLLY SHOULD ANYWAY.
CLICKT
PUT YOU OUT OF YOUR UGLY-ASS MISERY.
YOU GOT NO *IDEA* WHAT MISERY IS.
BUT YOU *WILL.*
SPACK
GONNA SQUEEZE YER HEAD CLEAN OFF.
CLEAN?
HAVEN'T YOU READ THE *SIGNS?*

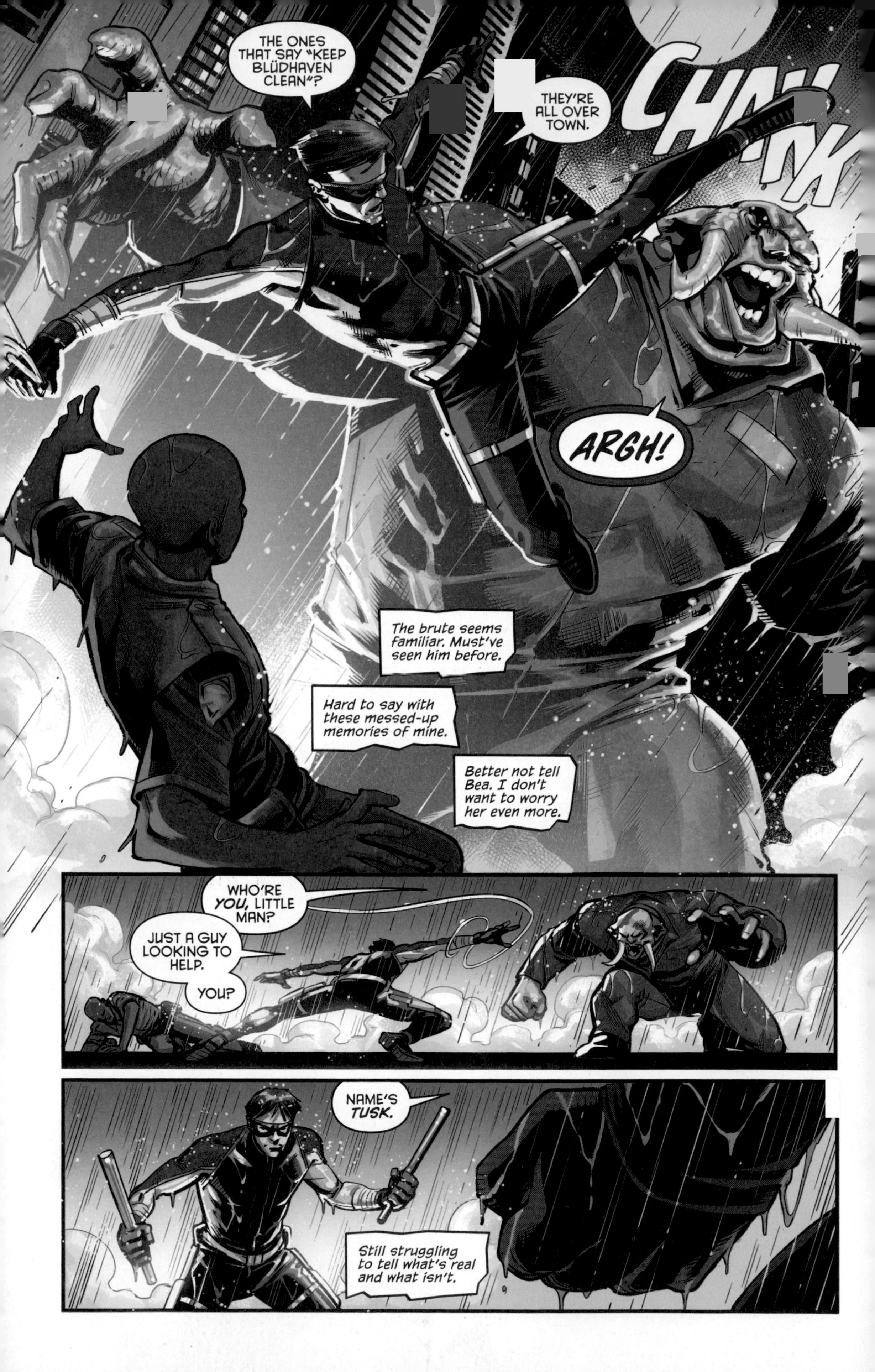
THE ONES THAT SAY "KEEP BLÜDHAVEN CLEAN"?
THEY'RE ALL OVER TOWN.
CHANK
ARGH!
The brute seems familiar. Must've seen him before.
Hard to say with these messed-up memories of mine.
Better not tell Bea. I don't want to worry her even more.
WHO'RE YOU, LITTLE MAN?
JUST A GUY LOOKING TO HELP.
YOU?
NAME'S TUSK.
Still struggling to tell what's real and what isn't.

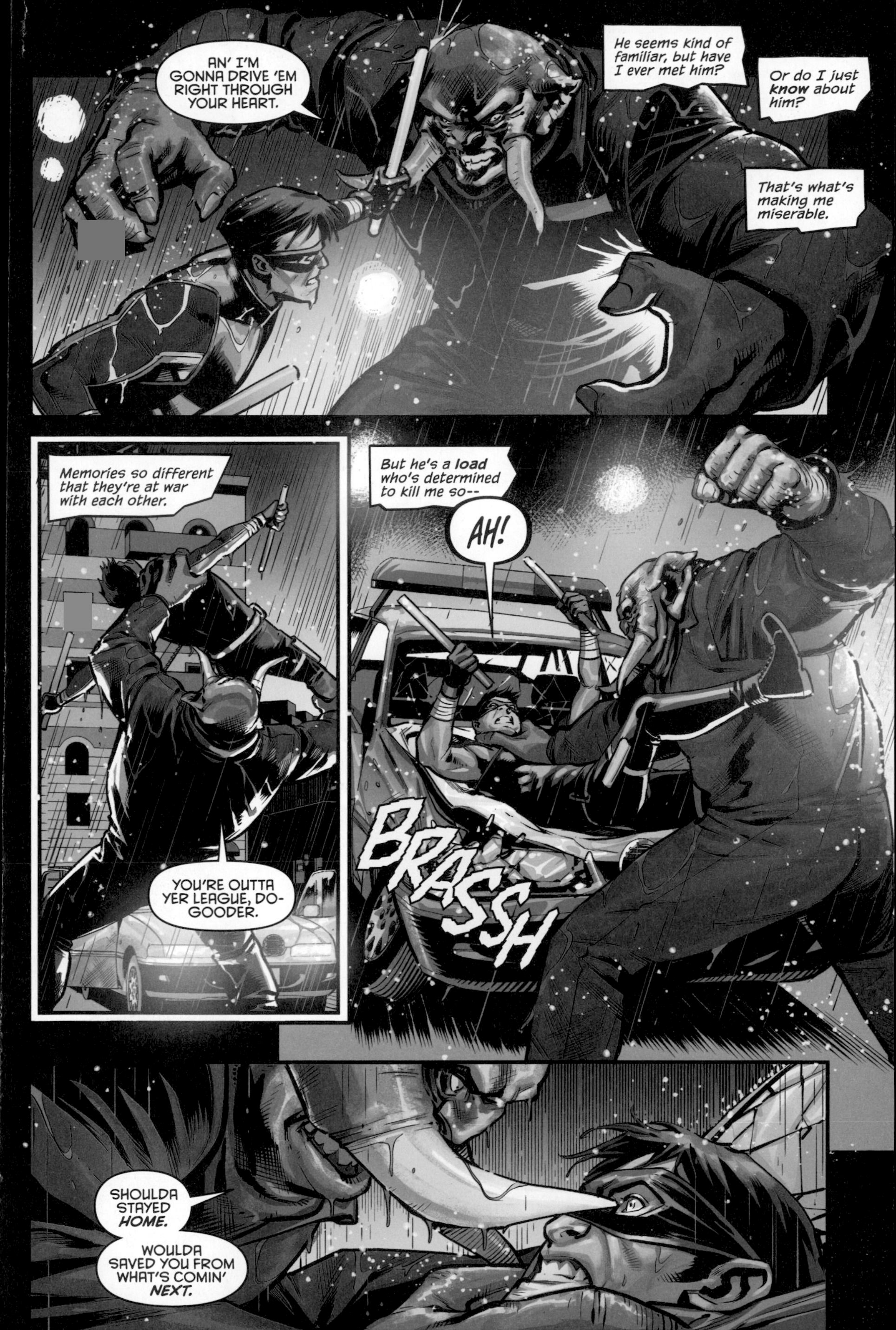
AN' I'M GONNA DRIVE 'EM RIGHT THROUGH YOUR HEART.
He seems kind of familiar, but have I ever met him?
Or do I just **know** about him?
That's what's making me miserable.
Memories so different that they're at war with each other.
YOU'RE OUTTA YER LEAGUE, DO-GOODER.
But he's a **load** who's determined to kill me so--
AH!
BRASSH
SHOULDA STAYED *HOME.*
WOULDA SAVED YOU FROM WHAT'S COMIN' *NEXT.*

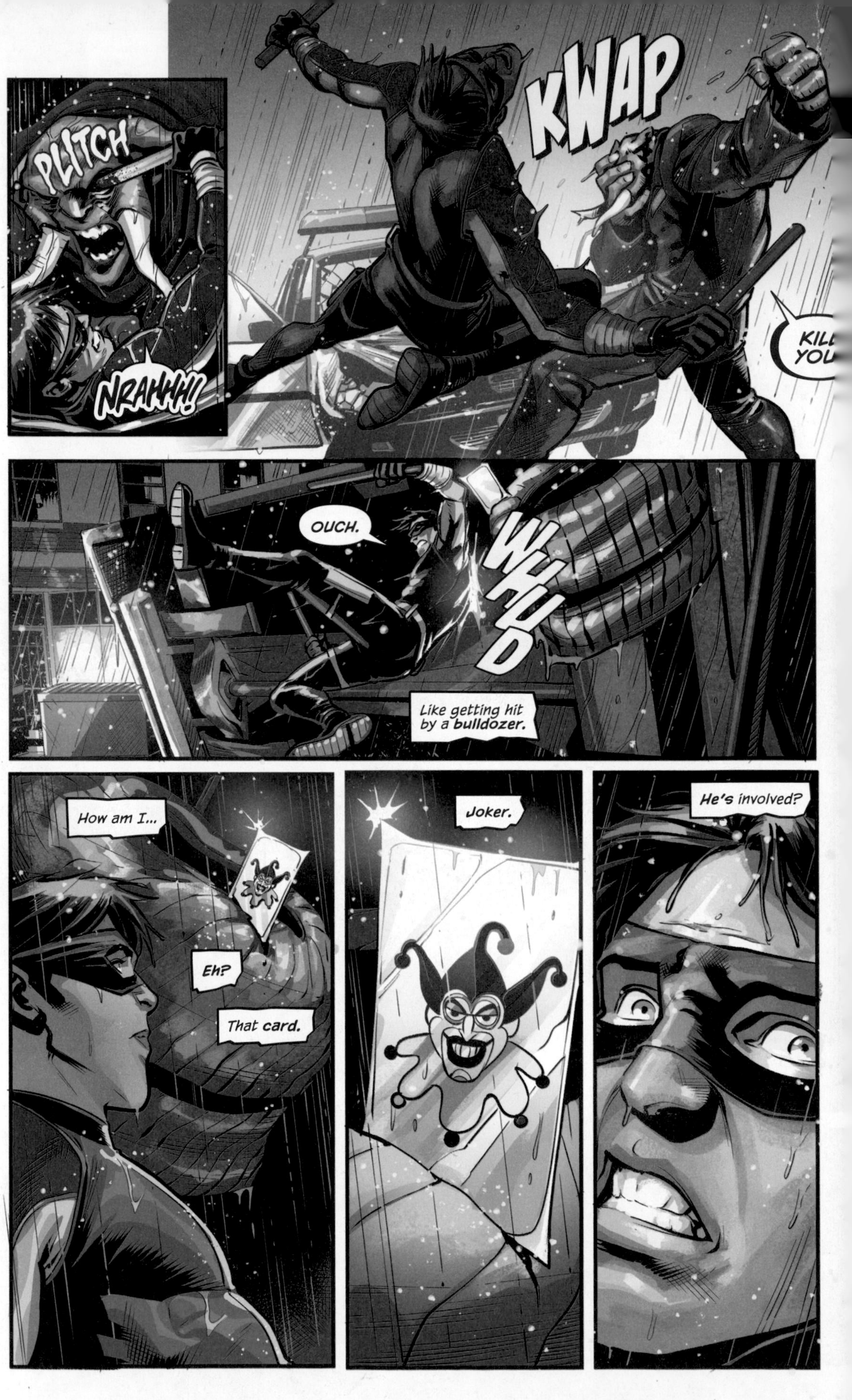
PLITCH
NRAHHH!
KWAP
KILL YOU
OUCH.
WHUD
Like getting hit by a bulldozer.
How am I...
Eh?
That card.
Joker.
He's involved?

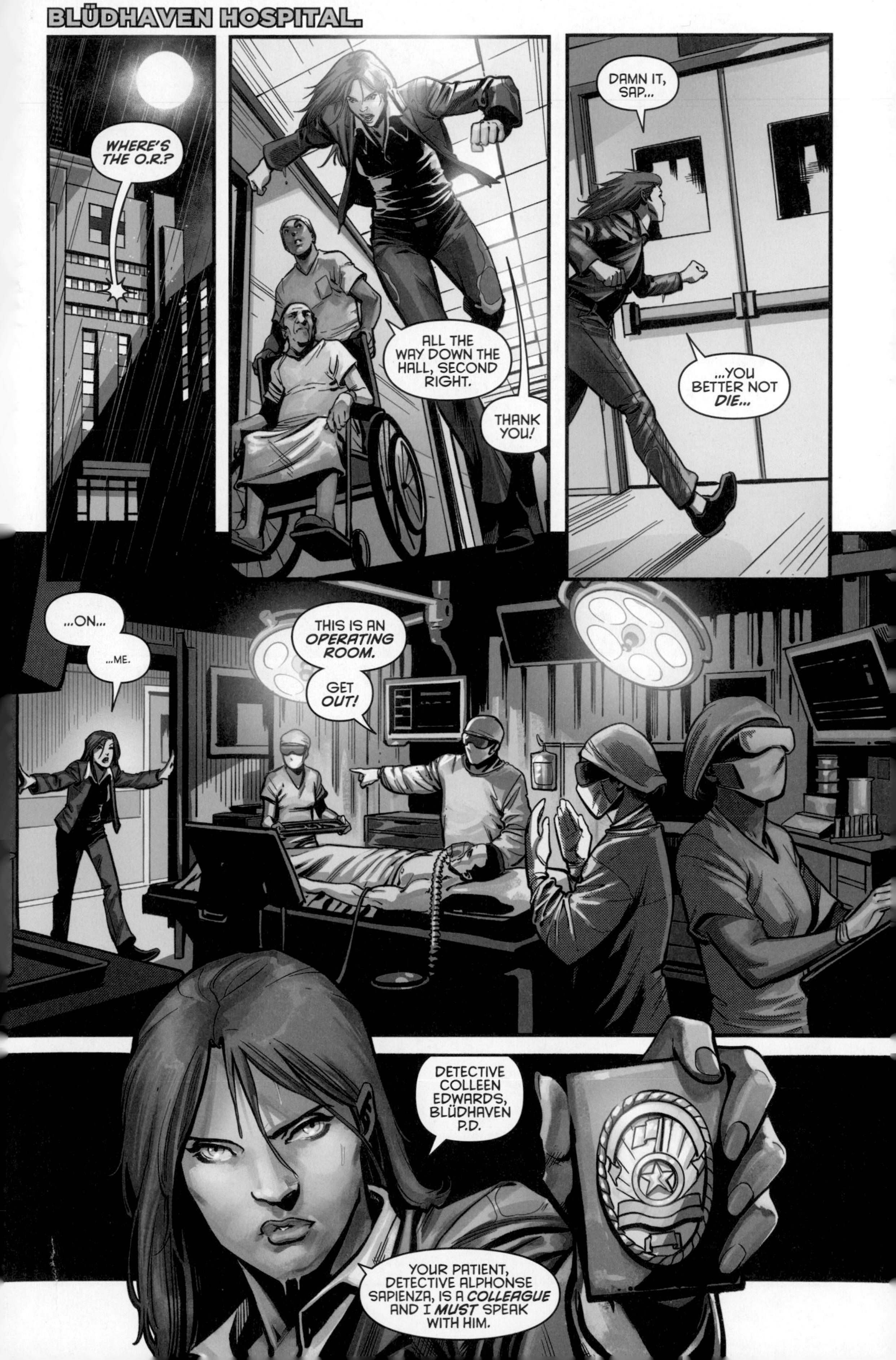

BLÜDHAVEN HOSPITAL.
WHERE'S THE O.R.?
ALL THE WAY DOWN THE HALL, SECOND RIGHT.
THANK YOU!
DAMN IT, SAP...
...YOU BETTER NOT DIE...
...ON...
...ME.
THIS IS AN OPERATING ROOM.
GET OUT!
DETECTIVE COLLEEN EDWARDS, BLÜDHAVEN P.D.
YOUR PATIENT, DETECTIVE ALPHONSE SAPIENZA, IS A COLLEAGUE AND I MUST SPEAK WITH HIM.

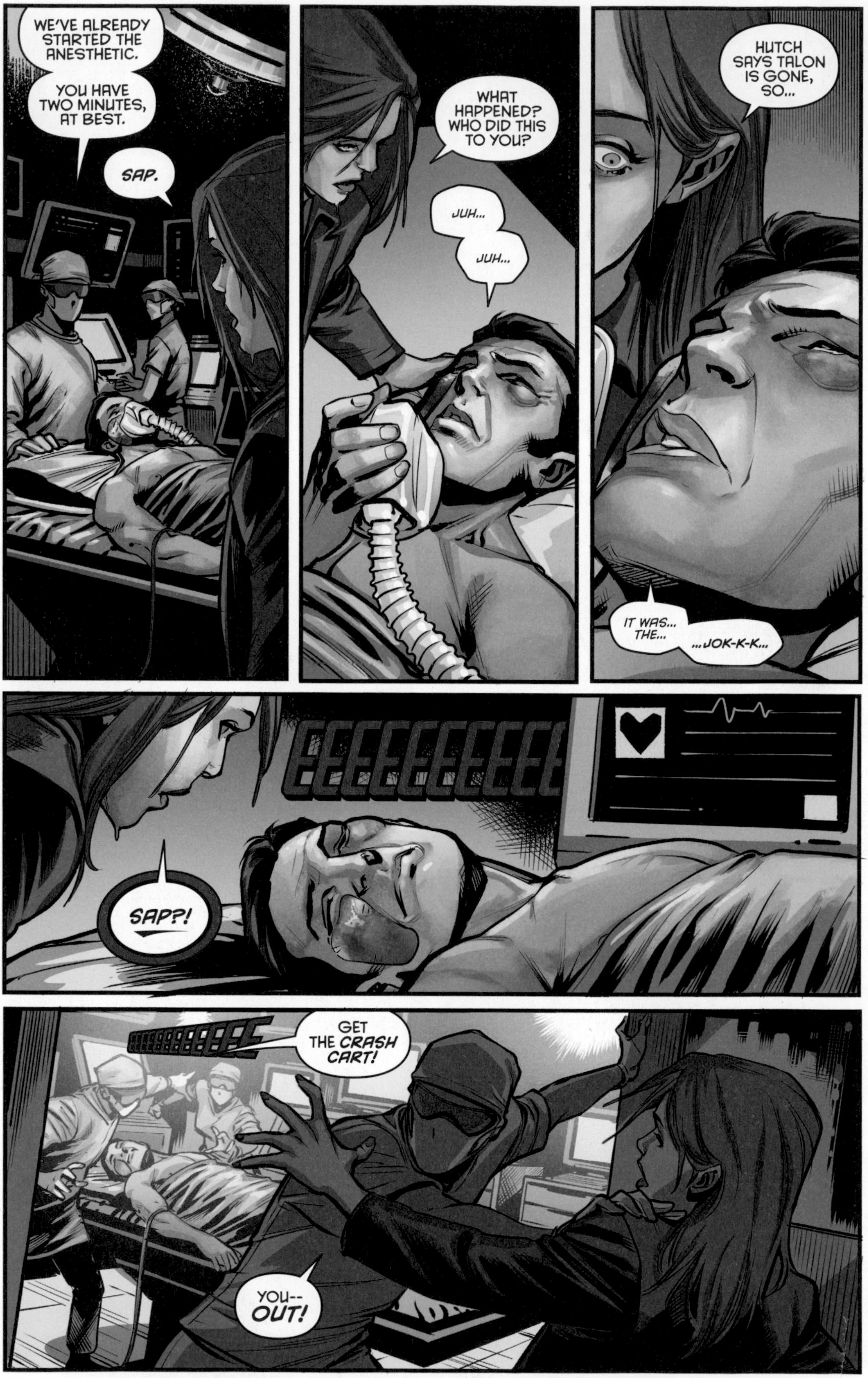
WE'VE ALREADY STARTED THE ANESTHETIC.
YOU HAVE TWO MINUTES, AT BEST.
SAP.
WHAT HAPPENED? WHO DID THIS TO YOU?
JUH...
JUH...
HUTCH SAYS TALON IS GONE, SO...
IT WAS... THE...
...JOK-K-K...
EEEEEEEEEEEE
SAP?!
EEEEEEEEEEEE
GET THE CRASH CART!
YOU-- OUT!

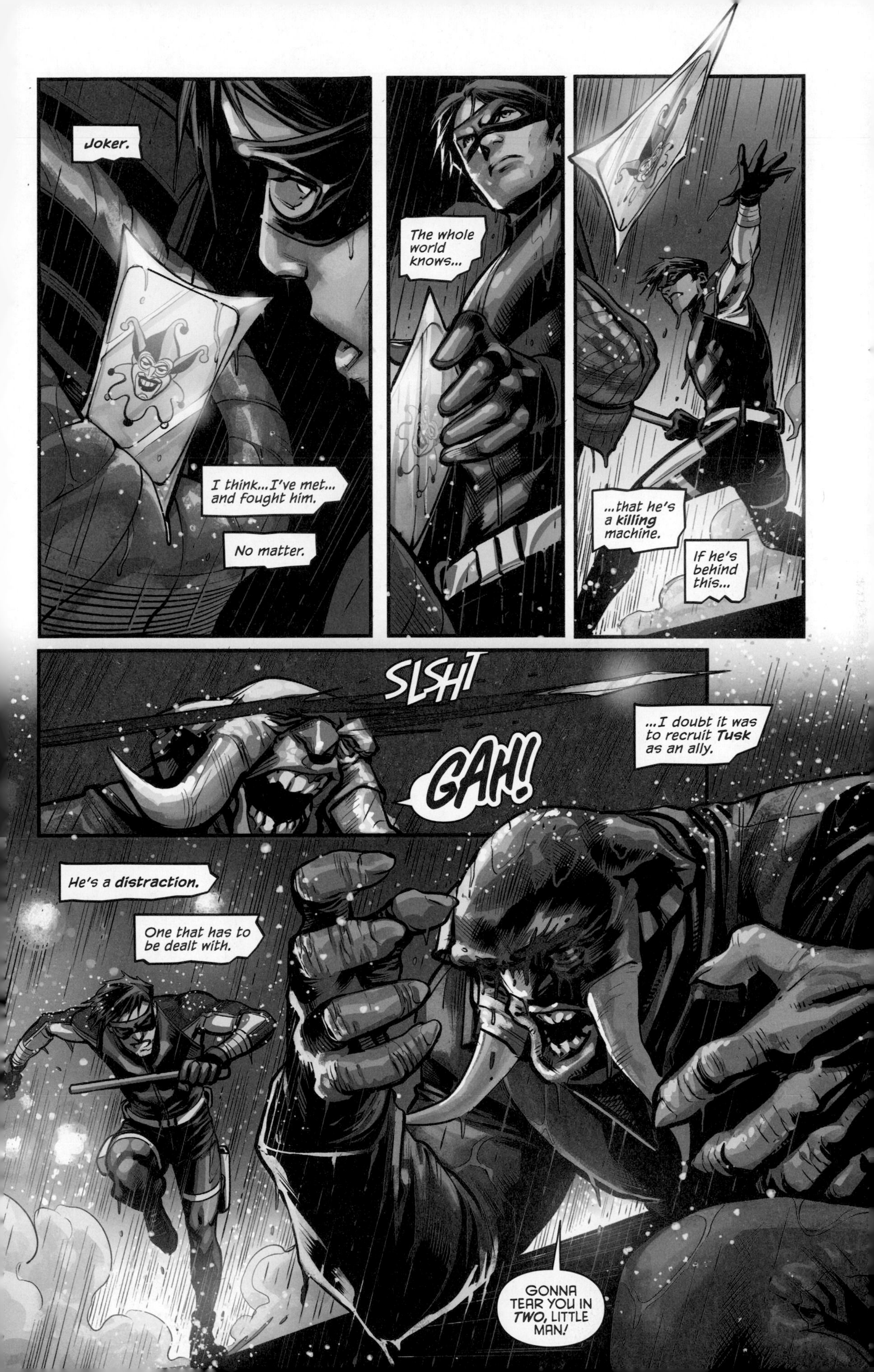
Joker.
I think...I've met... and fought him.
No matter.
The whole world knows...
...that he's a killing machine.
If he's behind this...
SLSHT
GAH!
...I doubt it was to recruit Tusk as an ally.
He's a distraction.
One that has to be dealt with.
GONNA TEAR YOU IN TWO, LITTLE MAN!

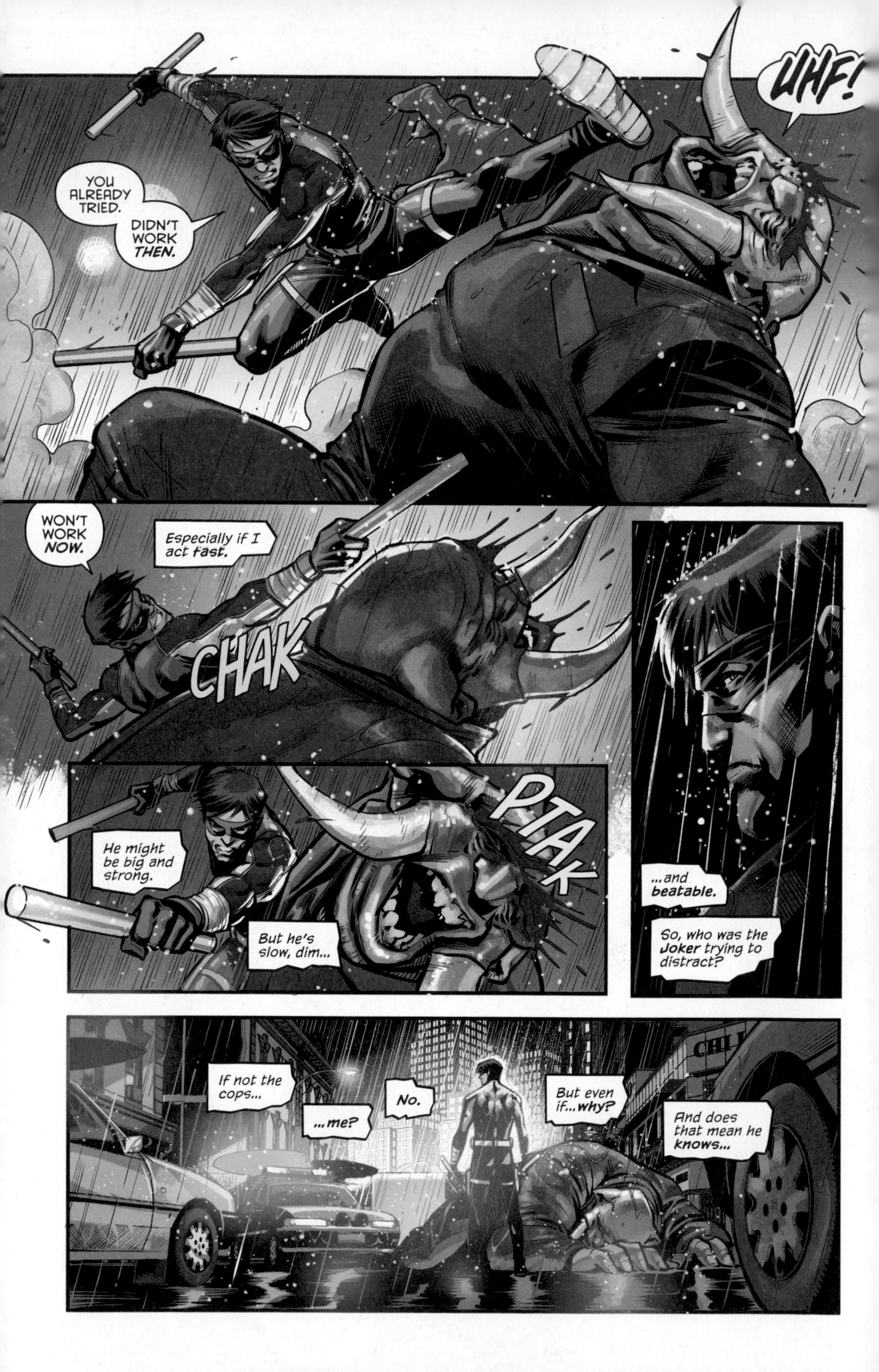

UHF!
YOU ALREADY TRIED.
DIDN'T WORK *THEN.*
WON'T WORK *NOW.*
*Especially if I act **fast**.*
CHAK
He might be big and strong.
PTAK
But he's slow, dim...
...and **beatable.**
So, who was the **Joker** trying to distract?
If not the cops...
...me?
No.
But even if... **why?**
And does that mean he **knows...**

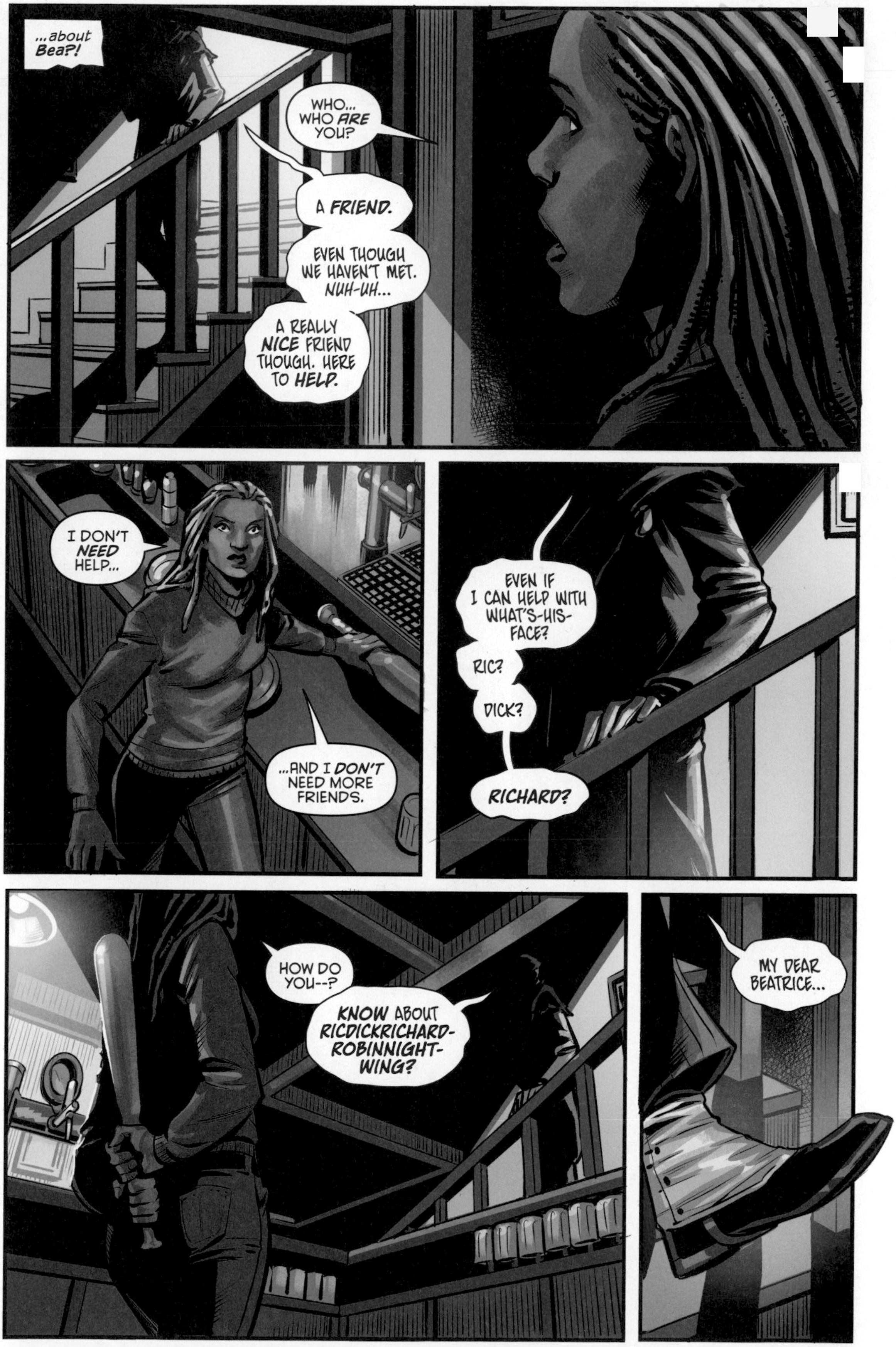

...about Bea?!
WHO... WHO ARE YOU?
A FRIEND.
EVEN THOUGH WE HAVEN'T MET. NUH-UH...
A REALLY NICE FRIEND THOUGH. HERE TO HELP.
I DON'T NEED HELP...
...AND I DON'T NEED MORE FRIENDS.
EVEN IF I CAN HELP WITH WHAT'S-HIS-FACE?
RIC?
DICK?
RICHARD?
HOW DO YOU--?
KNOW ABOUT RICDICKRICHARD-ROBINNIGHT-WING?
MY DEAR BEATRICE...

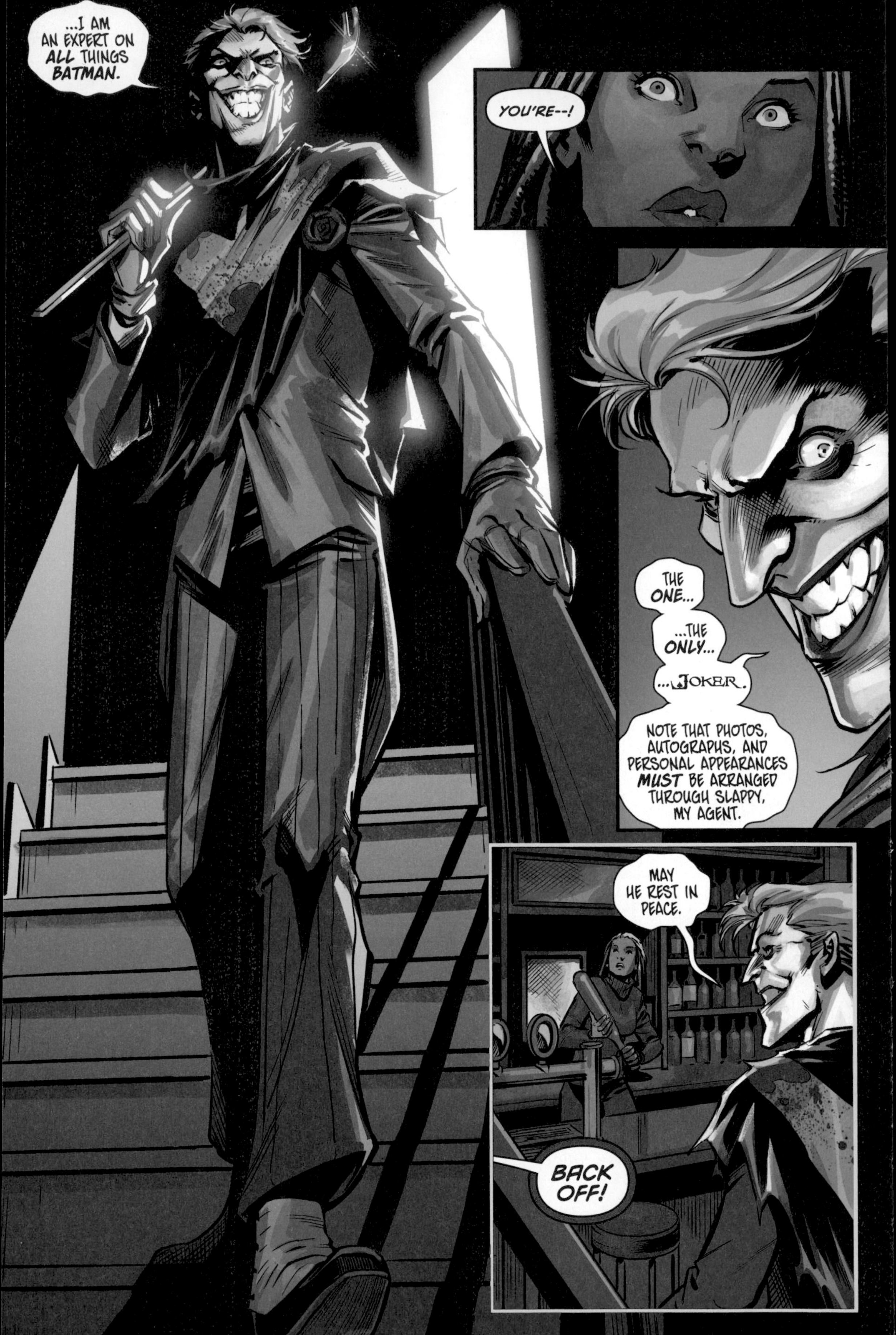
...I AM AN EXPERT ON ALL THINGS BATMAN.
YOU'RE--!
THE ONE...
...THE ONLY...
...JOKER.
NOTE THAT PHOTOS, AUTOGRAPHS, AND PERSONAL APPEARANCES MUST BE ARRANGED THROUGH SLAPPY, MY AGENT.
MAY HE REST IN PEACE.
BACK OFF!

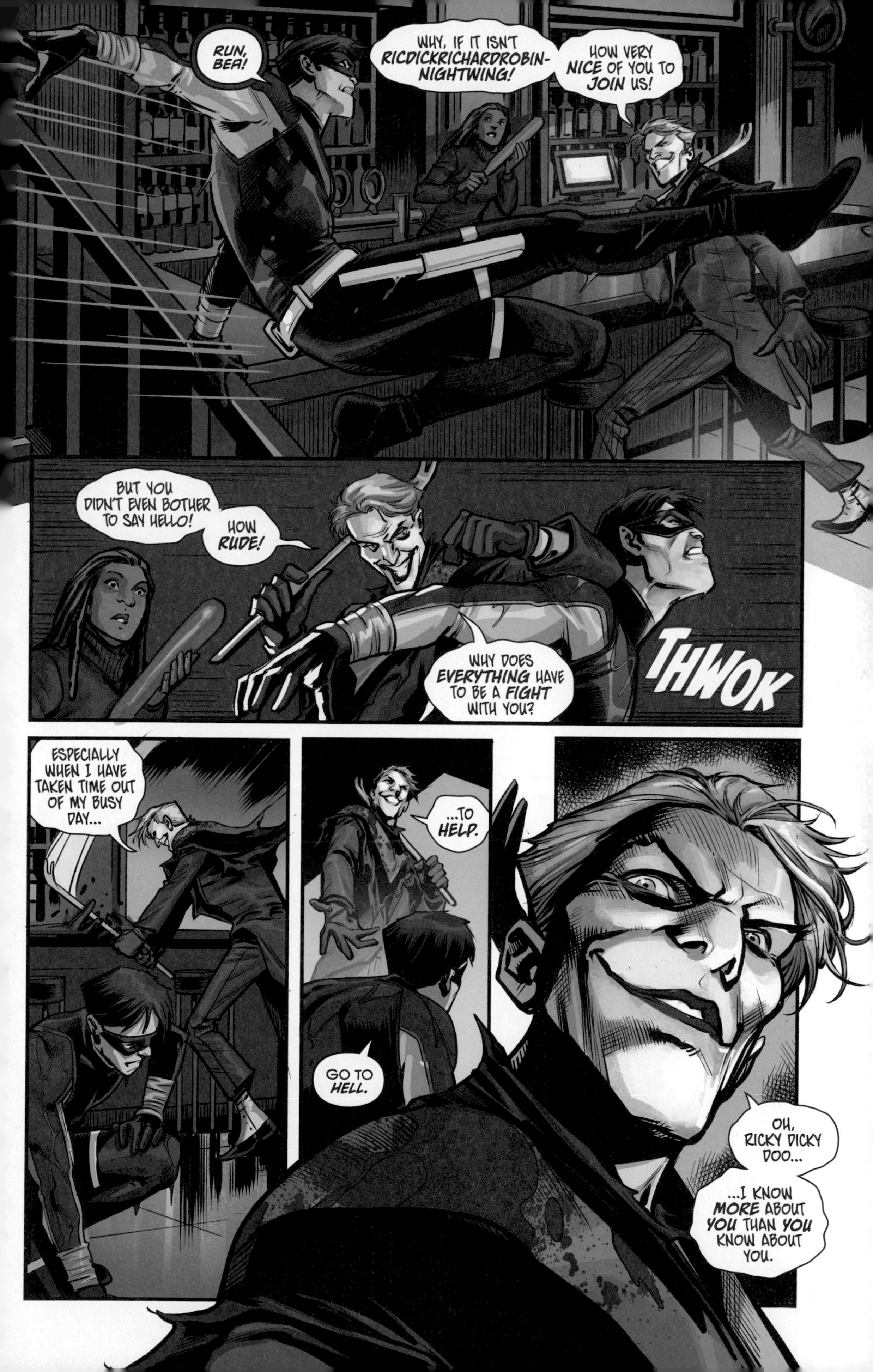
RUN, BEA!
WHY, IF IT ISN'T RICDICKRICHARDROBIN-NIGHTWING!
HOW VERY NICE OF YOU TO JOIN US!
BUT YOU DIDN'T EVEN BOTHER TO SAY HELLO!
HOW RUDE!
WHY DOES EVERYTHING HAVE TO BE A FIGHT WITH YOU?
THWOK
ESPECIALLY WHEN I HAVE TAKEN TIME OUT OF MY BUSY DAY...
...TO HELP.
GO TO HELL.
OH, RICKY DICKY DOO...
...I KNOW MORE ABOUT YOU THAN YOU KNOW ABOUT YOU.

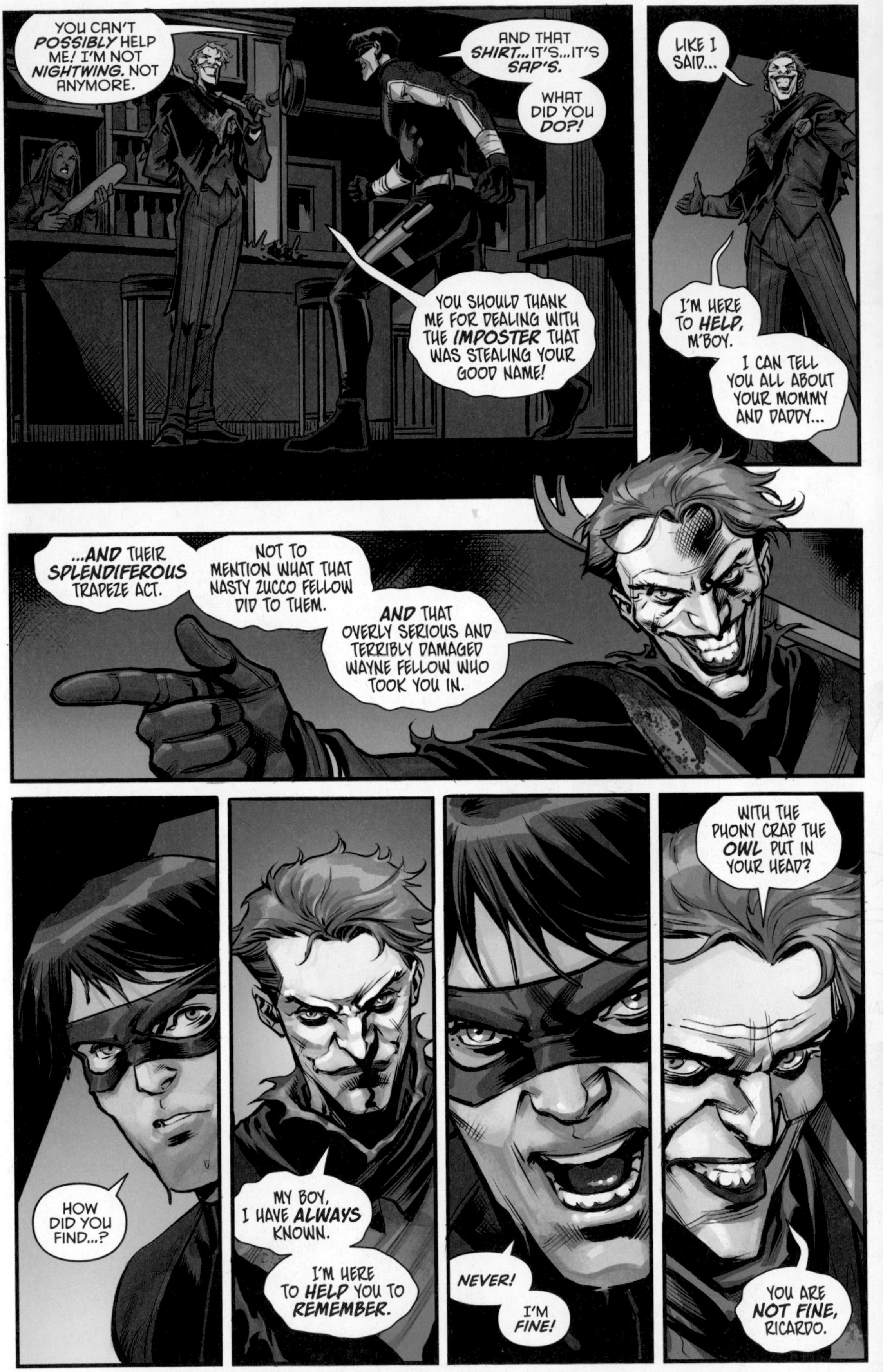
YOU CAN'T POSSIBLY HELP ME! I'M NOT NIGHTWING. NOT ANYMORE.
AND THAT SHIRT... IT'S...IT'S SAP'S.
WHAT DID YOU DO?!
YOU SHOULD THANK ME FOR DEALING WITH THE IMPOSTER THAT WAS STEALING YOUR GOOD NAME!
LIKE I SAID...
I'M HERE TO HELP, M'BOY.
I CAN TELL YOU ALL ABOUT YOUR MOMMY AND DADDY...
...AND THEIR SPLENDIFEROUS TRAPEZE ACT.
NOT TO MENTION WHAT THAT NASTY ZUCCO FELLOW DID TO THEM.
AND THAT OVERLY SERIOUS AND TERRIBLY DAMAGED WAYNE FELLOW WHO TOOK YOU IN.
HOW DID YOU FIND...?
MY BOY, I HAVE ALWAYS KNOWN.
I'M HERE TO HELP YOU TO REMEMBER.
NEVER!
I'M FINE!
WITH THE PHONY CRAP THE OWL PUT IN YOUR HEAD?
YOU ARE NOT FINE, RICARDO.

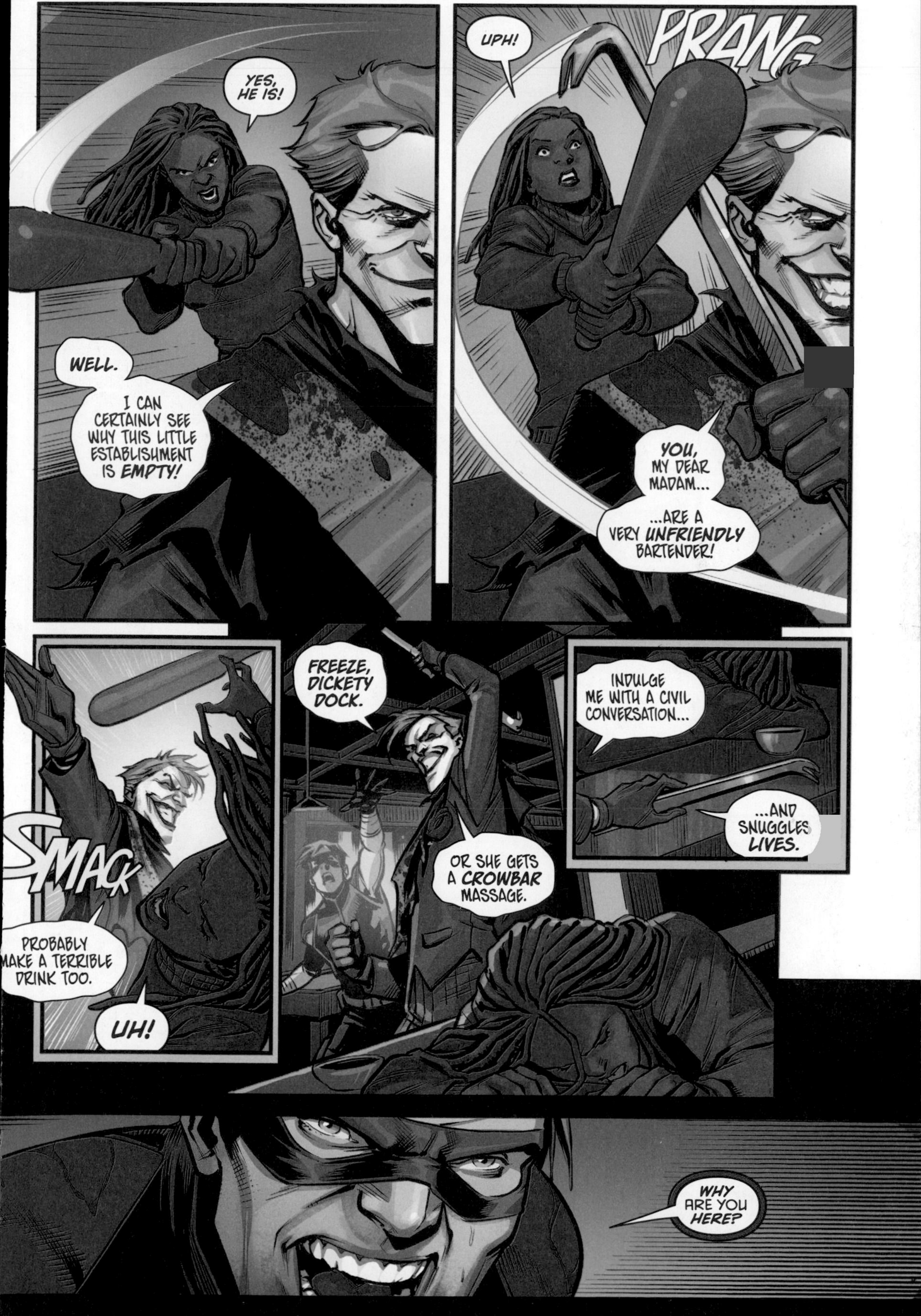
YES, HE IS!
WELL.
I CAN CERTAINLY SEE WHY THIS LITTLE ESTABLISHMENT IS EMPTY!
UPH!
PRANG
YOU, MY DEAR MADAM...
...ARE A VERY UNFRIENDLY BARTENDER!
SMACK
PROBABLY MAKE A TERRIBLE DRINK TOO.
UH!
FREEZE, DICKETY DOCK.
OR SHE GETS A CROWBAR MASSAGE.
INDULGE ME WITH A CIVIL CONVERSATION...
...AND SNUGGLES LIVES.
WHY ARE YOU HERE?

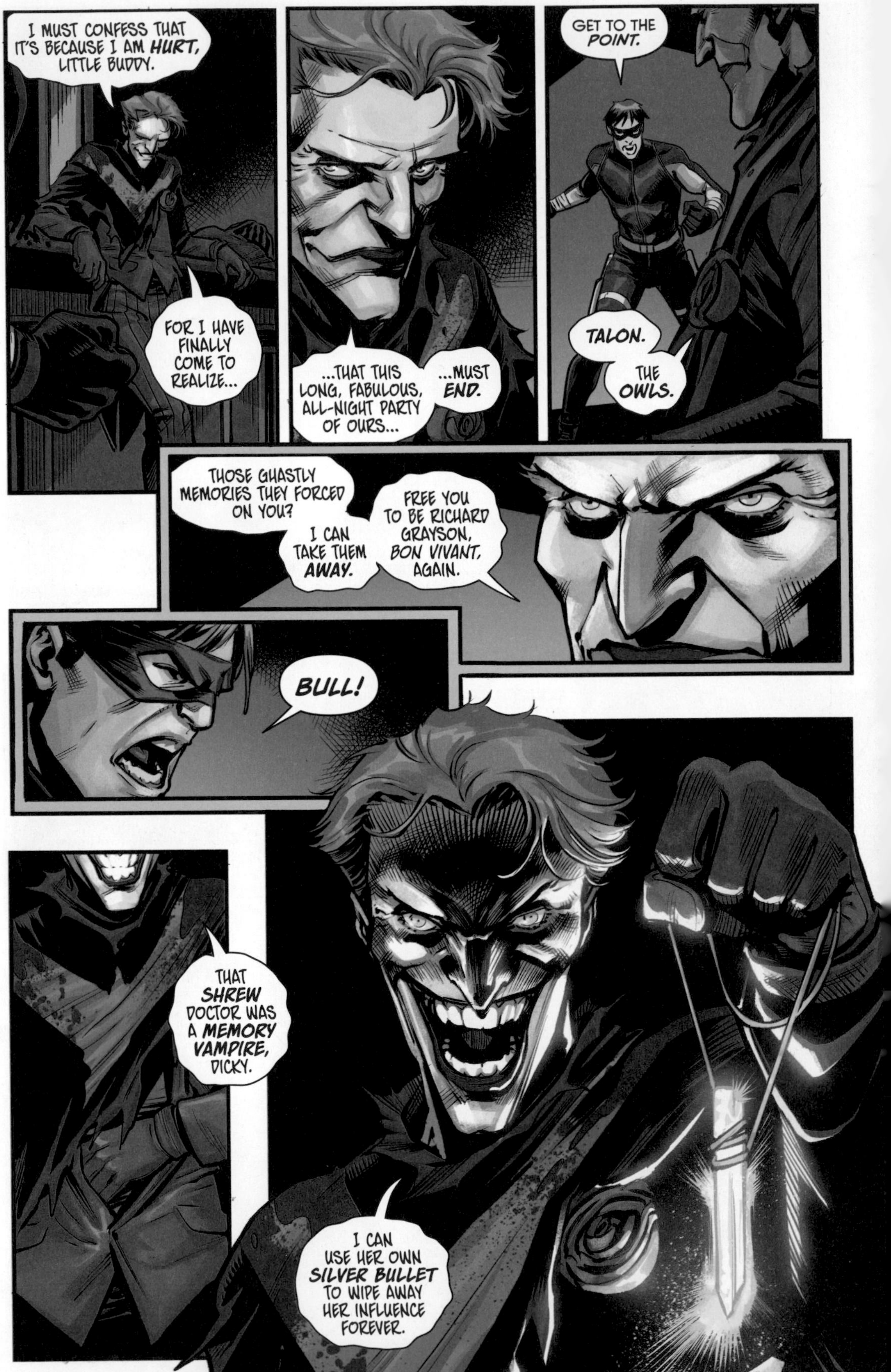
I MUST CONFESS THAT IT'S BECAUSE I AM **HURT**, LITTLE BUDDY.
FOR I HAVE FINALLY COME TO REALIZE...
...THAT THIS LONG, FABULOUS, ALL-NIGHT PARTY OF OURS...
...MUST **END.**
GET TO THE ***POINT.***
TALON.
THE ***OWLS.***
THOSE GHASTLY MEMORIES THEY FORCED ON YOU?
I CAN TAKE THEM ***AWAY.***
FREE YOU TO BE RICHARD GRAYSON, *BON VIVANT*, AGAIN.
BULL!
THAT ***SHREW*** DOCTOR WAS A ***MEMORY VAMPIRE,*** DICKY.
I CAN USE HER OWN ***SILVER BULLET*** TO WIPE AWAY HER INFLUENCE FOREVER.

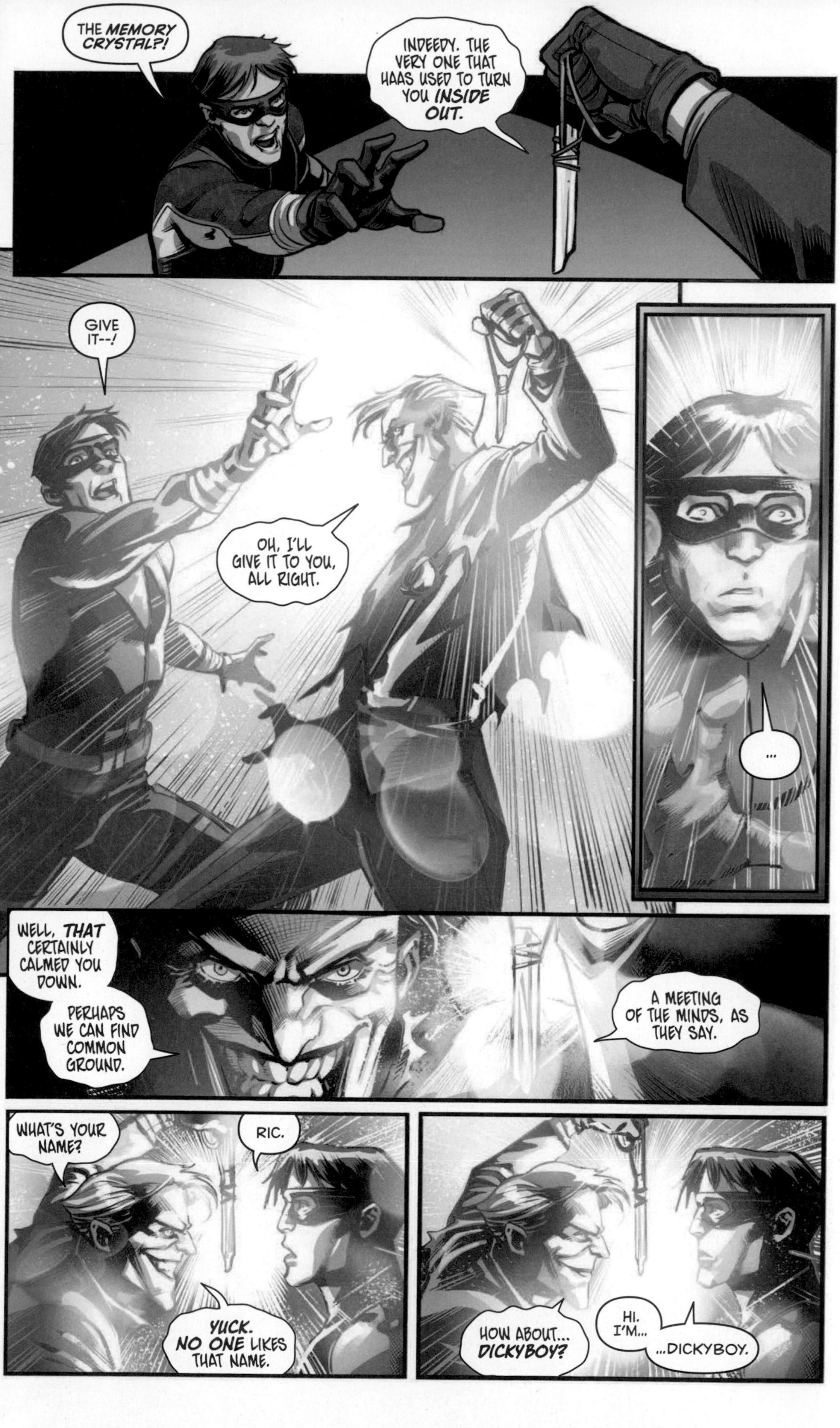

THE MEMORY CRYSTAL?!
INDEEDY. THE VERY ONE THAT HAAS USED TO TURN YOU INSIDE OUT.
GIVE IT--!
OH, I'LL GIVE IT TO YOU, ALL RIGHT.
...
WELL, THAT CERTAINLY CALMED YOU DOWN.
PERHAPS WE CAN FIND COMMON GROUND.
A MEETING OF THE MINDS, AS THEY SAY.
WHAT'S YOUR NAME?
RIC.
YUCK. NO ONE LIKES THAT NAME.
HOW ABOUT... DICKYBOY?
HI. I'M...
...DICKYBOY.

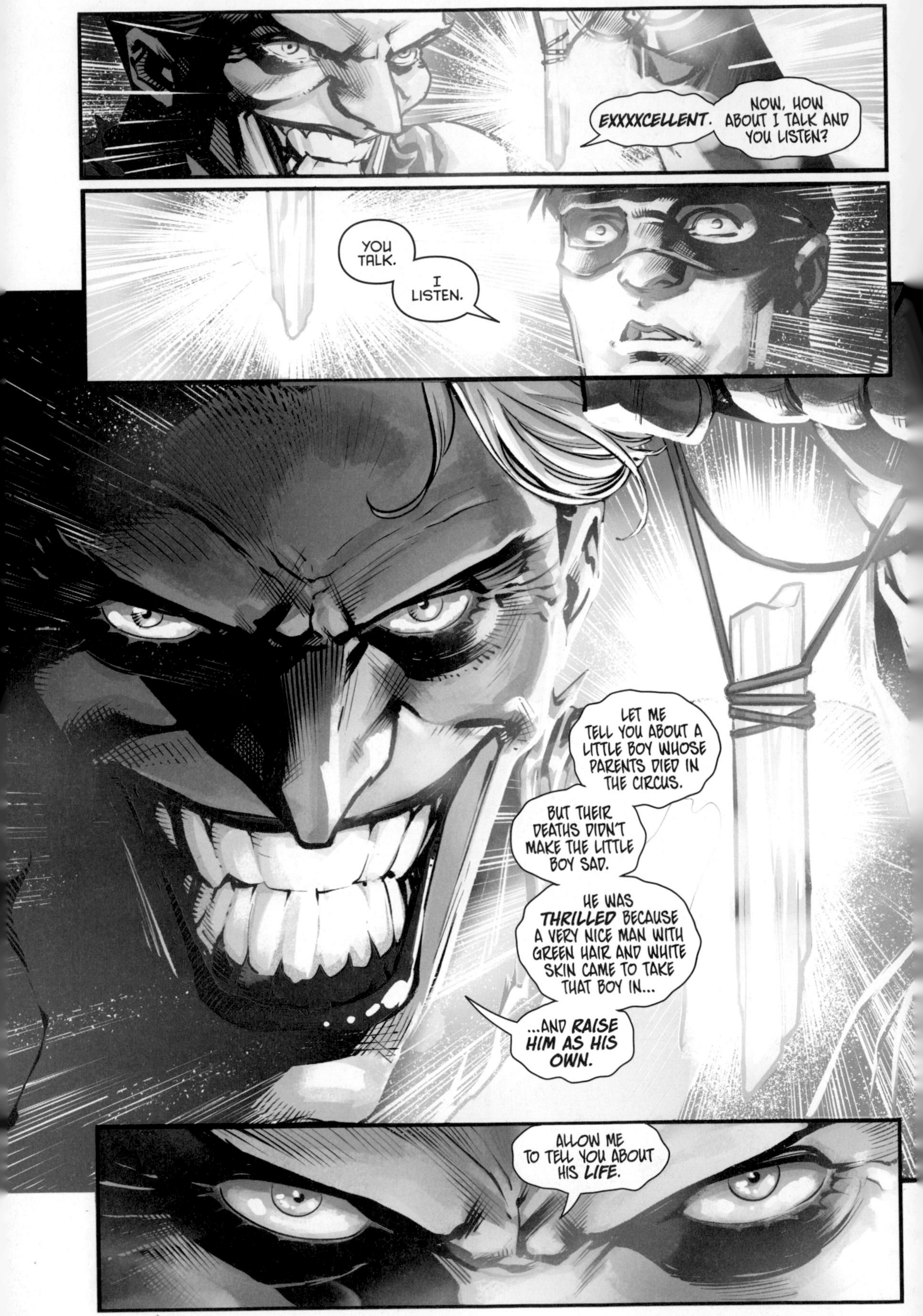
EXXXXCELLENT.
NOW, HOW ABOUT I TALK AND YOU LISTEN?
YOU TALK.
I LISTEN.
LET ME TELL YOU ABOUT A LITTLE BOY WHOSE PARENTS DIED IN THE CIRCUS.
BUT THEIR DEATHS DIDN'T MAKE THE LITTLE BOY SAD.
HE WAS THRILLED BECAUSE A VERY NICE MAN WITH GREEN HAIR AND WHITE SKIN CAME TO TAKE THAT BOY IN...
...AND RAISE HIM AS HIS OWN.
ALLOW ME TO TELL YOU ABOUT HIS LIFE.

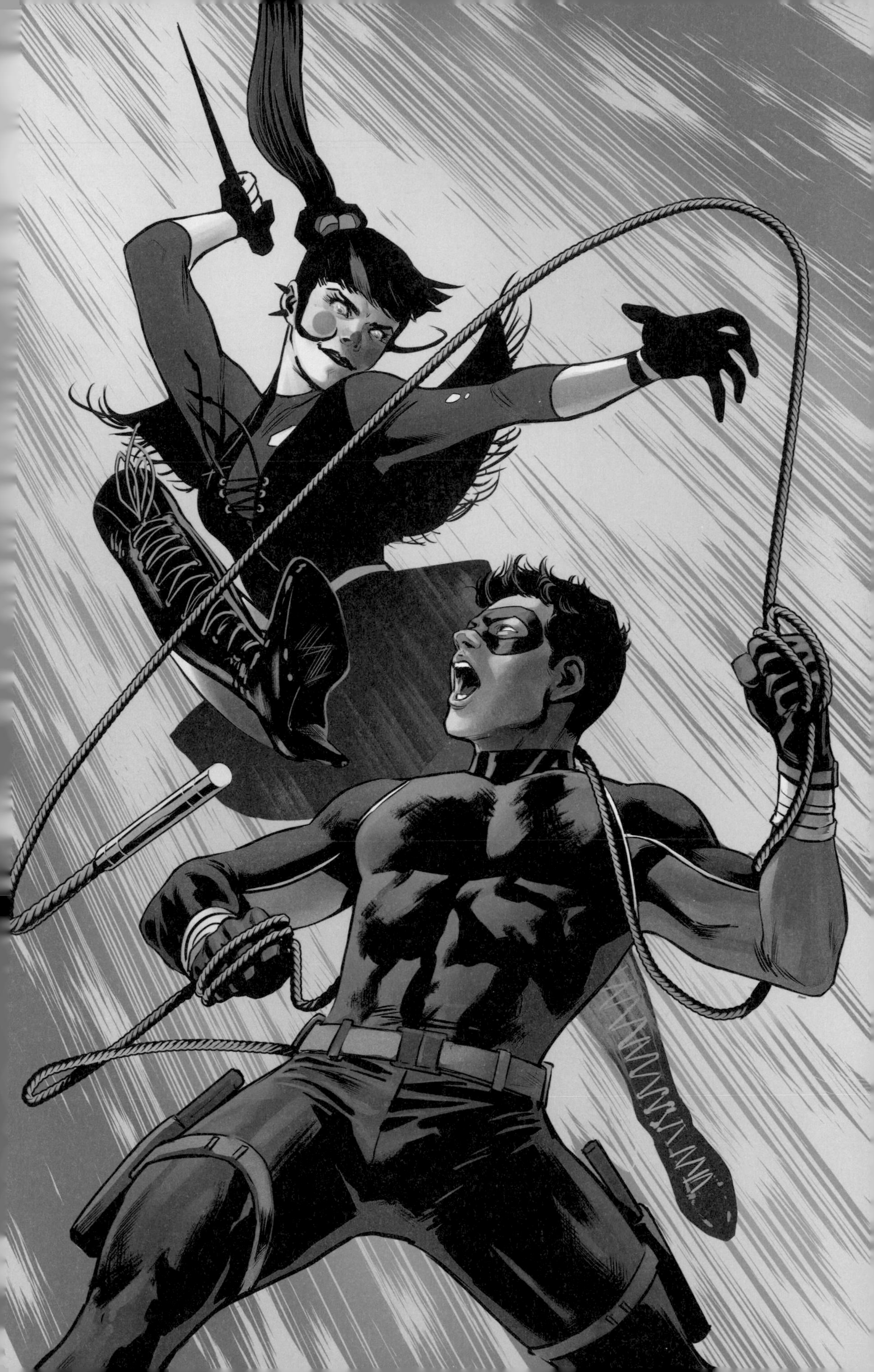

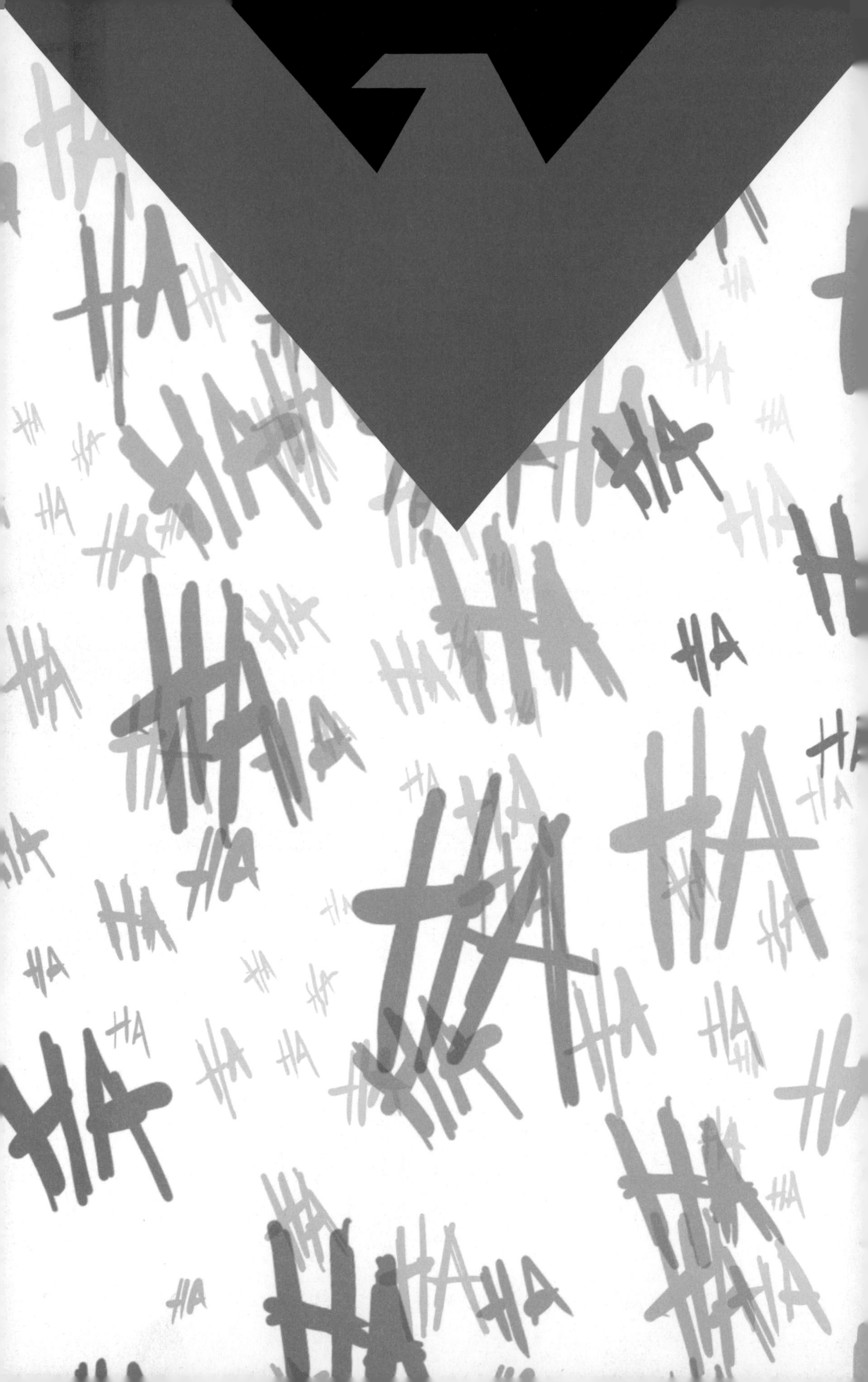

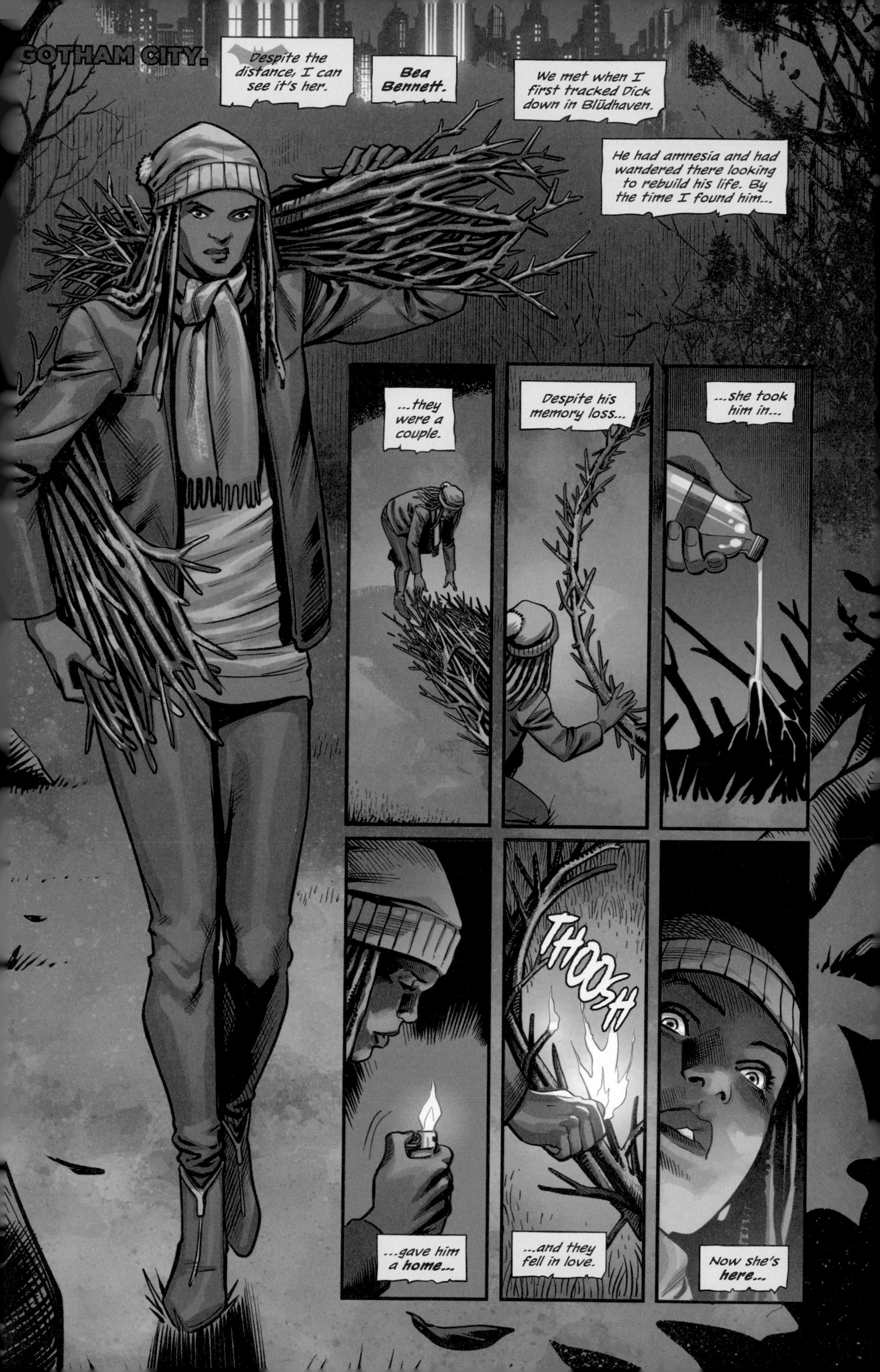
GOTHAM CITY.
Despite the distance, I can see it's her.
Bea Bennett.
We met when I first tracked Dick down in Blüdhaven.
He had amnesia and had wandered there looking to rebuild his life. By the time I found him...
...they were a couple.
Despite his memory loss...
...she took him in...
...gave him a home...
THOOSH
...and they fell in love.
Now she's here...

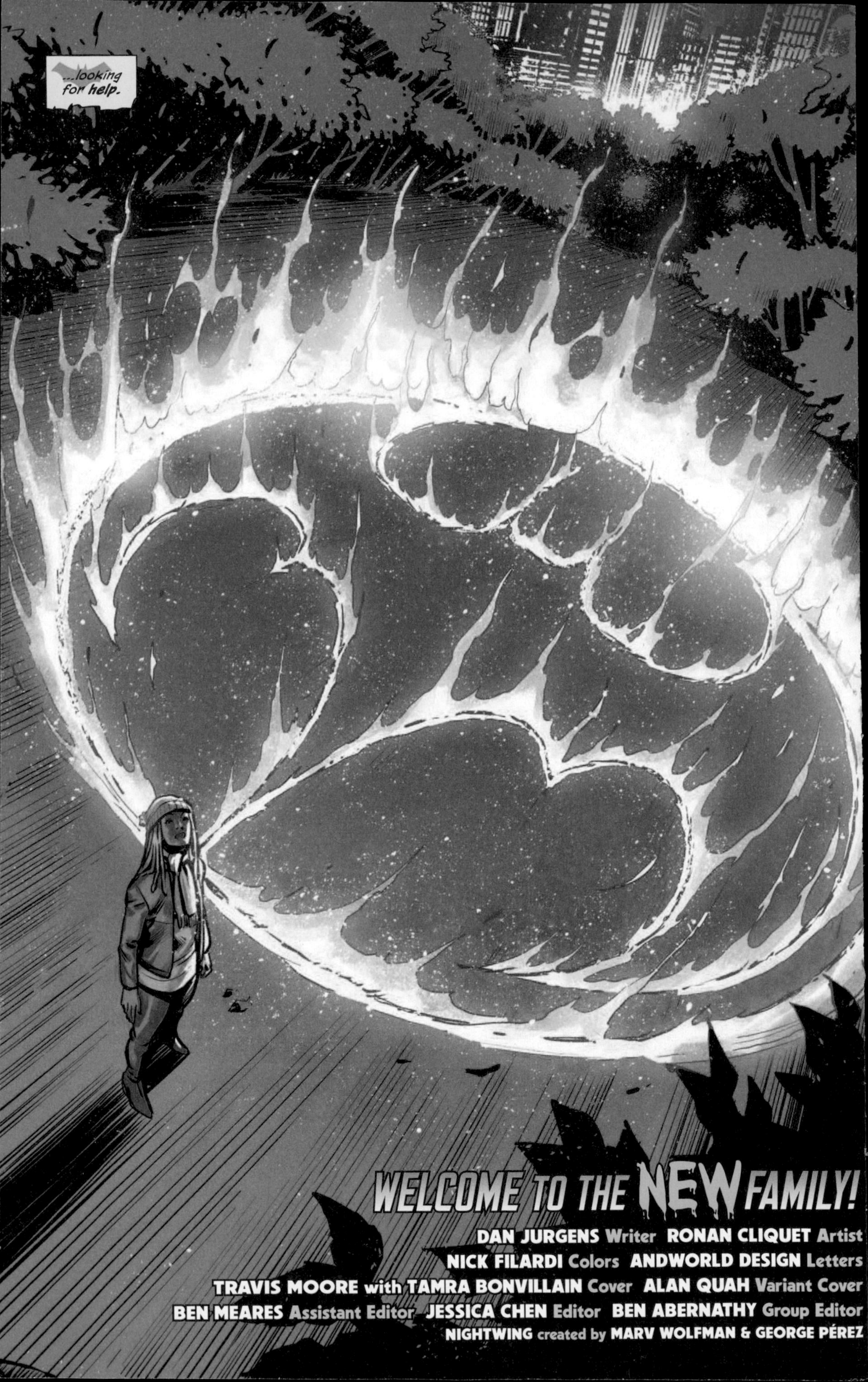

...looking for help.
WELCOME TO THE NEW FAMILY!
DAN JURGENS Writer RONAN CLIQUET Artist
NICK FILARDI Colors ANDWORLD DESIGN Letters
TRAVIS MOORE with TAMRA BONVILLAIN Cover ALAN QUAH Variant Cover
BEN MEARES Assistant Editor JESSICA CHEN Editor BEN ABERNATHY Group Editor
NIGHTWING created by MARV WOLFMAN & GEORGE PÉREZ

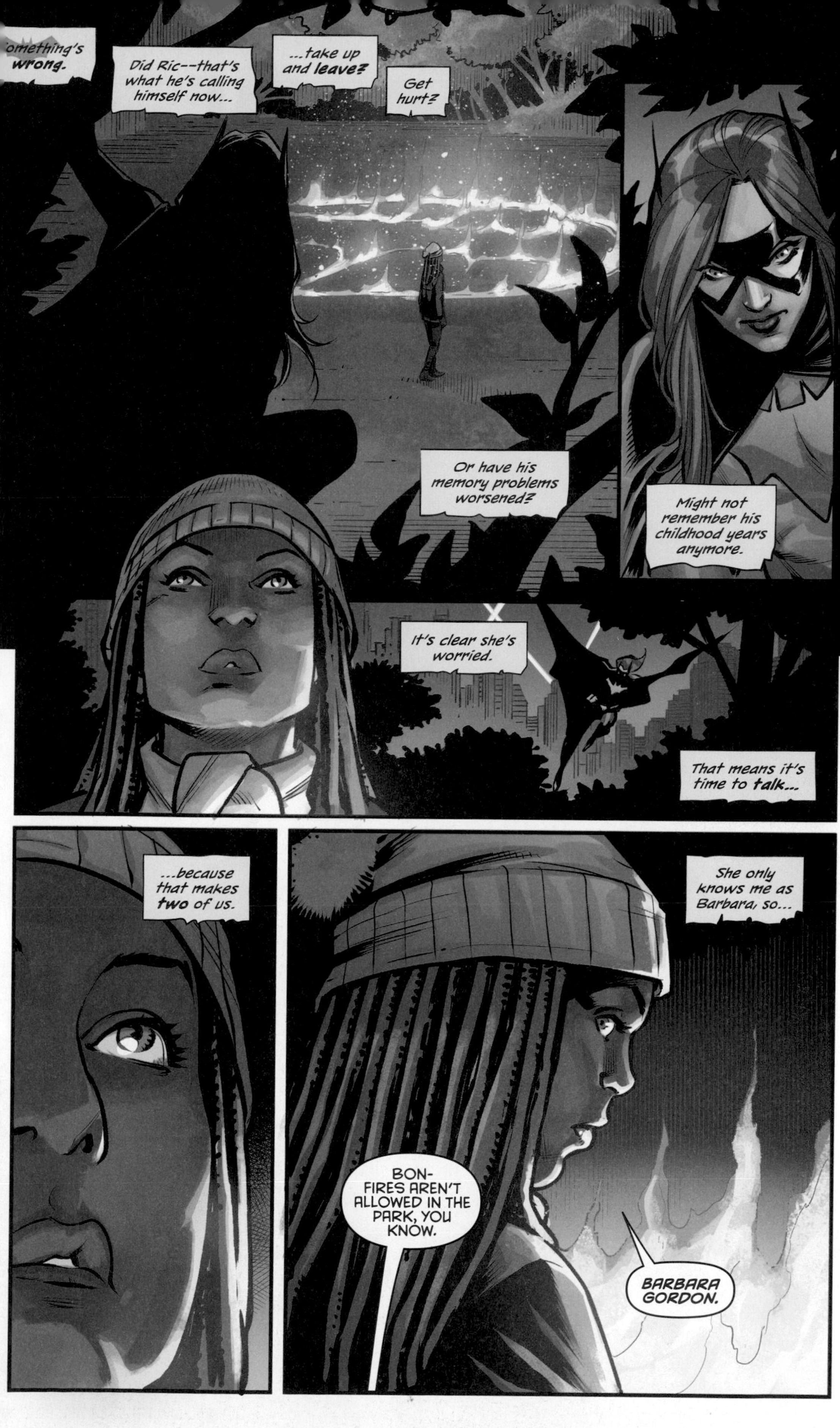

omething's wrong.
Did Ric--that's what he's calling himself now...
...take up and leave?
Get hurt?
Or have his memory problems worsened?
Might not remember his childhood years anymore.
It's clear she's worried.
That means it's time to talk...
...because that makes two of us.
She only knows me as Barbara, so...
BON-FIRES AREN'T ALLOWED IN THE PARK, YOU KNOW.
BARBARA GORDON.

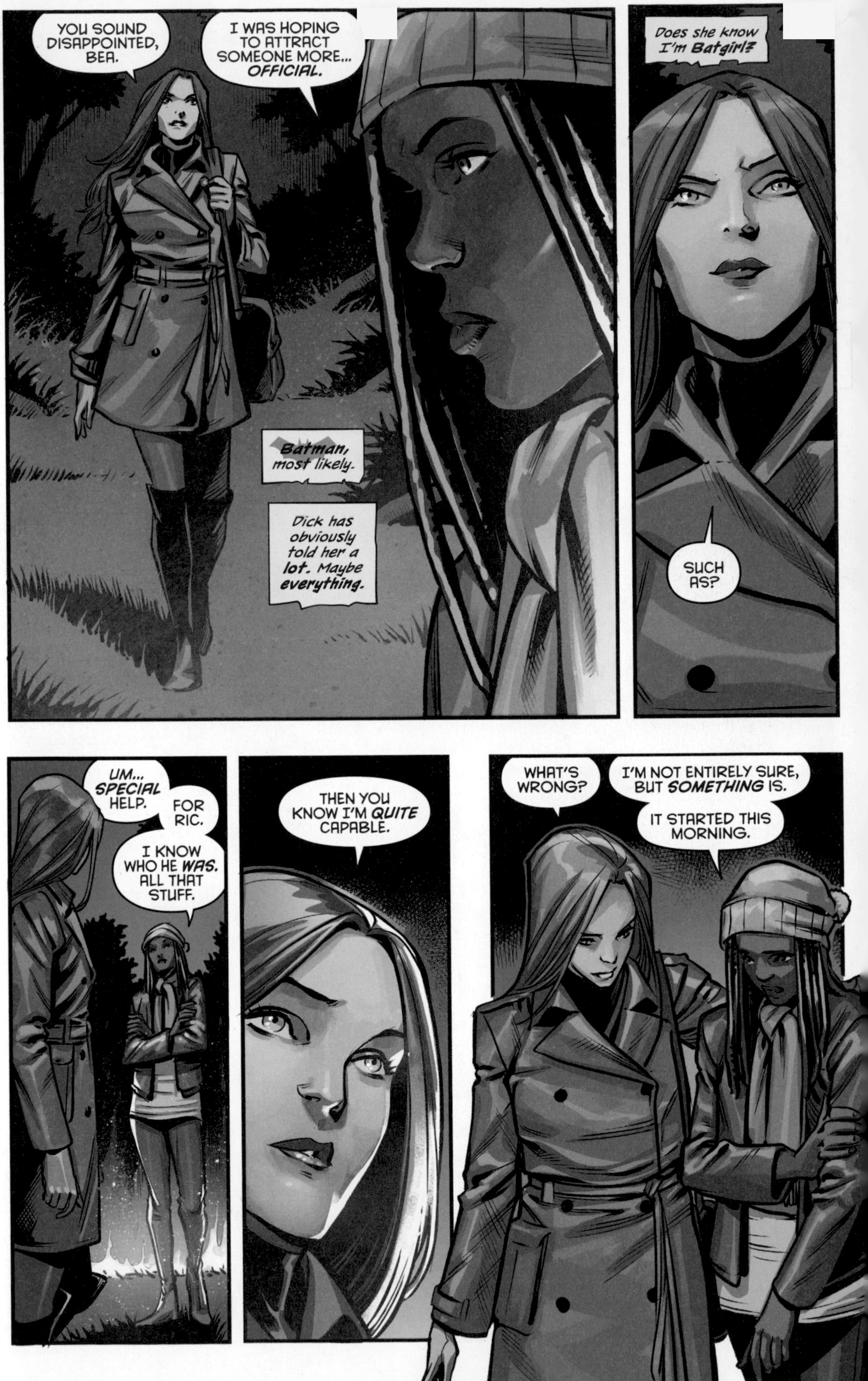
YOU SOUND DISAPPOINTED, BEA.
I WAS HOPING TO ATTRACT SOMEONE MORE... OFFICIAL.
Batman, most likely.
Dick has obviously told her a lot. Maybe everything.
Does she know I'm Batgirl?
SUCH AS?
UM... SPECIAL HELP.
FOR RIC.
I KNOW WHO HE WAS. ALL THAT STUFF.
THEN YOU KNOW I'M QUITE CAPABLE.
WHAT'S WRONG?
I'M NOT ENTIRELY SURE, BUT SOMETHING IS.
IT STARTED THIS MORNING.

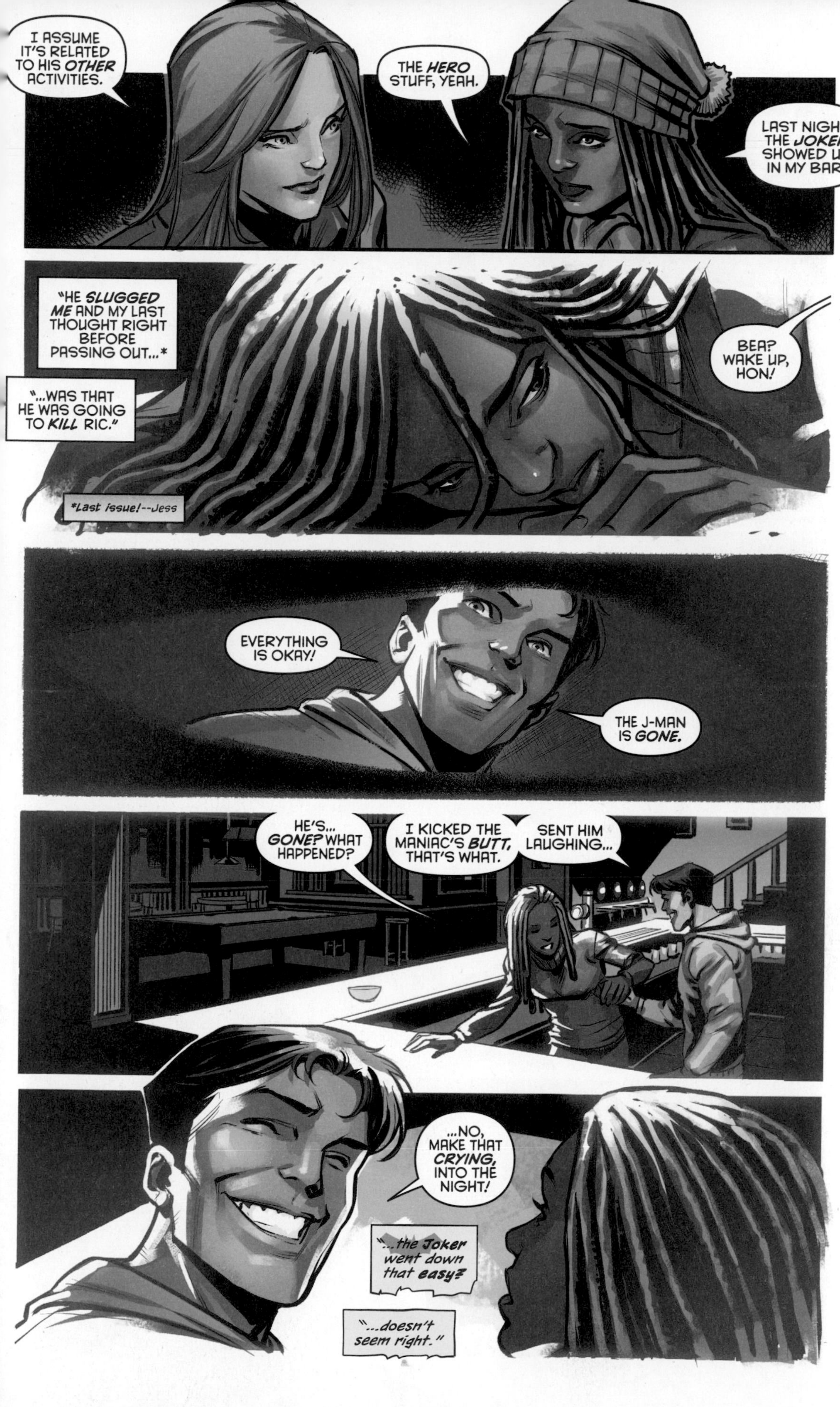
I ASSUME IT'S RELATED TO HIS OTHER ACTIVITIES.
THE HERO STUFF, YEAH.
LAST NIGHT, THE JOKER SHOWED UP IN MY BAR.
"HE SLUGGED ME AND MY LAST THOUGHT RIGHT BEFORE PASSING OUT...*
"...WAS THAT HE WAS GOING TO KILL RIC."
*Last issue!--Jess
BEA? WAKE UP, HON!
EVERYTHING IS OKAY!
THE J-MAN IS GONE.
HE'S... GONE? WHAT HAPPENED?
I KICKED THE MANIAC'S BUTT, THAT'S WHAT.
SENT HIM LAUGHING...
...NO, MAKE THAT CRYING, INTO THE NIGHT!
"...the Joker went down that easy?
"...doesn't seem right."

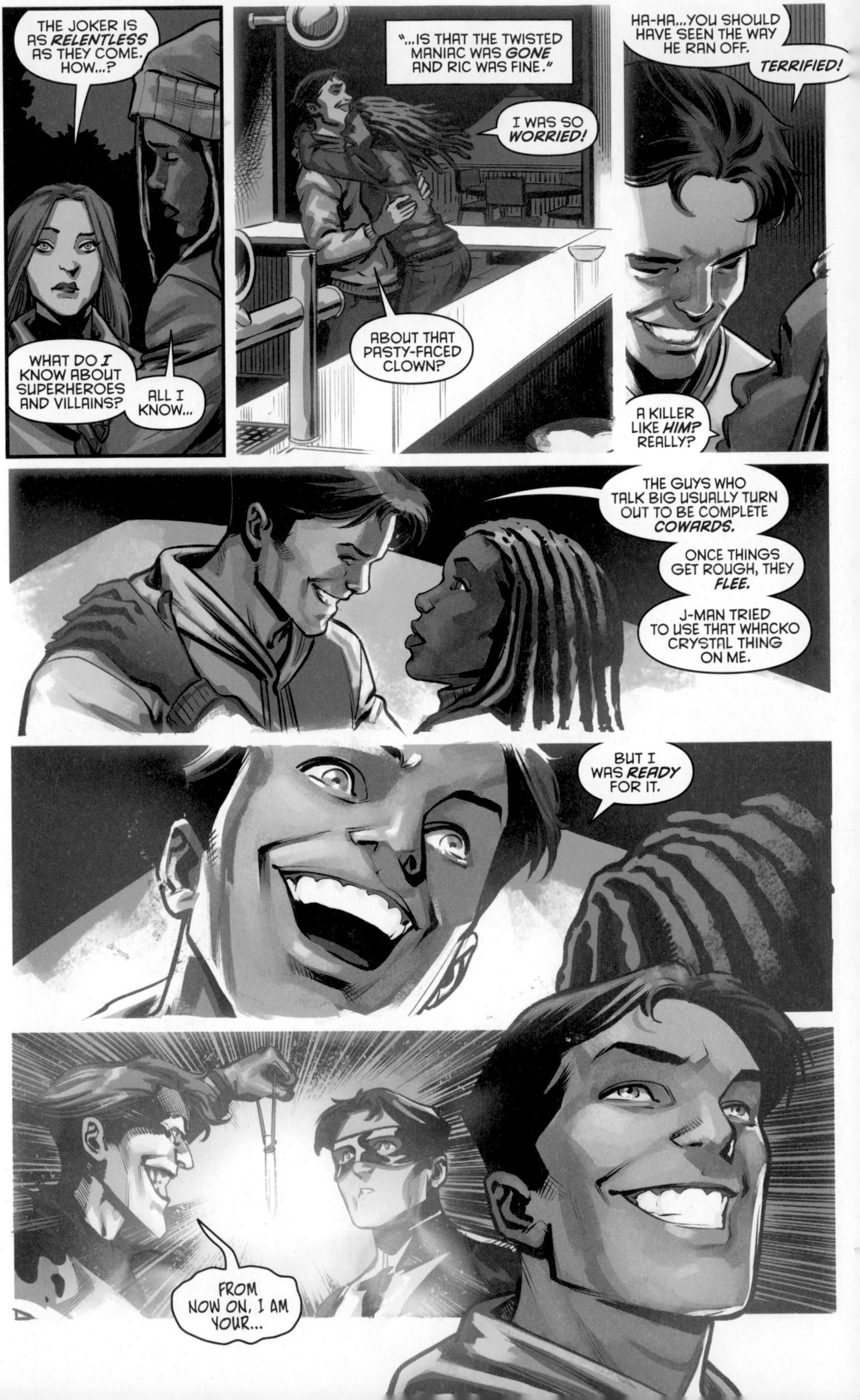
THE JOKER IS AS *RELENTLESS* AS THEY COME. HOW...?
WHAT DO *I* KNOW ABOUT SUPERHEROES AND VILLAINS?
ALL I KNOW...
"...IS THAT THE TWISTED MANIAC WAS *GONE* AND RIC WAS FINE."
I WAS SO *WORRIED!*
ABOUT THAT PASTY-FACED CLOWN?
HA-HA...YOU SHOULD HAVE SEEN THE WAY HE RAN OFF.
TERRIFIED!
A KILLER LIKE *HIM?* REALLY?
THE GUYS WHO TALK BIG USUALLY TURN OUT TO BE COMPLETE *COWARDS.*
ONCE THINGS GET ROUGH, THEY *FLEE.*
J-MAN TRIED TO USE THAT WHACKO CRYSTAL THING ON ME.
BUT I WAS *READY* FOR IT.
FROM NOW ON, I AM YOUR...

YOU ARE NOTHING!

KRAK

"HE SAID HE TOOK THE JOKER DOWN WITH ONE PUNCH AND SHATTERED THE CRYSTAL SO NO ONE WOULD EVER USE IT ON HIM AGAIN."

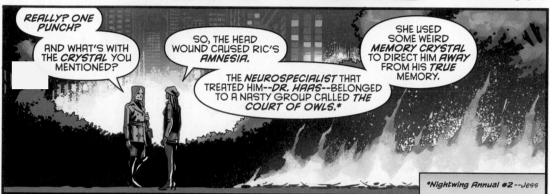

REALLY? ONE PUNCH?

AND WHAT'S WITH THE CRYSTAL YOU MENTIONED?

SO, THE HEAD WOUND CAUSED RIC'S AMNESIA.

THE NEUROSPECIALIST THAT TREATED HIM--DR. HAAS--BELONGED TO A NASTY GROUP CALLED THE COURT OF OWLS.*

SHE USED SOME WEIRD MEMORY CRYSTAL TO DIRECT HIM AWAY FROM HIS TRUE MEMORY.

*Nightwing Annual #2--Jess

WHAT?

EVEN BRAIN-WASHED HIM INTO FORGETTING HIS CHILDHOOD YEARS WHILE TRYING TO MAKE HIM A TALON.

AND THE JOKER GOT THE CRYSTAL?

TRIED TO USE IT ON HIM, TOO.

BUT RIC SAID HE GOT IT BACK AND SMASHED IT.

SEE? TOOK IT RIGHT OFF THE CLOWN'S NECK.

SMASHED TO PIECES.

WHY, THAT'S... WONDERFUL.

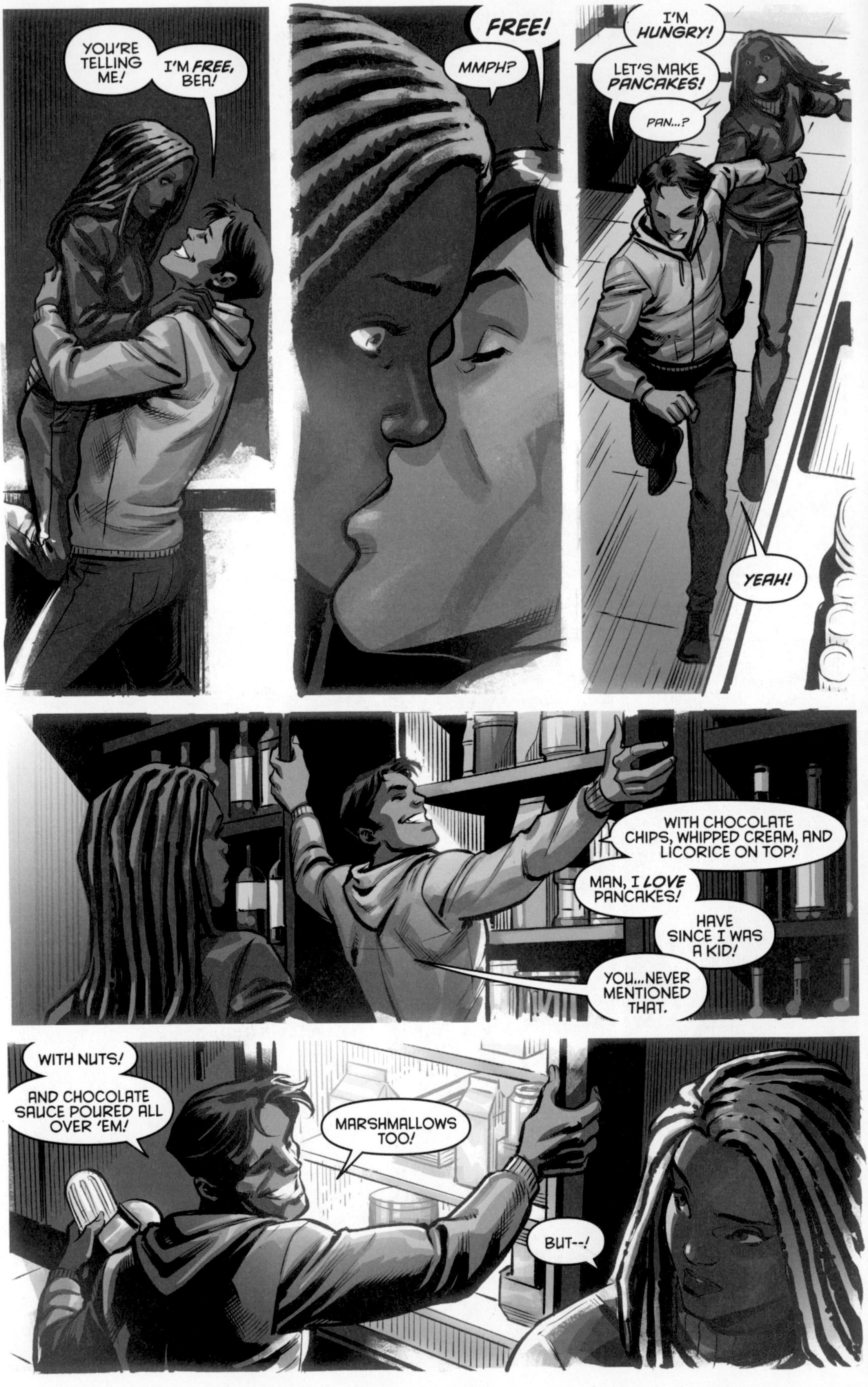
YOU'RE TELLING ME!
I'M FREE, BEA!
FREE!
MMPH?
I'M HUNGRY!
LET'S MAKE PANCAKES!
PAN...?
YEAH!
WITH CHOCOLATE CHIPS, WHIPPED CREAM, AND LICORICE ON TOP!
MAN, I LOVE PANCAKES!
HAVE SINCE I WAS A KID!
YOU...NEVER MENTIONED THAT.
WITH NUTS!
AND CHOCOLATE SAUCE POURED ALL OVER 'EM!
MARSHMALLOWS TOO!
BUT--!

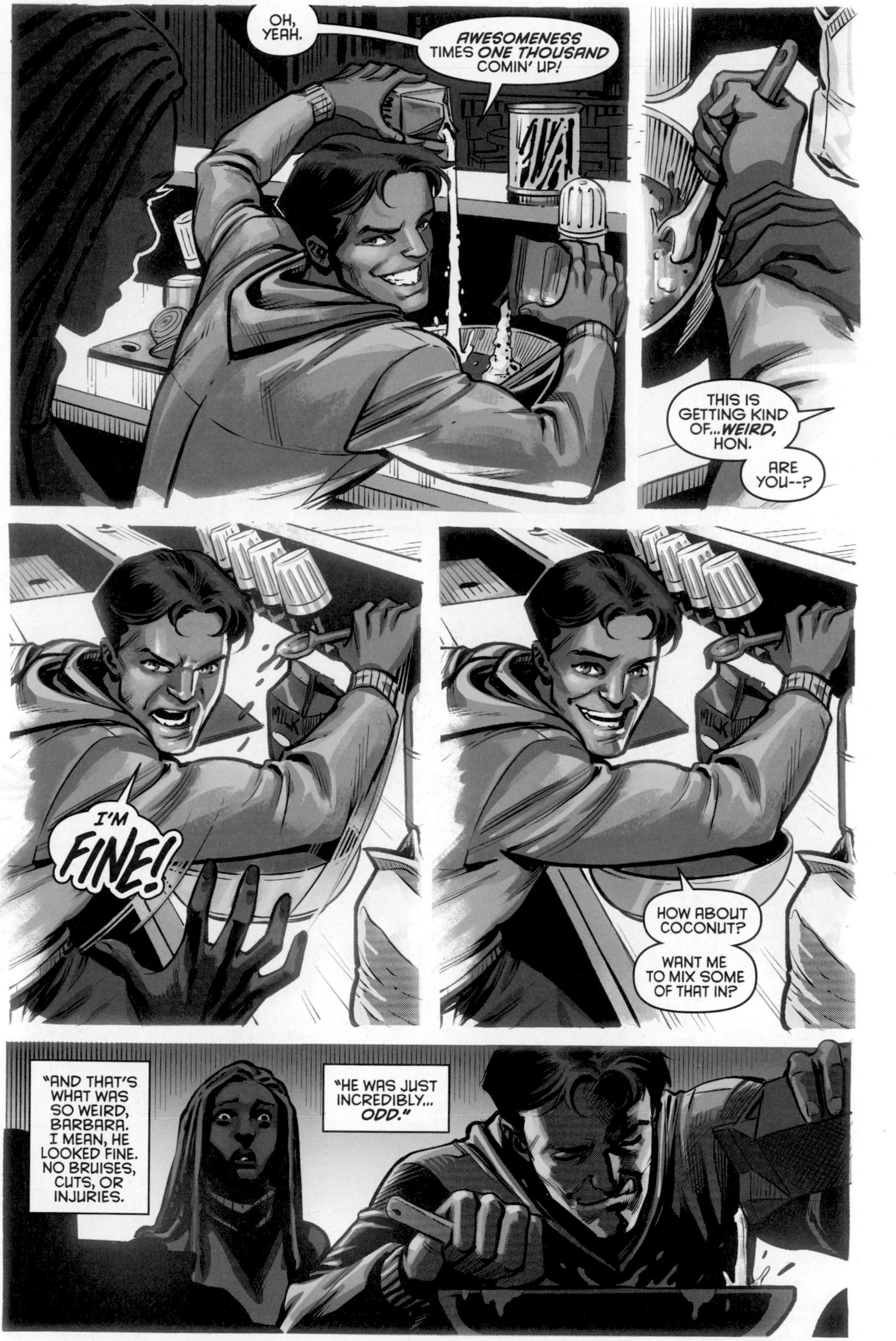
OH, YEAH.
AWESOMENESS TIMES ONE THOUSAND COMIN' UP!
THIS IS GETTING KIND OF...WEIRD, HON.
ARE YOU--?
I'M FINE!
HOW ABOUT COCONUT?
WANT ME TO MIX SOME OF THAT IN?
"AND THAT'S WHAT WAS SO WEIRD, BARBARA. I MEAN, HE LOOKED FINE. NO BRUISES, CUTS, OR INJURIES.
"HE WAS JUST INCREDIBLY... ODD."
MILK
MILK

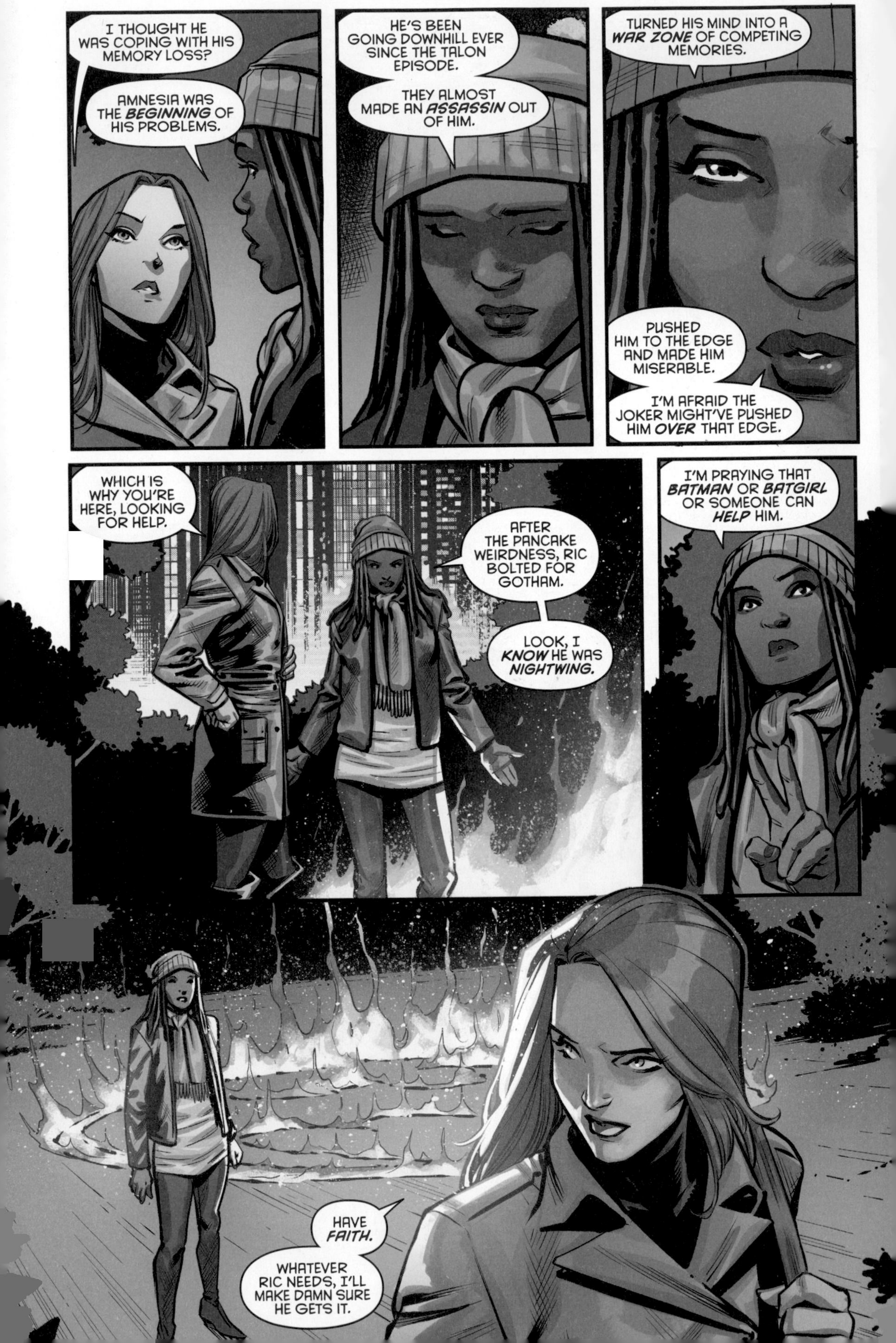
I THOUGHT HE WAS COPING WITH HIS MEMORY LOSS?
AMNESIA WAS THE BEGINNING OF HIS PROBLEMS.
HE'S BEEN GOING DOWNHILL EVER SINCE THE TALON EPISODE.
THEY ALMOST MADE AN ASSASSIN OUT OF HIM.
TURNED HIS MIND INTO A WAR ZONE OF COMPETING MEMORIES.
PUSHED HIM TO THE EDGE AND MADE HIM MISERABLE.
I'M AFRAID THE JOKER MIGHT'VE PUSHED HIM OVER THAT EDGE.
WHICH IS WHY YOU'RE HERE, LOOKING FOR HELP.
AFTER THE PANCAKE WEIRDNESS, RIC BOLTED FOR GOTHAM.
LOOK, I KNOW HE WAS NIGHTWING.
I'M PRAYING THAT BATMAN OR BATGIRL OR SOMEONE CAN HELP HIM.
HAVE FAITH.
WHATEVER RIC NEEDS, I'LL MAKE DAMN SURE HE GETS IT.

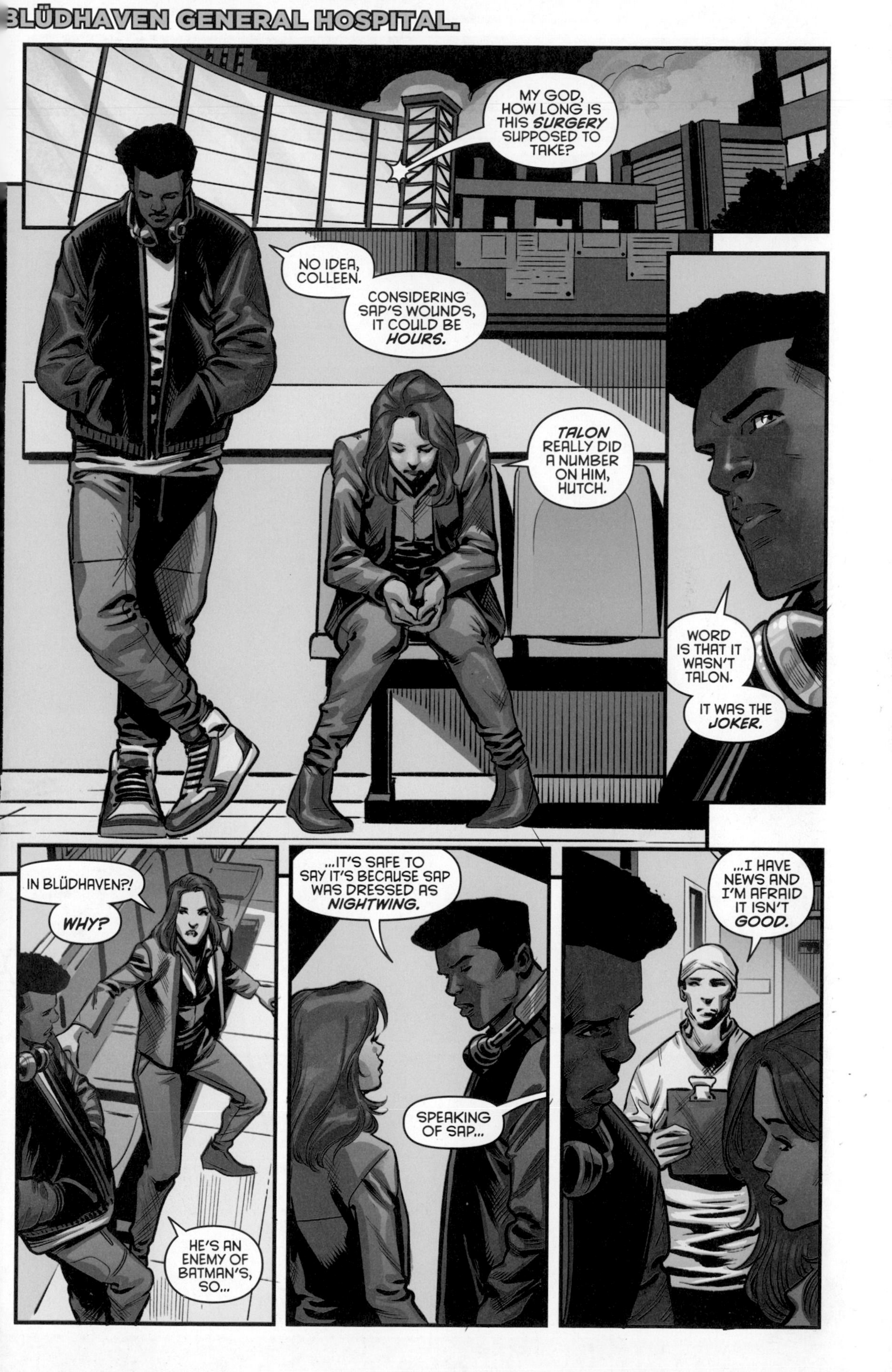
BLÜDHAVEN GENERAL HOSPITAL.
MY GOD, HOW LONG IS THIS SURGERY SUPPOSED TO TAKE?
NO IDEA, COLLEEN.
CONSIDERING SAP'S WOUNDS, IT COULD BE HOURS.
TALON REALLY DID A NUMBER ON HIM, HUTCH.
WORD IS THAT IT WASN'T TALON.
IT WAS THE JOKER.
IN BLÜDHAVEN?!
WHY?
HE'S AN ENEMY OF BATMAN'S, SO...
...IT'S SAFE TO SAY IT'S BECAUSE SAP WAS DRESSED AS NIGHTWING.
SPEAKING OF SAP...
...I HAVE NEWS AND I'M AFRAID IT ISN'T GOOD.

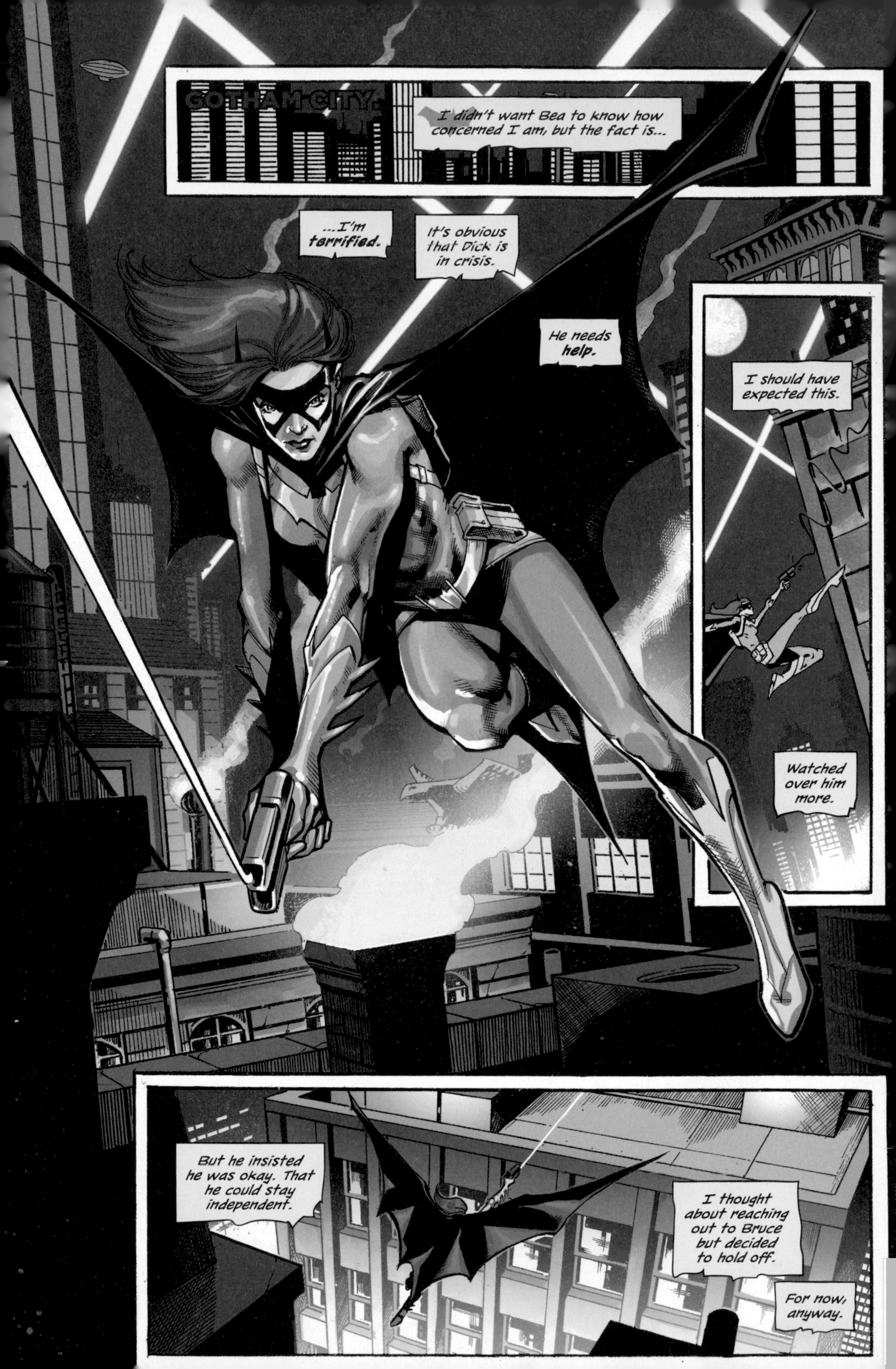

GOTHAM CITY.
I didn't want Bea to know how concerned I am, but the fact is...
...I'm terrified.
It's obvious that Dick is in crisis.
He needs help.
I should have expected this.
Watched over him more.
But he insisted he was okay. That he could stay independent.
I thought about reaching out to Bruce but decided to hold off.
For now, anyway.

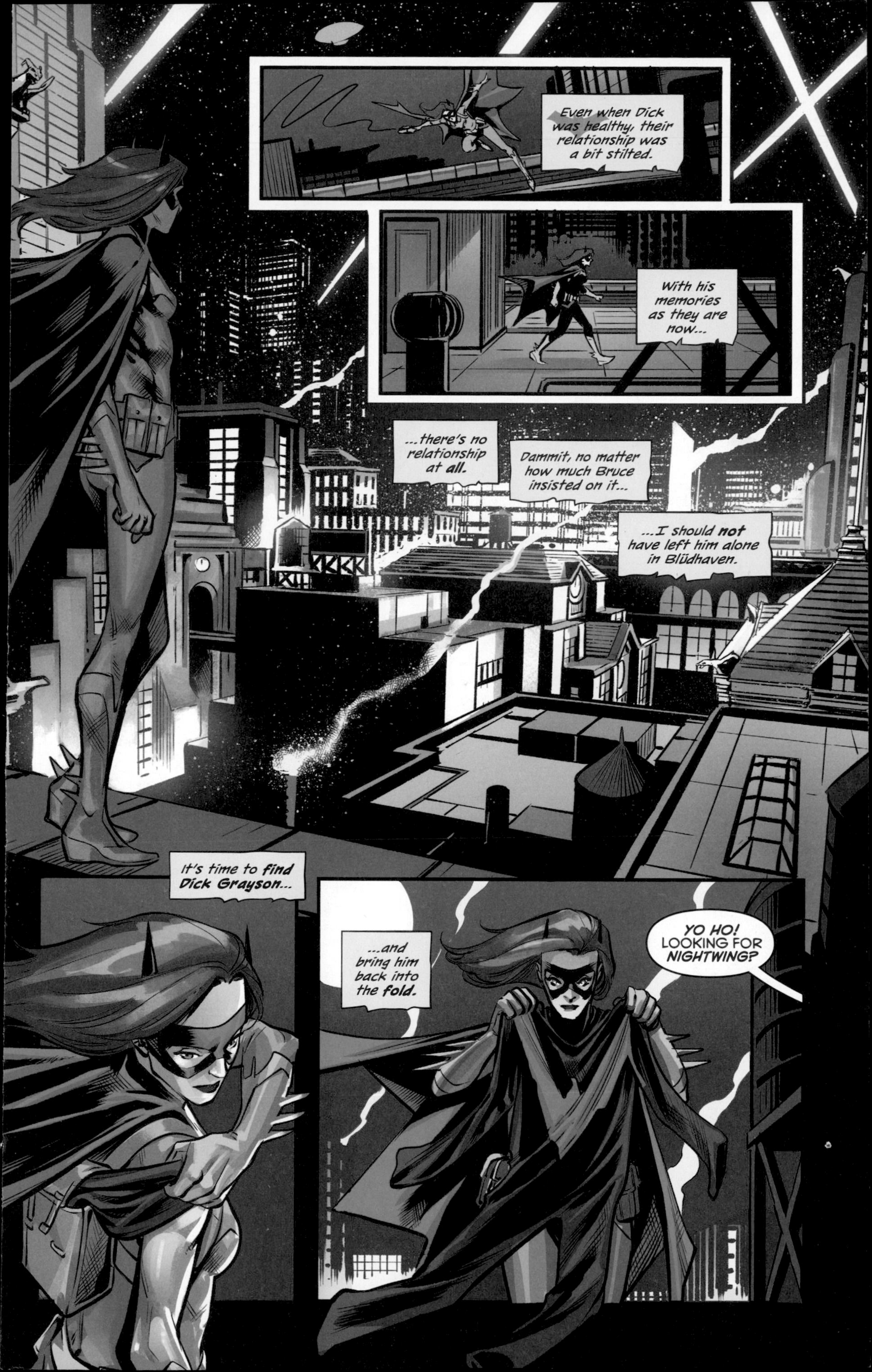
Even when Dick was healthy, their relationship was a bit stilted.
With his memories as they are now...
...there's no relationship at all.
Dammit, no matter how much Bruce insisted on it...
...I should not have left him alone in Blüdhaven.
It's time to find Dick Grayson...
...and bring him back into the fold.
YO HO! LOOKING FOR NIGHTWING?

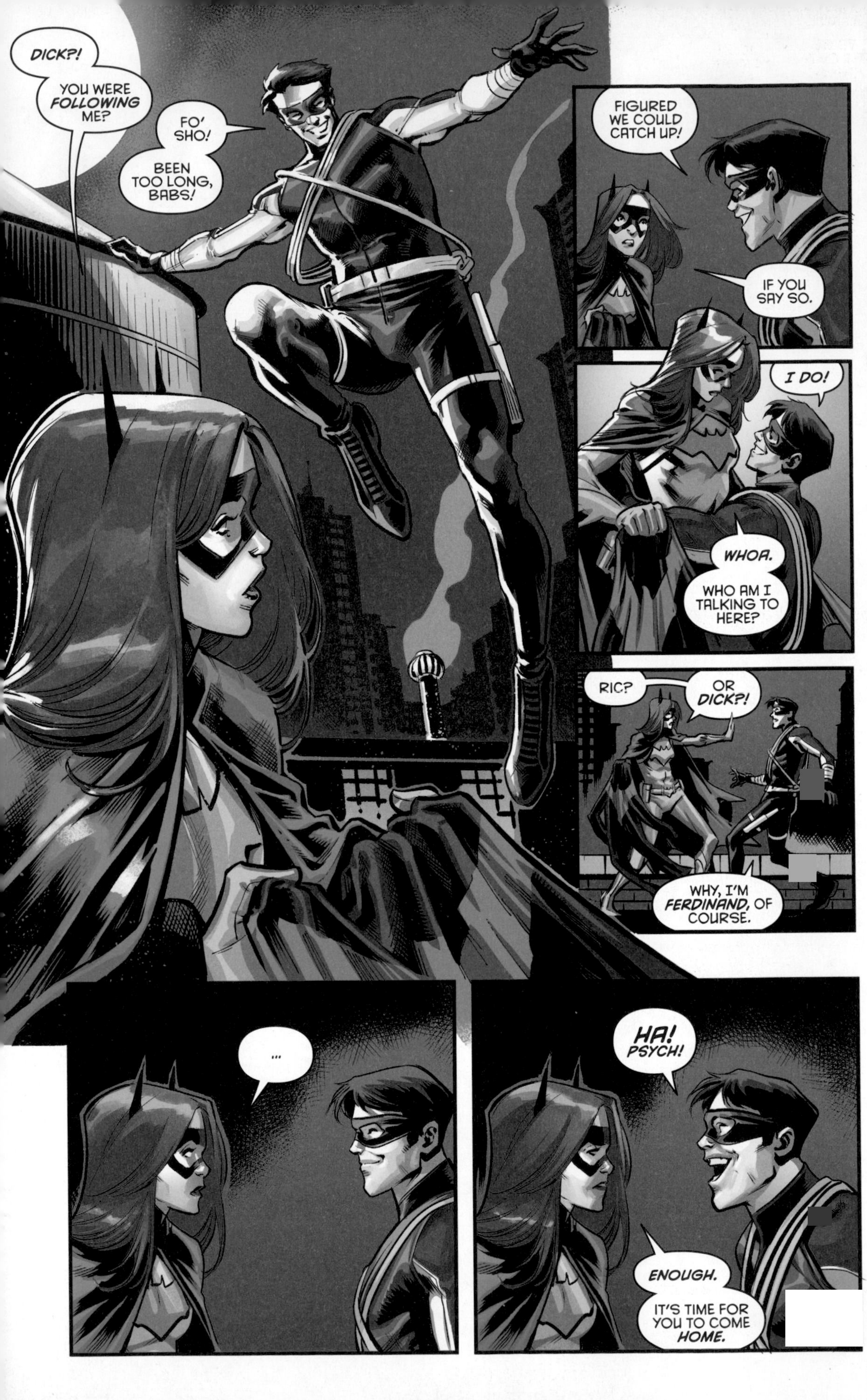
DICK?!
YOU WERE FOLLOWING ME?
FO' SHO!
BEEN TOO LONG, BABS!
FIGURED WE COULD CATCH UP!
IF YOU SAY SO.
I DO!
WHOA.
WHO AM I TALKING TO HERE?
RIC?
OR DICK?!
WHY, I'M FERDINAND, OF COURSE.
...
HA! PSYCH!
ENOUGH.
IT'S TIME FOR YOU TO COME HOME.

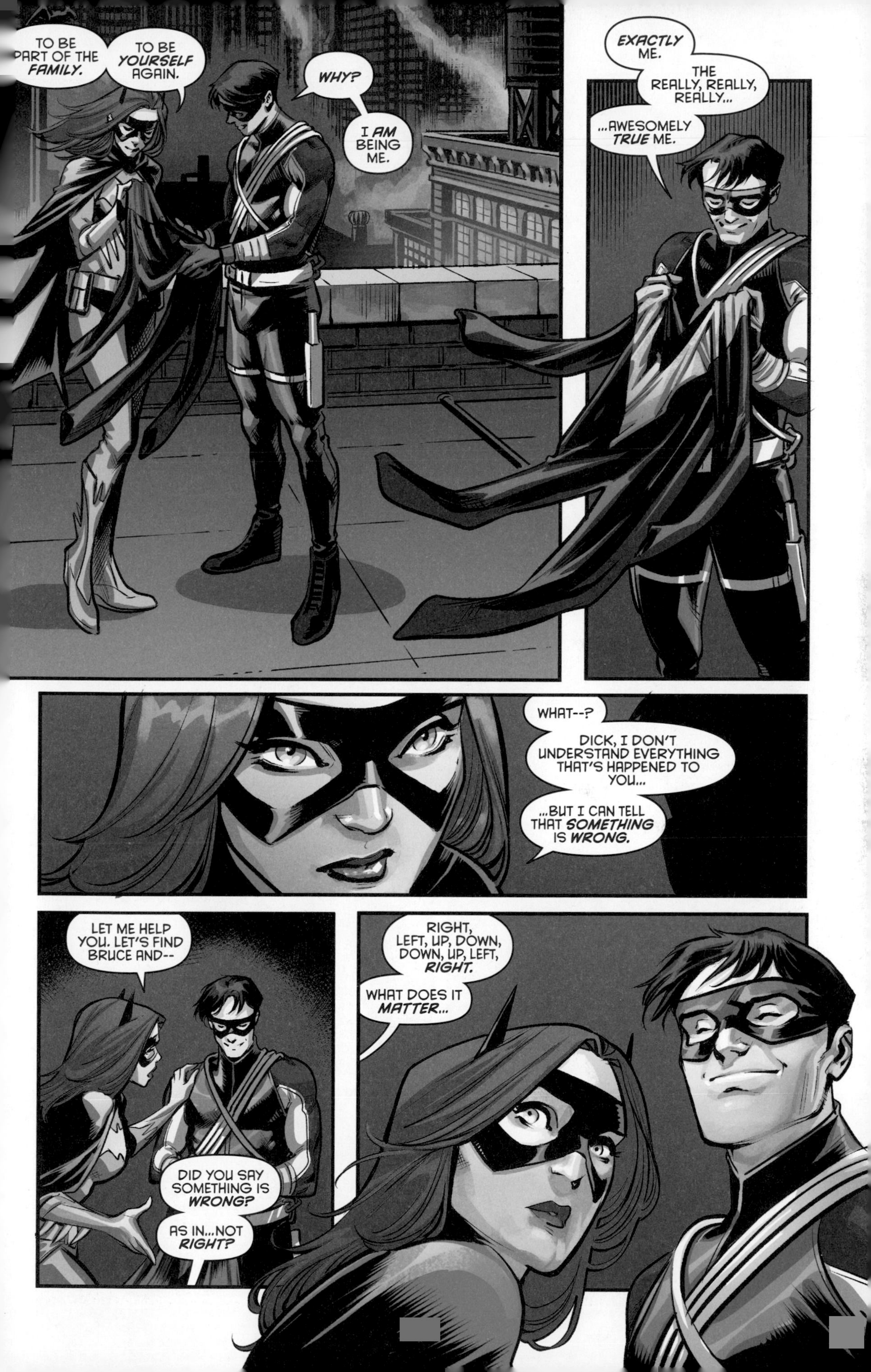
TO BE PART OF THE FAMILY.
TO BE YOURSELF AGAIN.
WHY?
I AM BEING ME.
EXACTLY ME.
THE REALLY, REALLY, REALLY...
...AWESOMELY TRUE ME.
WHAT--?
DICK, I DON'T UNDERSTAND EVERYTHING THAT'S HAPPENED TO YOU...
...BUT I CAN TELL THAT SOMETHING IS WRONG.
LET ME HELP YOU. LET'S FIND BRUCE AND--
DID YOU SAY SOMETHING IS WRONG?
AS IN...NOT RIGHT?
RIGHT, LEFT, UP, DOWN, DOWN, UP, LEFT, RIGHT.
WHAT DOES IT MATTER...

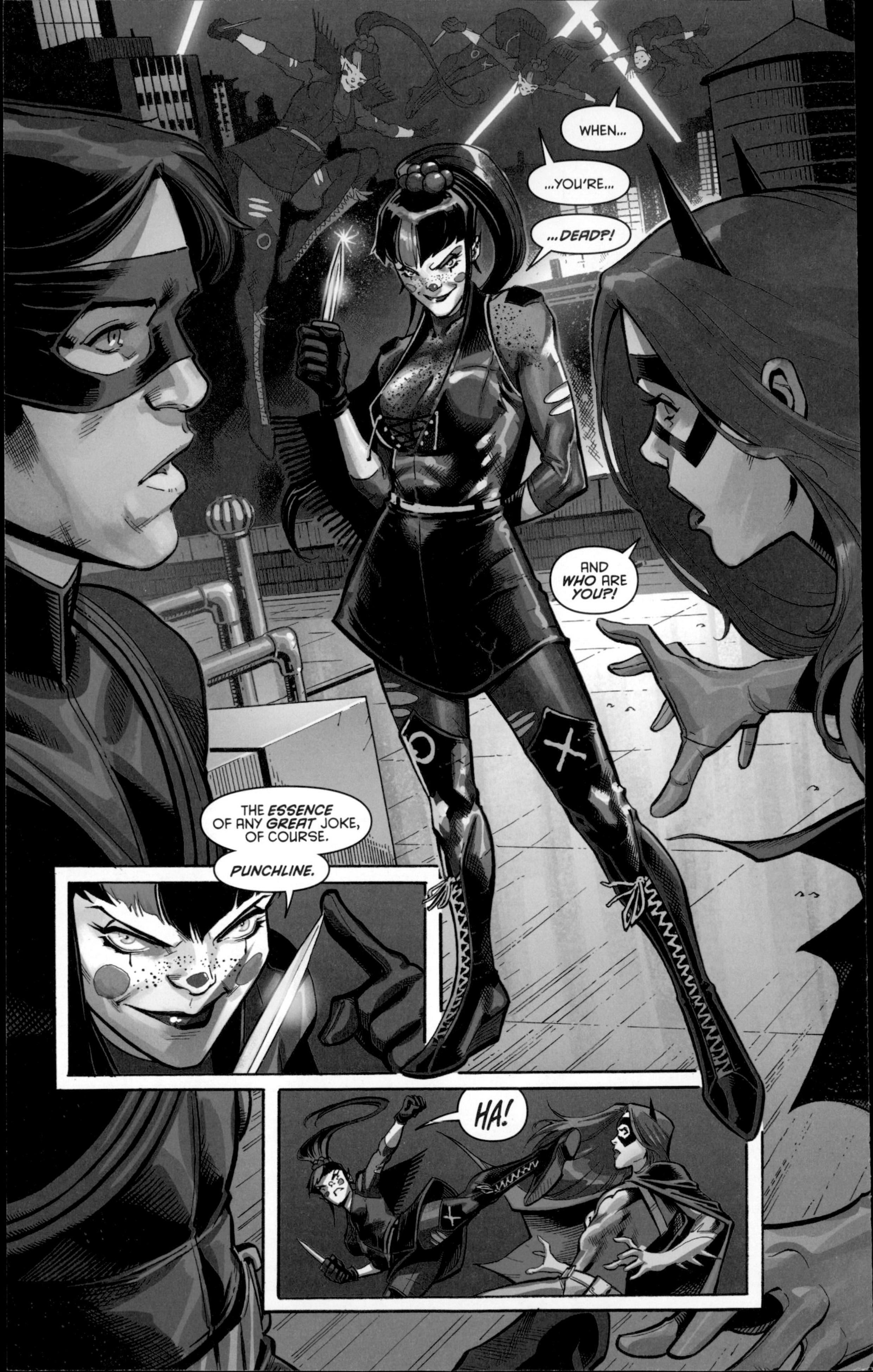
WHEN...
...YOU'RE...
...DEAD?!
AND WHO ARE YOU?!
THE ESSENCE OF ANY GREAT JOKE, OF COURSE.
PUNCHLINE.
HA!

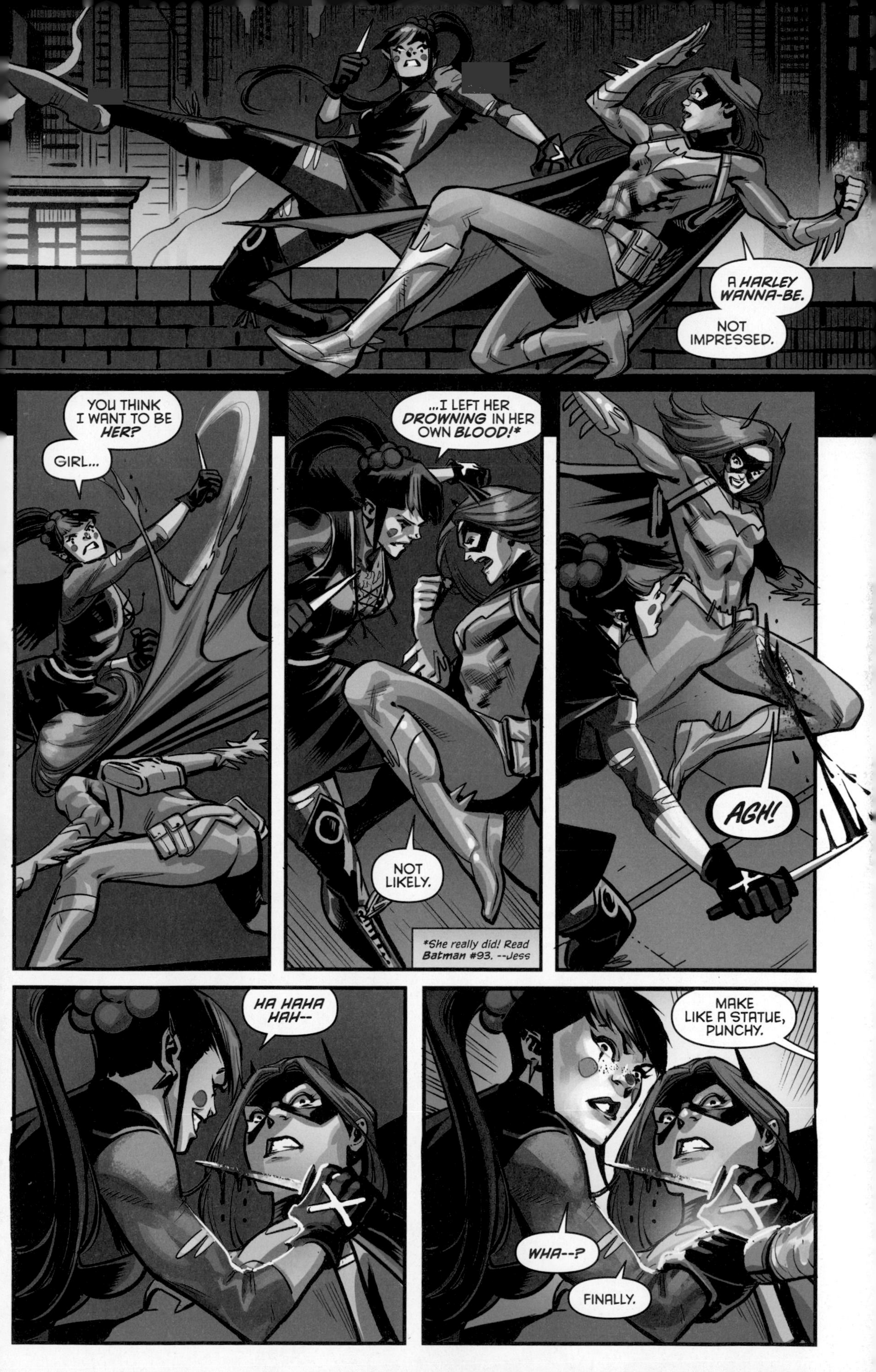
A HARLEY WANNA-BE.
NOT IMPRESSED.
YOU THINK I WANT TO BE HER?
GIRL...
...I LEFT HER DROWNING IN HER OWN BLOOD!*
NOT LIKELY.
*She really did! Read Batman #93. --Jess
AGH!
HA HAHA HAH--
MAKE LIKE A STATUE, PUNCHY.
WHA--?
FINALLY.

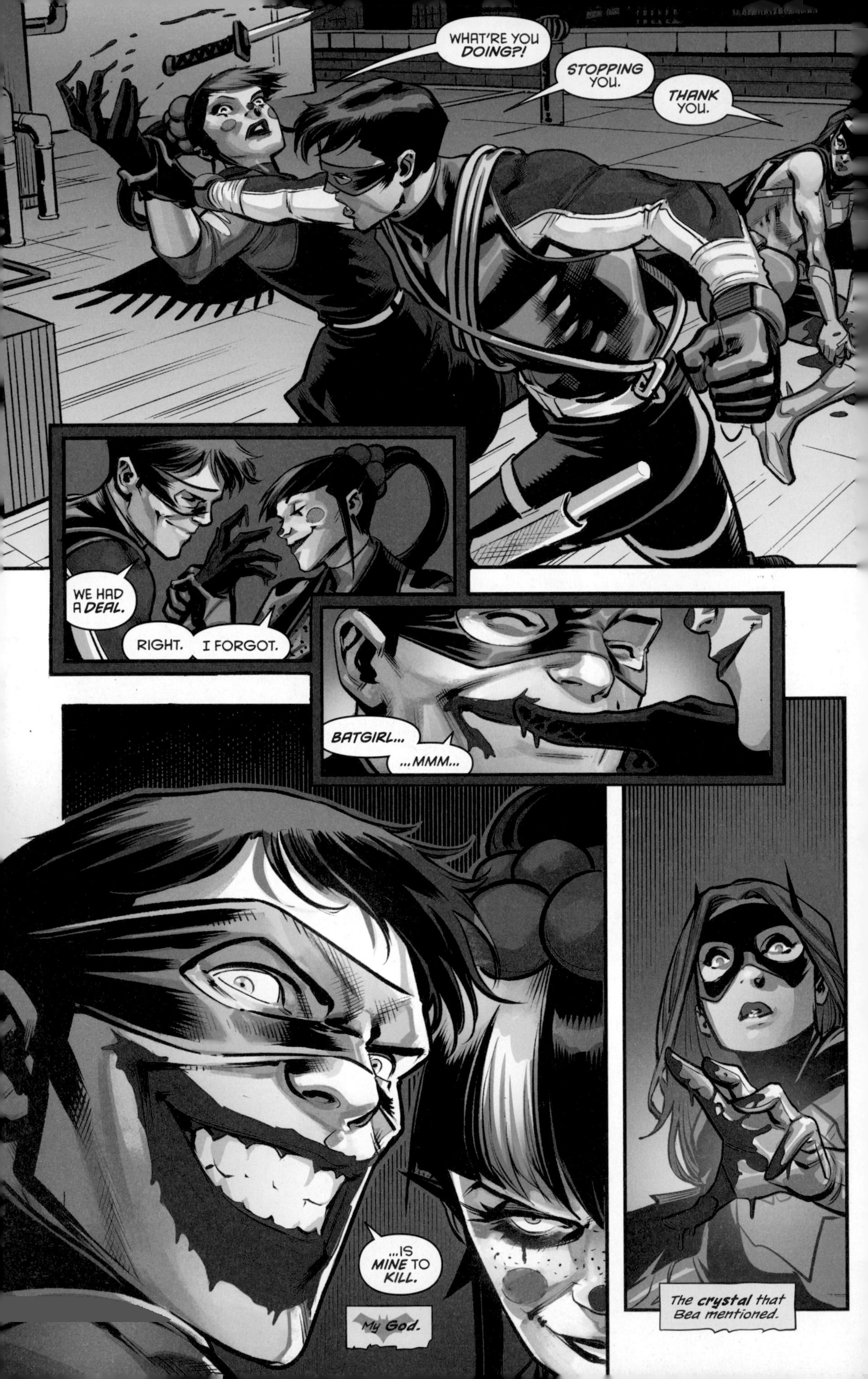
WHAT'RE YOU DOING?!
STOPPING YOU.
THANK YOU.
WE HAD A DEAL.
RIGHT.
I FORGOT.
BATGIRL...
...MMM...
...IS MINE TO KILL.
My God.
The crystal that Bea mentioned.

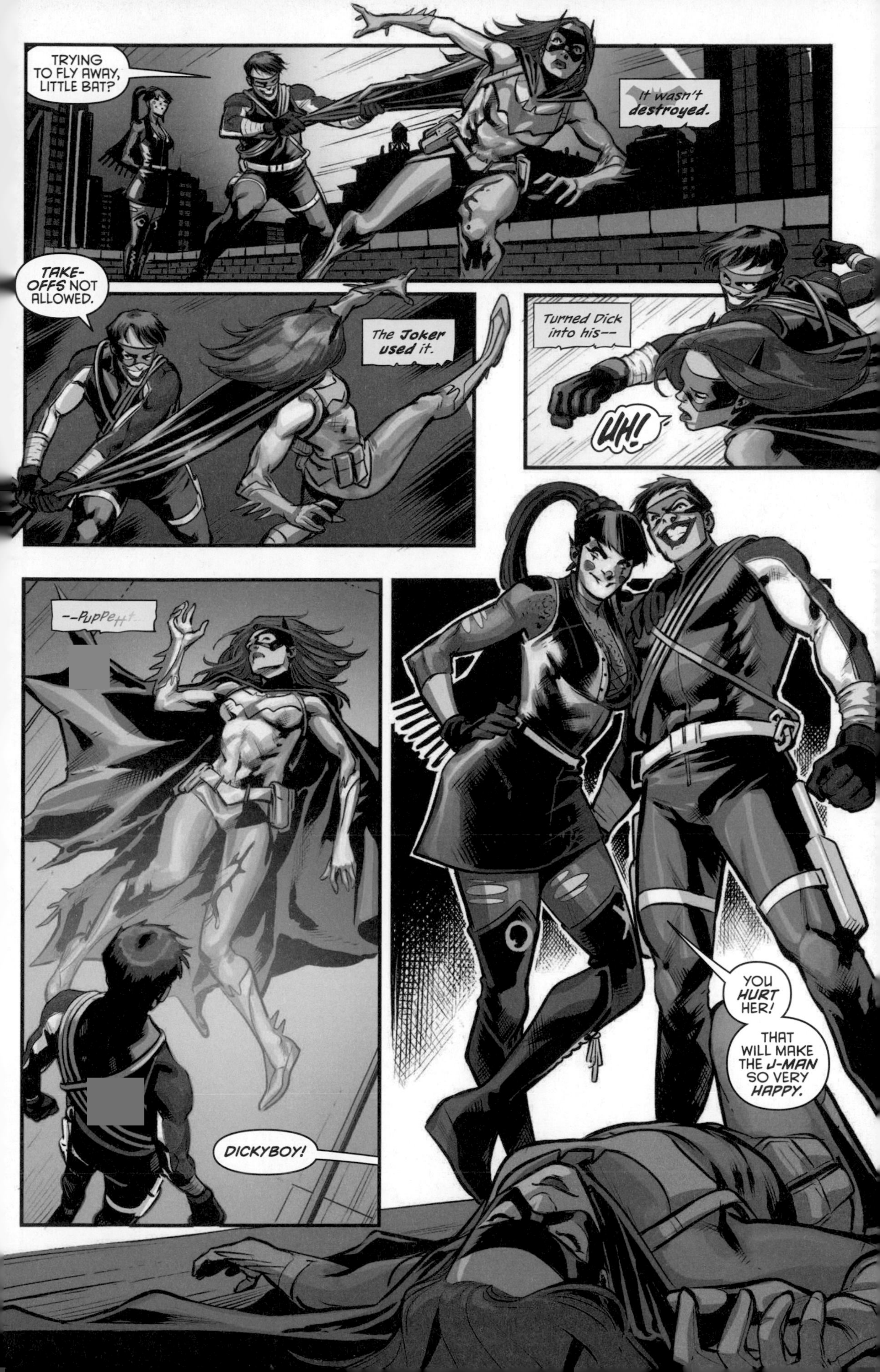
TRYING TO FLY AWAY, LITTLE BAT?
It wasn't destroyed.
TAKE-OFFS NOT ALLOWED.
The Joker used it.
Turned Dick into his--
UH!
--Puppett...
DICKYBOY!
YOU HURT HER!
THAT WILL MAKE THE J-MAN SO VERY HAPPY.

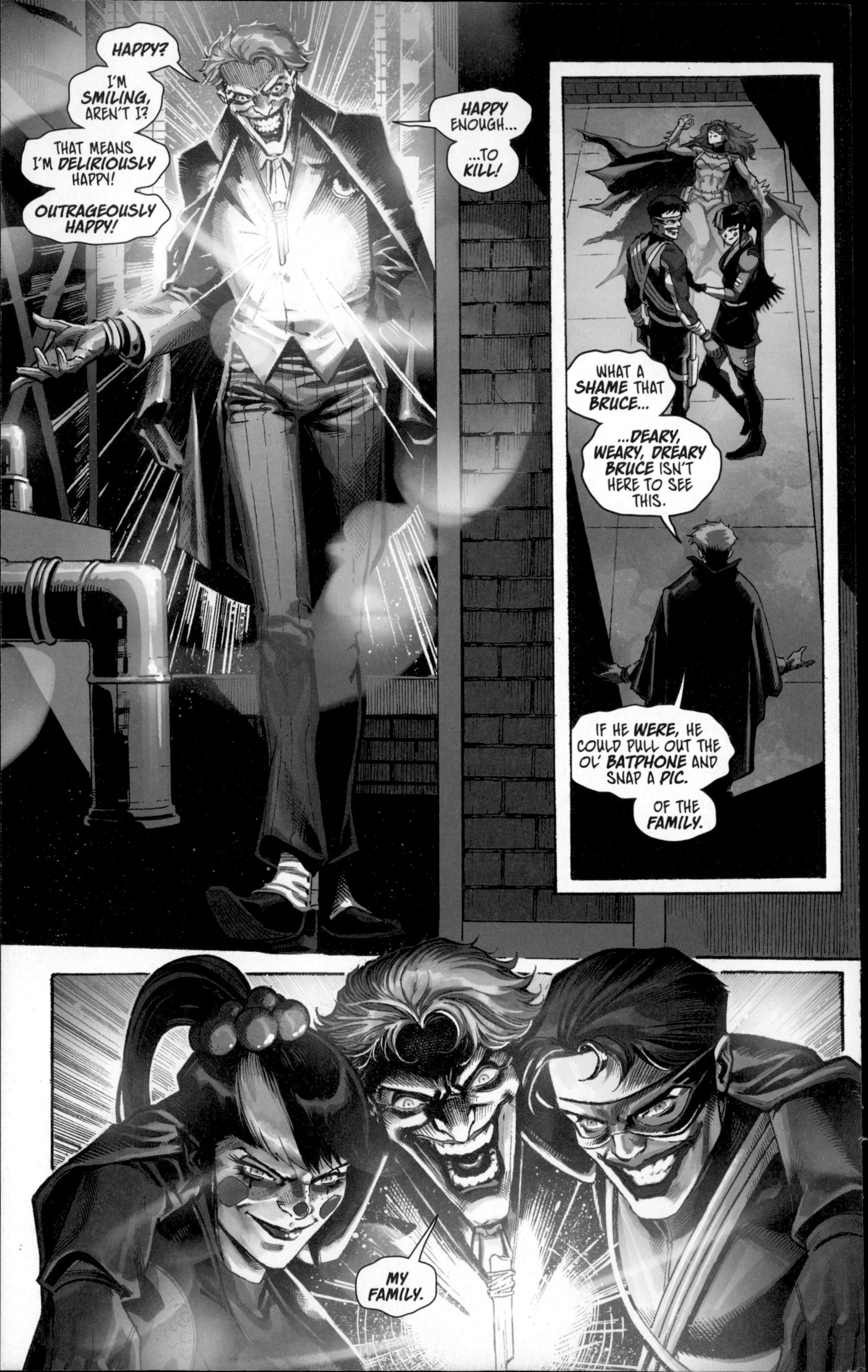
HAPPY?
I'M SMILING, AREN'T I?
THAT MEANS I'M DELIRIOUSLY HAPPY!
OUTRAGEOUSLY HAPPY!
HAPPY ENOUGH...
...TO KILL!
WHAT A SHAME THAT BRUCE...
...DEARY, WEARY, DREARY BRUCE ISN'T HERE TO SEE THIS.
IF HE WERE, HE COULD PULL OUT THE OL' BATPHONE AND SNAP A PIC.
OF THE FAMILY.
MY FAMILY.

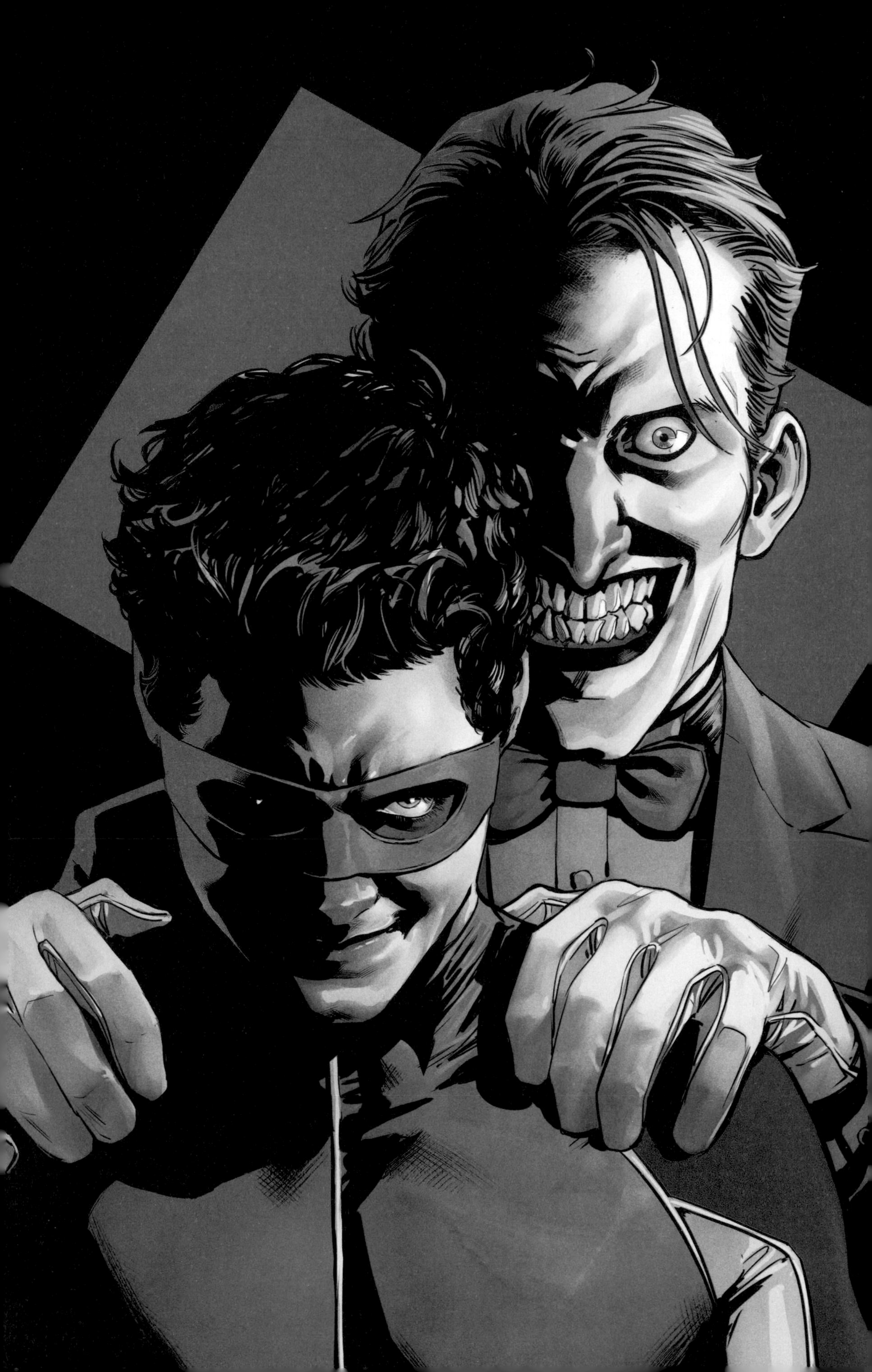

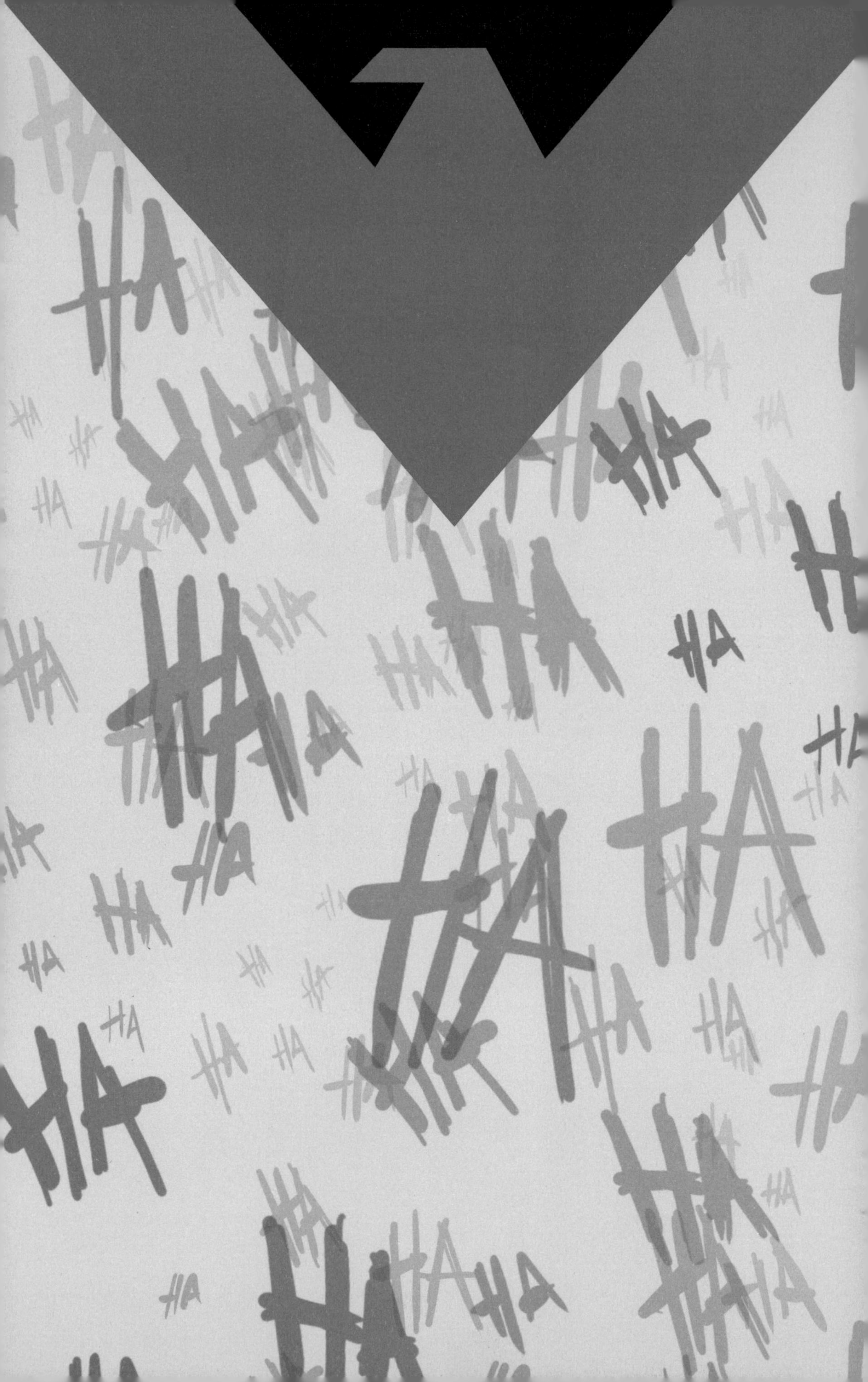

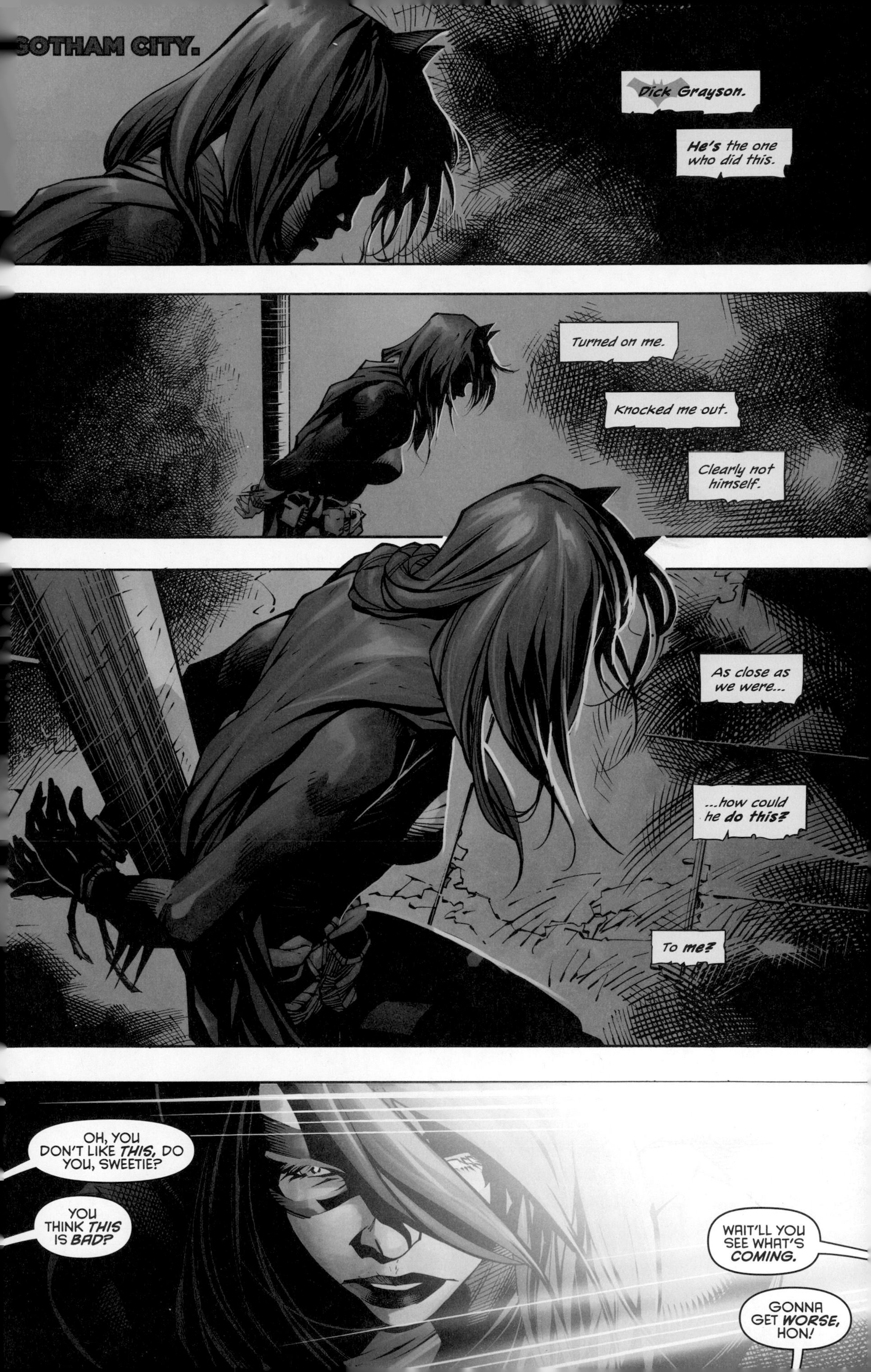
GOTHAM CITY.
Dick Grayson.
He's the one who did this.
Turned on me.
Knocked me out.
Clearly not himself.
As close as we were...
...how could he do this?
To me?
OH, YOU DON'T LIKE THIS, DO YOU, SWEETIE?
YOU THINK THIS IS BAD?
WAIT'LL YOU SEE WHAT'S COMING.
GONNA GET WORSE, HON!

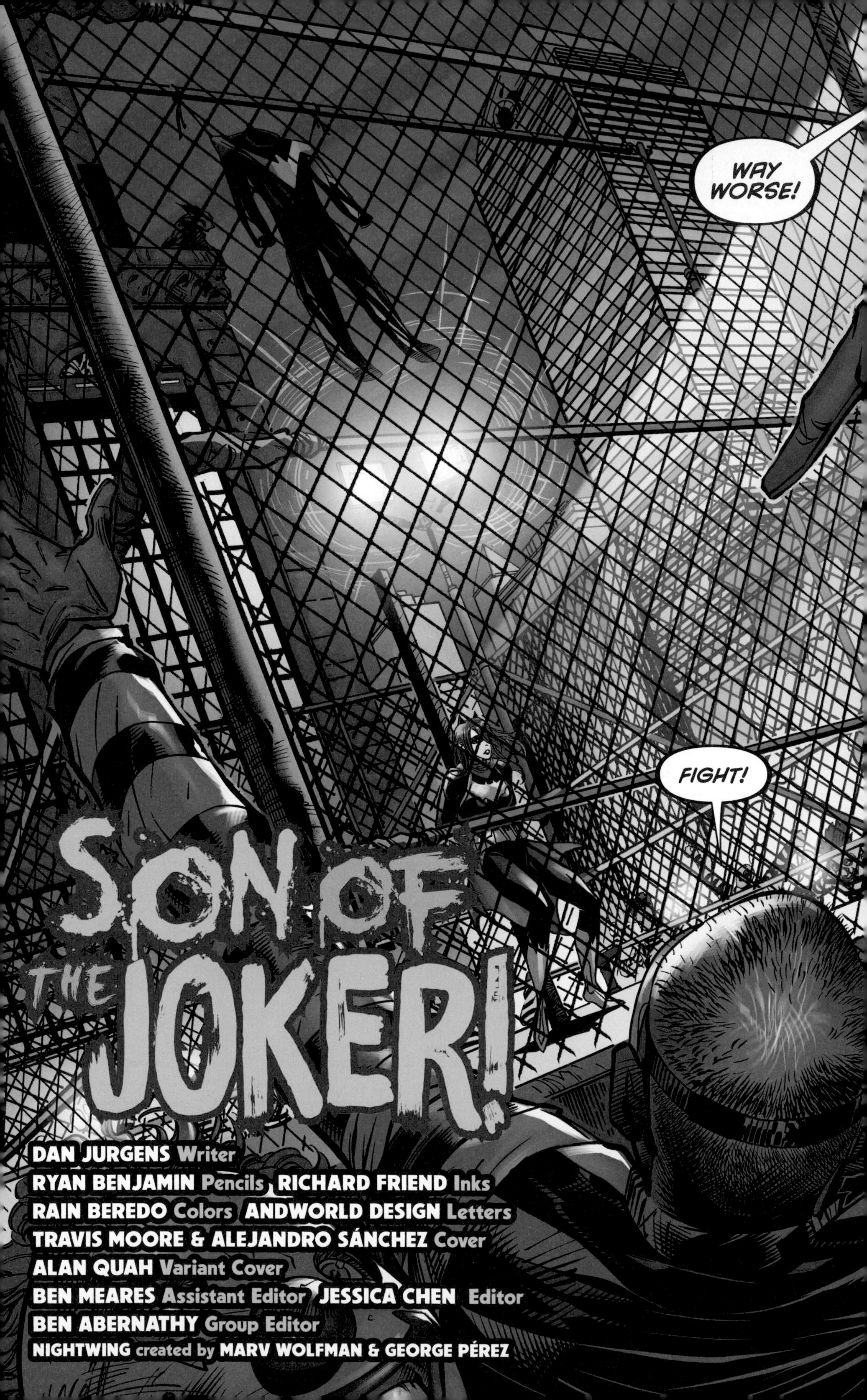
WAY WORSE!
FIGHT!
SON OF THE JOKER!
DAN JURGENS Writer
RYAN BENJAMIN Pencils RICHARD FRIEND Inks
RAIN BEREDO Colors ANDWORLD DESIGN Letters
TRAVIS MOORE & ALEJANDRO SÁNCHEZ Cover
ALAN QUAH Variant Cover
BEN MEARES Assistant Editor JESSICA CHEN Editor
BEN ABERNATHY Group Editor
NIGHTWING created by MARV WOLFMAN & GEORGE PÉREZ

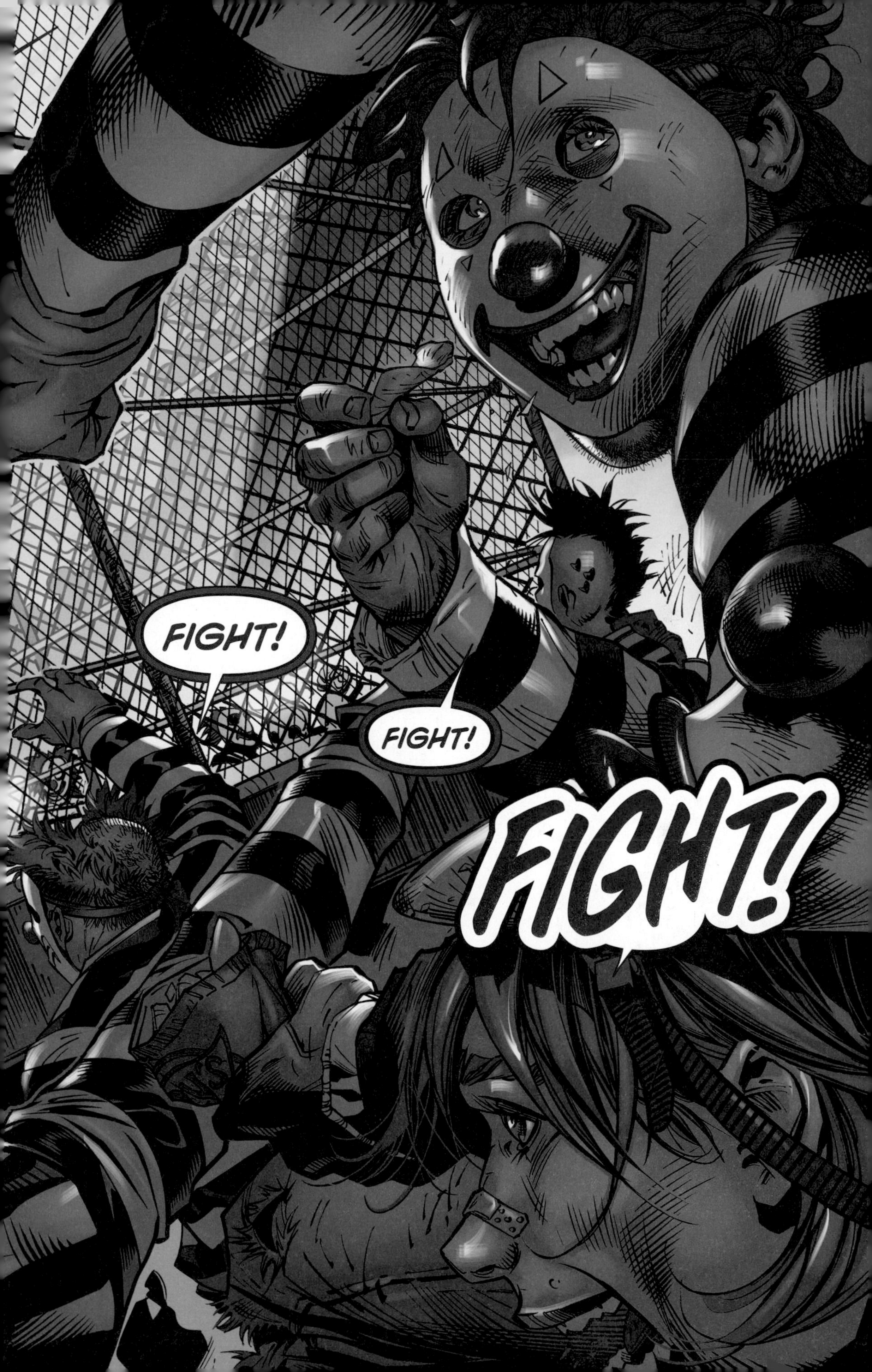
FIGHT!
FIGHT!
FIGHT!

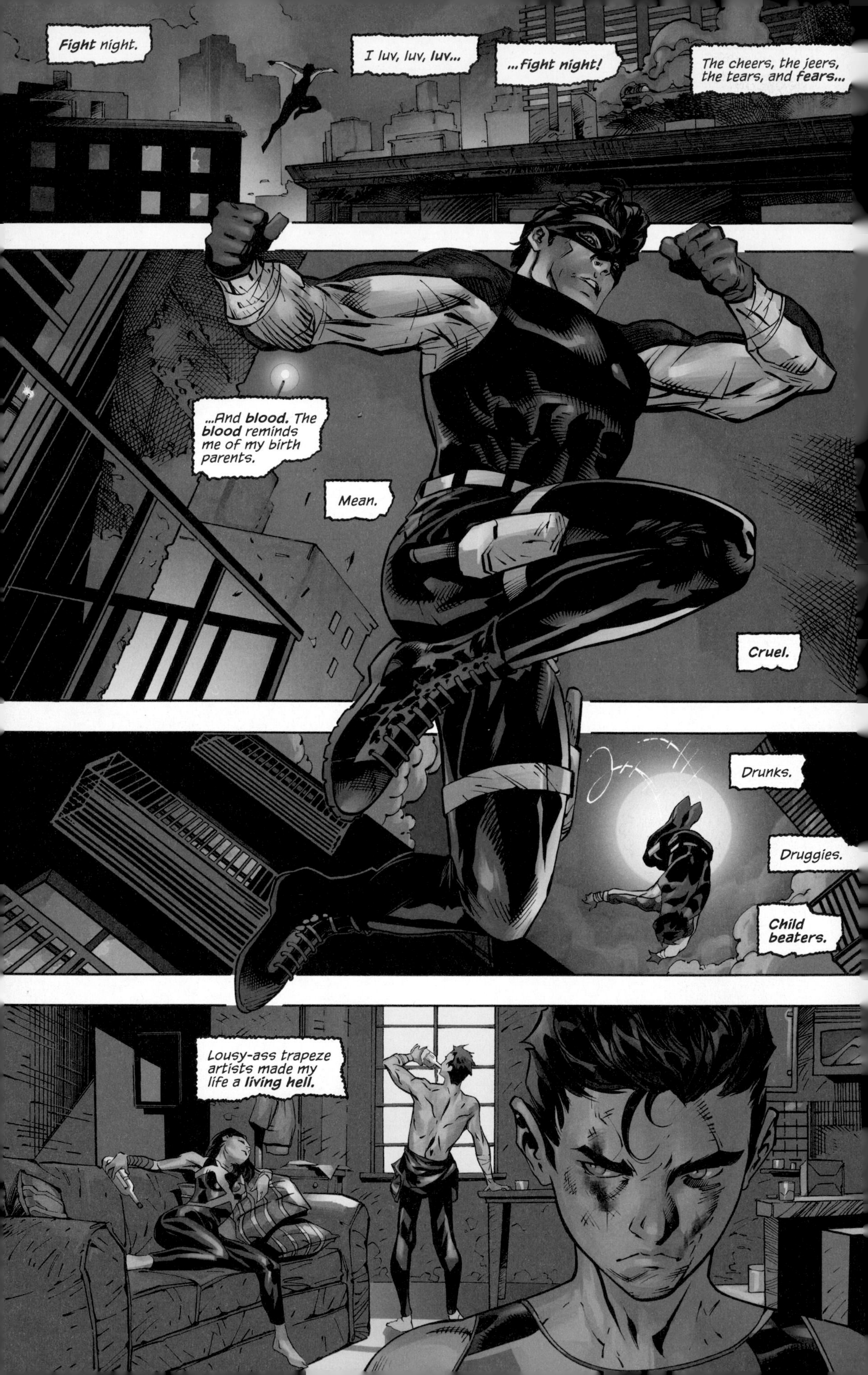
Fight night.
I luv, luv, luv...
...fight night!
The cheers, the jeers, the tears, and fears...
...And blood. The blood reminds me of my birth parents.
Mean.
Cruel.
Drunks.
Druggies.
Child beaters.
Lousy-ass trapeze artists made my life a living hell.

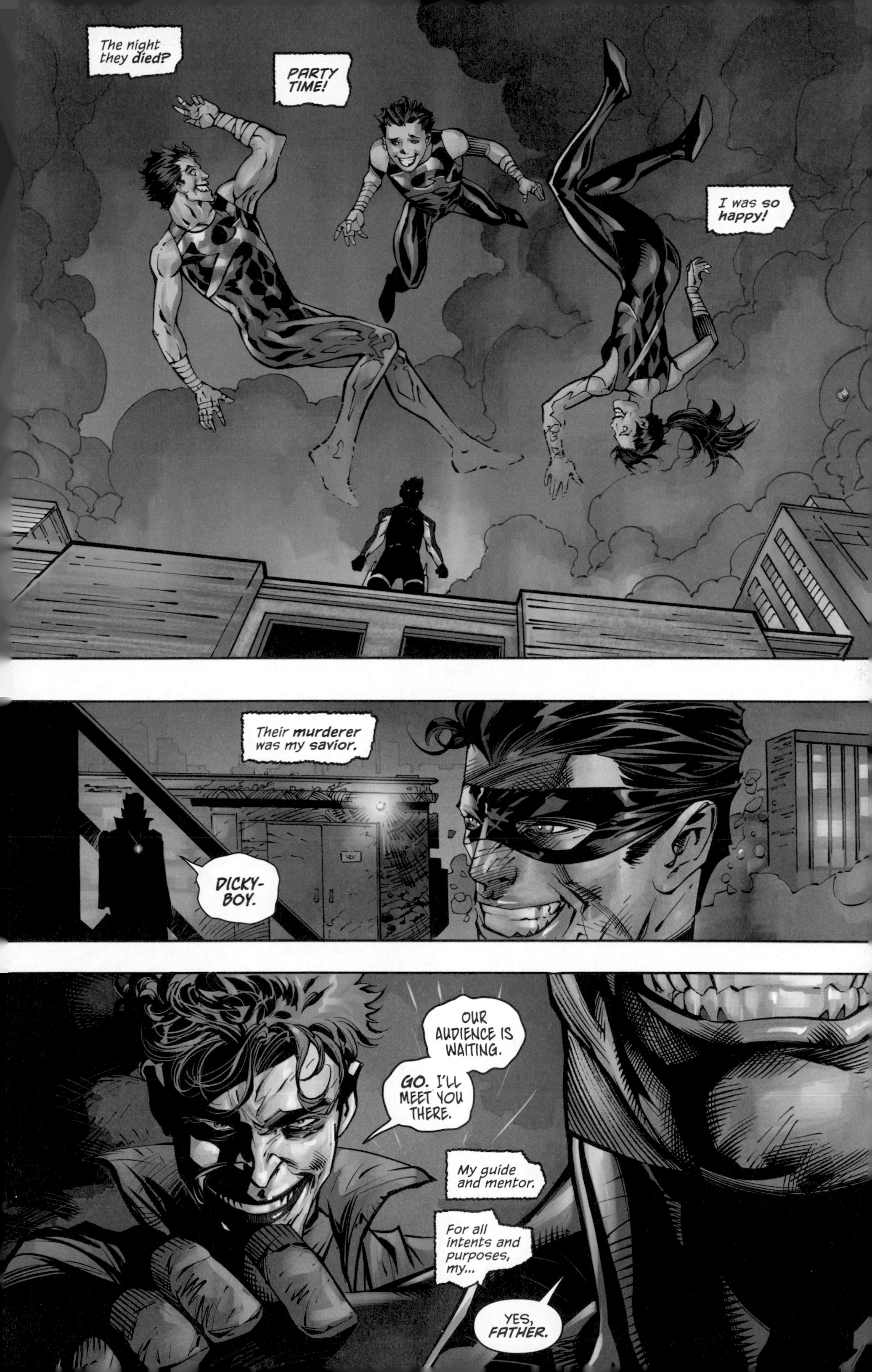

The night they died?
PARTY TIME!
I was so happy!
Their murderer was my savior.
DICKY-BOY.
OUR AUDIENCE IS WAITING.
GO. I'LL MEET YOU THERE.
My guide and mentor.
For all intents and purposes, my...
YES, FATHER.

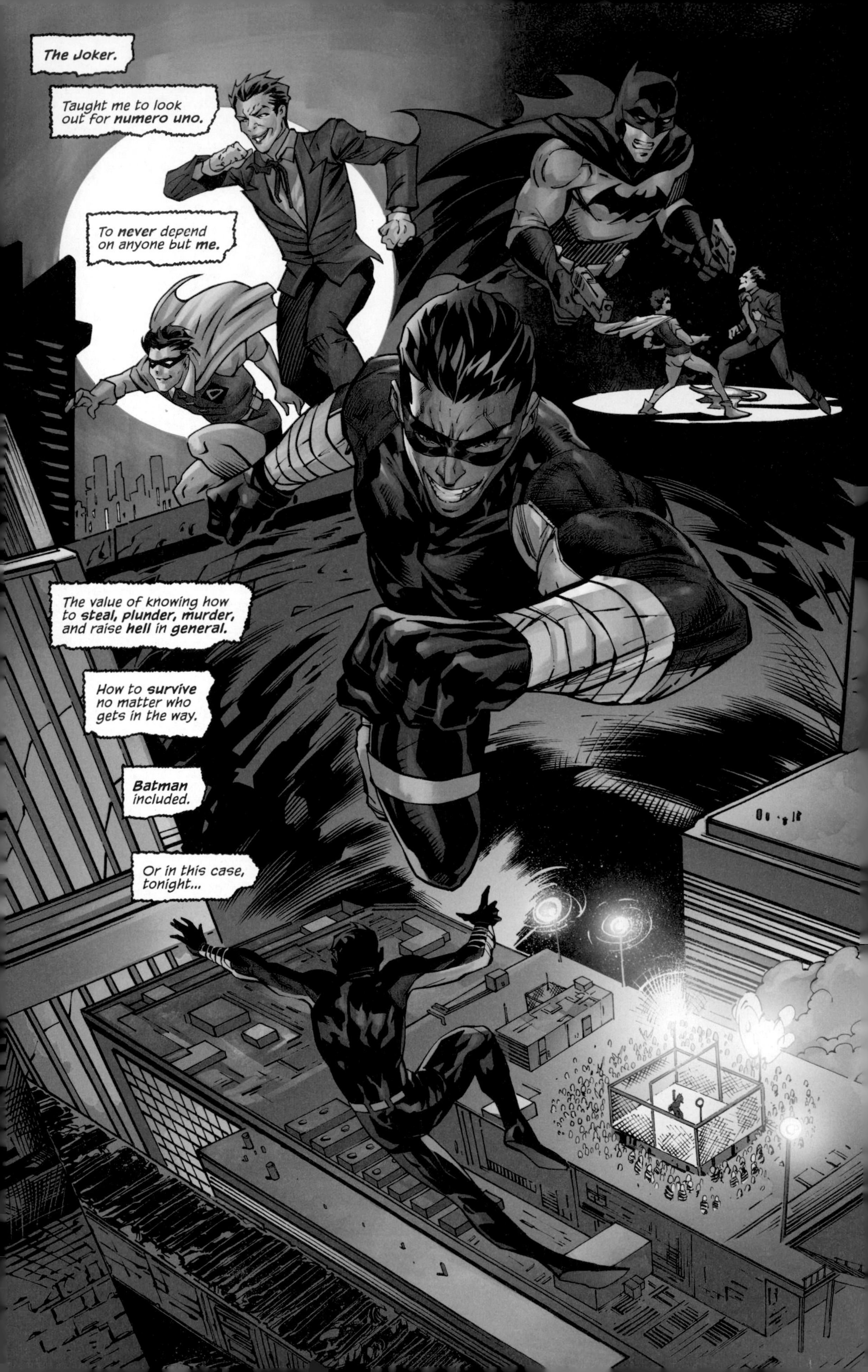
The Joker.
Taught me to look out for numero uno.
To never depend on anyone but me.
The value of knowing how to steal, plunder, murder, and raise hell in general.
How to survive no matter who gets in the way.
Batman included.
Or in this case, tonight...

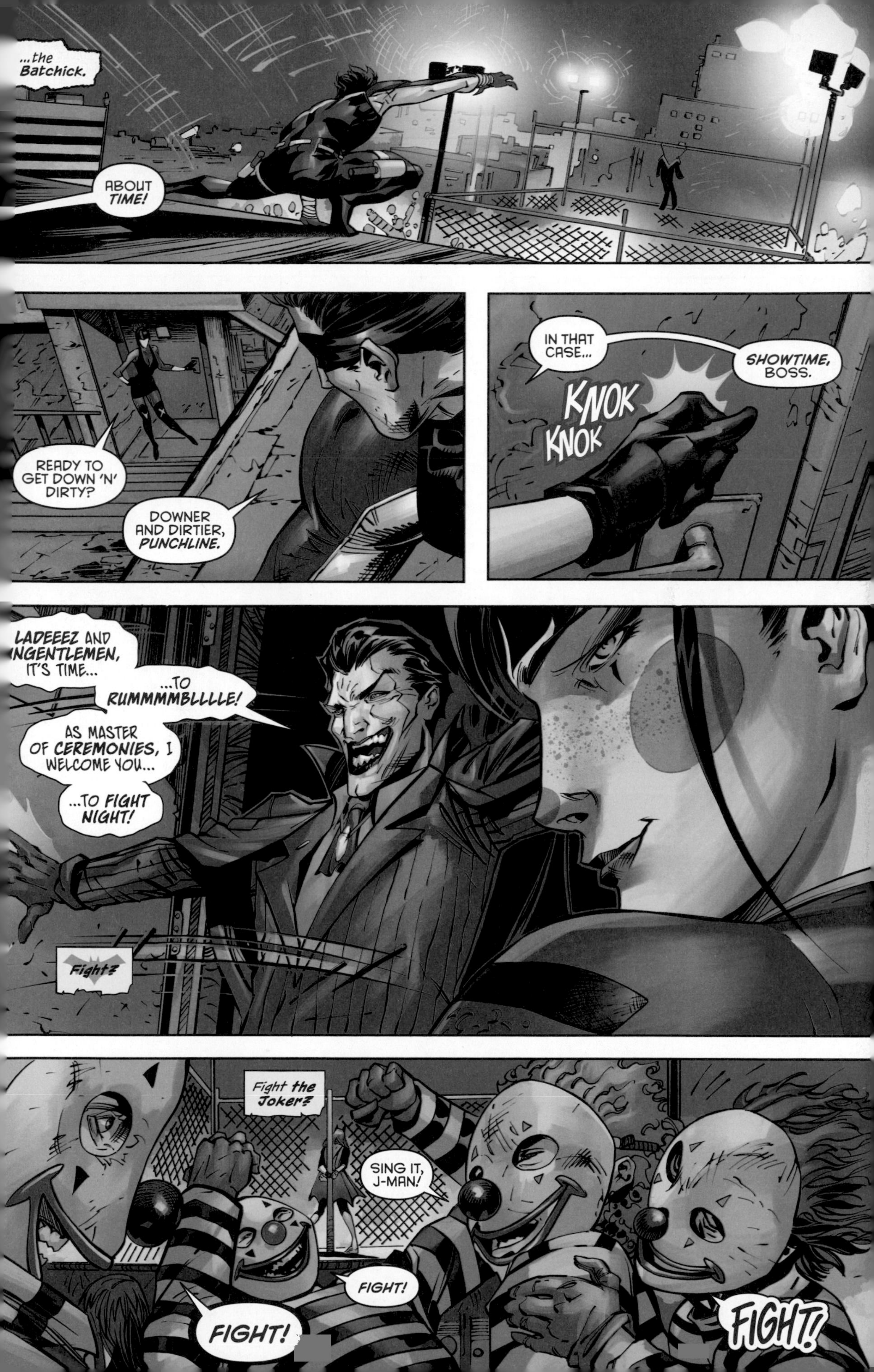

...the Batchick.
ABOUT TIME!
READY TO GET DOWN 'N' DIRTY?
DOWNER AND DIRTIER, PUNCHLINE.
IN THAT CASE...
SHOWTIME, BOSS.
KNOK KNOK
LADEEEZ AND NGENTLEMEN, IT'S TIME...
...TO RUMMMMBLLLLE!
AS MASTER OF CEREMONIES, I WELCOME YOU...
...TO FIGHT NIGHT!
Fight?
Fight the Joker?
SING IT, J-MAN!
FIGHT!
FIGHT!
FIGHT!

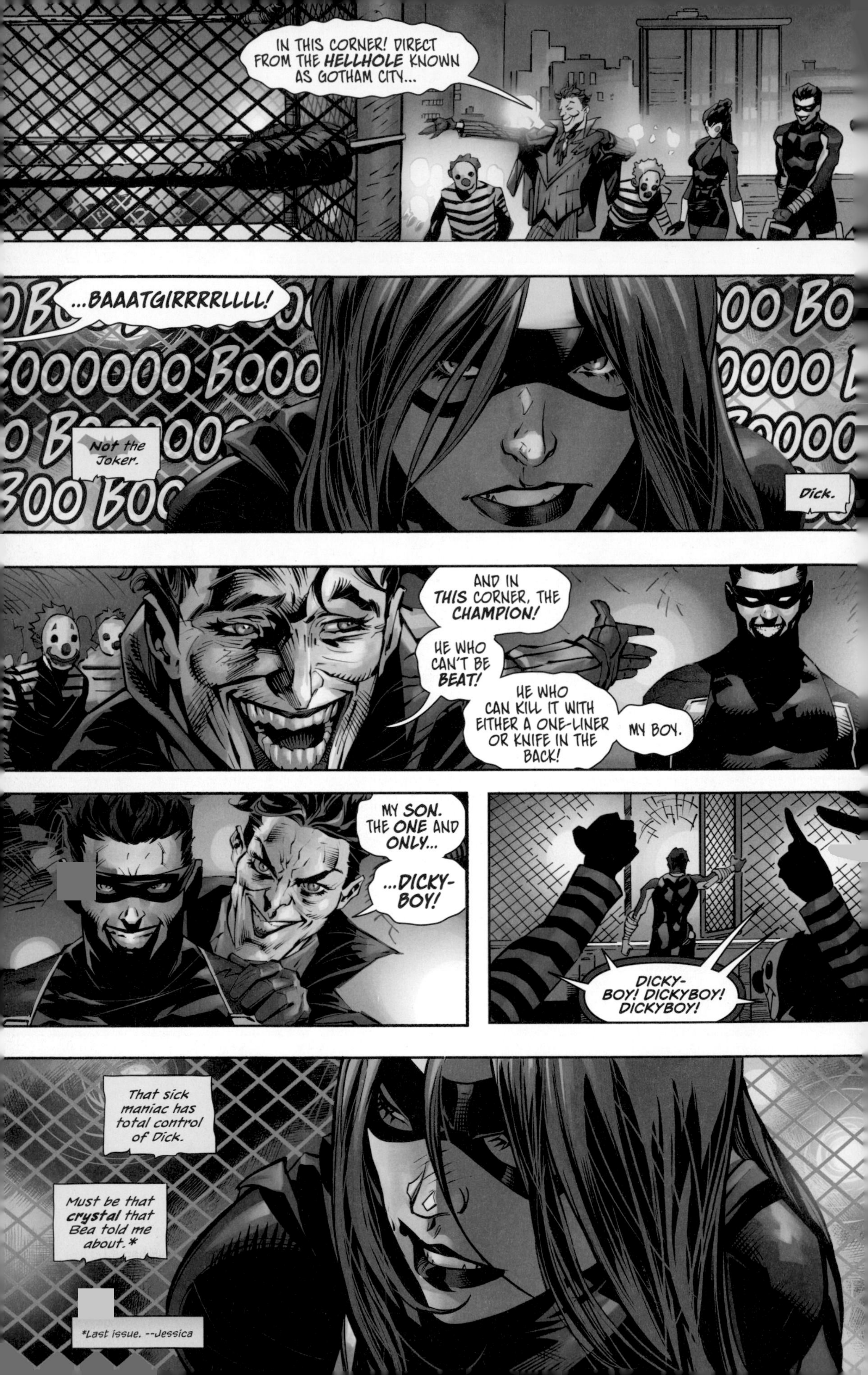

IN THIS CORNER! DIRECT FROM THE HELLHOLE KNOWN AS GOTHAM CITY...
...BAAATGIRRRRLLLL!
Not the Joker.
Dick.
AND IN THIS CORNER, THE CHAMPION!
HE WHO CAN'T BE BEAT!
HE WHO CAN KILL IT WITH EITHER A ONE-LINER OR KNIFE IN THE BACK!
MY BOY.
MY SON. THE ONE AND ONLY...
...DICKY-BOY!
DICKY-BOY! DICKYBOY! DICKYBOY!
That sick maniac has total control of Dick.
Must be that crystal that Bea told me about.*
*Last issue. --Jessica

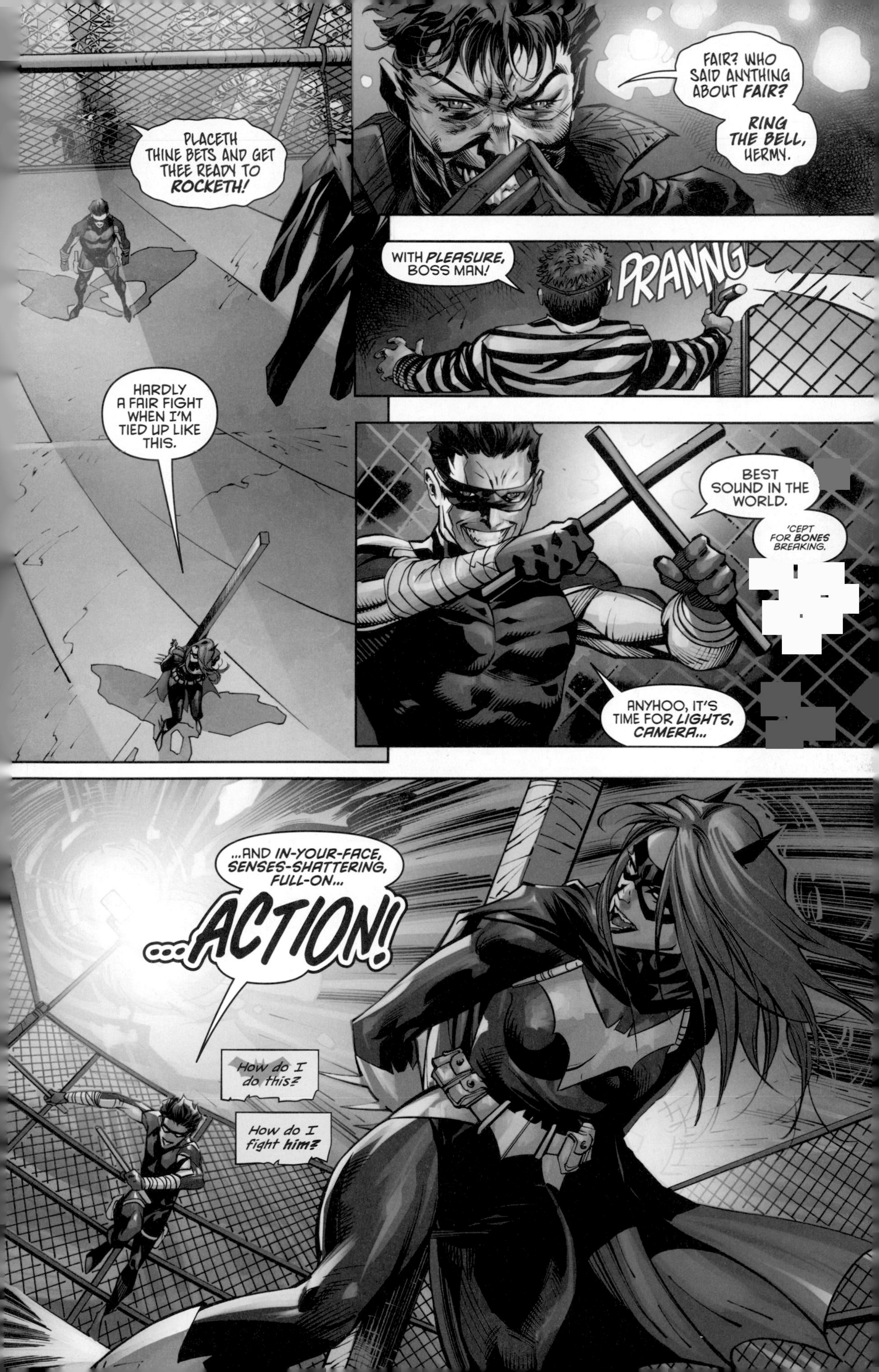

PLACETH THINE BETS AND GET THEE READY TO *ROCKETH!*
FAIR? WHO SAID ANYTHING ABOUT *FAIR?*
RING THE BELL, HERMY.
WITH *PLEASURE,* BOSS MAN!
PRANNG
HARDLY A FAIR FIGHT WHEN I'M TIED UP LIKE THIS.
BEST SOUND IN THE WORLD.
'CEPT FOR *BONES* BREAKING.
ANYHOO, IT'S TIME FOR *LIGHTS, CAMERA...*
...AND *IN-YOUR-FACE, SENSES-SHATTERING, FULL-ON...*
...ACTION!
How do I do this?
How do I fight *him?*

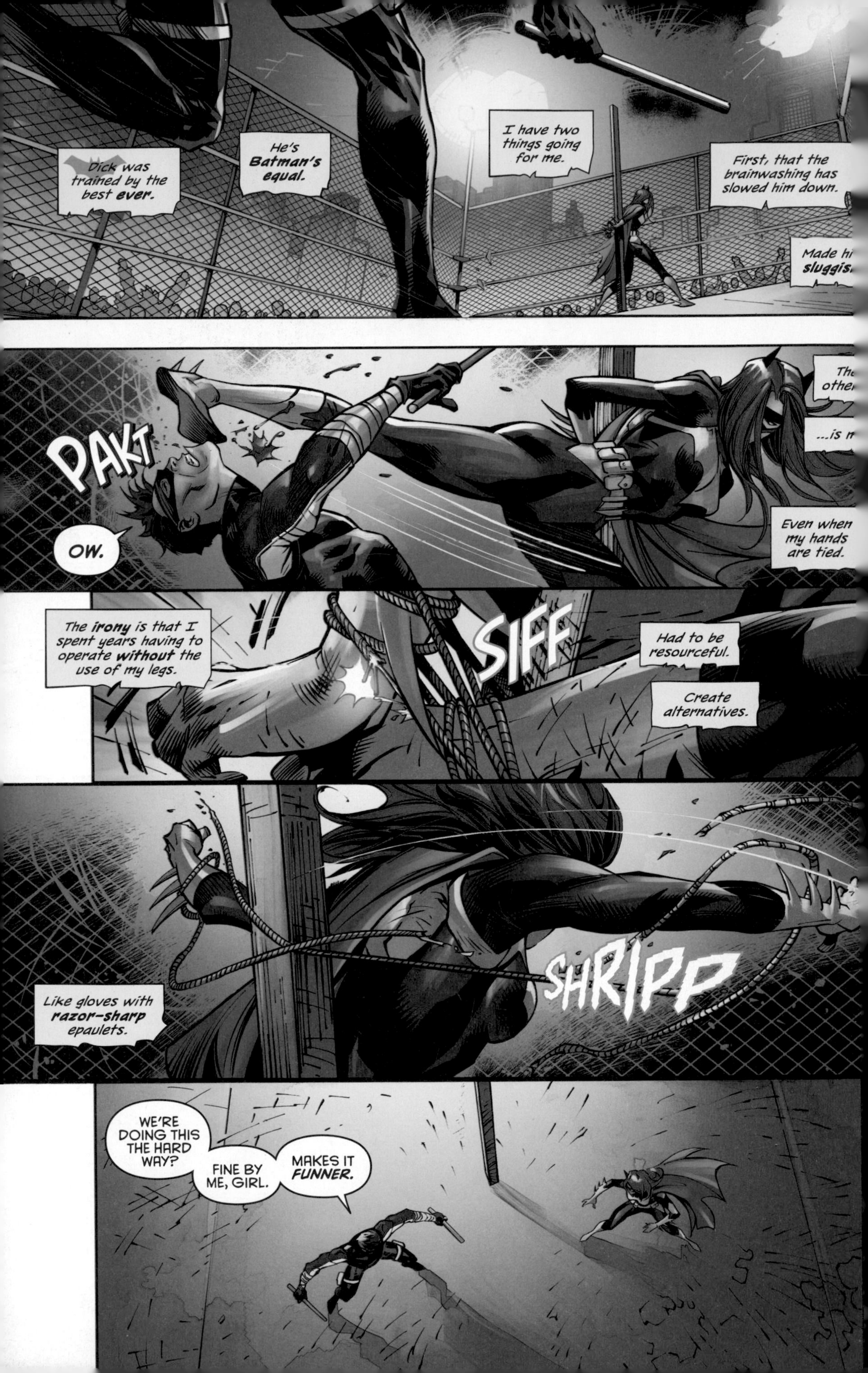
Dick was trained by the best ever.
He's Batman's equal.
I have two things going for me.
First, that the brainwashing has slowed him down.
PAKT
OW.
Even when my hands are tied.
The irony is that I spent years having to operate without the use of my legs.
SIFF
Had to be resourceful.
Create alternatives.
SHRIPP
Like gloves with razor-sharp epaulets.
WE'RE DOING THIS THE HARD WAY?
FINE BY ME, GIRL.
MAKES IT FUNNER.

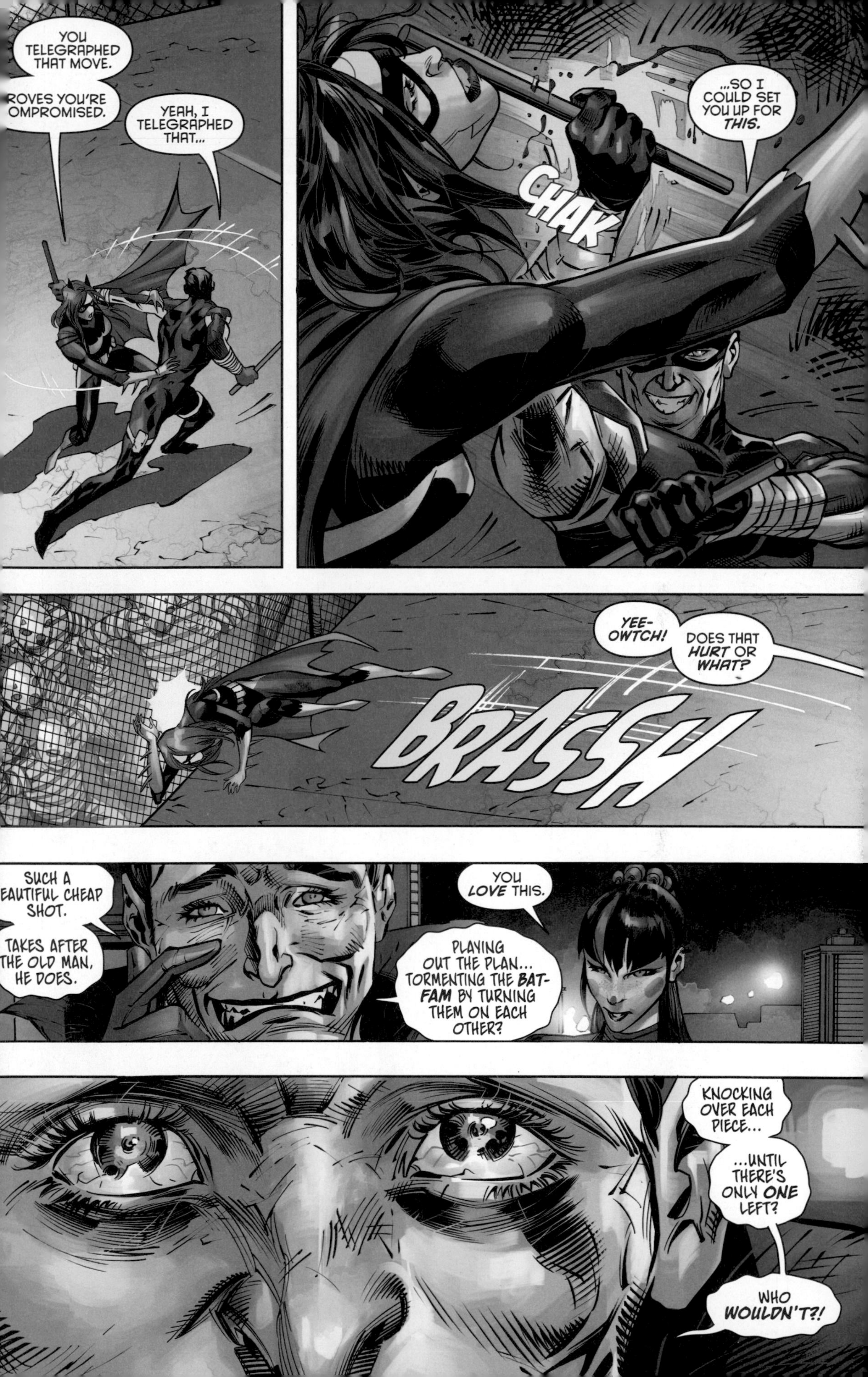
YOU TELEGRAPHED THAT MOVE.
ROVES YOU'RE OMPROMISED.
YEAH, I TELEGRAPHED THAT...
...SO I COULD SET YOU UP FOR THIS.
CHAK
YEE-OWTCH!
DOES THAT HURT OR WHAT?
BRASSH
SUCH A EAUTIFUL CHEAP SHOT.
TAKES AFTER THE OLD MAN, HE DOES.
YOU LOVE THIS.
PLAYING OUT THE PLAN... TORMENTING THE BAT-FAM BY TURNING THEM ON EACH OTHER?
KNOCKING OVER EACH PIECE...
...UNTIL THERE'S ONLY ONE LEFT?
WHO WOULDN'T?!

I KNOW THEM *ALL.*

BRUCE, DICK, BARBARA, TIMMY, LITTLE DAMIAN, AND EVEN SAD-SACK JASON.

WHEN YOU THINK ABOUT IT, WITH ALL I'VE DONE OVER THE YEARS...

"...I MEAN *MORE* TO THEM THAN THEY MEAN TO EACH OTHER!"

THE JOKER IS *CONTROLLING* YOU, DICK. YOU HAVE TO FIGHT *BACK!*

NOT DICK!

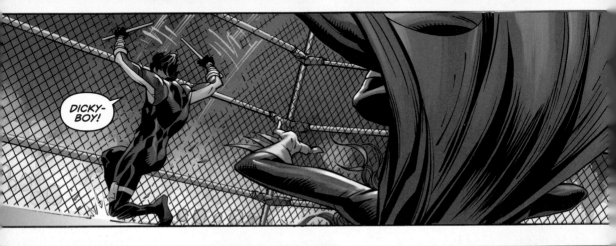

DICKY- BOY!

NO, YOU *AREN'T!*

YOU'RE *ENTHRALLED* TO THAT *MANIAC!*

I NEED YOU TO FOCUS ON THE PEOPLE YOU REALLY *KNOW...*

...THE ONES YOU *LOVE!*

I LOVE...

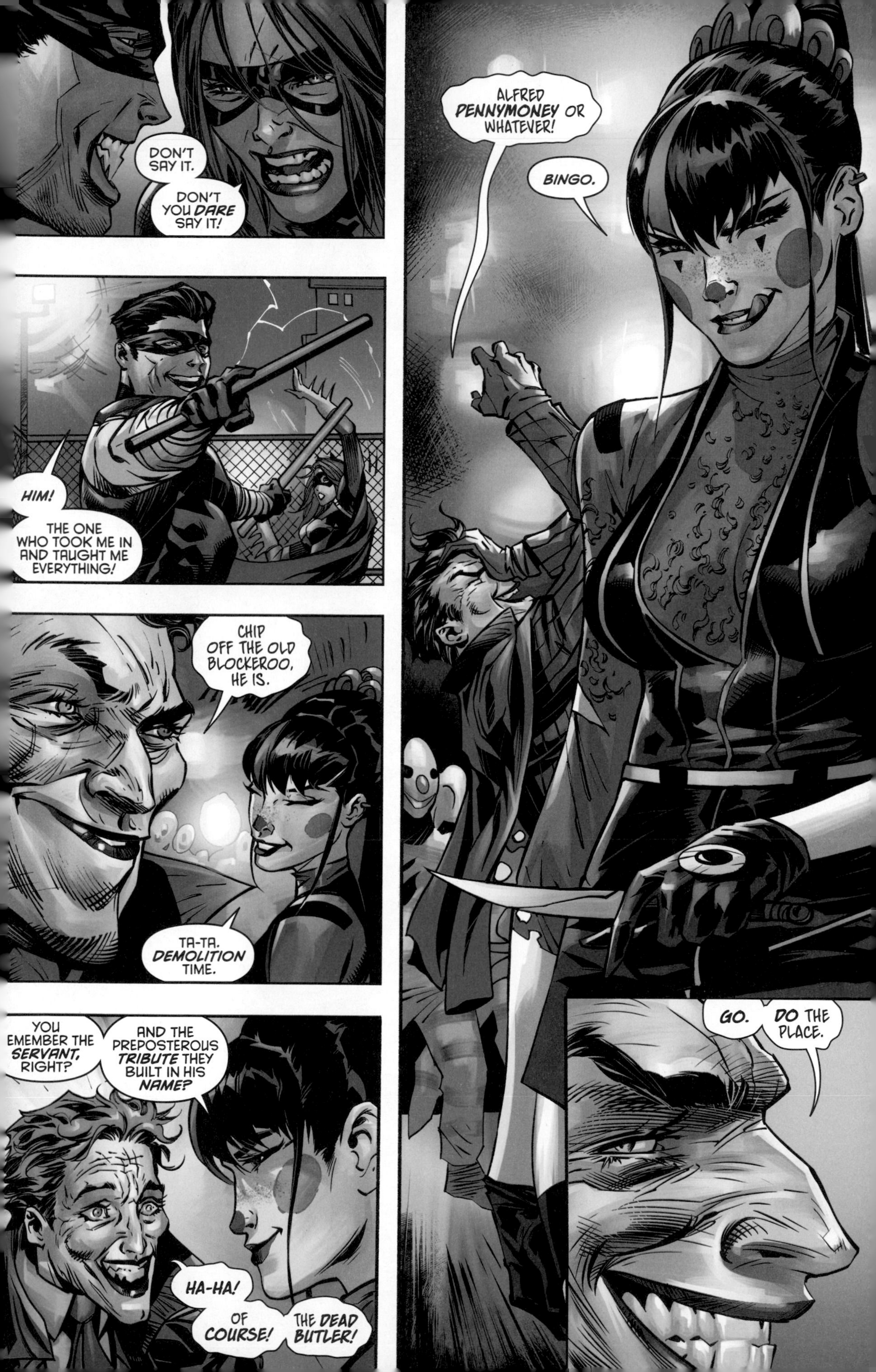
DON'T SAY IT.
DON'T YOU DARE SAY IT!
HIM!
THE ONE WHO TOOK ME IN AND TAUGHT ME EVERYTHING!
CHIP OFF THE OLD BLOCKEROO, HE IS.
TA-TA. DEMOLITION TIME.
YOU EMEMBER THE SERVANT, RIGHT?
AND THE PREPOSTEROUS TRIBUTE THEY BUILT IN HIS NAME?
HA-HA!
OF COURSE!
THE DEAD BUTLER!
ALFRED PENNYMONEY OR WHATEVER!
BINGO.
GO.
DO THE PLACE.

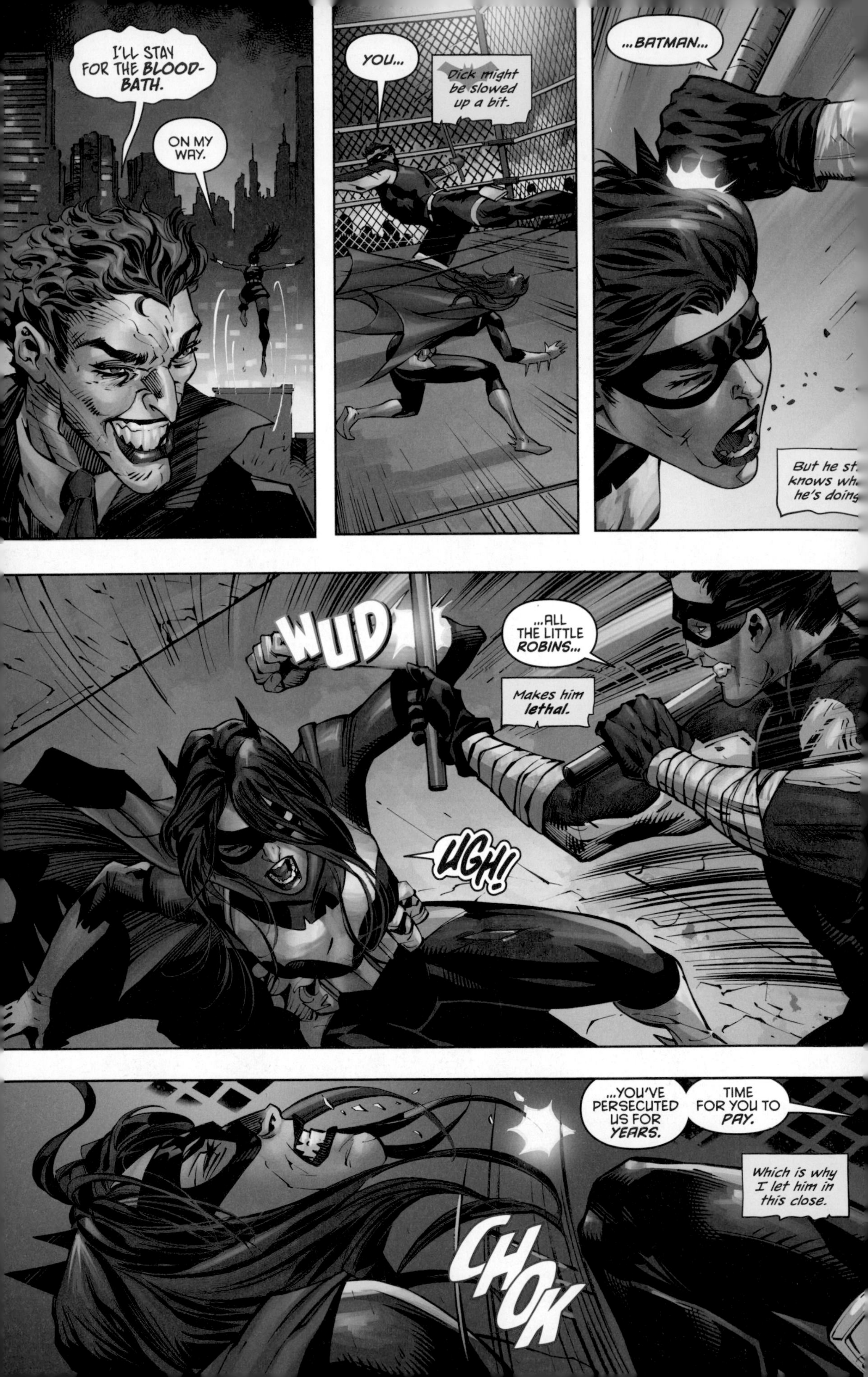
I'LL STAY FOR THE BLOOD-BATH.
ON MY WAY.
YOU...
Dick might be slowed up a bit.
...BATMAN...
But he st knows wh he's doing
WUD
...ALL THE LITTLE ROBINS...
Makes him lethal.
UGH!
...YOU'VE PERSECUTED US FOR YEARS.
TIME FOR YOU TO PAY.
Which is why I let him in this close.
CHOK

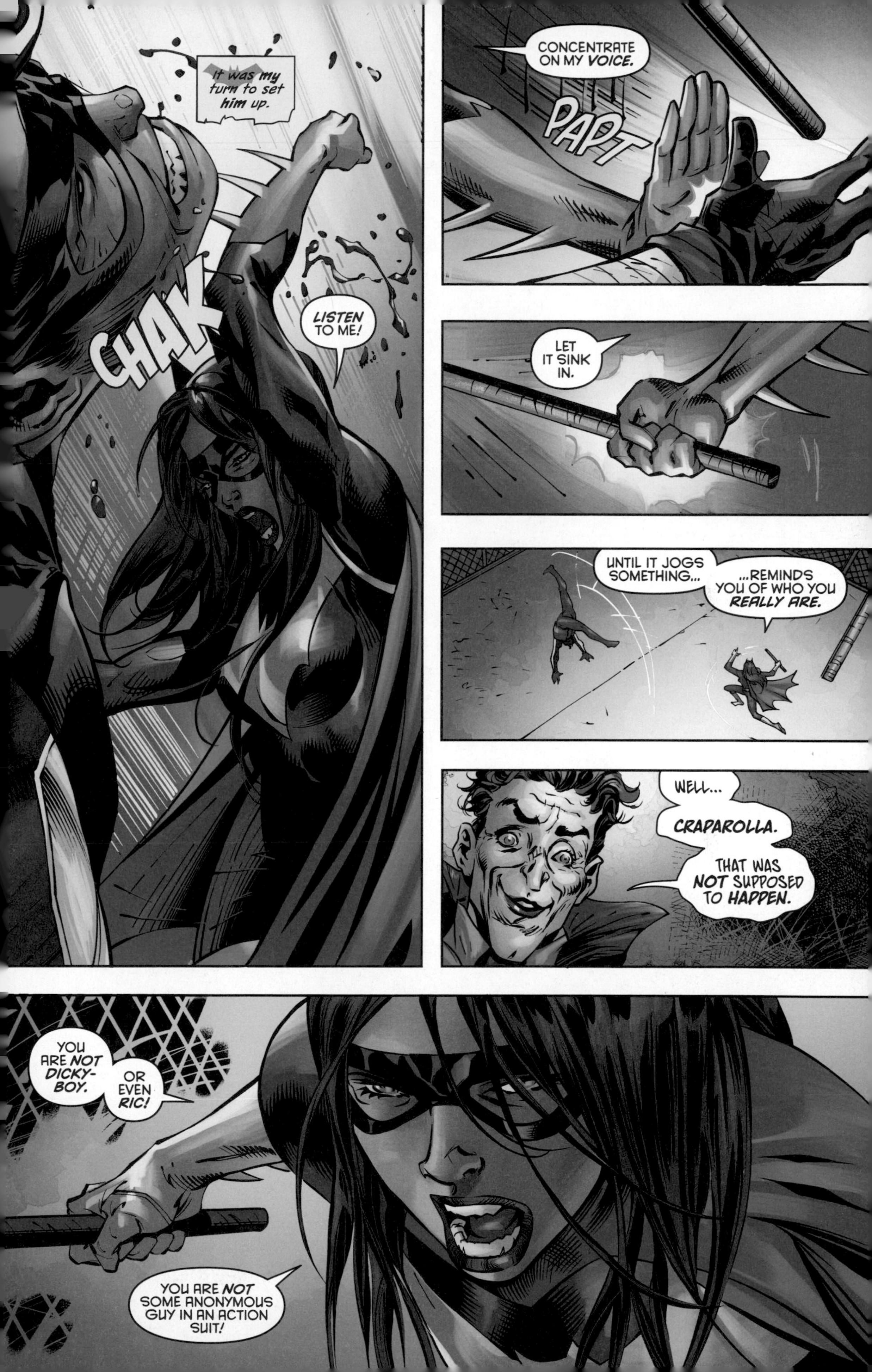
It was my turn to set him up.
CHAK
LISTEN TO ME!
CONCENTRATE ON MY VOICE.
PAPT
LET IT SINK IN.
UNTIL IT JOGS SOMETHING...
...REMINDS YOU OF WHO YOU REALLY ARE.
WELL...
CRAPAROLLA.
THAT WAS NOT SUPPOSED TO HAPPEN.
YOU ARE NOT DICKY-BOY.
OR EVEN RIC!
YOU ARE NOT SOME ANONYMOUS GUY IN AN ACTION SUIT!

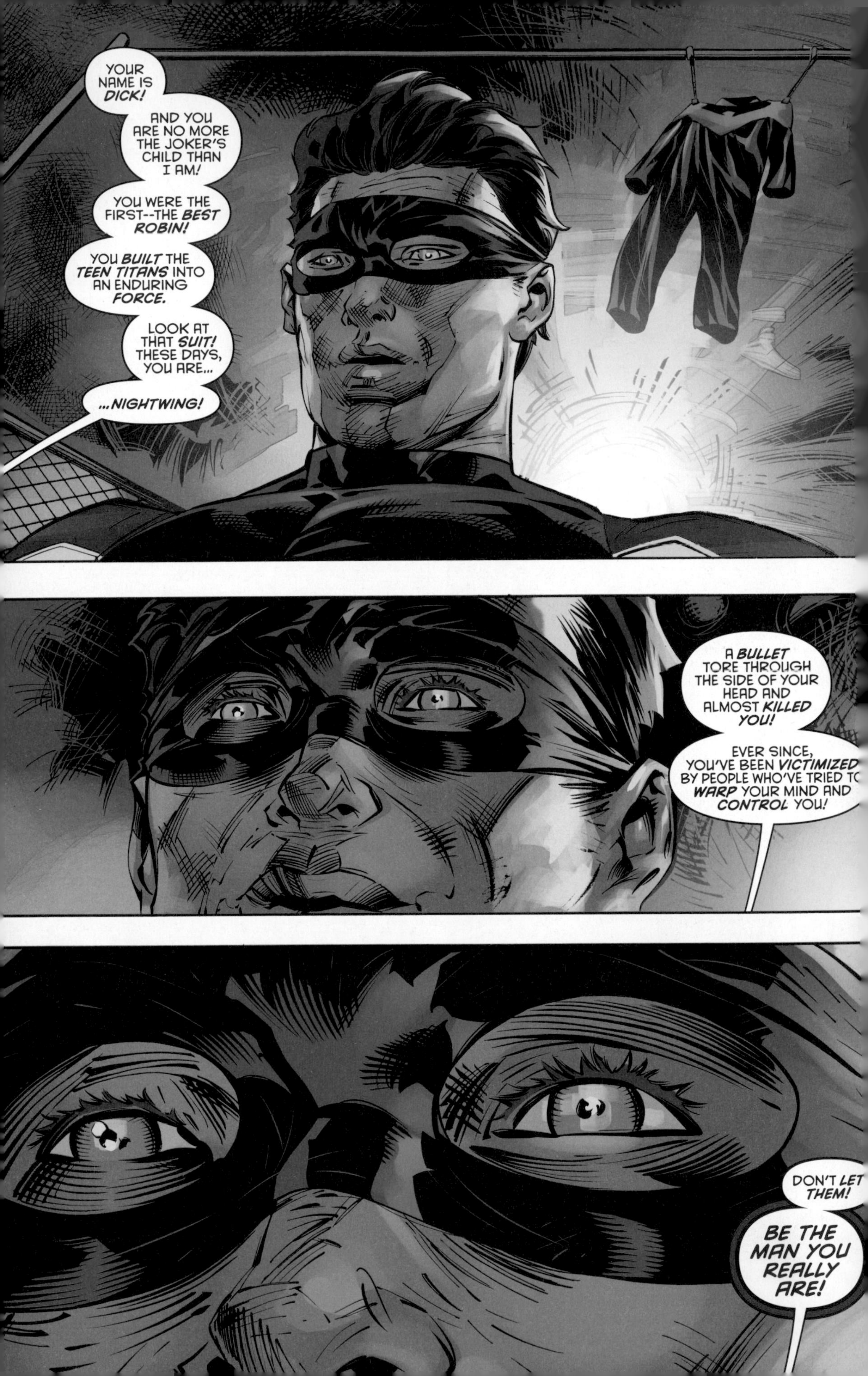
YOUR NAME IS DICK!
AND YOU ARE NO MORE THE JOKER'S CHILD THAN I AM!
YOU WERE THE FIRST--THE BEST ROBIN!
YOU BUILT THE TEEN TITANS INTO AN ENDURING FORCE.
LOOK AT THAT SUIT! THESE DAYS, YOU ARE...
...NIGHTWING!
A BULLET TORE THROUGH THE SIDE OF YOUR HEAD AND ALMOST KILLED YOU!
EVER SINCE, YOU'VE BEEN VICTIMIZED BY PEOPLE WHO'VE TRIED TO WARP YOUR MIND AND CONTROL YOU!
DON'T LET THEM!
BE THE MAN YOU REALLY ARE!

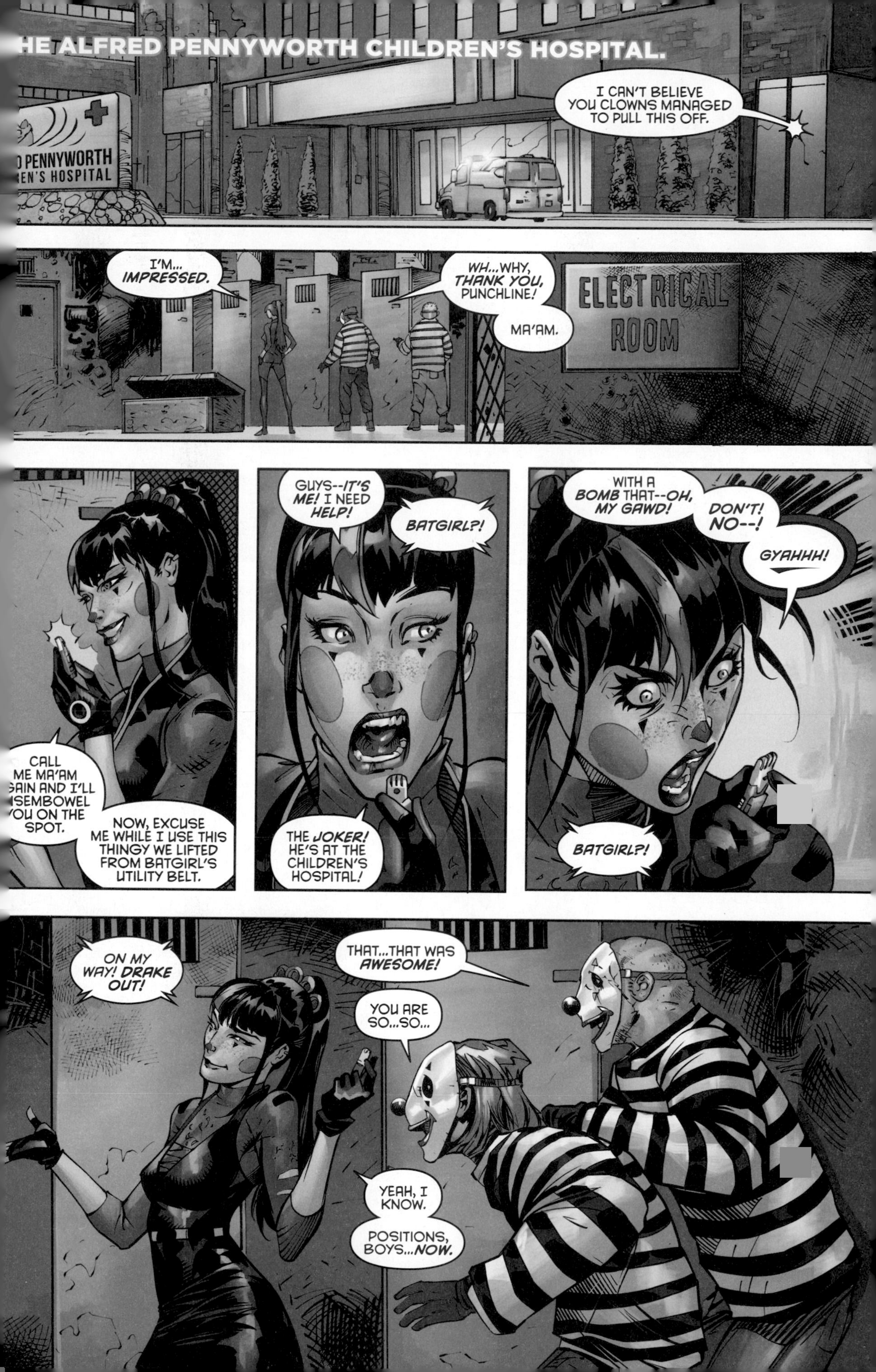
HE ALFRED PENNYWORTH CHILDREN'S HOSPITAL.
D PENNYWORTH
REN'S HOSPITAL
I CAN'T BELIEVE YOU CLOWNS MANAGED TO PULL THIS OFF.
I'M... IMPRESSED.
WH...WHY, THANK YOU, PUNCHLINE!
MA'AM.
ELECTRICAL ROOM
CALL ME MA'AM GAIN AND I'LL ISEMBOWEL YOU ON THE SPOT.
NOW, EXCUSE ME WHILE I USE THIS THINGY WE LIFTED FROM BATGIRL'S UTILITY BELT.
GUYS--IT'S ME! I NEED HELP!
BATGIRL?!
THE JOKER! HE'S AT THE CHILDREN'S HOSPITAL!
WITH A BOMB THAT--OH, MY GAWD!
DON'T! NO--!
GYAHHH!
BATGIRL?!
ON MY WAY! DRAKE OUT!
THAT...THAT WAS AWESOME!
YOU ARE SO...SO...
YEAH, I KNOW.
POSITIONS, BOYS...NOW.

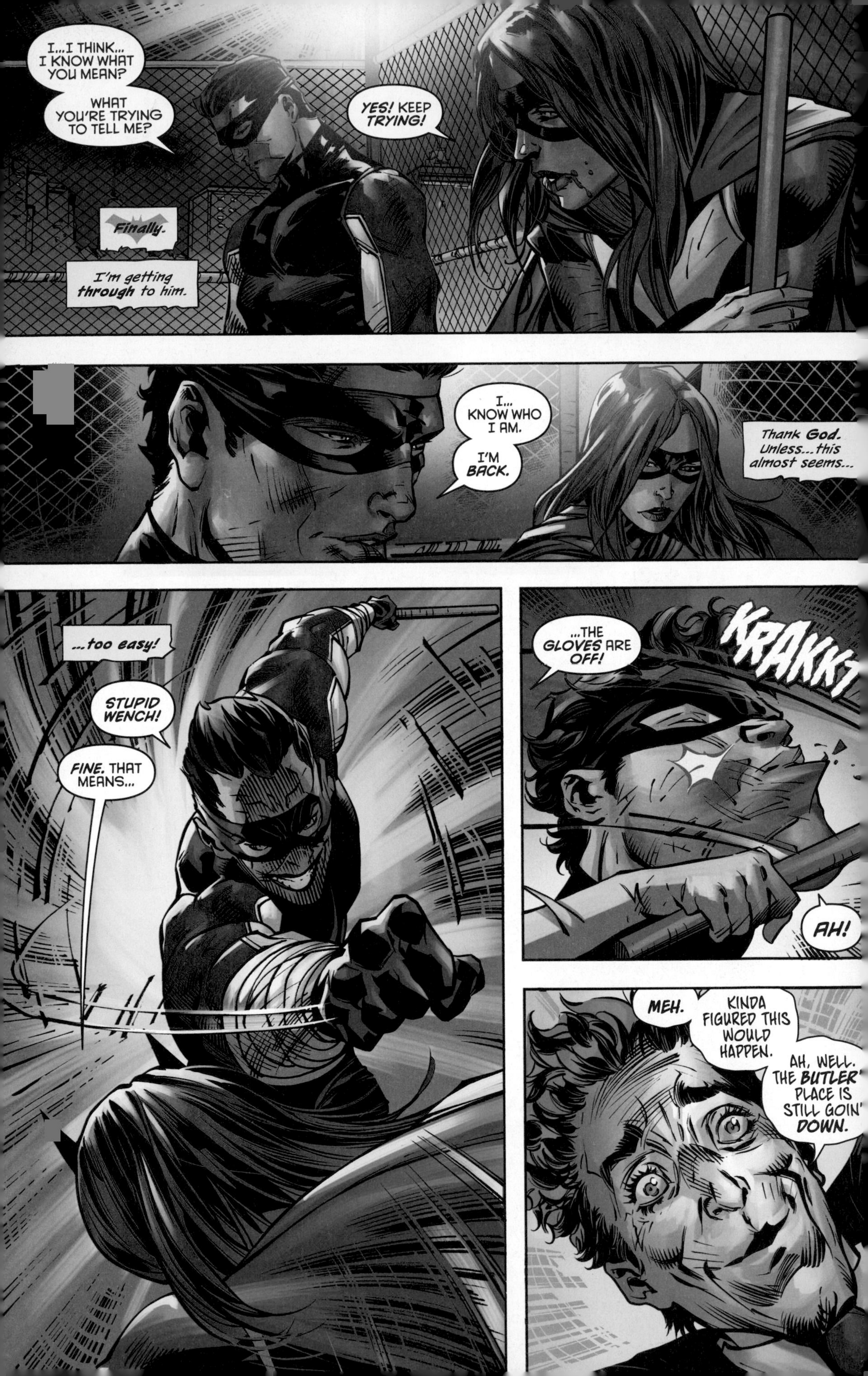
I...I THINK... I KNOW WHAT YOU MEAN?
WHAT YOU'RE TRYING TO TELL ME?
YES! KEEP TRYING!
Finally.
I'm getting through to him.
I... KNOW WHO I AM.
I'M BACK.
Thank God. Unless...this almost seems...
...too easy!
STUPID WENCH!
FINE. THAT MEANS...
...THE GLOVES ARE OFF!
KRAKK!
AH!
MEH.
KINDA FIGURED THIS WOULD HAPPEN.
AH, WELL. THE BUTLER' PLACE IS STILL GOIN' DOWN.

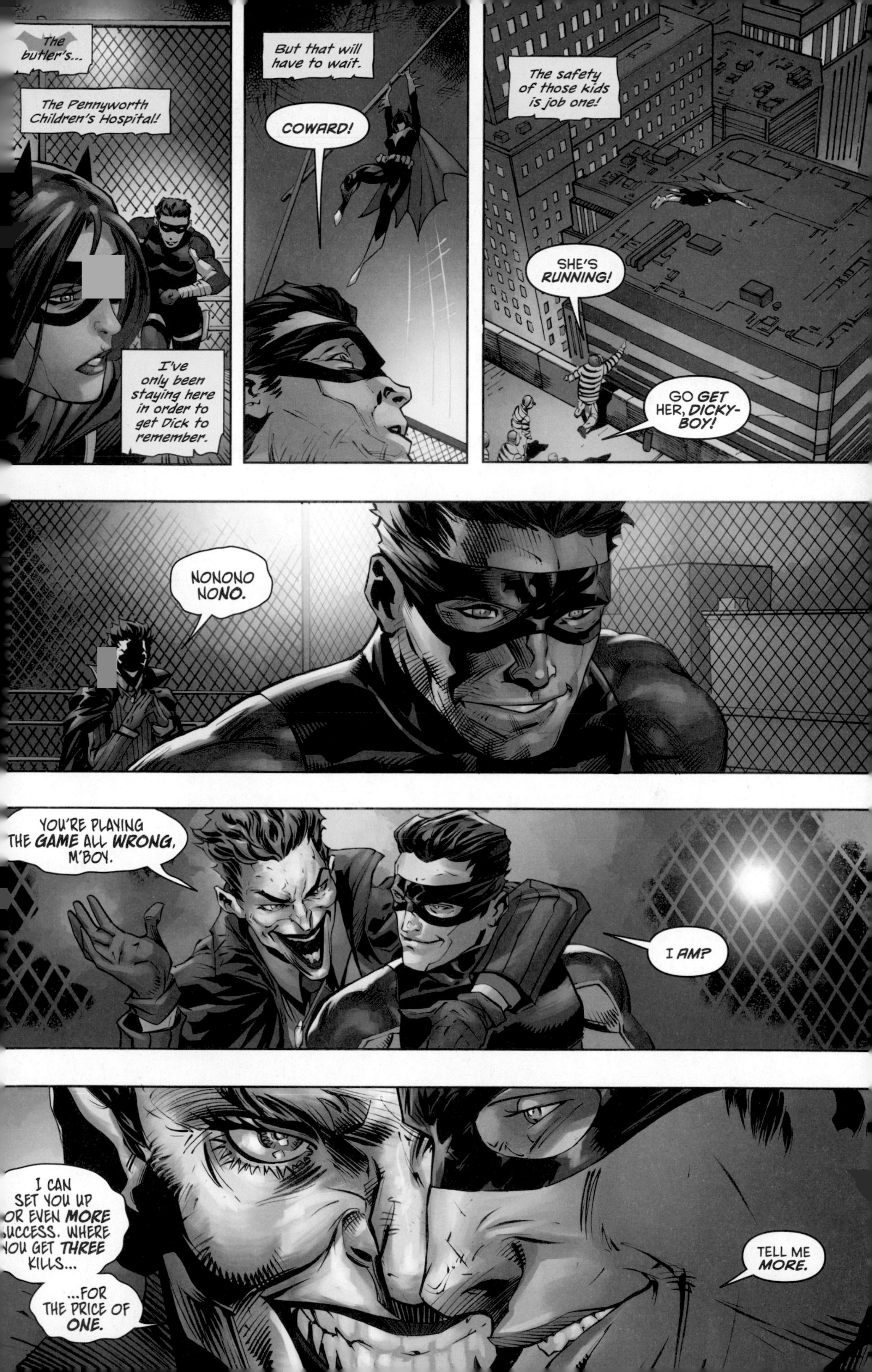
The butler's...
The Pennyworth Children's Hospital!
I've only been staying here in order to get Dick to remember.
But that will have to wait.
COWARD!
The safety of those kids is job one!
SHE'S RUNNING!
GO GET HER, DICKY-BOY!
NONONO NONO.
YOU'RE PLAYING THE GAME ALL WRONG, M'BOY.
I AM?
I CAN SET YOU UP
OR EVEN MORE
UCCESS. WHERE
OU GET THREE
KILLS...
...FOR THE PRICE OF ONE.
TELL ME MORE.

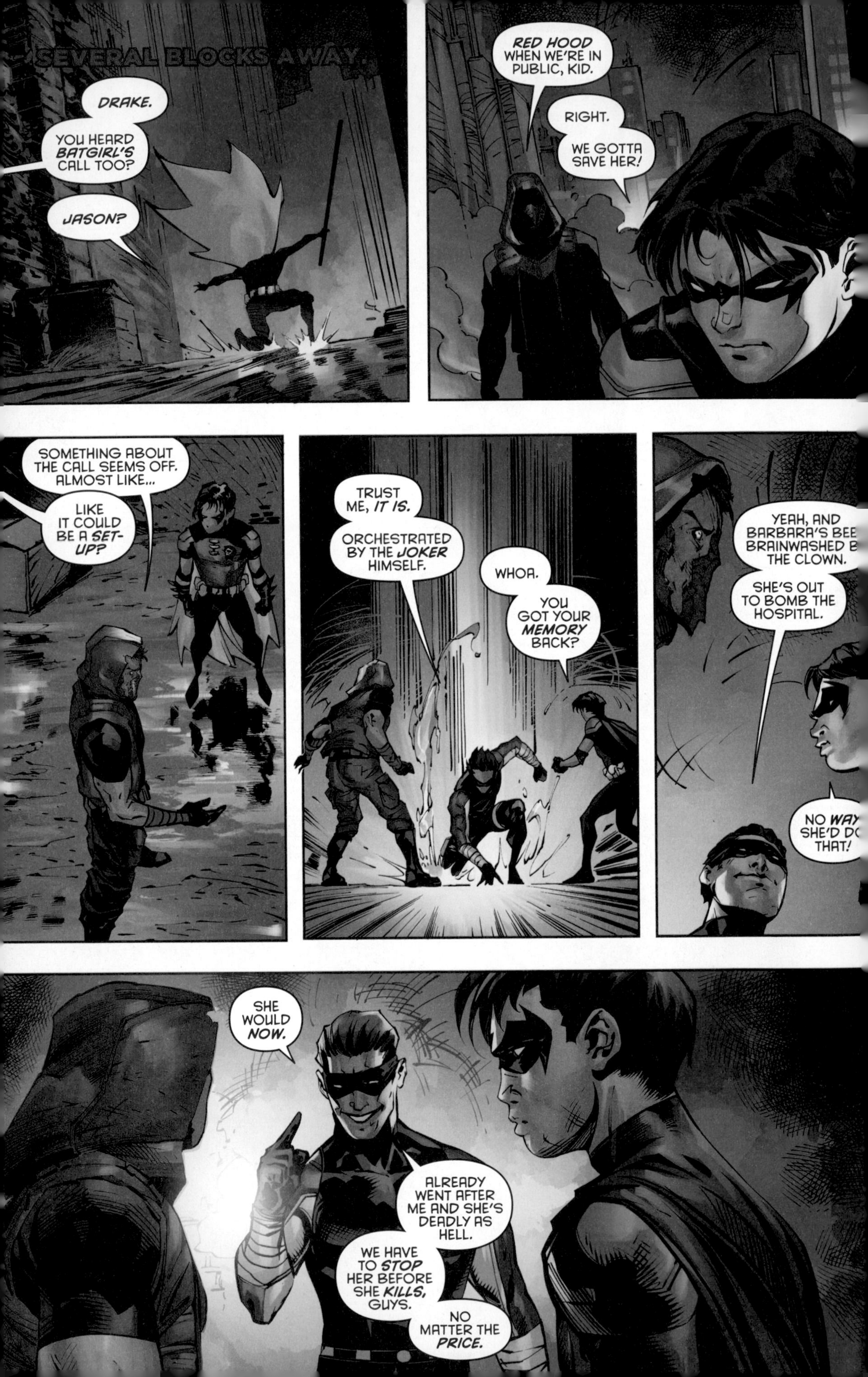
SEVERAL BLOCKS AWAY.
DRAKE.
YOU HEARD BATGIRL'S CALL TOO?
JASON?
RED HOOD WHEN WE'RE IN PUBLIC, KID.
RIGHT.
WE GOTTA SAVE HER!
SOMETHING ABOUT THE CALL SEEMS OFF. ALMOST LIKE...
LIKE IT COULD BE A SET-UP?
TRUST ME, IT IS.
ORCHESTRATED BY THE JOKER HIMSELF.
WHOA.
YOU GOT YOUR MEMORY BACK?
YEAH, AND BARBARA'S BEE BRAINWASHED B THE CLOWN.
SHE'S OUT TO BOMB THE HOSPITAL.
NO WAY SHE'D DO THAT!
SHE WOULD NOW.
ALREADY WENT AFTER ME AND SHE'S DEADLY AS HELL.
WE HAVE TO STOP HER BEFORE SHE KILLS, GUYS.
NO MATTER THE PRICE.

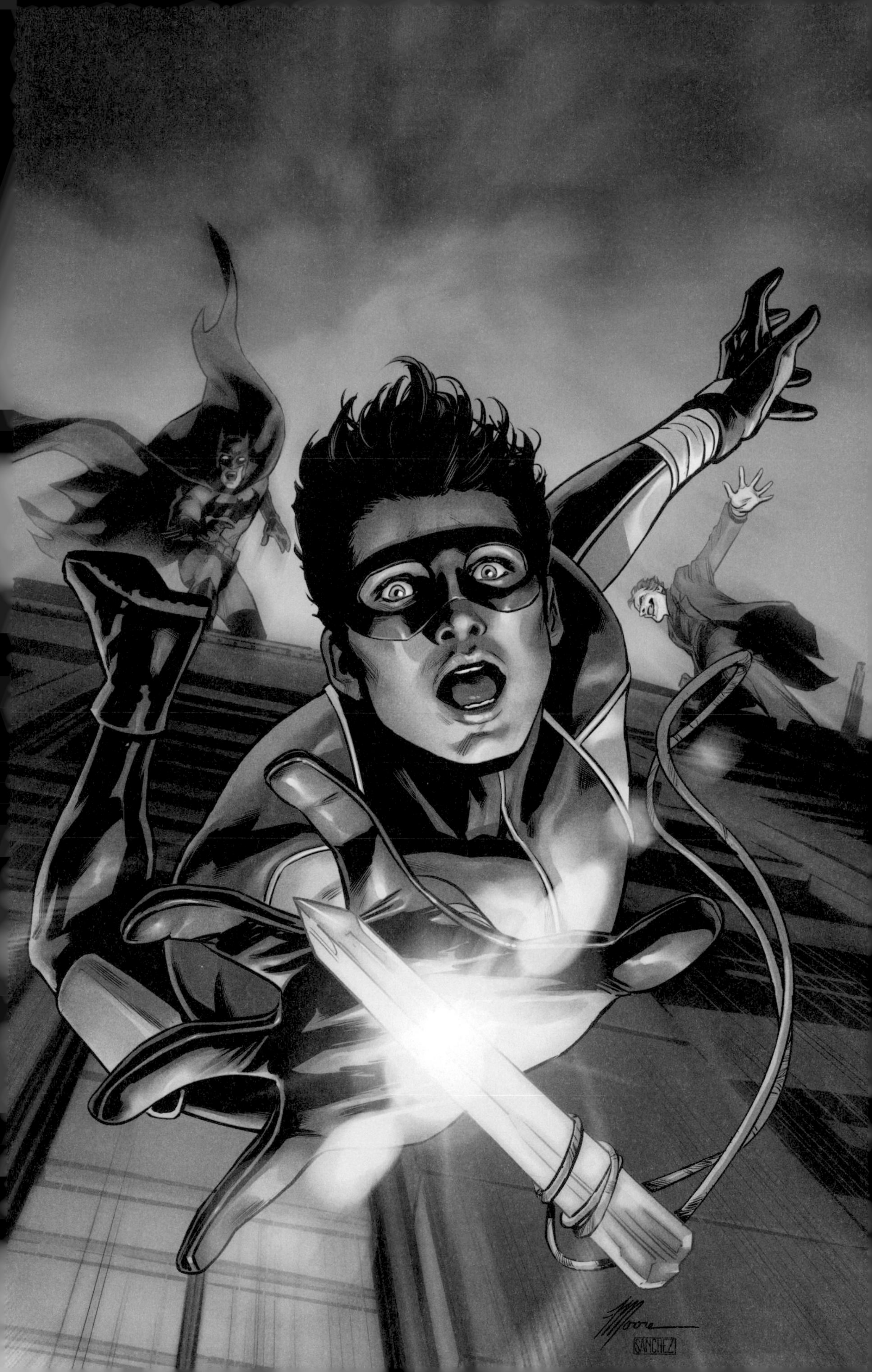
Moore
SANCHEZ

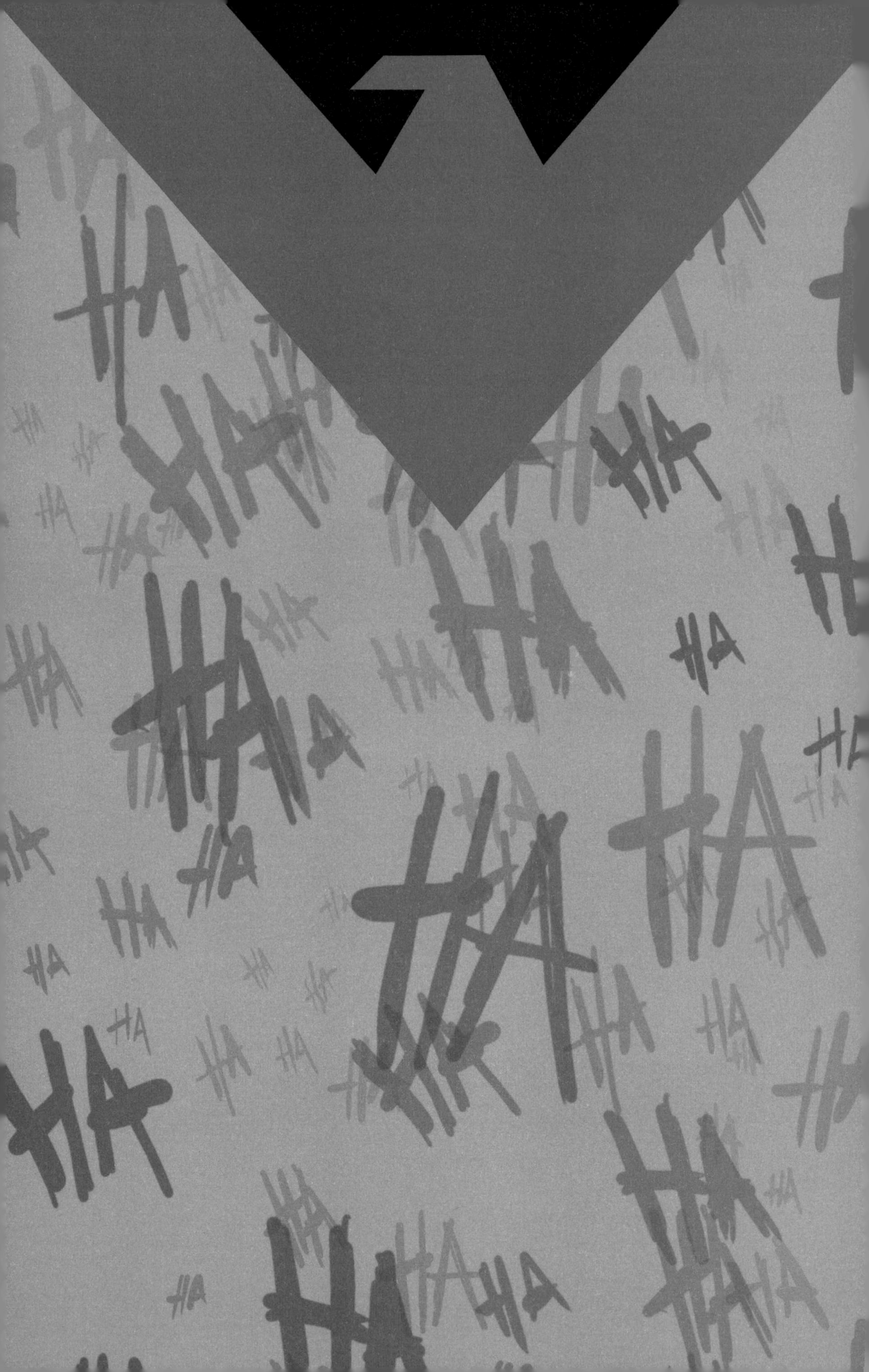

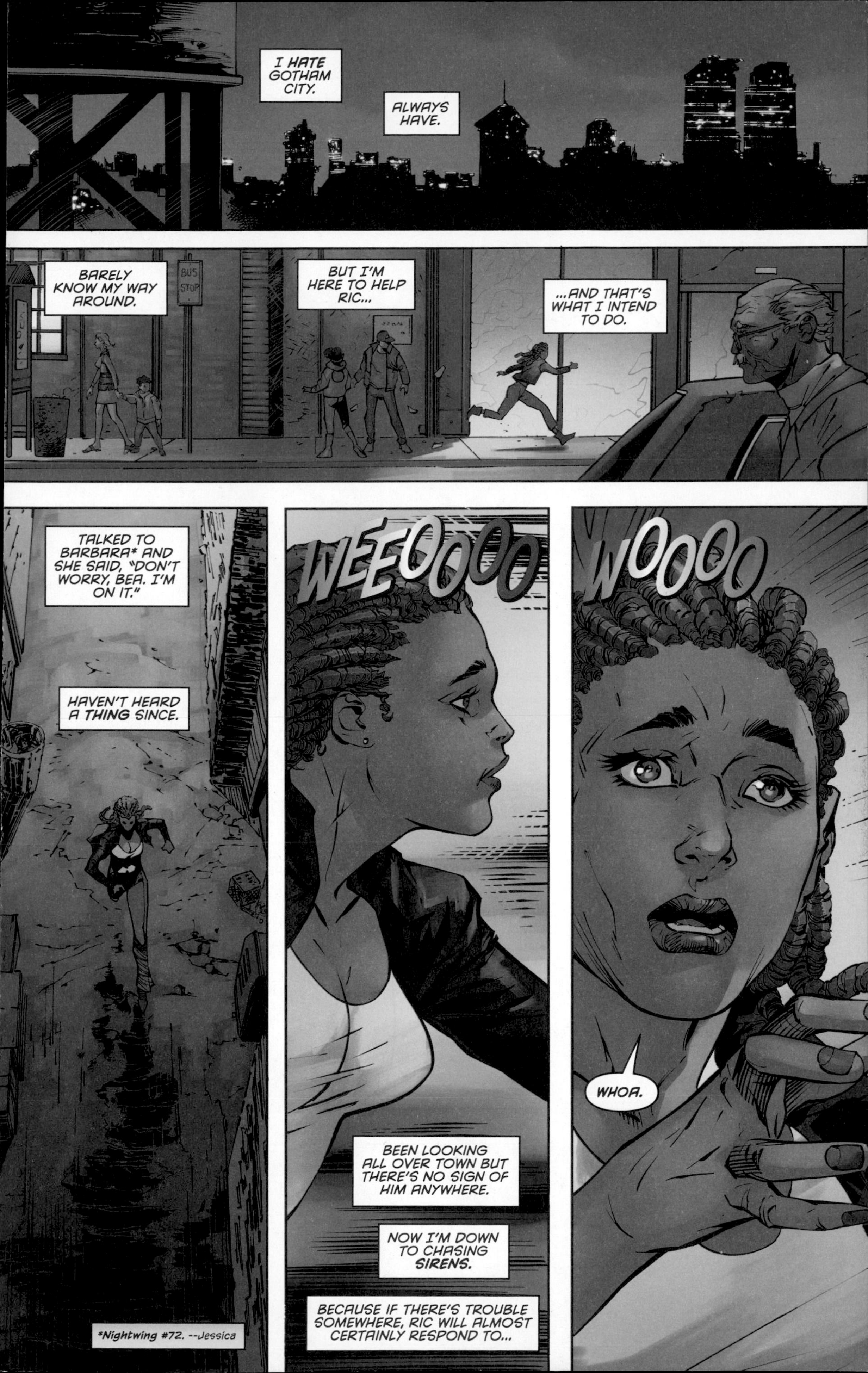
I HATE GOTHAM CITY.
ALWAYS HAVE.
BARELY KNOW MY WAY AROUND.
BUS STOP
BUT I'M HERE TO HELP RIC...
...AND THAT'S WHAT I INTEND TO DO.
TALKED TO BARBARA* AND SHE SAID, "DON'T WORRY, BEA. I'M ON IT."
HAVEN'T HEARD A THING SINCE.
*Nightwing #72. --Jessica
WEEOOOOO
BEEN LOOKING ALL OVER TOWN BUT THERE'S NO SIGN OF HIM ANYWHERE.
NOW I'M DOWN TO CHASING SIRENS.
BECAUSE IF THERE'S TROUBLE SOMEWHERE, RIC WILL ALMOST CERTAINLY RESPOND TO...
WOOOO
WHOA.

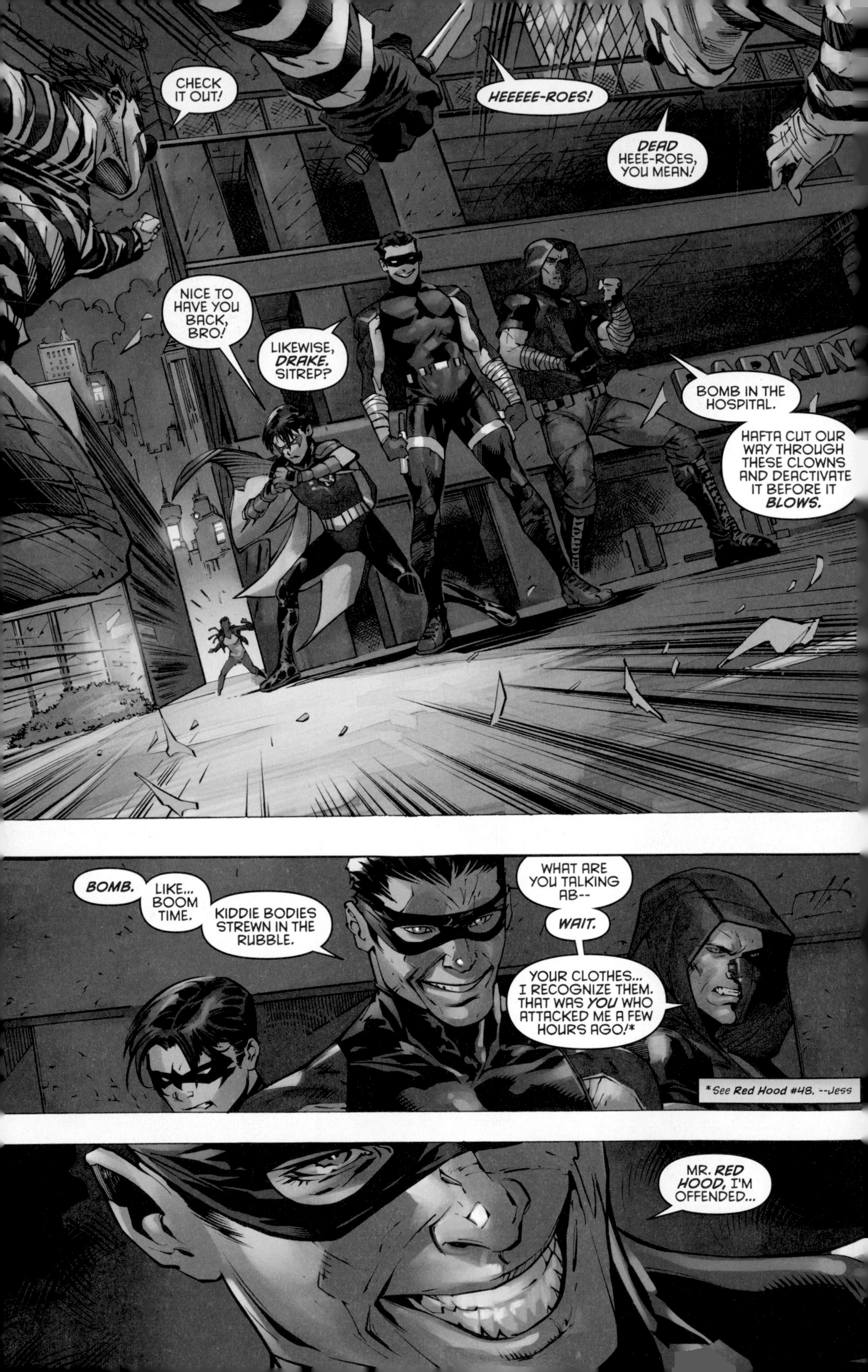
CHECK IT OUT!
HEEEEE-ROES!
DEAD HEEE-ROES, YOU MEAN!
NICE TO HAVE YOU BACK, BRO!
LIKEWISE, DRAKE. SITREP?
BOMB IN THE HOSPITAL.
HAFTA CUT OUR WAY THROUGH THESE CLOWNS AND DEACTIVATE IT BEFORE IT BLOWS.
BOMB.
LIKE... BOOM TIME.
KIDDIE BODIES STREWN IN THE RUBBLE.
WHAT ARE YOU TALKING AB--
WAIT.
YOUR CLOTHES... I RECOGNIZE THEM. THAT WAS YOU WHO ATTACKED ME A FEW HOURS AGO!*
*See Red Hood #48. --Jess
MR. RED HOOD, I'M OFFENDED...

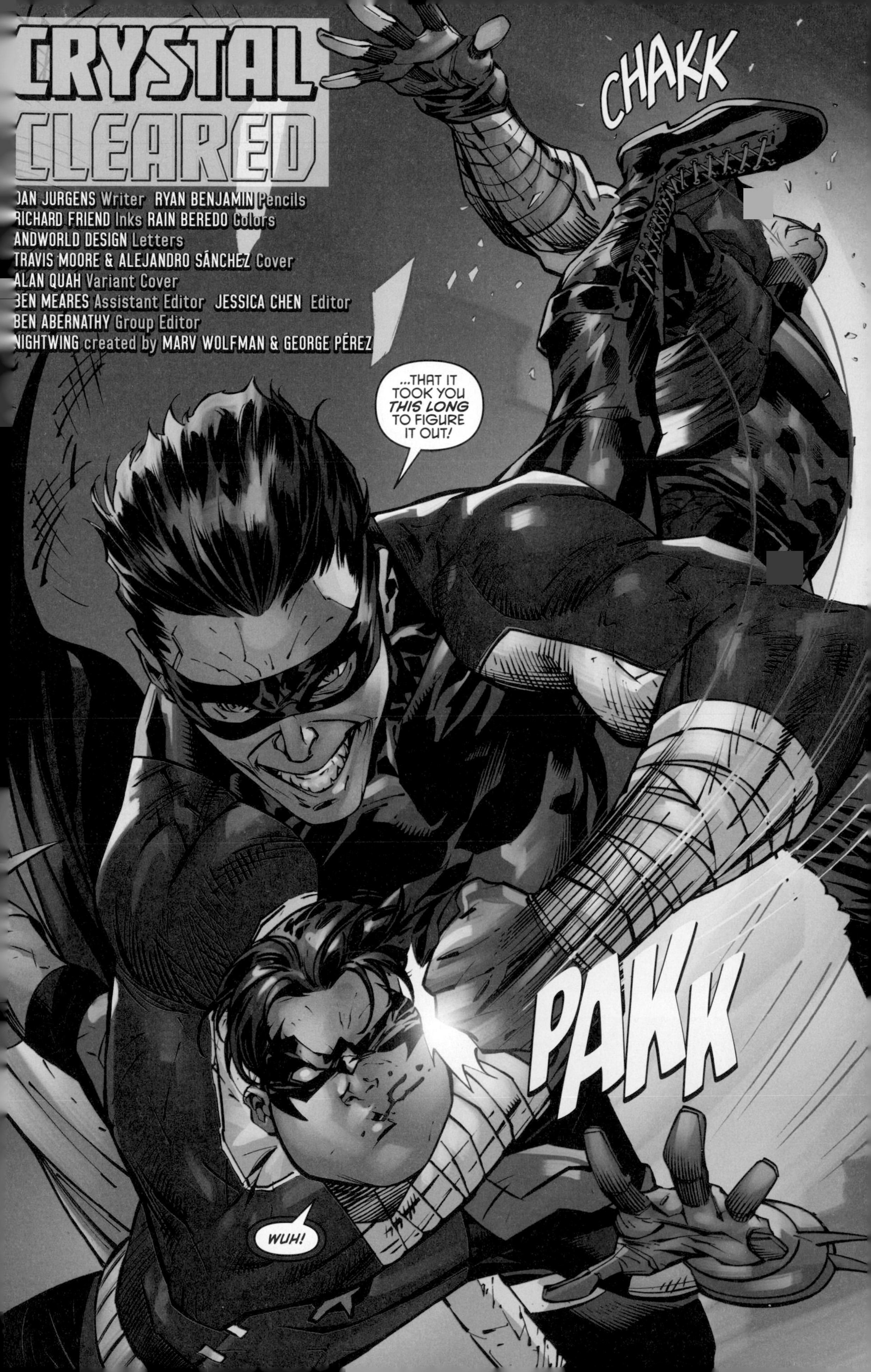
CRYSTAL CLEARED
DAN JURGENS Writer RYAN BENJAMIN Pencils
RICHARD FRIEND Inks RAIN BEREDO Colors
ANDWORLD DESIGN Letters
TRAVIS MOORE & ALEJANDRO SÁNCHEZ Cover
ALAN QUAH Variant Cover
BEN MEARES Assistant Editor JESSICA CHEN Editor
BEN ABERNATHY Group Editor
NIGHTWING created by MARV WOLFMAN & GEORGE PÉREZ
CHAKK
...THAT IT TOOK YOU *THIS LONG* TO FIGURE IT OUT!
PAKK
WUH!

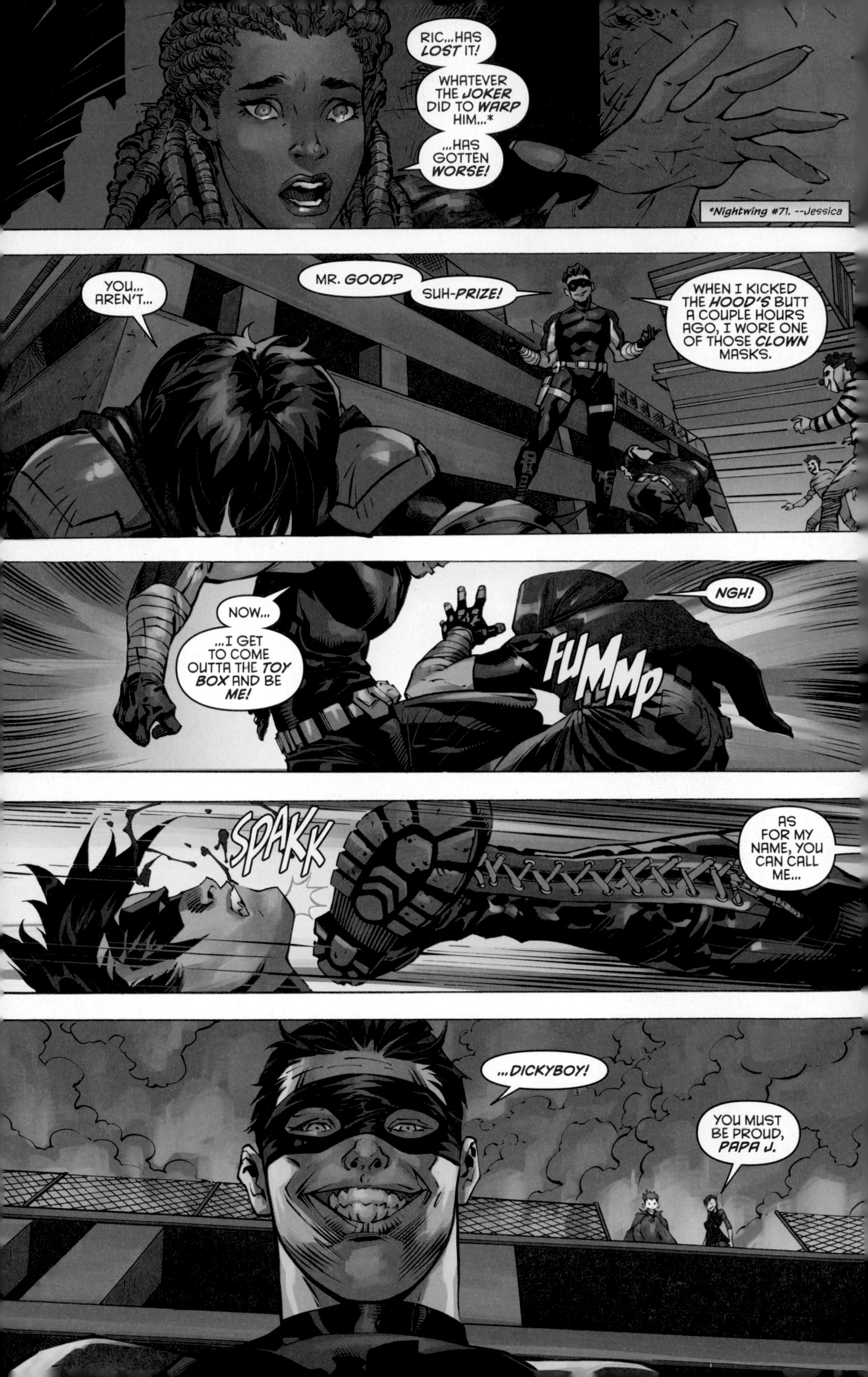
RIC...HAS LOST IT!
WHATEVER THE JOKER DID TO WARP HIM...*
...HAS GOTTEN WORSE!
*Nightwing #71. --Jessica
YOU... AREN'T...
MR. GOOD?
SUH-PRIZE!
WHEN I KICKED THE HOOD'S BUTT A COUPLE HOURS AGO, I WORE ONE OF THOSE CLOWN MASKS.
NOW...
...I GET TO COME OUTTA THE TOY BOX AND BE ME!
NGH!
FUMMP
SPAKK
AS FOR MY NAME, YOU CAN CALL ME...
...DICKYBOY!
YOU MUST BE PROUD, PAPA J.

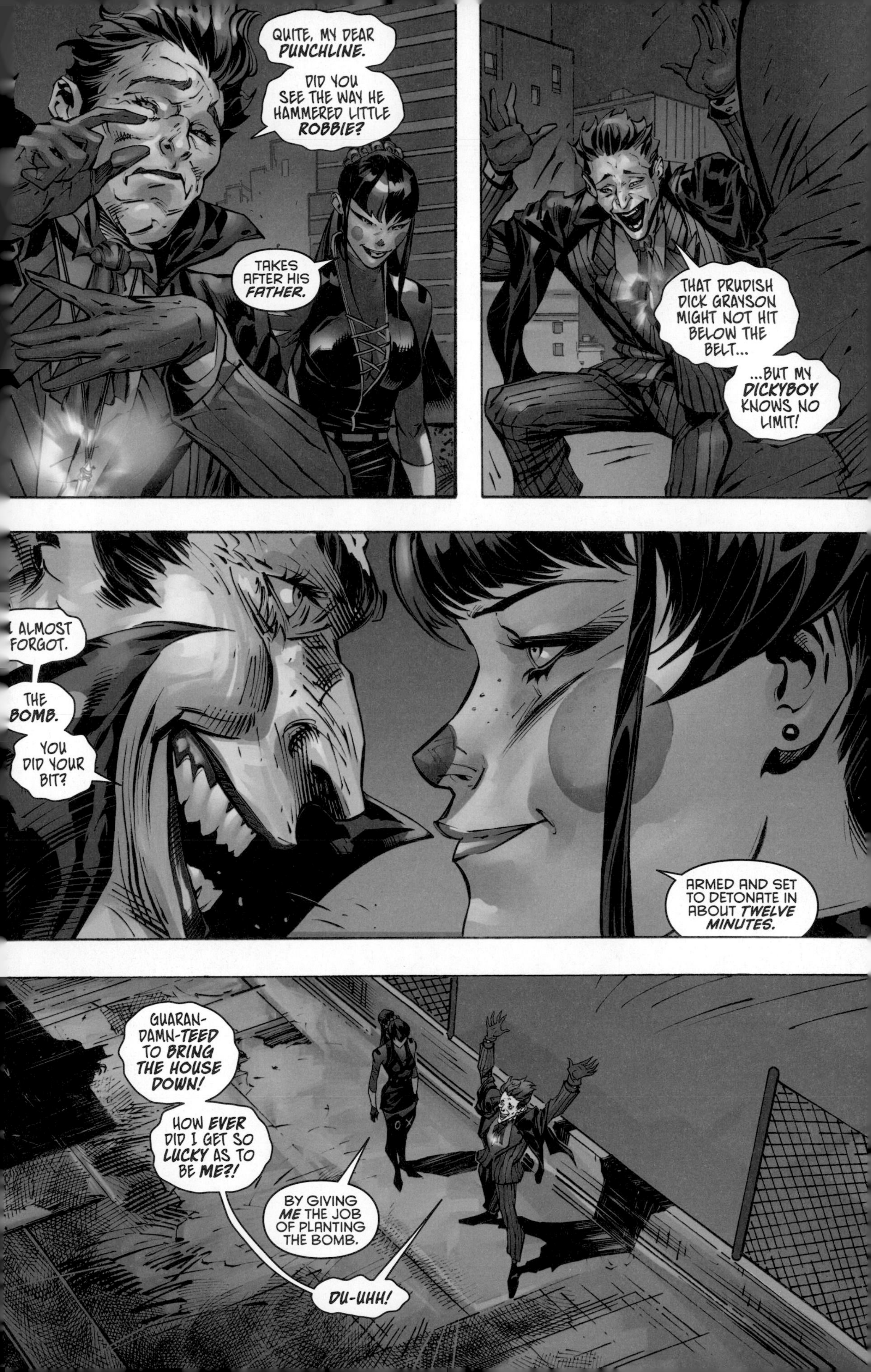
QUITE, MY DEAR PUNCHLINE.
DID YOU SEE THE WAY HE HAMMERED LITTLE ROBBIE?
TAKES AFTER HIS FATHER.
THAT PRUDISH DICK GRAYSON MIGHT NOT HIT BELOW THE BELT...
...BUT MY DICKYBOY KNOWS NO LIMIT!
I ALMOST FORGOT.
THE BOMB.
YOU DID YOUR BIT?
ARMED AND SET TO DETONATE IN ABOUT TWELVE MINUTES.
GUARAN-DAMN-TEED TO BRING THE HOUSE DOWN!
HOW EVER DID I GET SO LUCKY AS TO BE ME?!
BY GIVING ME THE JOB OF PLANTING THE BOMB.
DU-UHH!

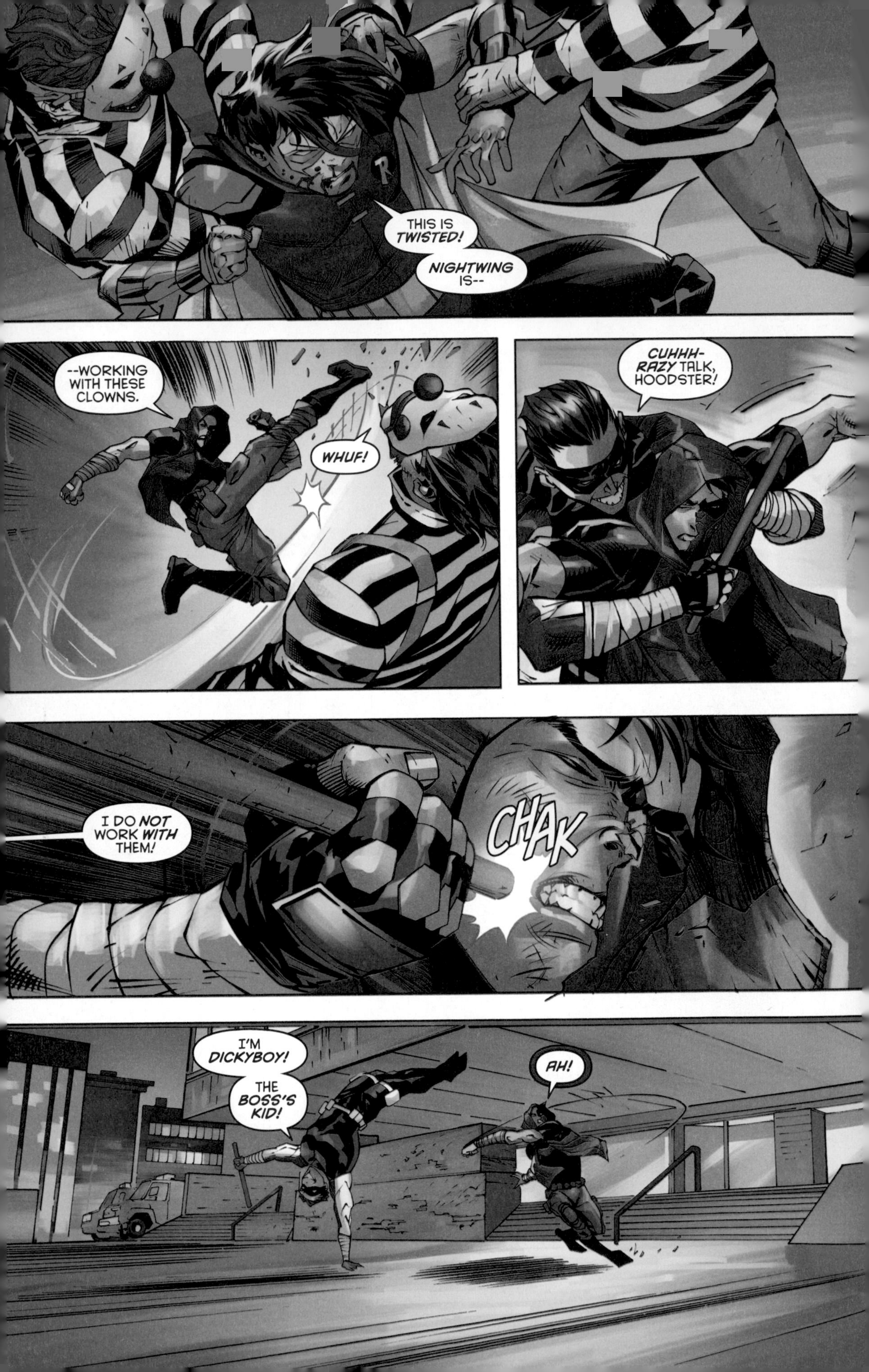
THIS IS TWISTED!
NIGHTWING IS--
--WORKING WITH THESE CLOWNS.
WHUF!
CUHHH-RAZY TALK, HOODSTER!
I DO NOT WORK WITH THEM!
CHAK
I'M DICKYBOY!
THE BOSS'S KID!
AH!

THAT MAKES *ME*...

...MANAGEMENT.

THIS IS GETTING MESSY, DRAKE. THE *BOMB* IS YOURS TO TAKE CARE OF.

ON IT!

DICKYBOY IS *MINE*.

REMEMBER-- HE'S *FAMILY*!

DON'T *HURT* HIM!

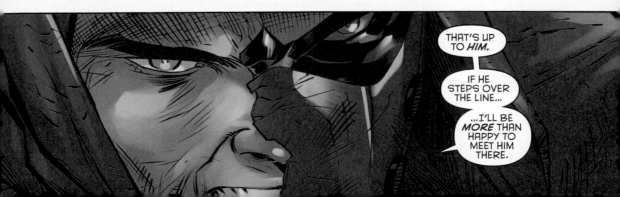

THAT'S UP TO *HIM*.

IF HE STEPS OVER THE LINE...

...I'LL BE *MORE* THAN HAPPY TO MEET HIM THERE.

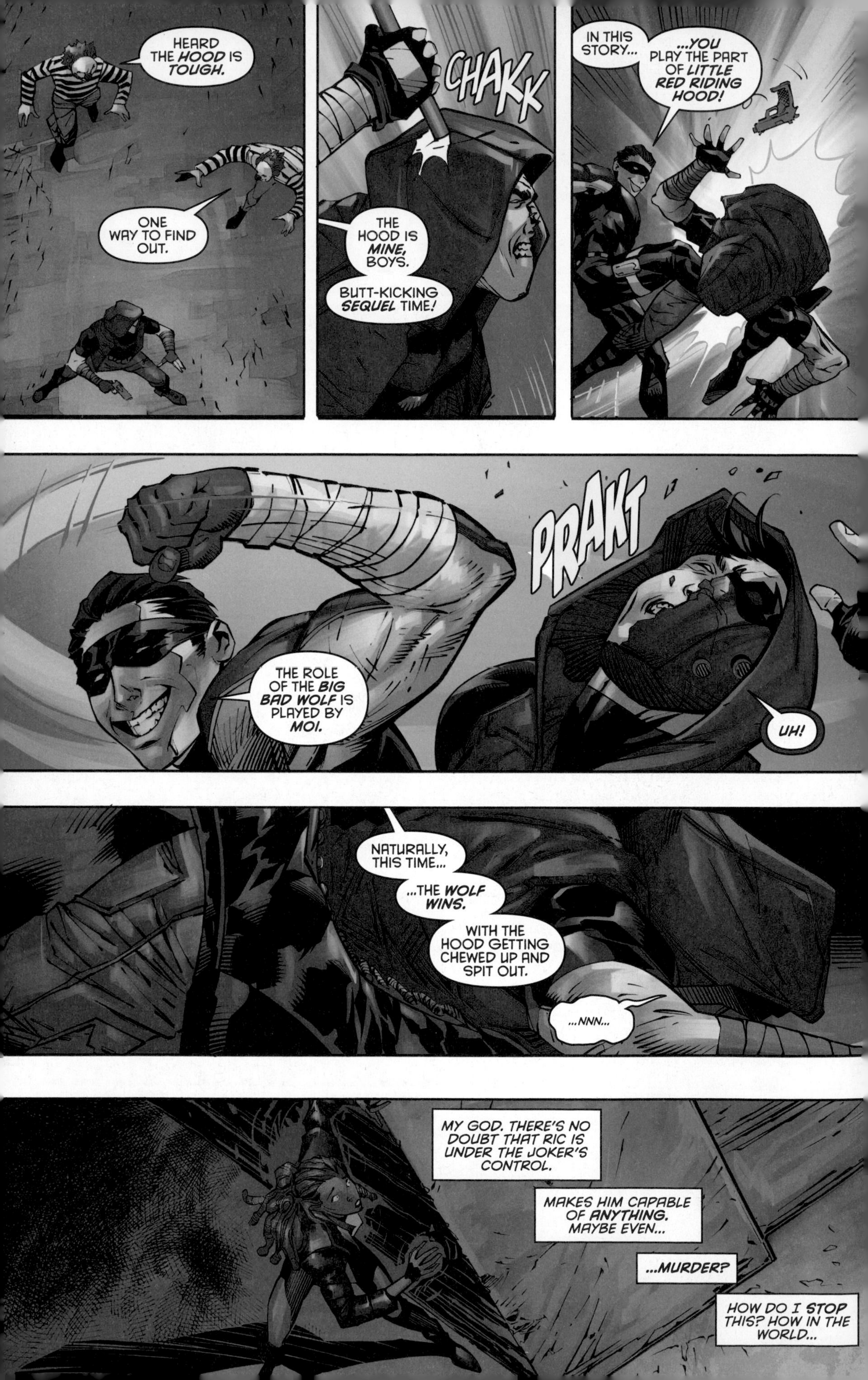
HEARD THE HOOD IS TOUGH.
ONE WAY TO FIND OUT.
CHAKK
THE HOOD IS MINE, BOYS.
BUTT-KICKING SEQUEL TIME!
IN THIS STORY...
...YOU PLAY THE PART OF LITTLE RED RIDING HOOD!
PRAKT
THE ROLE OF THE BIG BAD WOLF IS PLAYED BY MOI.
UH!
NATURALLY, THIS TIME...
...THE WOLF WINS.
WITH THE HOOD GETTING CHEWED UP AND SPIT OUT.
...NNN...
MY GOD. THERE'S NO DOUBT THAT RIC IS UNDER THE JOKER'S CONTROL.
MAKES HIM CAPABLE OF ANYTHING. MAYBE EVEN...
...MURDER?
HOW DO I STOP THIS? HOW IN THE WORLD...

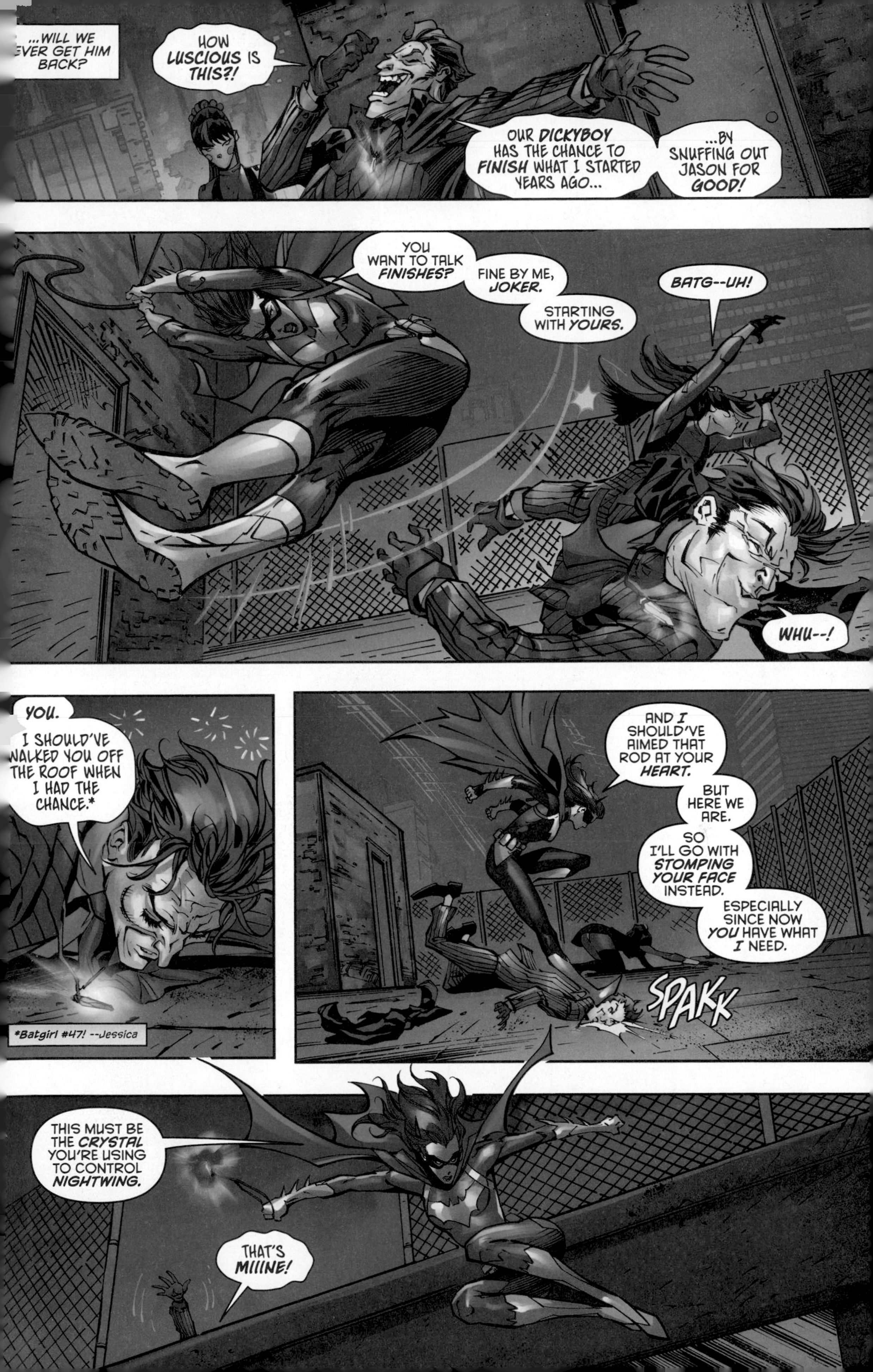

...WILL WE EVER GET HIM BACK?
HOW LUSCIOUS IS THIS?!
OUR DICKYBOY HAS THE CHANCE TO FINISH WHAT I STARTED YEARS AGO...
...BY SNUFFING OUT JASON FOR GOOD!
YOU WANT TO TALK FINISHES?
FINE BY ME, JOKER.
STARTING WITH YOURS.
BATG--UH!
WHU--!
YOU.
I SHOULD'VE WALKED YOU OFF THE ROOF WHEN I HAD THE CHANCE.*
*Batgirl #47! --Jessica
AND I SHOULD'VE AIMED THAT ROD AT YOUR HEART.
BUT HERE WE ARE.
SO I'LL GO WITH STOMPING YOUR FACE INSTEAD.
ESPECIALLY SINCE NOW YOU HAVE WHAT I NEED.
SPAKK
THIS MUST BE THE CRYSTAL YOU'RE USING TO CONTROL NIGHTWING.
THAT'S MIIINE!

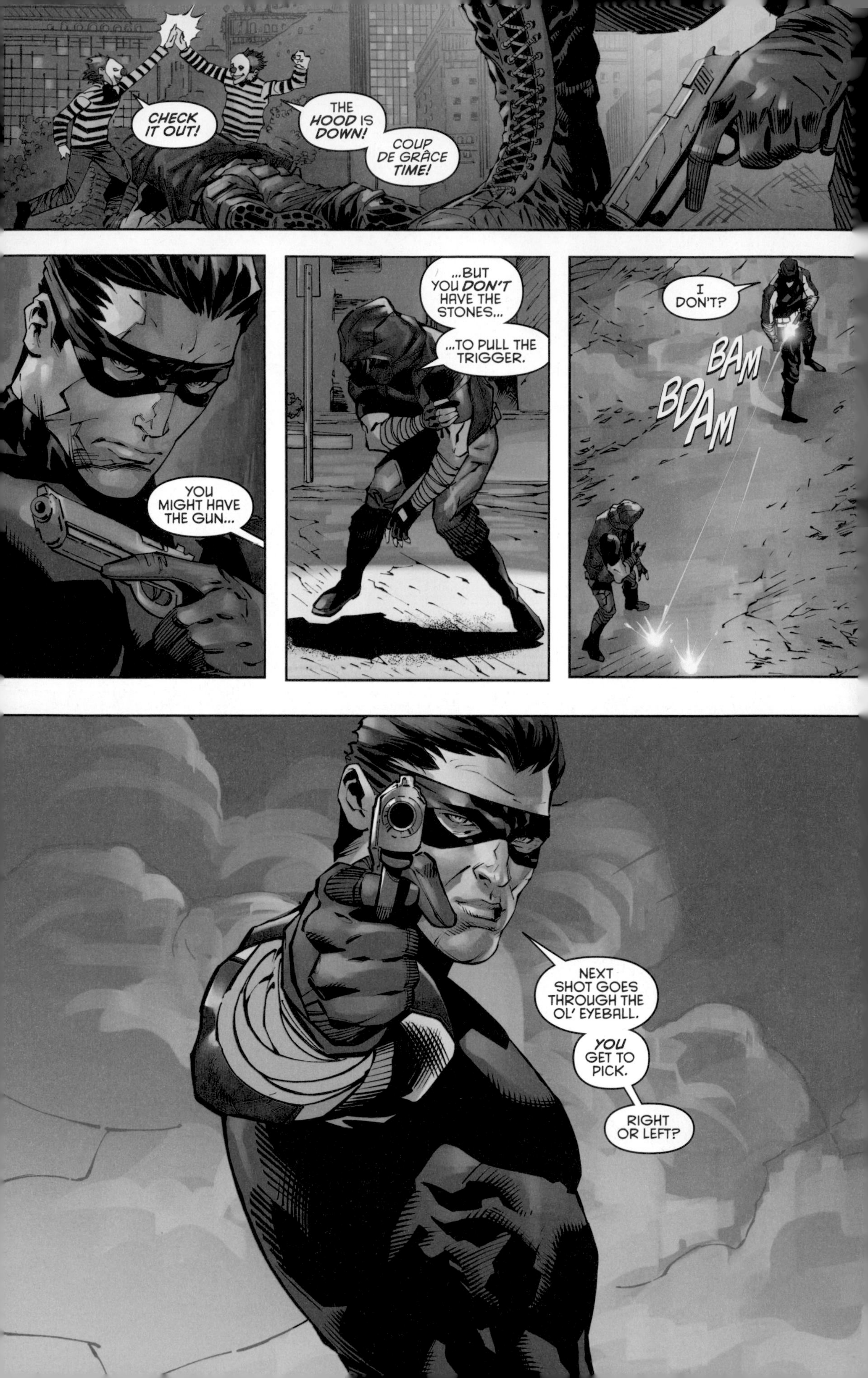
CHECK IT OUT!
THE HOOD IS DOWN!
COUP DE GRÂCE TIME!
YOU MIGHT HAVE THE GUN...
...BUT YOU DON'T HAVE THE STONES...
...TO PULL THE TRIGGER.
I DON'T?
BAM
BDAM
NEXT SHOT GOES THROUGH THE OL' EYEBALL.
YOU GET TO PICK.
RIGHT OR LEFT?

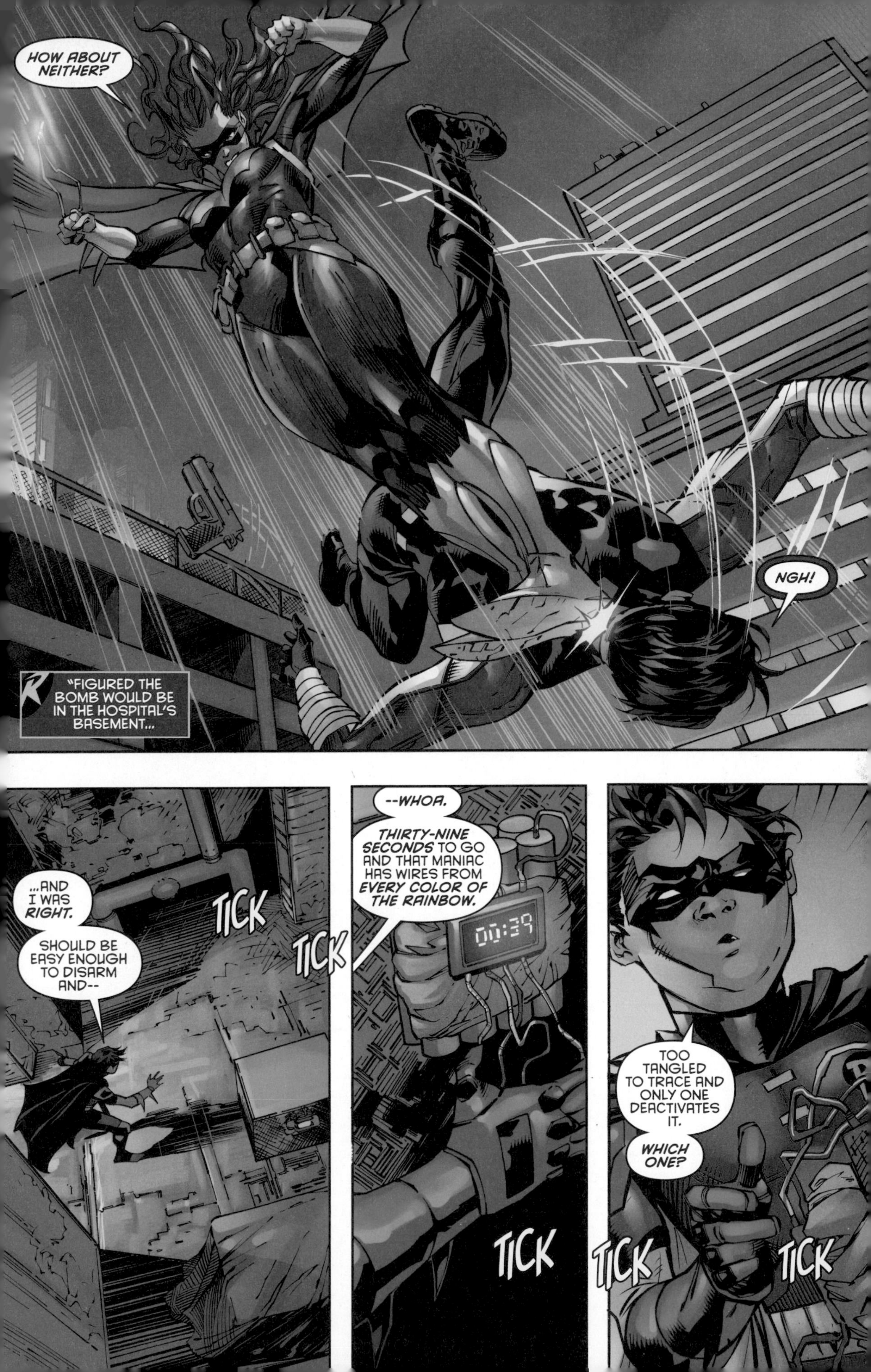
HOW ABOUT NEITHER?
NGH!
"FIGURED THE BOMB WOULD BE IN THE HOSPITAL'S BASEMENT...
...AND I WAS RIGHT.
SHOULD BE EASY ENOUGH TO DISARM AND--
TICK
TICK
--WHOA.
THIRTY-NINE SECONDS TO GO AND THAT MANIAC HAS WIRES FROM EVERY COLOR OF THE RAINBOW.
00:39
TICK
TOO TANGLED TO TRACE AND ONLY ONE DEACTIVATES IT.
WHICH ONE?
TICK
TICK

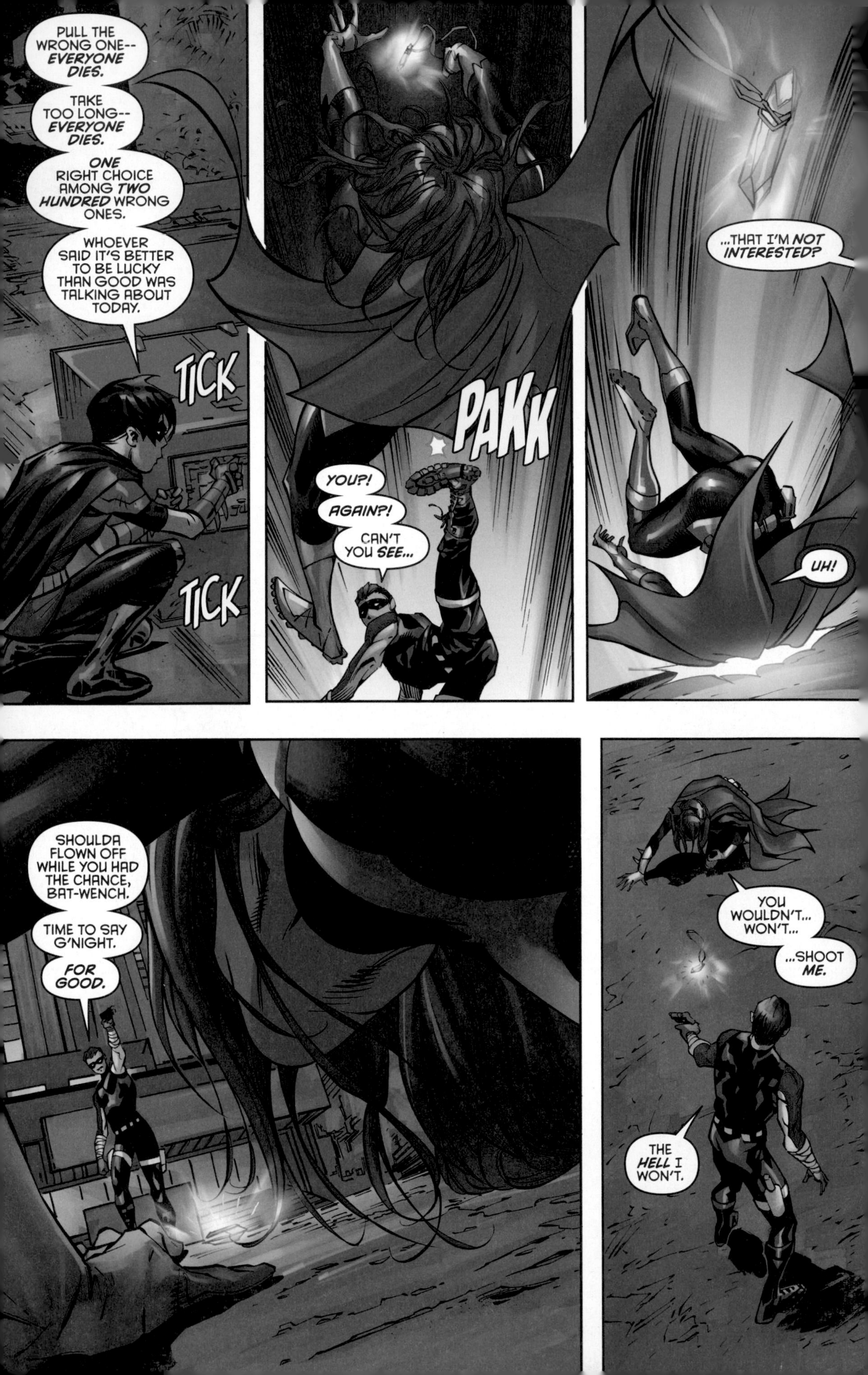
PULL THE WRONG ONE-- EVERYONE DIES.
TAKE TOO LONG-- EVERYONE DIES.
ONE RIGHT CHOICE AMONG TWO HUNDRED WRONG ONES.
WHOEVER SAID IT'S BETTER TO BE LUCKY THAN GOOD WAS TALKING ABOUT TODAY.
TICK
TICK
PAKK
YOU?!
AGAIN?!
CAN'T YOU SEE...
...THAT I'M NOT INTERESTED?
UH!
SHOULDA FLOWN OFF WHILE YOU HAD THE CHANCE, BAT-WENCH.
TIME TO SAY G'NIGHT.
FOR GOOD.
YOU WOULDN'T... WON'T...
...SHOOT ME.
THE HELL I WON'T.

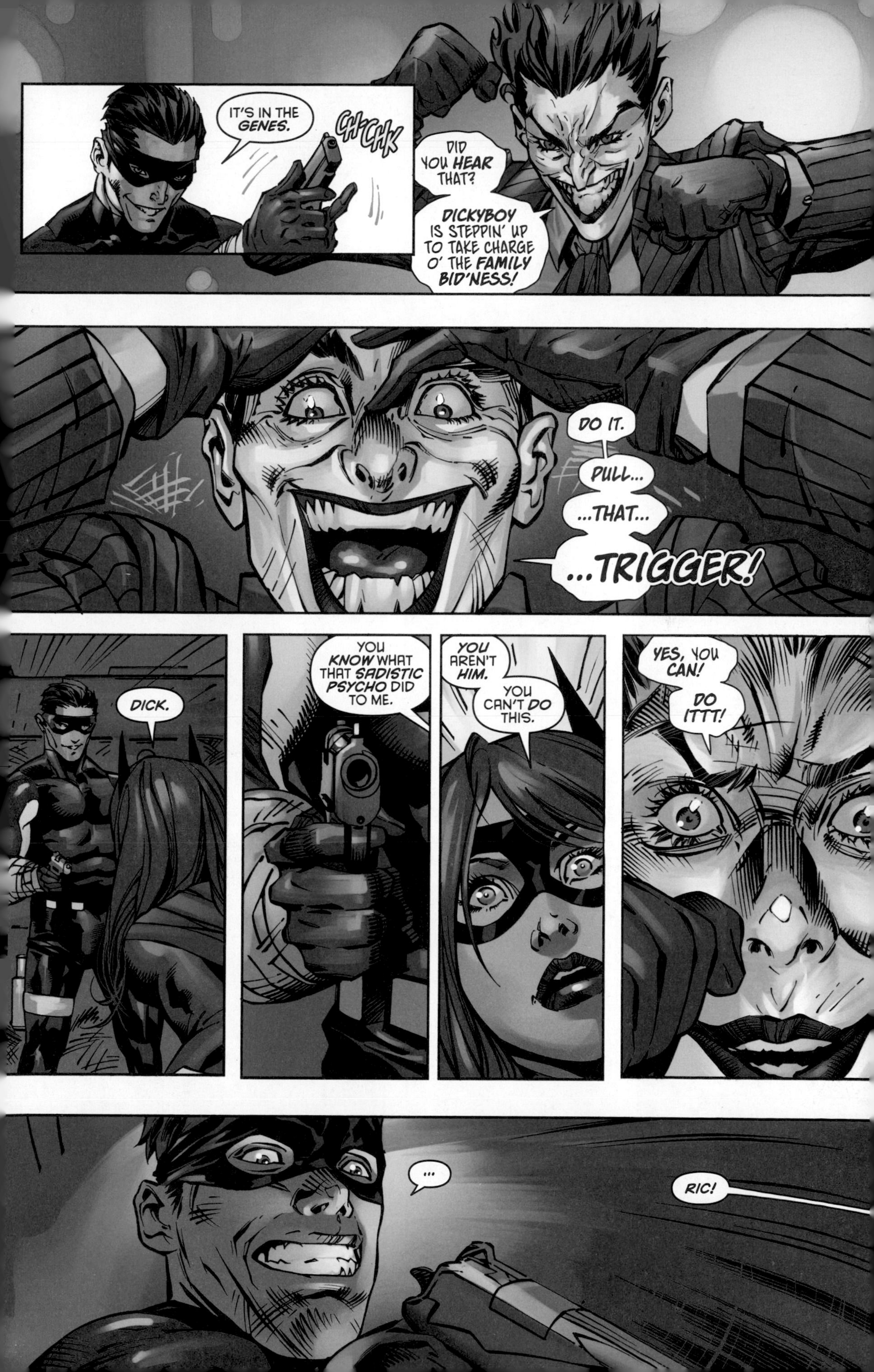
IT'S IN THE GENES.
CH-CHK
DID YOU HEAR THAT?
DICKYBOY IS STEPPIN' UP TO TAKE CHARGE O' THE FAMILY BID'NESS!
DO IT.
PULL...
...THAT...
...TRIGGER!
DICK.
YOU KNOW WHAT THAT SADISTIC PSYCHO DID TO ME.
YOU AREN'T HIM.
YOU CAN'T DO THIS.
YES, YOU CAN!
DO ITTT!
...
RIC!

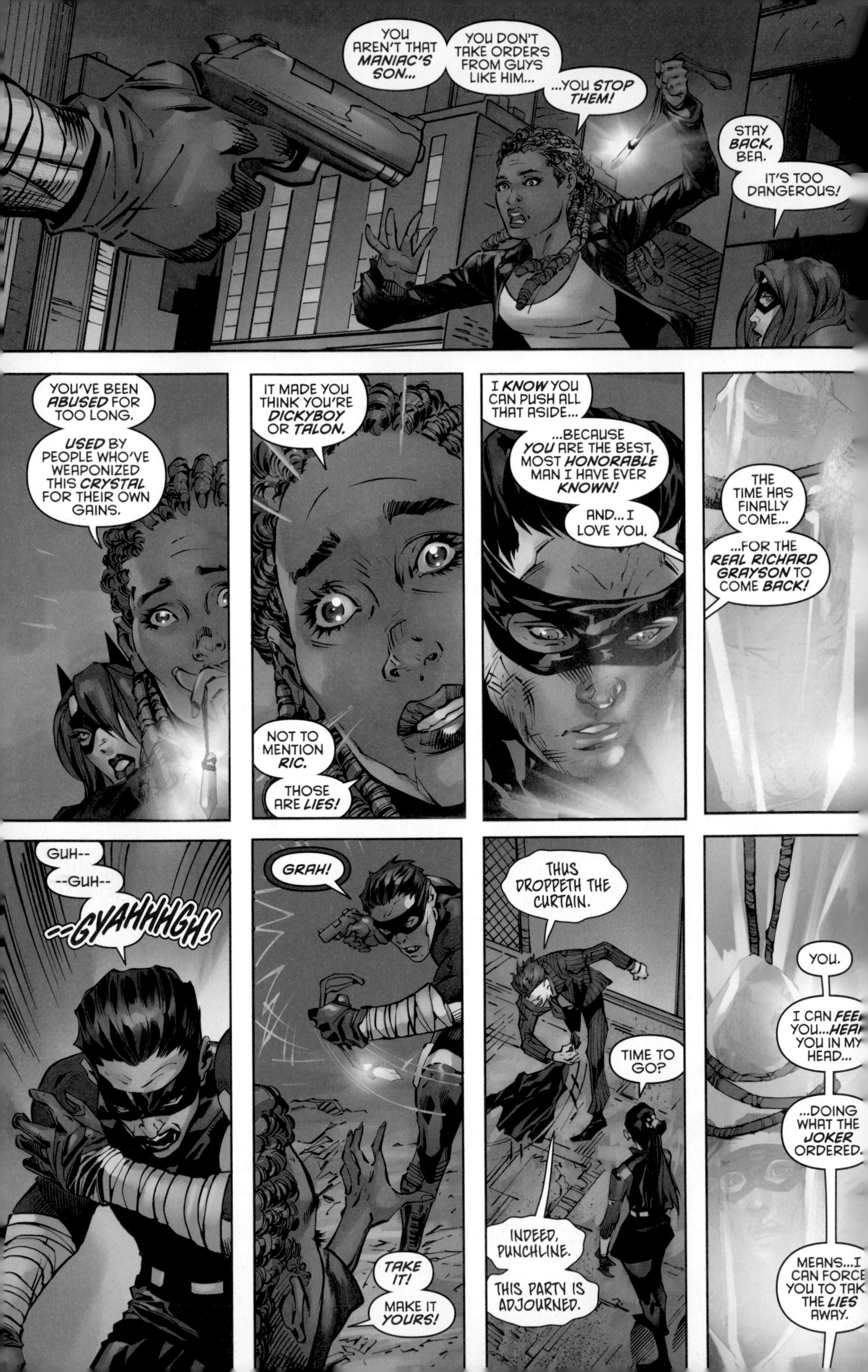
YOU AREN'T THAT MANIAC'S SON...
YOU DON'T TAKE ORDERS FROM GUYS LIKE HIM...
...YOU STOP THEM!
STAY BACK, BEA.
IT'S TOO DANGEROUS!
YOU'VE BEEN ABUSED FOR TOO LONG.
USED BY PEOPLE WHO'VE WEAPONIZED THIS CRYSTAL FOR THEIR OWN GAINS.
IT MADE YOU THINK YOU'RE DICKYBOY OR TALON.
NOT TO MENTION RIC.
THOSE ARE LIES!
I KNOW YOU CAN PUSH ALL THAT ASIDE...
...BECAUSE YOU ARE THE BEST, MOST HONORABLE MAN I HAVE EVER KNOWN!
AND... I LOVE YOU.
THE TIME HAS FINALLY COME...
...FOR THE REAL RICHARD GRAYSON TO COME BACK!
GUH--
--GUH--
--GYAHHHGH!
GRAH!
TAKE IT!
MAKE IT YOURS!
THUS DROPPETH THE CURTAIN.
TIME TO GO?
INDEED, PUNCHLINE.
THIS PARTY IS ADJOURNED.
YOU.
I CAN FEE YOU...HEA YOU IN MY HEAD...
...DOING WHAT THE JOKER ORDERED.
MEANS...I CAN FORCE YOU TO TAK THE LIES AWAY.

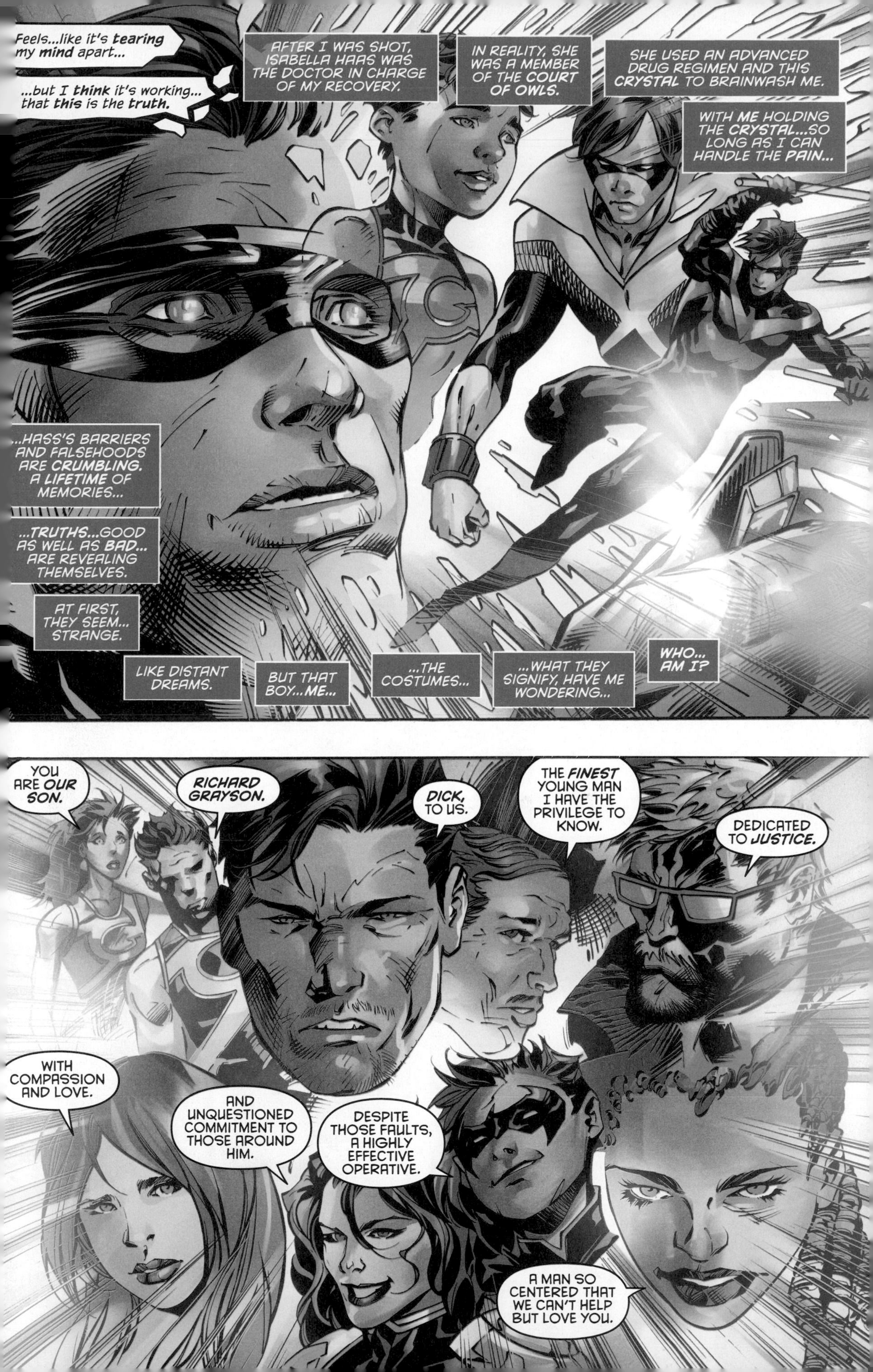
Feels...like it's tearing my mind apart...
...but I think it's working... that this is the truth.
AFTER I WAS SHOT, ISABELLA HAAS WAS THE DOCTOR IN CHARGE OF MY RECOVERY.
IN REALITY, SHE WAS A MEMBER OF THE COURT OF OWLS.
SHE USED AN ADVANCED DRUG REGIMEN AND THIS CRYSTAL TO BRAINWASH ME.
WITH ME HOLDING THE CRYSTAL...SO LONG AS I CAN HANDLE THE PAIN...
...HASS'S BARRIERS AND FALSEHOODS ARE CRUMBLING. A LIFETIME OF MEMORIES...
...TRUTHS...GOOD AS WELL AS BAD... ARE REVEALING THEMSELVES.
AT FIRST, THEY SEEM... STRANGE.
LIKE DISTANT DREAMS.
BUT THAT BOY...ME...
...THE COSTUMES...
...WHAT THEY SIGNIFY, HAVE ME WONDERING...
WHO... AM I?
YOU ARE OUR SON.
RICHARD GRAYSON.
DICK, TO US.
THE FINEST YOUNG MAN I HAVE THE PRIVILEGE TO KNOW.
DEDICATED TO JUSTICE.
WITH COMPASSION AND LOVE.
AND UNQUESTIONED COMMITMENT TO THOSE AROUND HIM.
DESPITE THOSE FAULTS, A HIGHLY EFFECTIVE OPERATIVE.
A MAN SO CENTERED THAT WE CAN'T HELP BUT LOVE YOU.

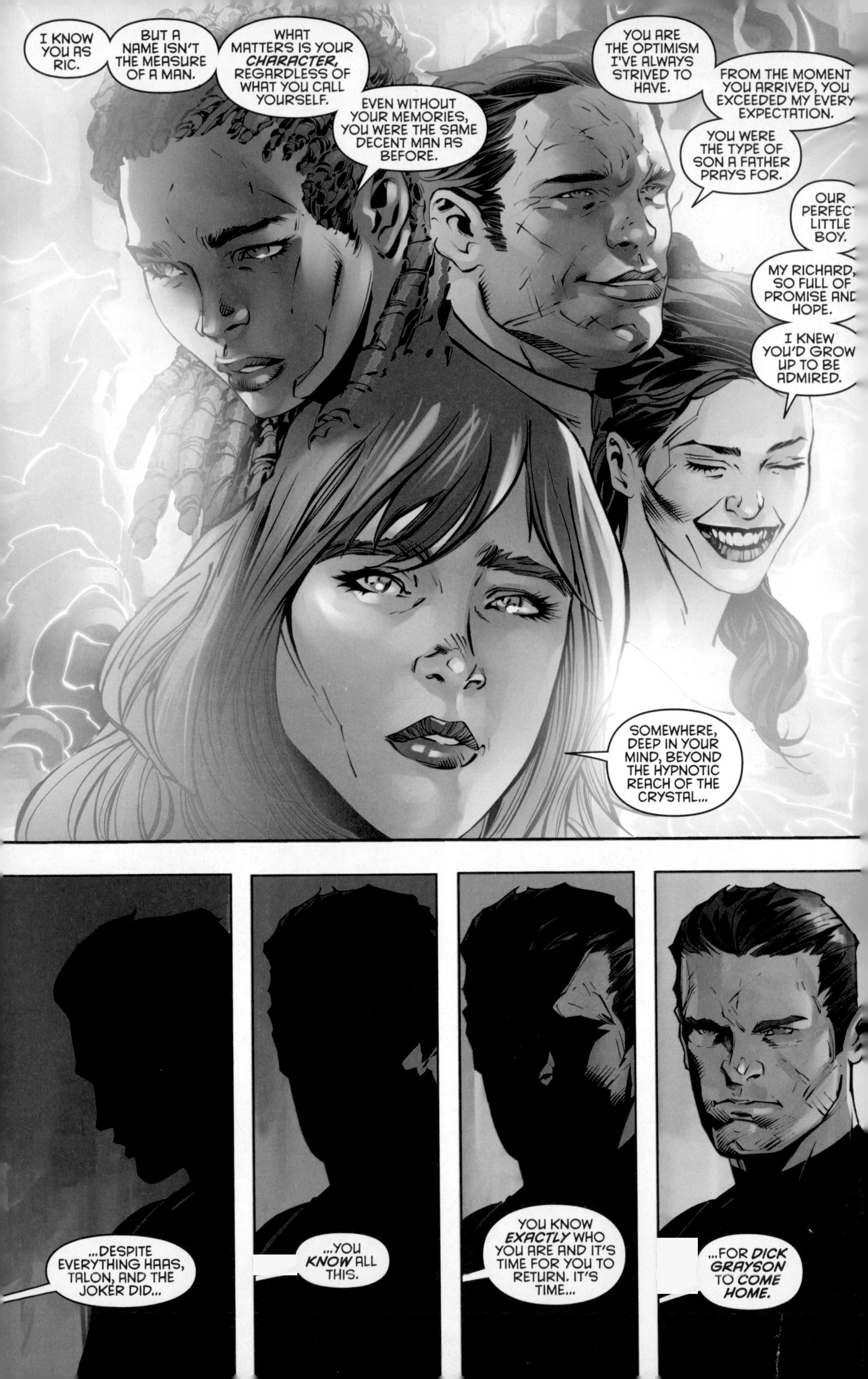
I KNOW YOU AS RIC.
BUT A NAME ISN'T THE MEASURE OF A MAN.
WHAT MATTERS IS YOUR *CHARACTER*, REGARDLESS OF WHAT YOU CALL YOURSELF.
EVEN WITHOUT YOUR MEMORIES, YOU WERE THE SAME DECENT MAN AS BEFORE.
YOU ARE THE OPTIMISM I'VE ALWAYS STRIVED TO HAVE.
FROM THE MOMENT YOU ARRIVED, YOU EXCEEDED MY EVERY EXPECTATION.
YOU WERE THE TYPE OF SON A FATHER PRAYS FOR.
OUR PERFECT LITTLE BOY.
MY RICHARD, SO FULL OF PROMISE AND HOPE.
I KNEW YOU'D GROW UP TO BE ADMIRED.
SOMEWHERE, DEEP IN YOUR MIND, BEYOND THE HYPNOTIC REACH OF THE CRYSTAL...
...DESPITE EVERYTHING HAAS, TALON, AND THE JOKER DID...
...YOU *KNOW* ALL THIS.
YOU KNOW *EXACTLY* WHO YOU ARE AND IT'S TIME FOR YOU TO RETURN. IT'S TIME...
...FOR *DICK GRAYSON* TO *COME HOME.*

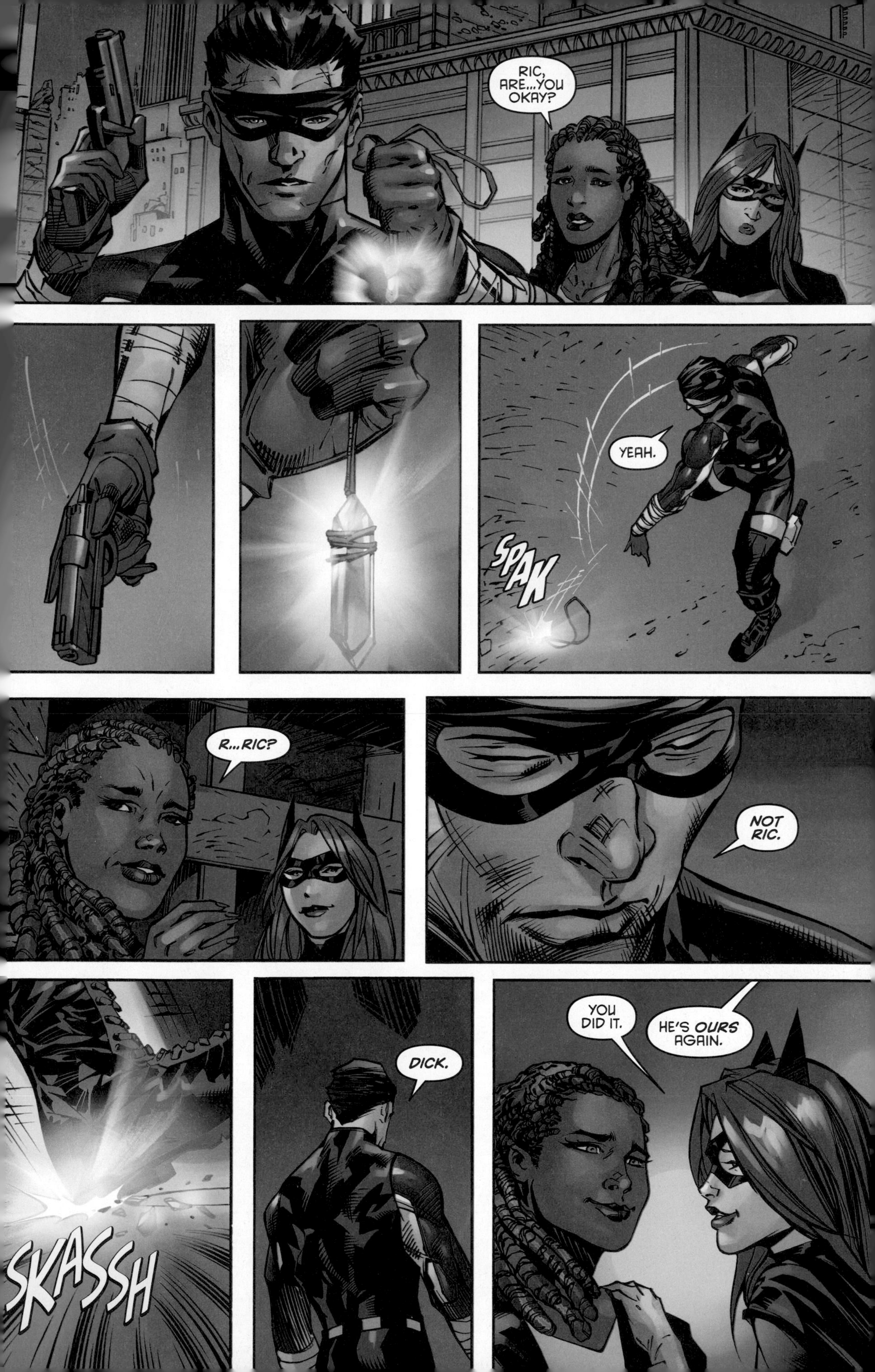
RIC, ARE...YOU OKAY?
YEAH.
SPAK
R...RIC?
NOT RIC.
SKASSH
DICK.
YOU DID IT.
HE'S OURS AGAIN.

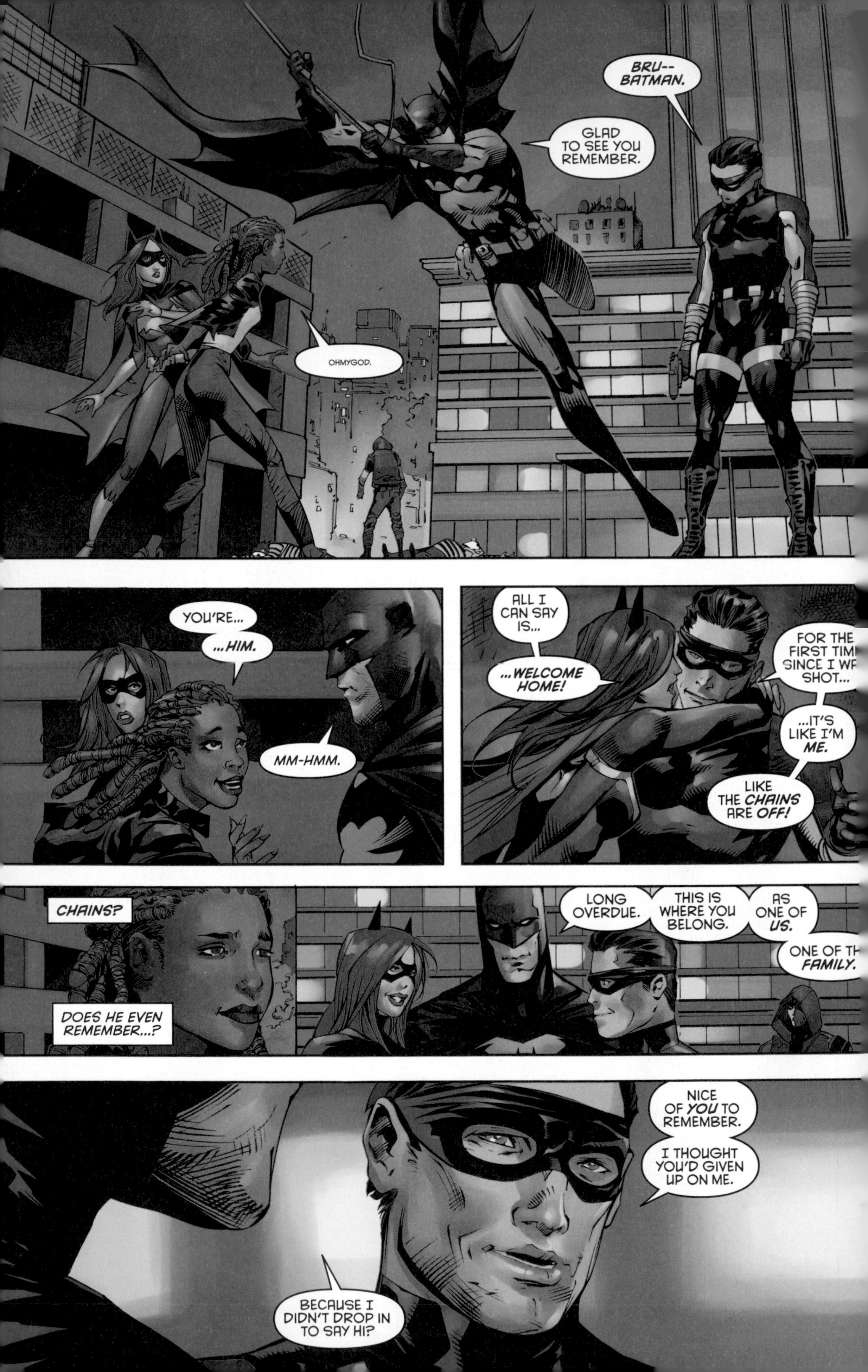
BRU--
BATMAN.
GLAD TO SEE YOU REMEMBER.
OHMYGOD.
YOU'RE...
...HIM.
MM-HMM.
ALL I CAN SAY IS...
...WELCOME HOME!
FOR THE FIRST TIM SINCE I WA SHOT...
...IT'S LIKE I'M ME.
LIKE THE CHAINS ARE OFF!
CHAINS?
DOES HE EVEN REMEMBER...?
LONG OVERDUE.
THIS IS WHERE YOU BELONG.
AS ONE OF US.
ONE OF TH FAMILY.
NICE OF YOU TO REMEMBER.
I THOUGHT YOU'D GIVEN UP ON ME.
BECAUSE I DIDN'T DROP IN TO SAY HI?

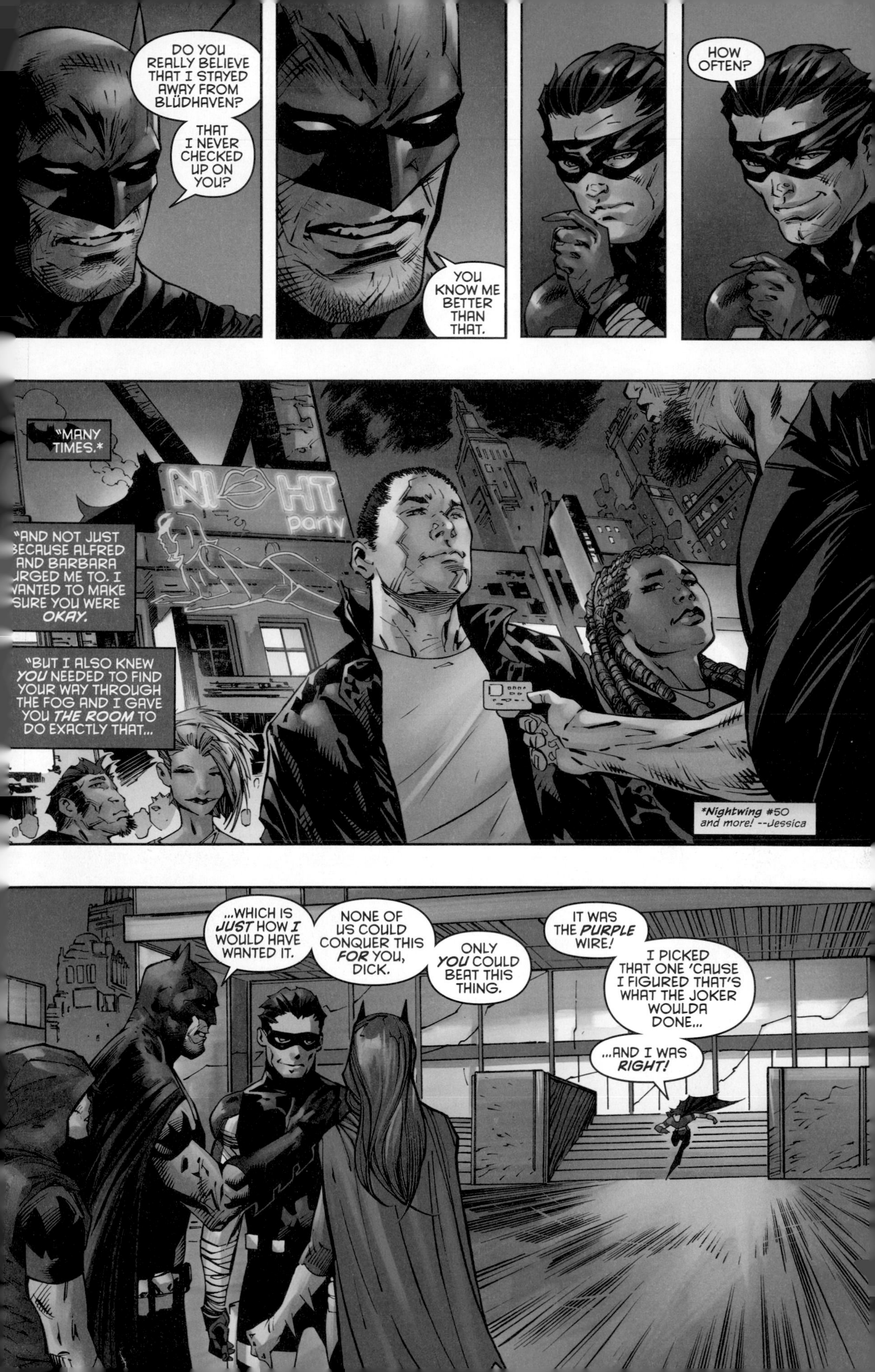
DO YOU REALLY BELIEVE THAT I STAYED AWAY FROM BLÜDHAVEN?
THAT I NEVER CHECKED UP ON YOU?
YOU KNOW ME BETTER THAN THAT.
HOW OFTEN?
"MANY TIMES.*
"AND NOT JUST BECAUSE ALFRED AND BARBARA URGED ME TO. I WANTED TO MAKE SURE YOU WERE OKAY.
"BUT I ALSO KNEW YOU NEEDED TO FIND YOUR WAY THROUGH THE FOG AND I GAVE YOU THE ROOM TO DO EXACTLY THAT...
*Nightwing #50 and more! --Jessica
...WHICH IS JUST HOW I WOULD HAVE WANTED IT.
NONE OF US COULD CONQUER THIS FOR YOU, DICK.
ONLY YOU COULD BEAT THIS THING.
IT WAS THE PURPLE WIRE!
I PICKED THAT ONE 'CAUSE I FIGURED THAT'S WHAT THE JOKER WOULDA DONE...
...AND I WAS RIGHT!

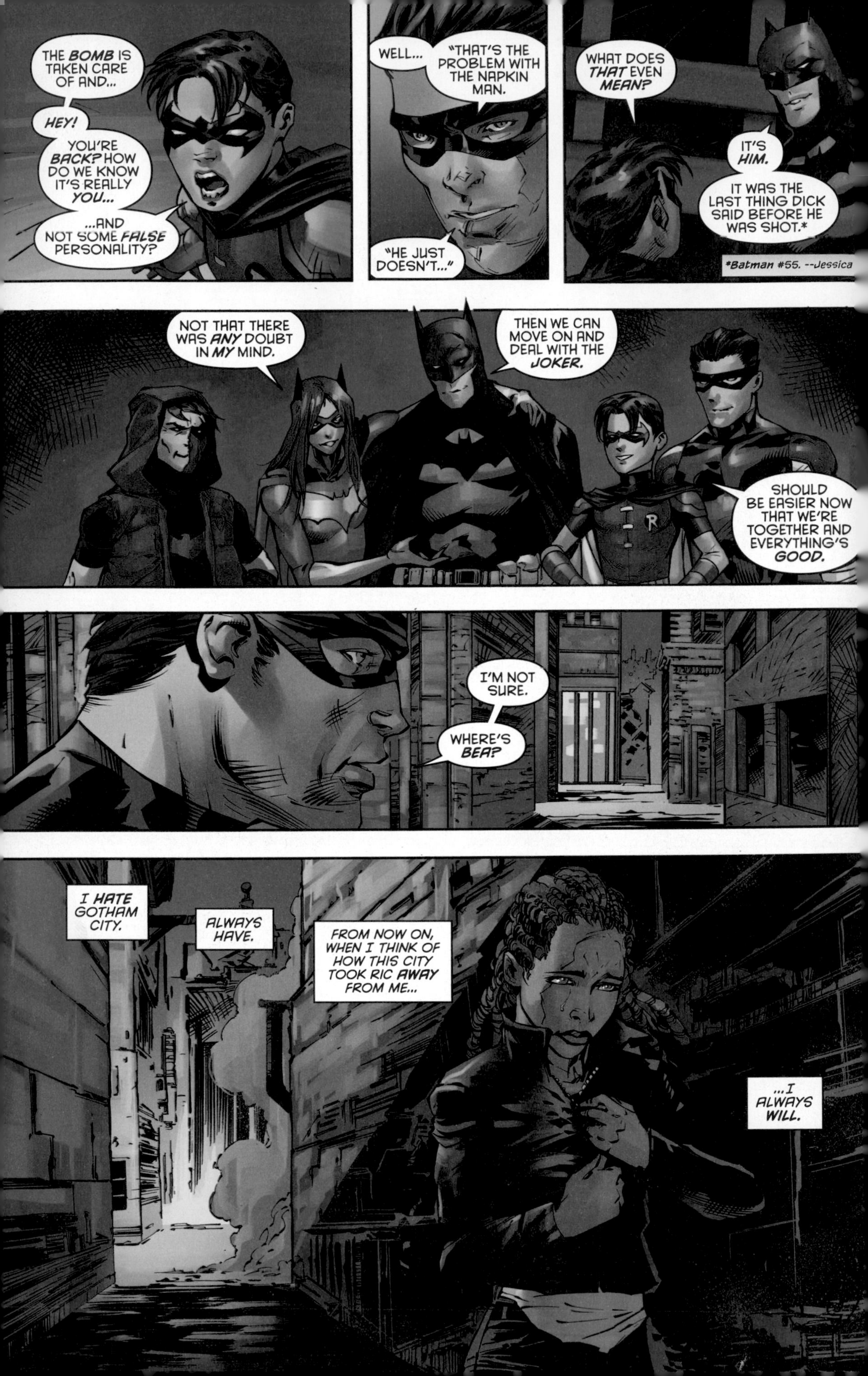
THE BOMB IS TAKEN CARE OF AND...
HEY!
YOU'RE BACK? HOW DO WE KNOW IT'S REALLY YOU...
...AND NOT SOME FALSE PERSONALITY?
WELL...
"THAT'S THE PROBLEM WITH THE NAPKIN MAN.
"HE JUST DOESN'T..."
WHAT DOES THAT EVEN MEAN?
IT'S HIM.
IT WAS THE LAST THING DICK SAID BEFORE HE WAS SHOT.*
*Batman #55. --Jessica
NOT THAT THERE WAS ANY DOUBT IN MY MIND.
THEN WE CAN MOVE ON AND DEAL WITH THE JOKER.
SHOULD BE EASIER NOW THAT WE'RE TOGETHER AND EVERYTHING'S GOOD.
I'M NOT SURE.
WHERE'S BEA?
I HATE GOTHAM CITY.
ALWAYS HAVE.
FROM NOW ON, WHEN I THINK OF HOW THIS CITY TOOK RIC AWAY FROM ME...
...I ALWAYS WILL.

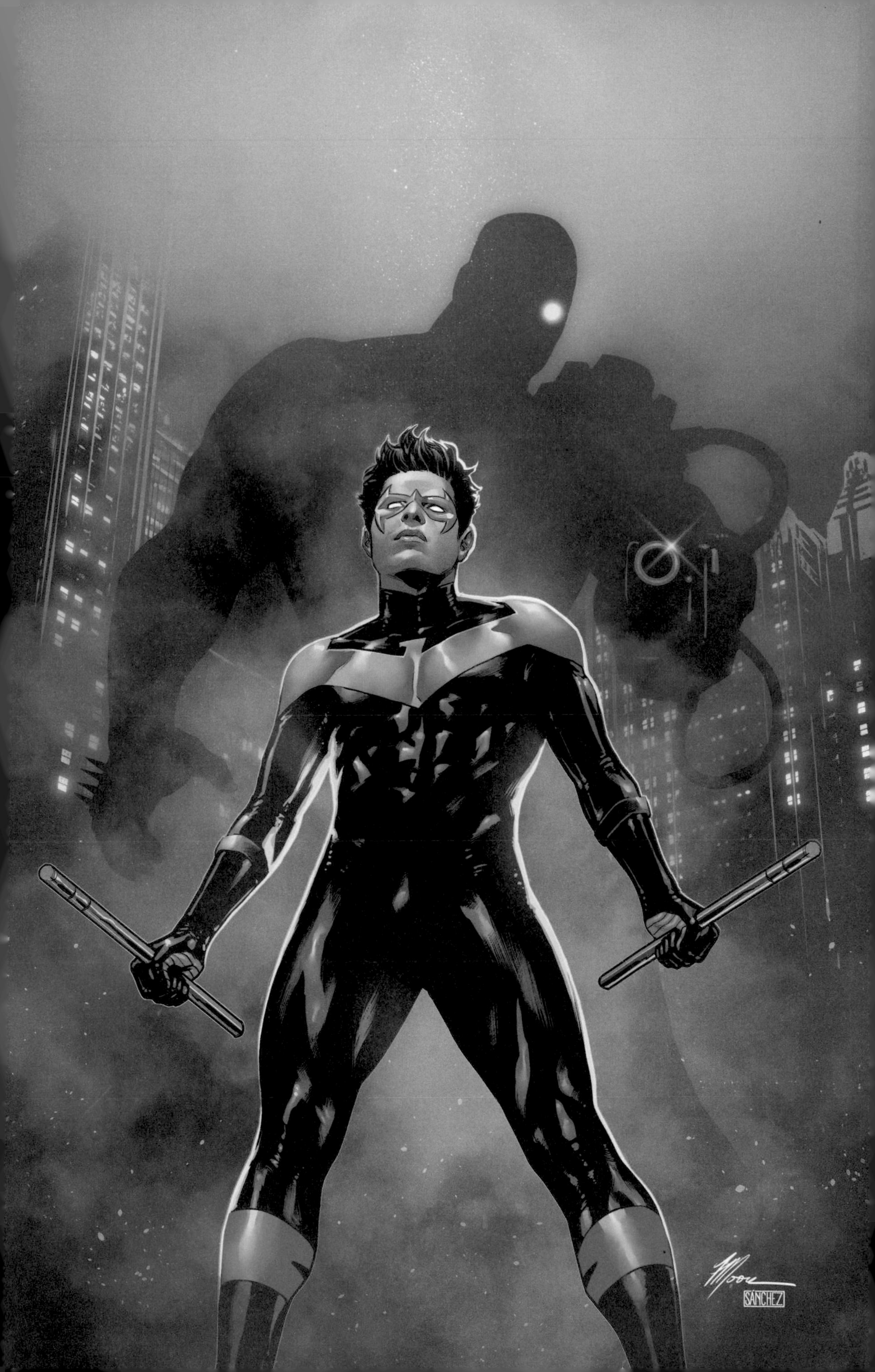
SÁNCHEZ

HA HA HA HA HA HA

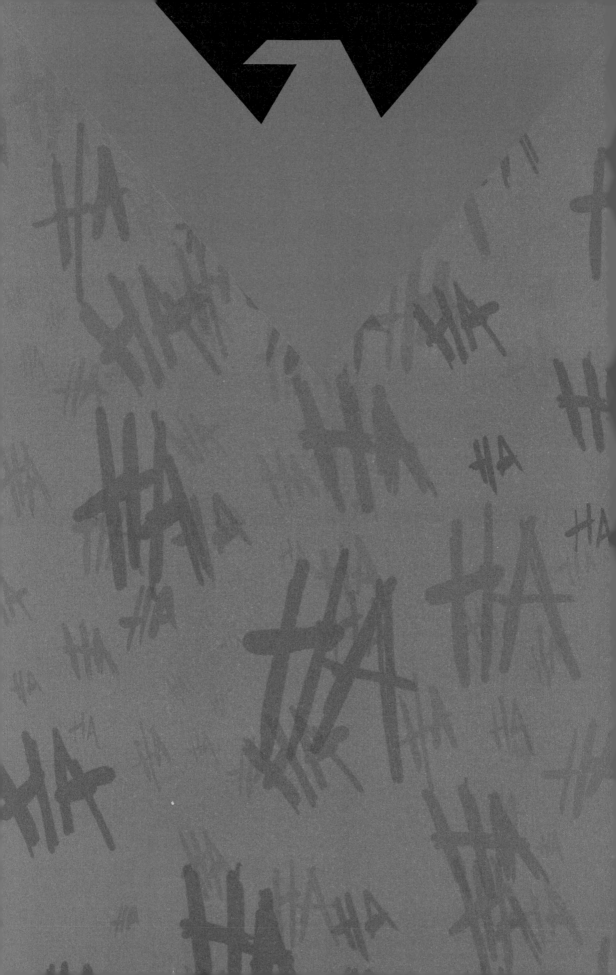

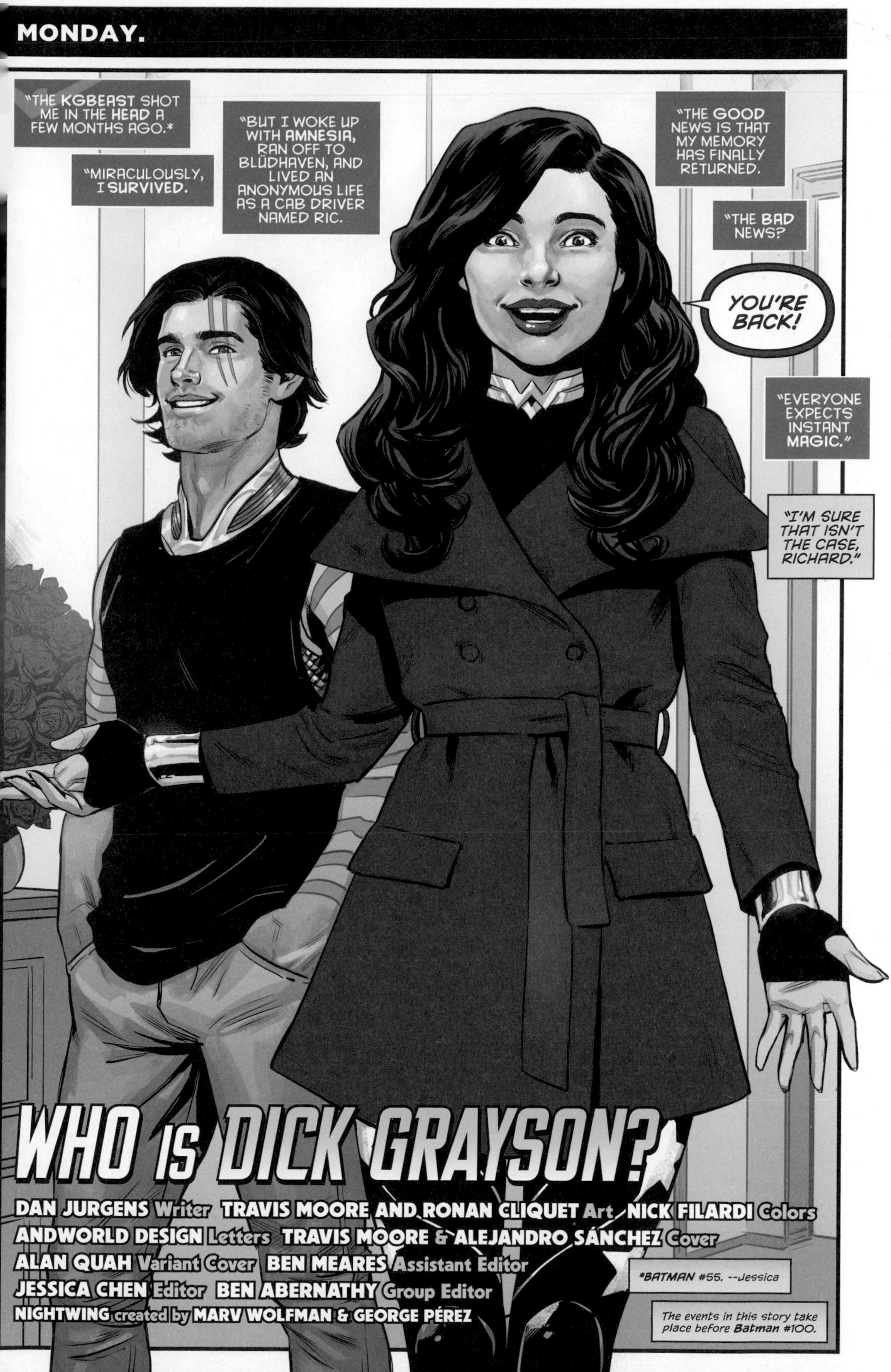
MONDAY.
"THE KGBEAST SHOT ME IN THE HEAD A FEW MONTHS AGO.*
"MIRACULOUSLY, I SURVIVED.
"BUT I WOKE UP WITH AMNESIA, RAN OFF TO BLÜDHAVEN, AND LIVED AN ANONYMOUS LIFE AS A CAB DRIVER NAMED RIC.
"THE GOOD NEWS IS THAT MY MEMORY HAS FINALLY RETURNED.
"THE BAD NEWS?
YOU'RE BACK!
"EVERYONE EXPECTS INSTANT MAGIC."
"I'M SURE THAT ISN'T THE CASE, RICHARD."
WHO IS DICK GRAYSON?
DAN JURGENS Writer TRAVIS MOORE AND RONAN CLIQUET Art NICK FILARDI Colors
ANDWORLD DESIGN Letters TRAVIS MOORE & ALEJANDRO SÁNCHEZ Cover
ALAN QUAH Variant Cover BEN MEARES Assistant Editor
JESSICA CHEN Editor BEN ABERNATHY Group Editor
NIGHTWING created by MARV WOLFMAN & GEORGE PÉREZ
*BATMAN #55. --Jessica
The events in this story take place before Batman #100.

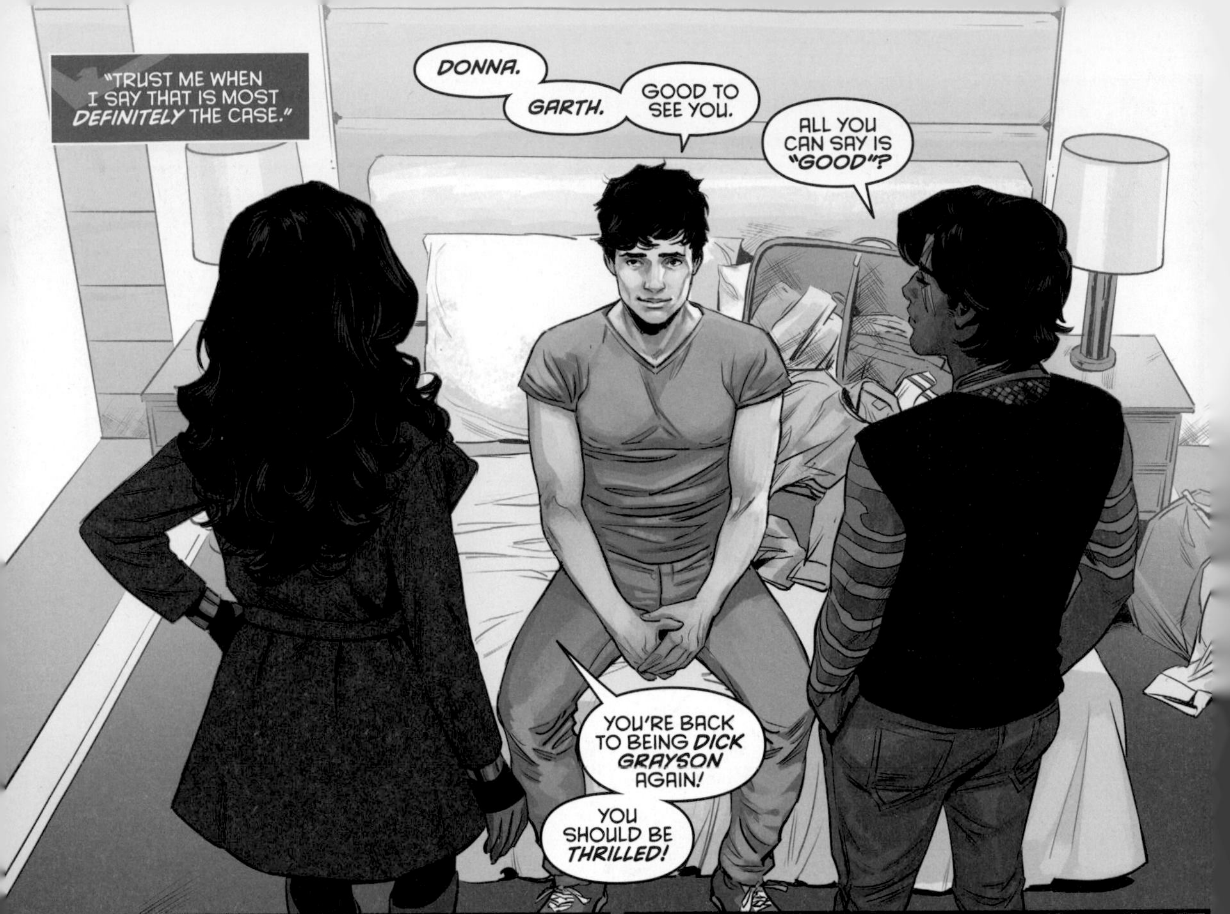
"TRUST ME WHEN I SAY THAT IS MOST DEFINITELY THE CASE."
DONNA.
GARTH.
GOOD TO SEE YOU.
ALL YOU CAN SAY IS "GOOD"?
YOU'RE BACK TO BEING DICK GRAYSON AGAIN!
YOU SHOULD BE THRILLED!

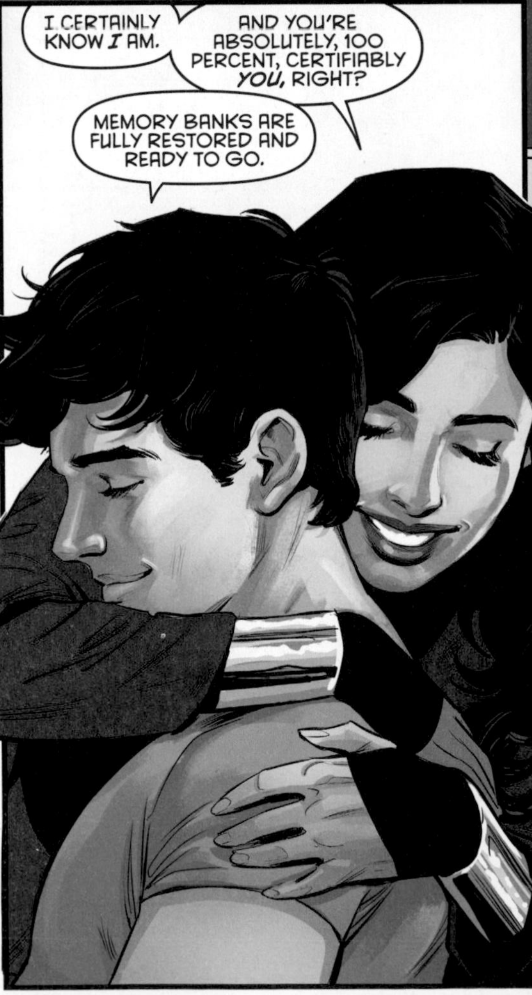
I CERTAINLY KNOW I AM.
AND YOU'RE ABSOLUTELY, 100 PERCENT, CERTIFIABLY YOU, RIGHT?
MEMORY BANKS ARE FULLY RESTORED AND READY TO GO.

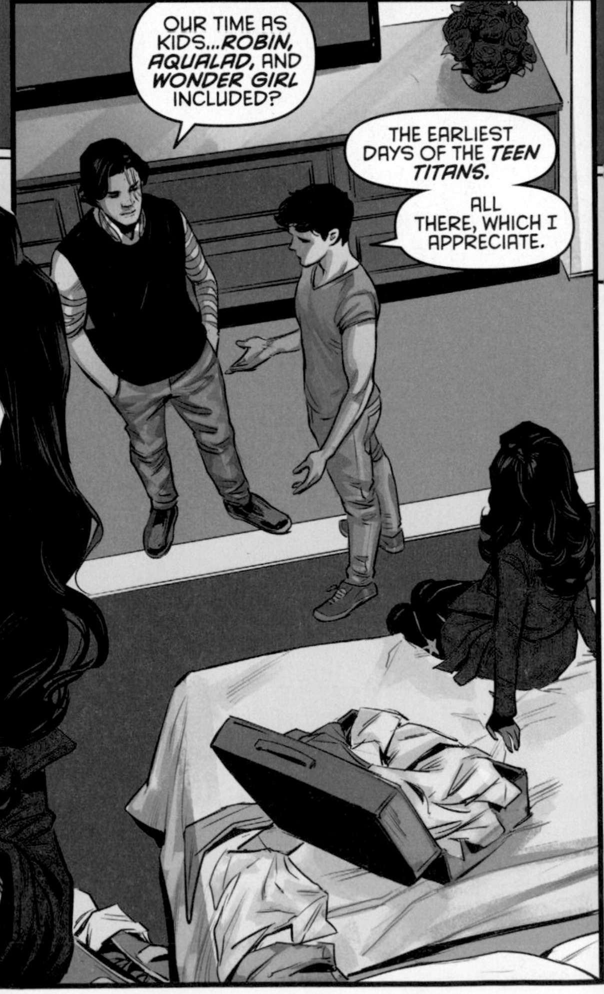
OUR TIME AS KIDS...ROBIN, AQUALAD, AND WONDER GIRL INCLUDED?
THE EARLIEST DAYS OF THE TEEN TITANS.
ALL THERE, WHICH I APPRECIATE.

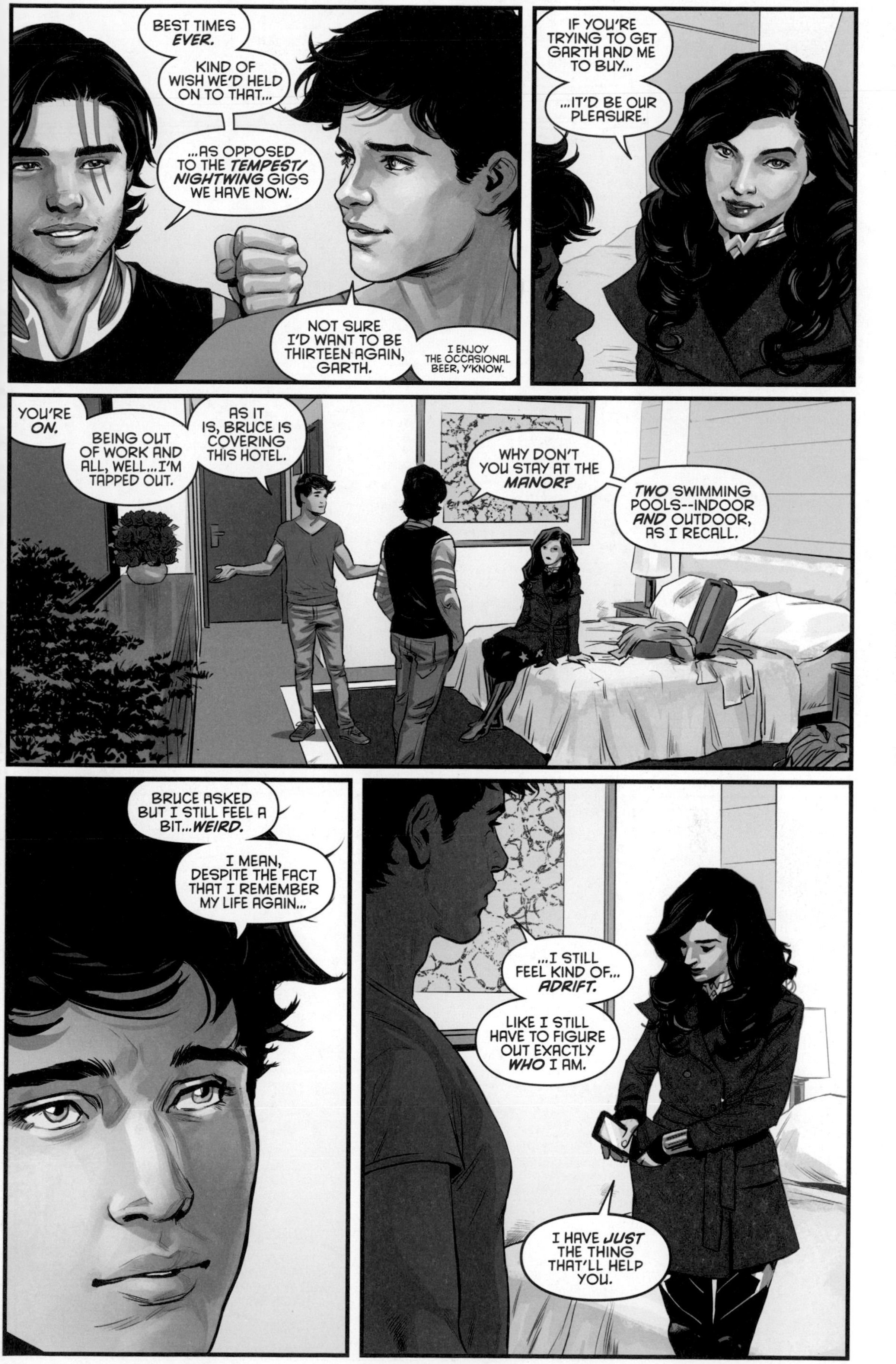

BEST TIMES *EVER.*
KIND OF WISH WE'D HELD ON TO THAT...
...AS OPPOSED TO THE *TEMPEST/ NIGHTWING* GIGS WE HAVE NOW.
NOT SURE I'D WANT TO BE THIRTEEN AGAIN, GARTH.
I ENJOY THE OCCASIONAL BEER, Y'KNOW.
IF YOU'RE TRYING TO GET GARTH AND ME TO BUY...
...IT'D BE OUR PLEASURE.
YOU'RE *ON.*
BEING OUT OF WORK AND ALL, WELL...I'M TAPPED OUT.
AS IT IS, BRUCE IS COVERING THIS HOTEL.
WHY DON'T YOU STAY AT THE *MANOR?*
TWO SWIMMING POOLS--INDOOR *AND* OUTDOOR, AS I RECALL.
BRUCE ASKED BUT I STILL FEEL A BIT...*WEIRD.*
I MEAN, DESPITE THE FACT THAT I REMEMBER MY LIFE AGAIN...
...I STILL FEEL KIND OF... *ADRIFT.*
LIKE I STILL HAVE TO FIGURE OUT EXACTLY *WHO* I AM.
I HAVE *JUST* THE THING THAT'LL HELP YOU.

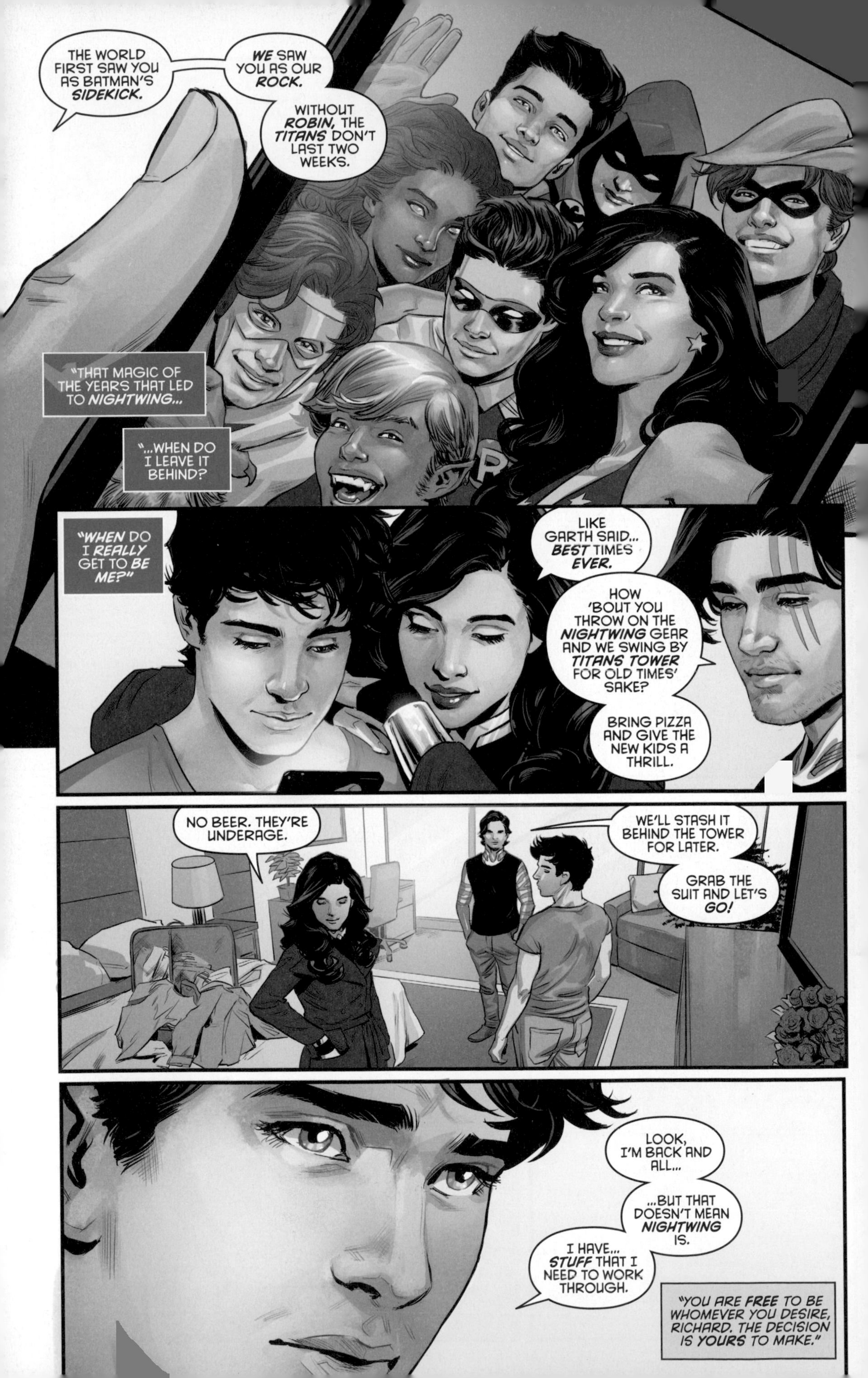
THE WORLD FIRST SAW YOU AS BATMAN'S *SIDEKICK.*
WE SAW YOU AS OUR *ROCK.*
WITHOUT *ROBIN,* THE *TITANS* DON'T LAST TWO WEEKS.
"THAT MAGIC OF THE YEARS THAT LED TO *NIGHTWING...*
"...WHEN DO I LEAVE IT BEHIND?
"*WHEN* DO I *REALLY* GET TO *BE ME?*"
LIKE GARTH SAID... *BEST* TIMES *EVER.*
HOW 'BOUT YOU THROW ON THE *NIGHTWING* GEAR AND WE SWING BY *TITANS TOWER* FOR OLD TIMES' SAKE?
BRING PIZZA AND GIVE THE NEW KIDS A THRILL.
NO BEER. THEY'RE UNDERAGE.
WE'LL STASH IT BEHIND THE TOWER FOR LATER.
GRAB THE SUIT AND LET'S *GO!*
LOOK, I'M BACK AND ALL...
...BUT THAT DOESN'T MEAN *NIGHTWING* IS.
I HAVE... *STUFF* THAT I NEED TO WORK THROUGH.
"YOU ARE *FREE* TO BE WHOMEVER YOU DESIRE, RICHARD. THE DECISION IS *YOURS* TO MAKE."

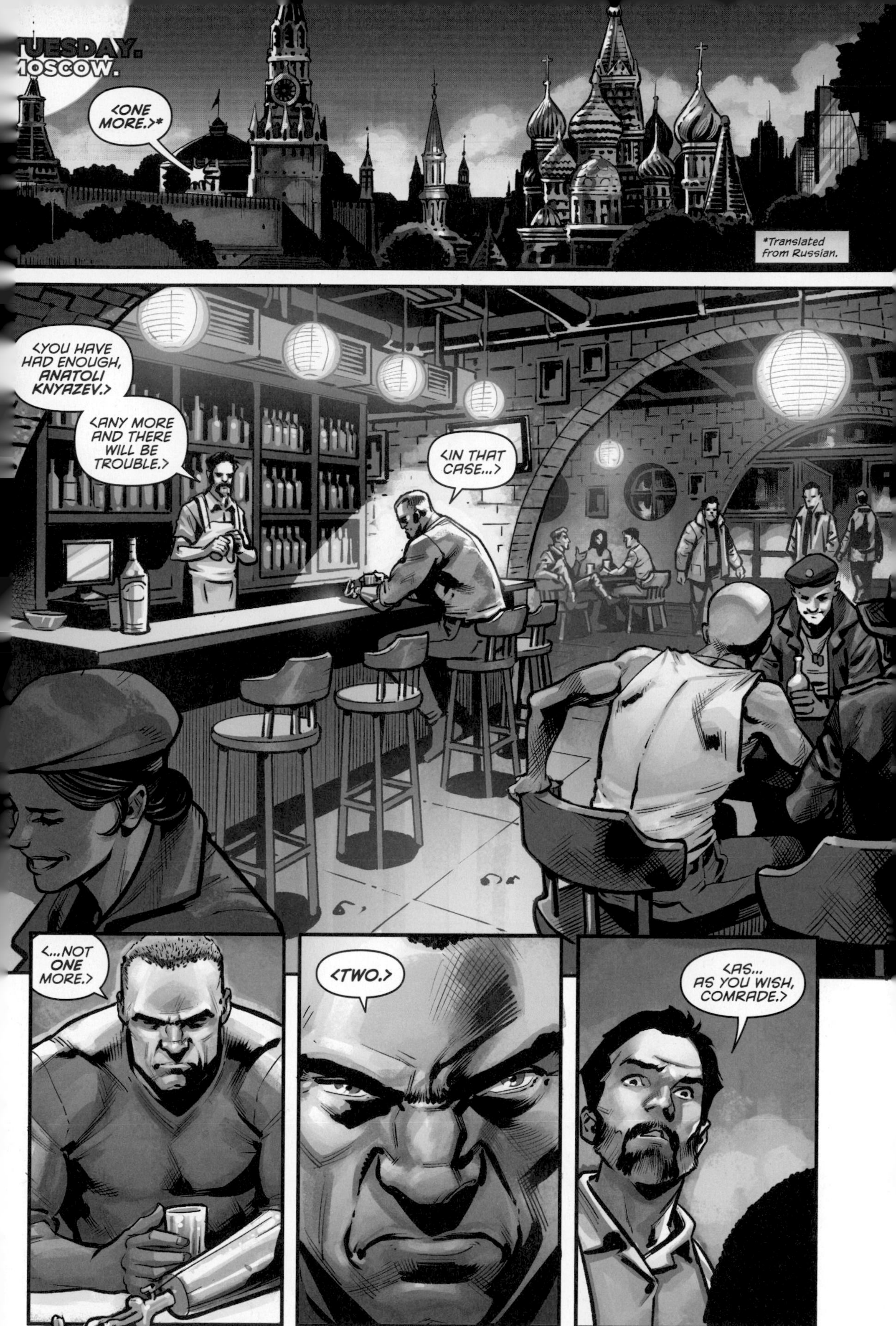

TUESDAY.
MOSCOW.
<ONE MORE.>*
*Translated from Russian.
<YOU HAVE HAD ENOUGH, ANATOLI KNYAZEV.>
<ANY MORE AND THERE WILL BE TROUBLE.>
<IN THAT CASE...>
<...NOT ONE MORE.>
<TWO.>
<AS... AS YOU WISH, COMRADE.>

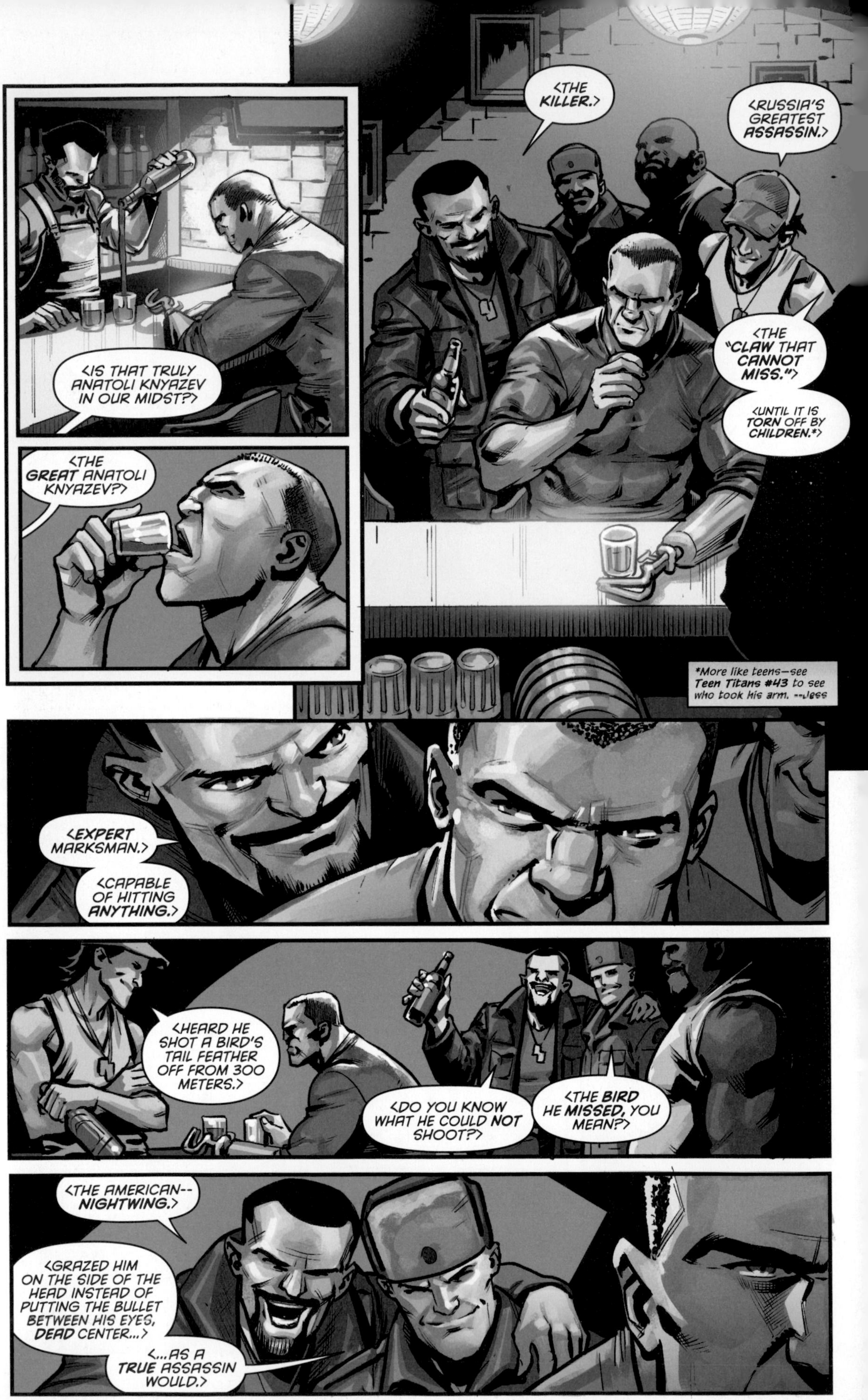
<IS THAT TRULY ANATOLI KNYAZEV IN OUR MIDST?>
<THE KILLER.>
<RUSSIA'S GREATEST ASSASSIN.>
<THE GREAT ANATOLI KNYAZEV?>
<THE "CLAW THAT CANNOT MISS.">
<UNTIL IT IS TORN OFF BY CHILDREN.*>
*More like teens—see Teen Titans #43 to see who took his arm. --Jess
<EXPERT MARKSMAN.>
<CAPABLE OF HITTING ANYTHING.>
<HEARD HE SHOT A BIRD'S TAIL FEATHER OFF FROM 300 METERS.>
<DO YOU KNOW WHAT HE COULD NOT SHOOT?>
<THE BIRD HE MISSED, YOU MEAN?>
<THE AMERICAN--NIGHTWING.>
<GRAZED HIM ON THE SIDE OF THE HEAD INSTEAD OF PUTTING THE BULLET BETWEEN HIS EYES, DEAD CENTER...>
<...AS A TRUE ASSASSIN WOULD.>

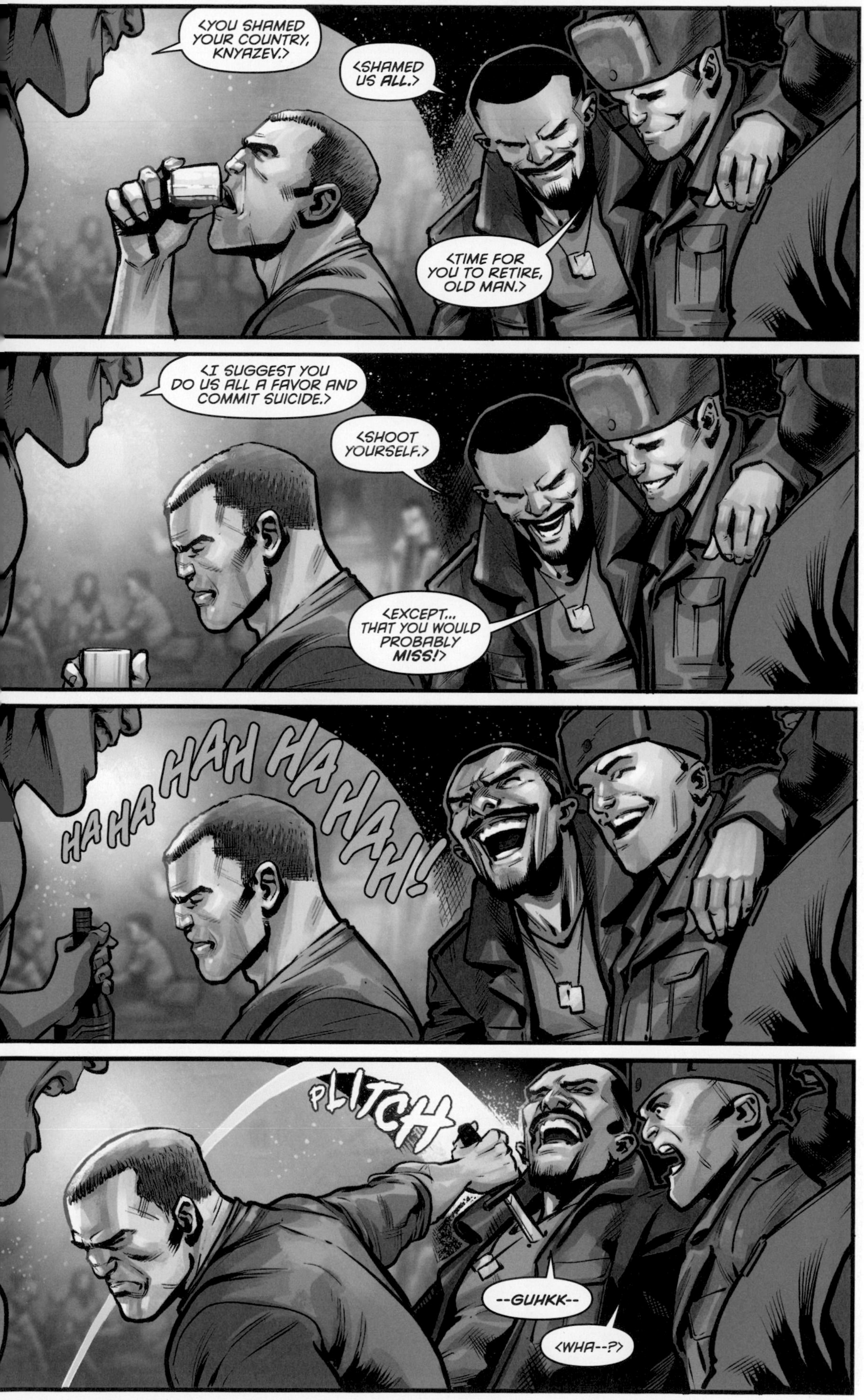
<YOU SHAMED YOUR COUNTRY, KNYAZEV.>
<SHAMED US ALL.>
<TIME FOR YOU TO RETIRE, OLD MAN.>
<I SUGGEST YOU DO US ALL A FAVOR AND COMMIT SUICIDE.>
<SHOOT YOURSELF.>
<EXCEPT... THAT YOU WOULD PROBABLY MISS!>
HA HA HAH HA HAH!
PLITCH
--GUHKK--
<WHA--?>

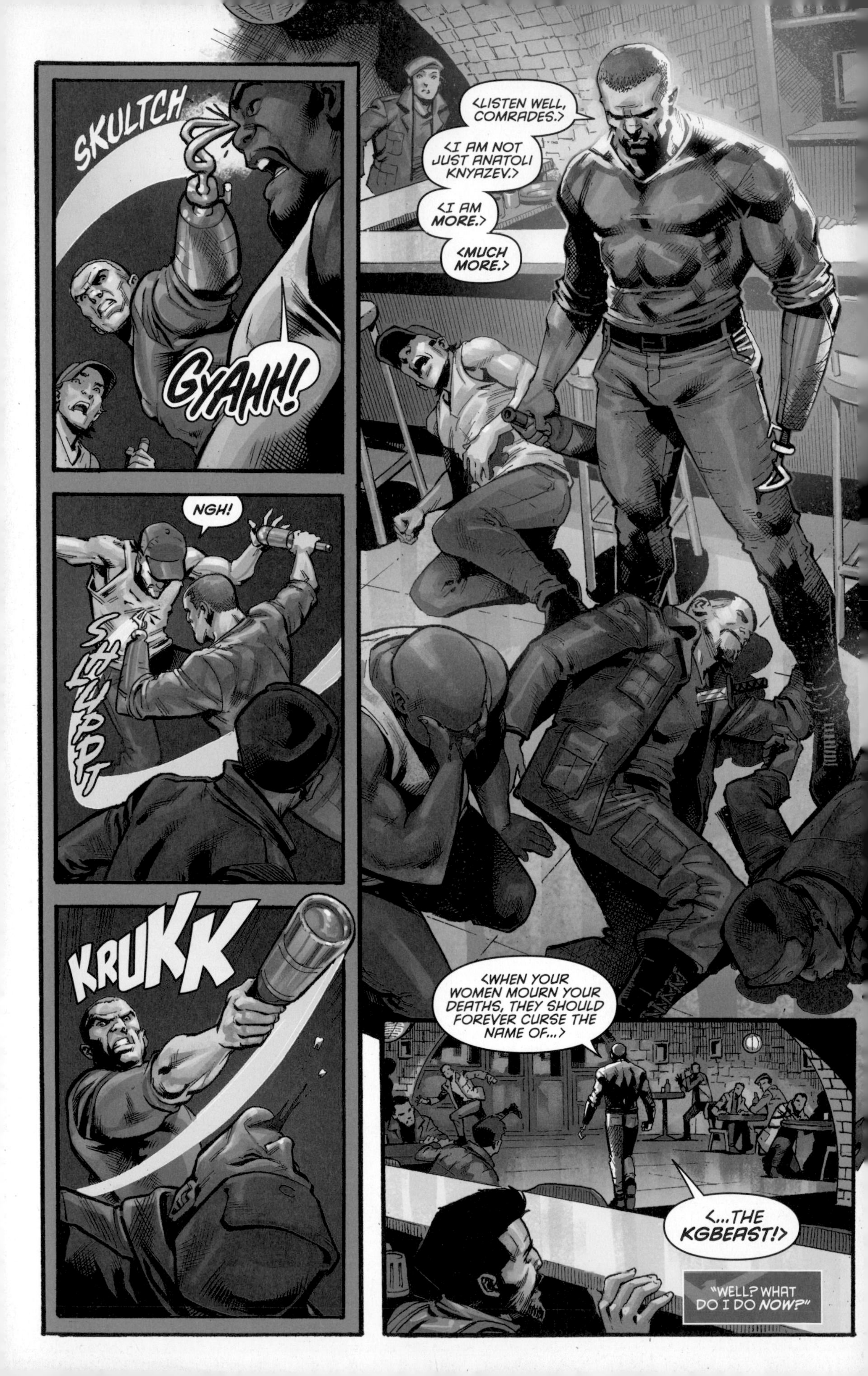
SKULTCH
GYAHH!
<LISTEN WELL, COMRADES.>
<I AM NOT JUST ANATOLI KNYAZEV.>
<I AM MORE.>
<MUCH MORE.>
NGH!
SHLUPPT
KRUKK
<WHEN YOUR WOMEN MOURN YOUR DEATHS, THEY SHOULD FOREVER CURSE THE NAME OF...>
<...THE KGBEAST!>
"WELL? WHAT DO I DO NOW?"

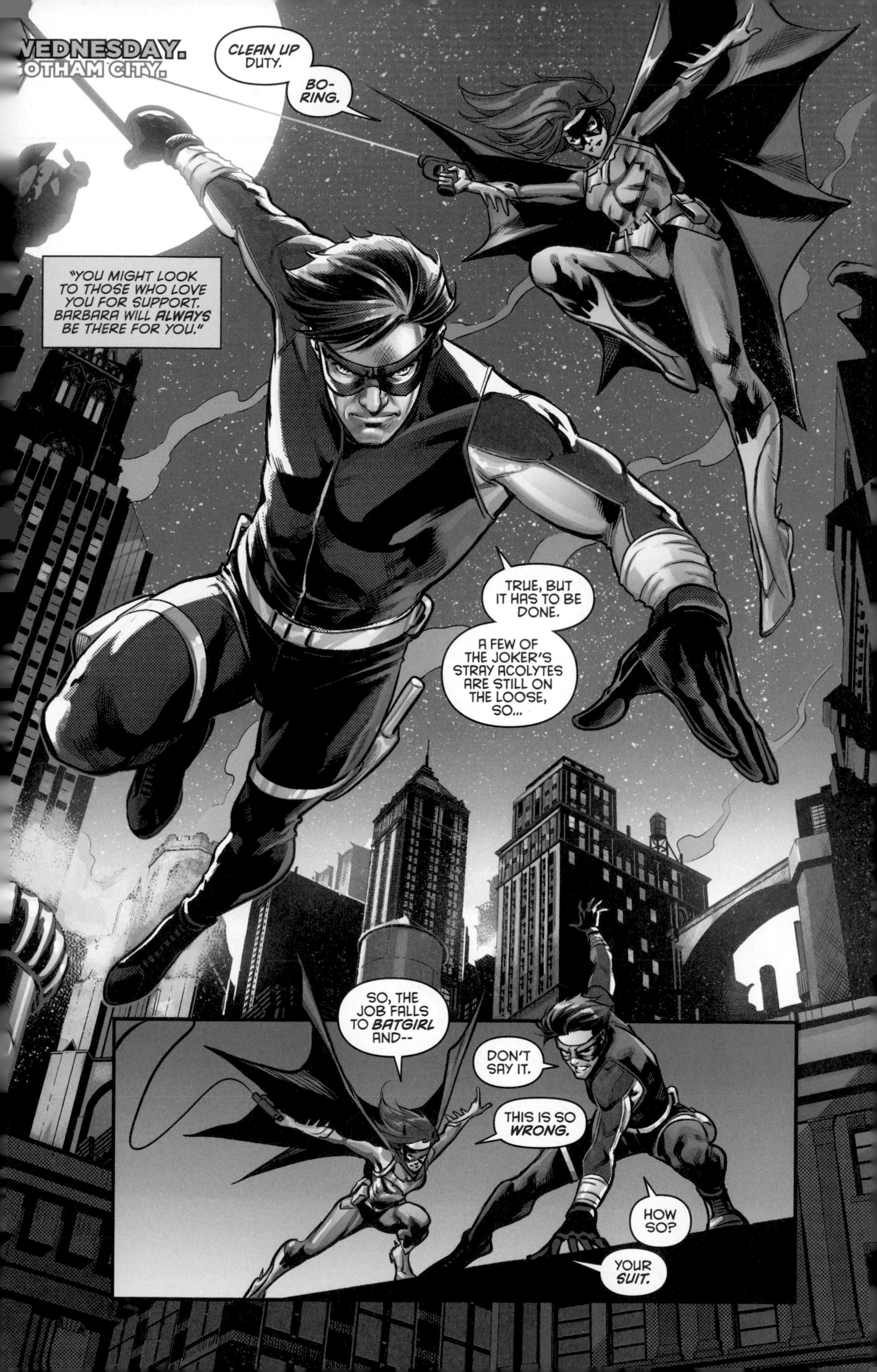
WEDNESDAY.
GOTHAM CITY.
CLEAN UP DUTY.
BO-RING.
"YOU MIGHT LOOK TO THOSE WHO LOVE YOU FOR SUPPORT. BARBARA WILL ALWAYS BE THERE FOR YOU."
TRUE, BUT IT HAS TO BE DONE.
A FEW OF THE JOKER'S STRAY ACOLYTES ARE STILL ON THE LOOSE, SO...
SO, THE JOB FALLS TO BATGIRL AND--
DON'T SAY IT.
THIS IS SO WRONG.
HOW SO?
YOUR SUIT.

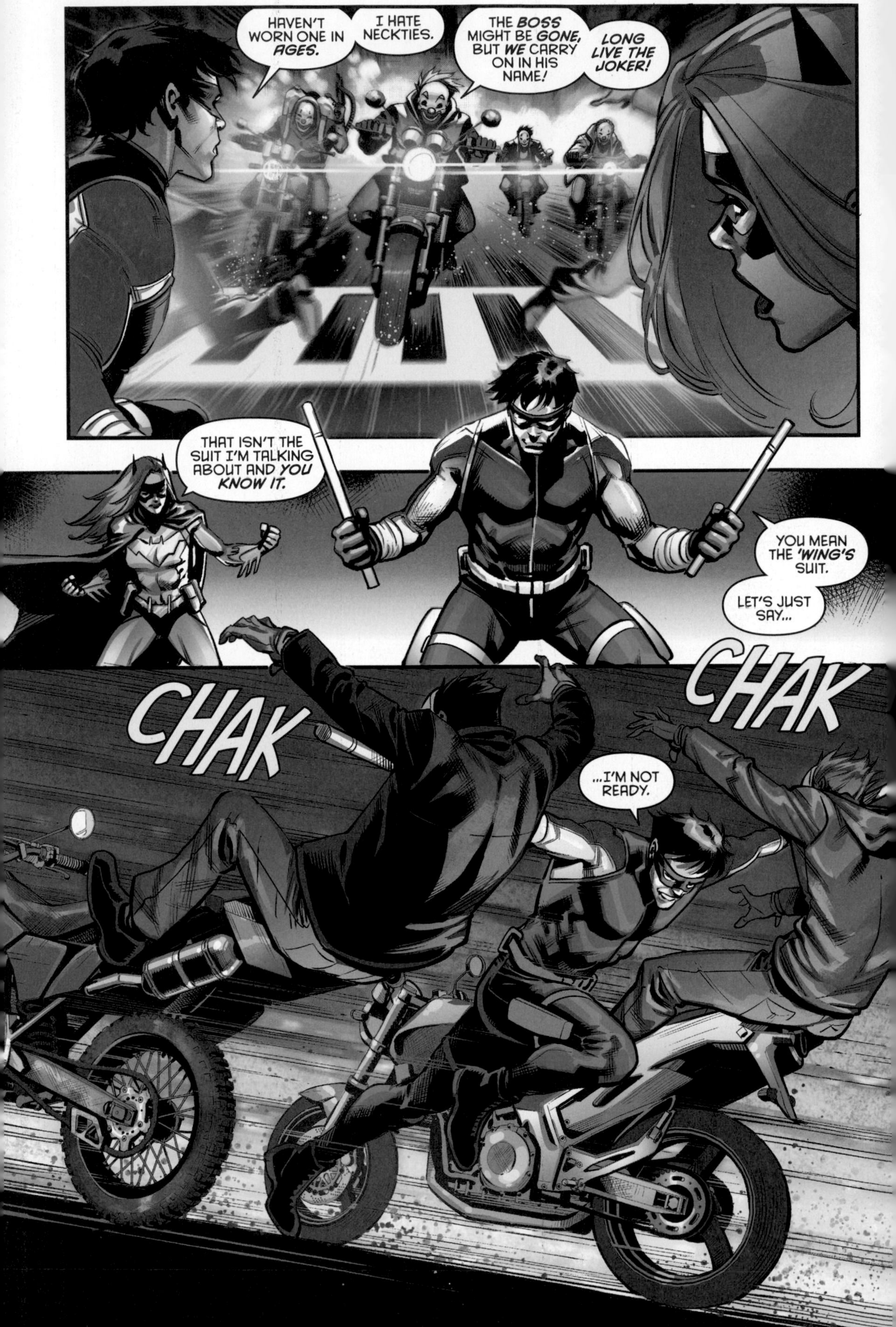
HAVEN'T WORN ONE IN AGES.
I HATE NECKTIES.
THE BOSS MIGHT BE GONE, BUT WE CARRY ON IN HIS NAME!
LONG LIVE THE JOKER!
THAT ISN'T THE SUIT I'M TALKING ABOUT AND YOU KNOW IT.
YOU MEAN THE 'WING'S SUIT.
LET'S JUST SAY...
CHAK
CHAK
...I'M NOT READY.

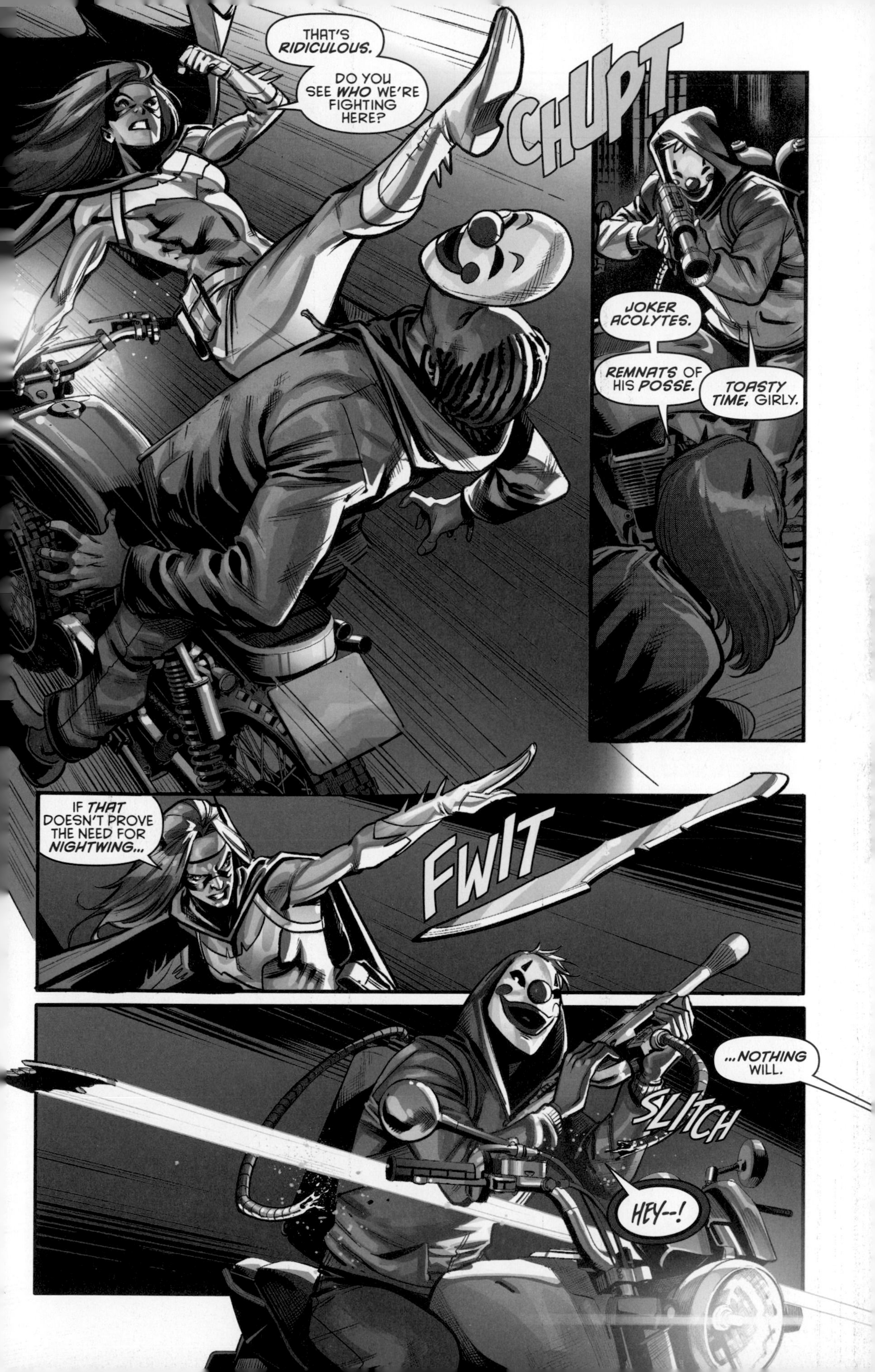
THAT'S *RIDICULOUS.*
DO YOU SEE *WHO* WE'RE FIGHTING HERE?
CHUPT
JOKER ACOLYTES.
REMNATS OF HIS *POSSE.*
TOASTY TIME, GIRLY.
IF *THAT* DOESN'T PROVE THE NEED FOR *NIGHTWING*...
FWIT
...*NOTHING* WILL.
SLITCH
HEY--!

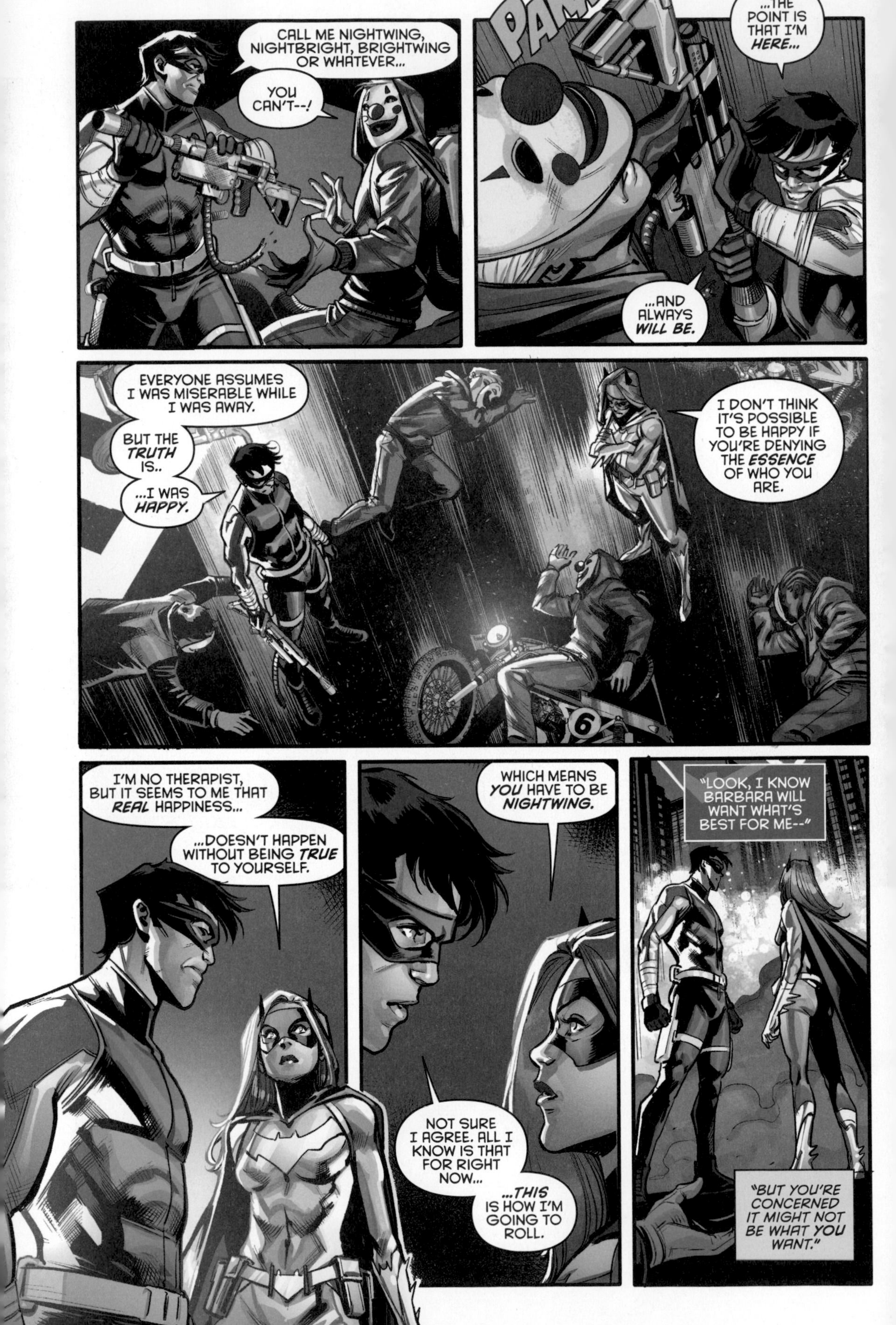
CALL ME NIGHTWING, NIGHTBRIGHT, BRIGHTWING OR WHATEVER...
YOU CAN'T--!
PAKK
...THE POINT IS THAT I'M HERE...
...AND ALWAYS WILL BE.
EVERYONE ASSUMES I WAS MISERABLE WHILE I WAS AWAY.
BUT THE TRUTH IS..
...I WAS HAPPY.
I DON'T THINK IT'S POSSIBLE TO BE HAPPY IF YOU'RE DENYING THE ESSENCE OF WHO YOU ARE.
I'M NO THERAPIST, BUT IT SEEMS TO ME THAT REAL HAPPINESS...
...DOESN'T HAPPEN WITHOUT BEING TRUE TO YOURSELF.
WHICH MEANS YOU HAVE TO BE NIGHTWING.
NOT SURE I AGREE. ALL I KNOW IS THAT FOR RIGHT NOW...
...THIS IS HOW I'M GOING TO ROLL.
"LOOK, I KNOW BARBARA WILL WANT WHAT'S BEST FOR ME--"
"BUT YOU'RE CONCERNED IT MIGHT NOT BE WHAT YOU WANT."

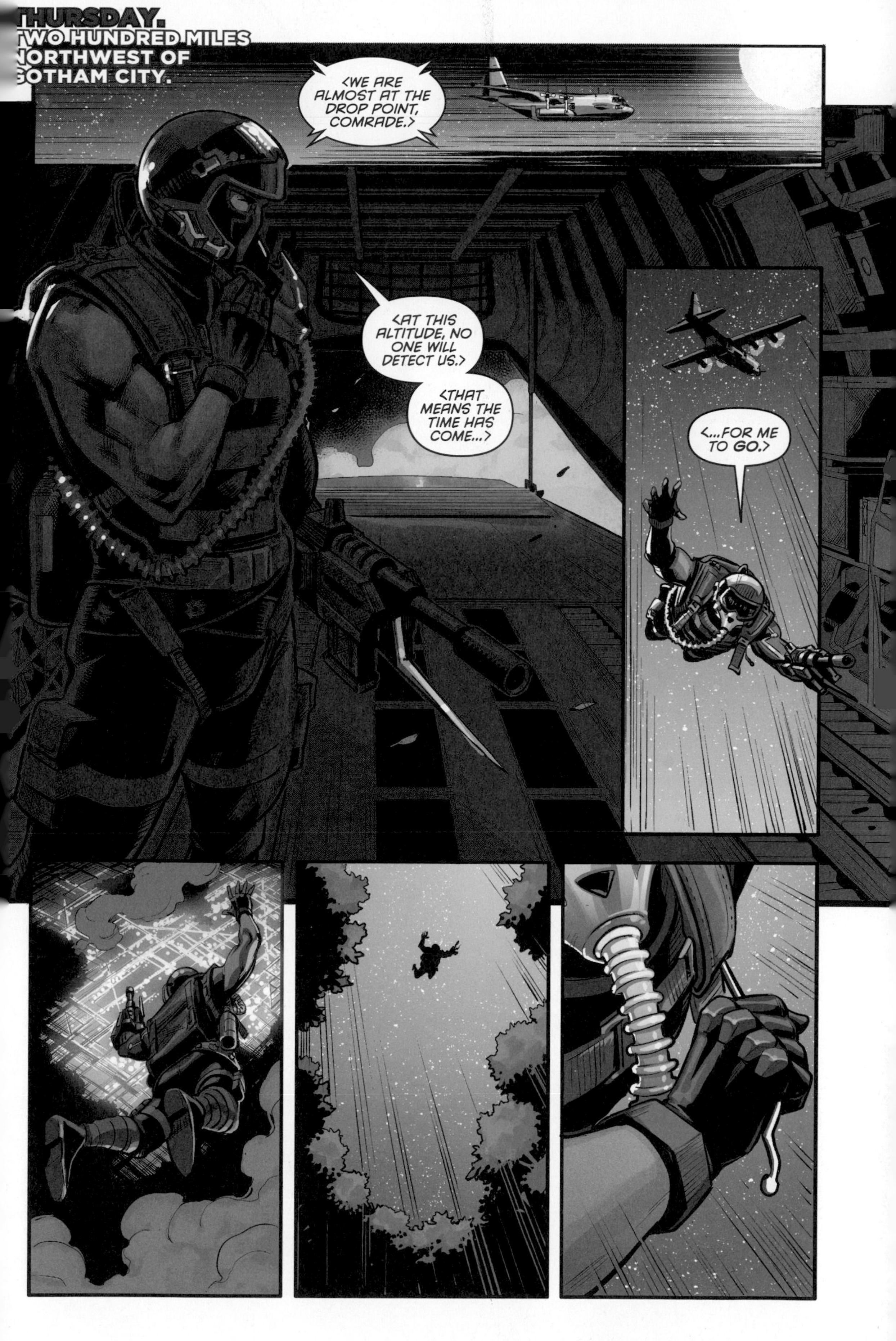
THURSDAY.
TWO HUNDRED MILES NORTHWEST OF GOTHAM CITY.
<WE ARE ALMOST AT THE DROP POINT, COMRADE.>
<AT THIS ALTITUDE, NO ONE WILL DETECT US.>
<THAT MEANS THE TIME HAS COME...>
<...FOR ME TO GO.>

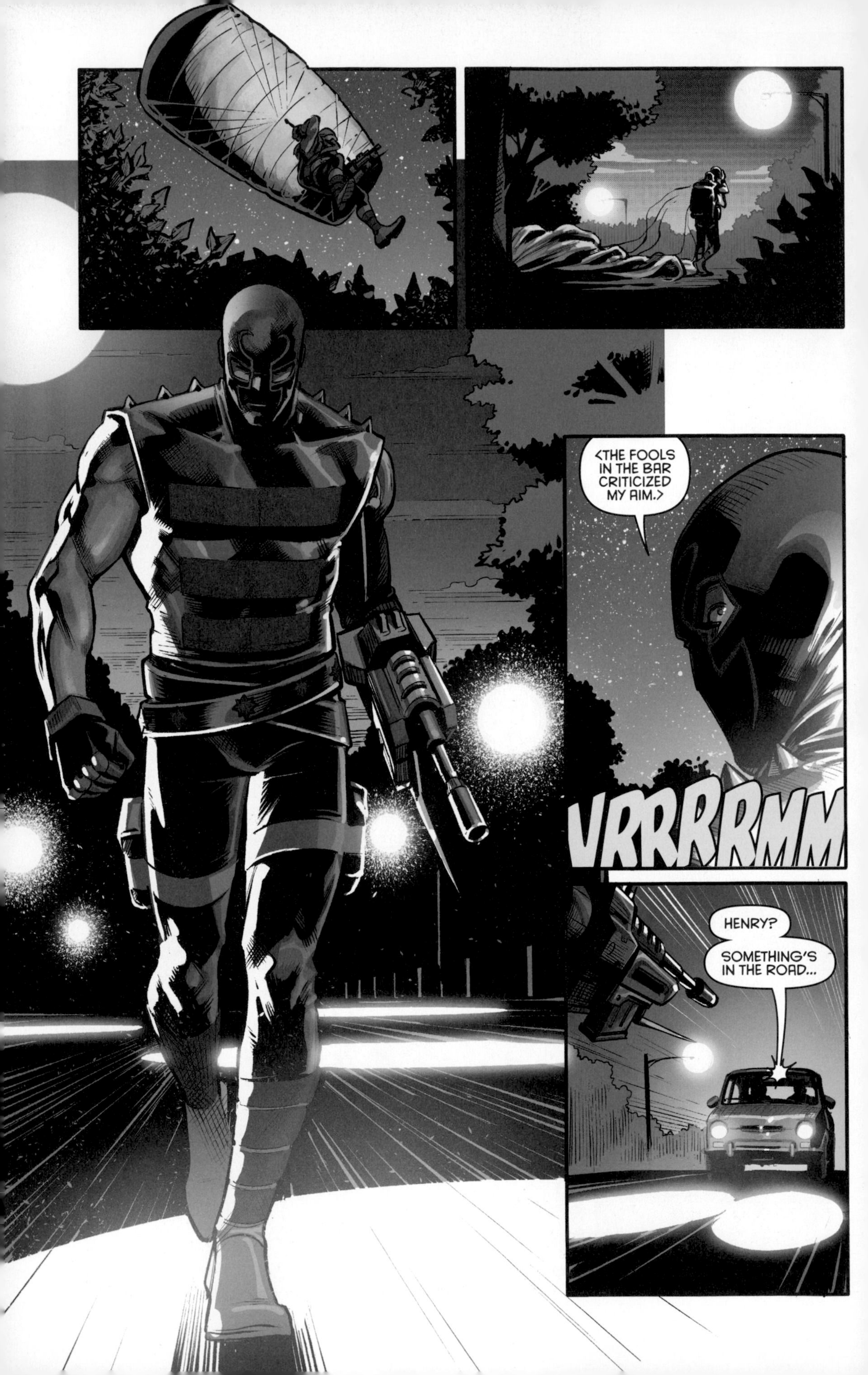
<THE FOOLS IN THE BAR CRITICIZED MY AIM.>
VRRRRMM
HENRY?
SOMETHING'S IN THE ROAD...

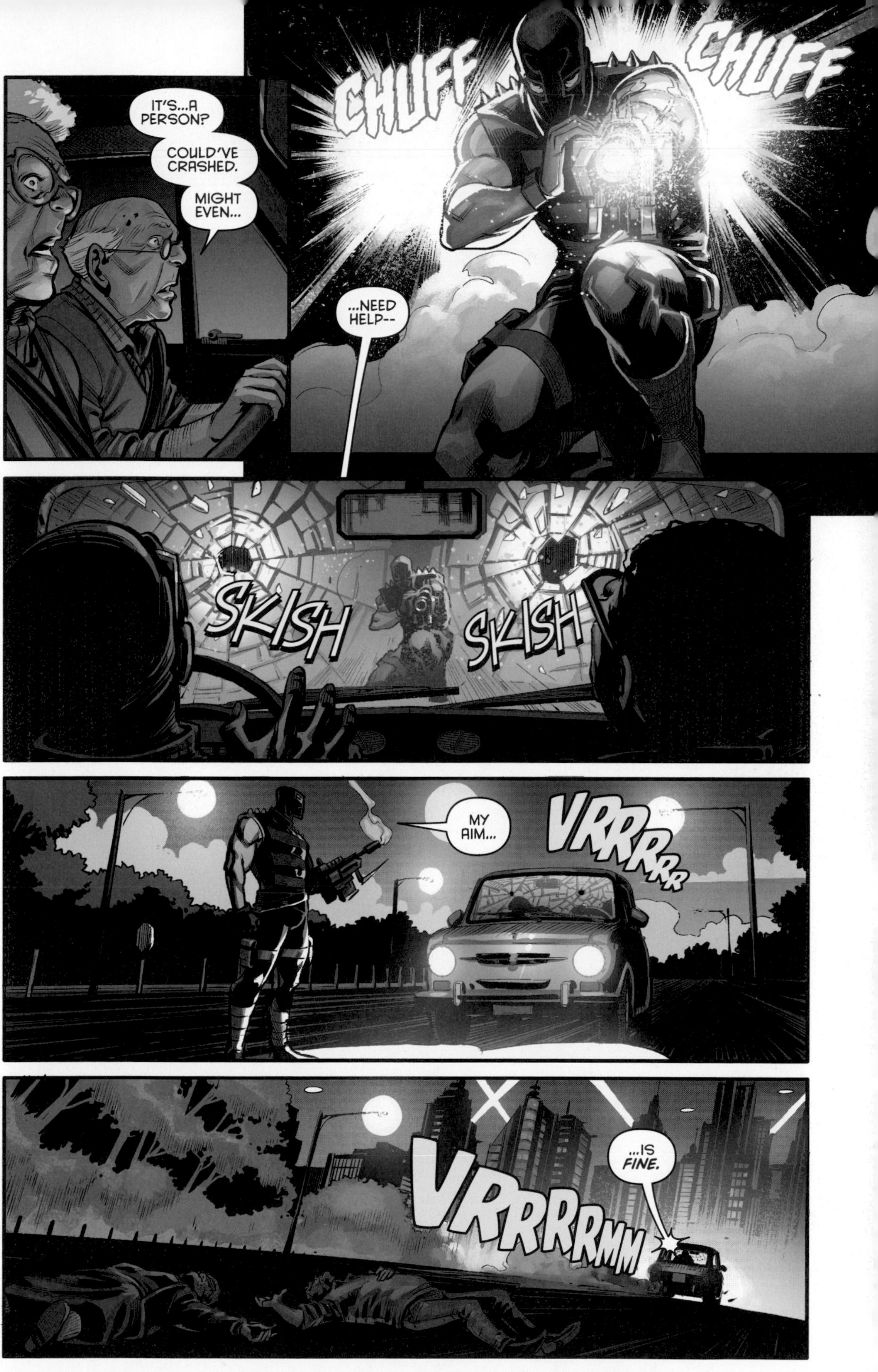
CHUFF
CHUFF
IT'S...A PERSON?
COULD'VE CRASHED.
MIGHT EVEN...
...NEED HELP--
SKISH
SKISH
MY AIM...
VRRRRRR
VRRRRRMM
...IS FINE.

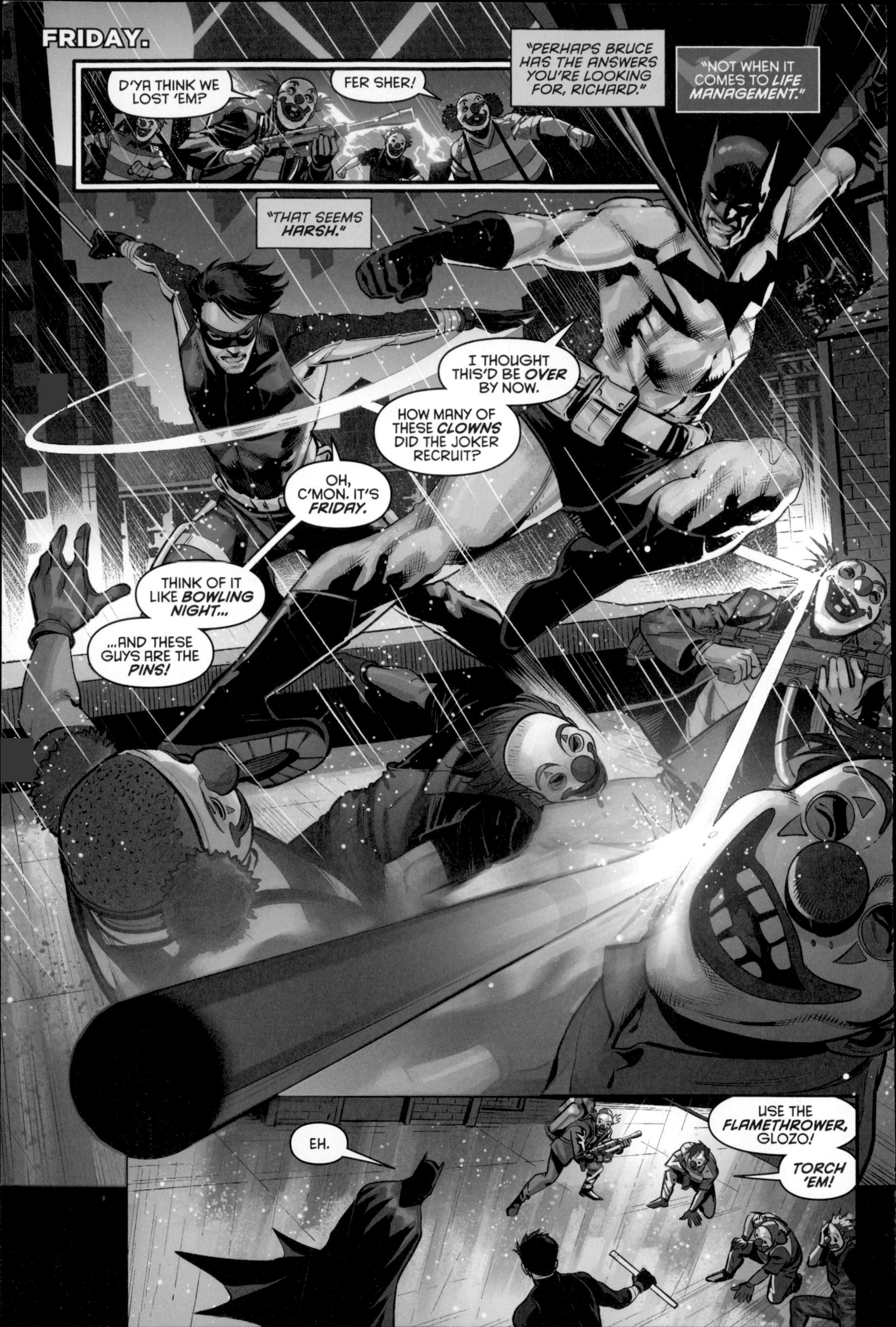
FRIDAY.
D'YA THINK WE LOST 'EM?
FER SHER!
"PERHAPS BRUCE HAS THE ANSWERS YOU'RE LOOKING FOR, RICHARD."
"NOT WHEN IT COMES TO LIFE MANAGEMENT."
"THAT SEEMS HARSH."
I THOUGHT THIS'D BE OVER BY NOW.
HOW MANY OF THESE CLOWNS DID THE JOKER RECRUIT?
OH, C'MON. IT'S FRIDAY.
THINK OF IT LIKE BOWLING NIGHT...
...AND THESE GUYS ARE THE PINS!
EH.
USE THE FLAMETHROWER, GLOZO!
TORCH 'EM!

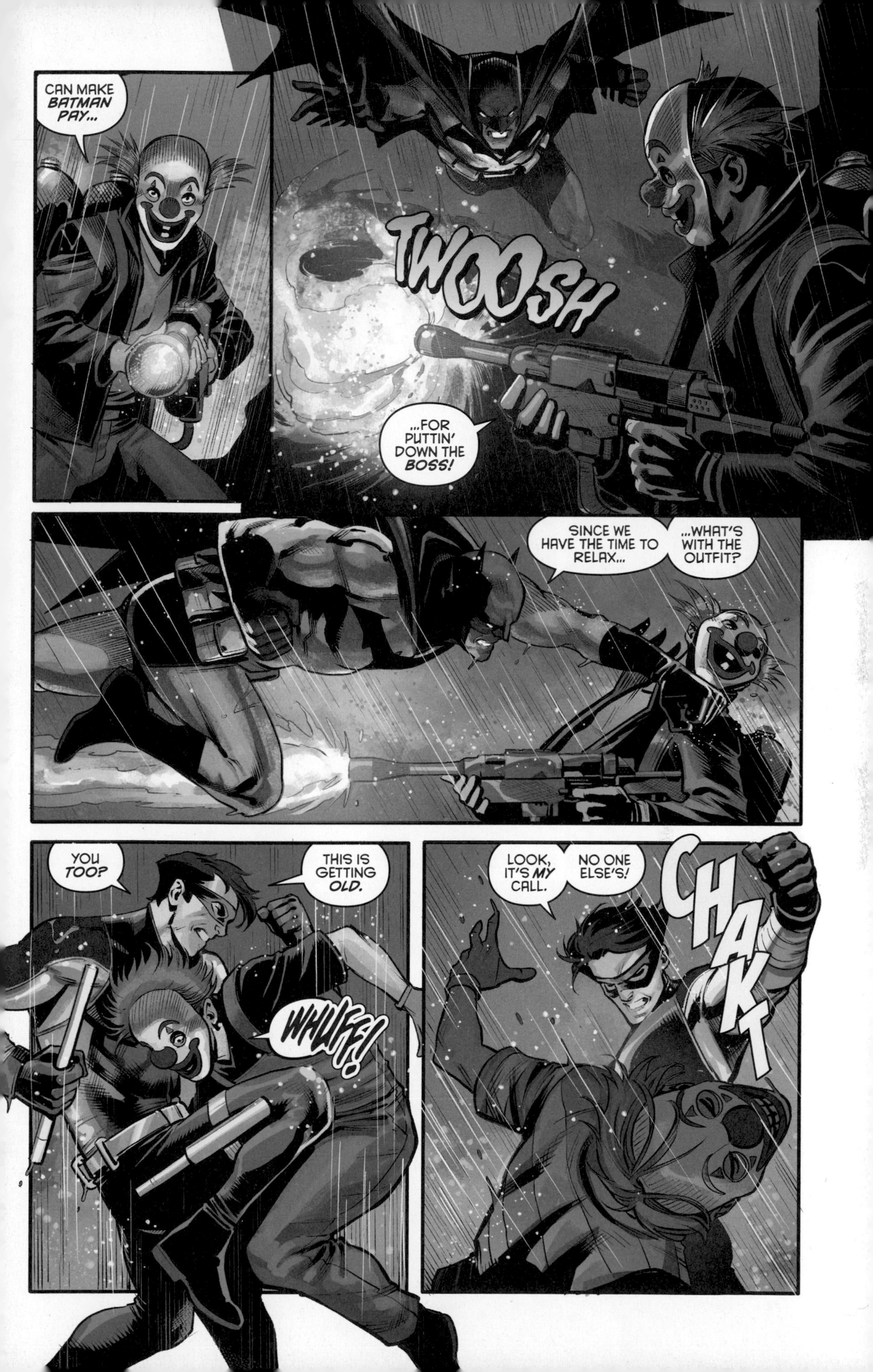
CAN MAKE BATMAN PAY...
TWOOSH
...FOR PUTTIN' DOWN THE BOSS!
SINCE WE HAVE THE TIME TO RELAX...
...WHAT'S WITH THE OUTFIT?
YOU TOO?
THIS IS GETTING OLD.
WHUFF!
LOOK, IT'S MY CALL.
NO ONE ELSE'S!
CHAKT

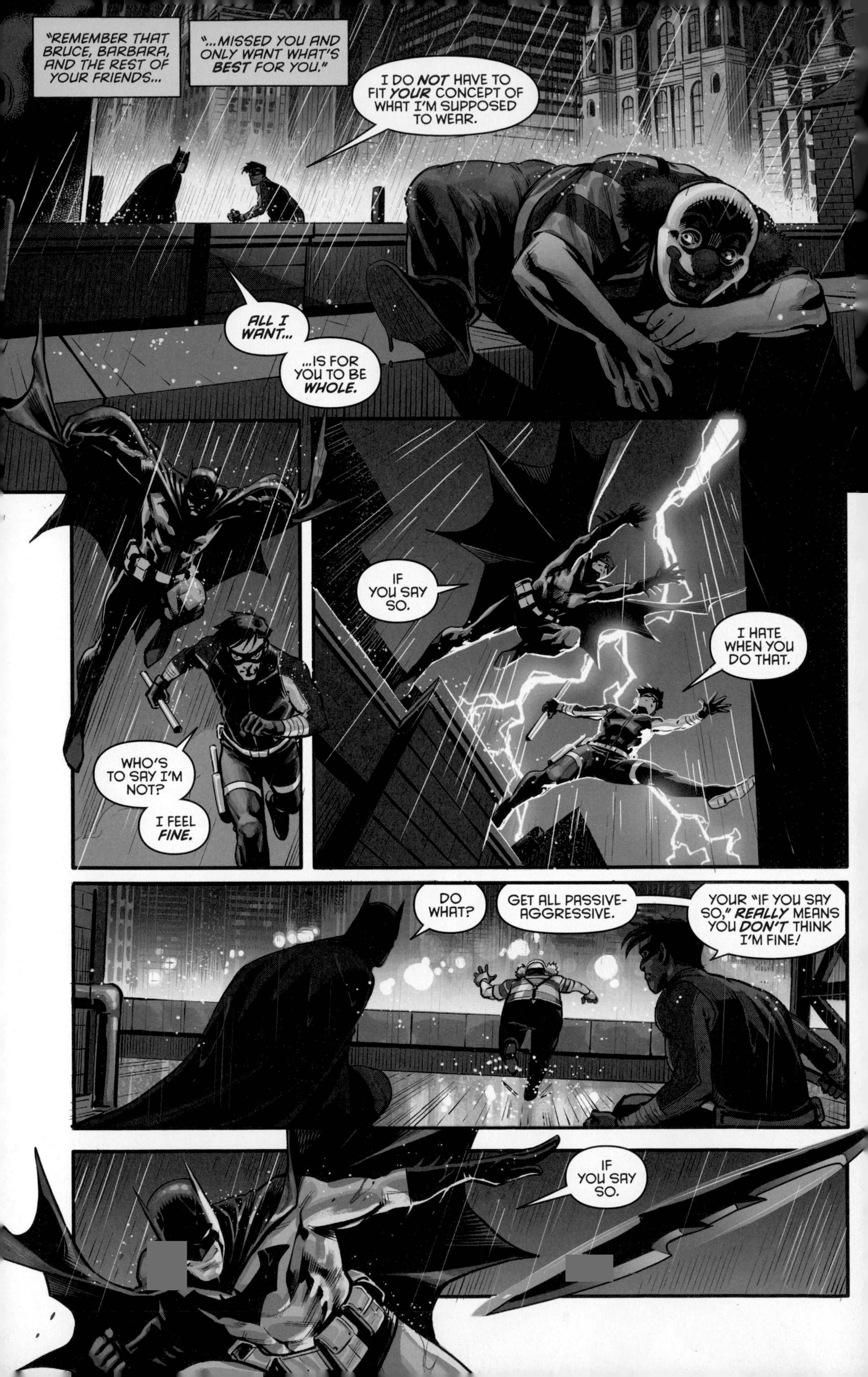
"REMEMBER THAT BRUCE, BARBARA, AND THE REST OF YOUR FRIENDS...
"...MISSED YOU AND ONLY WANT WHAT'S BEST FOR YOU."
I DO NOT HAVE TO FIT YOUR CONCEPT OF WHAT I'M SUPPOSED TO WEAR.
ALL I WANT...
...IS FOR YOU TO BE WHOLE.
WHO'S TO SAY I'M NOT?
I FEEL FINE.
IF YOU SAY SO.
I HATE WHEN YOU DO THAT.
DO WHAT?
GET ALL PASSIVE-AGGRESSIVE.
YOUR "IF YOU SAY SO," REALLY MEANS YOU DON'T THINK I'M FINE!
IF YOU SAY SO.

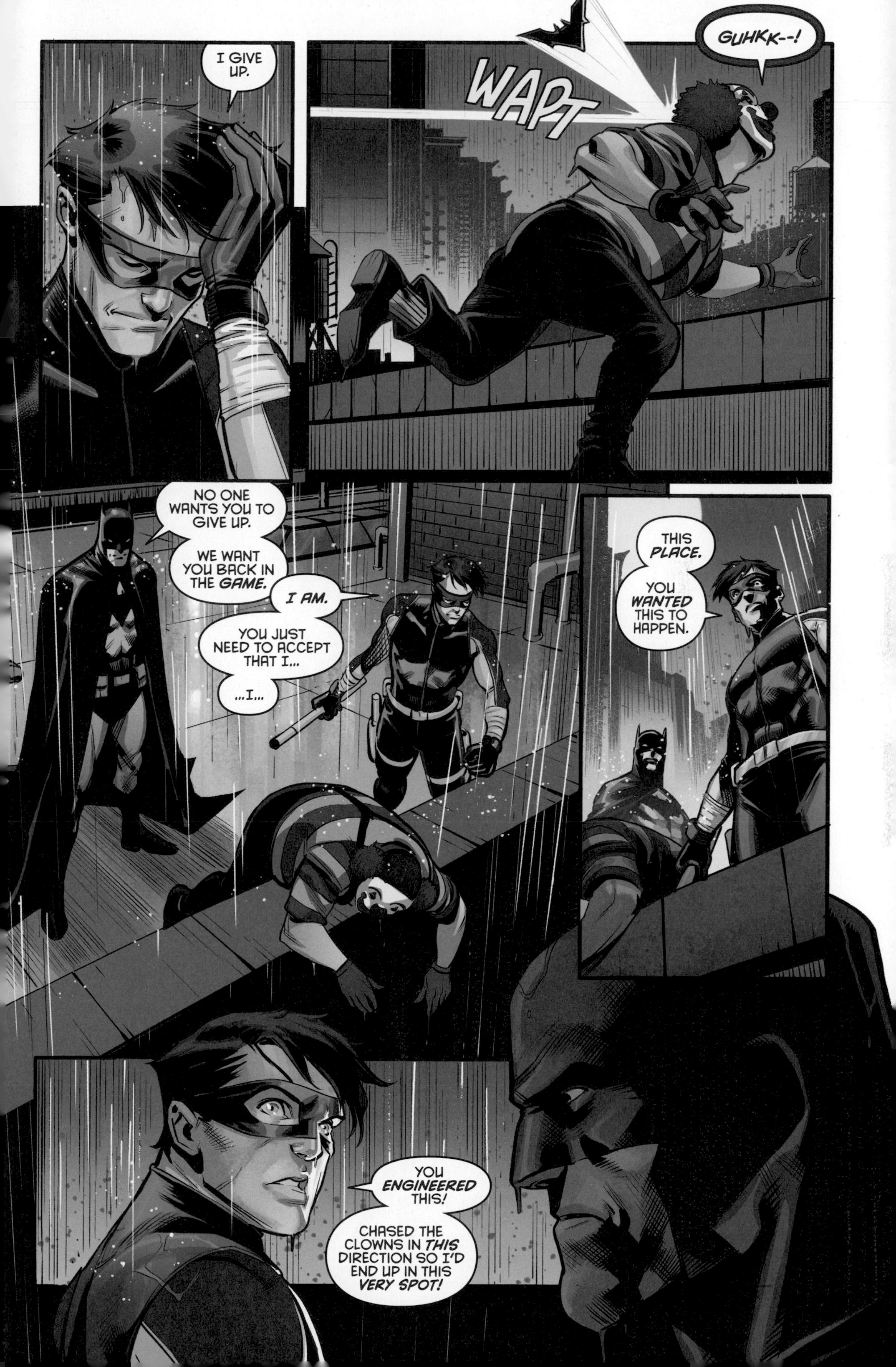
I GIVE UP.
WAPT
GUHKK--!
NO ONE WANTS YOU TO GIVE UP.
WE WANT YOU BACK IN THE *GAME.*
I AM.
YOU JUST NEED TO ACCEPT THAT I...
...I...
THIS *PLACE.*
YOU *WANTED* THIS TO HAPPEN.
YOU *ENGINEERED* THIS!
CHASED THE CLOWNS IN *THIS* DIRECTION SO I'D END UP IN THIS *VERY SPOT!*

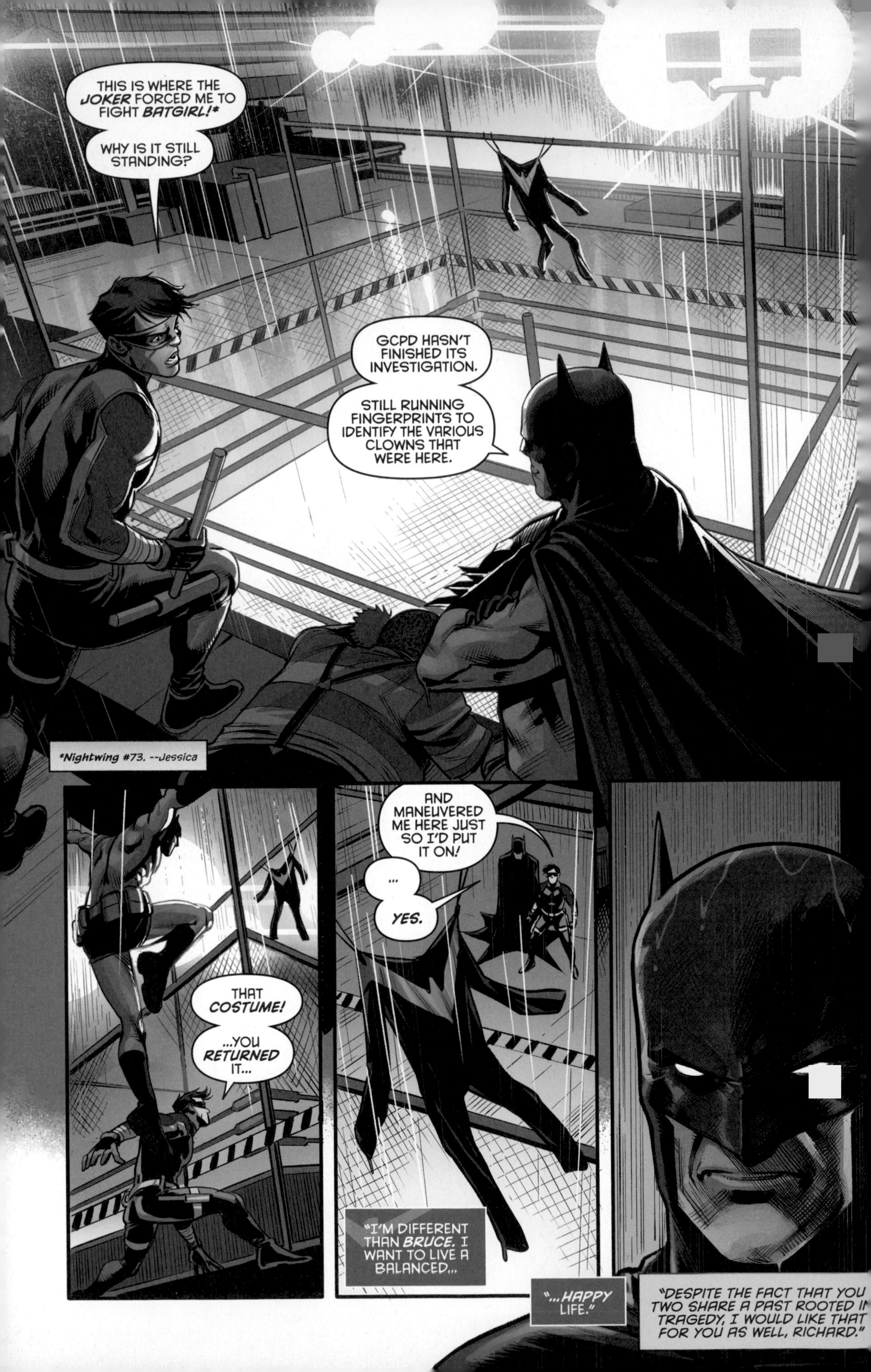
THIS IS WHERE THE JOKER FORCED ME TO FIGHT BATGIRL!*
WHY IS IT STILL STANDING?
GCPD HASN'T FINISHED ITS INVESTIGATION.
STILL RUNNING FINGERPRINTS TO IDENTIFY THE VARIOUS CLOWNS THAT WERE HERE.
*Nightwing #73. --Jessica
THAT COSTUME!
...YOU RETURNED IT...
AND MANEUVERED ME HERE JUST SO I'D PUT IT ON!
...
YES.
"I'M DIFFERENT THAN BRUCE. I WANT TO LIVE A BALANCED...
"...HAPPY LIFE."
"DESPITE THE FACT THAT YOU TWO SHARE A PAST ROOTED IN TRAGEDY, I WOULD LIKE THAT FOR YOU AS WELL, RICHARD."

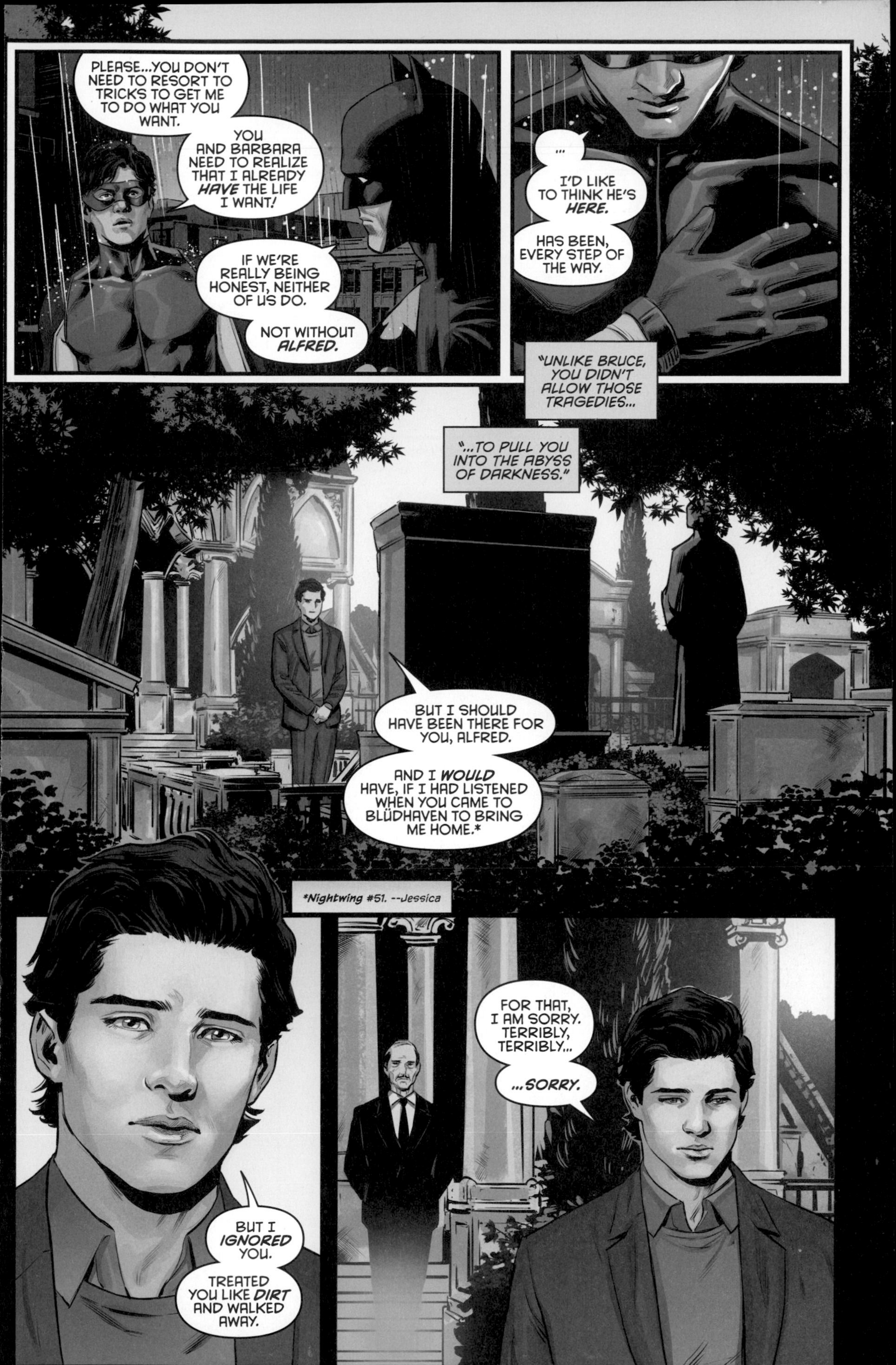
PLEASE...YOU DON'T NEED TO RESORT TO TRICKS TO GET ME TO DO WHAT YOU WANT.
YOU AND BARBARA NEED TO REALIZE THAT I ALREADY HAVE THE LIFE I WANT!
IF WE'RE REALLY BEING HONEST, NEITHER OF US DO.
NOT WITHOUT ALFRED.
...
I'D LIKE TO THINK HE'S HERE.
HAS BEEN, EVERY STEP OF THE WAY.
"UNLIKE BRUCE, YOU DIDN'T ALLOW THOSE TRAGEDIES...
"...TO PULL YOU INTO THE ABYSS OF DARKNESS."
BUT I SHOULD HAVE BEEN THERE FOR YOU, ALFRED.
AND I WOULD HAVE, IF I HAD LISTENED WHEN YOU CAME TO BLÜDHAVEN TO BRING ME HOME.*
*Nightwing #51. --Jessica
BUT I IGNORED YOU.
TREATED YOU LIKE DIRT AND WALKED AWAY.
FOR THAT, I AM SORRY. TERRIBLY, TERRIBLY...
...SORRY.

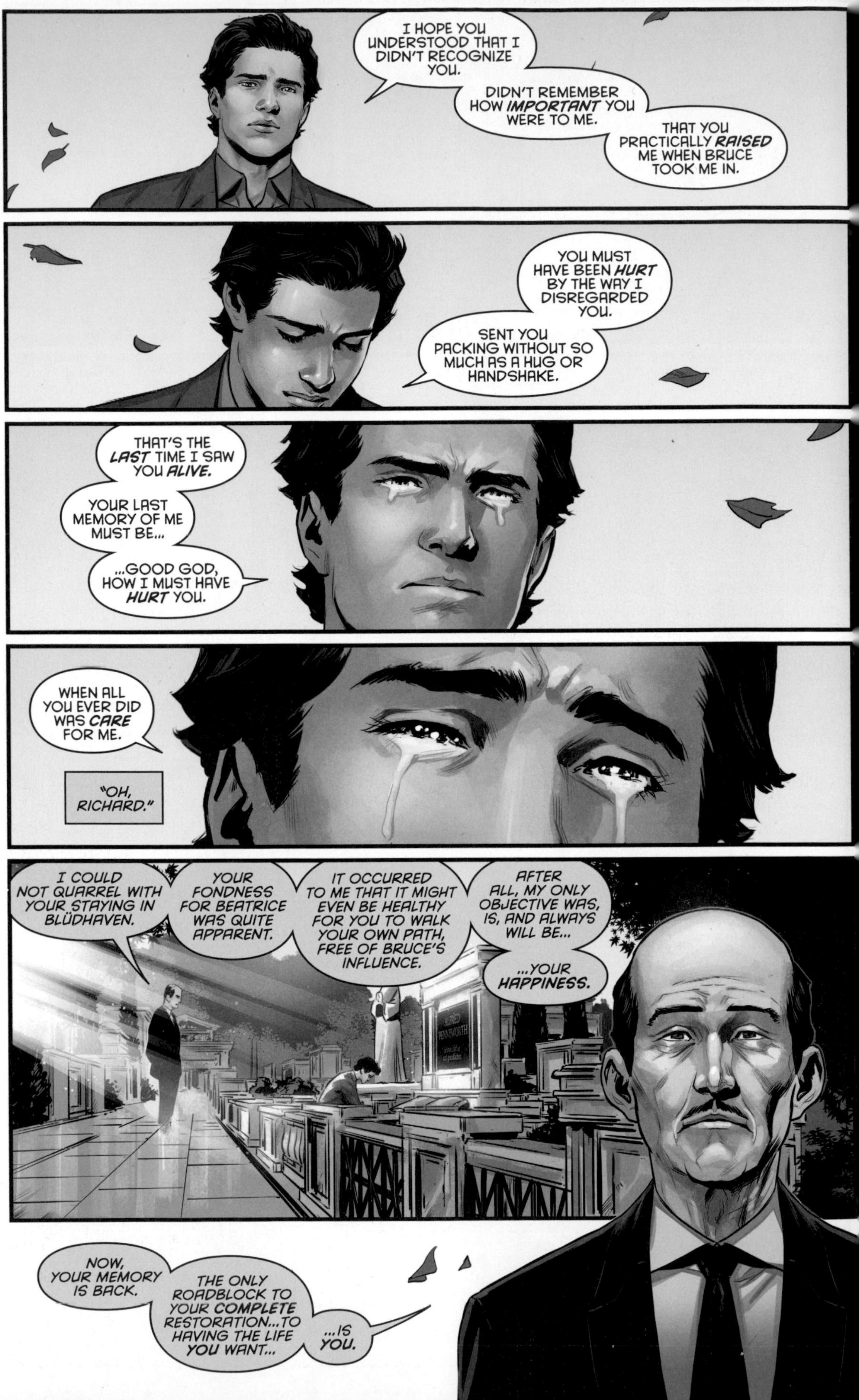
I HOPE YOU UNDERSTOOD THAT I DIDN'T RECOGNIZE YOU.
DIDN'T REMEMBER HOW IMPORTANT YOU WERE TO ME.
THAT YOU PRACTICALLY RAISED ME WHEN BRUCE TOOK ME IN.
YOU MUST HAVE BEEN HURT BY THE WAY I DISREGARDED YOU.
SENT YOU PACKING WITHOUT SO MUCH AS A HUG OR HANDSHAKE.
THAT'S THE LAST TIME I SAW YOU ALIVE.
YOUR LAST MEMORY OF ME MUST BE...
...GOOD GOD, HOW I MUST HAVE HURT YOU.
WHEN ALL YOU EVER DID WAS CARE FOR ME.
"OH, RICHARD."
I COULD NOT QUARREL WITH YOUR STAYING IN BLÜDHAVEN.
YOUR FONDNESS FOR BEATRICE WAS QUITE APPARENT.
IT OCCURRED TO ME THAT IT MIGHT EVEN BE HEALTHY FOR YOU TO WALK YOUR OWN PATH, FREE OF BRUCE'S INFLUENCE.
AFTER ALL, MY ONLY OBJECTIVE WAS, IS, AND ALWAYS WILL BE...
...YOUR HAPPINESS.
ALFRED PENNYWORTH
NOW, YOUR MEMORY IS BACK.
THE ONLY ROADBLOCK TO YOUR COMPLETE RESTORATION...TO HAVING THE LIFE YOU WANT...
...IS YOU.

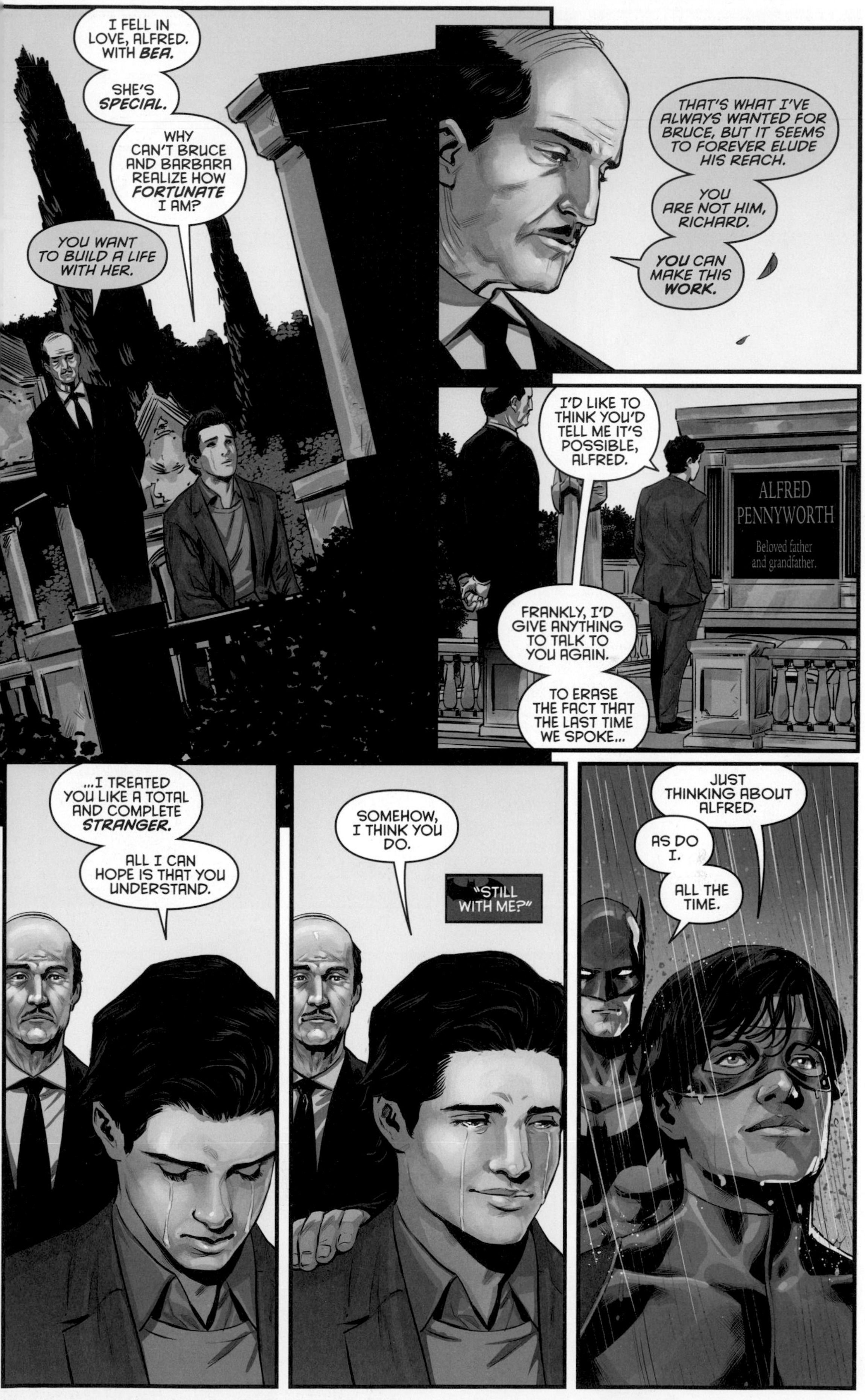
I FELL IN LOVE, ALFRED. WITH BEA.
SHE'S SPECIAL.
WHY CAN'T BRUCE AND BARBARA REALIZE HOW FORTUNATE I AM?
YOU WANT TO BUILD A LIFE WITH HER.
THAT'S WHAT I'VE ALWAYS WANTED FOR BRUCE, BUT IT SEEMS TO FOREVER ELUDE HIS REACH.
YOU ARE NOT HIM, RICHARD.
YOU CAN MAKE THIS WORK.
I'D LIKE TO THINK YOU'D TELL ME IT'S POSSIBLE, ALFRED.
ALFRED PENNYWORTH
Beloved father and grandfather.
FRANKLY, I'D GIVE ANYTHING TO TALK TO YOU AGAIN.
TO ERASE THE FACT THAT THE LAST TIME WE SPOKE...
...I TREATED YOU LIKE A TOTAL AND COMPLETE STRANGER.
ALL I CAN HOPE IS THAT YOU UNDERSTAND.
SOMEHOW, I THINK YOU DO.
"STILL WITH ME?"
JUST THINKING ABOUT ALFRED.
AS DO I.
ALL THE TIME.

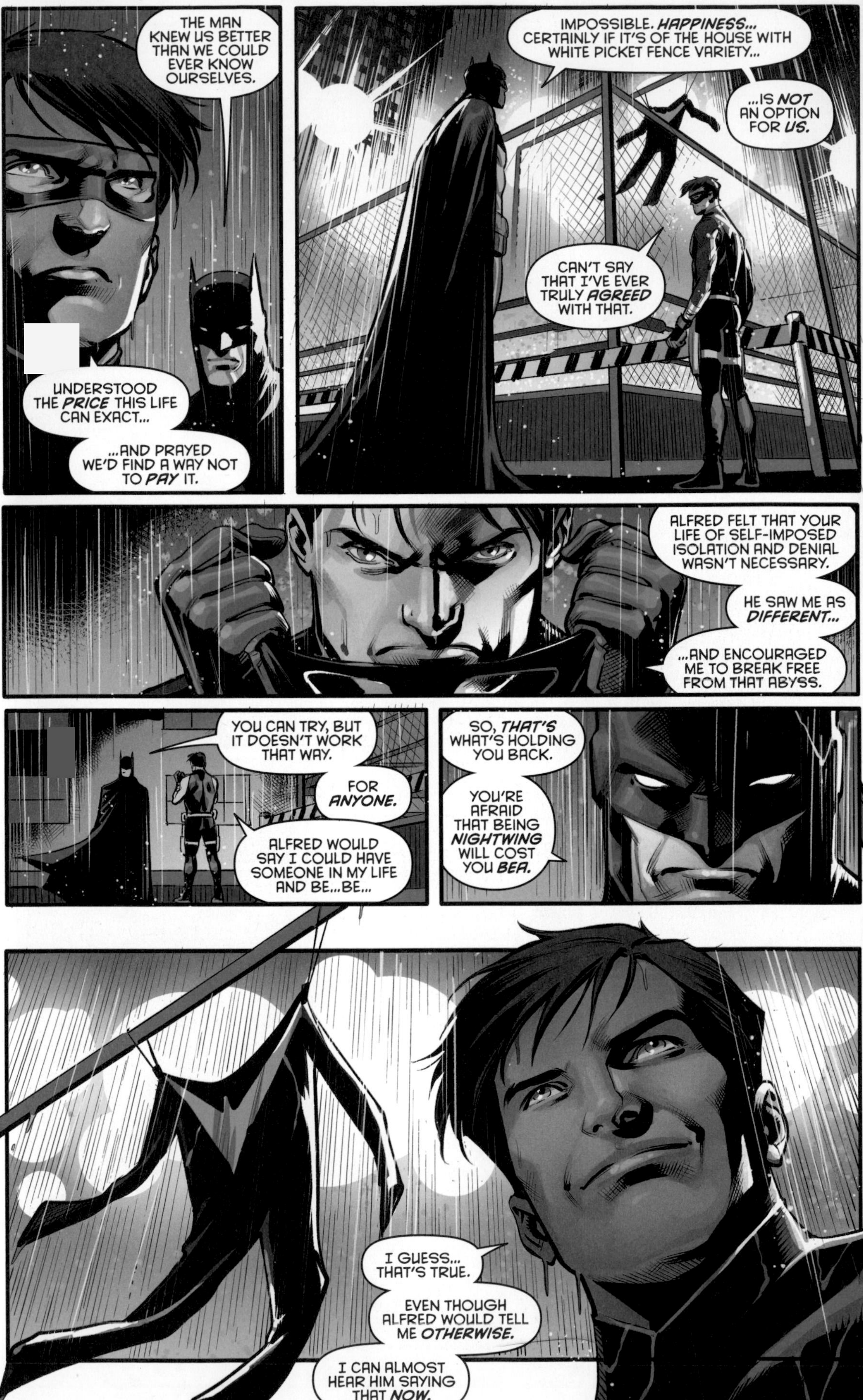
THE MAN KNEW US BETTER THAN WE COULD EVER KNOW OURSELVES.
UNDERSTOOD THE PRICE THIS LIFE CAN EXACT...
...AND PRAYED WE'D FIND A WAY NOT TO PAY IT.
IMPOSSIBLE. HAPPINESS... CERTAINLY IF IT'S OF THE HOUSE WITH WHITE PICKET FENCE VARIETY...
...IS NOT AN OPTION FOR US.
CAN'T SAY THAT I'VE EVER TRULY AGREED WITH THAT.
ALFRED FELT THAT YOUR LIFE OF SELF-IMPOSED ISOLATION AND DENIAL WASN'T NECESSARY.
HE SAW ME AS DIFFERENT...
...AND ENCOURAGED ME TO BREAK FREE FROM THAT ABYSS.
YOU CAN TRY, BUT IT DOESN'T WORK THAT WAY.
FOR ANYONE.
ALFRED WOULD SAY I COULD HAVE SOMEONE IN MY LIFE AND BE...BE...
SO, THAT'S WHAT'S HOLDING YOU BACK.
YOU'RE AFRAID THAT BEING NIGHTWING WILL COST YOU BEA.
I GUESS... THAT'S TRUE.
EVEN THOUGH ALFRED WOULD TELL ME OTHERWISE.
I CAN ALMOST HEAR HIM SAYING THAT NOW.

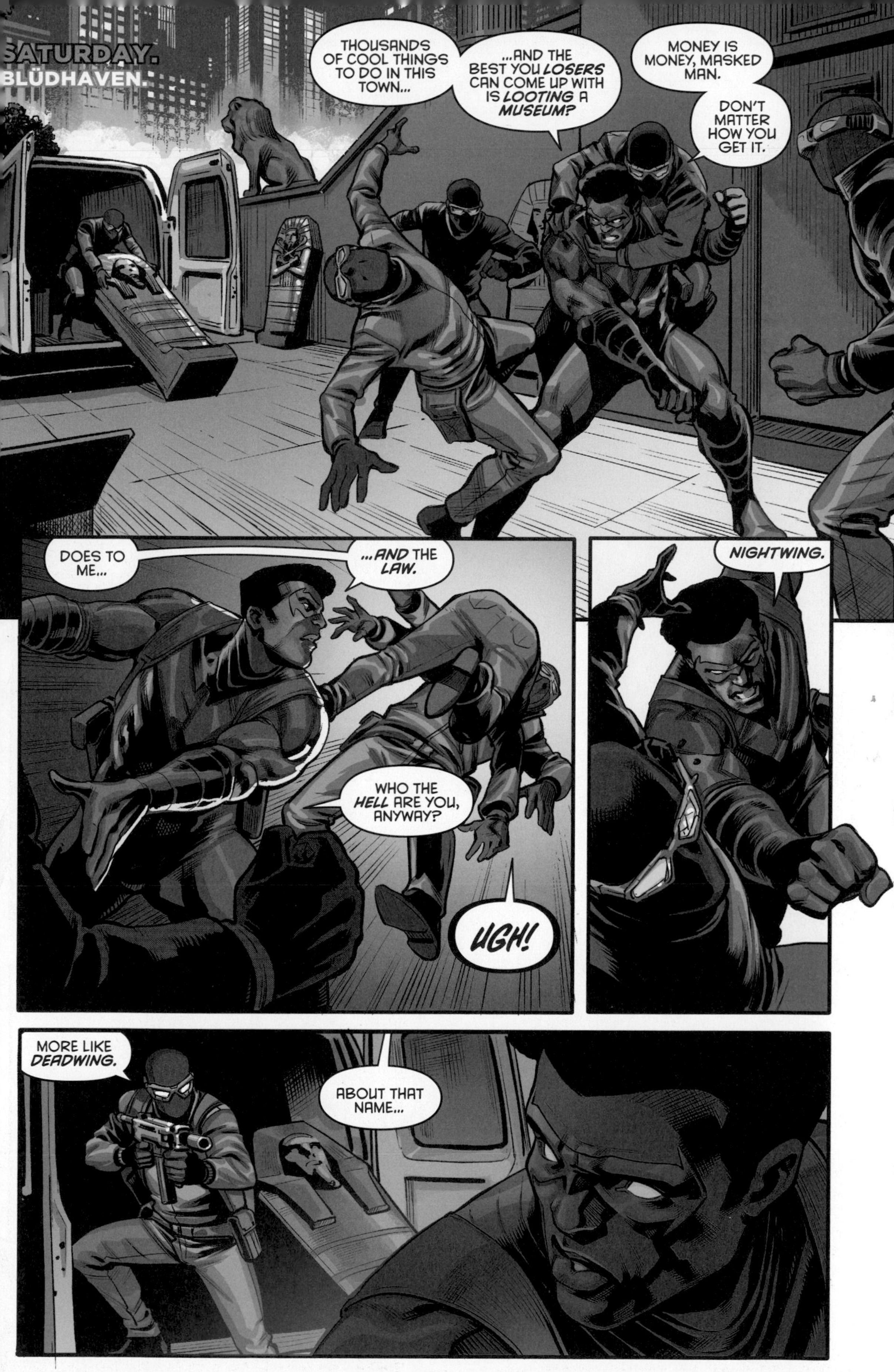
SATURDAY.
BLÜDHAVEN.
THOUSANDS OF COOL THINGS TO DO IN THIS TOWN...
...AND THE BEST YOU LOSERS CAN COME UP WITH IS LOOTING A MUSEUM?
MONEY IS MONEY, MASKED MAN.
DON'T MATTER HOW YOU GET IT.
DOES TO ME...
...AND THE LAW.
WHO THE HELL ARE YOU, ANYWAY?
UGH!
NIGHTWING.
MORE LIKE DEADWING.
ABOUT THAT NAME...

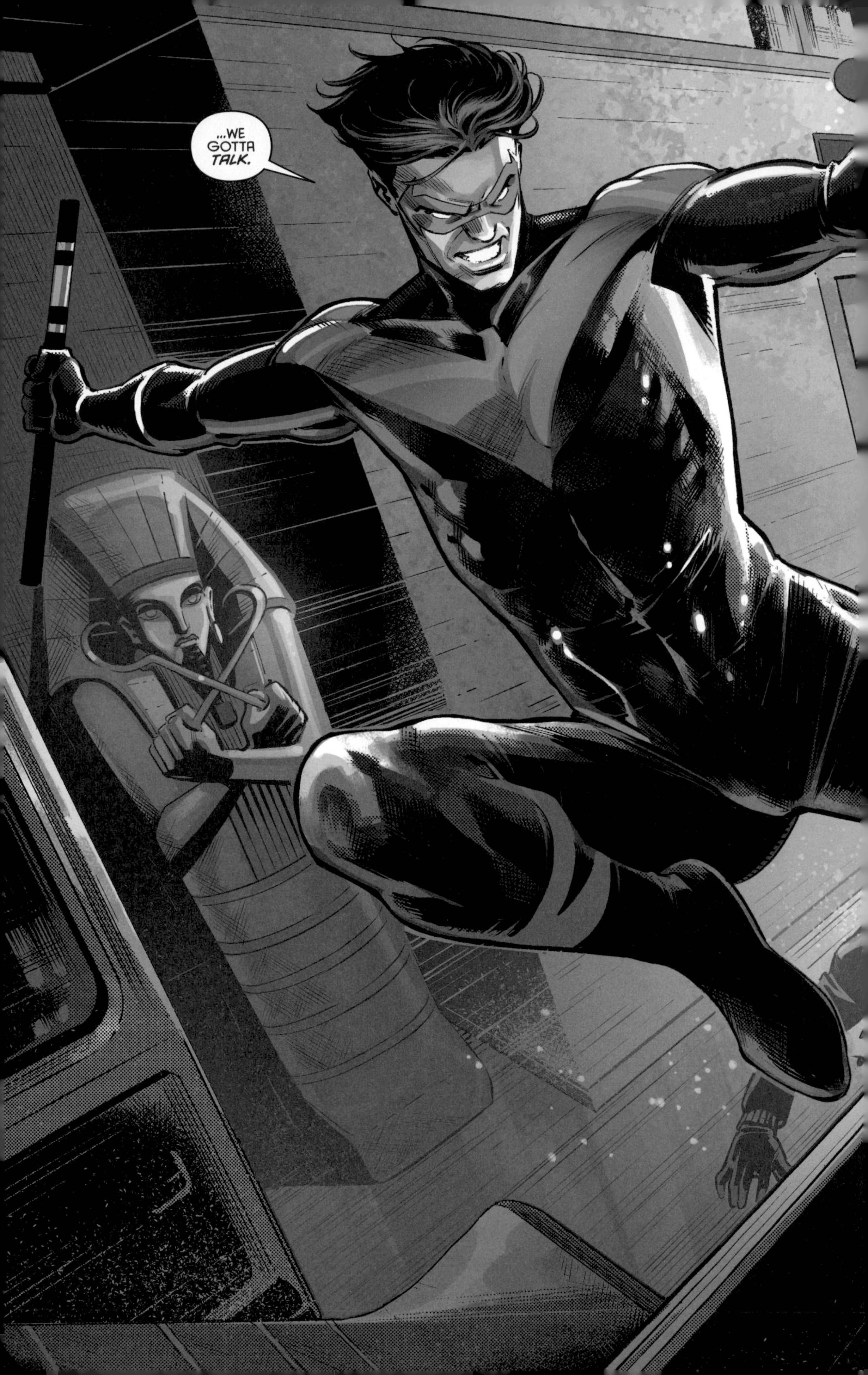
...WE GOTTA *TALK.*

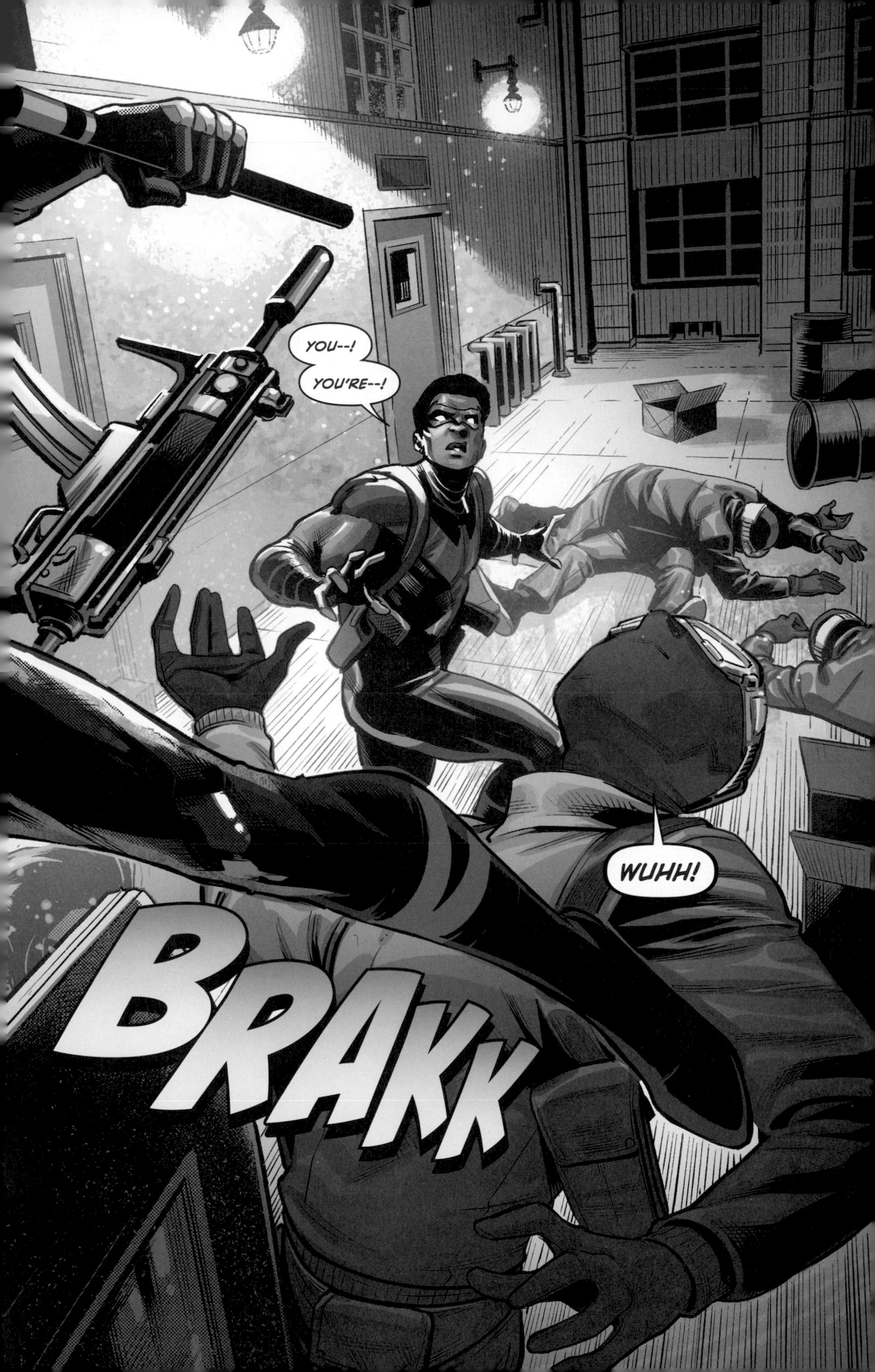
YOU--!
YOU'RE--!
WUHH!
BRAKK

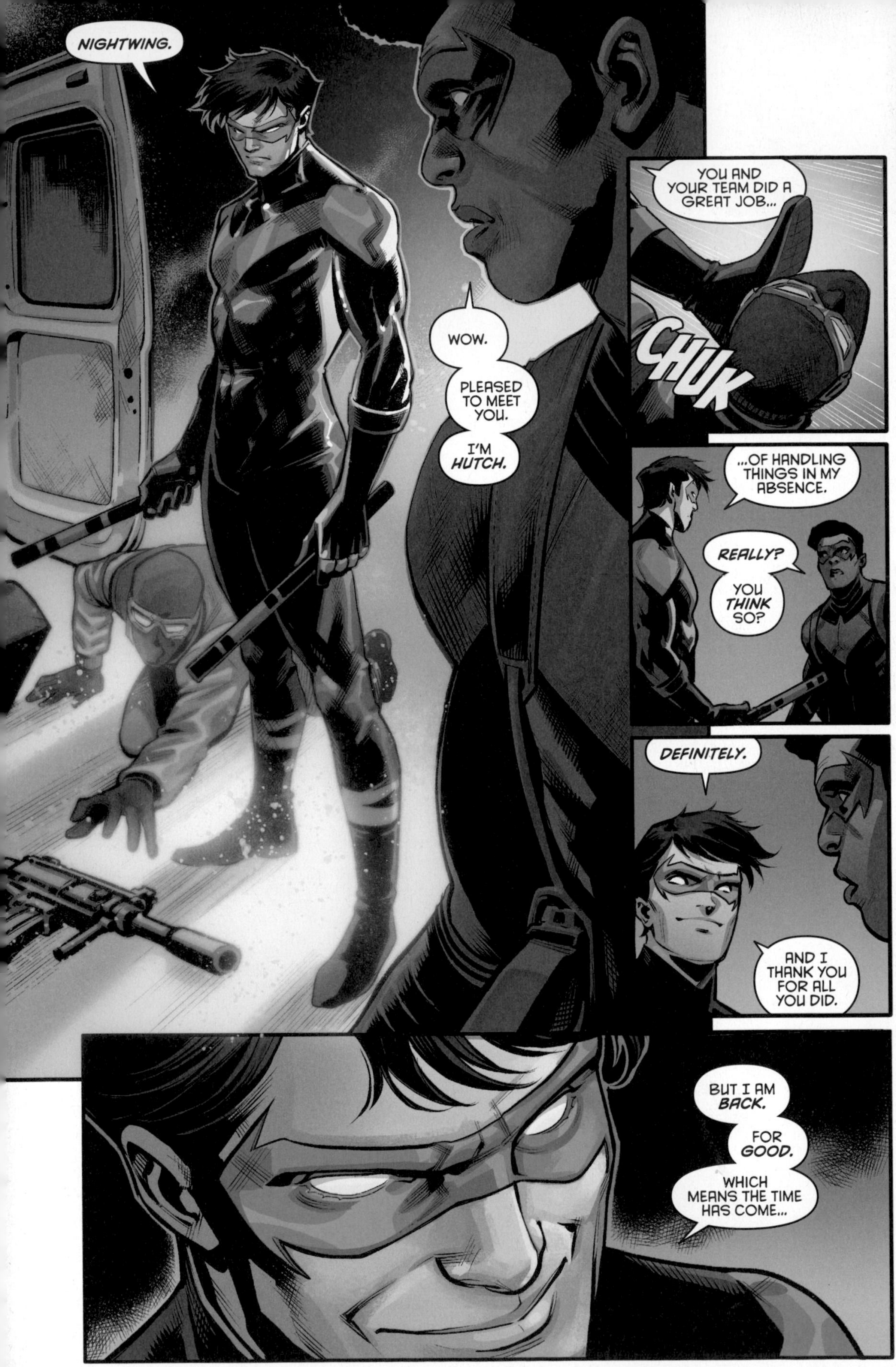
NIGHTWING.
WOW.
PLEASED TO MEET YOU.
I'M HUTCH.
YOU AND YOUR TEAM DID A GREAT JOB...
CHUK
...OF HANDLING THINGS IN MY ABSENCE.
REALLY?
YOU THINK SO?
DEFINITELY.
AND I THANK YOU FOR ALL YOU DID.
BUT I AM BACK.
FOR GOOD.
WHICH MEANS THE TIME HAS COME...

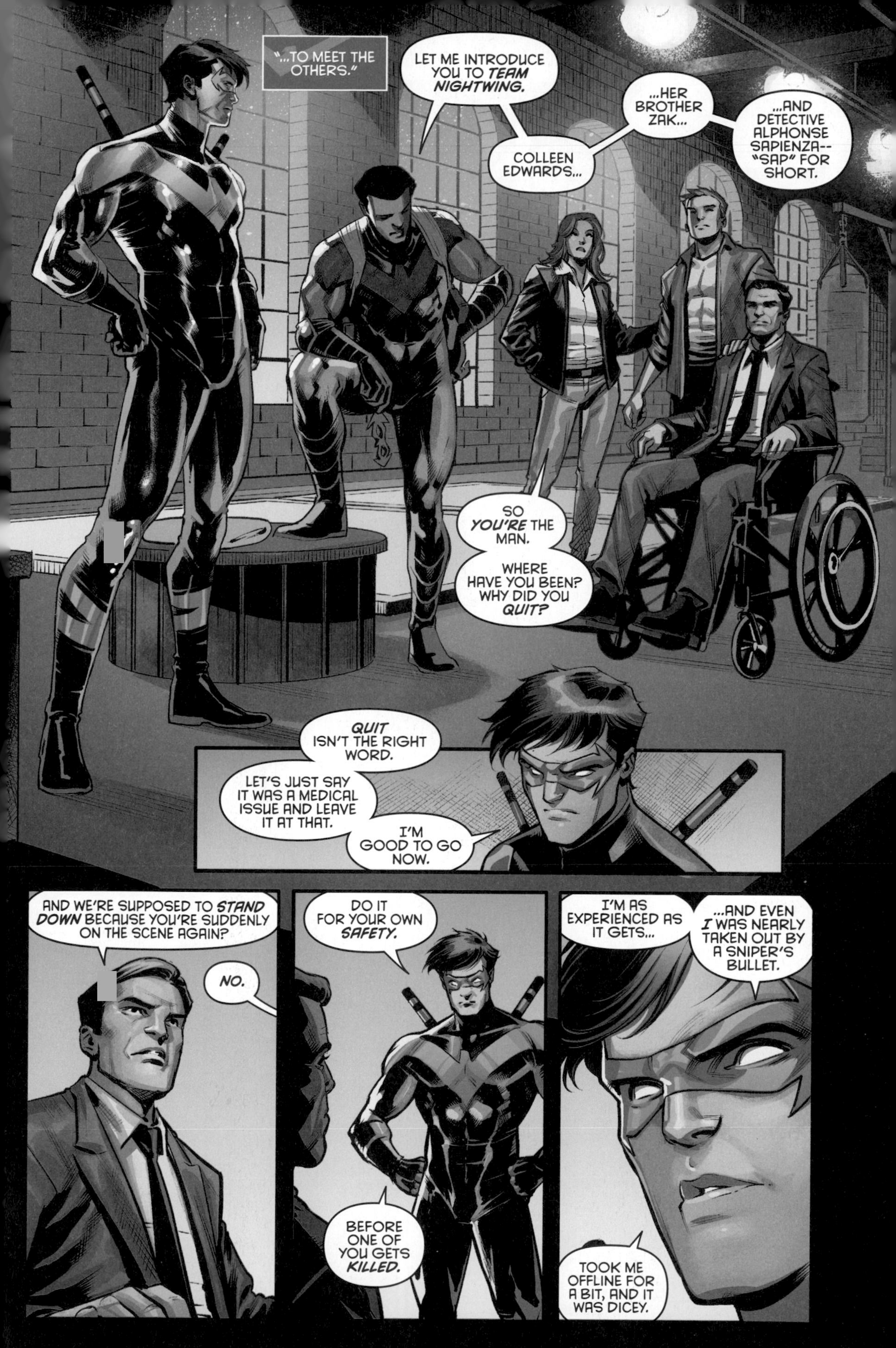
"...TO MEET THE OTHERS."
LET ME INTRODUCE YOU TO *TEAM NIGHTWING.*
COLLEEN EDWARDS...
...HER BROTHER ZAK...
...AND DETECTIVE ALPHONSE SAPIENZA-- "SAP" FOR SHORT.
SO *YOU'RE* THE MAN.
WHERE HAVE YOU BEEN? WHY DID YOU *QUIT?*
QUIT ISN'T THE RIGHT WORD.
LET'S JUST SAY IT WAS A MEDICAL ISSUE AND LEAVE IT AT THAT.
I'M GOOD TO GO NOW.
AND WE'RE SUPPOSED TO *STAND DOWN* BECAUSE YOU'RE SUDDENLY ON THE SCENE AGAIN?
NO.
DO IT FOR YOUR OWN *SAFETY.*
BEFORE ONE OF YOU GETS *KILLED.*
I'M AS EXPERIENCED AS IT GETS...
...AND EVEN *I* WAS NEARLY TAKEN OUT BY A SNIPER'S BULLET.
TOOK ME OFFLINE FOR A BIT, AND IT WAS DICEY.

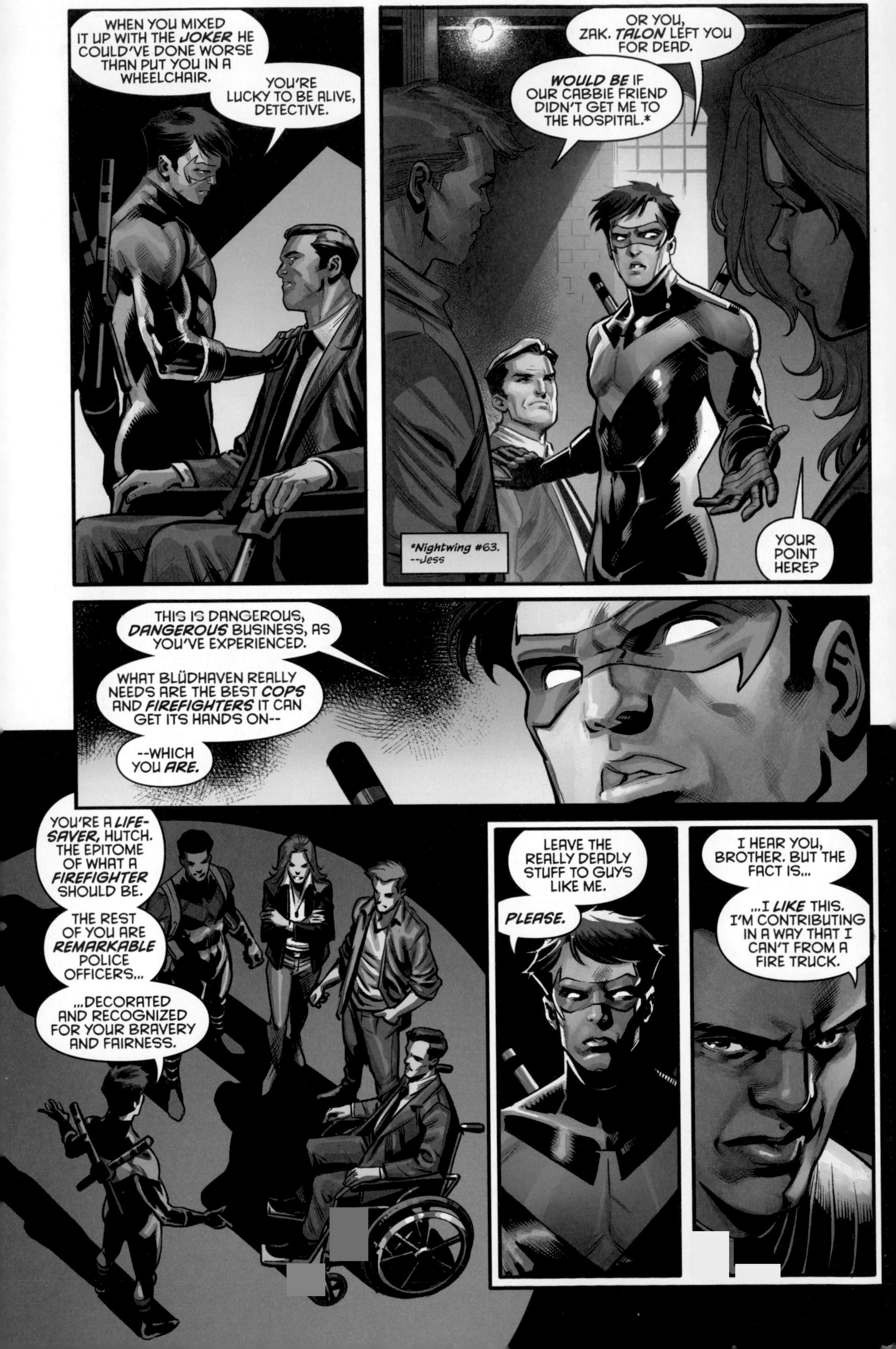
WHEN YOU MIXED IT UP WITH THE JOKER HE COULD'VE DONE WORSE THAN PUT YOU IN A WHEELCHAIR.
YOU'RE LUCKY TO BE ALIVE, DETECTIVE.
OR YOU, ZAK. TALON LEFT YOU FOR DEAD.
WOULD BE IF OUR CABBIE FRIEND DIDN'T GET ME TO THE HOSPITAL.*
*Nightwing #63. --Jess
YOUR POINT HERE?
THIS IS DANGEROUS, DANGEROUS BUSINESS, AS YOU'VE EXPERIENCED.
WHAT BLÜDHAVEN REALLY NEEDS ARE THE BEST COPS AND FIREFIGHTERS IT CAN GET ITS HANDS ON--
--WHICH YOU ARE.
YOU'RE A LIFE-SAVER, HUTCH. THE EPITOME OF WHAT A FIREFIGHTER SHOULD BE.
THE REST OF YOU ARE REMARKABLE POLICE OFFICERS...
...DECORATED AND RECOGNIZED FOR YOUR BRAVERY AND FAIRNESS.
LEAVE THE REALLY DEADLY STUFF TO GUYS LIKE ME.
PLEASE.
I HEAR YOU, BROTHER. BUT THE FACT IS...
...I LIKE THIS. I'M CONTRIBUTING IN A WAY THAT I CAN'T FROM A FIRE TRUCK.

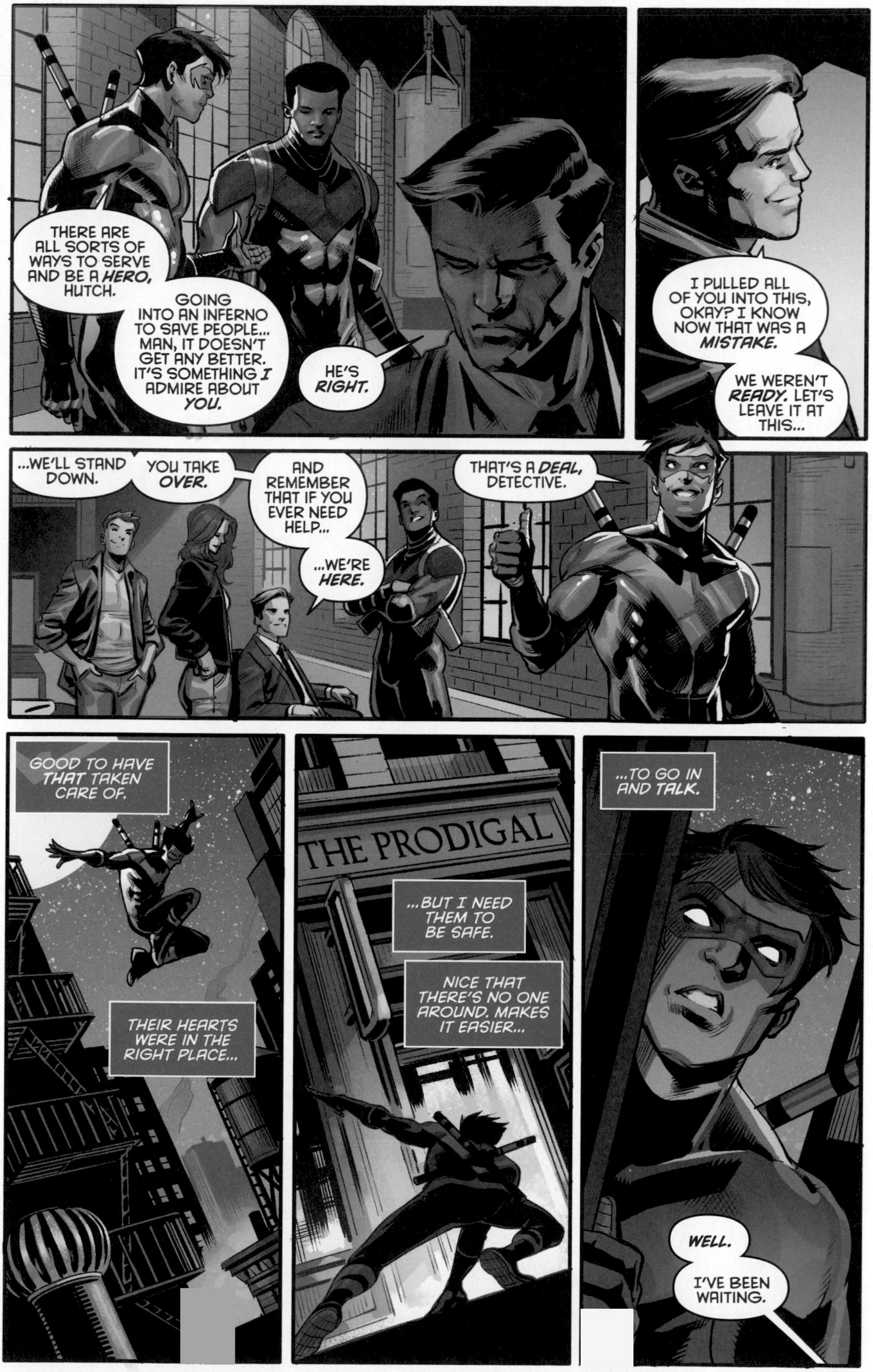

THERE ARE ALL SORTS OF WAYS TO SERVE AND BE A HERO, HUTCH.
GOING INTO AN INFERNO TO SAVE PEOPLE... MAN, IT DOESN'T GET ANY BETTER. IT'S SOMETHING I ADMIRE ABOUT YOU.
HE'S RIGHT.
I PULLED ALL OF YOU INTO THIS, OKAY? I KNOW NOW THAT WAS A MISTAKE.
WE WEREN'T READY. LET'S LEAVE IT AT THIS...
...WE'LL STAND DOWN.
YOU TAKE OVER.
AND REMEMBER THAT IF YOU EVER NEED HELP...
...WE'RE HERE.
THAT'S A DEAL, DETECTIVE.
GOOD TO HAVE THAT TAKEN CARE OF.
THEIR HEARTS WERE IN THE RIGHT PLACE...
THE PRODIGAL
...BUT I NEED THEM TO BE SAFE.
NICE THAT THERE'S NO ONE AROUND. MAKES IT EASIER...
...TO GO IN AND TALK.
WELL.
I'VE BEEN WAITING.

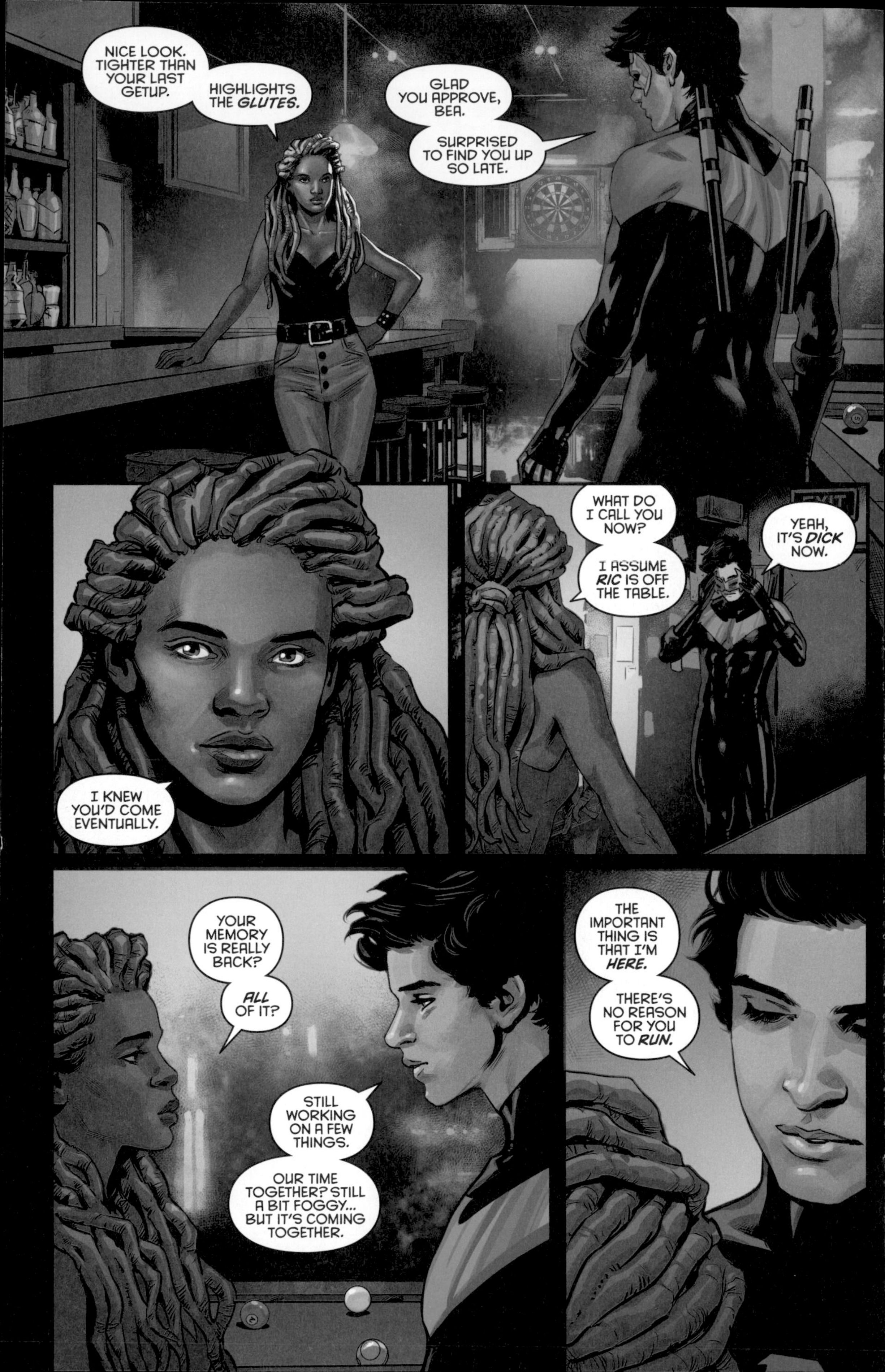
NICE LOOK. TIGHTER THAN YOUR LAST GETUP.
HIGHLIGHTS THE GLUTES.
GLAD YOU APPROVE, BEA.
SURPRISED TO FIND YOU UP SO LATE.
I KNEW YOU'D COME EVENTUALLY.
WHAT DO I CALL YOU NOW?
I ASSUME RIC IS OFF THE TABLE.
YEAH, IT'S DICK NOW.
YOUR MEMORY IS REALLY BACK?
ALL OF IT?
STILL WORKING ON A FEW THINGS.
OUR TIME TOGETHER? STILL A BIT FOGGY... BUT IT'S COMING TOGETHER.
THE IMPORTANT THING IS THAT I'M HERE.
THERE'S NO REASON FOR YOU TO RUN.

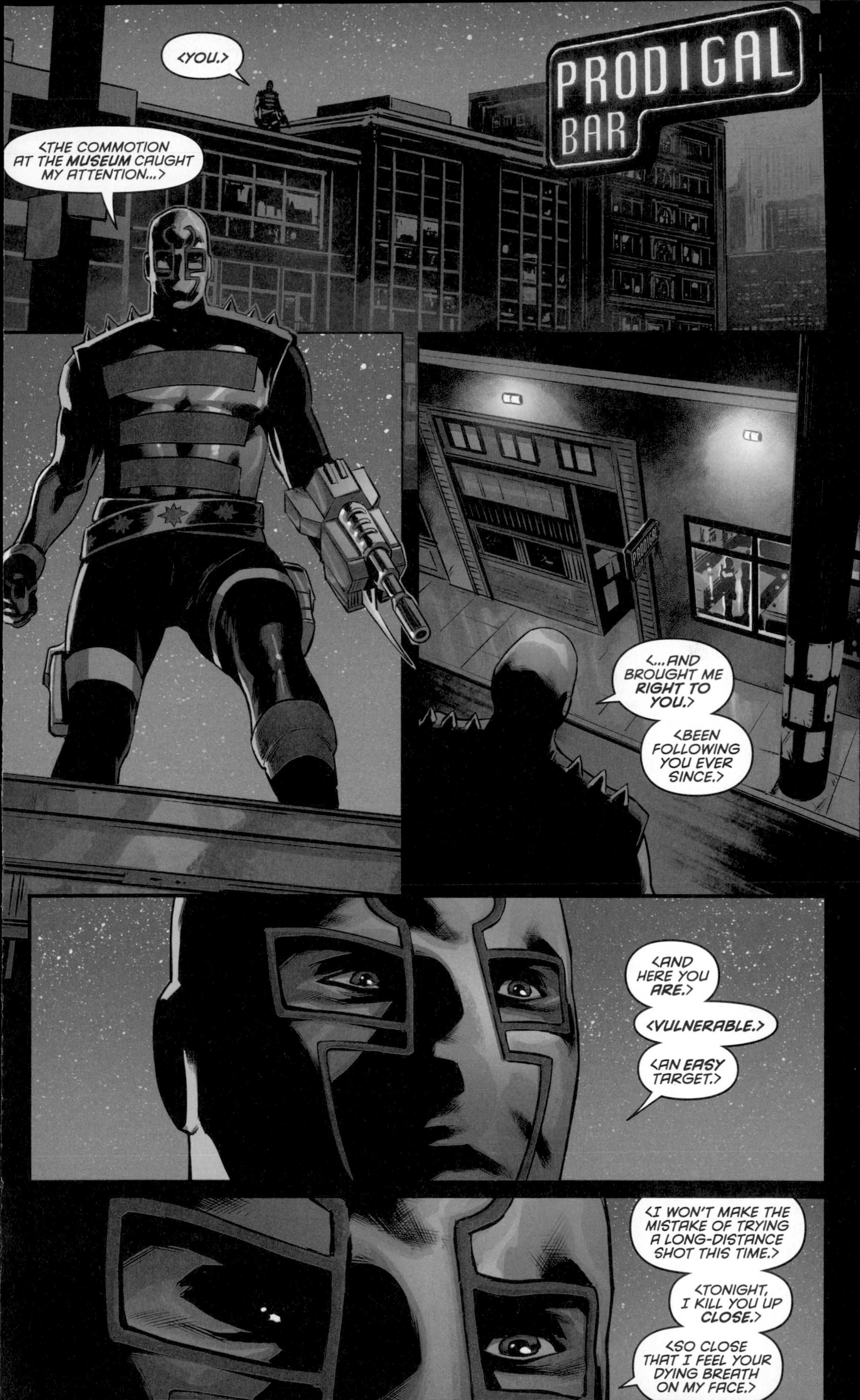
PRODIGAL BAR
<YOU.>
<THE COMMOTION AT THE MUSEUM CAUGHT MY ATTENTION...>
<...AND BROUGHT ME RIGHT TO YOU.>
<BEEN FOLLOWING YOU EVER SINCE.>
<AND HERE YOU ARE.>
<VULNERABLE.>
<AN EASY TARGET.>
<I WON'T MAKE THE MISTAKE OF TRYING A LONG-DISTANCE SHOT THIS TIME.>
<TONIGHT, I KILL YOU UP CLOSE.>
<SO CLOSE THAT I FEEL YOUR DYING BREATH ON MY FACE.>

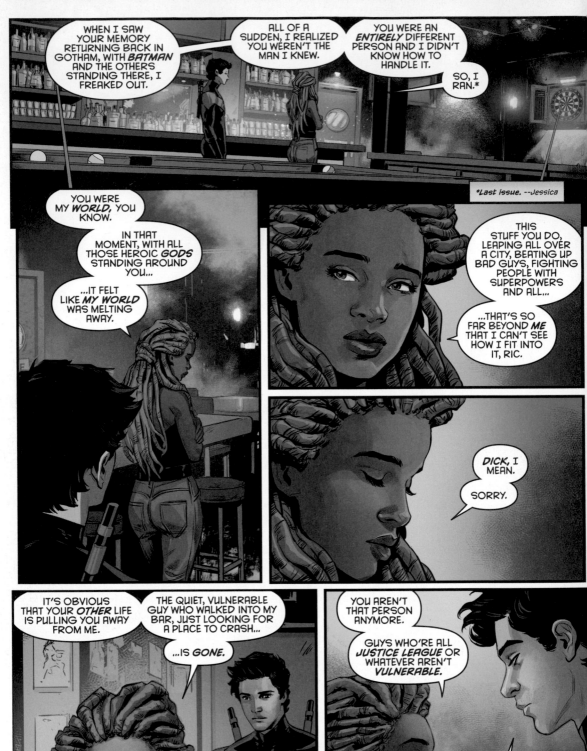

WHEN I SAW YOUR MEMORY RETURNING BACK IN GOTHAM, WITH *BATMAN* AND THE OTHERS STANDING THERE, I FREAKED OUT.

ALL OF A SUDDEN, I REALIZED YOU WEREN'T THE MAN I KNEW.

YOU WERE AN *ENTIRELY* DIFFERENT PERSON AND I DIDN'T KNOW HOW TO HANDLE IT.

SO, I RAN.*

*Last issue. --Jessica

YOU WERE MY *WORLD*, YOU KNOW.

IN THAT MOMENT, WITH ALL THOSE HEROIC *GODS* STANDING AROUND YOU...

...IT FELT LIKE *MY WORLD* WAS MELTING AWAY.

THIS STUFF YOU DO, LEAPING ALL OVER A CITY, BEATING UP BAD GUYS, FIGHTING PEOPLE WITH SUPERPOWERS AND ALL...

...THAT'S SO FAR BEYOND *ME* THAT I CAN'T SEE HOW I FIT INTO IT, RIC.

DICK, I MEAN.

SORRY.

IT'S OBVIOUS THAT YOUR *OTHER* LIFE IS PULLING YOU AWAY FROM ME.

THE QUIET, VULNERABLE GUY WHO WALKED INTO MY BAR, JUST LOOKING FOR A PLACE TO CRASH...

...IS *GONE*.

YOU AREN'T THAT PERSON ANYMORE.

GUYS WHO'RE ALL *JUSTICE LEAGUE* OR WHATEVER AREN'T *VULNERABLE*.

UH...I'M NOT IN THE LEAGUE...

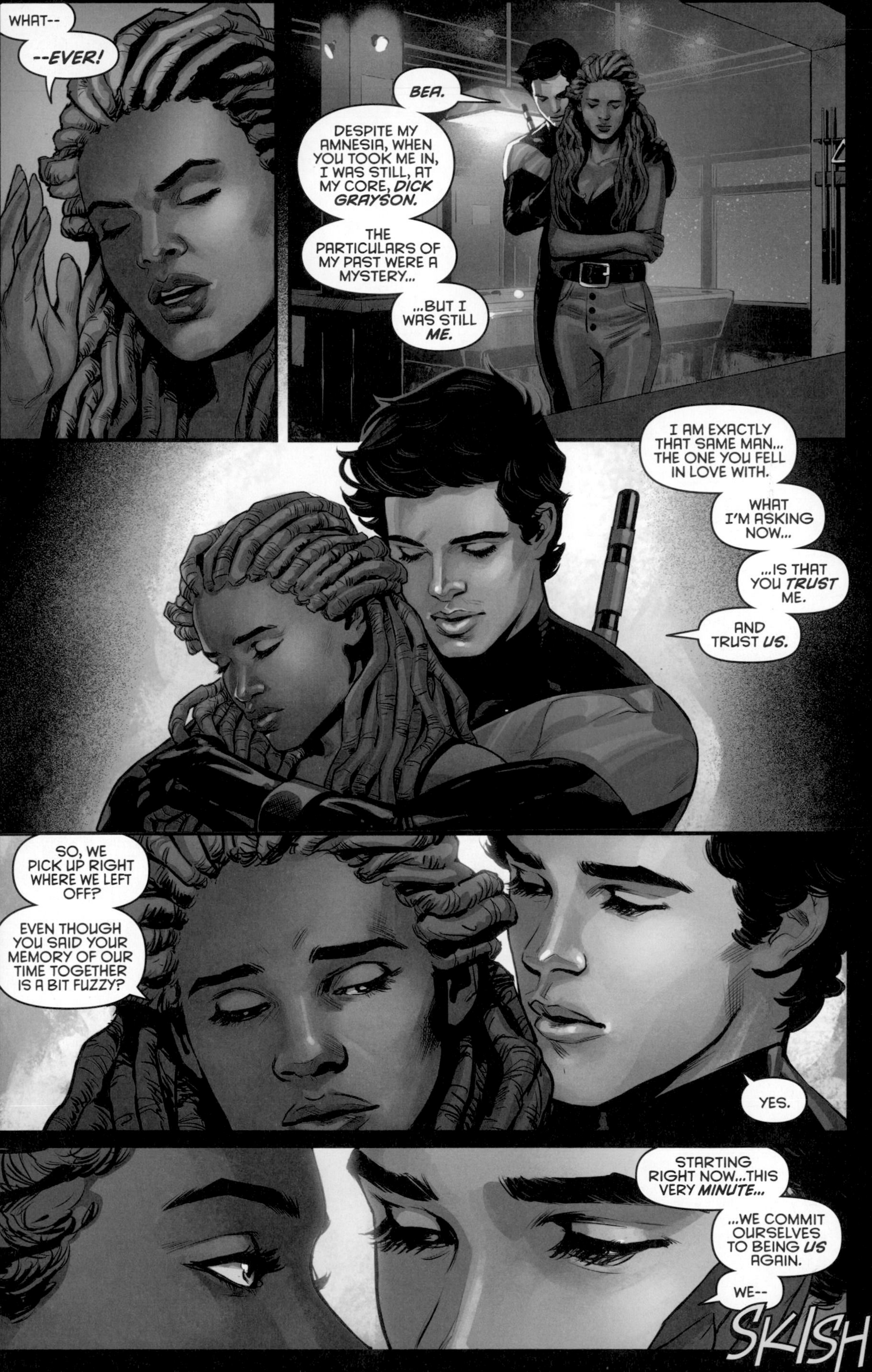
WHAT--
--EVER!
BEA.
DESPITE MY AMNESIA, WHEN YOU TOOK ME IN, I WAS STILL, AT MY CORE, DICK GRAYSON.
THE PARTICULARS OF MY PAST WERE A MYSTERY...
...BUT I WAS STILL ME.
I AM EXACTLY THAT SAME MAN... THE ONE YOU FELL IN LOVE WITH.
WHAT I'M ASKING NOW...
...IS THAT YOU TRUST ME.
AND TRUST US.
SO, WE PICK UP RIGHT WHERE WE LEFT OFF?
EVEN THOUGH YOU SAID YOUR MEMORY OF OUR TIME TOGETHER IS A BIT FUZZY?
YES.
STARTING RIGHT NOW...THIS VERY MINUTE...
...WE COMMIT OURSELVES TO BEING US AGAIN.
WE--
SKISH

CHAKKA CHAKKA CHAKKA CHAKKA CHAKKA
SKISH
SKISH
WHA--?!
DOWN!
SOMEONE'S SHOOTING AT US?!
CHAKKA CHAKKA CHAKKA CHAKKA CHAKKA
SKISH
STAY HERE.
STAY--?
WHAT'RE YOU DOING?!
YOU CAN'T GO OUT THERE!

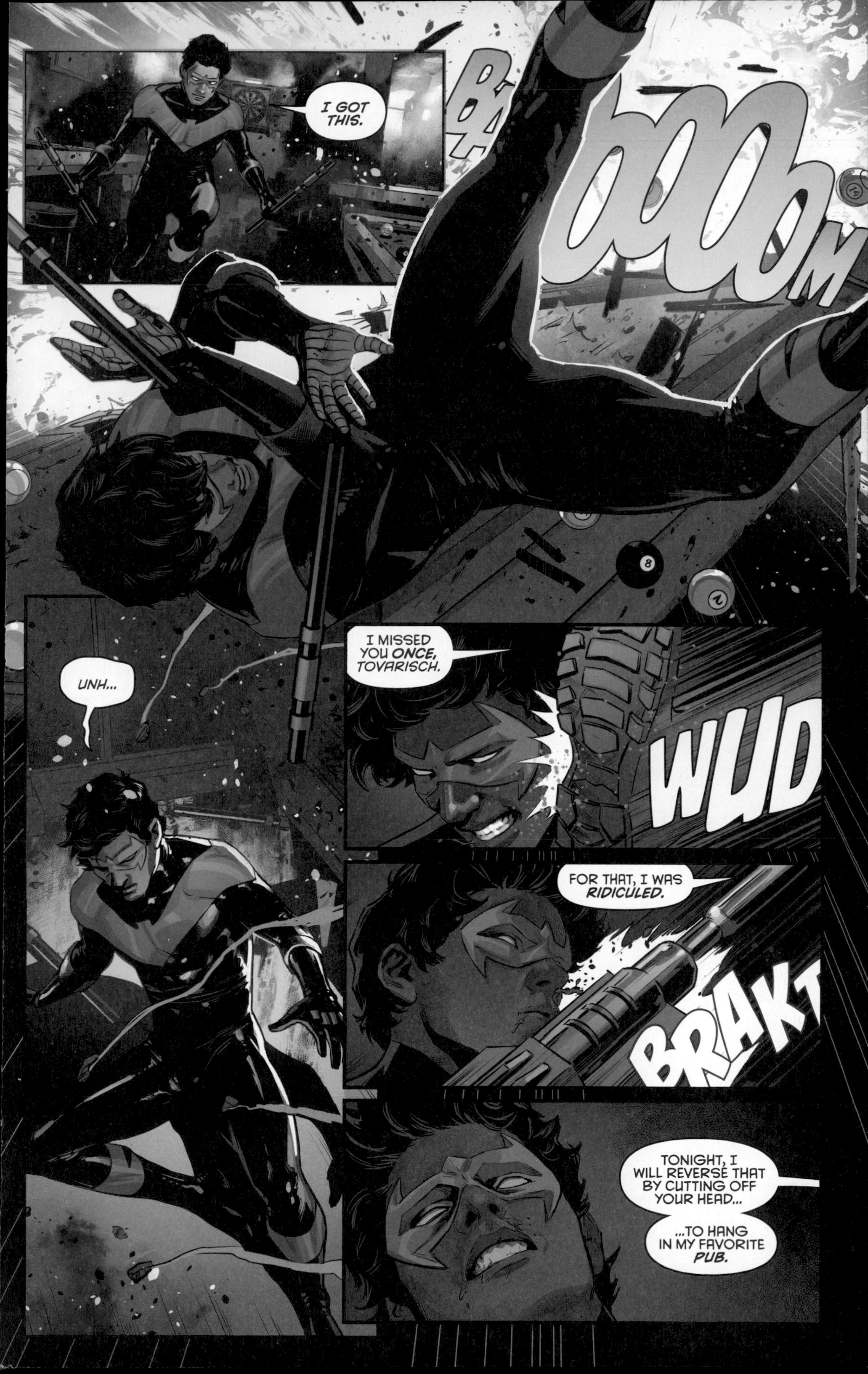
I GOT THIS.
BAbOOOOM
UNH...
I MISSED YOU ONCE, TOVARISCH.
WUD
FOR THAT, I WAS RIDICULED.
BRAKT
TONIGHT, I WILL REVERSE THAT BY CUTTING OFF YOUR HEAD...
...TO HANG IN MY FAVORITE PUB.

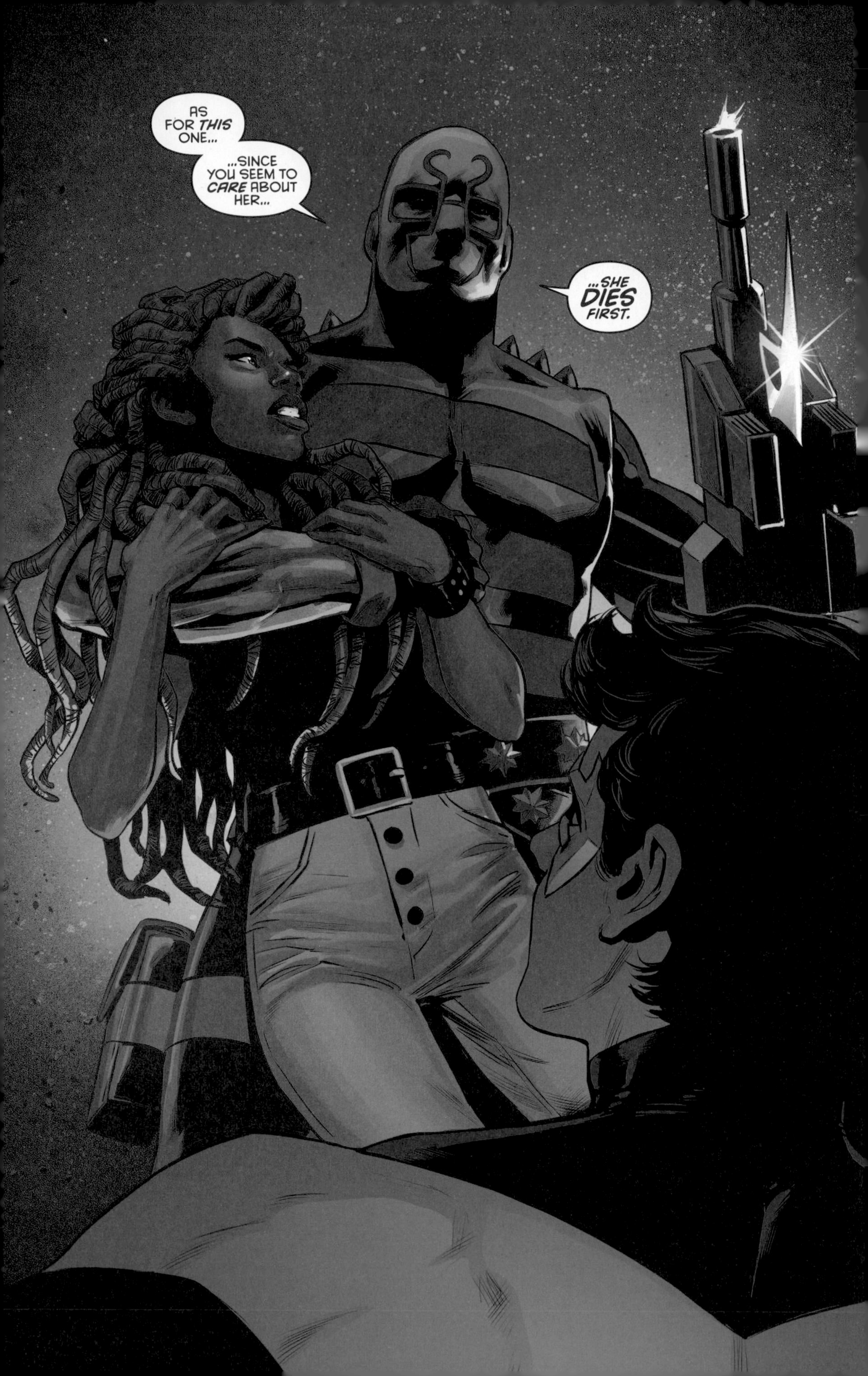
AS FOR THIS ONE...
...SINCE YOU SEEM TO CARE ABOUT HER...
...SHE DIES FIRST.

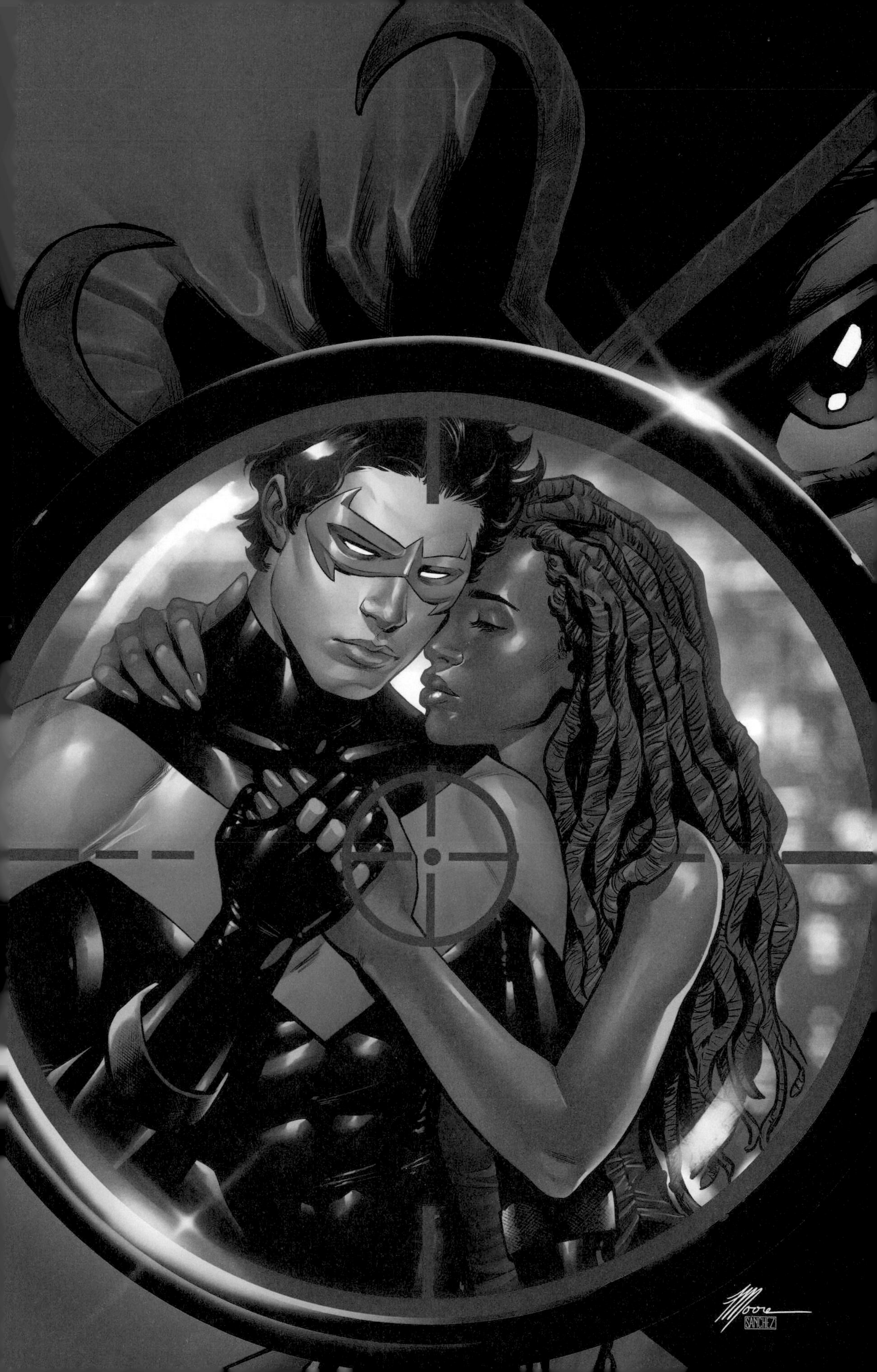
Moore
SANCHEZ

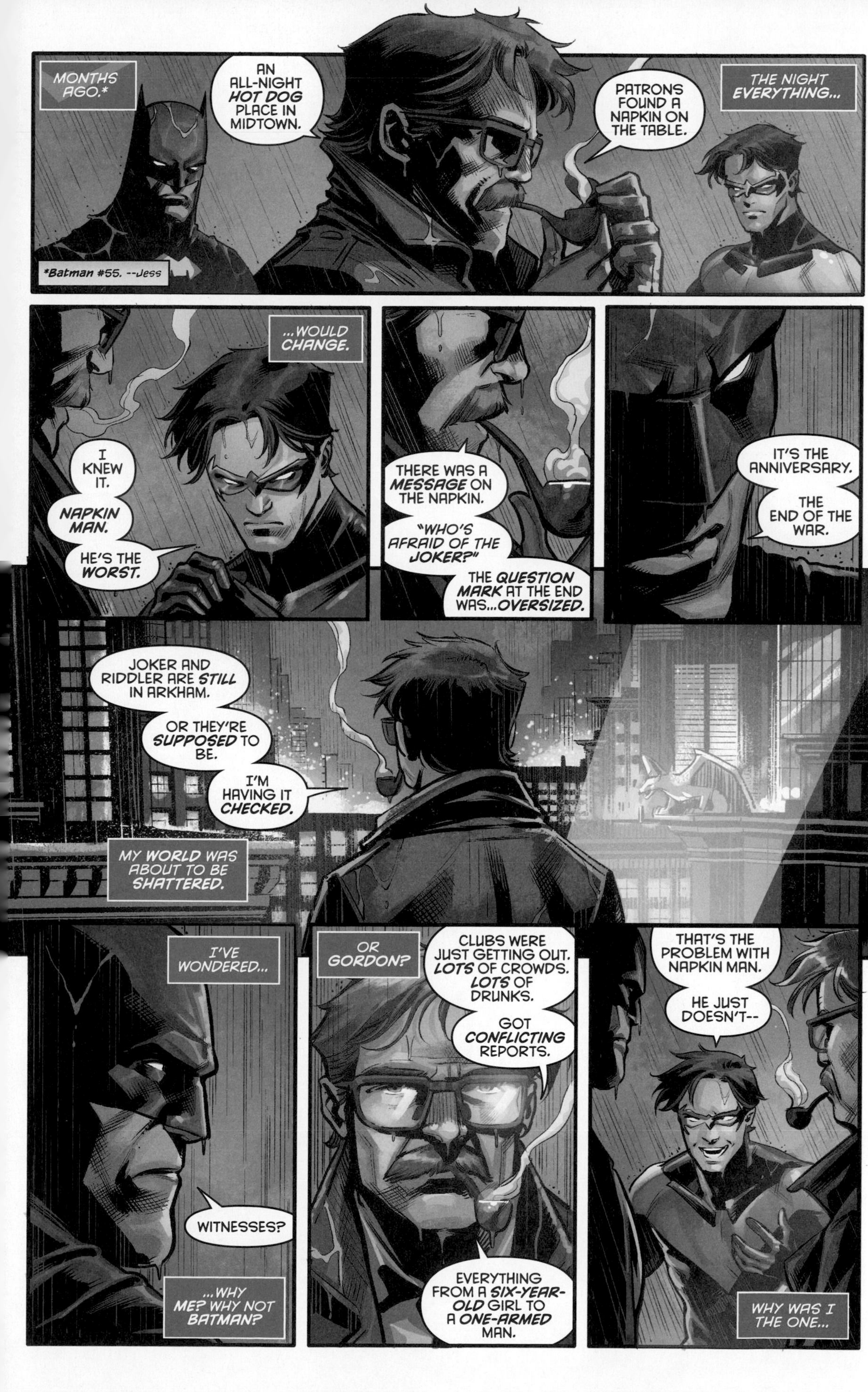
MONTHS AGO.*
AN ALL-NIGHT HOT DOG PLACE IN MIDTOWN.
PATRONS FOUND A NAPKIN ON THE TABLE.
THE NIGHT EVERYTHING...
*Batman #55. --Jess
...WOULD CHANGE.
I KNEW IT.
NAPKIN MAN.
HE'S THE WORST.
THERE WAS A MESSAGE ON THE NAPKIN.
"WHO'S AFRAID OF THE JOKER?"
THE QUESTION MARK AT THE END WAS...OVERSIZED.
IT'S THE ANNIVERSARY.
THE END OF THE WAR.
JOKER AND RIDDLER ARE STILL IN ARKHAM.
OR THEY'RE SUPPOSED TO BE.
I'M HAVING IT CHECKED.
MY WORLD WAS ABOUT TO BE SHATTERED.
I'VE WONDERED...
WITNESSES?
...WHY ME? WHY NOT BATMAN?
OR GORDON?
CLUBS WERE JUST GETTING OUT. LOTS OF CROWDS. LOTS OF DRUNKS.
GOT CONFLICTING REPORTS.
EVERYTHING FROM A SIX-YEAR-OLD GIRL TO A ONE-ARMED MAN.
THAT'S THE PROBLEM WITH NAPKIN MAN.
HE JUST DOESN'T--
WHY WAS I THE ONE...

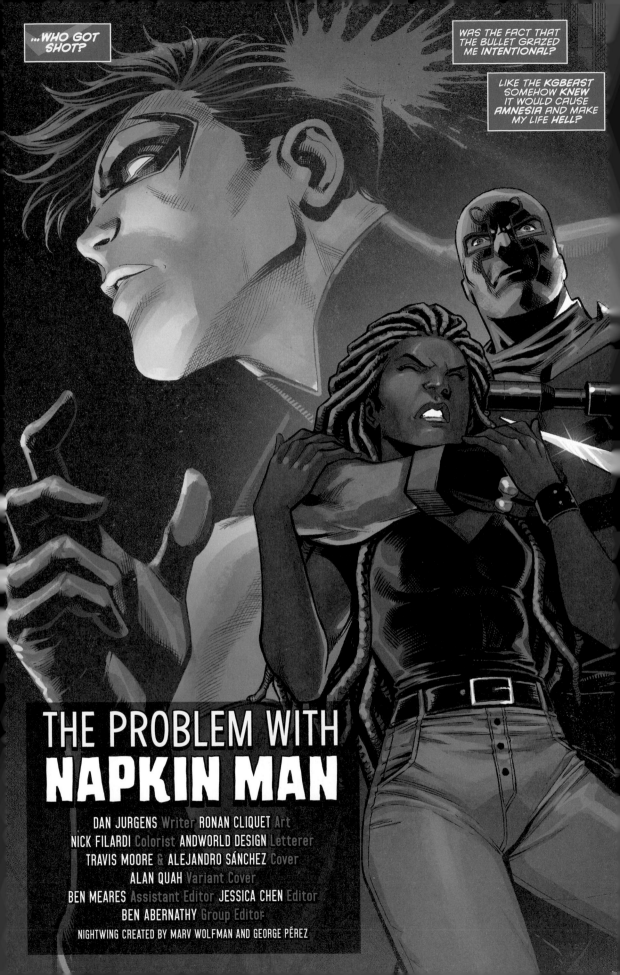

...WHO GOT SHOT?

WAS THE FACT THAT THE BULLET GRAZED ME INTENTIONAL?

LIKE THE KGBEAST SOMEHOW KNEW IT WOULD CAUSE AMNESIA AND MAKE MY LIFE HELL?

THE PROBLEM WITH
NAPKIN MAN

DAN JURGENS Writer RONAN CLIQUET Art

NICK FILARDI Colorist ANDWORLD DESIGN Letterer

TRAVIS MOORE & ALEJANDRO SÁNCHEZ Cover

ALAN QUAH Variant Cover

BEN MEARES Assistant Editor JESSICA CHEN Editor

BEN ABERNATHY Group Editor

NIGHTWING CREATED BY MARV WOLFMAN AND GEORGE PÉREZ

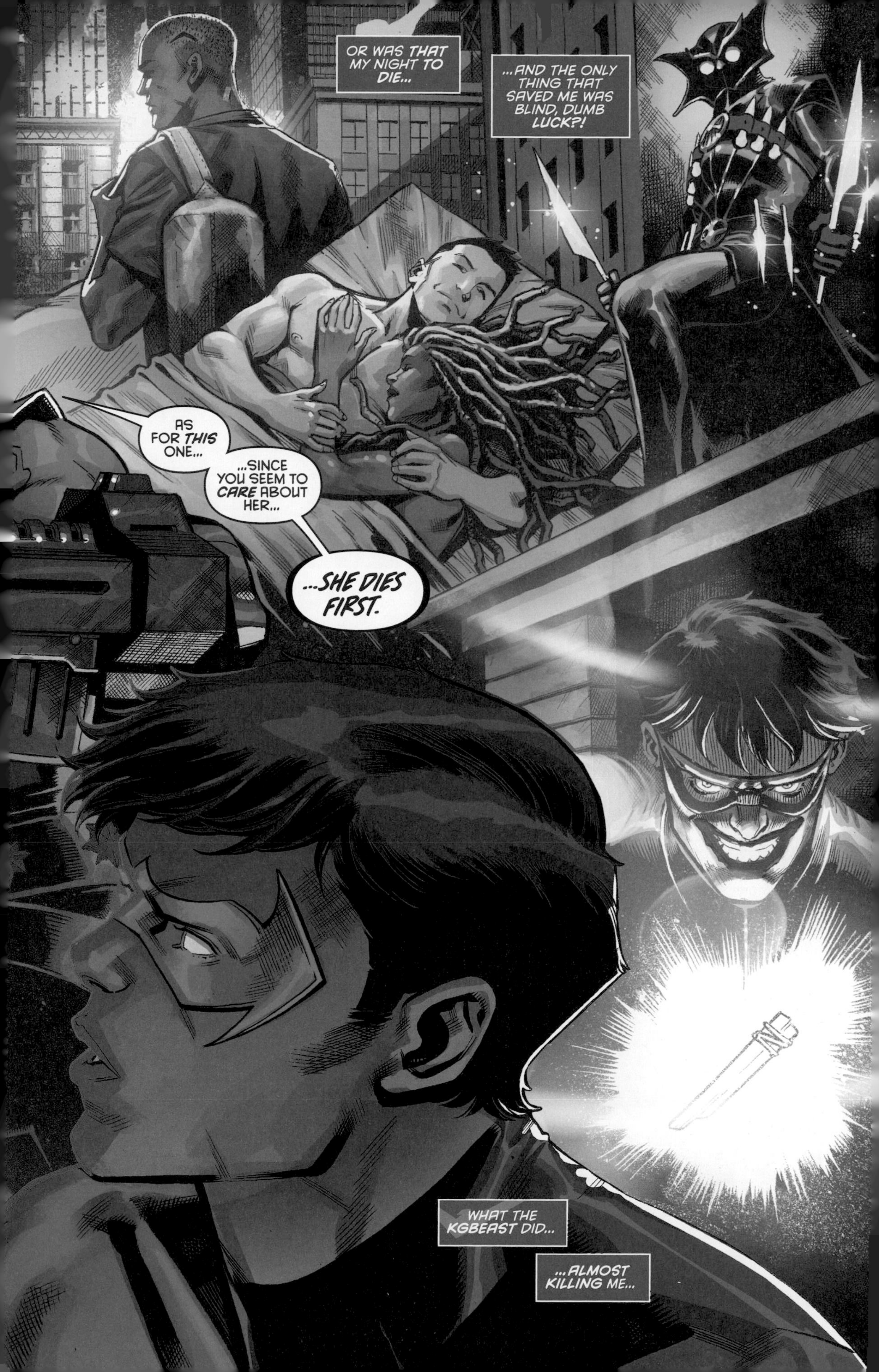

OR WAS THAT MY NIGHT TO DIE...
...AND THE ONLY THING THAT SAVED ME WAS BLIND, DUMB LUCK?!
AS FOR THIS ONE...
...SINCE YOU SEEM TO CARE ABOUT HER...
...SHE DIES FIRST.
WHAT THE KGBEAST DID...
...ALMOST KILLING ME...

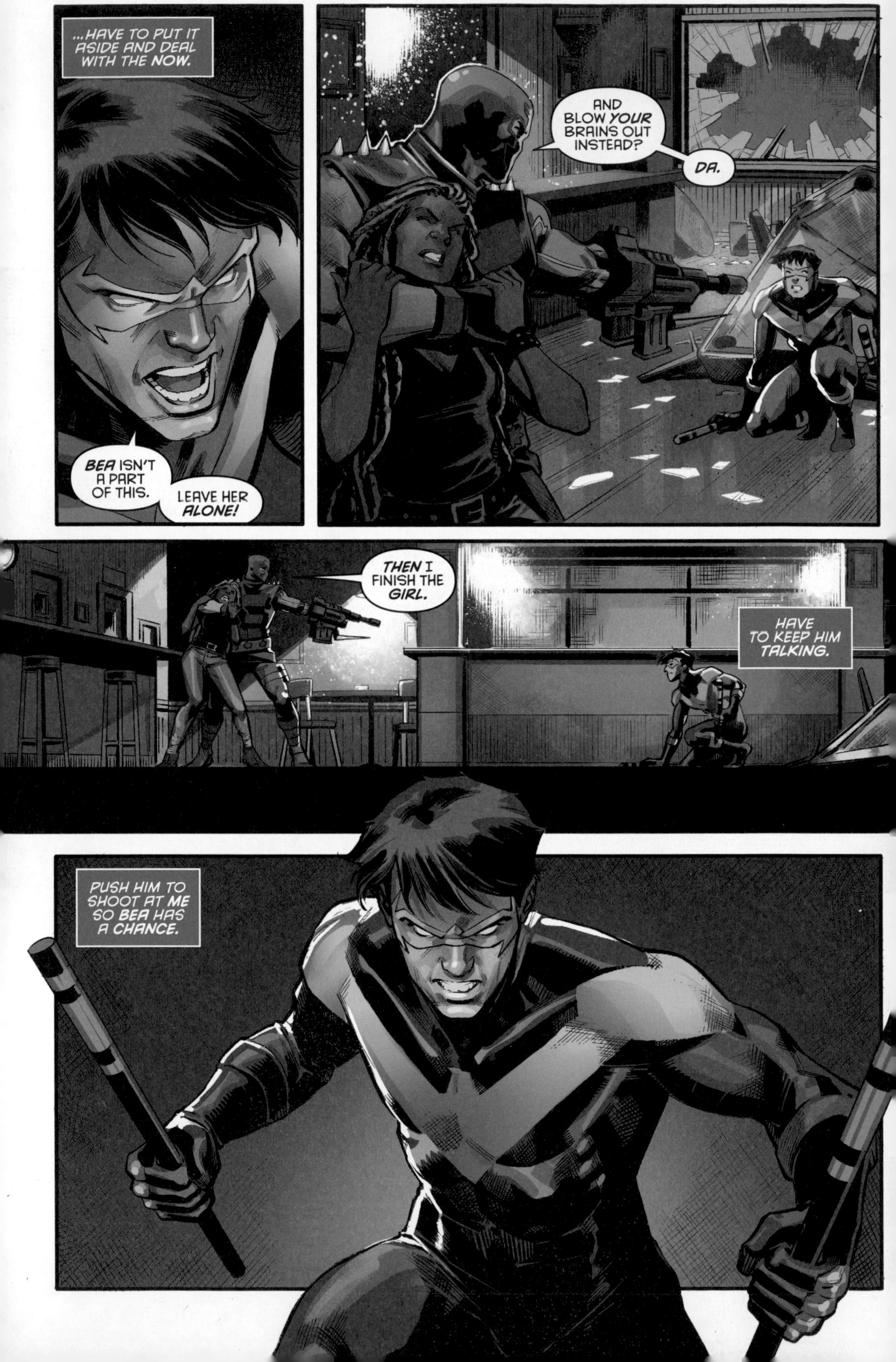
...HAVE TO PUT IT ASIDE AND DEAL WITH THE NOW.
BEA ISN'T A PART OF THIS.
LEAVE HER ALONE!
AND BLOW YOUR BRAINS OUT INSTEAD?
DA.
THEN I FINISH THE GIRL.
HAVE TO KEEP HIM TALKING.
PUSH HIM TO SHOOT AT ME SO BEA HAS A CHANCE.

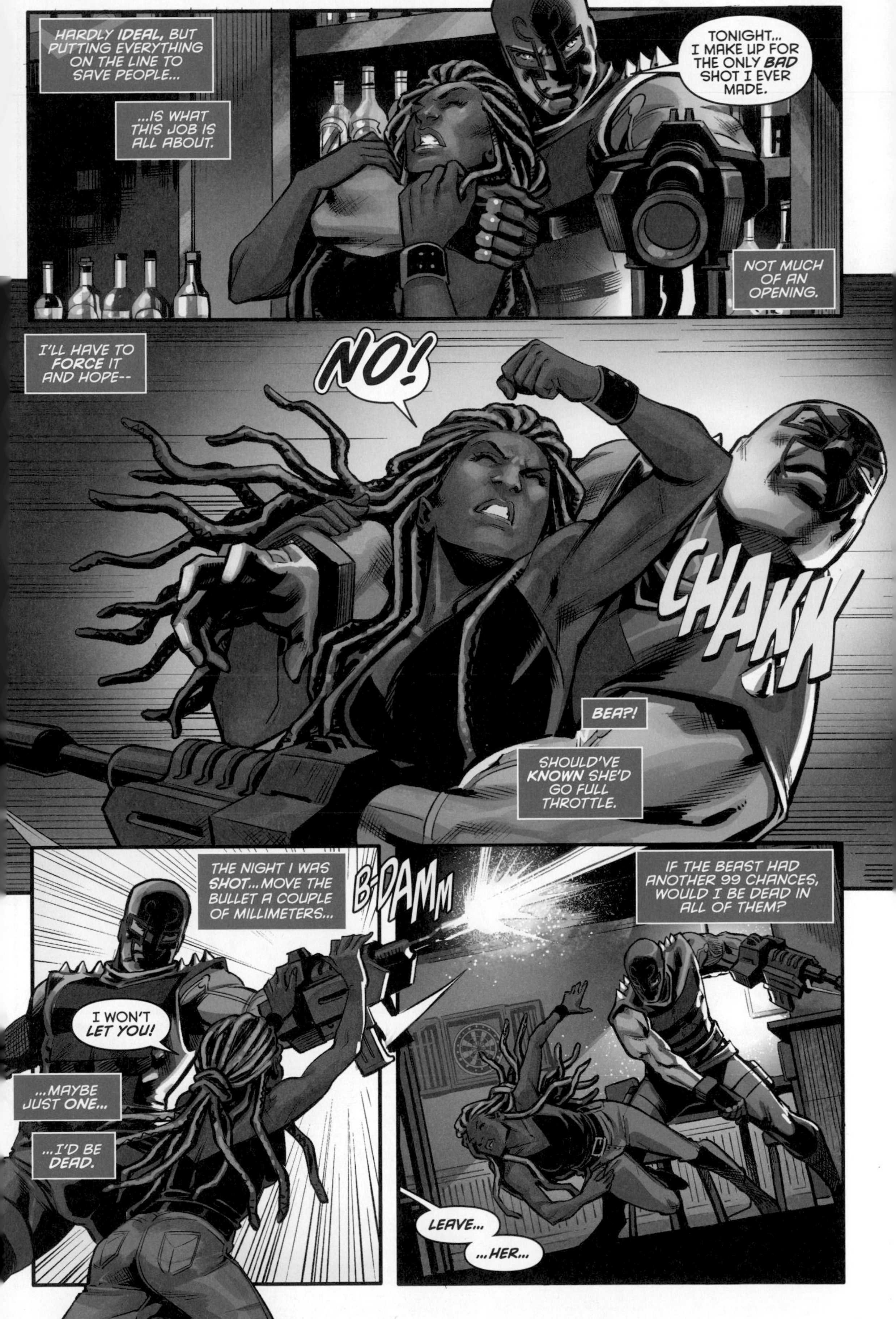
HARDLY IDEAL, BUT PUTTING EVERYTHING ON THE LINE TO SAVE PEOPLE...
...IS WHAT THIS JOB IS ALL ABOUT.
TONIGHT... I MAKE UP FOR THE ONLY BAD SHOT I EVER MADE.
NOT MUCH OF AN OPENING.
I'LL HAVE TO FORCE IT AND HOPE--
NO!
CHAKK
BEA?!
SHOULD'VE KNOWN SHE'D GO FULL THROTTLE.
THE NIGHT I WAS SHOT...MOVE THE BULLET A COUPLE OF MILLIMETERS...
B-DAMM
I WON'T LET YOU!
...MAYBE JUST ONE...
...I'D BE DEAD.
IF THE BEAST HAD ANOTHER 99 CHANCES, WOULD I BE DEAD IN ALL OF THEM?
LEAVE...
...HER...

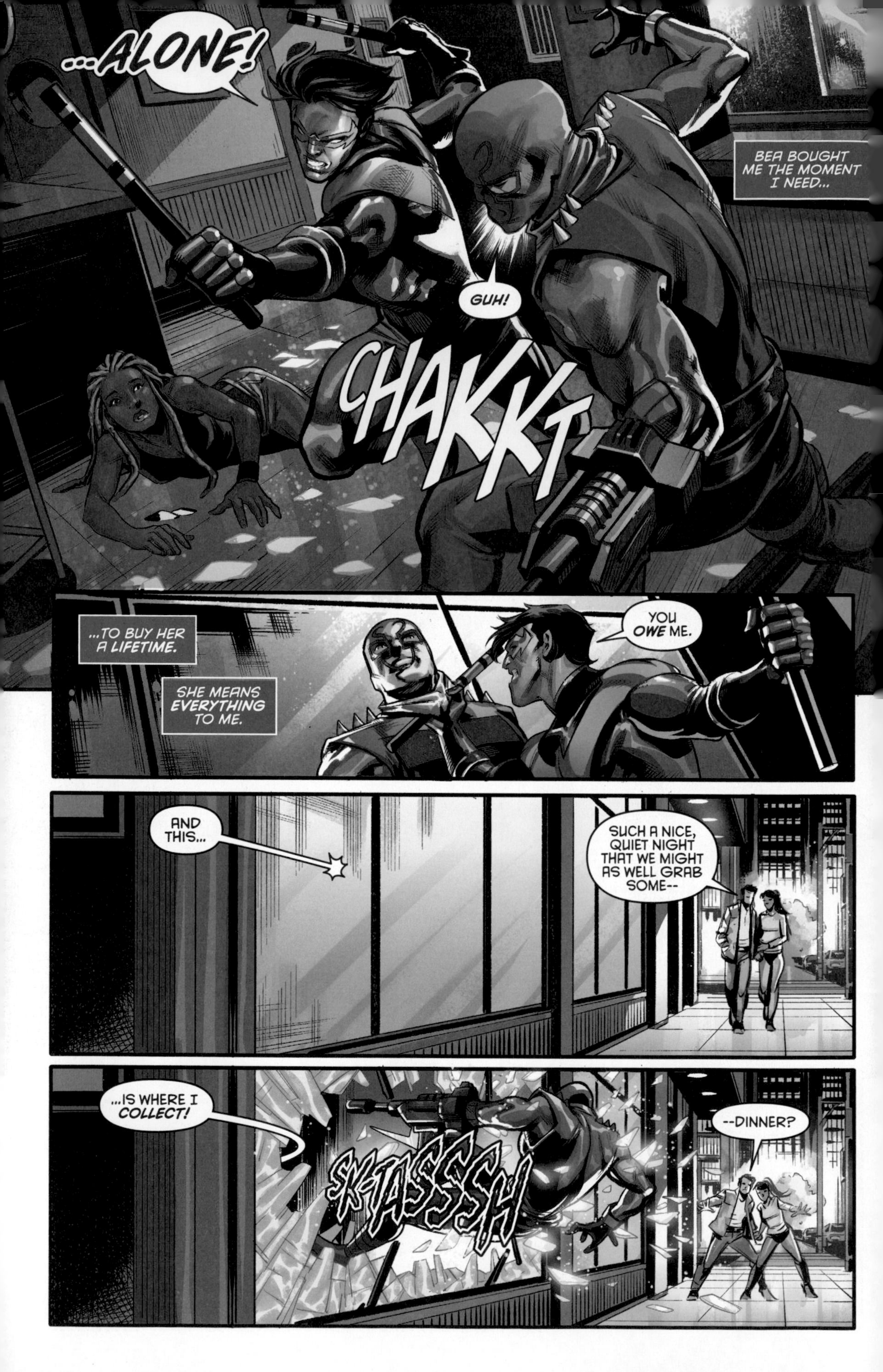
...ALONE!
BEA BOUGHT ME THE MOMENT I NEED...
GUH!
CHAKKT
...TO BUY HER A LIFETIME.
SHE MEANS EVERYTHING TO ME.
YOU OWE ME.
AND THIS...
SUCH A NICE, QUIET NIGHT THAT WE MIGHT AS WELL GRAB SOME--
...IS WHERE I COLLECT!
SK-TASSSH
--DINNER?

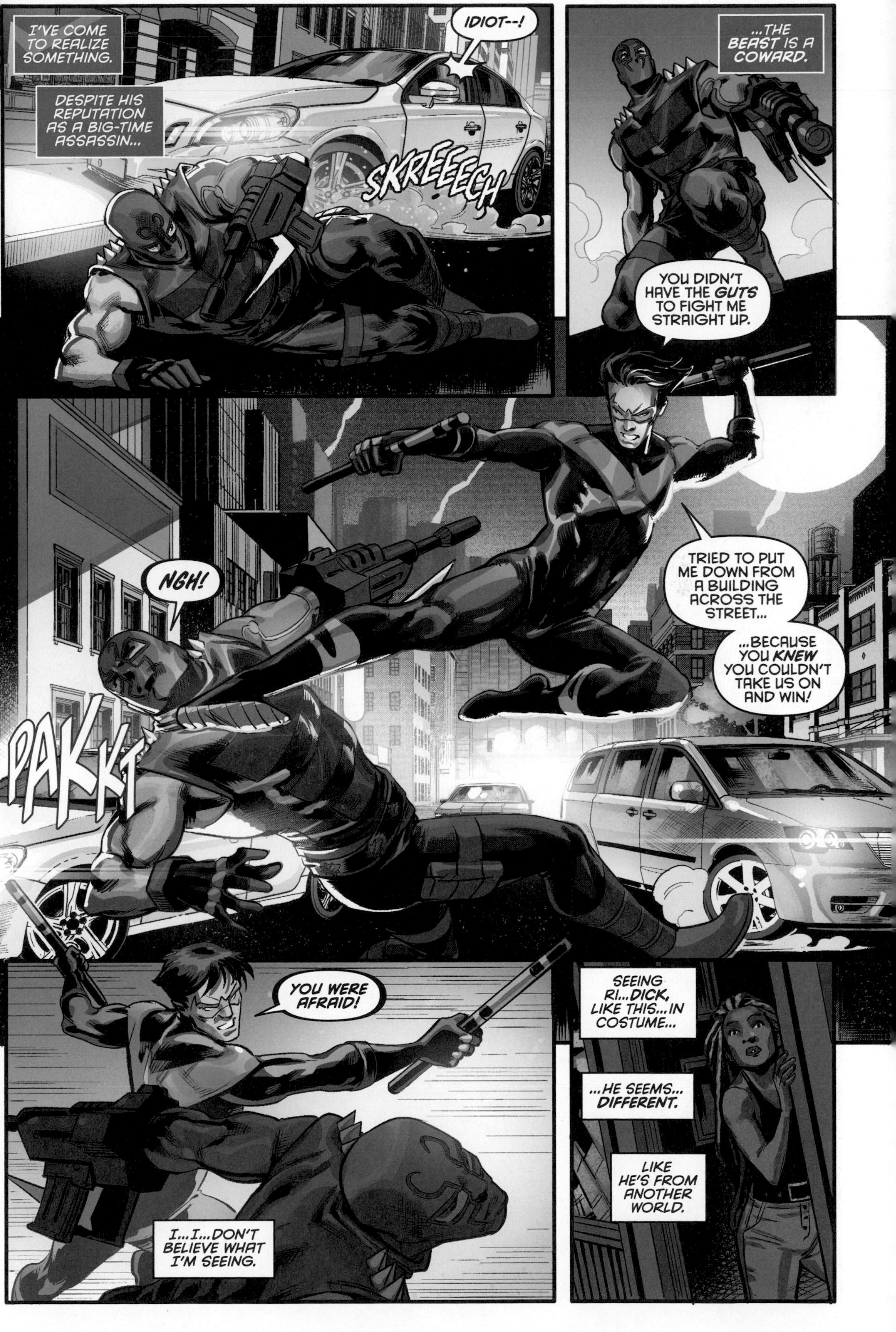
I'VE COME TO REALIZE SOMETHING.
DESPITE HIS REPUTATION AS A BIG-TIME ASSASSIN...
IDIOT--!
SKREEEECH
...THE BEAST IS A COWARD.
YOU DIDN'T HAVE THE GUTS TO FIGHT ME STRAIGHT UP.
TRIED TO PUT ME DOWN FROM A BUILDING ACROSS THE STREET...
...BECAUSE YOU KNEW YOU COULDN'T TAKE US ON AND WIN!
NGH!
PAKKT
YOU WERE AFRAID!
I...I...DON'T BELIEVE WHAT I'M SEEING.
SEEING RI...DICK, LIKE THIS...IN COSTUME...
...HE SEEMS... DIFFERENT.
LIKE HE'S FROM ANOTHER WORLD.

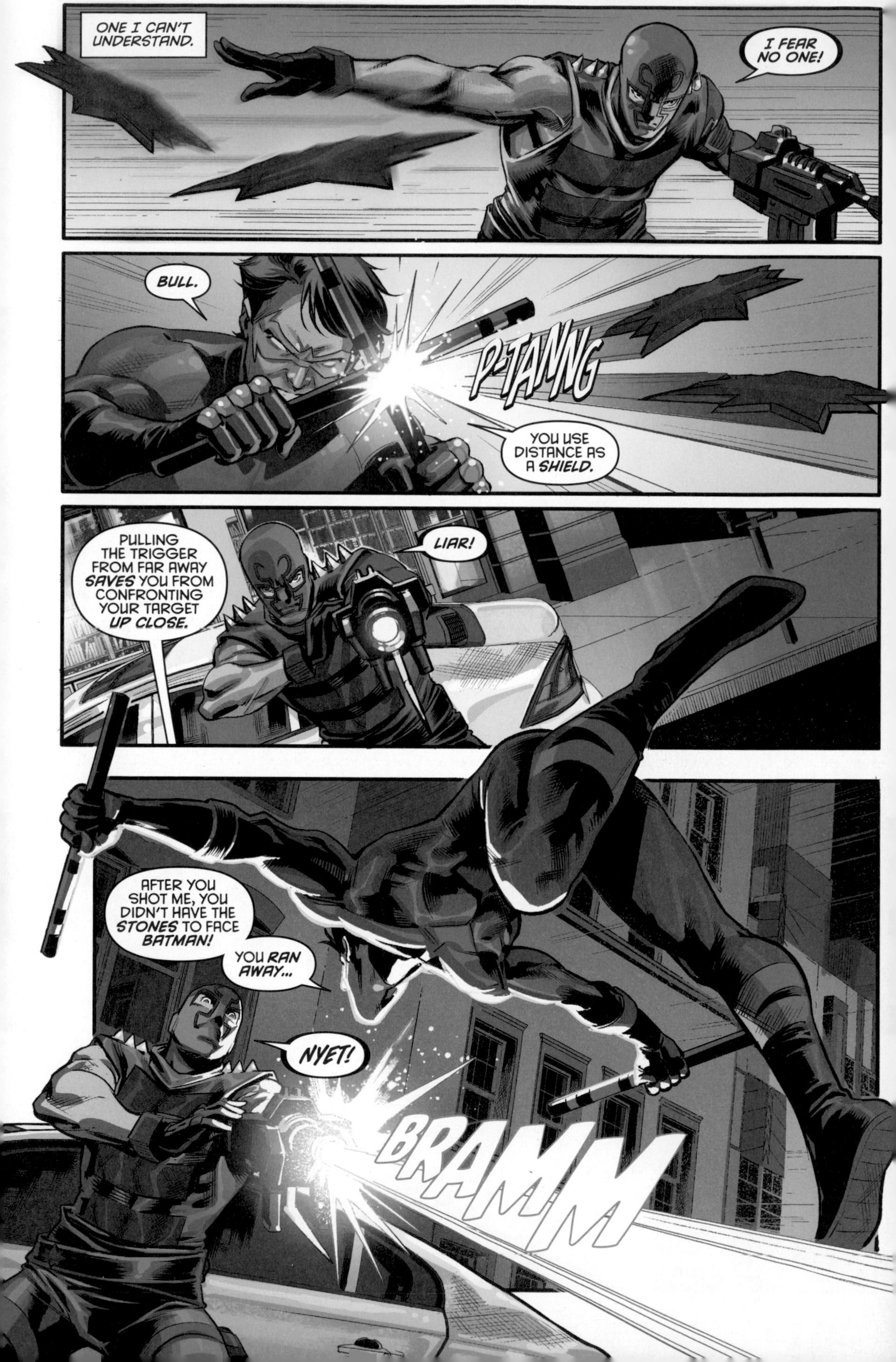

ONE I CAN'T UNDERSTAND.
I FEAR NO ONE!
BULL.
P-TANNG
YOU USE DISTANCE AS A SHIELD.
PULLING THE TRIGGER FROM FAR AWAY SAVES YOU FROM CONFRONTING YOUR TARGET UP CLOSE.
LIAR!
AFTER YOU SHOT ME, YOU DIDN'T HAVE THE STONES TO FACE BATMAN!
YOU RAN AWAY...
NYET!
BRAMM

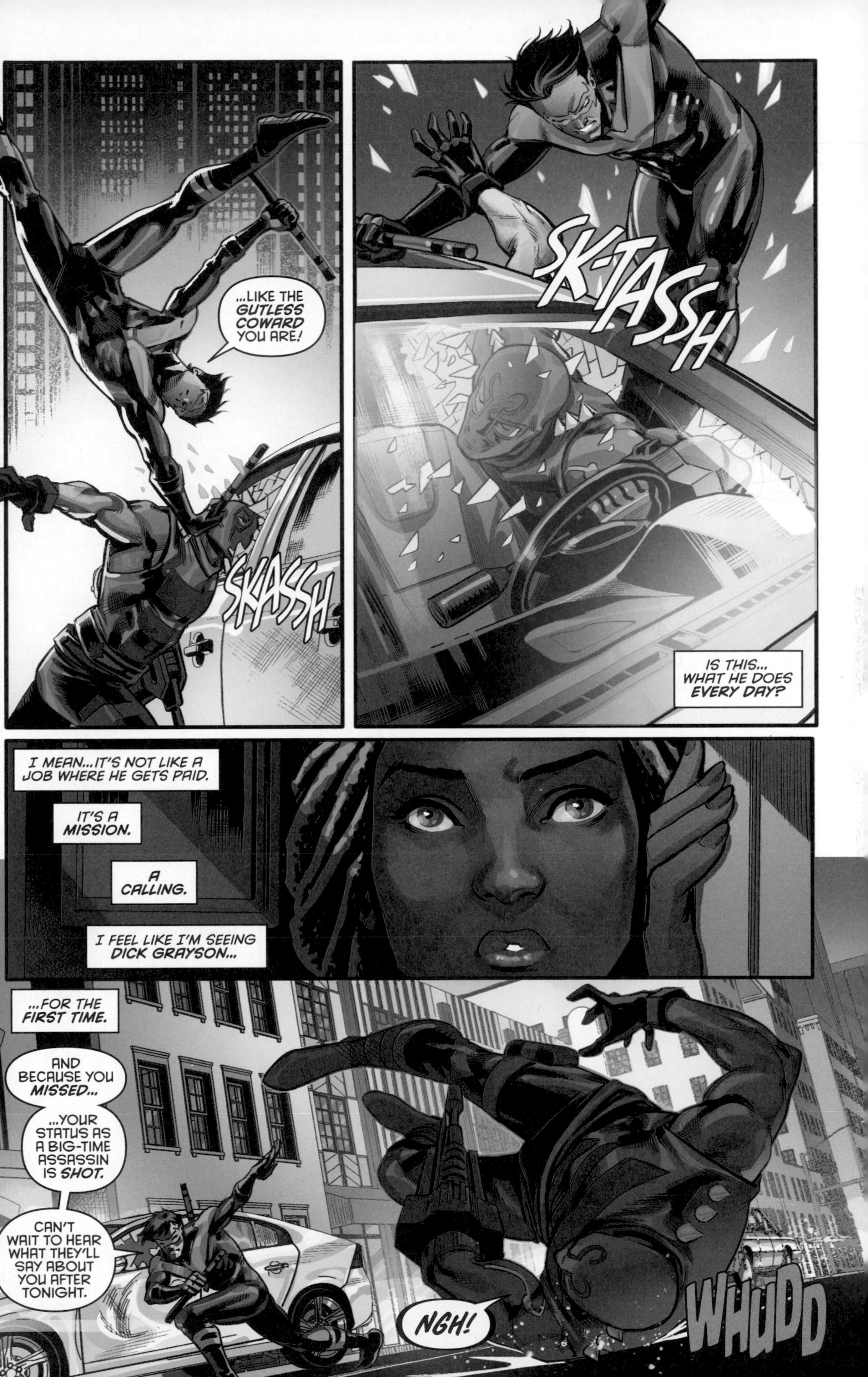

...LIKE THE GUTLESS COWARD YOU ARE!
SKASSH
SK-TASSH
IS THIS... WHAT HE DOES EVERY DAY?
I MEAN...IT'S NOT LIKE A JOB WHERE HE GETS PAID.
IT'S A MISSION.
A CALLING.
I FEEL LIKE I'M SEEING DICK GRAYSON...
...FOR THE FIRST TIME.
AND BECAUSE YOU MISSED...
...YOUR STATUS AS A BIG-TIME ASSASSIN IS SHOT.
CAN'T WAIT TO HEAR WHAT THEY'LL SAY ABOUT YOU AFTER TONIGHT.
NGH!
WHUDD

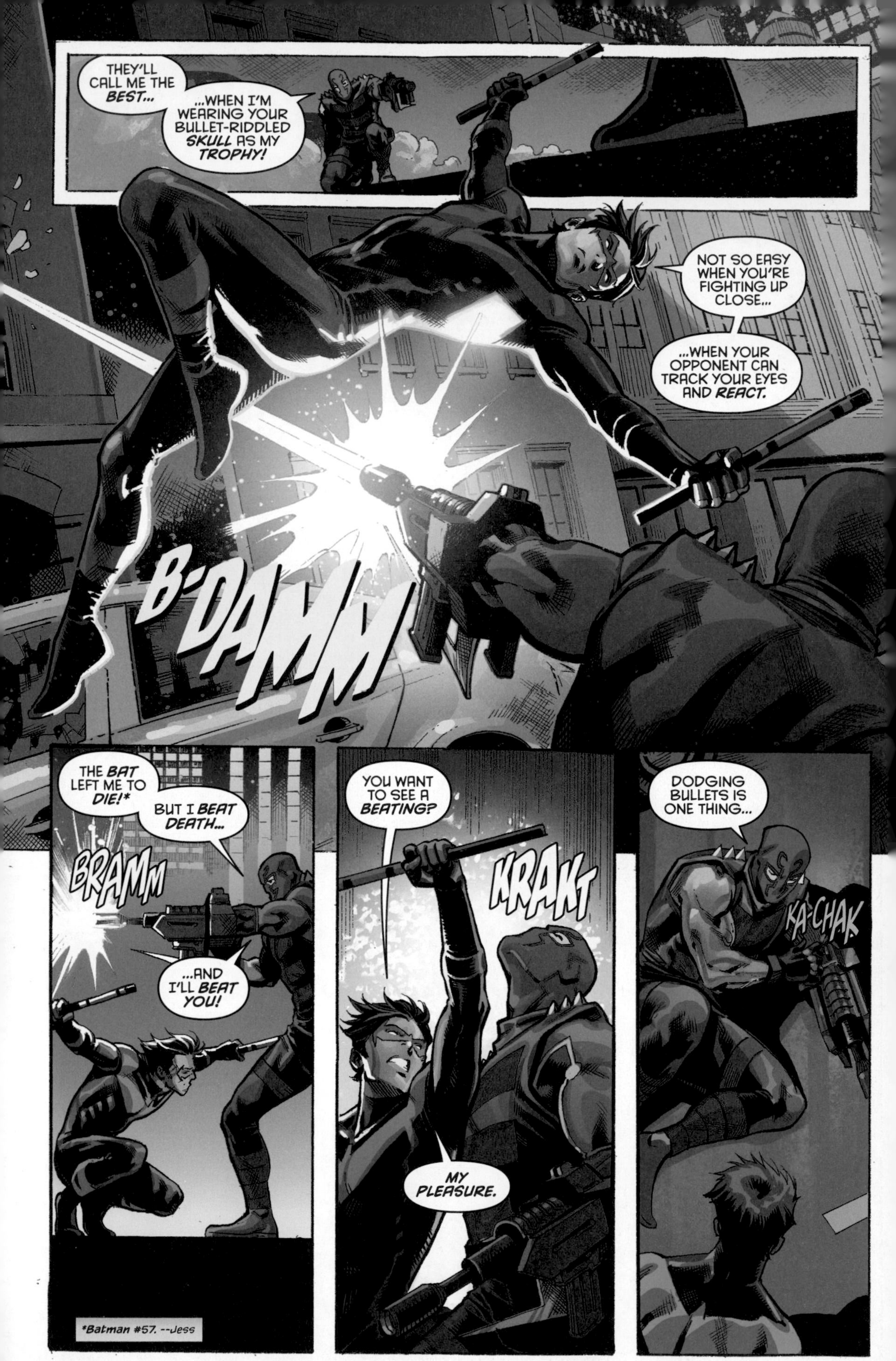
THEY'LL CALL ME THE BEST...
...WHEN I'M WEARING YOUR BULLET-RIDDLED SKULL AS MY TROPHY!
NOT SO EASY WHEN YOU'RE FIGHTING UP CLOSE...
...WHEN YOUR OPPONENT CAN TRACK YOUR EYES AND REACT.
B-DAMM
THE BAT LEFT ME TO DIE!*
BUT I BEAT DEATH...
BRAMM
...AND I'LL BEAT YOU!
*Batman #57. --Jess
YOU WANT TO SEE A BEATING?
KRAKT
MY PLEASURE.
DODGING BULLETS IS ONE THING...
KA-CHAK

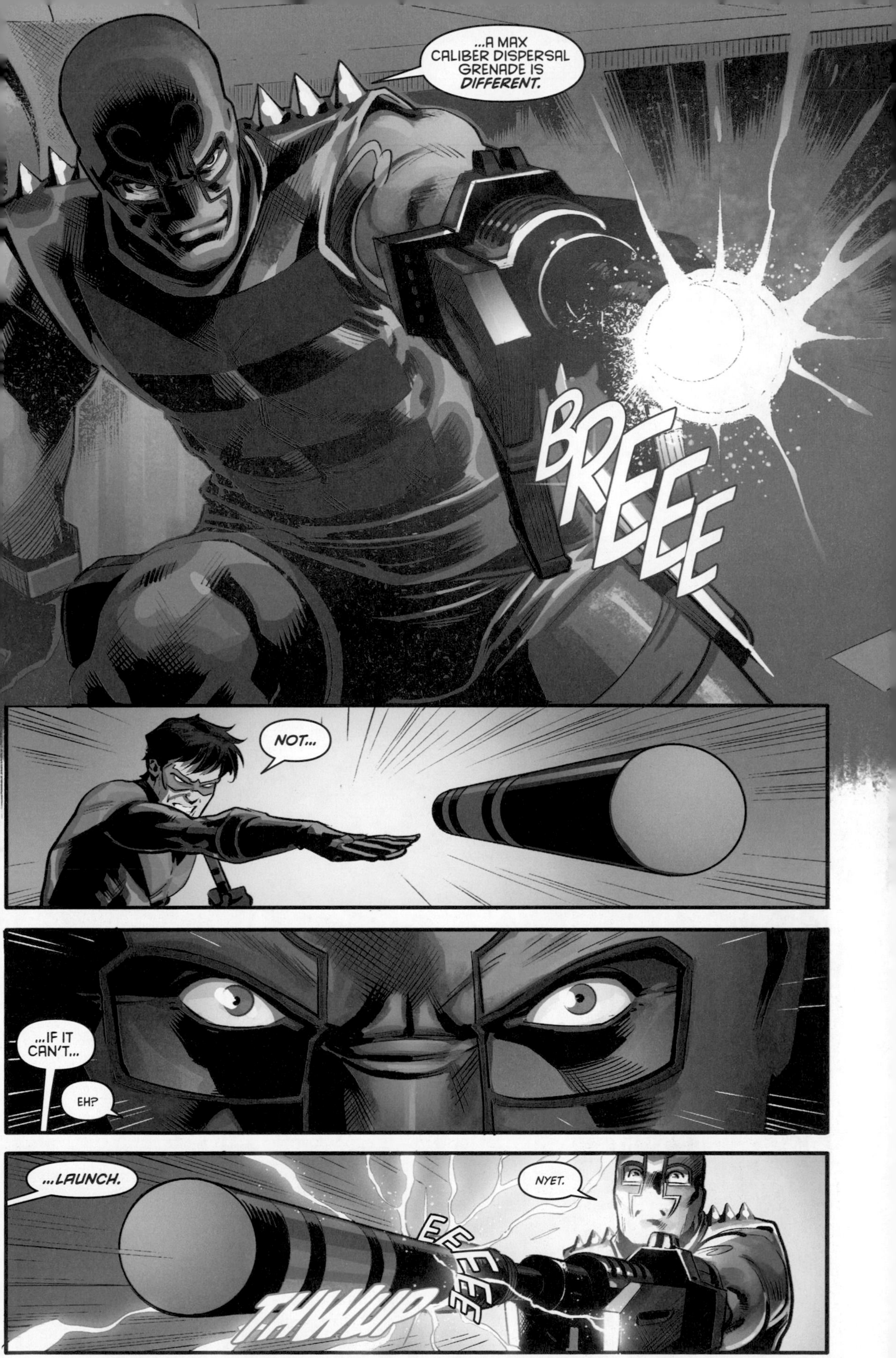
...A MAX CALIBER DISPERSAL GRENADE IS *DIFFERENT.*
BREEEE
NOT...
...IF IT CAN'T...
EH?
...LAUNCH.
NYET.
EEEEE
THWUP

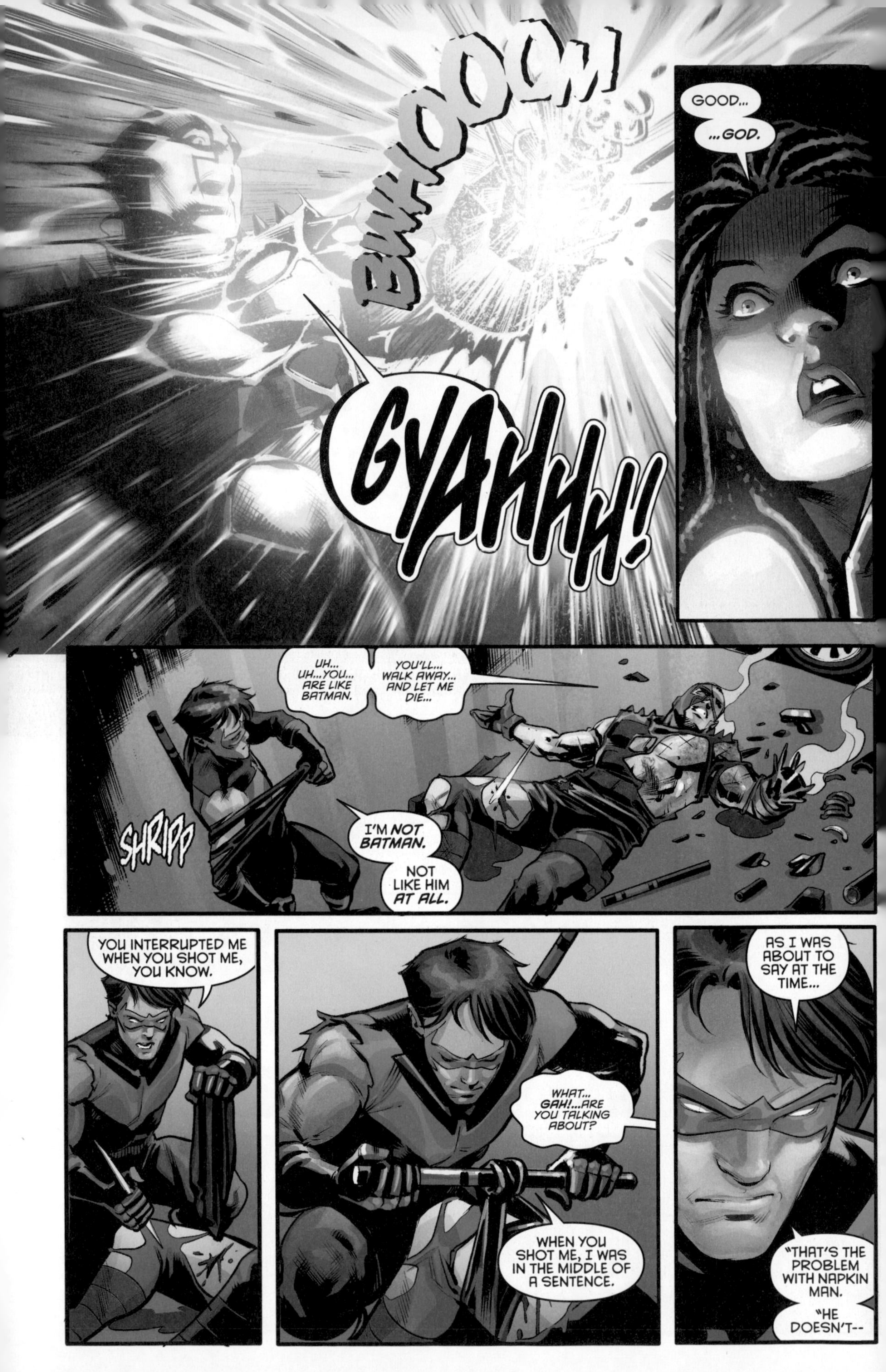
BWHOOOOM
GYAHHH!
GOOD...
...GOD.
UH... UH...YOU... ARE LIKE BATMAN.
YOU'LL... WALK AWAY... AND LET ME DIE...
SHRIPP
I'M NOT BATMAN.
NOT LIKE HIM AT ALL.
YOU INTERRUPTED ME WHEN YOU SHOT ME, YOU KNOW.
WHAT... GAH!...ARE YOU TALKING ABOUT?
WHEN YOU SHOT ME, I WAS IN THE MIDDLE OF A SENTENCE.
AS I WAS ABOUT TO SAY AT THE TIME...
"THAT'S THE PROBLEM WITH NAPKIN MAN.
"HE DOESN'T--

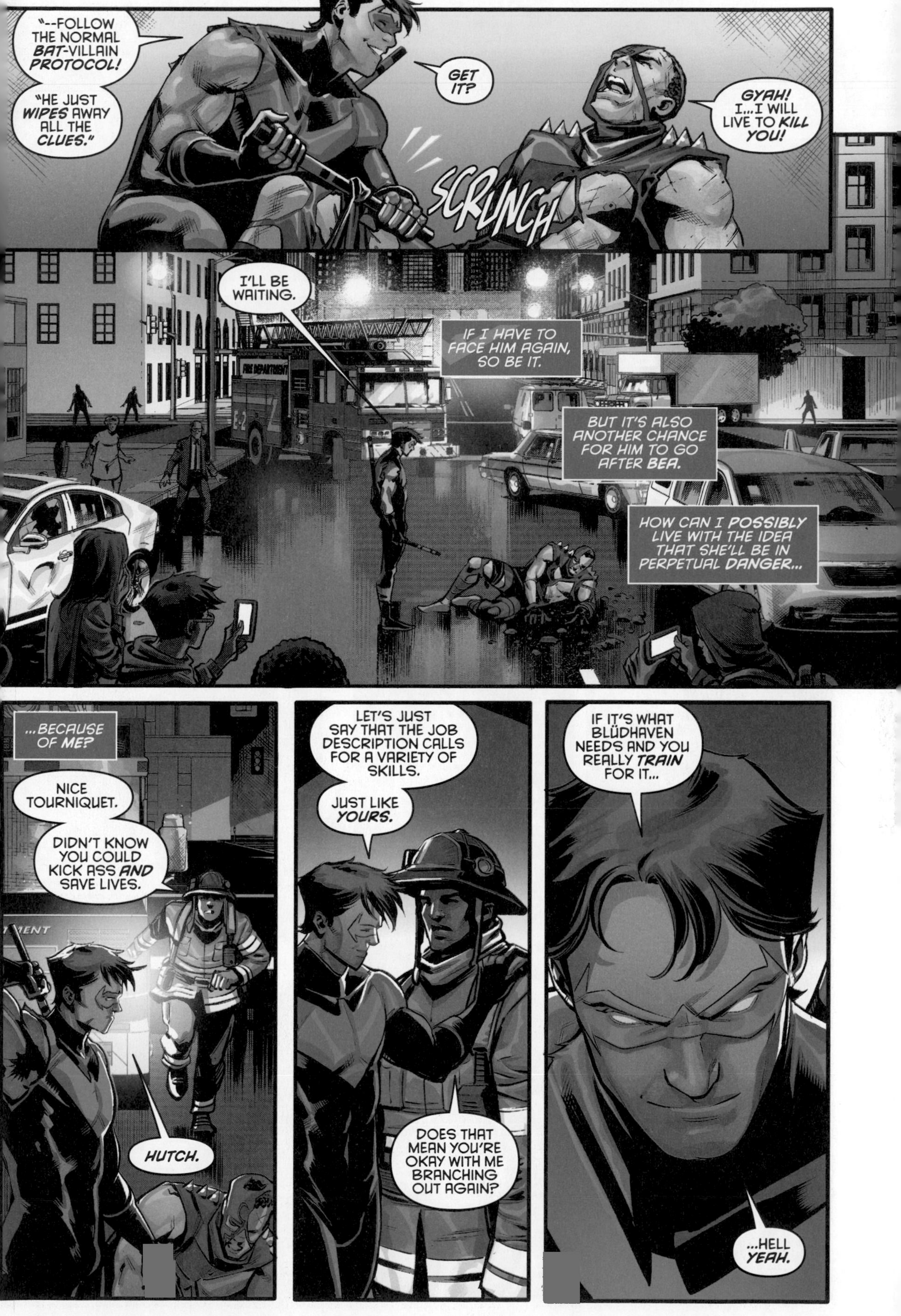
"--FOLLOW THE NORMAL BAT-VILLAIN PROTOCOL!
"HE JUST WIPES AWAY ALL THE CLUES."
GET IT?
GYAH! I...I WILL LIVE TO KILL YOU!
SCRUNCH
I'LL BE WAITING.
IF I HAVE TO FACE HIM AGAIN, SO BE IT.
BUT IT'S ALSO ANOTHER CHANCE FOR HIM TO GO AFTER BEA.
HOW CAN I POSSIBLY LIVE WITH THE IDEA THAT SHE'LL BE IN PERPETUAL DANGER...
FIRE DEPARTMENT
E-2
...BECAUSE OF ME?
NICE TOURNIQUET.
DIDN'T KNOW YOU COULD KICK ASS AND SAVE LIVES.
HUTCH.
LET'S JUST SAY THAT THE JOB DESCRIPTION CALLS FOR A VARIETY OF SKILLS.
JUST LIKE YOURS.
DOES THAT MEAN YOU'RE OKAY WITH ME BRANCHING OUT AGAIN?
IF IT'S WHAT BLÜDHAVEN NEEDS AND YOU REALLY TRAIN FOR IT...
...HELL YEAH.

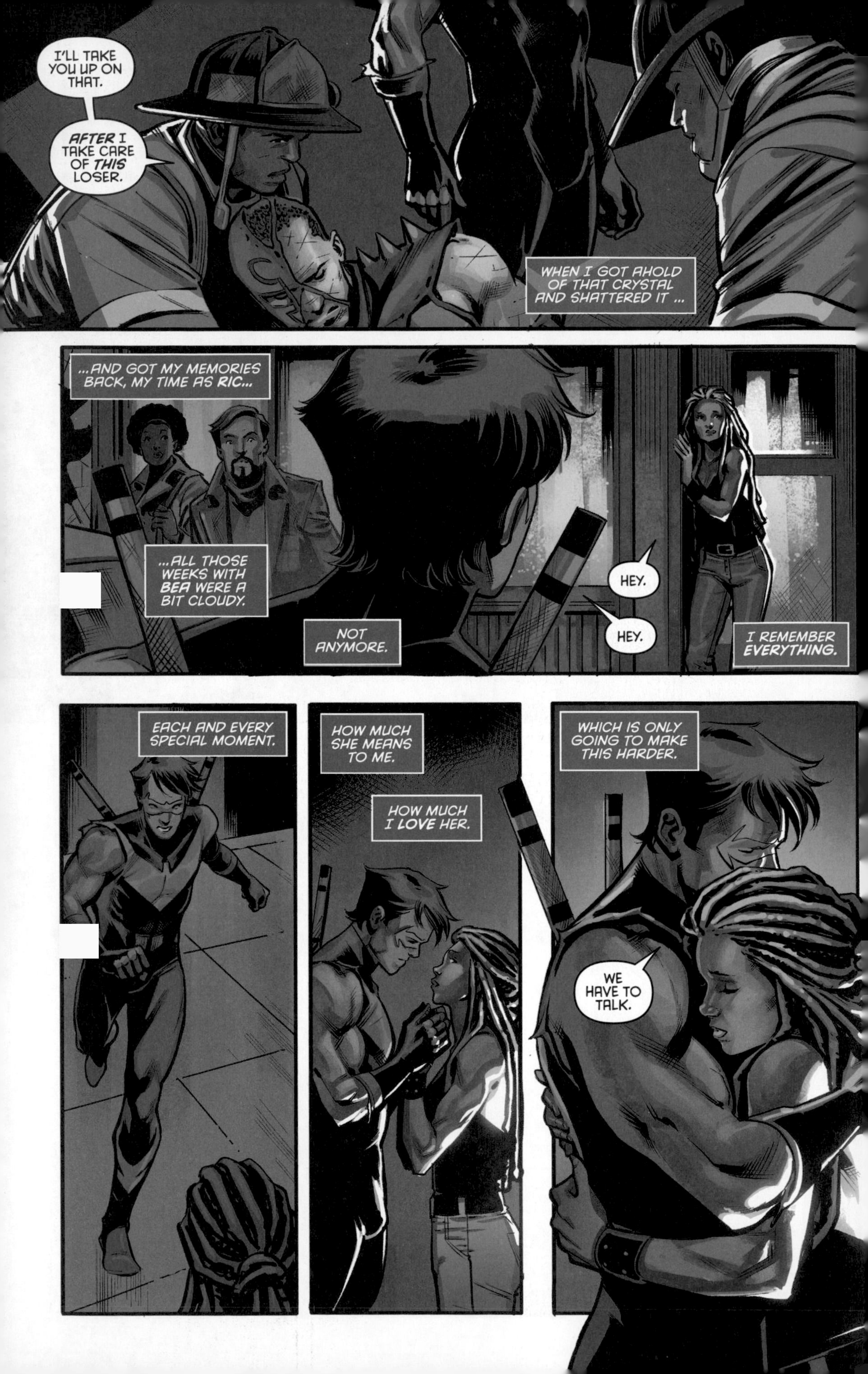
I'LL TAKE YOU UP ON THAT.
AFTER I TAKE CARE OF THIS LOSER.
WHEN I GOT AHOLD OF THAT CRYSTAL AND SHATTERED IT ...
...AND GOT MY MEMORIES BACK, MY TIME AS RIC...
...ALL THOSE WEEKS WITH BEA WERE A BIT CLOUDY.
NOT ANYMORE.
HEY.
HEY.
I REMEMBER EVERYTHING.
EACH AND EVERY SPECIAL MOMENT.
HOW MUCH SHE MEANS TO ME.
HOW MUCH I LOVE HER.
WHICH IS ONLY GOING TO MAKE THIS HARDER.
WE HAVE TO TALK.

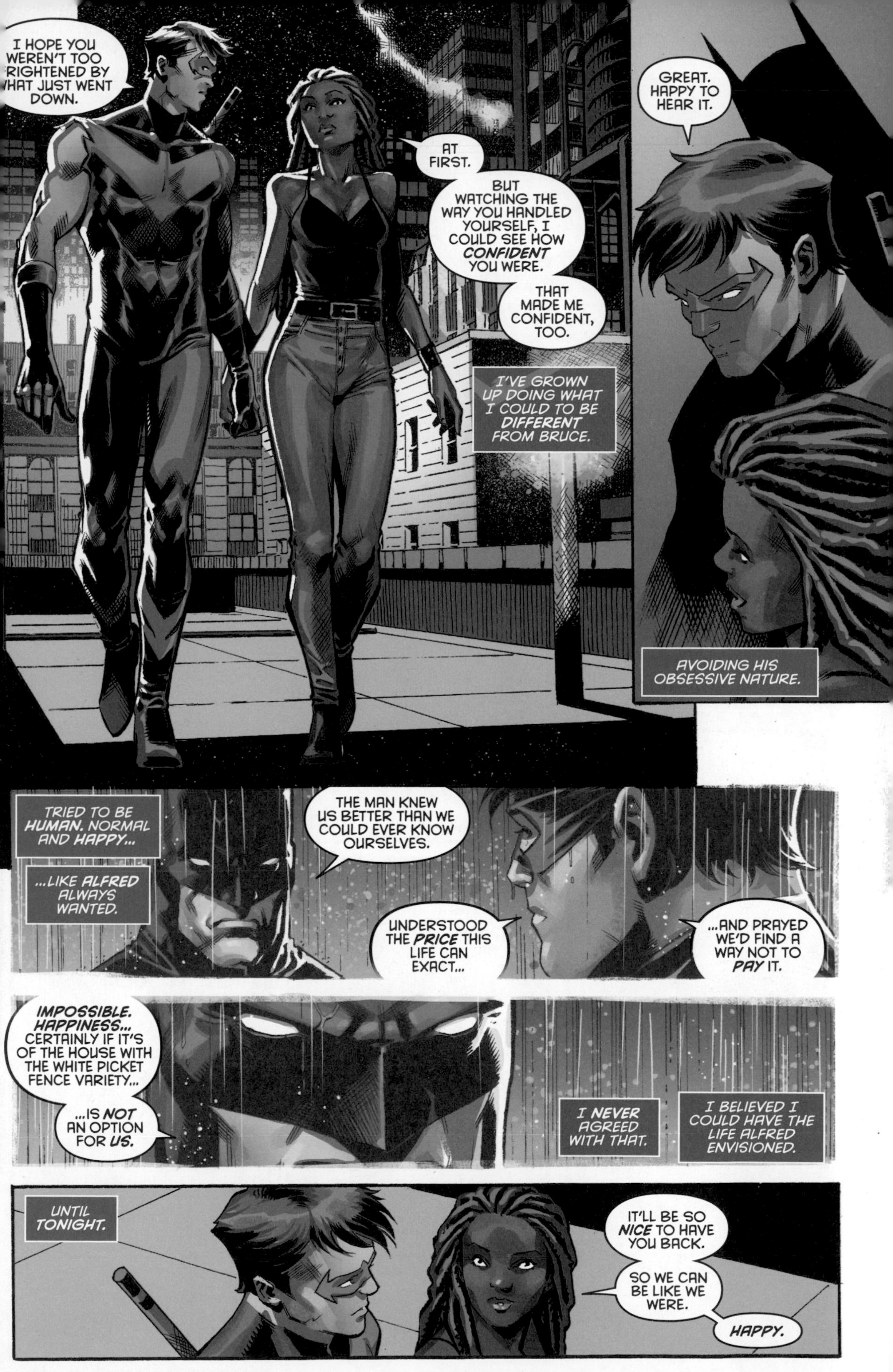

I HOPE YOU WEREN'T TOO FRIGHTENED BY WHAT JUST WENT DOWN.
AT FIRST.
BUT WATCHING THE WAY YOU HANDLED YOURSELF, I COULD SEE HOW CONFIDENT YOU WERE.
THAT MADE ME CONFIDENT, TOO.
I'VE GROWN UP DOING WHAT I COULD TO BE DIFFERENT FROM BRUCE.
GREAT. HAPPY TO HEAR IT.
AVOIDING HIS OBSESSIVE NATURE.
TRIED TO BE HUMAN. NORMAL AND HAPPY...
...LIKE ALFRED ALWAYS WANTED.
THE MAN KNEW US BETTER THAN WE COULD EVER KNOW OURSELVES.
UNDERSTOOD THE PRICE THIS LIFE CAN EXACT...
...AND PRAYED WE'D FIND A WAY NOT TO PAY IT.
IMPOSSIBLE. HAPPINESS... CERTAINLY IF IT'S OF THE HOUSE WITH THE WHITE PICKET FENCE VARIETY...
...IS NOT AN OPTION FOR US.
I NEVER AGREED WITH THAT.
I BELIEVED I COULD HAVE THE LIFE ALFRED ENVISIONED.
UNTIL TONIGHT.
IT'LL BE SO NICE TO HAVE YOU BACK.
SO WE CAN BE LIKE WE WERE.
HAPPY.

RIGHT?

...

RIGHT?

I MEAN, YOU DO *REMEMBER* US BEING TOGETHER?

EVERYTHING WE SHARED? WHAT WE *MEANT* TO EACH OTHER?

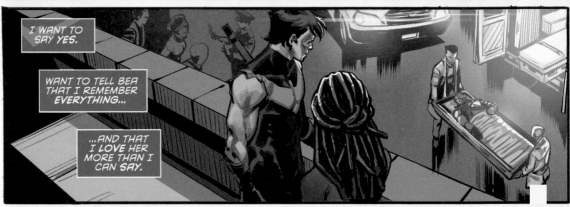

I WANT TO SAY YES.

WANT TO TELL BEA THAT I REMEMBER *EVERYTHING...*

...AND THAT I LOVE HER MORE THAN I CAN *SAY*.

BUT IT'S *BECAUSE I LOVE* HER SO MUCH...

...THAT I *CAN'T*.

I'M... SORRY, BEA.

THE MEMORIES OF US AS A COUPLE...YEAH. THEY CAME BACK.

BUT THE *FEELINGS* DIDN'T.

I HAVE NEVER *HATED* MYSELF...

...MORE THAN I DO RIGHT NOW.

WHEN I WAS RIC...AND WITH *YOU*...IT'S LIKE I WAS REALLY A DIFFERENT PERSON...

...AND THAT GUY NO LONGER EXISTS.

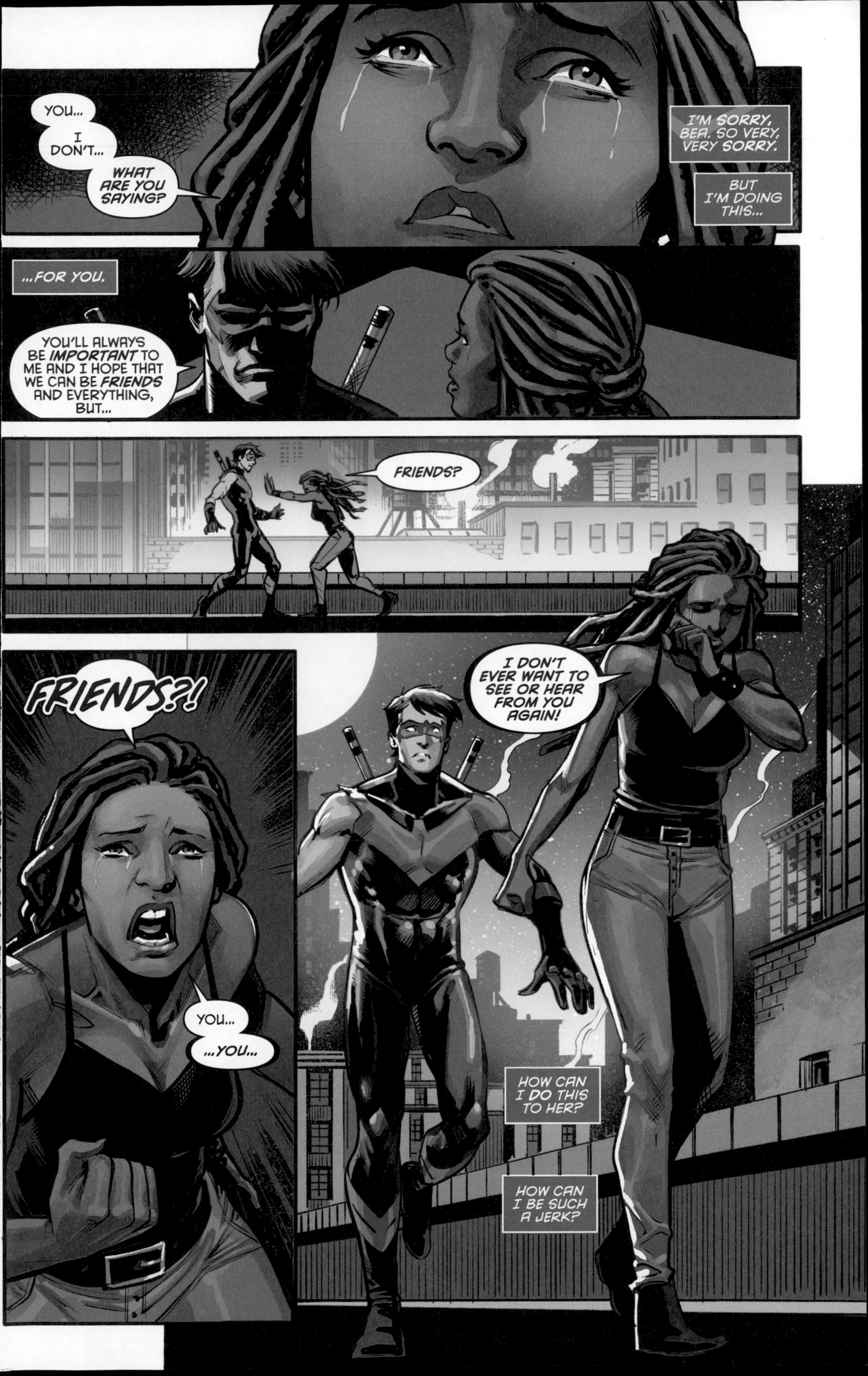

YOU...
I DON'T...
WHAT ARE YOU SAYING?
I'M SORRY, BEA. SO VERY, VERY SORRY.
BUT I'M DOING THIS...
...FOR YOU.
YOU'LL ALWAYS BE IMPORTANT TO ME AND I HOPE THAT WE CAN BE FRIENDS AND EVERYTHING, BUT...
FRIENDS?
FRIENDS?!
YOU...
...YOU...
I DON'T EVER WANT TO SEE OR HEAR FROM YOU AGAIN!
HOW CAN I DO THIS TO HER?
HOW CAN I BE SUCH A JERK?

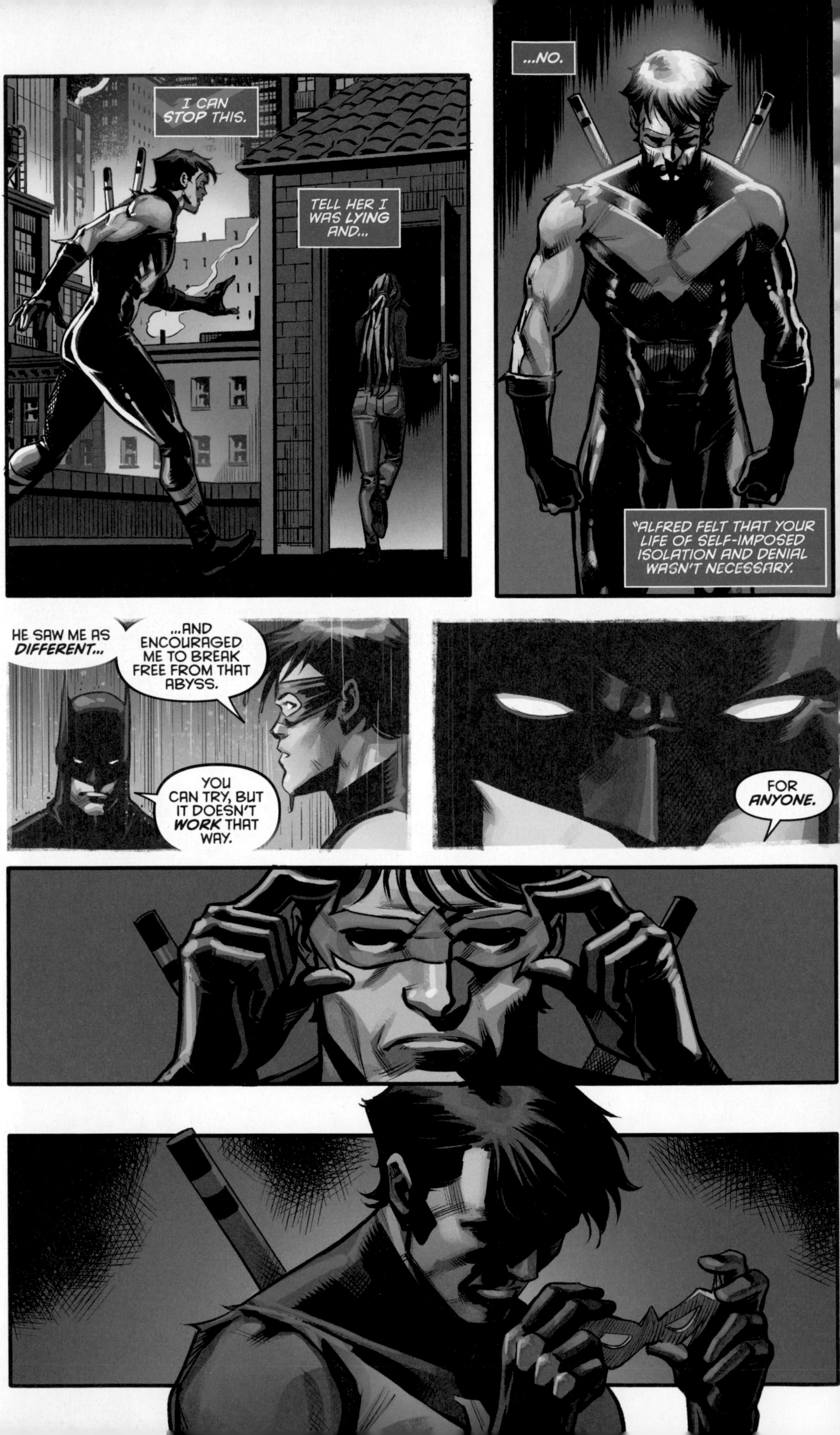

I CAN STOP THIS.
TELL HER I WAS LYING AND...
...NO.
"ALFRED FELT THAT YOUR LIFE OF SELF-IMPOSED ISOLATION AND DENIAL WASN'T NECESSARY.
HE SAW ME AS DIFFERENT...
...AND ENCOURAGED ME TO BREAK FREE FROM THAT ABYSS.
YOU CAN TRY, BUT IT DOESN'T WORK THAT WAY.
FOR ANYONE.

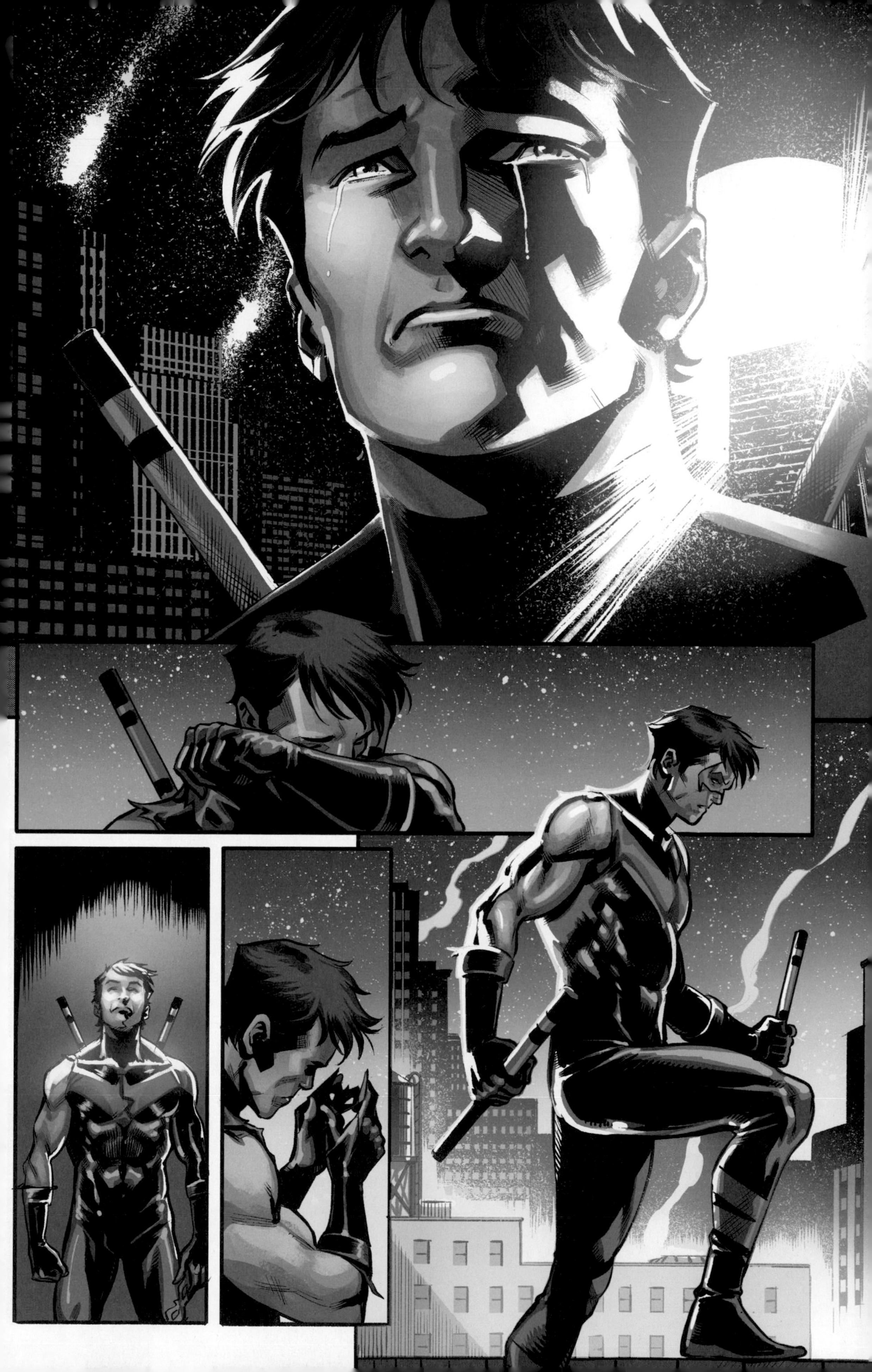

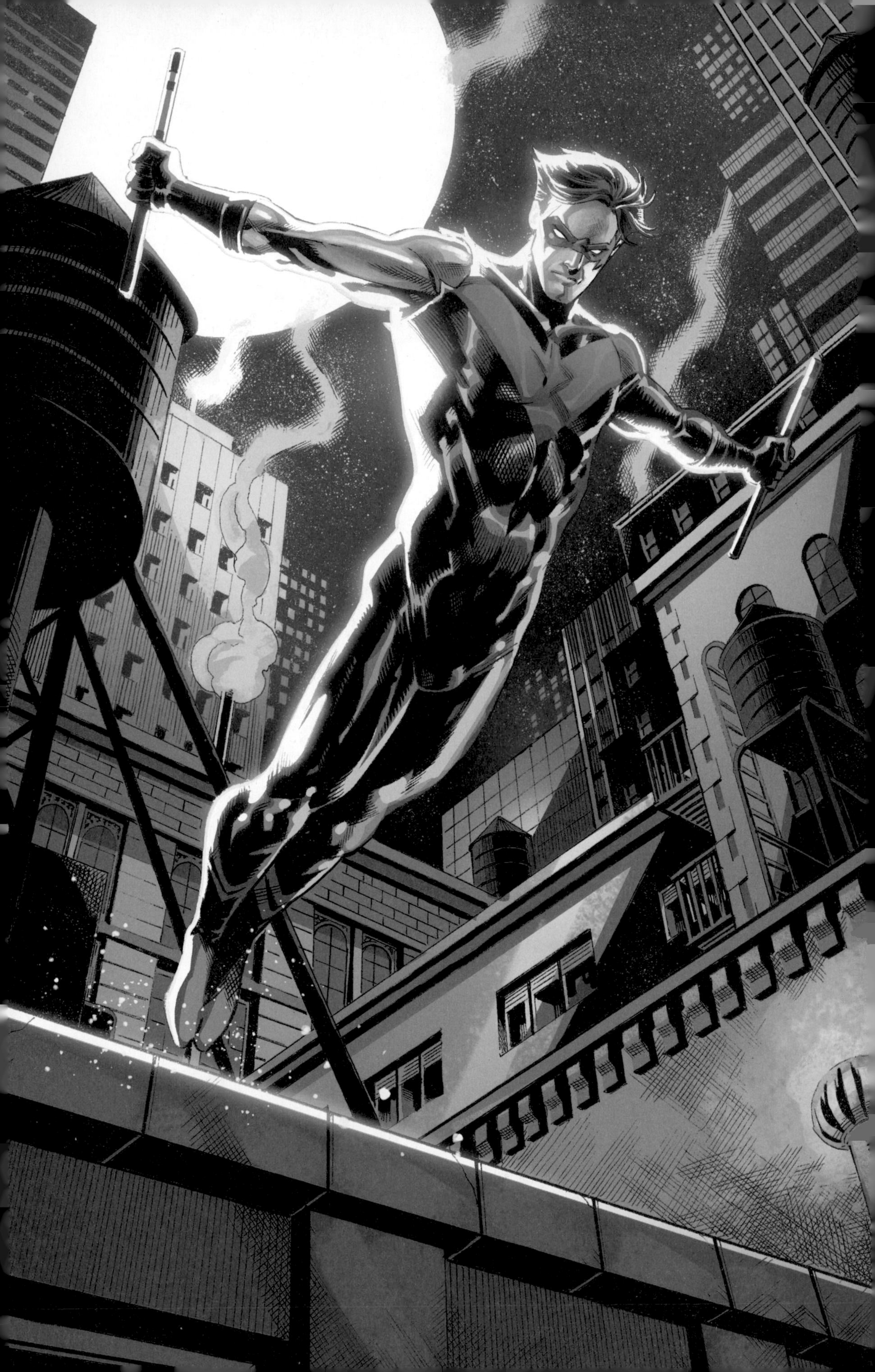

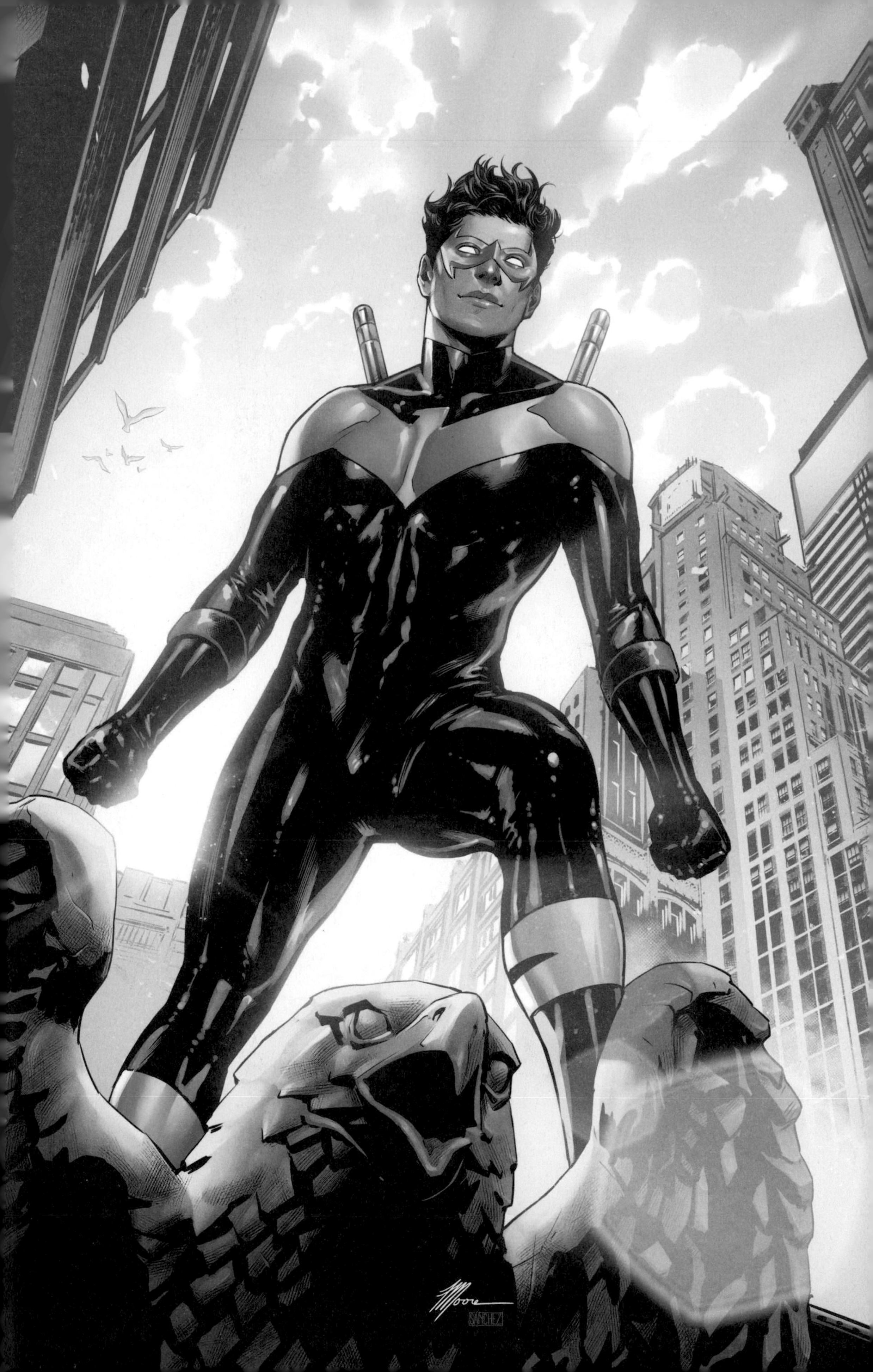
Moore
SANCHEZ

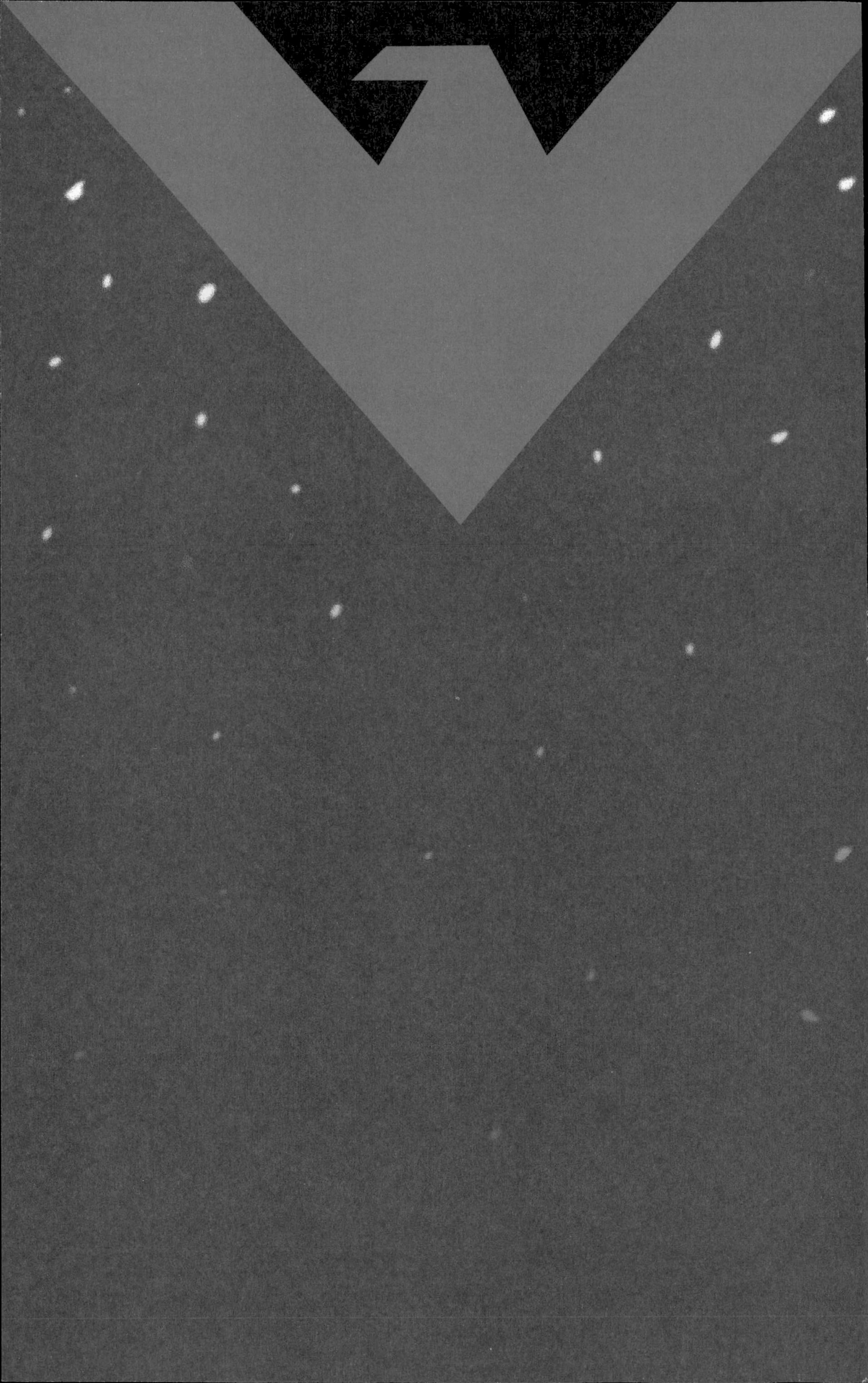

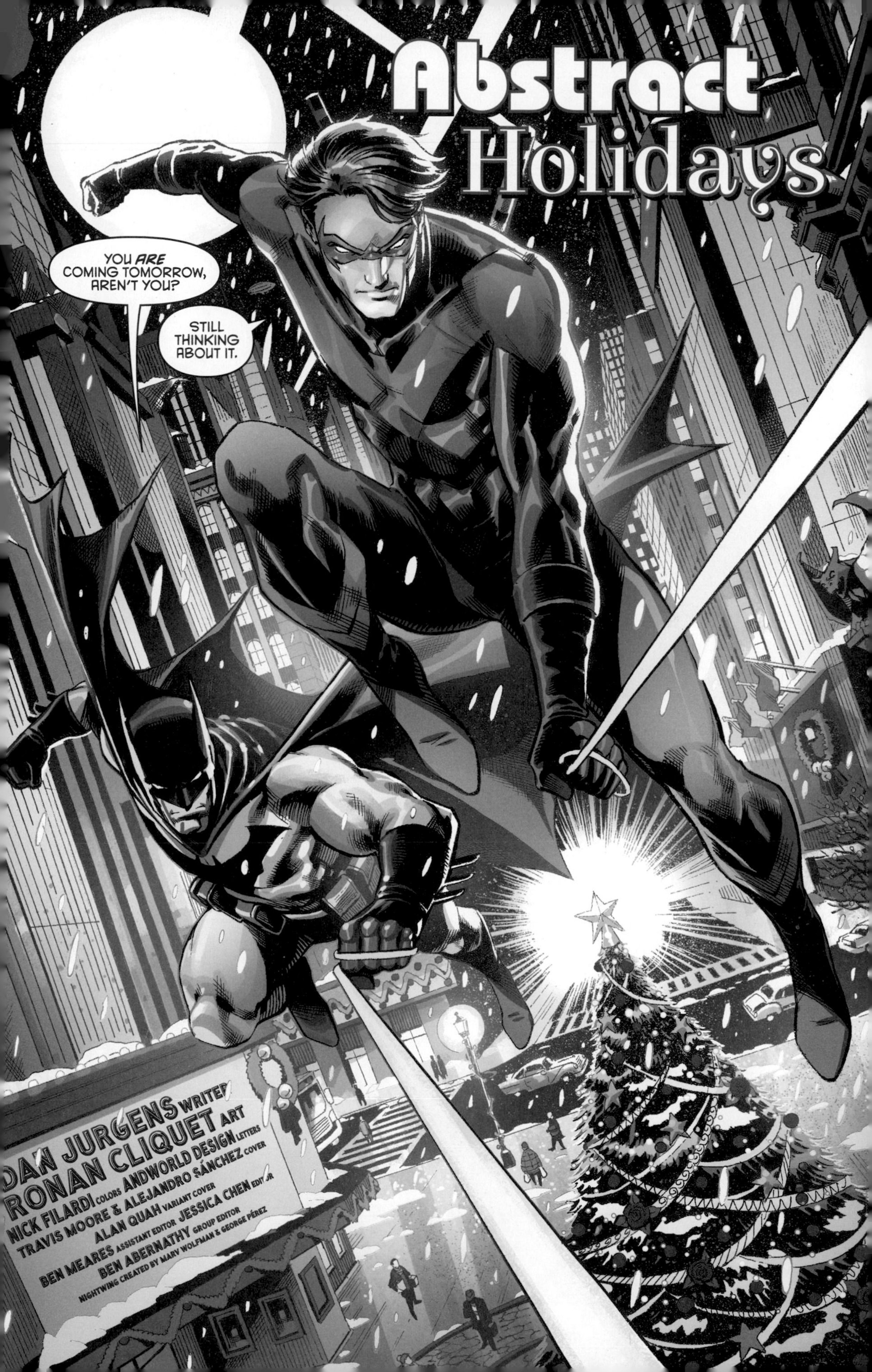
Abstract Holidays
YOU *ARE* COMING TOMORROW, AREN'T YOU?
STILL THINKING ABOUT IT.
DAN JURGENS WRITER
RONAN CLIQUET ART
NICK FILARDI COLORS ANDWORLD DESIGN LETTERS
TRAVIS MOORE & ALEJANDRO SÁNCHEZ COVER
ALAN QUAH VARIANT COVER
BEN MEARES ASSISTANT EDITOR JESSICA CHEN EDITOR
BEN ABERNATHY GROUP EDITOR
NIGHTWING CREATED BY MARV WOLFMAN & GEORGE PÉREZ

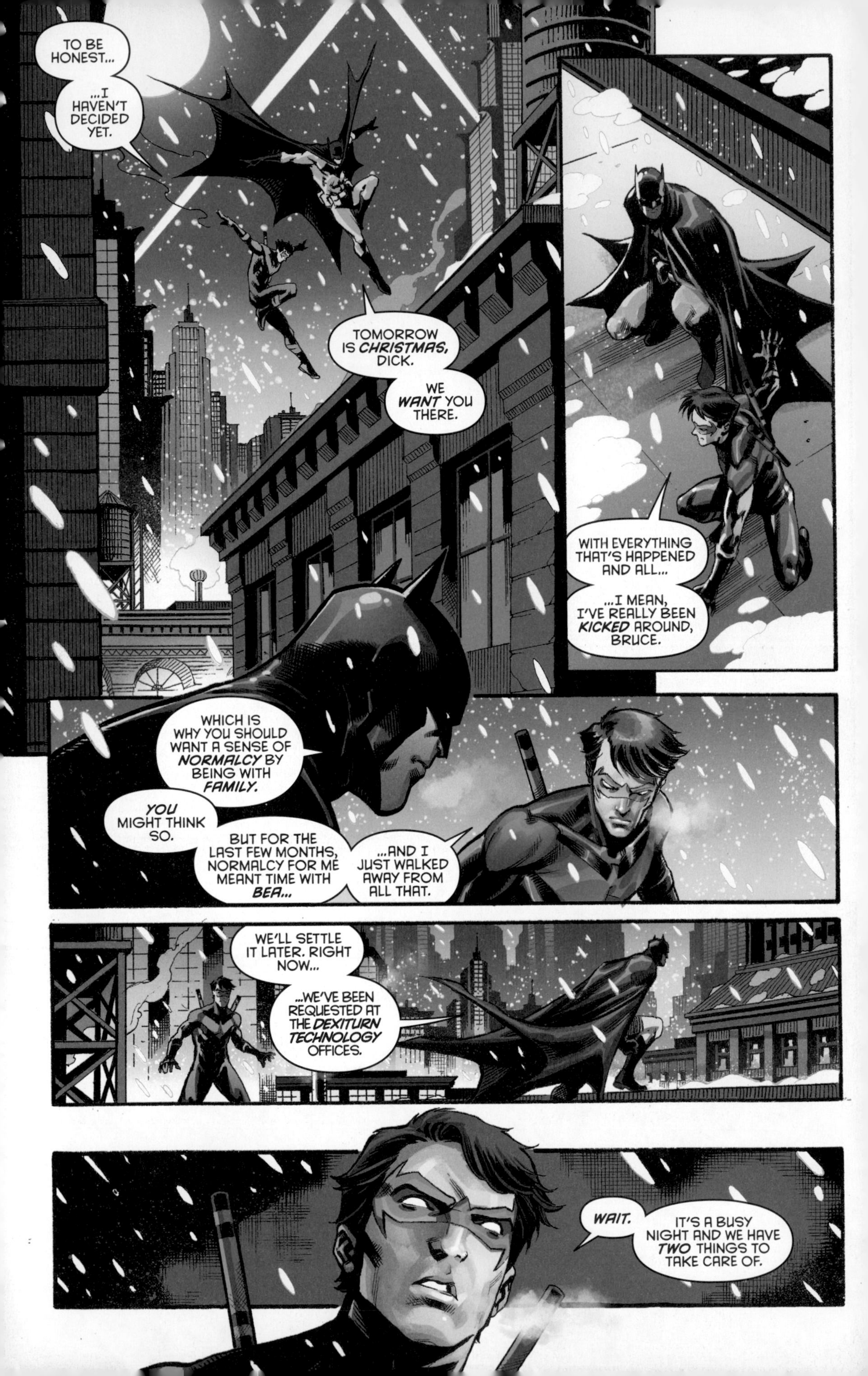

TO BE HONEST...
...I HAVEN'T DECIDED YET.
TOMORROW IS CHRISTMAS, DICK.
WE WANT YOU THERE.
WITH EVERYTHING THAT'S HAPPENED AND ALL...
...I MEAN, I'VE REALLY BEEN KICKED AROUND, BRUCE.
WHICH IS WHY YOU SHOULD WANT A SENSE OF NORMALCY BY BEING WITH FAMILY.
YOU MIGHT THINK SO.
BUT FOR THE LAST FEW MONTHS, NORMALCY FOR ME MEANT TIME WITH BEA...
...AND I JUST WALKED AWAY FROM ALL THAT.
WE'LL SETTLE IT LATER. RIGHT NOW...
...WE'VE BEEN REQUESTED AT THE DEXITURN TECHNOLOGY OFFICES.
WAIT.
IT'S A BUSY NIGHT AND WE HAVE TWO THINGS TO TAKE CARE OF.

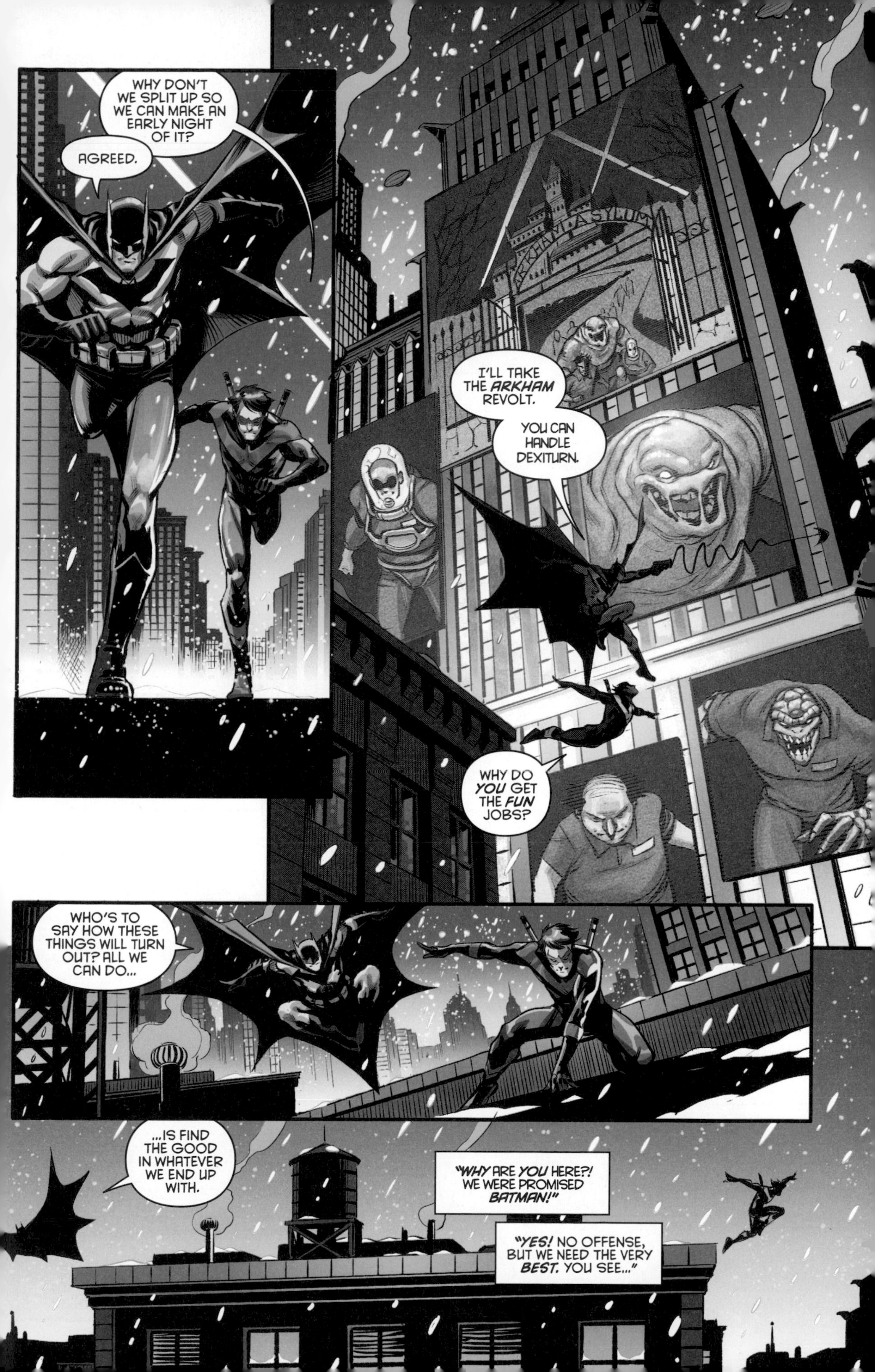
WHY DON'T WE SPLIT UP SO WE CAN MAKE AN EARLY NIGHT OF IT?
AGREED.
I'LL TAKE THE ARKHAM REVOLT.
YOU CAN HANDLE DEXITURN.
WHY DO YOU GET THE FUN JOBS?
WHO'S TO SAY HOW THESE THINGS WILL TURN OUT? ALL WE CAN DO...
...IS FIND THE GOOD IN WHATEVER WE END UP WITH.
"WHY ARE YOU HERE?! WE WERE PROMISED BATMAN!"
"YES! NO OFFENSE, BUT WE NEED THE VERY BEST. YOU SEE..."

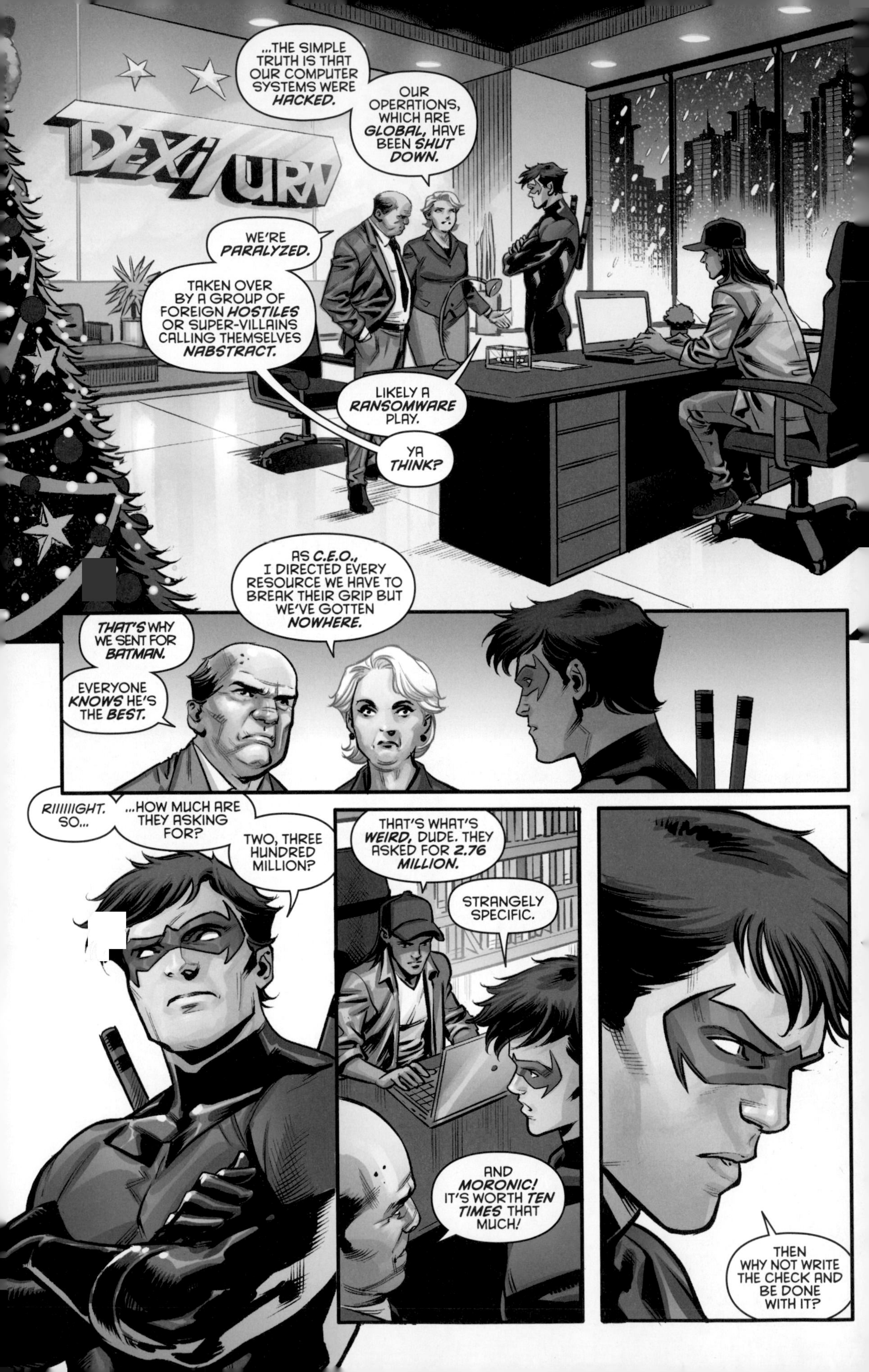

...THE SIMPLE TRUTH IS THAT OUR COMPUTER SYSTEMS WERE HACKED.
OUR OPERATIONS, WHICH ARE GLOBAL, HAVE BEEN SHUT DOWN.
WE'RE PARALYZED.
TAKEN OVER BY A GROUP OF FOREIGN HOSTILES OR SUPER-VILLAINS CALLING THEMSELVES NABSTRACT.
LIKELY A RANSOMWARE PLAY.
YA THINK?
AS C.E.O., I DIRECTED EVERY RESOURCE WE HAVE TO BREAK THEIR GRIP BUT WE'VE GOTTEN NOWHERE.
THAT'S WHY WE SENT FOR BATMAN.
EVERYONE KNOWS HE'S THE BEST.
RIIIIIGHT. SO...
...HOW MUCH ARE THEY ASKING FOR?
TWO, THREE HUNDRED MILLION?
THAT'S WHAT'S WEIRD, DUDE. THEY ASKED FOR 2.76 MILLION.
STRANGELY SPECIFIC.
AND MORONIC! IT'S WORTH TEN TIMES THAT MUCH!
THEN WHY NOT WRITE THE CHECK AND BE DONE WITH IT?

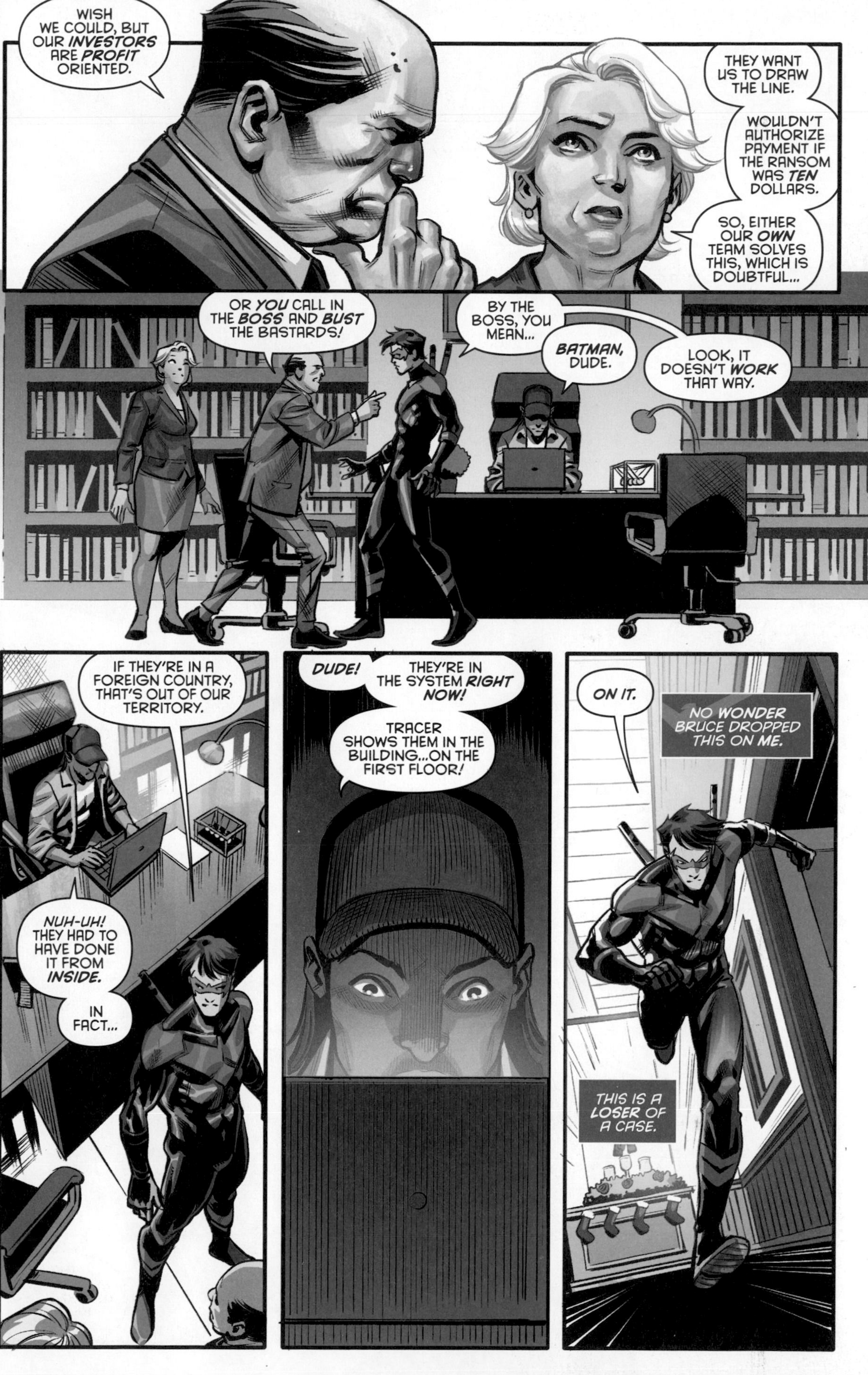

WISH WE COULD, BUT OUR *INVESTORS* ARE *PROFIT* ORIENTED.
THEY WANT US TO DRAW THE LINE.
WOULDN'T AUTHORIZE PAYMENT IF THE RANSOM WAS *TEN* DOLLARS.
SO, EITHER OUR *OWN* TEAM SOLVES THIS, WHICH IS DOUBTFUL...
OR *YOU* CALL IN THE *BOSS* AND *BUST* THE BASTARDS!
BY THE BOSS, YOU MEAN...
BATMAN, DUDE.
LOOK, IT DOESN'T *WORK* THAT WAY.
IF THEY'RE IN A FOREIGN COUNTRY, THAT'S OUT OF OUR TERRITORY.
NUH-UH! THEY HAD TO HAVE DONE IT FROM *INSIDE.*
IN FACT...
DUDE!
THEY'RE IN THE SYSTEM *RIGHT NOW!*
TRACER SHOWS THEM IN THE BUILDING...ON THE FIRST FLOOR!
ON IT.
NO *WONDER* BRUCE DROPPED THIS ON *ME.*
THIS IS A *LOSER* OF A CASE.

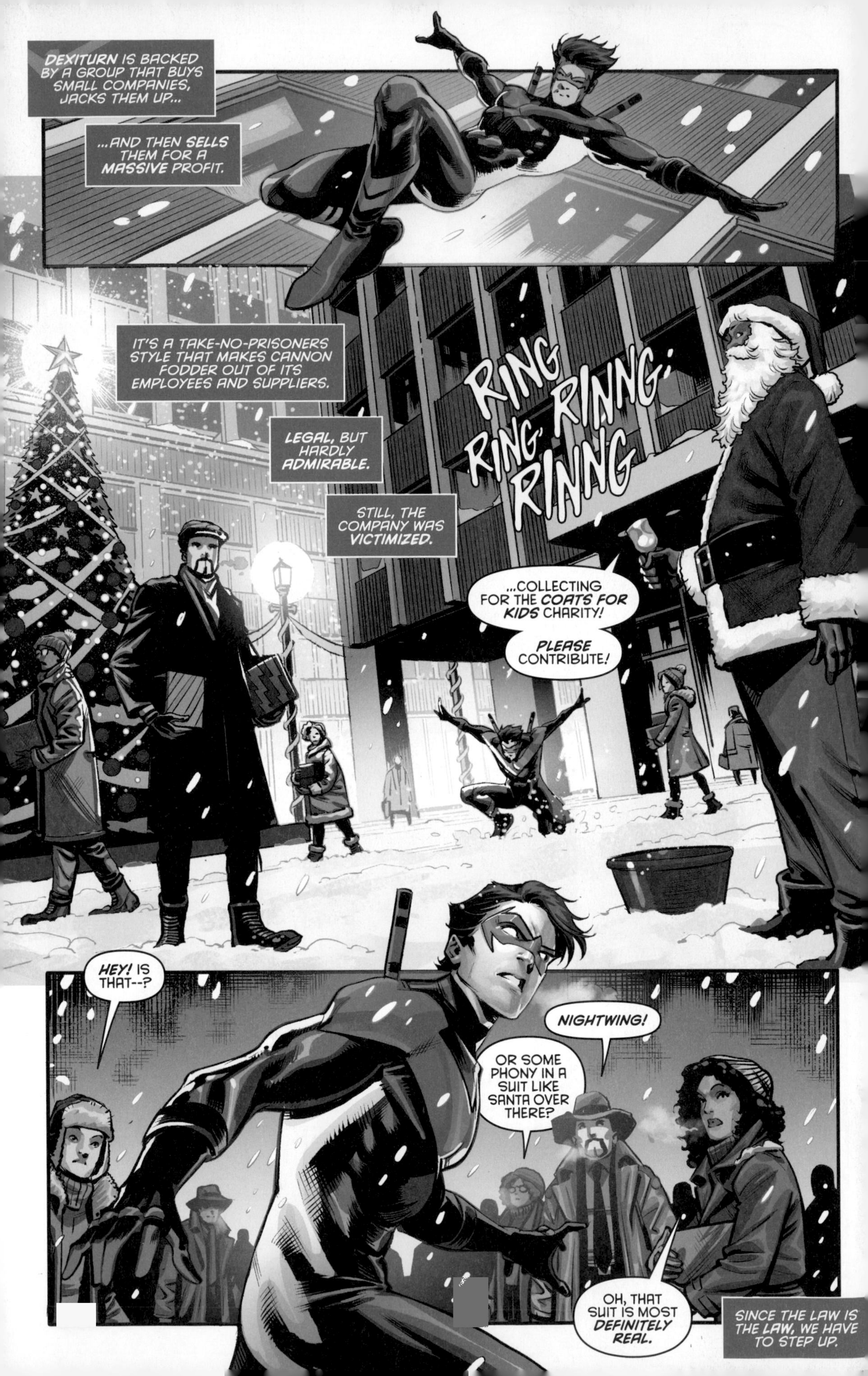

DEXITURN IS BACKED BY A GROUP THAT BUYS SMALL COMPANIES, JACKS THEM UP...
...AND THEN SELLS THEM FOR A MASSIVE PROFIT.
IT'S A TAKE-NO-PRISONERS STYLE THAT MAKES CANNON FODDER OUT OF ITS EMPLOYEES AND SUPPLIERS.
LEGAL, BUT HARDLY ADMIRABLE.
STILL, THE COMPANY WAS VICTIMIZED.
RING RING RINNG RINNG RINNG
...COLLECTING FOR THE COATS FOR KIDS CHARITY!
PLEASE CONTRIBUTE!
HEY! IS THAT--?
NIGHTWING!
OR SOME PHONY IN A SUIT LIKE SANTA OVER THERE?
OH, THAT SUIT IS MOST DEFINITELY REAL.
SINCE THE LAW IS THE LAW, WE HAVE TO STEP UP.

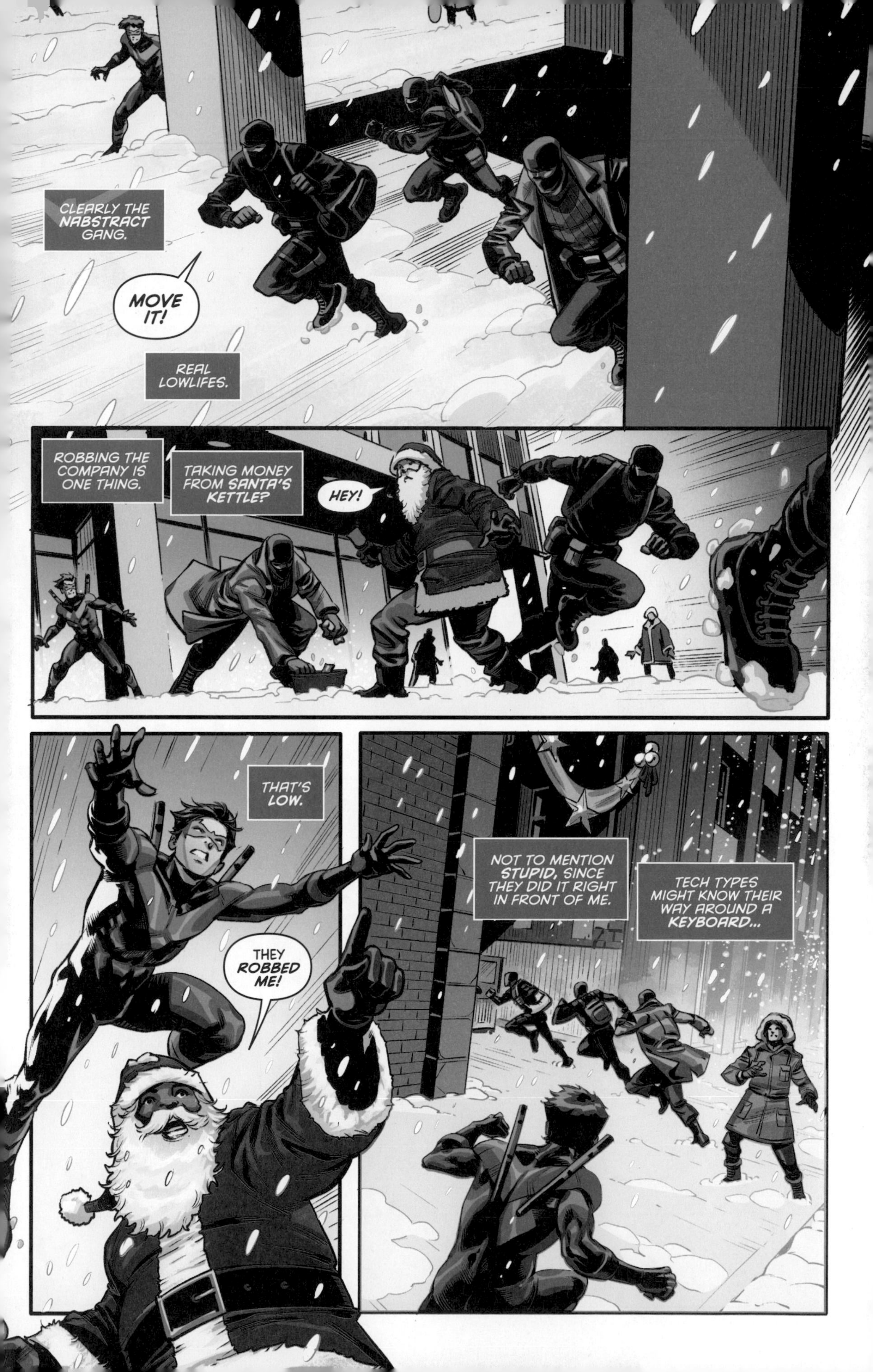
CLEARLY THE NABSTRACT GANG.
MOVE IT!
REAL LOWLIFES.
ROBBING THE COMPANY IS ONE THING.
TAKING MONEY FROM SANTA'S KETTLE?
HEY!
THAT'S LOW.
THEY ROBBED ME!
NOT TO MENTION STUPID, SINCE THEY DID IT RIGHT IN FRONT OF ME.
TECH TYPES MIGHT KNOW THEIR WAY AROUND A KEYBOARD...

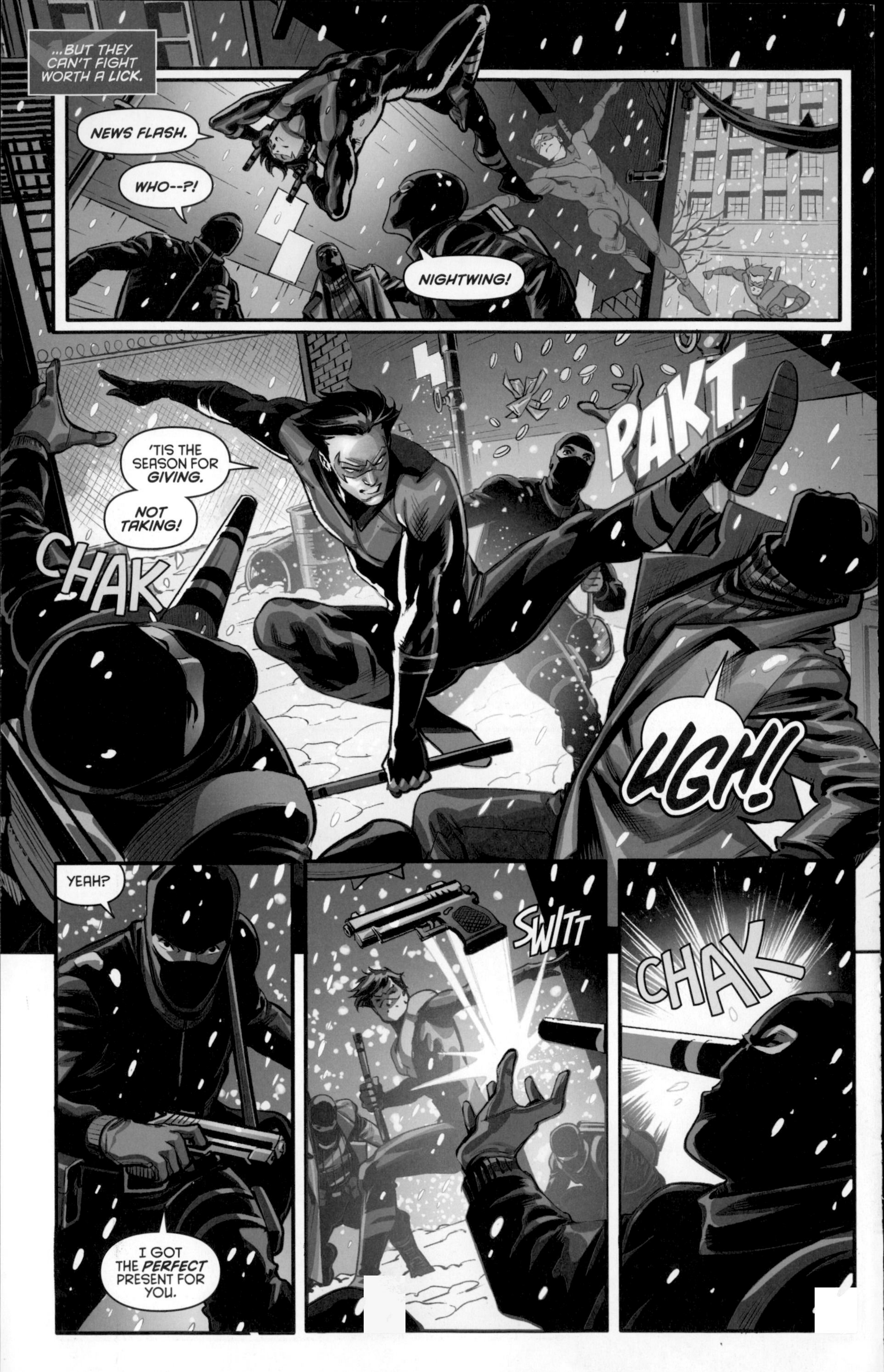

...BUT THEY CAN'T FIGHT WORTH A LICK.
NEWS FLASH.
WHO--?!
NIGHTWING!
'TIS THE SEASON FOR GIVING.
NOT TAKING!
PAKT
CHAK
UGH!
YEAH?
I GOT THE PERFECT PRESENT FOR YOU.
SWITT
CHAK

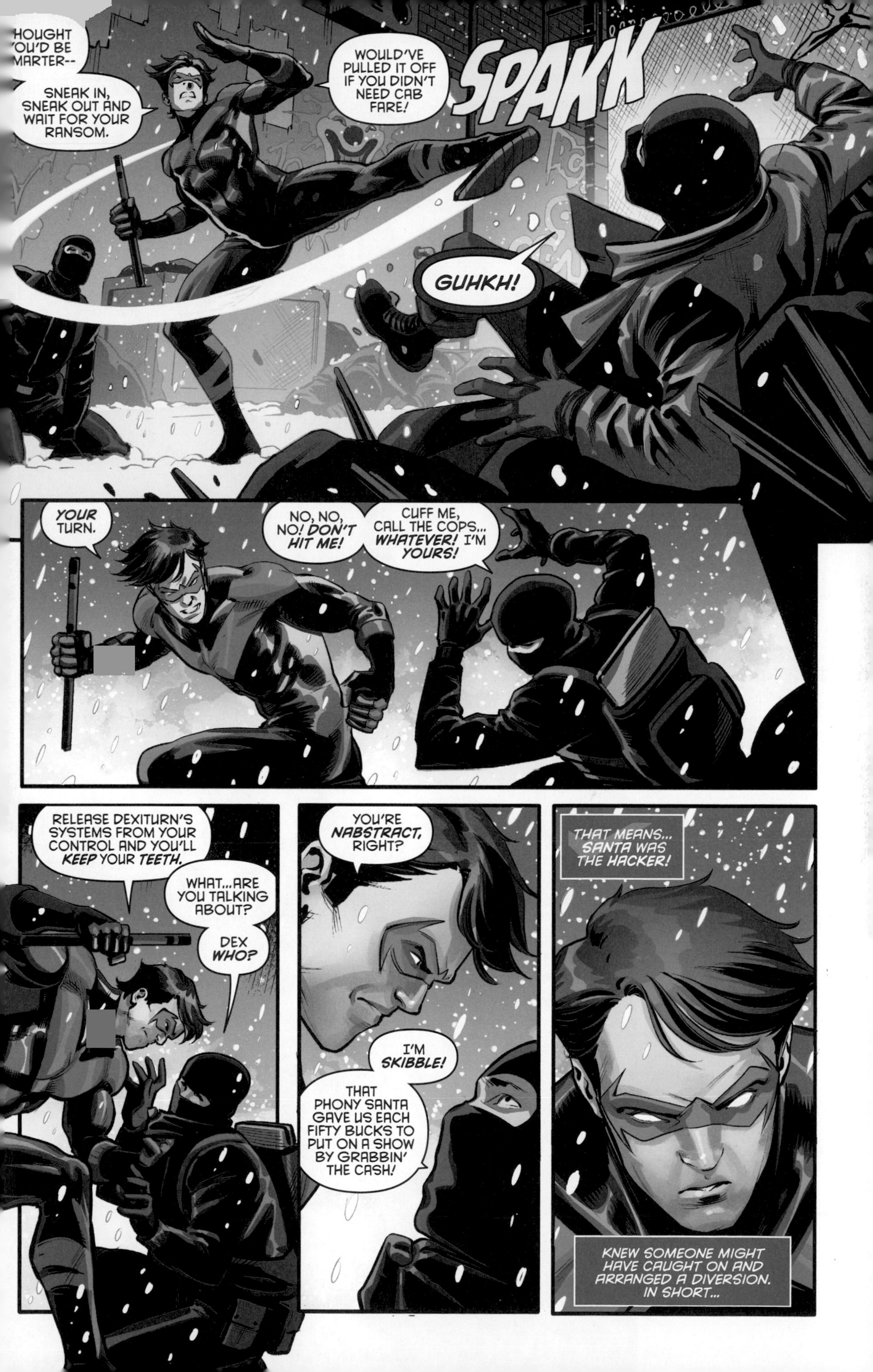

HOUGHT YOU'D BE MARTER--
SNEAK IN, SNEAK OUT AND WAIT FOR YOUR RANSOM.
WOULD'VE PULLED IT OFF IF YOU DIDN'T NEED CAB FARE!
SPAKK
GUHKH!
YOUR TURN.
NO, NO, NO! DON'T HIT ME!
CUFF ME, CALL THE COPS... WHATEVER! I'M YOURS!
RELEASE DEXITURN'S SYSTEMS FROM YOUR CONTROL AND YOU'LL KEEP YOUR TEETH.
WHAT...ARE YOU TALKING ABOUT?
DEX WHO?
YOU'RE NABSTRACT, RIGHT?
I'M SKIBBLE!
THAT PHONY SANTA GAVE US EACH FIFTY BUCKS TO PUT ON A SHOW BY GRABBIN' THE CASH!
THAT MEANS... SANTA WAS THE HACKER!
KNEW SOMEONE MIGHT HAVE CAUGHT ON AND ARRANGED A DIVERSION. IN SHORT...

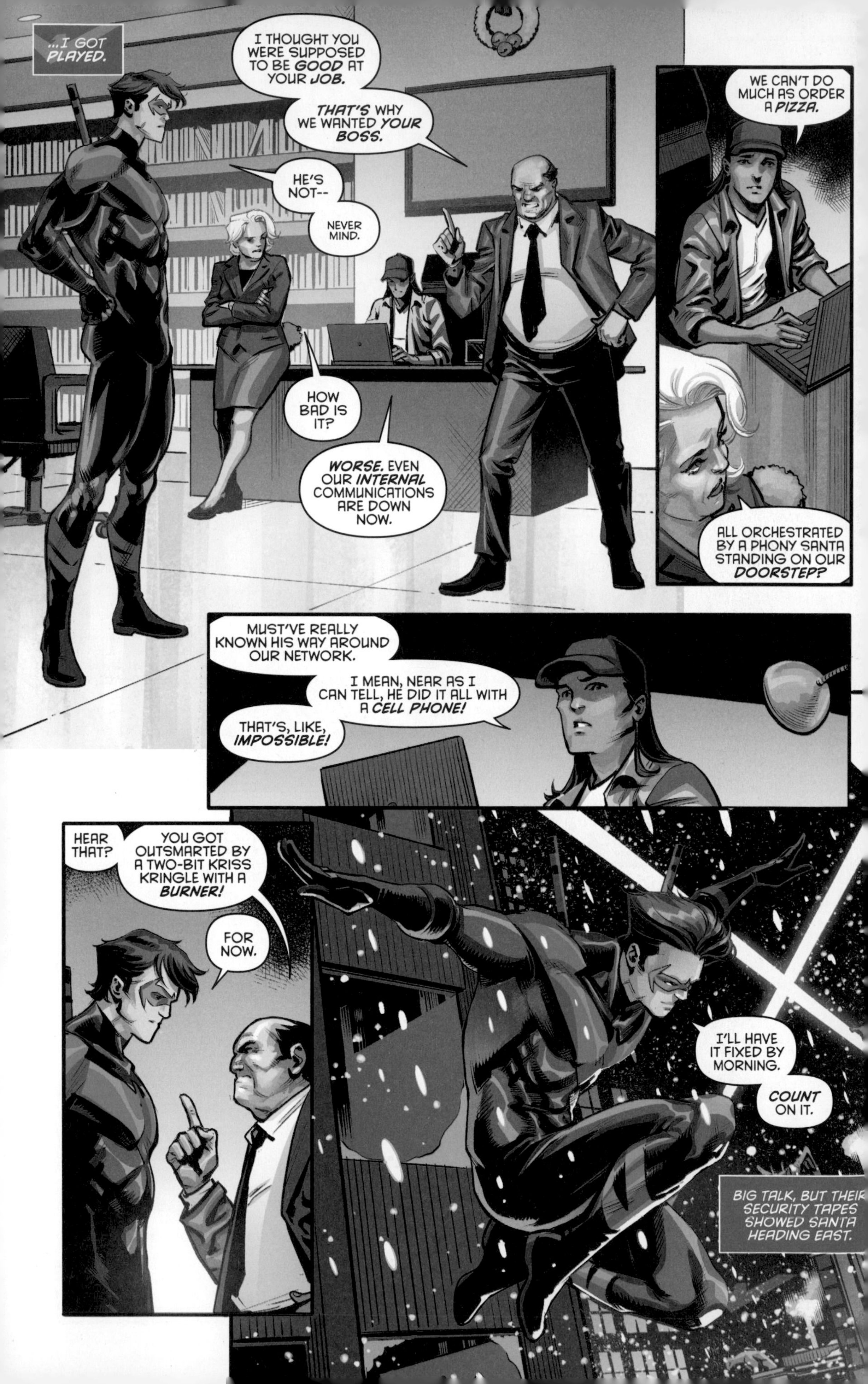
...I GOT PLAYED.
I THOUGHT YOU WERE SUPPOSED TO BE GOOD AT YOUR JOB.
THAT'S WHY WE WANTED YOUR BOSS.
HE'S NOT--
NEVER MIND.
HOW BAD IS IT?
WORSE. EVEN OUR INTERNAL COMMUNICATIONS ARE DOWN NOW.
WE CAN'T DO MUCH AS ORDER A PIZZA.
ALL ORCHESTRATED BY A PHONY SANTA STANDING ON OUR DOORSTEP?
MUST'VE REALLY KNOWN HIS WAY AROUND OUR NETWORK.
I MEAN, NEAR AS I CAN TELL, HE DID IT ALL WITH A CELL PHONE!
THAT'S, LIKE, IMPOSSIBLE!
HEAR THAT?
YOU GOT OUTSMARTED BY A TWO-BIT KRISS KRINGLE WITH A BURNER!
FOR NOW.
I'LL HAVE IT FIXED BY MORNING.
COUNT ON IT.
BIG TALK, BUT THEIR SECURITY TAPES SHOWED SANTA HEADING EAST.

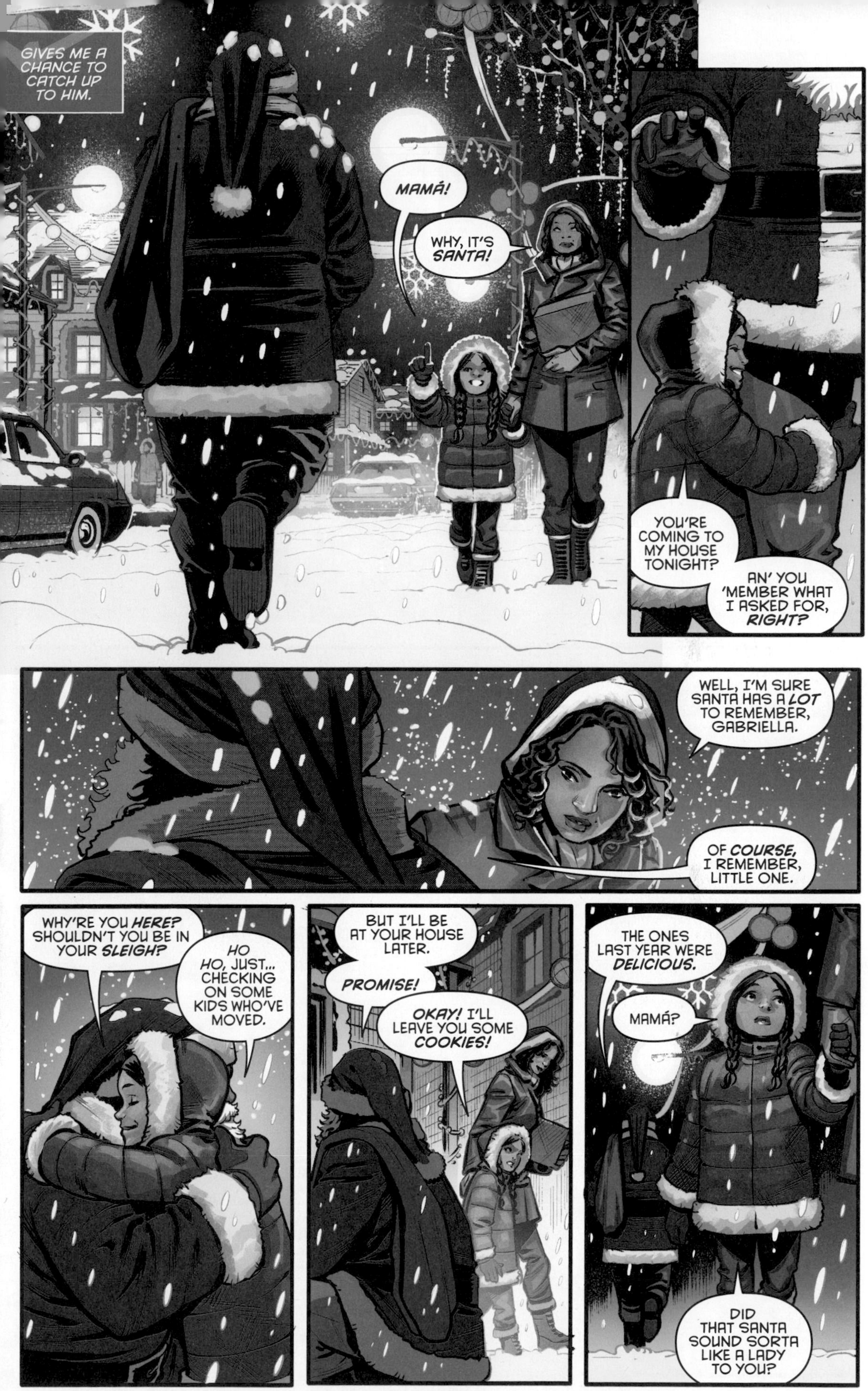

GIVES ME A CHANCE TO CATCH UP TO HIM.
MAMÁ!
WHY, IT'S SANTA!
YOU'RE COMING TO MY HOUSE TONIGHT?
AN' YOU 'MEMBER WHAT I ASKED FOR, RIGHT?
WELL, I'M SURE SANTA HAS A LOT TO REMEMBER, GABRIELLA.
OF COURSE, I REMEMBER, LITTLE ONE.
WHY'RE YOU HERE? SHOULDN'T YOU BE IN YOUR SLEIGH?
HO HO, JUST... CHECKING ON SOME KIDS WHO'VE MOVED.
BUT I'LL BE AT YOUR HOUSE LATER.
PROMISE!
OKAY! I'LL LEAVE YOU SOME COOKIES!
THE ONES LAST YEAR WERE DELICIOUS.
MAMÁ?
DID THAT SANTA SOUND SORTA LIKE A LADY TO YOU?

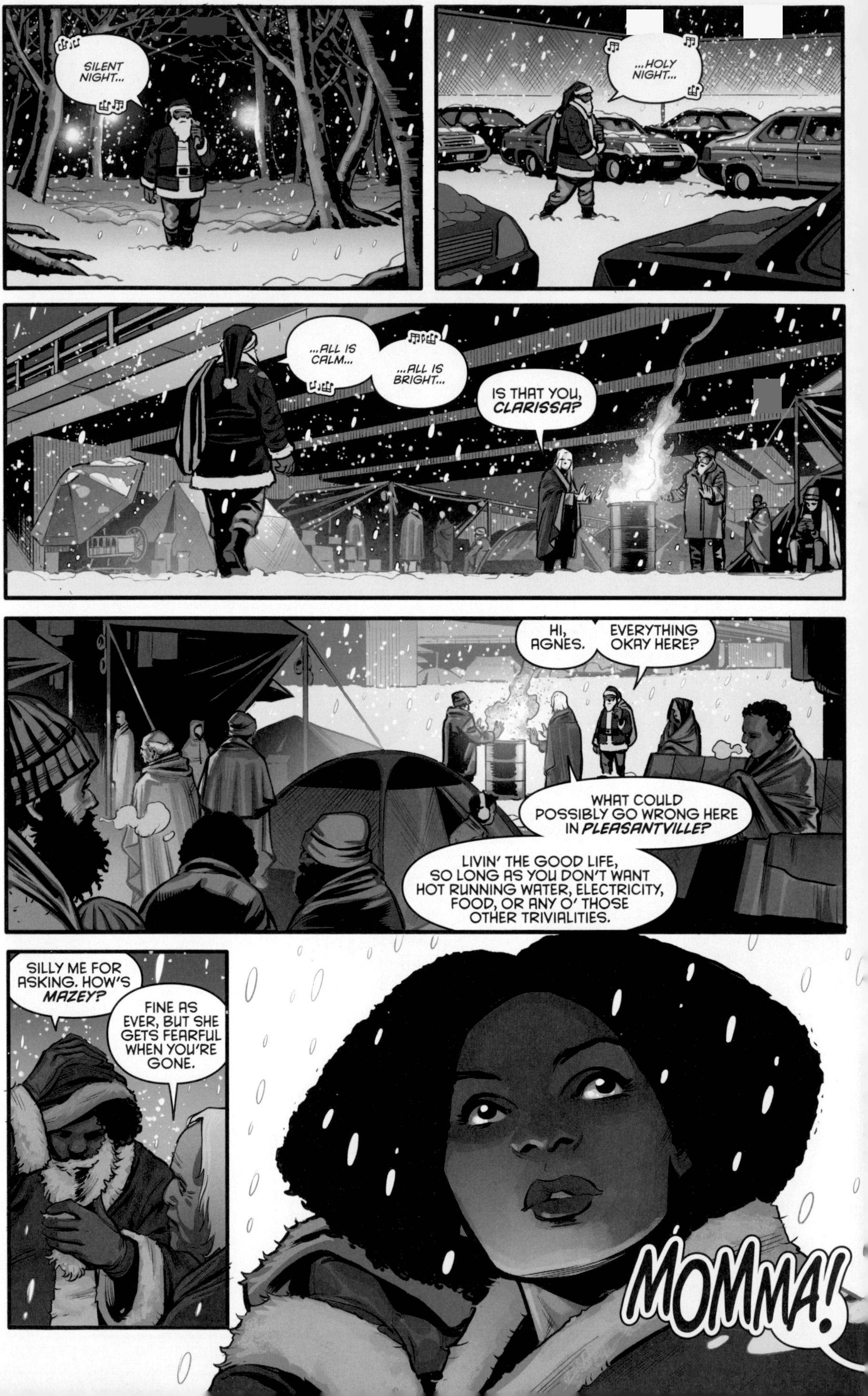
SILENT NIGHT...
...HOLY NIGHT...
...ALL IS CALM...
...ALL IS BRIGHT...
IS THAT YOU, CLARISSA?
HI, AGNES.
EVERYTHING OKAY HERE?
WHAT COULD POSSIBLY GO WRONG HERE IN PLEASANTVILLE?
LIVIN' THE GOOD LIFE, SO LONG AS YOU DON'T WANT HOT RUNNING WATER, ELECTRICITY, FOOD, OR ANY O' THOSE OTHER TRIVIALITIES.
SILLY ME FOR ASKING. HOW'S MAZEY?
FINE AS EVER, BUT SHE GETS FEARFUL WHEN YOU'RE GONE.
MOMMA!

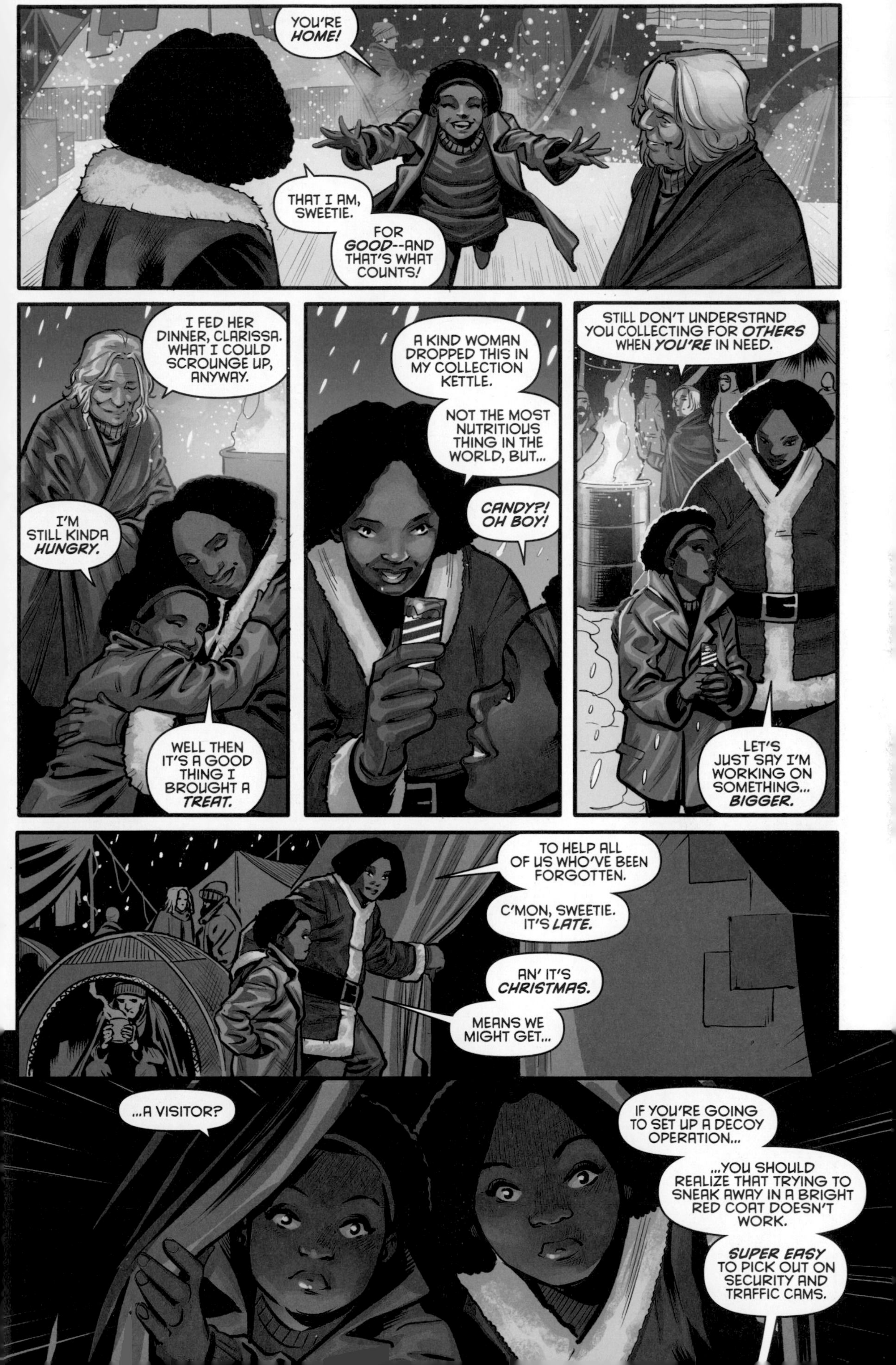
YOU'RE HOME!
THAT I AM, SWEETIE.
FOR GOOD--AND THAT'S WHAT COUNTS!
I FED HER DINNER, CLARISSA. WHAT I COULD SCROUNGE UP, ANYWAY.
I'M STILL KINDA HUNGRY.
WELL THEN IT'S A GOOD THING I BROUGHT A TREAT.
A KIND WOMAN DROPPED THIS IN MY COLLECTION KETTLE.
NOT THE MOST NUTRITIOUS THING IN THE WORLD, BUT...
CANDY?! OH BOY!
STILL DON'T UNDERSTAND YOU COLLECTING FOR OTHERS WHEN YOU'RE IN NEED.
LET'S JUST SAY I'M WORKING ON SOMETHING... BIGGER.
TO HELP ALL OF US WHO'VE BEEN FORGOTTEN.
C'MON, SWEETIE. IT'S LATE.
AN' IT'S CHRISTMAS.
MEANS WE MIGHT GET...
...A VISITOR?
IF YOU'RE GOING TO SET UP A DECOY OPERATION...
...YOU SHOULD REALIZE THAT TRYING TO SNEAK AWAY IN A BRIGHT RED COAT DOESN'T WORK.
SUPER EASY TO PICK OUT ON SECURITY AND TRAFFIC CAMS.

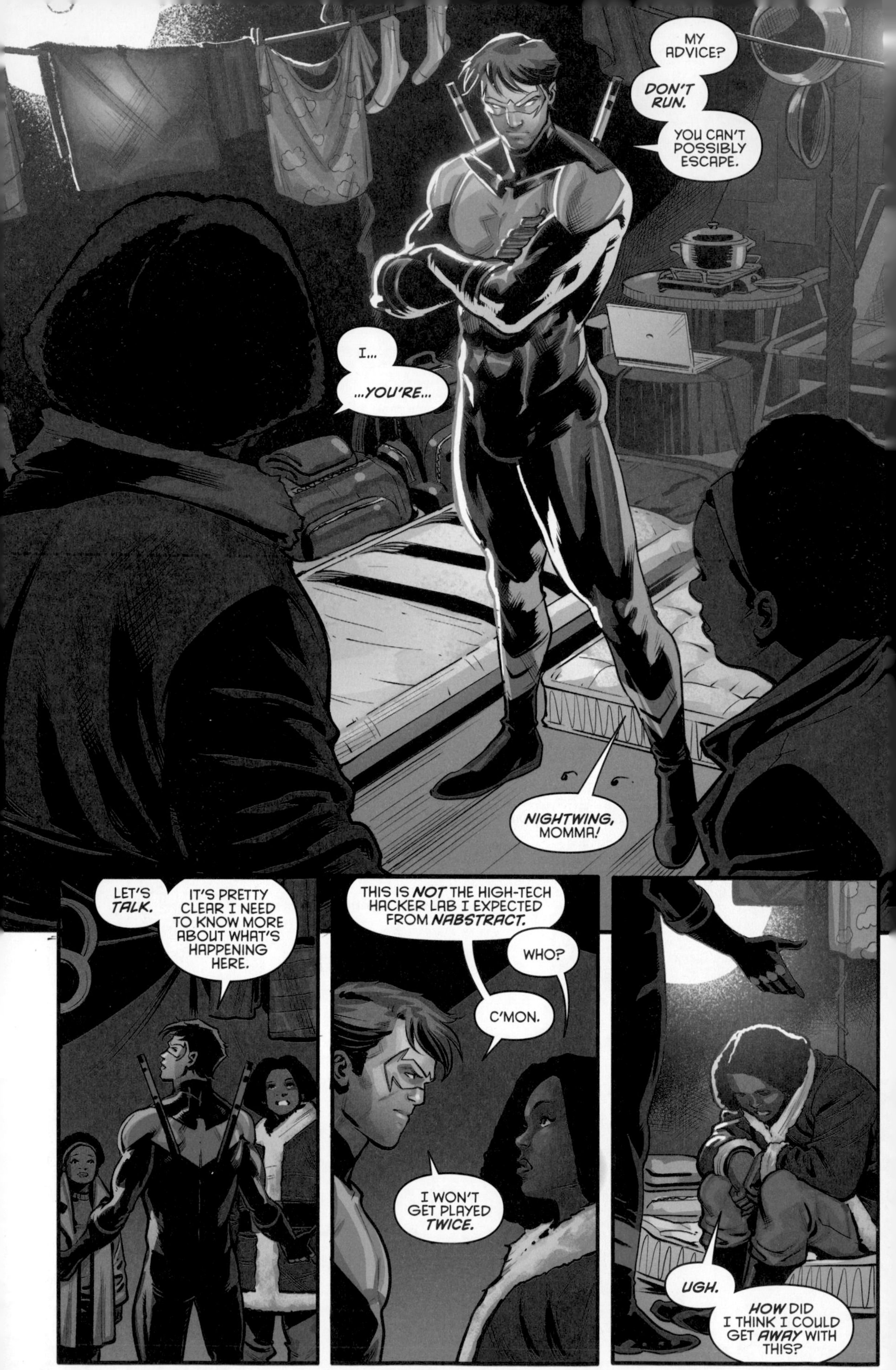
MY ADVICE?
DON'T RUN.
YOU CAN'T POSSIBLY ESCAPE.
I...
...YOU'RE...
NIGHTWING, MOMMA!
LET'S TALK.
IT'S PRETTY CLEAR I NEED TO KNOW MORE ABOUT WHAT'S HAPPENING HERE.
THIS IS NOT THE HIGH-TECH HACKER LAB I EXPECTED FROM NABSTRACT.
WHO?
C'MON.
I WON'T GET PLAYED TWICE.
UGH.
HOW DID I THINK I COULD GET AWAY WITH THIS?

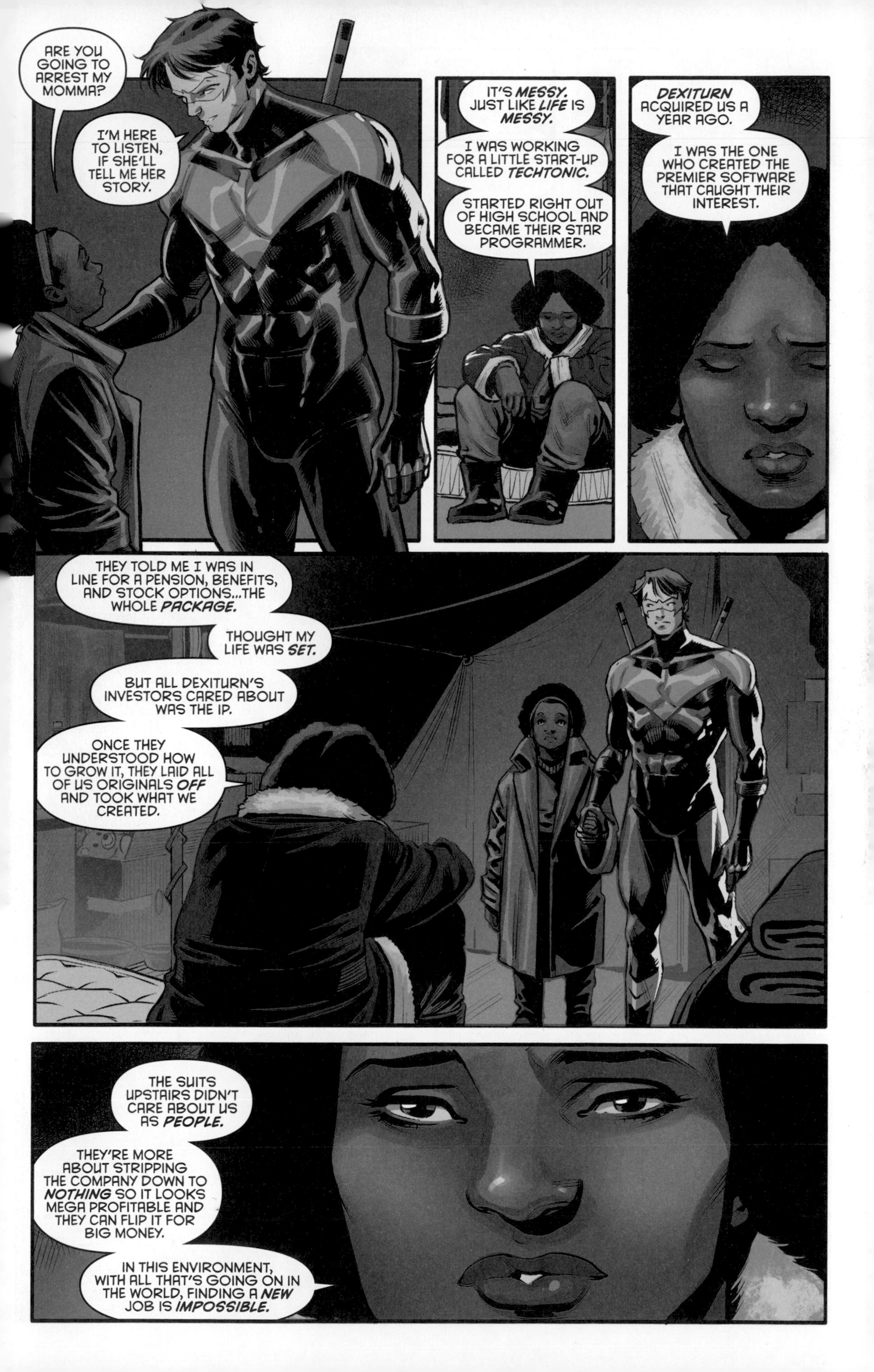
ARE YOU GOING TO ARREST MY MOMMA?
I'M HERE TO LISTEN, IF SHE'LL TELL ME HER STORY.
IT'S *MESSY.* JUST LIKE *LIFE* IS *MESSY.*
I WAS WORKING FOR A LITTLE START-UP CALLED *TECHTONIC.*
STARTED RIGHT OUT OF HIGH SCHOOL AND BECAME THEIR STAR PROGRAMMER.
DEXITURN ACQUIRED US A YEAR AGO.
I WAS THE ONE WHO CREATED THE PREMIER SOFTWARE THAT CAUGHT THEIR INTEREST.
THEY TOLD ME I WAS IN LINE FOR A PENSION, BENEFITS, AND STOCK OPTIONS...THE WHOLE *PACKAGE.*
THOUGHT MY LIFE WAS *SET.*
BUT ALL DEXITURN'S INVESTORS CARED ABOUT WAS THE IP.
ONCE THEY UNDERSTOOD HOW TO GROW IT, THEY LAID ALL OF US ORIGINALS *OFF* AND TOOK WHAT WE CREATED.
THE SUITS UPSTAIRS DIDN'T CARE ABOUT US AS *PEOPLE.*
THEY'RE MORE ABOUT STRIPPING THE COMPANY DOWN TO *NOTHING* SO IT LOOKS MEGA PROFITABLE AND THEY CAN FLIP IT FOR BIG MONEY.
IN THIS ENVIRONMENT, WITH ALL THAT'S GOING ON IN THE WORLD, FINDING A *NEW* JOB IS *IMPOSSIBLE.*

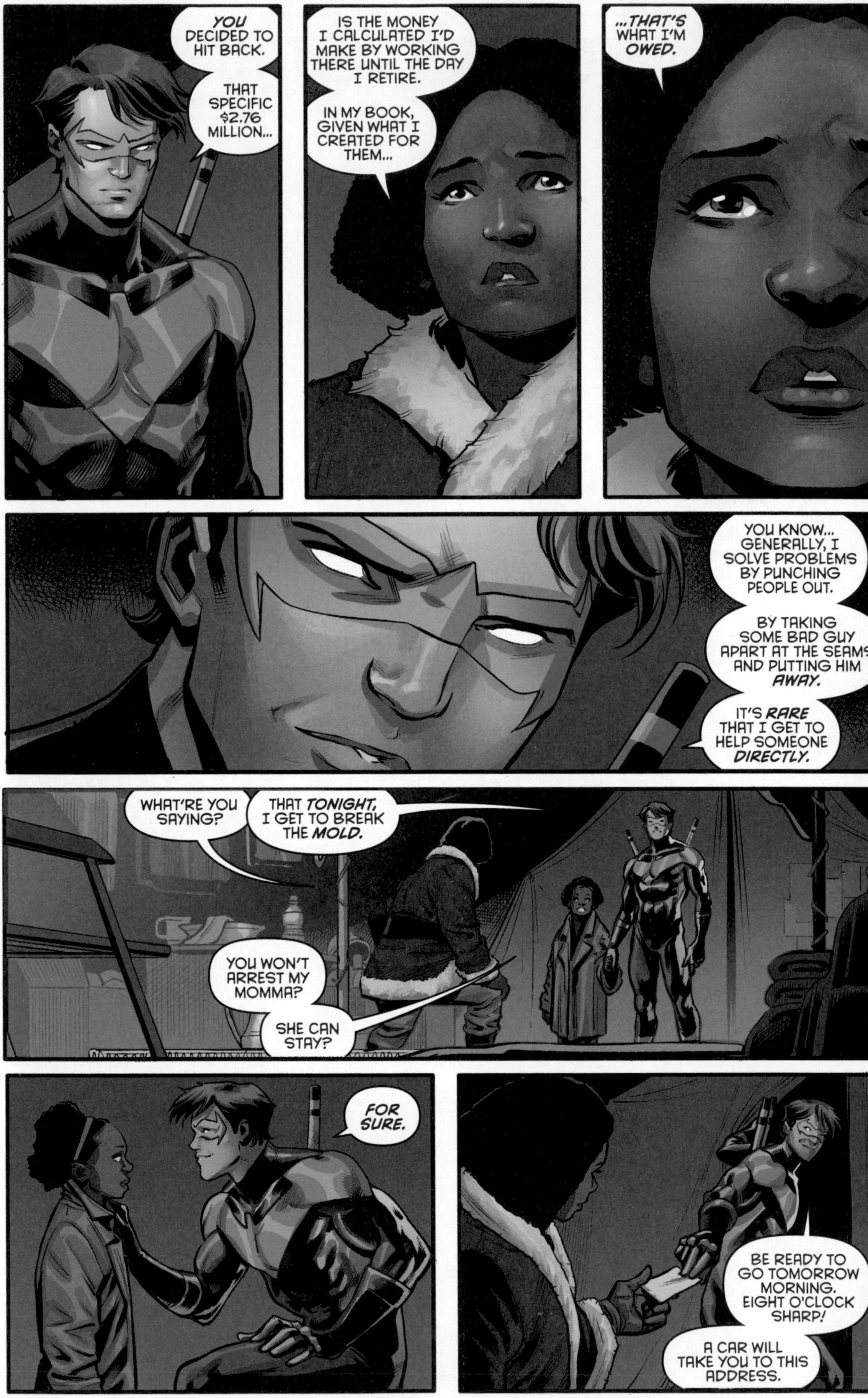
YOU DECIDED TO HIT BACK.
THAT SPECIFIC $2.76 MILLION...
IS THE MONEY I CALCULATED I'D MAKE BY WORKING THERE UNTIL THE DAY I RETIRE.
IN MY BOOK, GIVEN WHAT I CREATED FOR THEM...
...THAT'S WHAT I'M OWED.
YOU KNOW... GENERALLY, I SOLVE PROBLEMS BY PUNCHING PEOPLE OUT.
BY TAKING SOME BAD GUY APART AT THE SEAMS AND PUTTING HIM AWAY.
IT'S RARE THAT I GET TO HELP SOMEONE DIRECTLY.
WHAT'RE YOU SAYING?
THAT TONIGHT, I GET TO BREAK THE MOLD.
YOU WON'T ARREST MY MOMMA?
SHE CAN STAY?
FOR SURE.
BE READY TO GO TOMORROW MORNING. EIGHT O'CLOCK SHARP!
A CAR WILL TAKE YOU TO THIS ADDRESS.

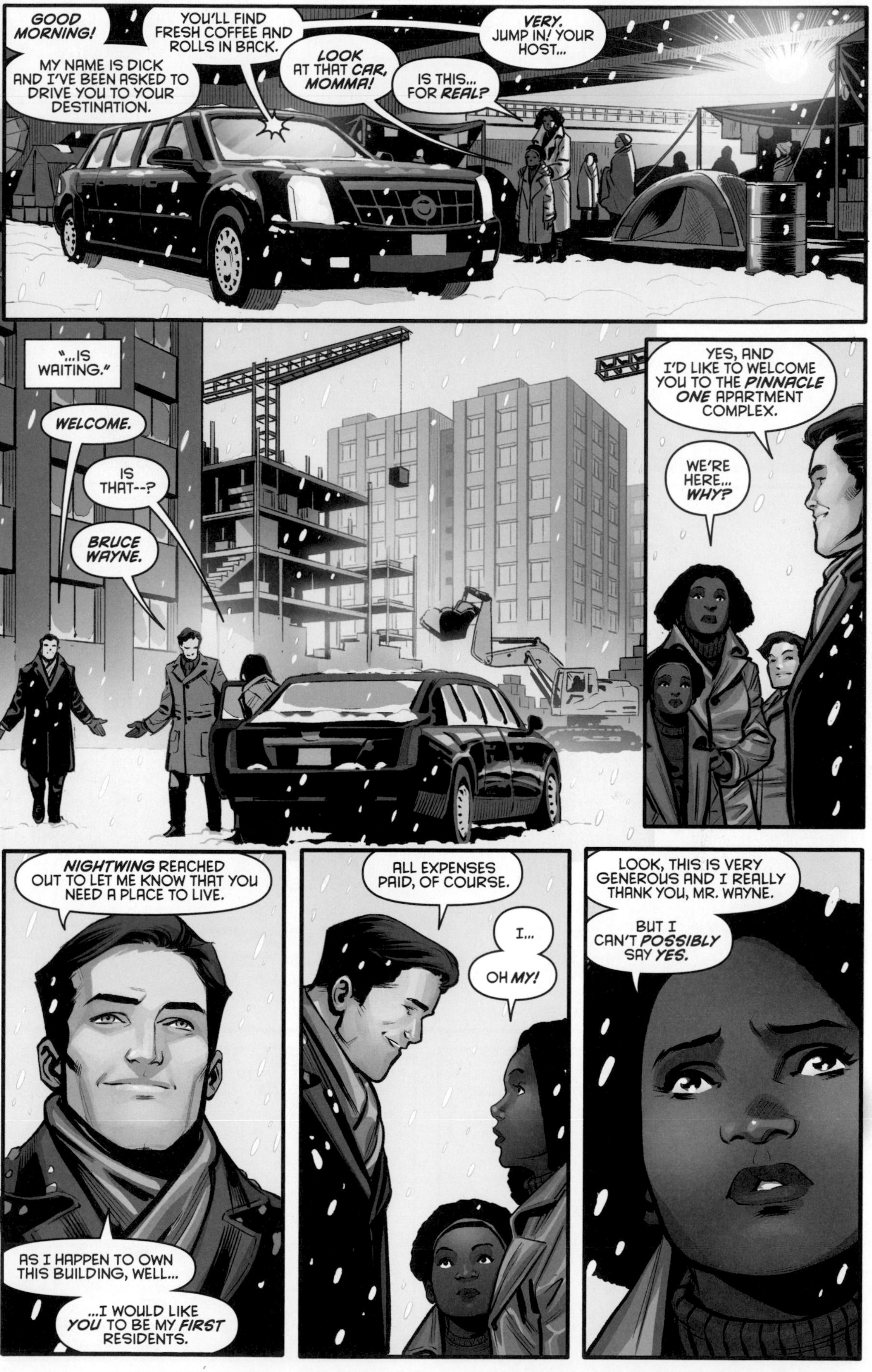
GOOD MORNING!
MY NAME IS DICK AND I'VE BEEN ASKED TO DRIVE YOU TO YOUR DESTINATION.
YOU'LL FIND FRESH COFFEE AND ROLLS IN BACK.
LOOK AT THAT CAR, MOMMA!
IS THIS... FOR REAL?
VERY. JUMP IN! YOUR HOST...
"...IS WAITING."
WELCOME.
IS THAT--?
BRUCE WAYNE.
YES, AND I'D LIKE TO WELCOME YOU TO THE PINNACLE ONE APARTMENT COMPLEX.
WE'RE HERE... WHY?
NIGHTWING REACHED OUT TO LET ME KNOW THAT YOU NEED A PLACE TO LIVE.
AS I HAPPEN TO OWN THIS BUILDING, WELL...
...I WOULD LIKE YOU TO BE MY FIRST RESIDENTS.
ALL EXPENSES PAID, OF COURSE.
I...
OH MY!
LOOK, THIS IS VERY GENEROUS AND I REALLY THANK YOU, MR. WAYNE.
BUT I CAN'T POSSIBLY SAY YES.

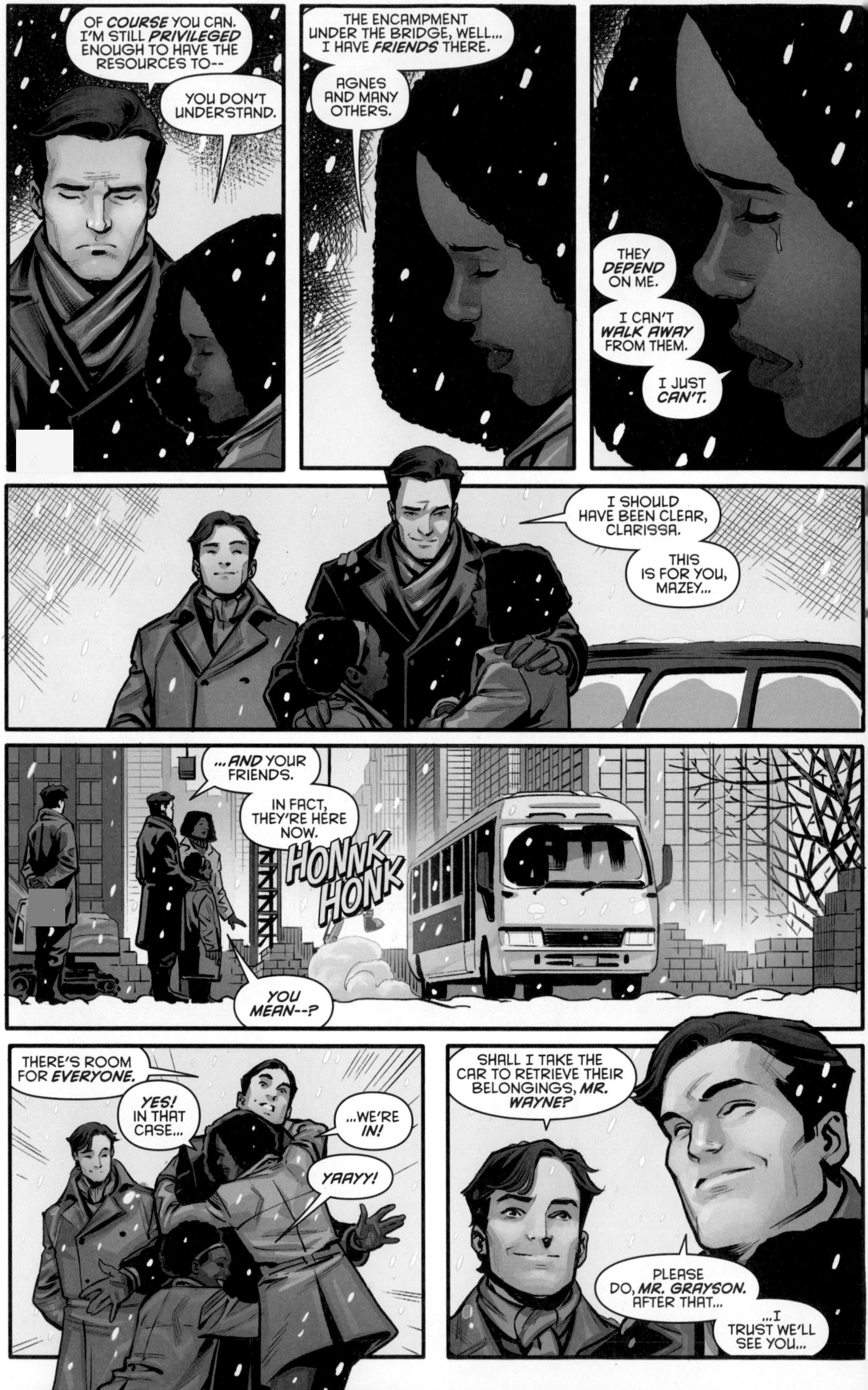
OF COURSE YOU CAN. I'M STILL PRIVILEGED ENOUGH TO HAVE THE RESOURCES TO--
YOU DON'T UNDERSTAND.
THE ENCAMPMENT UNDER THE BRIDGE, WELL... I HAVE FRIENDS THERE.
AGNES AND MANY OTHERS.
THEY DEPEND ON ME.
I CAN'T WALK AWAY FROM THEM.
I JUST CAN'T.
I SHOULD HAVE BEEN CLEAR, CLARISSA.
THIS IS FOR YOU, MAZEY...
...AND YOUR FRIENDS.
IN FACT, THEY'RE HERE NOW.
HONNK HONK
YOU MEAN--?
THERE'S ROOM FOR EVERYONE.
YES! IN THAT CASE...
...WE'RE IN!
YAAYY!
SHALL I TAKE THE CAR TO RETRIEVE THEIR BELONGINGS, MR. WAYNE?
PLEASE DO, MR. GRAYSON. AFTER THAT...
...I TRUST WE'LL SEE YOU...

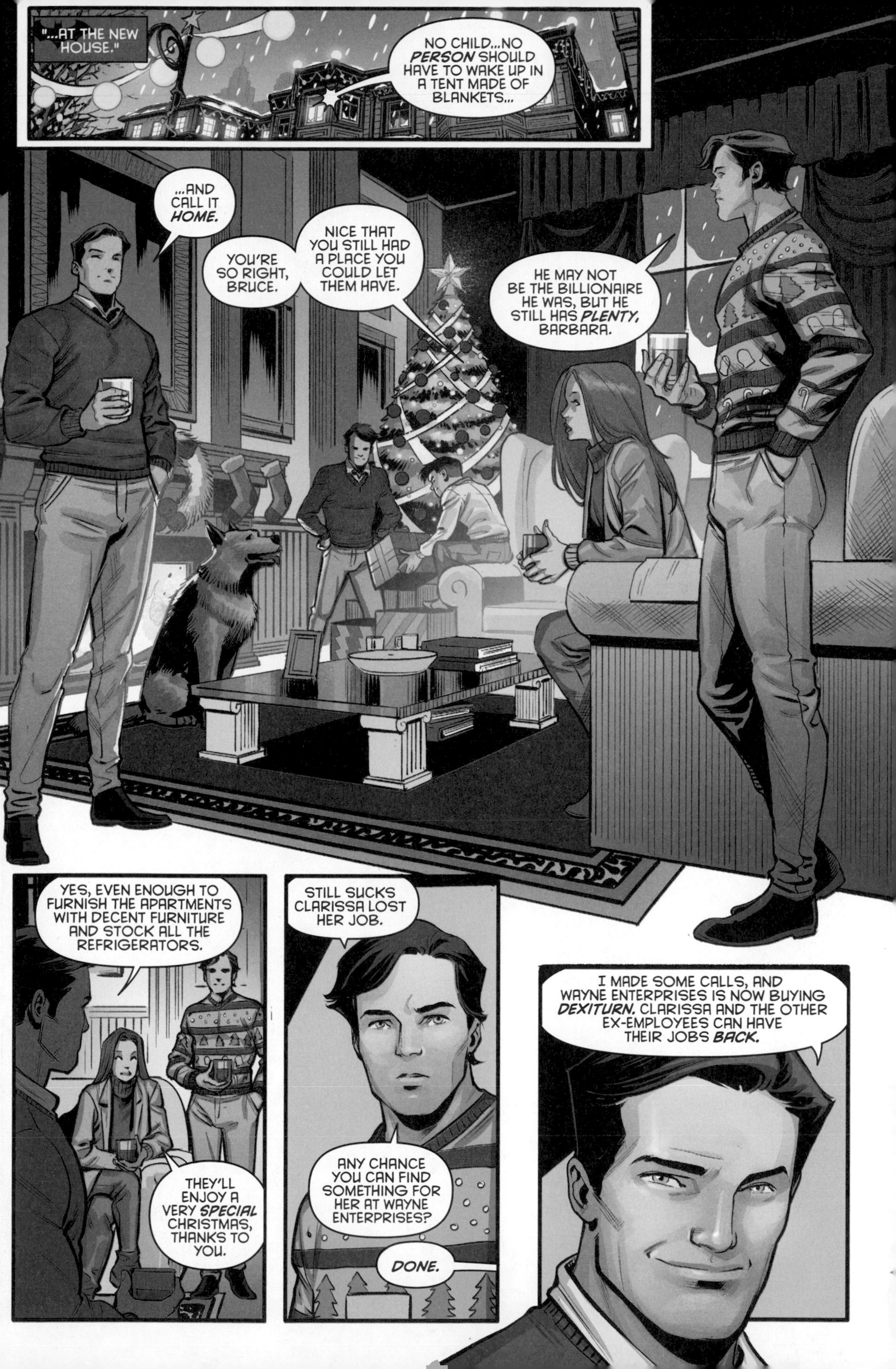
"...AT THE NEW HOUSE."
NO CHILD...NO *PERSON* SHOULD HAVE TO WAKE UP IN A TENT MADE OF BLANKETS...
...AND CALL IT *HOME.*
YOU'RE SO RIGHT, BRUCE.
NICE THAT YOU STILL HAD A PLACE YOU COULD LET THEM HAVE.
HE MAY NOT BE THE BILLIONAIRE HE WAS, BUT HE STILL HAS *PLENTY,* BARBARA.
YES, EVEN ENOUGH TO FURNISH THE APARTMENTS WITH DECENT FURNITURE AND STOCK ALL THE REFRIGERATORS.
THEY'LL ENJOY A VERY *SPECIAL* CHRISTMAS, THANKS TO YOU.
STILL SUCKS CLARISSA LOST HER JOB.
ANY CHANCE YOU CAN FIND SOMETHING FOR HER AT WAYNE ENTERPRISES?
DONE.
I MADE SOME CALLS, AND WAYNE ENTERPRISES IS NOW BUYING *DEXITURN.* CLARISSA AND THE OTHER EX-EMPLOYEES CAN HAVE THEIR JOBS *BACK.*

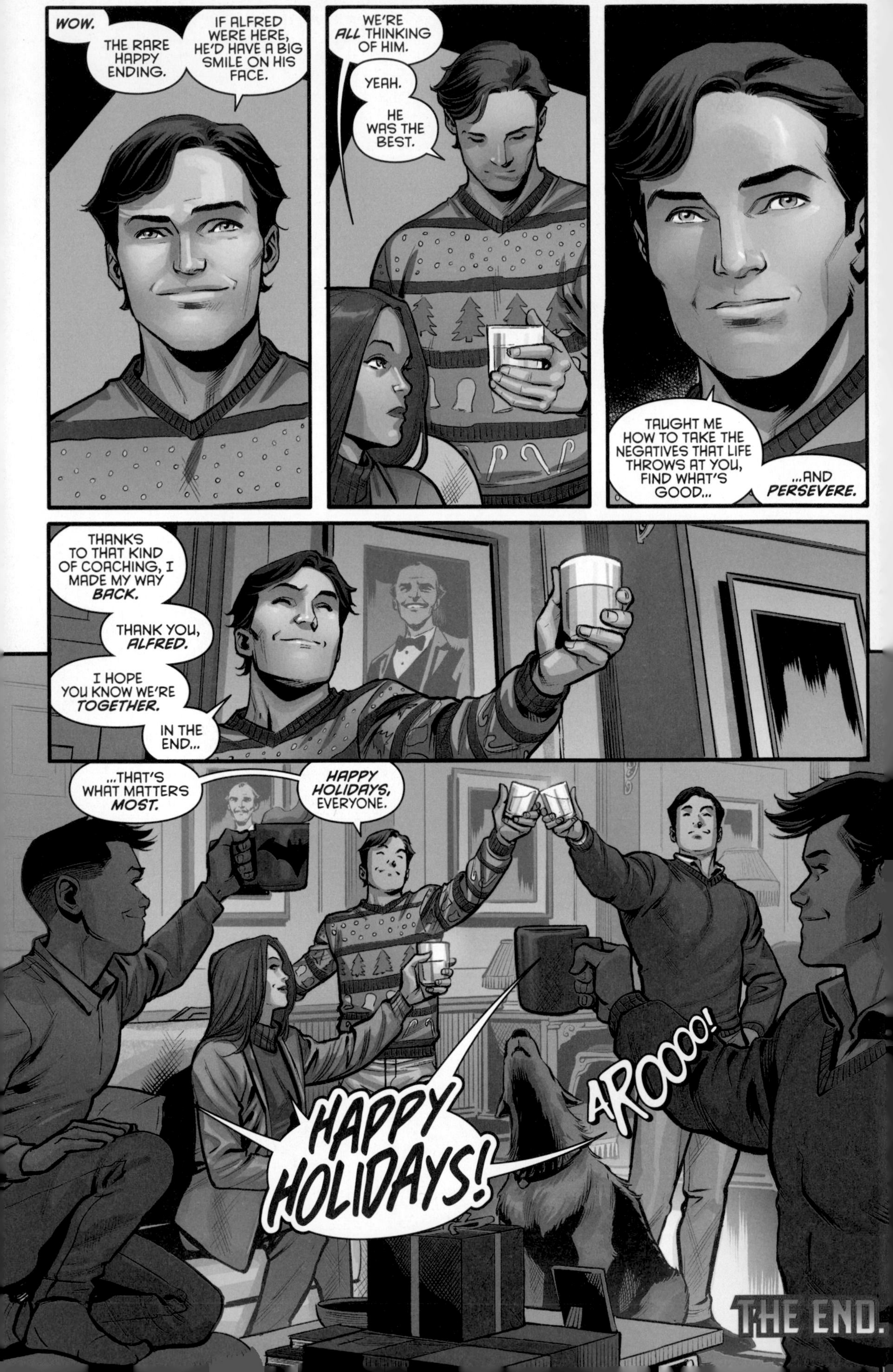
WOW.
THE RARE HAPPY ENDING.
IF ALFRED WERE HERE, HE'D HAVE A BIG SMILE ON HIS FACE.
WE'RE ALL THINKING OF HIM.
YEAH.
HE WAS THE BEST.
TAUGHT ME HOW TO TAKE THE NEGATIVES THAT LIFE THROWS AT YOU, FIND WHAT'S GOOD...
...AND PERSEVERE.
THANKS TO THAT KIND OF COACHING, I MADE MY WAY BACK.
THANK YOU, ALFRED.
I HOPE YOU KNOW WE'RE TOGETHER.
IN THE END...
...THAT'S WHAT MATTERS MOST.
HAPPY HOLIDAYS, EVERYONE.
HAPPY HOLIDAYS!
AROOOO!
THE END.

Variant Cover Gallery
by ALAN QUAH

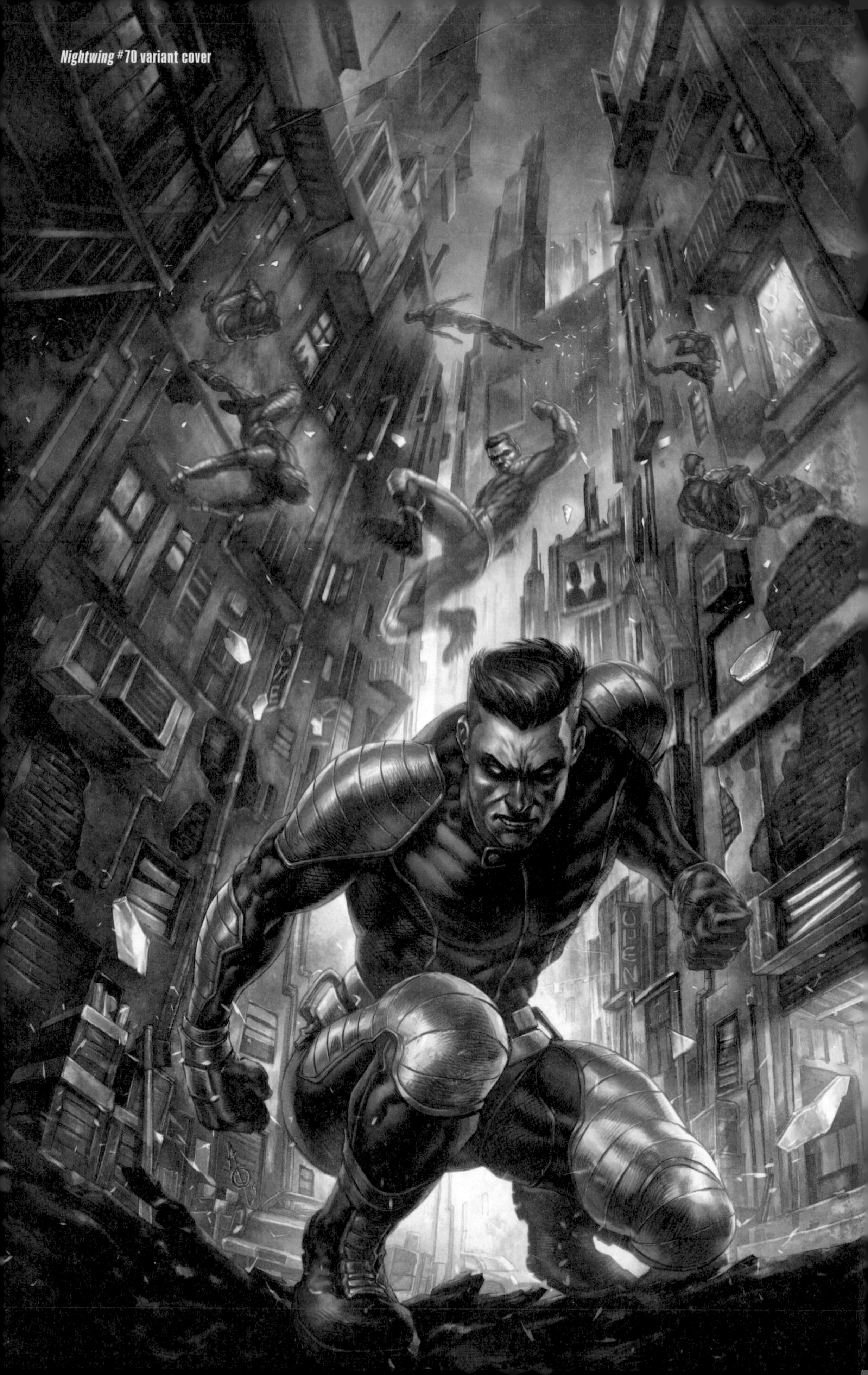
OPEN

Nightwing #70 variant cover

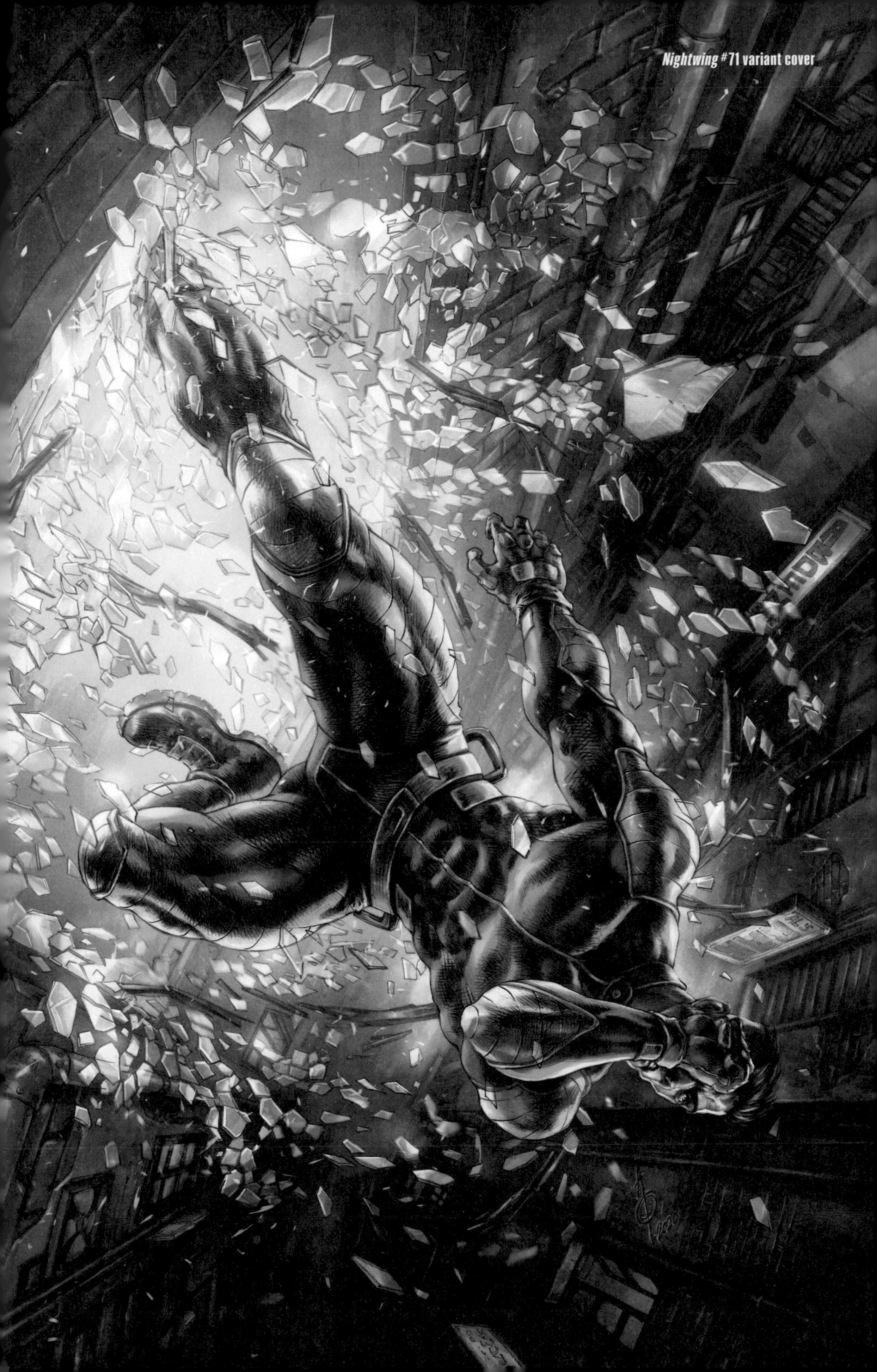

Nightwing #71 variant cover

Nightwing #72 variant cover

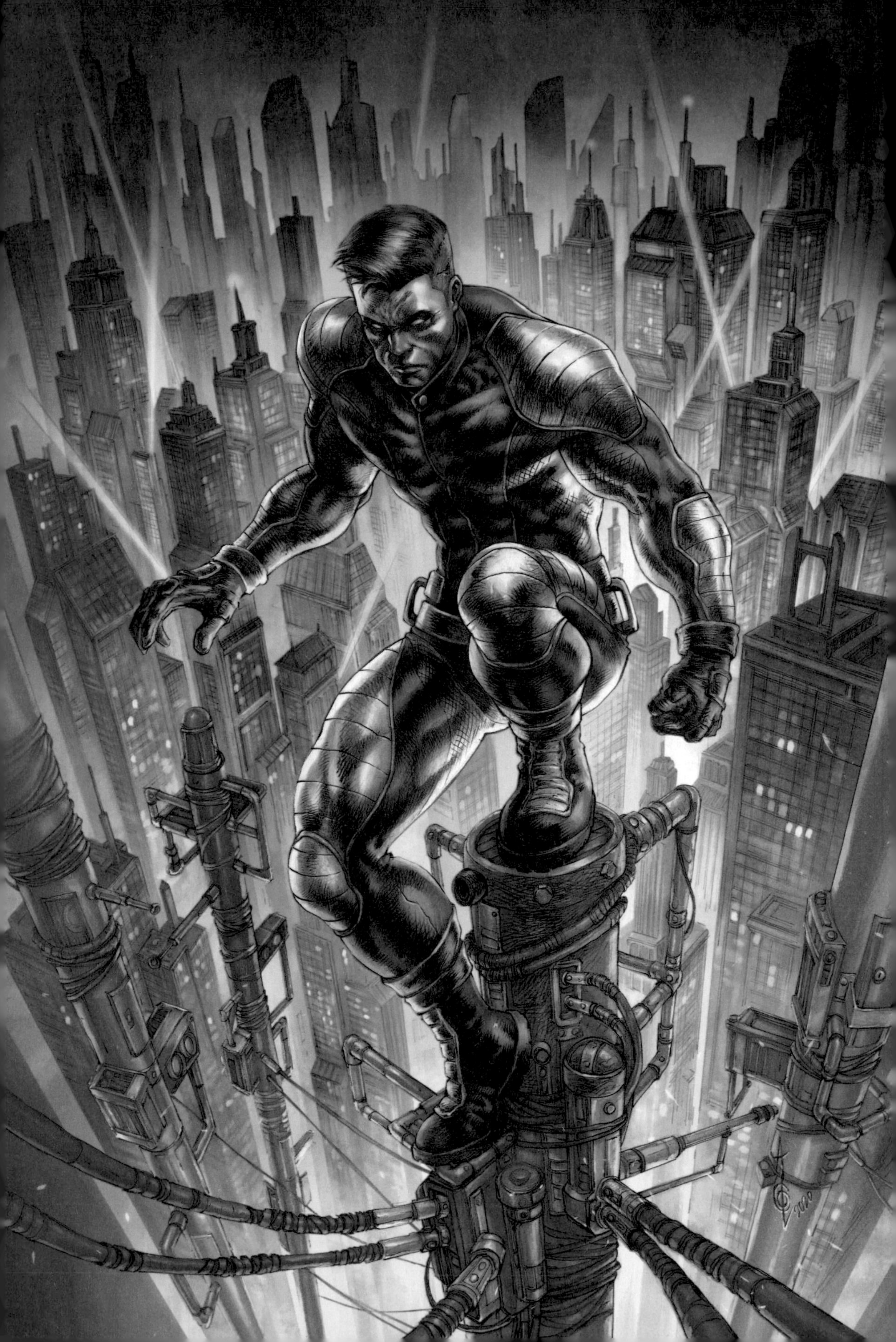

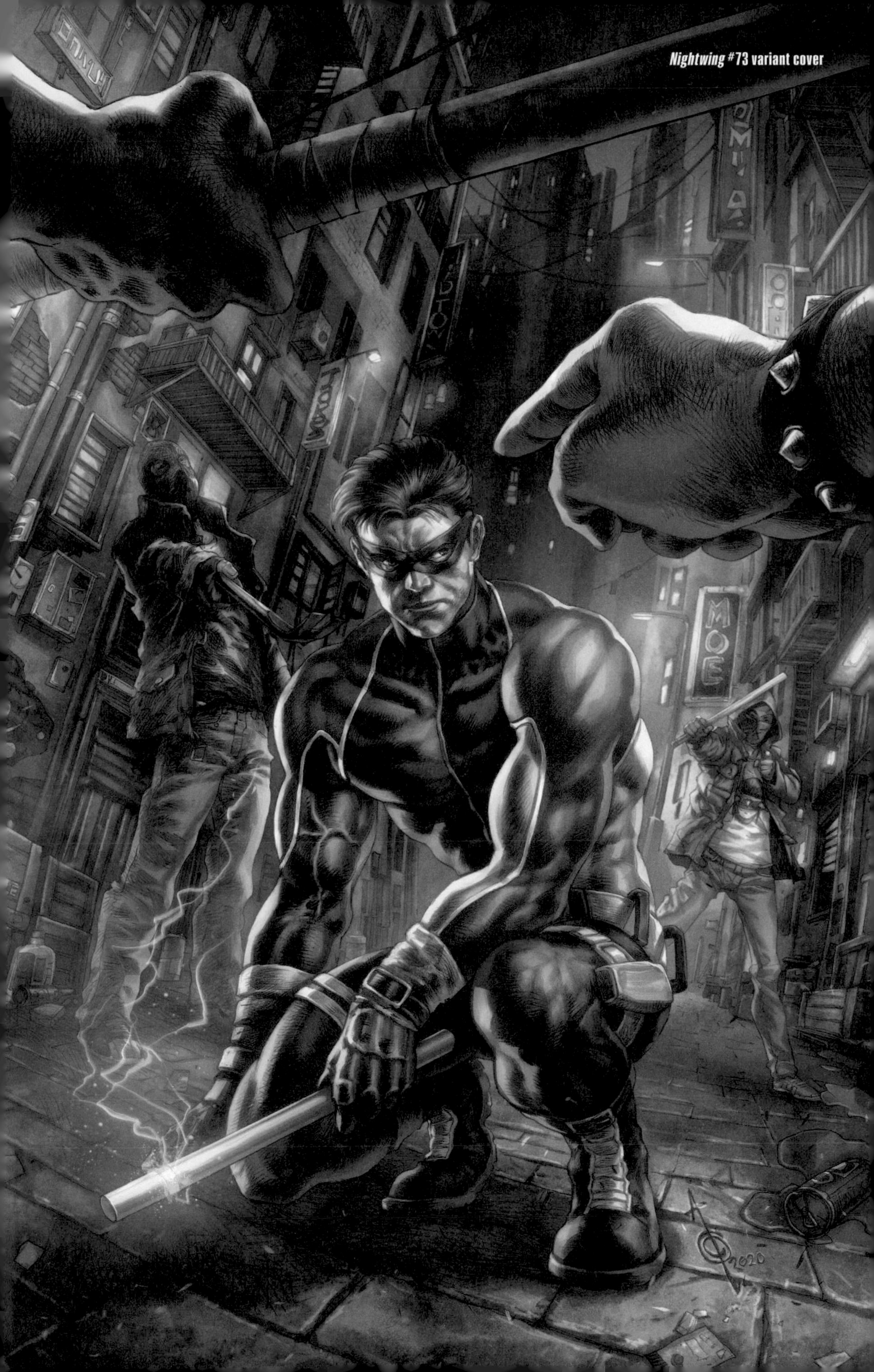
MOE

Nightwing #73 variant cover

Nightwing #74 variant cover

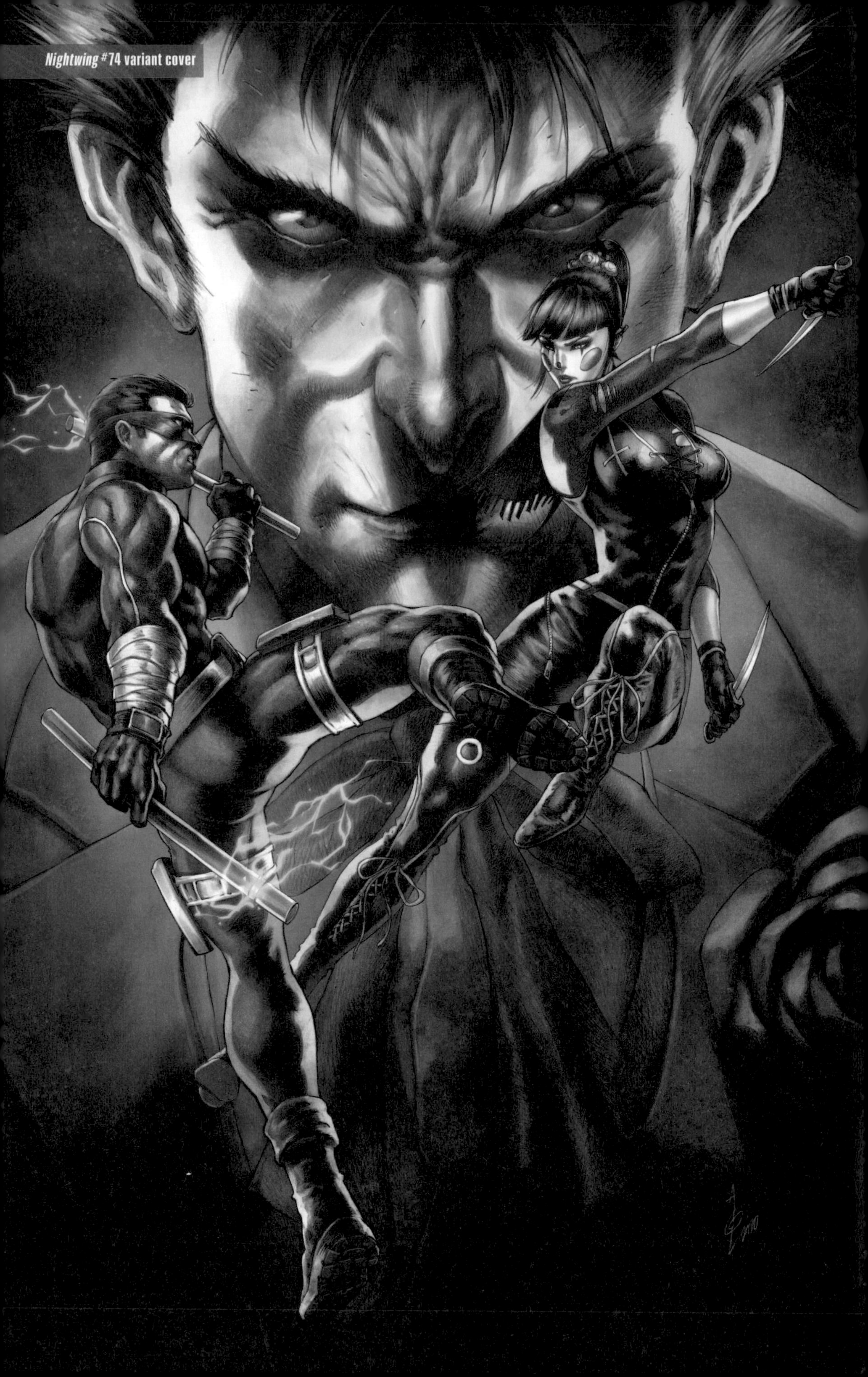

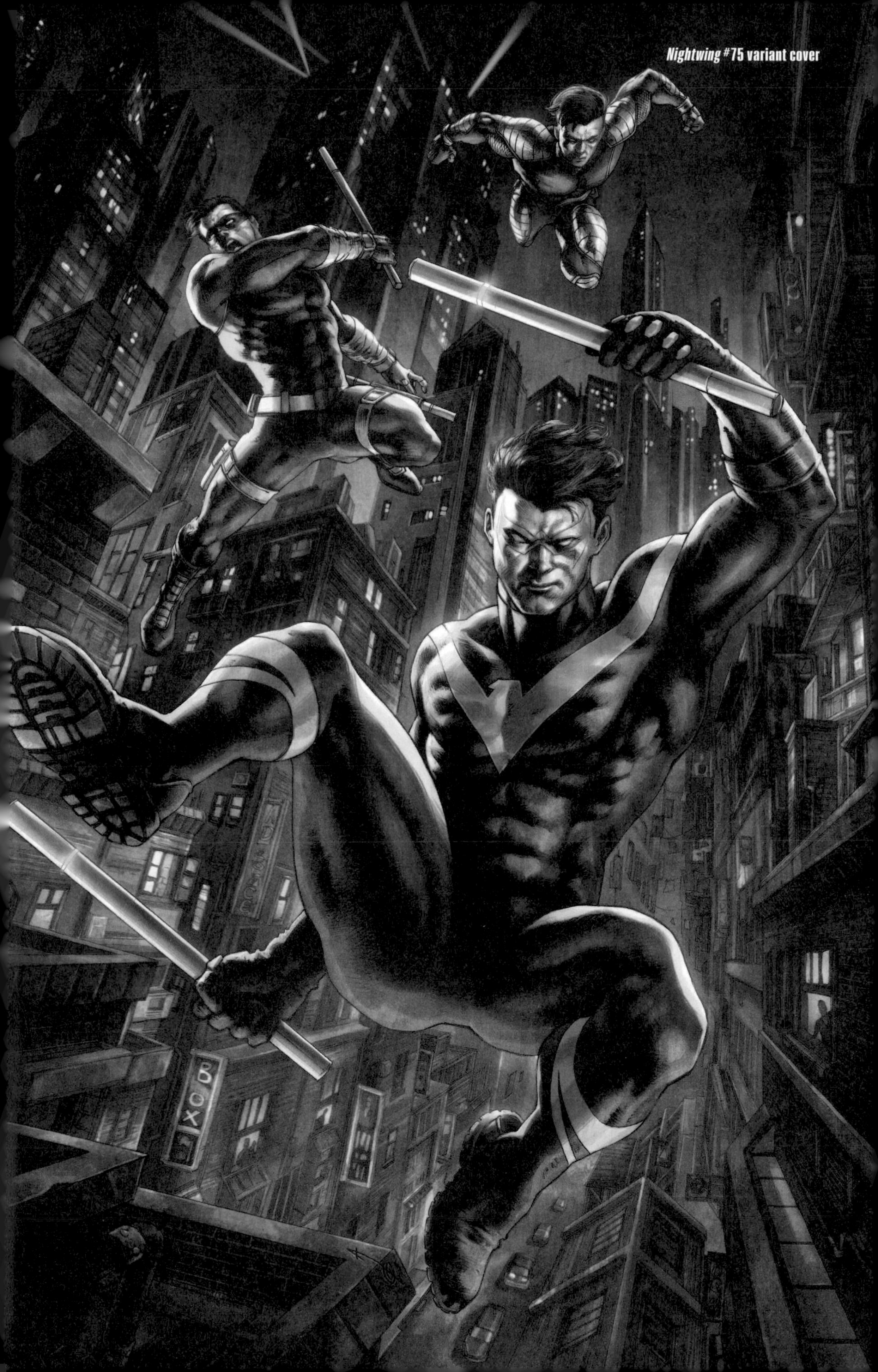
BOX

Nightwing #75 variant cover

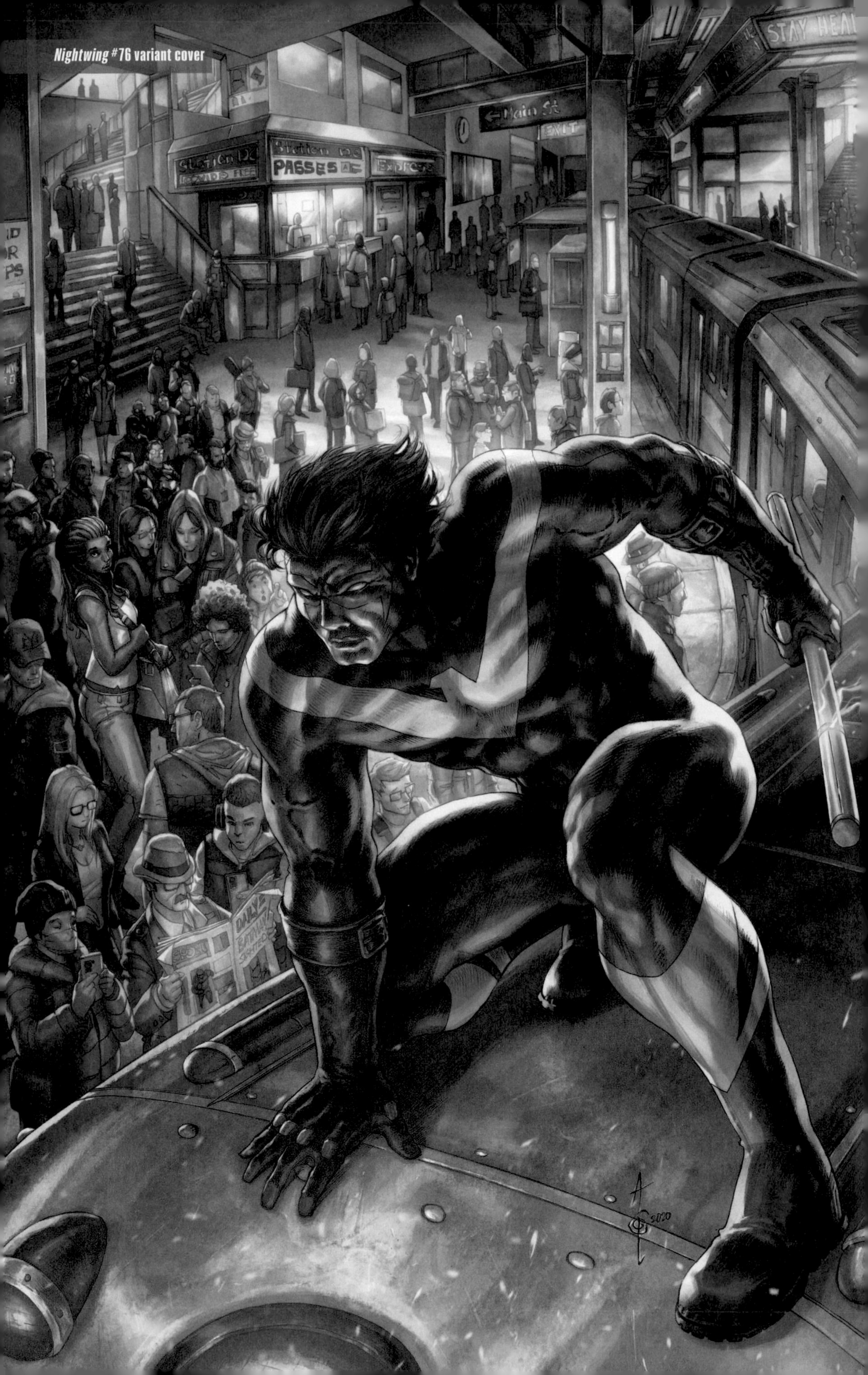
Main St
EXIT
PASSES

Nightwing #76 variant cover

Nightwing #77 variant cover

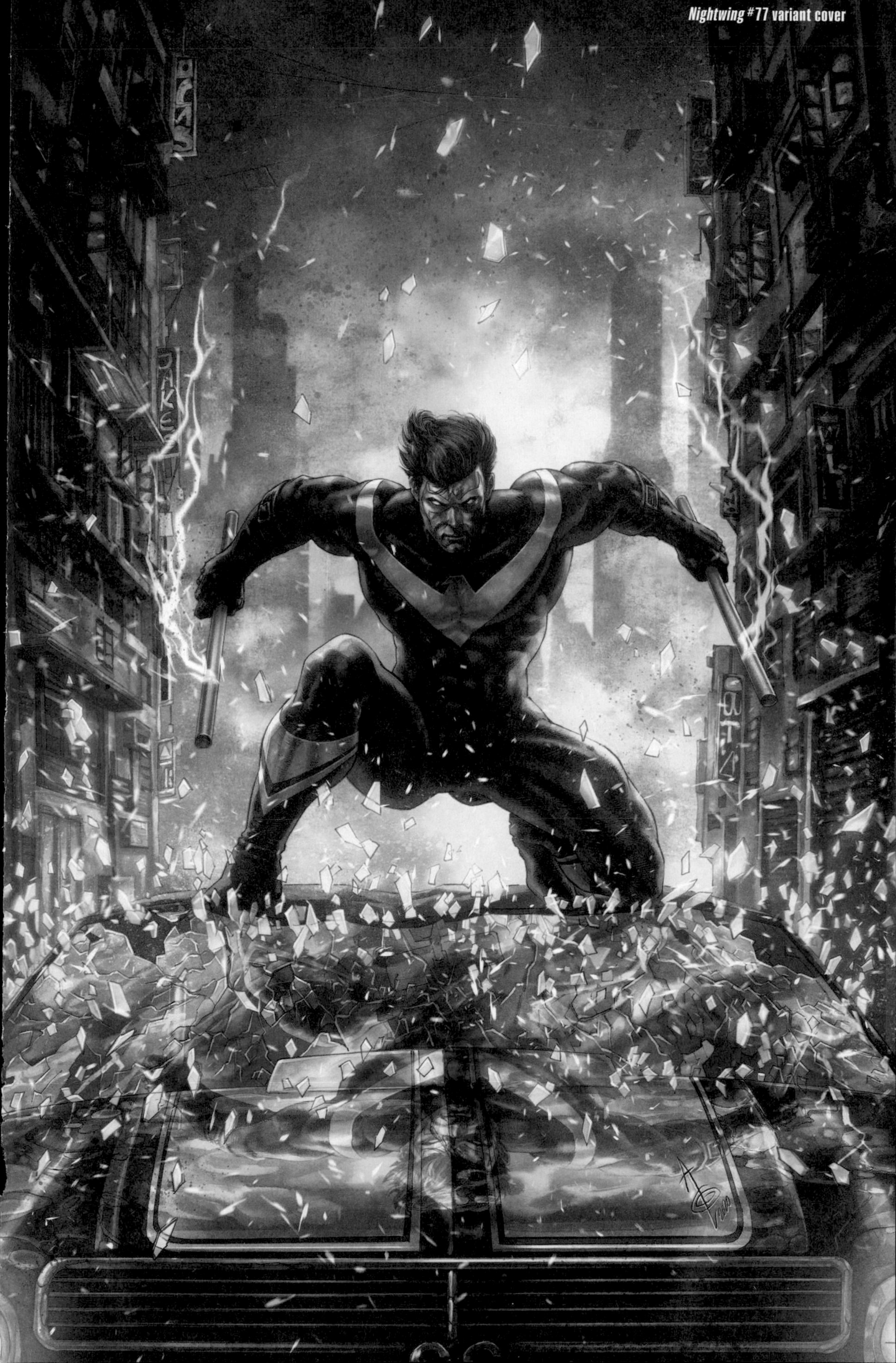

"There's just something about the idea of Dick Grayson returning to the role of Nightwing that feels right." – **IGN**

"Equally weighted between pulse-pounding and heartfelt drama."
– **NEWSARAMA**

DC UNIVERSE REBIRTH

NIGHTWING

VOL. 1: BETTER THAN BATMAN

TIM SEELEY
with JAVIER FERNANDEZ

NIGHTWING

VOL. 1 BETTER THAN BATMAN
TIM SEELEY • JAVIER FERNÁNDEZ • CHRIS SOTOMAYOR

TITANS

VOL. 1: THE RETURN OF WALLY WEST
DAN ABNETT • BRETT BOOTH • NORM RAPMUND • ANDREW DALHOUSE

**TITANS VOL. 1:
THE RETURN OF WALLY WEST**

BATGIRL

VOL. 1 BEYOND BURNSIDE
HOPE LARSON • RAFAEL ALBUQUERQUE

**BATGIRL VOL. 1:
BEYOND BURNDSIDE**

VOL. 1 I AM GOTHAM
TOM KING • DAVID FINCH

**BATMAN VOL. 1:
I AM GOTHAM**

Get more DC graphic novels wherever comics and books are sold!

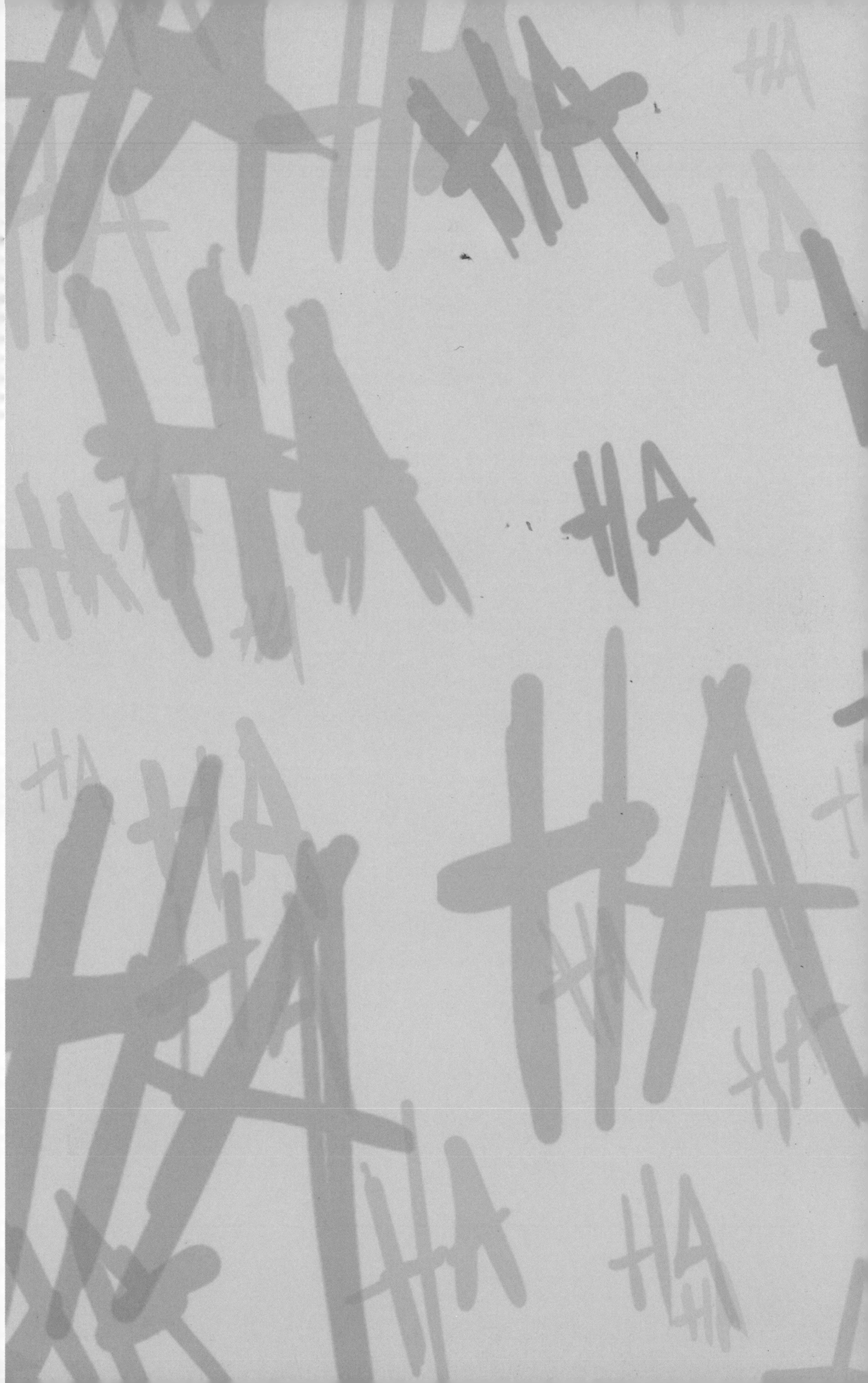
HA

HA
HA HA
HA HA